SWANSON

THE LIFE AND TIMES OF A
VICTORIAN DETECTIVE

ADAM WOOD

First edition published 2020

Copyright © Adam Wood, 2020

The right of Adam Neil Wood to be identified as the author of this work has been asserted in accordance with the Copyright, Designs & Patents Act 1988.

All rights reserved. No part of this book may be reprinted or reproduced or utilised in any form or by any electronic, mechanical or other means, now known or hereafter invented, including photocopying and recording, or in any information storage or retrieval system, without the prior permission in writing of the publishers.

ISBN: 978-0-9931806-1-3 (hardcover)
ISBN: 978-1-911273-86-8 (softcover)
ISBN: 978-0-9931806-2-0 (ebook)

Published by Mango Books
www.MangoBooks.co.uk
18 Soho Square
London W1D 3QL

SWANSON

THE LIFE AND TIMES OF A
VICTORIAN DETECTIVE

For

Jim Swanson

who once thought
his Grandfather
deserved a mention

and

Mary Berkin

who helped ensure
that he received it

Contents

Preface by Nevill Swanson i
Foreword by Paul Begg iii

Becoming a Detective through Magnetism 1
Whisky Makers and Booragtooners 5
Stench and the City 19
A Blue Tunic and Two Pairs of Boots 29
Crimes, Fines and The Veiled Lady of Loughton 51
The Lady Vanishes 68
Fall of the Detectives 80
Mrs. Swanson and the C.I.D. 93
The Duchess and the Showgirl 102
The Case of the Quarter-Million Pound Pearl 109
Lucky Swanson and the Murder of Mr. Gold 124
The Bodysnatchers 155
The Fenians are Coming! 179
Blood on the Square 231
Eyes and Ears 267
The Philosopher's Stone 381
City of the Plain 406
The Death is Reported of Detective Swanson 446
The Hero of Bow Street 460
Return of the Duchess 483
At the Going Down of the Sun 510

Appendix One: Continuing from Page 138 519
Appendix Two: Kosminski was the Suspect 538
Appendix Three: Donald Sutherland Swanson Timeline 587

Notes and References 589
Acknowledgements 687
Bibliography 691
Index 705

List of Illustrations

Donald Sutherland Swanson .... *frontis*
Rev. Dr. Francis Ward Monck 2
Thurso Harbour, 1864 7
High Street, Thurso, 1864 9
The Miller Institution, 1864 13
Miller Institution advertisement 14
Testimonial letter from Donald Swanson's Head Teacher 17
Seething Lane, and the entrance to Catherine Court 25
The attack on Mrs. Nunn 27
Metropolitan Police officers undergoing cutlass training 39
The Clerkenwell explosion 45
New recruits being fitted for uniforms 49
King Street police station 52
Lieutenant-Colonel Edmund Henderson 56
City of London Police record for Mary Ann Travers; 'Curly Poll' 59
Charley Ross 65
Carte-de-visite of the "Stolen Duchess" 71
Daniel Good 75
Frederick Adolphus Williamson 78
The Trial of the Detectives 92
Charles Edward Howard Vincent 95
The Harley Street mystery 108
Scenes in the Harley Street mystery 109
The Countess of Bective 111
The arrest of Michael Davitt 117
Sketch of the Sea Serpent Battling a Sperm Whale 120
Captain Drevar, Mr. Ward and Alfred Ward at Dover 123
Lefroy's lodgings, 32 Smith Street, Stepney 125
Mr. Gold in life and death 131
The original sketch of Lefroy made by someone who knew him 133
The handbill produced from the sketch 134
Lefroy at Lewes and Cuckfield 137

The murder and funeral of P.C. Frederick Atkins 141
The trial of Lefroy at Maidstone Assizes 145
The execution of Percy Lefroy Mapleton 149
Discovery of the Earl of Crawford's empty coffin 157
John Swanson, former Superintendent of the Aberdeen police 160
Dunecht House and Chapel 163
The 'Nabob' letter. 164
The recovery of the Earl of Crawford's body 169
Charles Soutar in later life. 171
Advertisement for Charles Soutar's verminist service. 172
The memorial marking where the Earl's body was found 173
Malcolm Fairfax *aka* Lochiel Lorimer Graham 177
The Phoenix Park murders. 185
The attempt to blow up Government offices in Westminster 198
Colonel Vivian Majendie, H.M. Chief Inspector of Explosives. 200
The mysterious death of John Broome Tower. 211
The bombing of Scotland Yard. 221
Assistant Commissioner (Crime) James Monro 222
The explosion at Westminster Hall 228
Sir Charles Warren tests the first war balloon used in the field 236
Sir Charles Warren: the newly-appointed Commissioner 241
The Life Guards patrol Trafalgar Square during Bloody Sunday 257
Robert Cunninghame Graham and John Burns at the Old Bailey 263
29 Hanbury Street, where the crime was committed. 281
Det. Inspector Frederick Abberline 282
Coroner Wynne Edwin Baxter. 290
The scene in Berner Street 303
The scenes of the recent murders 305
Dorset Street and Miller's Court. 323
Dr. George Farr 329
Dr. Thomas Bond 334
The attack on Annie Farmer. 344
Dr. L. Forbes Winslow 356
Westminster Bridge and New Scotland Yard 363
Sir Edward Bradford 369

James Sadler and Frances Coles 379
Edward Pinter: 'The Modern Alchemist' 386
Mrs. Florence Osborne... 390
Captain Osborne helps his wife from the Bow Street dock.......... 393
The attack on Emily Smith 398
The Railway Arms 403
The committal hearing of W.T. Stead and others 419
Charles Hammond and the messenger boys 426
The West End scandal: some further sketches 431
Ernest Parke.. 436
Donald Swanson's record of those found at the "Sods Ball"......... 441
Blackmailer Robert Cliburn 444
The Kensington Murder: A Madman's Crime...................... 450
Reginald Saunderson 454
Leonard Harper and Inspector Peter Pender 457
Map of South Africa in 1895.. 461
Dr. Leander Starr Jameson 463
Dr. Jameson and his officers aboard the *Victoria* 469
Det. Chief Inspector Jarvis and Det. Inspector Nutkins 481
C. Morland Agnew in later life....................................... 485
Adam Worth alias Harry Raymond and 'Piano' Charley Bullard..... 488
Lieutenant-Colonel Henry Smith and Dr. Robert Anderson......... 500
Drawing of Donald Swanson in his study 511
Donald Swanson Jr., James Swanson and Ada Swanson............. 514
Douglas Swanson, Alice Swanson and Peterishea Alexander 515
At home with Ada, 1920s 516
Charles Sandell, Chief Crime Reporter for the *News of the World* ... 525
Samuel Morley 541
Martin Mill railway station... 542
Postcard showing Morley House Convalescent Home 545
Entrance to Morley House, 1898 546
Det. Constable Henry Cox and Det. Sergeant Robert Sagar 554
Colney Hatch Asylum 563
Det. Sergeant James Nearn: the missing link?...................... 579
'Yours faithfully, Donald S. Swanson'................................. 586

Swanson personal photographs .... *centre section*

    The ruins of Geise Distillery, birthplace of Donald Swanson
    Donald Swanson aged around 10-years-old, fishing with his father
    Swanson family home at Durness Street, Thurso
    Donald Swanson in schoolmaster's robes, aged approximately 17
    Catherine Court, where Swanson worked as a clerk on arrival in London
    Rare photograph of Swanson without a moustache
    Donald Swanson's application to the Metropolitan Police
    Swanson circa 1871
    Julia Nevill and Donald Swanson in their courting days, mid-1870s
    Painting of Julia Nevill; her parents James and Sarah
    Marriage certificate of Donald Swanson and Julia Nevill
    Photograph album presented by A Division detectives
    Children of Donald and Julia Swanson
    Tranter pistol presented to Swanson by the Countess of Bective
    Swanson's arrest book showing capture of Percy Lefroy Mapleton
    Swanson mid-1870s
    Donald Swanson in 1882
    Swanson's personal address book
    Memorandum appointing Swanson to the Ripper case
    List of Whitechapel murder victims
    Swanson's list comparing witness descriptions of Jack the Ripper
    On duty at Epsom Races; Rare leisure activities; A well-earned rest
    Donald and Julia Swanson circa 1898, their 20th wedding anniversary
    Swanson boating in front of Thurso Castle during a holiday visit c.1900
    Sketch of Swanson by his niece Peterishea Alexander
    Det. Superintendent Donald Swanson's Pension Certificate
    In the back garden of 3 Presburg Road, 1920s
    Remembrance book for Donald Swanson
    Final resting place of Donald Sutherland Swanson
    Ada Swanson, Peg Swanson and Alice Swanson outside Orchard Cottage
    Swanson's copy of Sir Robert Anderson's autobiography
    Jim Swanson
    The Swanson Marginalia

Preface

By Nevill Swanson

I appreciated it when Adam invited me to write a short Preface to this book on the career of my Great Grandfather Donald Sutherland Swanson from the point of view of his "legend" within the family.

I never met him, but this Preface will, of necessity, be succinct anyway because, according to my father, he was always very reluctant to speak about his work as a point of principle, in accordance with the code by which he viewed and lived his professional life.

However, it was known family fact that, from a background that was not privileged, he had progressed in his chosen career from the lowest rung to become Scotland Yard's top detective.

He never divulged nor discussed any detail of his work, nor the cases he was involved with, but it was family lore that he had not only been in charge of the investigations into the Whitechapel murders but in fact knew the identity of the so-called 'Jack-the-Ripper' – personal knowledge that, in keeping with his moral code, came to light only decades after his death.

My father campaigned long and hard for proper recognition of his grandfather's achievements. This book provides it (and some) – my father would have been extremely proud and (finally) satisfied.

NEVILL SWANSON
November 2019

Foreword

By Paul Begg

Most biographies of Victorian policemen are usually nothing more than an excuse to re-hash the cases they investigated, which is understandable because policemen otherwise left little else but the usual bureaucratic records by which to remember them. Sometimes the biographer is lucky even to have a photograph to show what the policeman looked like. Fortunately, this is not the case with Donald Swanson. Through a fortuitous set of circumstances, Adam Wood had access to a goldmine of material – including the many photographs that liberally illustrate this book – and this has made it possible to describe Swanson's life and times, as well as the crimes he investigated and their context.

Swanson didn't leave much of a footprint in the sands of history, which is strange. He began his successful career as a uniformed constable pounding the relentlessly hard pavements of London and retired from the force as a detective superintendent, almost as high as one could get through the ranks in those days. Many famous cases came his way, including the Jack the Ripper murders in 1888, unquestionably the most infamous crime of the 19th century. Yet he escaped the attention of writers and researchers, including those who scour every document imaginable for the tiniest detail about the Ripper case. Then, one Monday in 1987, an article appeared in the *Daily Telegraph*.

The article, written by a distinguished journalist and author named Charles Nevin, was headed, 'Has This Man Revealed the Real Jack the Ripper?' Most readers probably read it with little enthusiasm. It appeared a few months short of the 100th anniversary of the Ripper's murders and several books anticipating the centenary had already appeared on the bookshop shelves, and revelations about the identity of Jack the Ripper were common and usually nonsense. So this article about a book belonging to Donald Swanson that contained some pencilled marginal notes naming Jack the Ripper had all the makings of a hoax.

As it turned out, the book's all-important provenance was impeccable, Swanson had owned the book, and it had never left the possession of the family. It was part of a small cache of papers and books, some of which also contained marginal comments, and there was no doubt that Donald Swanson would have known the facts of the Ripper case at a very senior level. Suddenly, Donald Swanson was hugely important to anyone interested in the identity of Jack the Ripper and research into his life and career began in earnest, ultimately leading to this absorbing book.

But this isn't a Jack the Ripper book. Only a tiny part of it involves the case. What has emerged from Adam Wood's research is a fully rounded account of Swanson's life and times, and the depth of detailed analysis – right down to what Swanson would have paid for lunch in his pre-police days as a City clerk! – is as remarkable as it is informative.

Donald Swanson was born on the north coast of Scotland, in a hamlet called Geise, although the word 'hamlet' makes it sound more extensive than it was. The place was nothing more than two farms and a small distillery, Donald being born in the adjoining house. After a couple of years, the family moved to nearby Thurso, where Donald received his education at the grand-sounding Miller Institution. Apparently, he was a brilliant student, and it looked like a career in teaching was mapped out for him, but in July 1867 he headed for London, which must have seemed as distant as the moon and just as alien.

Donald's sister, Mary, was living in London with her family, which may have made the move a little easier, and he also had a job as a clerk in the City waiting for him, so his future may have seemed secure and settled. But nine months later, the rug was pulled from beneath his feet when his employer decided to close the business and retire. Donald solved his unemployment problem by making what may have been a reluctant decision to join the Metropolitan Police. He applied, and as the time between application and acceptance was short, it wasn't long before Donald Swanson, P.C. 331A, paraded out from King Street Police Station to pound his first beat.

Donald Swanson had joined the Metropolitan Police at an interesting time. Since its creation in1829, the Metropolitan Police had been run subject to rigid military discipline, sever restrictions being placed on what a policeman could and couldn't do. They had to wear their uniform both on and off duty, they weren't allowed to have beards or moustaches, and they were not permitted to vote.

There were two commissioners, Lieutenant Colonel Charles Rowan and Richard Mayne, the former to oversee discipline and organisation, and the latter, a young barrister, for his legal knowledge and skills to the table. Rowan retired through ill-health in 1850 and died two years later. Mayne had been a difficult man, to put it mildly, and many people had fallen out with him, but he became increasingly insensitive, aloof, elitist and out of touch, and incompetent. Even Mayne recognised that it was time for him to go and he twice tendered his resignation, but each time it was refused. On 26th December 1868, it was taken out of human hands. Sir Richard Mayne died.

So, only a few months after Donald Swanson marched out of King Street Police Station, Lieutenant-Colonel Edmund Henderson assumed the role of new broom and set about sweeping away some of the stuffy rules that had undermined the Met's morale and efficiency. It won him the support of the rank and file, and the Metropolitan Police embarked on a new period in its history.

The population of London numbered about 3,507,828, a quite dramatic increase from 2,8400,843 just twelve years earlier, but the area within the jurisdiction of the Metropolitan Police had increased considerably. The number of policemen had risen too, from 3,341 shortly after the creation of the force, to 8,960 in 1868, two-thirds of whom were on duty at night. As for the detective force, in 1868 there were just 16 detectives, although this was about to be increased to 28. A man of Swanson's background and education would have quickly earmarked him to his Divisional Superintendent as a man with all the qualities necessary to undertake as and when needed investigations in plain clothes. In less than ten years he was back where he started at King Street, but this time as a fully-fledged detective sergeant!

The disparity between the number of uniformed policemen and plain-clothed detectives reflects how the authorities saw the purpose of policing at that time, which was primarily crime prevention. It was tantamount to an admission of failure to employ someone to investigate a crime that had already happened. From time to time, the detective force didn't even receive an acknowledgement in the annual report of the Commissioner of Police, as was once the case during the ill-fated commissionership of Sir Charles Warren. It was an attitude that was changing, brought about by Fenian bombings and other acts of terrorism and by the Jack the Ripper murders, crimes which were beyond the ordinary experience of the police. Warren's departure as commissioner following the debacle of the Ripper investigation and the succession of James Monro, formerly head of the detective Criminal Investigation Department, brought about a fundamental change in how the role of the police was perceived. Swanson couldn't have been closer to the heart of this.

His career witnessed lots of changes. Crime-detection came to the fore, the detective slowly becoming a figure of widespread interest and almost superstar status. Science and technology were beginning to play a part in crime detection. Swanson was associated with an early example when a newspaper for the first time published a picture (albeit a composite drawn by an artist) of a wanted man – the railway murderer, Percy Lefroy Mapleton – that resulted in his arrest. By the time Swanson retired in 1903, having achieved the rank of Superintendent (C.I.D.), Scotland Yard had opened a Fingerprint Bureau and achieved its first conviction based on fingerprint evidence. The Metropolitan Police would soon be a very different force.

Swanson witnessed and was active in the maturing of the Metropolitan Police into what would come to be considered one of the finest police organisations in the world, the headquarters at Scotland Yard a byword for expertise and excellence.

That's the story Adam Wood tells in this hugely detailed biography of a fascinating life and the exciting and changing times through which it was lived.

PAUL BEGG
January 2020

INTRODUCTION

Becoming a Detective through Magnetism

The ghostly hand floated across the room and played a tattoo on a tambourine, while peals rang out from unseen bells. Around a table in Mr. Hepplestone's parlour, a group comprising five men and four women watched transfixed as a small music box responded to questions put to it by one of their number by tinkling once for 'yes' and twice for 'no'.

It was Wednesday, 25th October 1876. At the modest house in Arthur Street, Huddersfield, the séance was going to plan for the spiritualist medium Rev. Dr. Francis Ward Monck. However, as the evening drew to a close one of the attendees, a Mr. H. B. Lodge,[1] suspected trickery on the part of Monck and challenged him to let the guests see the contents of a large box which the spiritualist had brought to the meeting. Monck became indignant and made as if to leave, but, finding his way blocked by Mr. Lodge, ran upstairs to a bedroom, locking the door behind him.

All efforts to persuade Monck to open the door failed. The services of a passing policeman were secured and the door was broken open to reveal that Monck had disappeared – not through spirit assistance, but by means of a bedsheet tied to a waterspout near a window. The doctor had made the mistake of leaving behind his box of tricks, which when opened revealed several 'spirit hands' – stuffed gloves – and a machine for floating these around the room, a second machine for table knocking and a 'spirit face' painted on muslin, along with several pieces of elastic and silk thread.[2]

Two days later the 34-year-old Monck was apprehended by Chief Constable Hilton of the Huddersfield Police and appeared before magistrates on 28th October 1876, where he was found guilty of deception and fraud and sentenced to three months' hard labour.

Monck's solicitor, however, contested that the phrase "palmistry or otherwise" contained in the Vagrancy Act under which his client was charged did not apply in this case and Dr. Monck was accordingly released on bail of £250 on 14th November while the Court considered the appeal.[3]

Rev. Dr. Francis Ward Monck

Taking advantage of his temporary freedom, Monck appeared at a spiritualist meeting in Manchester on 1st January 1877, where he entertained the congregation by asking his spirit guide "Sammy" for his thoughts on those who were prosecuting him. Sammy offered his considered opinion that they were "noodles".[4]

What Sammy thought of events at the appeal hearing is not recorded, but at the High Court of Justice on 6th February, Barons Cleasby and Pollock upheld the original verdict and Monck was ordered to serve his sentence at Wakefield Gaol.[5] Unfortunately, by this time he had vanished from Huddersfield and fled to London, accepting an invitation to appear at a spiritualist meeting held at Doughty Hall, Bedford Row, Holborn on 21st January.[6]

Chief Constable Hilton applied for a warrant at Bow Street Magistrates' Court[7] and on 7th February 1877 sought the assistance of the Metropolitan Police, in the form of Detective Sergeant Donald Swanson.

Armed with the warrant, Swanson and Hilton went to 15 Southampton Row,[8] the offices of the spiritualist journal *Medium and Daybreak*,[9] where they suspected Monck was hiding.

Swanson recorded what happened next:

> I went to the office of *Medium & Daybreak* newspaper kept by a crafty Scotchman named Burns, a pretended phrenologist and physiognomist, who carefully scrutinised me and told me the Doctor could not be seen.
>
> I had represented my case as that of lethargy and was desirous of trying his healing powers. The Doctor's case was explained to me by the shopman, and the difficulty of seeing him. My friend, who accompanied me, nearly spoiled my dodge by laughing – luckily it was not observed.
>
> I wrote a letter to the Doctor, purporting to come from the east [of London] and asking to see him, and the bait took admirably. Next day I called as per arrangement, and with my friend the solicitor waited in the secretary's room for the Doctor's arrival.
>
> At length he came and professionally took his gloves and hat off and began questioning me as to my malady. Here my friend left to reacquaint Hilton, and just as the Doctor commenced to magnetise me Hilton made his appearance. Having told him that by magnetism I had become a detective officer, I produced the warrant. The Doctor jumped completely out of his chair and said "Good God". We soon pacified him and took him away. His secretary's hair stood on end and he looked as pale as death. The others seemed petrified.
>
> The whole was an amusing scene. The solicitor friend of mine enjoyed it immensely.[10]

Monck was taken by Hilton back to Huddersfield on 9th February 1877, where on arrival he was "hooted by a large crowd, to whom he bowed with mock politeness",[11] then on to Wakefield Gaol to serve his sentence.

Such was the life of a Victorian detective, hunting villains with names like Piano Charley, Captain George and Pudding.

While Donald Sutherland Swanson would go on to become Detective Superintendent of the Metropolitan Police's C.I.D. and is today chiefly remembered as the officer in overall charge of the Jack the Ripper investigation, he was involved in several sensational cases of the day and his 35 year career spanned a period of great change within the Metropolitan Police and the methods of detection it employed.

This book is a history of the Metropolitan Police force in the mid to late Victorian era, told from the viewpoint of one detective.

Within these pages are the details behind major points in the development of the Met, from its creation in 1829 to the fall of the corrupt Detective Department and the rise of its successor, the C.I.D.; the Fenian campaigns of the 1860s and 1880s; riots in Trafalgar Square and other parts of the metropolis; homosexual scandals involving the highest in the land; and the hunt for criminals committing crimes as mundane as fraud and forgery to sensational cases of railway murders, bodysnatching and, of course, the crimes of 'Jack the Ripper'.

Linking it all together is Donald Swanson, whose application letter to the Metropolitan Police spoke of a desire for "a good opening". After reading his story, the reader will be left in little doubt that he made the most of the opportunities which came his way.

It begins not in London, but in the far north of Scotland.

ONE

Whisky Makers and Booragtooners

On Saturday, 16th September 1886, in a field at the village of Halkirk in the northern Scottish county of Caithness, a group of young men stood shoulder to shoulder preparing to compete in sixteen events of strength and agility ranging from the shot put and pole vault to a three-legged race and tug of war.[1]

It was the first ever Halkirk Highland Games, with the local athletic club staging their version of the famed Games established centuries earlier.

Adjoining the field was the newly-built Gerston II Distillery. It had been opened that year to replace the old Gerston I, a large, successful distillery established in 1796 and from 1825 run by two brothers named James and John Swanson.[2]

Situated on the banks of the Thurso River, the original Gerston was the first licensed whisky distillery in an area notorious for illicit establishments, some fifteen being recorded in the parish of Halkirk alone in the late eighteenth century.[3]

The Gerston Distillery, part of a 220-acre estate which included farmlands,[4] would go from strength to strength, to the extent that by the 1840s its whisky was extremely popular in London and supposedly a favourite of Prime Minister Sir Robert Peel.[5]

One of many other distilleries in the vicinity was a much smaller establishment five miles to the north at the nearby Newlands of Geise, a small settlement comprising two farms, Henderland and Janetstown.[6] The Geise Distillery, stone-built and comprising just two rooms, was situated in the shade of trees at the bottom of a short, steep hill, drawing water from the Geise Burn.[7]

It was run from the early 1840s by another John Swanson, of no relation to the Gerston family,[8] who lived in the farmhouse above with wife Mary Thomson, whom he married on Christmas Day 1828,[9] and their seven surviving children, five of whom had been born prior to the family arriving at Geise.[10] Two sons were born while John operated the Geise Distillery: James, on 8th March 1844, and Donald, on 12th August 1848.[11]

Four months before the birth of his youngest son, John Swanson was involved in a terrible accident at the distillery when, on 1st April, his clothing became caught in the machinery and he was pulled into it, his left arm being completely wrenched off. Despite the *John O'Groat Journal* reporting on 7th April that his injuries were life-threatening, John would in fact make a full recovery, albeit no doubt reliant on his elder sons to help with the running of the distillery.

With the birth of Donald, the family was complete. However, the elder children were fast growing up, with eldest son John Thomson Swanson marrying Elizabeth Gair on 13th December 1850.[12] He initially worked for his father as Distillery Manager,[13] but shortly afterwards left Caithness for London and joined the City of London Police.[14] Although he would serve in that Force for just a year, John Swanson remained a police officer and joined the Edinburgh Police force in 1853, working his way up to Second Lieutenant. In October 1868 he successfully applied for the position of Superintendent of the Aberdeen Police, beating 23 other candidates to the post, and retired in 1879 after eleven years in the role, and twenty-seven in total as a policeman.[15] It was a choice of career which would eventually have a profound effect on his youngest brother, Donald.

With their eldest son leaving Geise and their youngest not yet three years old, John and Mary abandoned the Distillery and moved the family seven miles north to what would become their long-standing home at 30 Durness Street, Thurso.[16]

Thurso is the most northerly town on the British mainland, closer to Norway than London. It is possible to observe Aurora Borealis, the Northern Lights, from Thurso, and the *John O'Groat Journal* of 22nd March 1860 reported that during a week-long display of the Lights a large school of whales had also been spotted in the Bay.

Despite the town's remote location, Thurso enjoyed a prolific export trade in the 17th and 18th centuries, initially in fish, beef and hides, and gained a reputation as one of the cheapest weekly markets in the north, drawing sellers from as far away as Edinburgh, with traders also arriving from the Continent, especially Scandinavia, sailing into Thurso

Thurso harbour in 1864
Courtesy Alan McIvor

harbour with cargoes such as pine and other types of wood, the scent filling the air.

The early main industry was supplied by Thurso's large fishing community, where boats would be sent out to the Pentland Firth, a hazardous stretch of water between Caithness and the Orkney Islands, to land herring, haddock, cod, salmon and lobster. Once ashore, the catch would be taken in baskets by fisherwomen to various selling points throughout the town.

These markets were still thriving in the early nineteenth century when the Caithness flagstone industry took off, seeing Thurso become the major exporter of paving stones in the United Kingdom. Flagstone was worked at the mouth of the River Thurso and exported throughout the world, with cities and towns from Australia to America having buildings and roads constructed from warm-grey Caithness stone. The noise from the flagstone works of George Craig & Son[17] and others filled the air, their chimneys puffing thick black smoke.

The oldest part of the town grew close to the shore in a haphazard manner, with no planning authorities existing at the time to dictate how houses should be built. They therefore followed the natural shape of the land, resulting in odd-shaped, narrow streets, which were mostly occupied by those working in the fishing industry. This resulted in that area of town being called the Fisherbiggins, 'biggins' being an old Scots word for 'residence'.

In the last days of the eighteenth century the philanthropic Sir John

Sinclair,[18] landlord of much of Caithness county and its Member of Parliament, devised a plan for the development of the town based on a grid system. Over the next century, the 'Newtown' of Thurso spread southwards from the coast, with wide, long, straight roads and open squares purposely built as public meeting places. Buildings on busy junctions were often built with radius rather than right-angled corners to allow for greater visibility. It is claimed that the redevelopers of New York followed Sir John's scheme when devising their Commissioners' Plan of 1811.

As with any bustling town in Victorian times, the people of Thurso enjoyed a wide variety of services, such as the Post Office on Traill Street run by Donald McKay, where letters sent to the town's inhabitants would arrive on the mail coach every morning at 04.00, and those being sent to the outside world deposited before eight o'clock each evening. There were several churches and schools, blacksmiths, booksellers and bakers – including the famous geologist and botanist Robert Dick – and, unsurprisingly given the presence of the River Thurso, a salmon curer.[19]

Crime in Thurso was virtually unknown, with the vast majority of offences being relatively minor misdemeanours such as breaches of the peace, unstamped measures or cruelty to animals. While convictions in the town weren't recorded until 1858, the Caithness Constabulary Conviction Book records fewer than 350 arrests in Thurso over the ten-year period 1858-1868.

Police officers employed in keeping the peace were in the main labourers such as George Swanson, recruited in 1856 and who at 6ft 2in tall was exceptionally tall for the era, and P.C. William Ronaldson, 6ft 1in, appointed in 1858. In the 1850s a total of seven officers covered Caithness county under the direction of Chief Constable Mitchell,[20] arresting people such as James Anderson, a rag gatherer aged 20 who was brought in by Sergeant Swanson for 'malicious mischief' on 23rd August 1858 and sentenced to 48 hours detention, and Elizabeth Young, a young lady aged 20 whose occupation was given as 'Prostitute', arrested in consecutive years from 1860-62, once for breach of the peace and twice for theft. For her trouble she earned custodial sentences of 15, 30 and 60 days, after which she disappears from the record books having either learned her lesson or more likely moved elsewhere.[21] These sentences would have been served at the county gaol 21 miles away in Wick, as Thurso had just a lock-up-house where criminals were confined until they could be sent to Wick.[22]

By the time the Swanson family arrived at Durness Street in the early 1850s, Thurso was well-established and had a close-knit, thriving

High Street, Thurso in 1864
Courtesy Alan McIvor

community, with a population of around 3,000.

Durness Street, just one row back from the beach, was one of the old, original streets and had its own nickname – Booragtoon. 'Boorag' was the Scots word for peat, which residents would burn as a fuel in the absence of any natural coal in the area. It was a common sight for piles of peat to be stacked alongside the houses in Durness Street, greyish-black smoke drifting from the chimneys.[23]

Like the vast majority of houses in Thurso in the 1850s, there was neither gas nor a fresh water supply. Water for washing was either saved rainwater or that collected from the river; drinking water had to be drawn from the town's main well, the Meadow Well on Manson's Lane.[24] Water-carriers offered their services to those unable to walk to the Well for a 'reasonable' fee, although it was not unknown for complaints to be made that water-carriers were simply filling their buckets from the river in order to avoid a long journey. As one of the hubs of the town, the Well was the place to hear the latest gossip, much like today's office water coolers.

The Swanson family paid an annual rent of £6 15s[25] to their landlord, the Trustees of the late William Sinclair of Freswick, for the house at 30 Durness Street.[26] Although it was in the main a residential street, in the same road were a tailor named William Innes, painters A & D McLeod, and the Thurso Benevolent Institution, an educational facility run by Elizabeth Gilbertson.[27]

Also living nearby was Helen Swanson,[28] a widow whose son Donald, a former draper born in Thurso, had joined London's Metropolitan Police in 1843 with a testimonial from Sir George Sinclair, son of Sir John.[29] He would later prove instrumental in the fledgling career of John and Mary's youngest son.

As the years passed, the couple's children began to fly the nest.

Alexander, their second son, married Annie Chalmers in 1856 and became a millwright.[30]

John and Mary's eldest daughter, Margaret Sutherland Swanson, married an English fireman named Peter Alexander in London on 27th August 1861. Alexander was stationed at Watling Street fire station,[31] and later introduced a colleague named John Bailey to Margaret's sister Mary Thomson Swanson. The latter couple married on 1st January 1864, also in London.[32]

Jannet Shearer Swanson married George Gunn, a tailor, on 20th June 1856 at the Free Church of Scotland, Thurso.[33]

James Swanson remained unmarried and moved to Edinburgh where he worked as a joiner.[34]

As the youngest child, Donald Sutherland Swanson would no doubt have personally benefitted from his brothers and sisters leaving home as it would have resulted in more time with his parents, whom surviving family papers show to have been affectionate and caring. It is therefore not surprising that they were keen for their son to obtain an education, even though it was not compulsory until the Education Act of 1872. By contrast, many parents at that time preferred to keep their children at home to help with work and household chores.

Early education in Thurso parish was either offered by the Church or in private schools set up by those seeking to make a profit. Occasionally schooling was organised on a charitable founding by individuals.[35] A report made in 1840 estimated that of 950 Thurso parish children between the ages of six and fifteen, 200 were unable to read and 600 could not write.[36]

Donald first attended the Parish School in Market Place, a two-minute walk from his home at Durness Street.[37] There was one teacher, Robert Meikle, in 1860 a 27-year-old living on the premises with his wife Margaret.[38] It was a fee-paying school, offering lessons in subjects such as Reading, Writing, Arithmetic, History, Geography, Grammar, Latin and French.[39]

Donald proved to be an exceptional pupil. At Edinburgh Caithness Association's annual examination of pupils from across the parish held at Thurso's Benevolent Institution Hall on 19th May 1860, he achieved first place in the Under-12 categories for Arithmetic (15 competitors), Geography (13), and Scripture History (23).[40]

Like all young boys, however, Donald enjoyed his leisure time spent with friends as much as his education, if not more so. With the superb salmon fishing to be had in the area, just a few weeks after his success in the examination he was out angling with a friend at nearby Scrabster when he fell and broke an arm.[41]

This would most likely not have been his only injury; a contemporary recalled the intense rivalry between the Thurso boys, who

> observed a species of caste which would have done credit to India. They ranged themselves into companies answering to the localities in which they resided. There were Fisherbiggins, Ellanders, Coogaters, Booragtooners and Newtooners, each heartily hating the other.
>
> I was once the somewhat unwitting cause of a bloody affray between Fisherbigginers and Newtooners. It was at a cricket match played on the sand, in proximity to the wooden breakwater, and therefore in Fisherbiggin' territory. I was the last to go in for the Newtoon team, and we required nine runs to win. My side regarded the match as lost, as I was thought a hopeless hope. The wicket was a slab of pavement, bat and ball cost a sixpence each, but we took our sport in grim earnest.
>
> As first ball, the bowler sent me up a fast 'grub', which I promptly cut to cover point for two. The Fisherbigginers scowled darkly, and my own side cheered. I can't recall my other hits, but I proved invincible, and we won by a wicket and two.
>
> Then the fun began. Our opponents closed in upon us, and having the majority of spectators in their favour, we had a peppery time of it. Noses bled freely, and I got my share – naturally! We escaped at last, with many threatenings of revenge, when our opportunity came.[42]

As a Booragtooner, Donald would have experienced his share of 'tribal warfare' and he joined another 'gang' a couple of years later when he started attending school at the Miller Institution.

The Institution, which would become the most important addition to educational facilities in Thurso,[43] was founded by local merchant Alexander Miller, who used the considerable fortune inherited from his uncle Henry Miller to provide funds for several charitable causes.

In June 1859 it was reported that local builder Duncan Donald had been awarded the contract, with plans being drawn up by an architect from Edinburgh named Scott, assisted by local architect David Smith.

The anticipated cost was between £1,200 and £1,500.[44] The school would be built on land gifted by Sir George Sinclair.[45]

The foundation stone was laid with great ceremony on 1st June 1860, causing tremendous excitement in Thurso:

> Pennons flew from the masts of the ships in the river and flags from Thurso Castle and Pennyland. The shops were closed and even at 11 o'clock the streets assumed an air of bustle and excitement. Workmen were hurrying home to don their holiday attire and boys in considerable numbers were bustling about wearing rosettes while the Rifle and Artillery Volunteers could be seen making their way to the Court House... with drums beating and colours flying they marched to the Parish Church where the other parts of the Procession were assembling.
>
> The Procession went through Caithness Street, up the 'Maul', and down Janet Street till they arrived at the residence of Mr. Miller where the Volunteers presented arms, the Band played the Queen's Anthem and the crowd gave three cheers for Mr. Miller.
>
> The site of the building was reached at 12.45 and Sgt. Swanson of the Police had no trouble in preserving order... there were about 4,000 present.
>
> At 1.10 Sir George Sinclair accompanied by the Chief Magistrate, Dr. Mill, most of the ministers of the town and many of the prominent people from town and county appeared, the Band played the National Anthem while the troops presented arms.
>
> A bottle was inserted into a cavity of the Foundation Stone containing copies of the *John O'Groat Journal* and the *Northern Ensign* of 31st May 1860, one of all the coins of Her Majesty's reign, a guinea of the year of Mr. Miller's birth and a parchment giving an account of the donation of the Academy with the name of the donor. The stone having been fixed in its place, the mallet was handed to Sir George Sinclair, who, having hit upon it three times declared it laid.[46]

The Institution took just under two years to build. It was, and still is, an impressive building in a Roman Gothic style, with a polished ashlar frontage and pillars made from white St. Andrews stone, the roof topped with a dome and clock tower.

For some weeks early in 1862 an advertisement ran in the *Northern Ensign* stating an opening date of 1st April 1862 and quoting the various quarterly tuition fees: English Reading, Writing and Arithmetic 3s 0d; the above plus Grammar and Geography 4s 0d; the above plus History, Writing and Arithmetic 5s 0d. Additional classes in the Classics were

The Miller Institution in 1864
Courtesy Alan McIvor

ADVERTISEMENT.

THE
MILLER INSTITUTION

Was Opened on the 1st day of April, and put under the direction of Two Teachers, both capable and respectable, determined to Teach effectively, at the following Rates per Quarter, viz. :—

For English Reading, Writing, and Arithmetic,	3s. 0d.
For all the above, with Grammar and Geography,	4s. 0d.
For all the above, with History, Writing, and Arithmetic to its full extent, including Book-keeping,	5s. 0s.

In the Rector's Class.

English Reading, with Composition, Latin, Greek, and Mathematics,	10s. 0d.
Or for Mathematics and French,	7s. 6d.
Navigation,	7s. 6d.

Thurso, April 1, 1862.

PRINTED AT THE NORTHERN ENSIGN OFFICE, WICK.

Courtesy Alan McIvor

available in the Rector's class,[47] although a contemporary of Donald Swanson's recalled that "few of us went in for 'fancy' subjects, but I obtained a smattering of Latin and French, which I promptly lost after starting to work".[48]

The first classes were held on 8th April 1862, with around 20 pupils being taught by Rev. Andrew Miller, a nephew of the founder, assisted by Robert Harvey.[49] Numbers steadily increased but both Miller and Harvey left their posts after little more than a year, with James Waters becoming Headmaster on 17th September 1863, with no assistant for three years. He was to retain the post until dying in office on 9th April 1886.[50]

Rivalry with other schools was intense:

> Boys were boys in the true sense of the term. That is to say, they were healthy, fighting young animals. At stated intervals pitched battles were fought between the different schools, and some of these encounters were sanguinary enough. Between the boys of the Miller Institution and the boys attending Docherty's School [the Free Church School] an especially keen feud existed.
>
> The latter thought the former "swanks", and there was some justification for the idea. I remember, for example, several of the bigger boys coming to the [Miller] Academy wearing beaded slippers as foot gear! I have now a shrewd suspicion that the elegant slippers belonged to fathers who knew little the duty their evening wear was made to serve during the day.
>
> Docherty's pupils were mostly bare footers, but what they lacked in dignity they made up for in bravery. They were nearly always the attacking party. Leaving their school in extended battle array, they would march up Duncan Street to the top, and then charge down the hill with challenging cheers.
>
> The Academy boys would hastily form into column and meet the attackers on Princes Street. In winter, snowballs formed the ammunition, but in summer sticks or fail runts were effectively used.
>
> The honours were fairly evenly divided as a rule. The best fighter the Academy had in my day – he was the commanding officer as long as he was with us – was Hugh Mackay, youngest son of Sergeant-Instructor Mackay. Fighting seemed to have been bred in Hugh's bones, for he would face Docherty's legions single-handed sooner than turn his back on the enemy. If I am not mistaken he got an arm broken in one of the fusillades.

Altogether, it was hot work attending school in those days – you never knew the moment when you would be called upon to uphold by 'force majeure' the dignity of your hall of learning. We developed a respect for each other which the unification of school life does little to foster today.[51]

It's not known exactly when Donald Swanson first attended the Miller Institution, but his name appears on pupil lists for 1863 alongside classmates such as Daniel and James Begg, Angus McKay and George Innes.[52] A famous attendee was William Smith, founder of the Boys' Brigade.[53] Again, Donald distinguished himself. At the Edinburgh Caithness Association examination for 1864, he secured first place in Grammar, Geography and Bible History.[54]

By this time approaching his sixteenth birthday, Donald became a Pupil Teacher at the Miller Institution, still receiving an education while at the same time assisting the Head Teacher.[55] Although not formally qualified, Pupil Teachers received on-the-job training from Head Teachers, usually an hour in the morning and 30 minutes at the end of the school day and earned a salary of £10 per annum in the first year,[56] rising by increments of £2.50 over the usual five-year training period to a maximum of £20 per annum.[57]

Donald would probably have taught the younger pupils in the Infant Department, with James Waters teaching older pupils.[58]

In most cases a Pupil Teacher would complete their five-year apprenticeship and become employed as Assistant Teachers, or move to a training college to become fully certificated.[59] Donald, however, secured a position as Second Master at the Miller Institution late in 1866, under Waters.

Donald Swanson would not teach for long, in fact just nine months.[60] Disillusioned with his prospects, in the summer of 1867 he decided to end his fledgling teaching career and find work in London.[61]

On 24th July, James Waters wrote a glowing testimonial letter:

> I have much pleasure in certifying that Mr. Donald Swanson has acted as Second Master in this Institution for the last nine months & that he discharged the duties of his office with ability, conscientiousness & success.
>
> While by his correct & varied scholarship, teaching power, & mild but firm discipline, his pupils made very creditable progress under his care, he at the same time won their affections by his kindly manner.
>
> As he now leaves, much to my regret, with the view of obtaining a

> Miller Institution
> Thurso, 24th July, 1867
>
> I have much pleasure in certifying that Mr Donald Swanson has acted as Second Master in this Institution for the last nine months & that he discharged the duties of his office with ability, conscientiousness & success. While by his correct & varied Scholarship, teaching power, & mild but firm discipline, his pupils made very creditable progress under his care, he at the same time won their affections by his

First page of a testimonial letter by James Waters, Head Teacher at the Miller Institution
Swanson family archives

situation in the mercantile line, I can fully testify to his proficiency in all the ordinary branches of a commercial education, as well as Latin & French, & from my knowledge of his punctual habits, obliging disposition, good manners, & trustworthy character, he will, I feel assured, give satisfaction to any who may secure his services.[62]

It was a character description which would resonate time and again in the future.

The fact that his sisters Margaret and Mary lived in the capital no doubt made Donald's decision easier, and he would in fact initially live with Mary and her family. Sadly, not long after his arrival tragedy would strike for his sister Margaret, when on 18th September 1867 his brother-in-law Peter Alexander died in London aged 32, unable to pass a kidney stone,[63] just days after his wife Margaret had given birth to their fourth child, Peterishea.[64]

Margaret returned to Thurso and Durness Street with her young family.[65]

Although the railway was expanding across the country at a furious rate, it wasn't until July 1874 that the first train arrived at Thurso. Anyone wanting to leave the town in the 1860s would have to endure a seventeen-hour stagecoach journey to Inverness, from where a train to the south could be taken.

As Donald stood at the doorway of the Royal Hotel on Thurso's Traill Street, waiting for the mail coach which departed at precisely 10.28am each day,[66] he clutched his ticket for one of the few passenger seats tightly in his hand.

The coach, with a magnificent livery of black and maroon with royal cipher in gold on its panels, was loaded with passengers and mail as its four horses were harnessed and the driver and guard, bedecked in a uniform of blue and red,[67] prepared for departure.[68]

156 miles, two ferry crossings and one change of horses later,[69] the coach arrived at the Caledonian Hotel in Inverness at 03.40 in the morning.

Probably travelling on a Third Class train ticket costing 25 shillings,[70] Donald Swanson left Scotland for a new life in the Metropolis. What went through his mind? He was just 18 years old, and had left behind a small town full of friends and family, a place where doors could be left unlocked and everyone knew your name.

When he stepped off the train at London's King's Cross station the following day,[71] things were very different.

TWO

Stench and the City

When Donald Swanson walked out of King's Cross station it was in to an overwhelming mix of buildings, noise, smells and people.

Having left behind Thurso, where the tallest building was a mere three storeys high and a ten-minute walk in any direction would take you to open fields or the beach, by contrast the never-ending skyline of London's vast monuments, offices, housing and churches would have left Swanson open-mouthed in amazement.

As the British Empire had expanded at a great rate since the turn of the nineteenth century, so too had the population of the capital which controlled it through its governing bodies, banks and merchant houses.

Workers, merchants and refugees alike flocked to London, its population doubling from a little over one million in 1801 to two million in 1851. By 1871, 3.9 million people were living in the capital, many refugees from poorer parts of the country, Europe and the colonies. It is estimated that a fifth of London's population consisted of Irish settlers escaping the Great Famine of the 1840s.

As the vast majority of these immigrants were labourers, they were perfectly suited to working on the myriad construction projects constantly underway in mid-Victorian London: Euston, Paddington, Fenchurch Street, Waterloo, King's Cross and St. Pancras railway stations were all built during a period of a little over 20 years. The railway might not have arrived in Thurso by 1867, but by contrast, in the capital Swanson would have been able to catch an underground train to stations including Baker Street, Hammersmith and Moorgate.

While all this construction work on transport links was taking place, another project of vital importance was completed beneath the capital's streets.

Twenty years before Swanson's arrival, London relied on an estimated 200,000 cesspools to control human waste. Although these could be emptied by professional 'night soil men' at a cost of one shilling per cesspit, it was an expense beyond the majority of people and cesspits were therefore often left unemptied, overflowing onto the streets.

In a misguided attempt to resolve the considerable risk to health, not to mention stench, in 1848 the Metropolitan Commission of Sewers ordered that London's cesspits were to be closed and that house drains connected to sewers should empty untreated human waste directly into the Thames, the water from which was then pumped back into houses and businesses for drinking, washing and cooking. Over the following year almost 15,000 people died in a cholera epidemic, and a further 10,000 in 1853 during another outbreak.

The final straw came during an exceptionally hot summer in 1858, when raw sewage overflowed in the Thames and the resulting bacteria caused an intolerable smell across the majority of central London, becoming known as The Great Stink. Members of Parliament attempted to cope with the stench by draping curtains soaked in chloride of lime from the windows of the House of Commons.[1]

At long last Parliament decided to tackle the problem once and for all, and in July 1858 passed the Metropolis Management Amendment Act, which approved a plan presented two years earlier by Joseph Bazalgette, Chief Engineer of the Metropolitan Board of Works, the body which had succeeded the Metropolitan Commission of Sewers in 1856.

Over the next decade Bazalgette oversaw the construction of more than 1,200 miles of underground sewers, which collected raw sewage from London's streets and outflows which had previously been deposited directly into the Thames. Major steam-powered pumping stations, initially at Deptford and Crossness, took the sewage downstream.

The system was opened by the Prince of Wales in 1865, although it would be another ten years before the scheme was completed. Some 52 acres of land were reclaimed as the Albert, Chelsea and Victoria Embankments were built to contain the huge pipework, avoiding the need to dig up much of London. The track which would become London Underground's District Line was constructed at the same time, alongside the sewage tunnels.

As Bazalgette's system commenced operation, water supplies improved and the foul blanket hanging over the capital gradually subsided – at least from human waste.

Victorian London was home to many thousands of working animals, as well as those destined for the slaughterhouse.[2] Social commentator Henry Mayhew estimated that each of London's 50,000 horses,[3] essential for providing power, deposited 45lb of dung onto London's streets each day – almost 37,000 tons per year. The cattle, sheep and pigs being driven through the streets to Smithfield and other markets left 40,000 tons of faeces behind them each year.[4] The stench of the capital would have been overpowering for someone brought up in a fishing town with a purifying sea breeze.

Another problem was the smoke constantly billowing out from locomotives, and the chimneys of house fires, gas works, bakeries, potteries and even bone-boiling factories, with furnaces consuming hundreds of tons of coal each day. Some 1,654 cases of Smoke Nuisance were reported in 1867.[5]

The appearance of this smoke was described by the meteorologist Hon. Francis Albert Rollo Russell:

> A London fog is brown, reddish-yellow, or greenish, darkens more than a white fog, has a smoky, or sulphurous smell, is often somewhat drier than a country fog, and produces, when thick, a choking sensation. Instead of diminishing while the sun rises higher, it often increases in density, and some of the most lowering London fogs occur about midday or late in the afternoon. Sometimes the brown masses rise and interpose a thick curtain at a considerable elevation between earth and sky. A white cloth spread out on the ground rapidly turns dirty, and particles of soot attach themselves to every exposed object.
>
> Haziness, if not fog, prevails in London on nearly every day in the year. It is absent only during part of the night and early morning. Every one who has seen the metropolis in the small hours of a fine morning knows the totally changed and unfamiliar appearance of the town when nothing interrupts the vision. On fine, hot, breezy Sundays in summer, when factories are stopped and fires not so much used for cooking, the clearness is so unusual that prominent objects such as St. Paul's Cathedral and the Albert Hall may be seen from distant suburbs.
>
> Smoke-haze is bluish, dirty-grey, or brown in colour, may be smelt if thick, and renders the outlines of clouds murky and ill-defined. The last distinction is the best, and if clouds are overhead, the peculiar grey dirtiness of smoke blurring their edges is almost unmistakable.[6]

In addition to the noise from the never-ending construction works, steam trains and thousands of horses' hooves, the everyday sounds of people going about their work would have been almost overbearing for Swanson. Mayhew reported that some 13,000 vehicles and horse-riders crossed London Bridge alone on an average weekday.[7]

Costermongers, coffee stall keepers, food sellers, newsboys, knife sharpeners, chimney sweeps, flower sellers, shoeblacks... all proclaiming their wares in the streets, all trying to eke out a living from day to day.

While life was tough for the vast majority of ordinary Londoners, the welfare of their Queen was for the most part not a concern. 1867 saw the 30th year of Victoria's reign, during which time six attempts had been made on her life, the most recent in 1850.[8] At the time these had resulted in an increase in popularity for the Sovereign, but following the death of her husband Prince Albert in 1861 Victoria became a recluse and her self-imposed isolation distanced the monarchy from the public, so that in 1867 the Royal family was far from popular.

On 30th May of that year, however, Victoria made a rare London appearance when she laid the foundation stone of the planned Central Hall of Arts and Sciences. The Queen had other ideas, changing the name of the building during the ceremony to the Royal Albert Hall. It was situated on the grounds of Gore House, at one time occupied by William Wilberforce, and was purchased in 1851 by the Royal Commission as the intended site for a permanent public exhibition following the success of the Great Exhibition. This proposal was scrapped following Albert's death to be replaced by the Hall, with the Albert Memorial situated opposite in Kensington Gardens. The Royal Albert Hall was opened by the Prince of Wales on 29th March 1871, and the Albert Memorial by Victoria in July 1872.

It was into this maelstrom of activity, which could scarcely be more different to Thurso, that Donald Swanson took up lodgings with his sister Mary and her husband John Bailey at 39 King Street,[9] the fire station where Bailey was stationed.[10]

Built between 1677 and 1692,[11] King Street ran from Prince's Street on its eastern end (now the southern extension of Wardour Street) to Crown Street (now Charing Cross Road) to the west, running parallel to Old Compton Street and Lisle Street. The Fire Station backed onto St. Anne's Church, consecrated in 1686 and built to a design believed to be by William Talman, a pupil of Sir Christopher Wren.

To the east side of Crown Street was the notorious rookery of St. Giles, for fifty years one of the worst slums in the country. It was visited in 1860 by Henry Mayhew, who wrote:

> The parish of St. Giles, with its nests of close and narrow alleys and courts inhabited by the lowest class of Irish costermongers, has passed into a byword as the synonym of filth and squalor.
>
> They [are] a noisy and riotous lot, fond of street brawls, equally 'fat, ragged and saucy;' and the courts abound in pedlars, fish-women, newscriers, and corn-cutters.[12]

An area popular with criminals of every class due to its close proximity with the West End and the possibility of easy pickings, the warrens of St. Giles offered ample opportunity for thieves to evade capture:

> The houses in Jones Court were connected by roof, yard and cellar with those in Bainbridge and Buckeridge Streets, and with each other in such a manner that the apprehension of an inmate or refugee in one of them was almost a task of impossibility to a stranger, and difficult to those well acquainted with the interior of the dwellings. In one of the cellars was a large cess-pool, covered in such a way that a stranger would likely step into it. In the same cellar was a hole about two foot square, leading to the next cellar, and thence by a similar hole into the cellar of a house in Scott's Court, Buckeridge Street. These afforded a ready means of escape to a thief, but effectually stopped the pursuer, who would be put to the risk of creeping on his hands and knees through a hole two feet square in a dark cellar in St. Giles's Rookery, entirely in the power of dangerous characters.[13]

With the expansion of the railways, and improved transport routes and sanitation across London, several plans had been suggested to clear the capital's slums, and in 1847 New Oxford Street was built right through the heart of the St. Giles rookery, displacing some 5,000 residents. Those who remained were finally driven out of the slum when work began on Shaftesbury Avenue, designed by architect George Vulliamy and engineered by Joseph Bazalgette for the Metropolitan Board of Works.

Although approval had been granted in 1877 for the construction of both Shaftesbury Avenue and Charing Cross Road, work did not begin for seven years due to legal discussions over the rehousing of some 5,497 impoverished people who would be made homeless by the works.

King Street was demolished in 1883 to make way for Shaftesbury Avenue, which was finally completed in 1886. The buildings on the north side of King Street were retained for several years as the northern side of the new road.[14] Charing Cross Road eventually opened in February 1887.[15]

Back in 1867, on his arrival in London Donald Swanson began working as a clerk for Meikle & Co., Commission Merchants.[16] The owner, Scottish-born John Meikle,[17] had known of Swanson for many years[18] and was probably related to the latter's former teacher in Thurso, Robert Meikle. It's likely that once Swanson had decided to leave Thurso, employment was found for him in his extended network. In 1867 occupying offices at 4 Savage Gardens in the City,[19] the company moved to rooms at nearby 8 Catherine Court at the beginning of 1868,[20] sharing the building with John Clifford Petrie & Co., Adolphus Italiener & Co., and John Bridgeman, wine importer.[21]

The City was still recovering from Black Friday, the culmination of months of nervousness amongst its finance houses caused by the situation at Overend, Gurney & Co., a finance company with a previously solid 60-year reputation. A string of reckless investments had seen the firm accrue bad debts, until it was forced to close its doors on Thursday, 10th May, owing some £5million.[22] The City panicked. The following day, 'Black Friday', bank rates rose to 10% and many financial firms were ruined.[23]

As with all Londoners, those working in the City benefitted from the advances with the railways and other transport links. Over twenty years the resident population of the Square Mile shrank from 129,000 in 1851 to 75,000 in 1871, as merchants and bankers took advantage of newly-opened stations in close proximity to the City such as Blackfriars (1864), Broad Street (1865) and Cannon Street (1866) to relocate to suburbs including Hampstead, Richmond and Clapham, with location very much dependent on income.[24]

Catherine Court was a narrow pedestrian court accessed on its west side via Seething Lane and by Trinity Square to the east. It was built between 1720 and 1725 as residential houses and comprised eight single-fronted and two double-fronted buildings of three floors and an attic room, all constructed from red brick in keeping with houses built in the period, but out of place visually with the grey City offices of 150 years later, by which time most of Catherine Court had long been used for commercial purposes. No. 8 was situated halfway down the Court on the northern side, and in keeping with its neighbours the interior was fitted from floor to ceiling with eighteenth century painted panelling.[25]

Getting to Catherine Court from King Street wouldn't have been as straightforward as it is today, a 20 minute tube journey.[26] Although the London Underground had opened in 1863 and lines and stations were

Seething Lane, with the entrance to Catherine Court on the right underneath the lamp
Courtesy London Metropolitan Archives

being built at a frantic rate, in March 1868 there were just ten stations operating.[27] By the end of the year commuters would be able to travel to destinations such as Victoria, Westminster and St. James's Park, but only the Metropolitan Line was available to Swanson in his early days in London. He could have travelled from Great Portland Street or Gower Street to Moorgate then walked down London Wall, Bevis Marks and the Minories to Tower Hill, but the ticket price of one penny per single journey would have made a large dent in a junior clerk's income.

An alternative was the omnibus. Several routes ran from Regent Street to the City, including the green No. 1 (Bayswater), the blue No. 2 (Blackwall) and the white No. 6 (Brompton), each of which required eight to ten horses in harness. Again, the fare of 3d per journey would have been prohibitive.[28]

In all likelihood Swanson would have walked to his work, in common with thousands of Londoners in lower paid jobs.

His most direct route would have taken in some of London's most historic streets. From King Street he would have walked along Lichfield Street, then Garrick and Bedford Streets before turning left onto the

Strand, the ancient thoroughfare.

From here Swanson would have continued along busy Fleet Street, the home of Britain's press, before passing the ongoing roadworks at Ludgate Hill.[29] Cannon Street was next, at the time made up of large wholesale warehouses containing mainly cotton goods, then past Wren's Monument to the Great Fire of London before finally turning left at Seething Lane, passing through the ornamental iron-gated entrance to Catherine Court.[30]

If the life of a clerk in the City was uninspiring, that of a general clerk was one of monotony. Being required to possess few skills other than the ability to read and write, a clerk of Swanson's position would be expected to spend nine hours a day, six days a week, preparing receipts, invoices and correspondence, where every letter was written, copied and filed by hand. The pay was a standard 25 shillings per week, paid quarterly.

Despite being allowed an hour for lunch, the culinary offerings available to a clerk at the numerous City eating houses were less than appetising, as described in a chapter entitled "The Life of City Clerks" in *Tempted London: Young Men*:

> The daily dinners of clerks have been improved by the competition amongst restaurants, but even now a large proportion can only afford to frequent the dirty coffee-shop, where "a good dinner may be obtained for 6d" and where the tablecloths are unchanged for a week, the knives smell of stale onions, the cabbage has always a long hair lying across it, and the meat consists of a piece of fat embedded in muddy hot water.[31]

It wouldn't have been a surprise had Mary Bailey provided her brother's lunch each day.

In March 1868 John Meikle decided to close the company.[32] He was at that time 56-years-old, and had married Charlotte Mellor in Staffordshire in 1833.[33] Moving to London by the time their first child, Thomas, was born in 1835, the family grew steadily until it eventually moved north to near Manchester, John dividing his business interests between there and London.[34]

By giving up business in 1868, it meant a well-earned rest for Meikle, who retired to Lancashire,[35] but a dilemma for Donald Swanson. Should he return home to Thurso and take up another teaching role, or seek other employment in the capital?

The answer came on Friday, 20th March, when, looking through the Situations Vacant classifieds in the *Daily Telegraph*, he spotted an advertisement placed by the Metropolitan Police seeking candidates.[36]

No doubt thinking of his eldest brother John's position at that time in the Edinburgh Police force, Swanson saw this as a good opportunity and, taking a sheet of pale blue paper headed '8 Catherine Court', dipped his pen and began to write.[37]

Just six weeks after Swanson wrote to the Metropolitan Police an incident occurred in Catherine Court which would have benefitted from his later detective skills.

On Friday, 1st May 1868, two young boys hid in the coal cellar of 2 Catherine Court, diagonally opposite No. 8. Their intention was to rob the housemaid, a 75-year-old widow named Mary Ann Nunn. Hearing her go out around 7.00pm, the boys crept up to her room and began to force open her moneybox. Mrs. Nunn returned unexpectedly and the boys, startled, rendered her unconscious by striking her repeatedly with a wooden mallet which they had brought up with them from the cellar. With Mrs. Nunn unconscious on the first floor landing, the assailants climbed out of a window and slid down a drainpipe, escaping via Seething Lane.

The housemaid's son-in-law later discovered her sitting on the doorstep covered in blood and semi-coherent. He alerted the City of

The attack on Mrs. Nunn, and the arrest of Arthur and Hector Smith from The Illustrated Police News, 9th May 1868

London Police who, led by Superintendent Foster and P.C.s Tillcock and Moss, examined the premises and, with the aid of doctors, established that Mrs. Nunn had been hit on the head and face at least 20 times, with her arms also beaten.

Fortunately Mrs. Nunn recovered and was able to tell police that her assailants had been brothers Arthur and Hector Smith, aged 15 and 13, the sons of her daughter's brother-in-law. She said she had always been very kind to them and on friendly terms.

The boys, just 4ft 10in and 4ft 6in, were arrested two days later and admitted that they had planned the robbery after reading a series of lurid stories such as *The Detective* and *The Young Apprentice*, in which young robbers were depicted as romantic figures. Despite losing her means of making a living as both her hands had been broken in the attack, and therefore her home at Catherine Court, at the trial on 10th July 1868 Mrs. Nunn asked the Court to be lenient. Lord Chief Justice Bovill, telling the boys he hoped their case would act as a warning to other youngsters considering a life of crime after reading similar stories, sentenced Arthur Smith to seven years' penal servitude and his brother Hector to 18 months, the Court believing he had been led astray by the older boy.[38]

THREE

A Blue Tunic and Two Pairs of Boots

8 Catherine Court
London EC

Sir

I beg respectfully to offer myself for the vacancy in your establishment advertised in the *Daily Telegraph* of today. I am now and have been for several months past clerk at the above address; but unfortunately for me my employer will give up business in a few weeks and I am thus compelled to look out for another situation.

Should you kindly grant me an interview I shall be happy to furnish you with most unexceptional references as to character, education & ability. I am 19 years of age and do not so much desire a large salary as a good opening at a moderate one.

I remain Sir
Yours obediently
Donald S Swanson[1]

The Metropolitan Police, Swanson's prospective employer, was in 1868 approaching the fortieth year of its existence.

Long before he developed a taste for John and James Swanson's Gerston whisky, Robert Peel had twice been appointed Home Secretary, first in 1822 under Prime Minister Lord Liverpool, and then under the Duke of Wellington.[2]

Soon after his appointment to the position for the second time on 26th January 1828, Peel formed a Committee at the House of Commons to conduct an enquiry into the possibility of forming a single police force governing the whole of London.[3] Previous committees had investigated the subject several times in the preceding years, on each occasion as a result of some major event. As the alarm had subsided, however, the committees had disbanded with no decision made.

On 15th April 1829 Peel spoke to the House of Commons to move the second reading of the New Police Bill. He informed the House that crime in the capital was very high compared to that in the rest of England and Wales, and was increasing. In 1828, one person per 383 living in London and Middlesex had been charged with a criminal offence, compared to one in 822 in the rest of the country.

Peel's proposal was to create "an efficient police," with "unity of design and responsibility of its agents." The new single force would be subject to the control of the Home Secretary, established in Westminster and subsequently extended to adjoining districts.[4]

The Bill went through committee on 19th May, barely a month having elapsed since its introduction, and on 5th June passed through the House of Lords.

Objections were voiced that the City was excluded, some predicting that crooks

> would assemble in [the City of] London as an asylum. When they throw a dog into the water, the fleas all get onto the head to avoid drowning, and in the same way all the thieves would get into the City to avoid hanging.[5]

Peel's public response was that the City of London had not been included because the City nightly police was much superior to that at Westminster.[6]

On 7th July 1829 the appointments were made: Lieutenant-Colonel Charles Rowan[7] and Richard Mayne[8] as the Joint Commissioners, and John Wray[9] as Receiver for the Metropolitan Police District, responsible for financial matters and police properties.[10]

Working from temporary accommodation at the Home Office, Rowan, Mayne and Wray drew up plans for the Metropolitan Police force in an incredibly short space of time: eight days after their appointments, papers detailing the proposals were in Peel's hands. They were soon approved.

Rowan and Mayne set the area under their jurisdiction as that part of the Metropolis within a radius of seven miles around Charing Cross,[11] to be divided into 17 Divisions, each designated a letter of the alphabet. One superintendent would be appointed to each Division to oversee the area.

Every Division would have its own headquarters, in the form of a 'station', which would be run by four inspectors. The Divisions would be further sub-divided into eight sections, each section having eight clearly-defined beats.

16 sergeants and 144 constables would patrol the beats, in day or night shifts, and every officer was to bear the letter of his Division and his unique number, so that he could be known to the public.[12]

On 20th July, Peel wrote to Rowan, Mayne and Wray to approve their plans, and the force was established. The commissioners would be allowed three clerks, and the Receiver two; superintendents would be paid £200 per annum, inspectors £100, sergeants 22s 6d per week and constables 21s per week.[13]

Vacant premises at 4 Whitehall Place was purchased and renovated; police officers would occupy the ground floor, with the clerks on the first floor and the Commissioners on the third. The rear of 4 Whitehall Place housed an office called the Back Hall, which was manned by officers to receive public enquiries. The entrance to the Hall was via an area known as Great Scotland Yard; in time the office and eventually the whole building became known to the public as the abbreviated 'Scotland Yard'.[14]

On 29th August, Rowan and Mayne were sworn in as Justices of the Peace by Lord Chief Baron Sir William Alexander, and on 16th September the pair personally swore in the 1,011 new police at the Foundling Hospital.[15] The majority of men had previously been employed as labourers, while others came from trades such as servants, shoemakers, clerks and carpenters. In terms of nationality, for every ten Englishmen there were five Irishmen and one Scotsman.[16]

Incredibly, the Metropolitan Police force had been created within just twelve weeks. The men were drilled and equipped with a uniform consisting a blue single-breasted swallow-tailed coat with eight gilt buttons down the front, each embossed with a crown and the words 'Police Force', blue trousers, strapped-over boots and a black leather top hat.[17] They were armed with truncheons, rattles and lanterns. Each officer was issued with a copy of the *Provisional Instructions for the Different Ranks of the Police Force*, which detailed the legal standing and powers of a police officer, and the law he was required to enforce.

The Commissioners issued notices to the watchmen who had previously policed London that their roles would be discontinued on Tuesday, 29th September 1829,[18] and that same day, with a minimum of training, the new police force first took to the streets.

They endured a very shaky start. P.C. William Atkinson, who had been awarded the prestigious warrant number "1", was dismissed just four hours into the new regime after being found drunk on duty.[19]

A few weeks later an innocent man was arrested and charged with murder for no reason other than to be found sitting on a doorstep 100 yards from the scene of the crime, two hours after the murder had been committed.[20] Arrests on the flimsiest of evidence were common in those early days, with constables eagerly memorising the section in the *Instructions* which promised "good conduct will be noticed by rewards and promotion".

Nevertheless, it was apparent that the new Metropolitan Police force was "a standing army, drilled like soldiers, and acting independently of the ratepayers."[21]

On 28th June 1830, P.C. Joseph Grantham became the first Metropolitan officer killed on duty when he intervened in a fight between two drunken Irishmen. Grantham, whose wife had given birth to twins the previous day, was knocked to the floor and a kick to the temple from Michael Duggan ended his life. At the inquest the jury cleared the defendants and returned a verdict of 'justifiable homicide', stating that Grantham had contributed to his own death by "over-exertion in the discharge of his duty",[22] an indication of the unpopularity of the New Police, who were given unflattering nicknames such as 'Blue Devils', 'Raw Lobsters' and 'Peel's Bloody Gang'.

Constables on the street were regularly the target of verbal abuse and often physically assaulted or pelted with fruit or stones, as seen by this incident which occurred just two weeks after the start of the new system:

> At an early hour on Sunday morning, crowds of drunken and disorderly persons of both sexes assembled as usual in and about Seven Dials, and the approach of a small body of policemen who had been ordered there in addition to the regular patrols was the signal for the commencement of a "row", the men being assailed by remarks such as "There go the bloody policemen". These tauntings were accompanied with groans and hootings, and the men were followed by knots of vagabonds, some of whom pushed each other against the officers...
>
> At last they were compelled to take two or three of the worst into custody. This act operated as a signal for a general attack upon the police... but Mr. Thomas, the supervisor, with Preece and Giles, the inspectors, was soon on the spot, and reinforcement of forty or fifty men was in a few minutes procured, and in a short time the ringleaders were secured. In a quarter of an hour, the whole neighbourhood was quiet and orderly.[23]

Two days later an incident occurred near Kensington Church in which an officer came close to losing his life:

> The policeman did not at first notice the abuse so unsparingly levelled at him. But at length, encouraged by the black-guard behaviour... the rest of the go-cart men joined in the tumult, following close upon the heels of the policeman. The ringleader seized him by the collar and endeavoured to throw him down, upon which the policeman drew forth his staff to protect himself: but it was speedily wrested from him. And there is no doubt he would have suffered severely from his assailants, had not another policeman run to his aid and succeeded, after a desperate resistance, in placing the ringleader in the watch-house.[24]

Constables had been instructed not to pay attention to "any ignorant or silly expressions that may be made use of towards them personally", and this attitude, along with their general behaviour, saw the New Police gradually accepted and even grudgingly respected.

The first constables may have become hardened to the taunts of the public, but they still succumbed to the temptation of alcohol: of the first 2,800 men enlisted, 2,238 were dismissed within two years, 1,790 for drunkenness on duty.[25]

New recruits were enlisted to replace these men who, in turn, were discharged and themselves replaced, until, at last, by 1833 the force consisted of reliable officers whose conduct was, by comparison, exemplary.

In the years that followed, as the reign of King George IV ended and that of William IV began, the Metropolitan Police firmly established itself and crime rates dropped.

In June 1837, a week after an 18-year-old Queen Victoria assumed the throne, a Committee recommended that the City of London be placed under the control of the Metropolitan Police, which was again rejected.[26]

In December 1849, Charles Rowan announced his wish to retire after nearly 21 years as Commissioner,[27] formally doing so on 5th January 1850 aged 67.[28]

Richard Mayne expected to assume the role of sole Commissioner, but the Home Office felt that a military man was still required and on the day Rowan retired Captain William Hay, who had been appointed Inspecting Superintendent just months earlier, was promoted to Second Commissioner.

Another soldier, Captain Douglas Labalmondière, was approached for the vacant role of Inspecting Superintendent, essentially assistant to the Commissioners. Descended from an aristocratic French family, Labalmondière was given permission by his regiment, the 83rd Foot, to return to London in April 1850 to attend an interview,[29] and subsequently retired from the army on half-pay.[30] His appointment as Inspecting Superintendent was announced[31] and he officially started work in his new position on 8th May.

Rather embarrassingly for the new Metropolitan Police officer, a few months later he found himself at Marlborough Street Magistrates' Court giving evidence in the trial of 15-year-old Sarah Boness, who was accused of stealing items of clothing from 20 Duke Street, where she had previously been employed. Labalmondière, who had rooms at the address, appeared in court to confirm that around 20th July he had missed a coat and a pair of trousers; Boness later confirmed she had stolen these and other items and pledged them with pawnbroker Thomas Cloud of 1 Lower John Street, Golden Square. The trousers were reclaimed, the coat never found.[32]

Labalmondière's appointment wasn't popular with everyone, and one of his new charges would later complain about the strict regime:

> When I joined the police there was no such thing known as drill, but since this great Captain Labalmondière (a name which sounds like German) joined the force, we have never known what one day or night's rest is.[33]

If the relationship between Mayne and Hay had got off to a bad start with the former not being awarded the sole Commissionership, things became worse when plans for the Great Exhibition were announced the following year. Hay, who had served during the Peninsular War and at Waterloo, felt that the policing of the event required a military hand, and complained bitterly when Mayne took personal control in supervising the Police presence. In the event, Mayne's planning was so successful that he was raised to K.C.B., and Inspecting Superintendent Labalmondière, who implemented the plans, made Companion of the Bath.

More friction between the two Commissioners occurred following the Duke of Wellington's death in 1852, when crowds at the Iron Duke's lying-in-state became unruly and the police were blamed when several people were injured. In response, Hay wrote to the newspapers claiming that Mayne had been solely responsible for arrangements, infuriating his senior colleague.

The final straw in the pair's fractured relationship came in 1853, when Hay submitted proposals to the Home Office for a reorganisation of the Police without showing them to Mayne.

Two years later, a Bill introduced by Lord Robert Grosvenor which prohibited all forms of trading on Sundays was met with considerable complaint and a small group of traders met in Hyde Park on Sunday 24th June in an orderly protest.

Sarcastic handbills were produced, advertising a tongue-in-cheek meeting in the Park the following week:

> Hyde Park – On Sunday the open air féte and monstre concert, under the patronage of the 'Leave-Us-Alone-Club', will be repeated on Sunday next. The *private property* will be open to the public on the occasion. Hot water for parties supplied by Lord Robert Grosvenor, who is in plenty of it. Dinners, pale ale, wines, and spirits of the choicest quality will be provided at the West End Clubs during the hours when the Licensed Victuallers' houses are closed by law. Admission gratia to members of the legislature, the clergy, bishops, etc.[34]

Home Secretary Lord Palmerston, attempting to suppress any public protests, ordered Mayne to ban further gatherings in the Park. The press, against the Sunday Trading Bill, took the opportunity to attack the police, and Mayne in particular, and widely publicised the ban.

The result was that on Sunday, 1st July, a mob of 40,000 gathered in the Park.

The day started peacefully enough, until the police attempted to arrest a speaker who was in middle of announcing that Lord Grosvenor had left London, leaving his home guarded by 200 police officers. Those nearby shouted taunts at the constables attempting to move the speaker on, who were further provoked when

> some of the mob managed to get an enormous eel out of the Serpentine and they commenced throwing it over the heads of the people, and, at last, at the police; two of the constables of the A Division at length secured the eel, and carried it to headquarters.[35]

When protestors began throwing stones at carriages passing through the Park, Superintendent Samuel Hughes had had enough and ordered a baton charge which resulted in injuries to numerous people, including 49 policemen.

The crowd began to move on, some making their way to Lord Grosvenor's home where, despite displaying no violence, they were dispersed by a police baton charge led by Superintendent Nassau Smith O'Brian.

The Hyde Park Riot may have resulted in hostility towards the Police, but the protestors achieved their goal: the following day, Lord Grosvenor told the House of Commons that he wished to withdraw the Bill.[36]

Although the force was in the main cleared at a subsequent Commission inquiry into the actions of the police, both Hughes and O'Brian were reprimanded and six other officers dismissed.

Mayne told the Commission that his instructions had been for his officers to 'move on' the crowd. Of his colleagues, he said that Captain Labalmondière was absent on the day of the Riot, on Foreign Legion duty at Shorncliffe,[37] and that Commissioner Hay had not given any order or instruction, having been absent from duty for some time due to illness.[38]

Mayne's version of events was challenged, however, by an anonymous policeman who was on duty during the Riot, who wrote to the *Daily News*:

> As a policeman of several years' standing, I blush to think that I and my comrades should have been compelled to turn round upon our fellow-citizens, in the manner so fully described by the witnesses before the commission. According to Sir R. Mayne's evidence, he admits that the police exceeded their duty. But I say we did not exceed our dirty duty. We were told to charge the people by Superintendent Hughes, and other mad-brained officers, and had we refused, instead of appearing against inoffensive parties at Marlborough Street on Monday morning, we should have been drilled down to Scotland Yard and dismissed from the service. Had we more intelligent officers at our head, I am positive that not a blow would have been struck on that day.
>
> Let the superintendents and inspectors who were left at home on the 1st July be asked their opinion as to what steps they would have taken, and whether they would back out Sir R. Mayne in his plans; and I think, instead of throwing the blame upon us constables, as Sir R. Mayne did yesterday, the public will see that our case is not quite so black as it now appears.
>
> Sir R. Mayne was in the park himself on that day, and so was our drill superintendent, as he is called amongst us, Captain Labalmondière, to whom we are indebted for being so expert in using our staves in the broadsword fashion, as described by one or two of the witnesses; and yet Sir R. Mayne tells the commissioners that he was in his office on that day, and that his instructions to the police were to advise the people to move

on, and that he did not know but that these instructions were carried out.[39]

While Mayne and Labalmondière may well have been in the thick of things, Captain Hay certainly was ill: he died from bronchitis on 28th August 1855 at the age of 61,[40] but not before having his name dragged into a scandal when a 25-year-old fraudster named Mary Sawyer St. Vincent claimed on her arrest by a local constable that she was 'intimate' with Captain Hay, and that he had not long left her lodgings and would soon return. The arresting officer was undaunted by this veiled threat, and took her into custody. No proof of any wrongdoing by the married Captain Hay was presented.[41]

Given the problems Mayne had complained of when required to work with a colleague of the same rank, following Hay's death it was announced that in future the Metropolitan Police would have just one Commissioner, with two assistants. Labalmondière was appointed as Assistant Commissioner (Administrative), responsible for administration and discipline, and Captain William Harris, the long-serving Chief of the Hampshire Constabulary, appointed Assistant Commissioner (Executive). Mayne assumed the title of Chief Commissioner.[42] The rank of Inspecting Superintendent was abolished.

Captain Harris, although greatly admired, possessed a prickly side. On one occasion receiving a letter in which the writer said he had been "out of an engagement for many months, and being unable to obtain employment of any kind, as a last resource I beg to apply for the position of constable in the Metropolitan Police", Harris told a clerk to

> inform the applicant that the Police Force of the Metropolis is not a refuge for the destitute.[43]

John Wray had been quietly building the Office of the Receiver, increasing the number of clerks and improving facilities. He appointed Lyons, Barnes and Ellis as the official Police Solicitors, and Joseph Morris as the force's Surveyor, responsible for identifying suitable property to serve as offices, stations and accommodation. Wray eventually retired in 1860 after 31 years in the role, to be replaced by Maurice Drummond.[44]

Another riot in Hyde Park in 1866 almost resulted in the departure of the increasingly aloof and autocratic Commissioner Mayne.

Demonstrations in Trafalgar Square on 29th June and 2nd July by the Reform League saw increasing levels of violence, and a third meeting on a much larger scale planned for 23rd July at Hyde Park promised trouble. As with Lord Palmerston in 1855, the Home Secretary, Spencer Walpole, banned the event and ordered Mayne to police the Park's perimeter. The gates were chained, and more than 3,000 police officers were on duty under Mayne's personal command.

Respectable Reform League members abandoned attempts to access Hyde Park and made their way to Trafalgar Square, but a mob estimated as in excess of 200,000 removed railings and attacked the police; Mayne, on horseback, was hurt and 28 policemen injured for life. Mayne realised he had lost control, and for the first time in the history of the Metropolitan Police the military were called in to restore order.

The riot, which became known as 'The Hyde Park Railings Affair', was blamed fully on the police. Mayne offered his resignation, which was refused by Walpole.

The Commissioner was determined that his men would be better prepared in the event of another riot:

> Sir Richard Mayne has begun to exercise the police force in battalion drill with some vigour. A few days ago a large number of policemen were marched to the Wellington Barracks, and subjected to three hours' skeleton battalion drill. It appears that the "Bobbies", unused to such hard work, by no means relished the innovation, and many were exhausted by it – one man being carried off the ground in a fainting state. It was rather hard, too, that the men, immediately on leaving the ground, had to go back to their regular eight hours' work. Much prejudice exists in various quarters against this development of military organisation among the police; but in these days of outdoor meetings it is highly necessary that they should be prepared to act with effect against great masses of people.[45]

By the time of Swanson's application letter of March 1868, then, London and the Metropolitan Police had changed significantly, as had the punishments meted out to wrongdoers. It was the year that penal transportation to Australia was finally ended, and a year later the Debtors Act of 1869 began reforms which saw those owing money no longer detained indefinitely in debtors' prisons.

Although the population of the capital had risen by more than one million in the twenty-year period to 1868, with over 200,000 new homes built and 1,000 miles of new streets laid, the combined strength of the Metropolitan Police had risen by just 1,500 to 6,672 in the same

Metropolitan Police officers undergoing cutlass training at Wellington Barracks from the Illustrated London News, 19th October 1867

period.[46]

A return to Parliament at the same time by James Fraser, Commissioner of the City of London Police, gave a snapshot not only of the strength of that force, but also of the declining population of the City. While the total number of officers had increased from 536 in 1841 to 658 in 1865, during the same period the number of people living in the City had fallen from 125,000 to 110,000, although it was estimated that almost one million people inhabited the area during the day. In 1867 the City was policed by a total of 684 men; records show that almost a third had been assaulted while performing their duty.[47]

Calls for an amalgamation of the City of London Police into the Metropolitan force, discussed frequently over the years, came loudest in 1863 following the disastrous policing by the City during the wedding procession of Prince Edward and Princess Alexandra, resulting in *The Times* leading a campaign for the amalgamation of the two forces:

> The occurrences of Saturday... give a sufficient condemnation of the present system. To anyone who applies common sense and judgment to the question it is not necessary that street rows and fatal accidents should take place in order to convince him that a separate Police jurisdiction, isolating about a twentieth part of the metropolis from the

rest, must be an absurd arrangement.

The Princess Alexandra, within a few minutes after entering those sacred precincts which no metropolitan policemen is allowed to violate, was, with her future husband, her parents, her family, and all her attendants, completely in the power of a London mob. The Corporation, which had vaingloriously refused the assistance proffered to them by the Duke of Cambridge and Sir R. Mayne, was unable to get the Prince and Princess past its own Mansion House. The City Police were quite inadequate in numbers to control the mass of rough and eager sightseers... the small force which the City can command was perfectly unable to keep the line along the whole distance from London Bridge to Temple Bar. The consequence was that the mob rushed in, surrounded the Royal carriage, clambered on to it, got between the horses, and, in short, brought the procession to a standstill. Had it not been for a few artillerymen, whose services had been almost forced on the City, it is probable that the Bride would never have passed through Westminster at all.[48]

The following week *The Times* reported that Lord Dalhousie had risen in the House of Lords to enquire whether the Government "intended to take any steps with respect to the consolidation of the Metropolitan and City Police."[49]

The answer came on 14th April, when the *Globe* reported that Sir George de Lacy Evans was to submit a motion to the House of Commons which would hand control of the City of London Police to the Government.[50] The Bill was unopposed in its first stage[51] but quietly disappeared shortly afterwards. The Metropolitan Police, perhaps expecting the amalgamation to happen at some stage in the near future, opened an official file to collate newspaper mentions of combining the two forces.[52]

The uneasy existence between the two neighbouring forces was perfectly illustrated in this amusing recollection by a Metropolitan Police officer:

> I was keeping observation in the vicinity of the City boundary, keeping well out of view, as I was on the track of two dangerous criminals.
>
> It was about two o'clock in the morning, when from my hiding-place I saw two uniform constables carrying what appeared to be a heavy bundle from one side of the road to the other. When they got on the further side they gently laid the bundle down, and then hurried back to the spot from which they had brought it. Watching very intently, for I thought it might possibly be connected with the matter in which I was connected, I saw

the bundle move.

I didn't have long to wait for confirmation of my belief, as another policeman arrived, and as he gently pushed the bundle with his foot, there emanated from it as fine a flow of "best Whitechapel" as I have ever heard. It was a woman, and failing to get her on her feet, the officer quietly disappeared, and presently returned with another.

The two lifted her up and were halfway back across the road, when a voice called out: "No you don't, you take her back on your own side." The first two policemen, who were members of the H Division, now came into view, and with all the cheek and temerity possible, threatened to report the other two – who were, of course, City men – if they didn't take the woman back. There looked like being trouble at first, but cheek won and the two City men retired discomfited with their undeserved "drunk".[53]

The increase in population across the metropolis naturally brought with it a rise in crime, mostly minor offences such as fraud and theft. But as Swanson's letter made its way to Hatton Garden police court in March 1868,[54] it was one of many answering an appeal for help in dealing with a far more sinister threat.

Formed in Dublin on St. Patrick's Day 1858 by the revolutionary James Stephens, the Irish Republican Brotherhood had one aim: to free Ireland from British rule. Unsurprisingly, it quickly gained a large following in Ireland and beyond, boasting an estimated 100,000 members by 1865. A branch was formed in America, and named the Fenian Brotherhood. The Fenians attacked British army forts and other settlements, on one occasion in 1866 attempting to invade Canada. These incidents were all calculated to impose pressure on Britain to withdraw from Ireland.[55]

As 1866 drew to a close, a lack of progress saw Stephens replaced as leader of the Brotherhood by Colonel Thomas J. Kelly, an Irish-American veteran of the American Civil War.

The Fenian Rising of March 1867 saw a poorly-organised attempt at insurrection. Kelly and another leading member, Timothy Deasy, were eventually arrested by chance on 11th September in Manchester, and a week later were transported to Belle Vue Gaol by horse-drawn police van. As the van passed under a railway arch, a man stepped into the road and ordered it to stop, pointing a pistol at the driver. Immediately, a gang of more than 30 Fenians appeared from behind a wall and surrounded the van, attempting to break in using an assortment of tools including sledgehammers and a hatchet. After Police Sergeant Charles Brett, travelling inside with the keys, refused to unlock the doors, one of the mob placed his pistol on the keyhole with the intention of blowing open the lock. At the same moment Brett bent to look through the keyhole and the bullet passed through his eye into his brain, killing him immediately and earning Brett the unwanted tag of the first Manchester police officer to be killed on duty.

A woman among four other prisoners inside the van with Kelly and Deasy took the keys from Brett's body and passed them out via a ventilator, enabling the Fenians to free the pair.

Kelly and Deasy fled to America and were never recaptured, but a police raid on Manchester's Irish quarter resulted in 28 Irishmen being arrested on suspicion of involvement in the rescue, with five 'principal offenders' tried under one indictment on 28th October 1867.

Perhaps related, around the same time a former officer of the Manchester Police who had more recently been acting as an informant contacted the Chief Constable with news of an 'audacious' Fenian plot to kidnap Queen Victoria from her Balmoral estate and hold her hostage at a remote cottage until Republicans being held in jails in Ireland and the mainland were released.[56]

The information was forwarded to Scotland Yard, who sent dozens of armed undercover officers to Balmoral. After a few days the operation was scaled down as no kidnap attempt was made, the Fenians either realising their plans were known or losing their nerve.

The plot might have failed, but Mayne recognised that his officers needed to be better equipped, and ordered intense cutlass drill:

> The frequent repetition of murderous attacks on the police in these days of Fenian fury makes it highly expedient that the civil guardians of our peace should be taught how to use more formidable weapons than the truncheon, in case of need, for the purposes of self defence. Arrangements have, indeed, been made for the instruction of the officers and constables of the Metropolitan Police Force in the cutlass exercise, and a portion of the ground belonging to the Wellington Barracks, St. James's Park, has been placed at the disposal of Sir Richard Mayne, being more convenient than any space which was available at Scotland-yard. A squad of twenty or thirty of the police sergeants and inspectors now assemble there daily to be instructed by Inspectors Fraser and Robinson, who have already been initiated in the exercise. The sergeants and inspectors will communicate similar instruction to the constables under their command.[57]

At the trial of those arrested in the aftermath of P.S. Brett's murder, all five were found guilty and sentenced to death by hanging but two,

Thomas Maguire and Edward O'Meagher Condon, were reprieved. The remaining three men – William Allen, Michael Larkin and Michael O'Brien – were hanged by executioner William Calcraft on 23rd November. The trio became known as the Manchester Martyrs.

Following the trial several meetings had been attended on Clerkenwell Green in London by thousands of people appalled at the sentencing. Their appeals for clemency came to nothing and on Sunday, 24th November 1867, the day after the hangings, a march left Clerkenwell Green to Hyde Park in complaint.

The route took them away from the Middlesex House of Detention, better known as Clerkenwell Prison, where ironically a leading arms organiser of the Brotherhood, Irish-American Ricard O'Sullivan Burke, had been taken following his arrest with colleague Joseph Casey in London's Woburn Square four days earlier for supplying weapons to Fenians in Birmingham.

On 11th December the Home Office received information of a plot to free Burke, which was scheduled to take place the following day. The plan was

> to blow up the exercise walls by means of gunpowder – the hour between 3 and 4pm; and the signal for 'all right', a white ball thrown up outside when he is at exercise.[58]

The report was sent to Scotland Yard and seen first by Assistant Commissioner Labalmondière in Mayne's absence. When the Commissioner arrived, his orders were for the prison walls to be examined and watched by five police constables and three officers in plain clothes. Labalmondière personally examined the prison, and the prison Governor placed additional armed prison guards on the rooftop.[59]

At 3.30pm a man approached the prison, wheeling a handcart bearing a large barrel which he unloaded and placed next to the wall adjoining the exercise yard. He then threw a white rubber ball into the air, lit the fuse and ran for cover. Burke, having seen the signal, did the same and waited for the explosion which never came. The fuse had gone out; a second attempt to light it also failed, and with not enough length of fuse remaining for a third attempt, the man placed the barrel back on his cart and departed.

Unbelievably, a police constable had watched the whole thing but failed to consider it 'suspicious'. A prison guard, having seen the white ball thrown over the wall, put it in his pocket and took it home for his son.[60]

At 3.45pm the following day, 13th December 1867, a horse and cart were driven up Corporation Row to the prison and two men unloaded a covered barrel, which they placed against the wall. Sitting opposite, playing with burning paper, were two small boys. One of the men placed a firework on the pavement, which the boys picked up, and positioned a second into the barrel. Declining the boys' offer of their burning paper, the man lit a match and held it to the firework; as soon as it began to flare both men and the two boys ran. A Constable Moriarty approached the barrel just as it exploded.[61]

The prison wall – 60 feet long, 25 feet tall and 2 feet thick – was demolished seconds later. The fronts of houses and shops along Corporation Row were also blown down, more than 50 inhabitants buried under rubble. Burke and Casey were at the time locked in their cells, the authorities having changed their exercise allowance to that morning as a precaution. Twelve members of the public died, and over 120 people were injured.

Anne Justice, a Fenian sympathiser who had visited Casey pretending to be his aunt,[62] was quickly arrested along with two men found at a rented room in nearby Woodbridge Street from which Justice had been seen observing the prison. The men, Timothy Desmond and Jeremiah Allen, were charged with murder along with Anne Justice. The latter chose to cooperate with the police rather than face the death penalty, and told them that a man named Michael Barrett had arrived from Glasgow two days earlier, and that he was known to Desmond and Allen. Barrett was found back in Glasgow on 3rd January 1868, in the home of James O'Neil. Both men were arrested for murder.

At a government enquiry on 9th March 1868, the Home Secretary, Gathorne Hardy, offered a farcical explanation for the police inactivity:

> It appeared that the mode of carrying out the design of which they had received information did not strike those who were set to watch the outside of the prison... What their attention was apparently directed to was the undermining of the wall; they thought it would probably be blown up from underneath, and had no conception that it would be blown down in the way is really was done.[63]

Mayne once more offered his resignation; again it was refused. By this time 72-years-old, tired and embittered by increasing public vilification, it seemed the right time to leave. The press certainly thought so, the *Daily News* urging the Home Office to appoint another civilian as Mayne's successor following his seemingly imminent retirement;[64] a

*The Clerkenwell explosion
from the Illustrated Police News, 21st December 1867*

fortnight later the *Pall Mall Gazette* went so far as to publish a 'rumour' that Alexander Knox, a Magistrate at Marlborough Street police court, was in line to replace the Commissioner.[65] Mayne remained in office.

Three months before the bombing the Home Office had decided to create a special department to deal with the growing Fenian threat, although nothing had been done yet. The day following the attack, Chancellor of the Exchequer Benjamin Disraeli wrote to Prime Minister Lord Derby, warning that the situation was serious and that action needed to be taken; the Counter Revolutionary Secret Service Department was born. Intended as a temporary branch, Colonel William Feilding was installed as its head, assisted by Captain William Whelan and a young Dublin-based barrister named Robert Anderson. All three had experience of Fenianism in Ireland.

Anderson arrived in London on 19th December to find a city in fear:

> The panic which prevailed in London at this time was absolutely ludicrous. When I took up *The Times* on the morning of my arrival, I learned that, the night before, "a great number of detective police were sent out on duty into different parts of the city." And further, that "the South Kensington Museum, the British Museum, the gas factories, the powder magazines etc, were all protected by officers of the police and military." By every post Ministers received letters from panic-stricken folk, or from lunatics or cranks, reporting suspicious incidents, or giving

warning of plots upon public or private property.⁶⁶

The trial of Barrett, O'Neil, Desmond, Allen and Justice opened on 20th April, each charged with the murder of Sarah Ann Hodgkinson, one of those killed in the explosion.⁶⁷ Anne Justice was quickly acquitted, followed by James O'Neil. Timothy Desmond and Jeremiah Allen turned Queen's Evidence and testified against Michael Barrett, who alone was found guilty of the bombing and subsequent deaths.

Defending Anne Justice was Montagu Williams Q.C., who described Barrett:

> On looking at the dock, one's attention was principally attracted by the appearance of Barrett, for whom I must confess I subsequently felt great commiseration. He was a square-built fellow, scarcely five feet eight in height, and dressed something like a well-to-do farmer. The resemblance was certainly increased by the frank, open expression of his face. A less murderous countenance than Barrett's, indeed, I do not remember to have seen. Good-humour was latent in every feature.
>
> The only time I saw Barrett's face change was during the examination of the informers and the look of disgust, scorn, and hatred that turned upon those two miserable creatures was a thing to be remembered.⁶⁸

On 26th May 1868, Barrett became the last man to be publicly hanged in England when William Calcraft dispatched him outside Newgate Prison.

The Counter Revolutionary Secret Service Department was disbanded at the end of the trial, with Feilding and Whelan returning to their duties. Anderson was invited by Home Secretary Hardy to remain at the Home Office as Home Office Advisor on Political Crime.⁶⁹

The Clerkenwell Outrage resulted in widespread panic and anger towards the Irish, and more specifically the Fenians. The bombing had been carried out not by the Brotherhood, but by a small gang of London Irish, but the result was a sharp decline of public sympathy for the Fenian cause.

In the immediate aftermath, Irishmen in London were called 'Mick Barretts' as an insult; this, in time, became shortened to simply 'Micks'.⁷⁰

During the trial Sir Richard Mayne had been quoted in the *Pall Mall Gazette* as saying there were "ten thousand armed Fenians in London". Faced with this overreaction and obviously concerned that a prolonged campaign was underway, the Metropolitan Police had started a recruitment drive by placing advertisements in newspapers, seeking temporary Special Constables and full-time policemen.[71]

It was this appeal to which Donald Swanson responded.

Although the formal response to Swanson's letter of application has not survived, his communication was evidently of interest to the Metropolitan Police as at ten o'clock on the morning of Tuesday, 31st March 1868, he attended an interview with William Staples, 2nd Class Clerk of the Candidates Department.[72]

The initial qualifications for entry to the Metropolitan Police were few: a candidate had to be under 35 years of age, and to stand clear 5 feet 7 inches without his shoes.[73] He had to be able to read and write, and to be "free from bodily complaint, of strong constitution, and equal to the performance of Police Duty." He would be examined by the Chief Surgeon of the Police, who would also judge his general intelligence. Finally, a candidate could not be accepted if he had more than two dependent children.[74]

As an intelligent, single 19-year-old, Swanson easily met these requirements.

He was examined by Superintendent George Rose, a Scot appointed to the Preparation Class in 1865 following five years' service with the Met,[75] and was recorded as being 5 feet 8½ inches tall, with hazel eyes, dark brown hair and a dark complexion.[76]

Having passed the initial examination, Swanson was required to provide details of two respectable people who could attest to his good character, both of whom had to have known him for at least five years. These referees had to be known to a third person, to whom the Form of Recommendation had to be sent for approval.

Swanson gave as referees his brother-in-law George Gunn, recorded as living at High Street, Thurso, and childhood friend James McLeod of Brabster Street, Thurso. Both men reported that they had known Swanson for the required five year period, i.e. since 1862 to the time of his leaving Thurso in 1867.

The completed form was then sent to Inspector Donald Swanson of A Division, whose mother Helen still lived in Thurso. The Inspector had joined the Metropolitan Police in April 1843, but obviously returned to his hometown as he knew not only George Gunn and James McLeod, but also the younger Swanson. He signed the Form of Recommendation on 8th April 1868.[77]

The young Swanson had been accepted into the Metropolitan Police, but before he was ready to pound the beat he had to undergo three weeks' drill and training. Along with the other recruits, he was sent to the Candidates' Section House at Kennington Lane, where he underwent a "School of Instruction", learning the Instructions to Police and how to operate an A.B.C. Machine, the form of telegraph used by the police at that time.

For a force drilled in a military style, exercise was extremely important, and the recruits were taught how to stand straight and walk at a measured pace under the watchful eye of Inspector Robinson.[78] The physical nature of the drill was recounted by a later contemporary of Swanson:

> Every morning after breakfast we made our way to Wellington Barracks, and there on the Guards' drill-ground we were put through a very tiring two hours a day drill, much to the amusement of the guardsmen and civilian onlookers. We were a mixed lot, farm labourers, ploughmen, waggoners and the like from every county in the British Isles.
>
> There were three squads with three instructors, and how on earth these latter managed to qualify for the jobs I really do not know. Their knowledge of drill was not much better than our own.[79]

At the time constables were not permitted to wear facial hair. John Littlechild, who joined the Police around the same time as Swanson and who would rise to the position of Detective Chief Inspector, recalled:

> I remember how amused I was at being told on the first day I went to learn drill that I must shave, no hair being permitted on the upper lip in those days. I really had no idea myself that I had any hirsute adornment to take off, and felt somewhat proud that someone else seemed to think I had; but the next moment I felt very foolish, as I fancied the drill instructor was just "getting at me" on account of my youthful appearance.[80]

At the end of the three week period the recruits were sent to Scotland Yard to be affirmed by the Commissioner or one of the Assistant Commissioners, and given their uniform: one great coat, one dress tunic, one cape, two pairs of trousers, two pairs of boots, a helmet, a stock and an armlet. A Constable was required to wear his uniform at all times, even when off duty,[81] although the quality did not meet with universal approval:

> There were plenty of uniforms, each of us having two complete outfits.

A Blue Tunic and Two Pairs of Boots

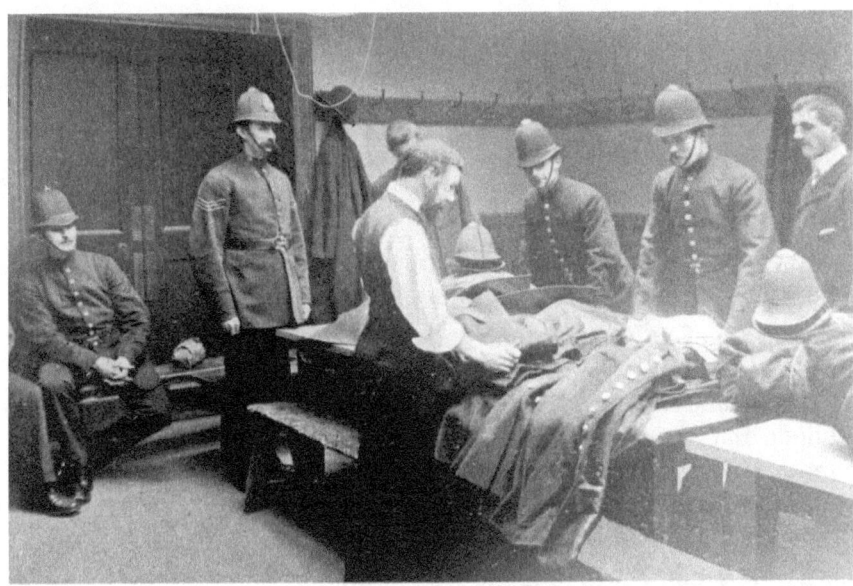

*New recruits being fitted for uniforms
from The Police Encyclopaedia by Hargrave L Adam*

The material of these was good, but they were poorly made and ill-fitting; no padding, and in some cases no lining either; so bad, in fact, that by holding the uniform to the light you could see between the seams.

And the boots! Convict-made, and instruments of torture. You were required to take them two sizes too large for you, in order to make room for the toes.

Can you wonder that a PC was known as "flatfoot"?[82]

Now drilled, uniformed and possessing a basic knowledge of the law, each recruit swore the Oath:

I swear that I will well and truly to the best of my knowledge and ability act as a Constable for the Metropolitan Police district and within the Royal Palaces of Her Majesty Queen Victoria and ten miles thereof for preserving the peace and preventing robberies and other felonies and apprehending offenders against the peace and that I will well and truly execute such office of Constable and all powers and duties which I may be authorised or required to execute by virtue on an Act of Parliament passed in the tenth year of the reign of His Majesty King George the seventh for improving the police in and near the Metropolis or by virtue of an Act of Parliament passed in the third year of the reign of Her

Majesty Queen Victoria for further improving the police in and near the Metropolis.

So help me God

Swanson was assigned to A Division (Whitehall). As well as the Division in which Scotland Yard was situated, many of the most important Branches were situated there.

A Division covered an area totalling 1.43 square miles, comprised of 3 superintendents, 35 inspectors, 96 sergeants and 414 constables.[83]

Under Chief Superintendent Robert Walker, A Division was where the likes of Frederick Adolphus Williamson, Richard Tanner, James Thomson and George Clarke of the Detective Department worked; William Harris, Timothy Cavanagh and Thomas Howe operated from Scotland Yard, and Inspectors Denning, Starr and Grant were based at King Street police station.[84]

As well as being the base for Police headquarters, the men assigned here were seen to be among the top recruits:

> It was found that in some of the worst districts, such as St. Giles and Covent Garden, the Division in charge could not always handle disturbances, through insufficiency of men. A Division... therefore became the 'general reserve' from which reinforcements could be sent out on special orders from the Commissioners. Because of this, there was a tendency to make A Division... into a corps d'elite, by seeing that it was composed of some of the best men in the force.[85]

In April 1868, Donald Swanson was given warrant number 50282 and sent to King Street station as Police Constable 331A.[86]

FOUR

Crimes, Fines and the Veiled Lady of Loughton

King Street, before being demolished in the late 1890s to make way for the widening of Parliament Street, ran south from the junction of Downing Street and Whitehall. The police station had been built in 1847 at 22 King Street, a large imposing building with a narrow frontage to King Street itself but extensive development to the rear.[1] One immediate neighbour was The Star and Garter public house, attendance at which may well have been the cause of misdemeanours by certain constables.[2]

The station reflected the importance of A Division, comprising 13 rooms including a charge room, offices for a Superintendent and two Inspectors, a library, living accommodation for two Inspectors and four Sergeants, stables for 16 horses with rooms for the groom, and a Section House accommodating 104 single officers.[3]

As an unmarried constable, Swanson was required to live in the Section House. A mess room, kitchen and washing facilities were located in the basement with scant light and fresh air; a library and recreation room was available on the ground floor, with a dormitory bedroom on the upper level.[4]

If Swanson was in any doubt that his new occupation carried the threat of great personal danger, he was to receive an immediate stark reminder. He had been at King Street for less than a fortnight and was no doubt still adjusting to his new lifestyle, when at 10.30pm on 7th May a "diminutive, wild looking" man was brought in and charged with breaking two beer glasses at another nearby public house, The Mitre and Dove. On hearing the charge, the man, a 32-year-old tailor named James Smith, shouted "Murder! Murder! They are after me!"

Although Smith seemed sober, the Divisional Surgeon examined him and recommended that he be carefully watched. Smith was placed in a cell and observed by Inspector David Baldwin.

In the early hours of the following day, Inspector Daniel Bradstock

King Street police station just prior to its demolition in 1899

arrived with P.C. Alex Brown to check on the prisoner. When Brown went to fetch water for Smith, the latter suddenly rushed at Bradstock, brandishing a large pair of scissors and shouting "I will kill you, I will kill you." The Inspector was stabbed twice in the neck and once on his right arm, and collapsed to the cell floor with blood gushing from a one inch-deep wound at the angle of his right jaw, saturating his tunic. He was immediately taken to Westminster Hospital.

Although Bradstock initially appeared to be making a good recovery, he died from his wounds on 2nd June. When Smith appeared at Bow Street Court on 11th June charged with the Inspector's murder, his statement that "for the last nine months snares have been laid for me, and I have been followed everywhere I went by men who wished to destroy me" led the jury to conclude that the prisoner was of unsound mind and unfit to plead. Smith was ordered to be detained in safe custody at Her Majesty's pleasure.[5]

Swanson joined the 400 other constables who patrolled A Division. By this time, the 6,708 miles of streets comprising the Metropolitan Police district were divided into 921 Day Beats and 3,126 smaller Night Beats.[6] Perhaps in recognition of the miles walked each shift, on 17th June 1868 an Order was given granting one day's leave per week, double the previous allowance of one day per fortnight.

A contemporary recalls his own first night on the beat:

> There was one street I didn't like the look of at all, neither were the odours emanating from it at all agreeable. However, police duty is police duty, and likes and dislikes had to be borne equally. The name of the thoroughfare alluded to was Ewer Street [in the Borough]... it was inhabited at the time by the lowest type of thieves and prostitutes, with a few Borough Market porters thrown in. I had gone over this ground two or three times, and [arrived at] The Pig and Whistle just before closing time. What a motley crew emerged therefrom as the gas was turned down and the shutters went up. Poor squalid creatures, men and women saturated up to the neck with what was termed "gin".

> Not one that came out of that hostelry had a decent appearance. All were more or less inebriated, the language made use of was something to remember, and as they rolled home, the ribaldry, horseplay etc was something appalling. They nearly all made for Ewer Street.

> Within half-an-hour (that was the time if took me to work my beat) I was in the street once more. As I entered it I could tell at once there was a tremendous row on at the farther end. I was about to quicken my steps,

when I found someone tugging at my coat-tails. It was [an old Irishman, who I had befriended earlier that night], who implored me for the love of St. Anthony to stay where I was or I would be murdered. Although I had a strong sense of duty, I had also a slight regard for my life, and yielding to the old man's persuasions I allowed him to gently draw me into the passage of his house, from whence I could see all that passed without being noticed. What tumult! Men and women skull-dragging each other all over the place; pokers, flat-irons, bellows etc in free use everywhere. Women pulling the hair out by the roots from others... and I certainly felt I was neglecting my duty by remaining in the passage of the chandler's shop, but, as the old chap said, "It will be all over in a minute," and as I could do nothing, I stayed where I was. He was right; the row collapsed as suddenly as it commenced, and had it not been for an odd skirt or two lying about, no one would have known that Ewer Street on that night had not worn its customary calm. I now began to feel I was somebody. Yes, I was a policeman and had seen service!

But the night was not over yet. I trudged round and round the beat with the greatest regularity until about three a.m., when feeling thoroughly tired, I sat down on a low window-ledge for a rest, and to ruminate my first night out. No one, not having gone through the ordeal, can possibly imagine the dreary work it is tramping about for eight long hours in such a filthy neighbourhood. There was nothing much worth recording after one o'clock, for by that time the streets belong to the police. A solitary wayfarer going home, or to work of some kind was all one met with; and nothing disturbed the stillness of the night except the steady tramp of the policeman, or the customary "all right" to the sergeant.[7]

Swanson seems to have found the strictness of the Met difficult to cope with in those early days. On 3rd October 1868, after six months' service, he was absent from the Section House and subsequently late for roll call, finally appearing 25 minutes later but out of uniform. He was subsequently fined for being in plain clothes without authorised leave, and further cautioned for being late.[8]

This didn't harm his progress, however, and three weeks later, on 24th October, he completed his probationary period and was advanced Third Class Police Constable.[9]

While the raw recruits were learning the ropes, at the top of the force a major change was coming.

Katherine Mayne, youngest daughter of Sir Richard, had suffered an enlarged spleen since April of 1868 and after six months of pain died of "exhaustion" on 28th September[10] at the family home Nuthurst Lodge, Horsham.[11]

The death of his 16-year-old daughter affected the Commissioner greatly. By now 72-years-old and becoming increasingly worn out through his work after 39 years in the role, Mayne developed an infection in an existing rheumatic hip-joint[12] and died of a pelvic abscess on Boxing Day 1868.[13]

The private funeral took place on 30th December. Following the hearse were three mourning coaches, in which travelled Mayne's sons Robert and William, along with Assistant Commissioners Labalmondière and Harris. They were met at Kensal Green cemetery by several hundred police officers.[14]

Assistant Commissioner Labalmondière was appointed as Acting Chief Commissioner while a replacement for Mayne was sought.

Plans for a memorial which required subscriptions from police officers (not to exceed one day's pay) was met with a muted response,[15] most likely due to Mayne becoming more remote from his men in the years before his death. A monument was eventually unveiled in Kensal Green cemetery on 25th January 1871, more than two years later.

Labalmondière lost no time exerting his particular area of expertise. Two days after his temporary promotion, he issued an order that Military Drill was to be resumed. Selected inspectors and sergeants were told to attend a series of instruction in drill at Wellington Barracks,[16] and it can be imagined that the officers were keen for a permanent Commissioner to be appointed.

This happened five weeks later on 5th February 1869, when Lieutenant-Colonel Edmund Y. W. Henderson was named as Mayne's successor.[17]

Born near Christchurch, Hampshire, Henderson was the perfect candidate given the debate following Mayne's death about whether the new Commissioner should be a military man or a civilian. Aged 47, he had served extensively with the Royal Engineers but since 1850 had been employed overseeing prisons, first in Australia and then from the Home Office. He was virtually unknown to the public, and therefore able to enter the position with an unblemished reputation.

Henderson immediately endeared himself to the force by relaxing some of the rigid rules set by Rowan and Mayne. One of the first orders issued by the new Commissioner, who boasted a fine set of whiskers, was to allow officers to wear facial hair, as long as it didn't obscure their collar number. It is easy to imagine the vast majority of the force

Lieutenant-Colonel Edmund Henderson
© *Illustrated London News Ltd/Mary Evans*

turning almost overnight from smooth-cheeked officers into an army of moustachioed law enforcers, and the 20-year-old Donald Swanson was no exception. For the rest of his life the Scotsman proudly sported a large moustache.

Henderson began a long battle to increase the wages of his men, initially achieving just 3 shillings extra per week for sergeants and 1 shilling for constables, but his efforts made him popular with his men, as did the Order allowing officers to wear plain clothes when off duty.

He established the fixed-point system, making his constables more available to the public, and also instituted the Commissioner's Report, an annual survey of crime statistics from each Division. The first report, for the year ended 31st December 1868, revealed that in those twelve months a total of 66,870 people had been apprehended, with a conviction rate of just 56%. More than half of these arrests were for drunkenness, assaults or petty larceny.

Just six people were taken into custody charged with murder, of whom three were acquitted. 56 were arrested for manslaughter, of which 39 cases were dismissed by magistrates. Of the remaining 17 trials, just nine people were convicted.[18]

Amongst the hundreds of cases of petty theft, the arrest by P.C. Swanson of a tailor named Jack Williams would reveal a sorry tale in the thief's domestic arrangements which would become all too familiar.

On investigating the tailor's background, Swanson discovered he was the common-law husband of Sarah Wyath. Wyath had left home at 16 to become the mistress of a Colonel at Southampton until she met Jack Williams two years later, and the couple absconded to London. Before long Williams forced Wyath to earn a living for them both through prostitution, at which point she adopted the name Agnes Williams.

'Agnes' next persuaded her younger sister, Mary Wyath, to move to London to join her in prostitution; Mary was introduced to "a dirty old Frenchman given to unnatural practices" and just a fortnight later was sent to the infamous Lock Hospital suffering from a "loathsome disease", never to be discharged.[19]

A friend of Agnes Williams named Julia Beauchamp, whom Swanson described as having been "sent to London by her family to learn millinery but obviously learned something else", sent for her own sister at the same time. Luckily, the young Emma Beauchamp was rescued from leading an immoral life by a young man from Balham who subsequently married her.

Agnes Williams continued prostitution for a further five years until she became so diseased that she was unable to work and, deserted by Jack Williams, became destitute. After a spell in St. James's Workhouse she went home to her parents and died a miserable death.[20]

Shortly after arresting Jack Williams, Swanson was assigned to assist a clergyman who had gone to King Street police station asking for help in locating his missing daughter, a young lady named Bella Hart. Swanson quickly ascertained that the 23-year-old Miss Hart had run away from the family home some three years earlier after her father had forbidden her to marry a young army officer of dubious character.

The father had recently discovered that his daughter was in London leading a party lifestyle and armed with her photograph, Swanson and the clergyman visited the Alhambra Music Hall, Leicester Square, and after several enquiries were directed to Walham Green, South West London where they found Miss Hart, who promptly fainted at the sight of her father.

It transpired that she was being kept in style by a young banker and despite her father's pleading, Miss Hart refused to return to the family home. The clergyman had no choice but to leave his daughter to the life she enjoyed. Less than two years later, however, she became infatuated with a Frenchman named Le Comte and the banker stopped her support. With no way of supporting herself other than prostitution, Bella Hart became a regular sight on Regent Street until she became riddled with disease and died in Lock Hospital shortly afterwards.[21]

Despite rapidly gaining experience in his first year as a Police Constable, Swanson continued to find the strict rules difficult to adhere to.

In April 1869 he was cautioned for accepting a shilling from a prisoner at King Street station in an attempt to procure bail. Although partially explaining his reasons, at a time when police corruption was commonplace Swanson had shown his naïvety. A year later he was again late for roll call and climbed over the Section House railings in an attempt to avoid being detected; the ruse failed and he was fined two shillings and again cautioned.

Swanson's policing skills had been noticed however, and less than a week after scaling the King Street railings he was advanced Second Class. Unusually, he was then advanced First Class (Special Duty) just eight days later.[22]

Around this time the Habitual Criminals Act was passed. Rudimentary records of criminals had previously been kept at Bow Street police station, and the new Act of 1869 created a single register of habitual criminals which recorded details of their physical appearance, the name of the prison in which a sentence was served, its length and date of discharge. Each convicted criminal was to be photographed. It was reported that at the time of the register's creation, some 4,336 people in London were known to the police.[23]

One of those undoubtedly recorded on the register was Edward 'Ned' Hines, alias 'Pudding'. Hines, described as 5ft 10in tall with a sallow complexion, dark hair and occasional dundreary whiskers,[24] was a career burglar and housebreaker who in 1870 attempted to rob George Attenborough, a pawnbroker in Fleet Street, with the notorious shutter-borer Tom Skinner and an accomplice named Thomas Hagerty. While Hines and a 26-year-old woman named Mary Ann Travers kept watch, Skinner bored small holes through the shutters in an attempt to steal two diamond necklaces worth £1,700 (£80,000 today). The bore holes were too small to extract the necklaces however, and the gang had to be content with gold chains worth £40 (£2,000).

While Tom Skinner escaped, Hines, Hagerty and Travers were traced by Swanson to an address in the City and arrested by Detective John

City of London Police record of Mary Ann Travers; 'Curly Poll'
Courtesy Amanda Harvey Purse

Carney; a file and length of bent wire were discovered at Mary Ann Travers' lodgings in Star Street, Commercial Road, which convinced Judge Carden that they had been used in the attempted robbery, and on 4th April 1870 each received three months' imprisonment.

After serving their sentences, Hines went to live in a brothel on Oxford Street and was later sentenced to seven years for highway robbery; Hagerty was apprehended again for housebreaking and sentenced to ten years, during which he died, and Mary Ann Travers (given the alias 'Curly Poll' by Swanson) became a prostitute patrolling the Minories and Tower of London area.[25]

Swanson's career continued to flourish. On 9th September 1870 he was transferred to North London's Y Division (Highgate)[26] and spent the next 15 months based at Kentish Town, a much smaller station than King Street, manned by fewer than 30 constables.

At the time of the 1871 census, taken on 2nd April, Swanson was recorded as staying with a cousin named John McDonald, south of the Thames at New Wellington Terrace, Kennington. McDonald, also a Scottish policeman, had two years earlier married a local girl and the couple had a year-old son at the time of Swanson's visit.[27]

In October of that year, a series of advertisements had trumpeted the reopening of Astley's Theatre on Westminster Bridge Road, Lambeth, under the management of Messrs. Sanger, managers of a travelling company of riders and gymnasts. The theatre, redecorated "in the most liberal fashion" and illuminated by some 200,000 gas jets, now took the form of a circus. The early part of each performance would commence with feats of gymnastics and horsemanship, with equine members of the troupe performing quadrilles, walking on their hind legs and kneeling to the audience.[28]

Reviews of the evening's opening night, on 21st October, were lacklustre, to say the least, most notably regarding a play written by one of the brothers, 'Lord' George Sanger. Entitled 'The Last of the Race, or The Warrior Women', the storyline revolved around a prolonged war between Afghanistan and Georgia, the mood of the play being lightened for the benefit of the audience by the inclusion of a character named Sadak, the proprietor of a performing monkey and a dancing bear. Unfortunately, the reviewer from the *Pall Mall Gazette* was less than impressed with the showman's performance:

> This comic personage boasts the name of Sadak, but his manners and conversation are rather of the East End than the East Indies.

The grand climax arrived just as the Prince of Georgia was about to be beheaded by an executioner, only for the city gates to suddenly burst open and the Warrior Women rode in to save the day. Again, the *Pall Mall Gazette*'s reporter could scarcely believe his eyes:

> Mounted Amazons in spangled armour gleam and prance about the stage, the ladies not being all of one mind, however, as to the advantages of the side-saddle.[29]

The *Standard* concurred, lamenting the absence of writer and producer George Sanger through 'sudden illness'.[30]

Precisely when Mr. Sanger had developed his sudden illness is unknown, but it was quite possibly related to his appearance the previous day at Clerkenwell Police Court before Mr. Barker, where he had been charged with putting on illegal plays in public without a licence the previous month while at the Winchester Music Hall, Islington, following a complaint from the Metropolitan Police.

Advertisements stated that admission was free, but that patrons must purchase a programme for 2d. On the night in question, between 300 and 400 people had attended and been made to buy a programme.[31]

The court heard how, as a result of a complaint, local Y Division officers Sergeant Frederick Abberline and P.C. Donald Swanson had been sent to the Winchester Hall in July, and the pair duly attended a performance in plain clothes, witnessing such delights as a farce entitled 'The Bellringer Who Had the Hump; or, the Mischievous Monk(ey) of Notre Dame'. Other performances included dancing and a cornet and harp player.

Whether the officers enjoyed the evening's entertainment is unknown, but also in attendance, observed by Abberline and Swanson, were several drunks, men of a 'doubtful character', and ladies of an 'immoral character' causing a nuisance to the public.[32]

Mr. Barker ordered Sanger to pay £5 5s, warning that should the impresario appear again in the future on a similar charge, he would be fined the full penalty of £10 for each occasion he offended.[33]

The two police officers returned to their duties, and would work together again in a case of a much higher profile case some seventeen years later.

Sergeant Frederick Abberline would soon be promoted Detective Inspector and transferred to H Division, Whitechapel.[34]

As for Donald Swanson, on 11th December, aged 23, he successfully passed his Sergeant examinations and was promoted Police Sergeant 71.

The following day he was sent to K Division (Bow) at the eastern perimeter of London, where he would remain for the next five years.[35] It was a move which would have positive repercussions both professionally and personally.

Among Swanson's first cases in K Division was a heartbreaking story of child neglect. Following complaints to police by neighbours, Swanson attended a house in North Street, Limehouse, with Mr. Neagle of the Stepney Union and discovered two young girls in an extremely emaciated condition. 8-year-old Clara Wheeler was found in a wretched state, lying in a box covered with rags. Her sister, 10-year-old Rose, was found elsewhere in the house in a similar condition.

The girls were children from the first marriage of wine porter Joseph Wheeler; his children with second wife Maria were found to be fat and healthy. Neighbours told Swanson they often saw Rose and Clara picking up potato peelings and crumbs from the street in an attempt to find nourishment.

Despite being severely malnourished, they were not suffering from any disease and were therefore taken immediately to Limehouse Workhouse to be properly cared for. It was reported that by the time of their parents' trial a few weeks later they had already gained weight after receiving proper food. The judge decided that Maria Wheeler was responsible for the girls' poor treatment, and she was sentenced to a fortnight in prison with hard labour.[36]

Tragedy would strike closer to home for Swanson when on 8th May 1873 his mother Mary died at the family home in Thurso aged 66, having suffered a chronic bowel complaint for the previous six weeks.[37]

In February the following year Swanson was fined yet again, after being seen standing outside The Lion public house in Carlton Square, Stepney Green, at midday with fellow officers Sergeants 22K and 70K with his armlet off while on duty. He was fined 5 shillings and severely reprimanded, it being recorded in Police Orders that he was not to be employed in any senior capacity for three months.[38]

It was to be the last time he would be cautioned.

On 3rd October 1874 he was appointed Station Sergeant at Plaistow, at the far eastern edge of K Division on Barking Road.[39] As the role carried some authority over an officer's peers, it was usual to appoint a Sergeant from a different station to avoid jealousy and insubordination.

It would seem to have been a temporary placement, for Swanson was back on the streets after a few months.

While his career was now seemingly on the rise after six years with the force, the Scot, by now 26-years-old, appears to have begun contemplating settling down. He entered into a fledgling romance with local girl Ruth Darby, which unfortunately failed to blossom.[40]

But he would not have long to wait before meeting his future wife.

It was common practice for policemen to get to know those who ran the public houses in their district, as these were meeting places for criminals and therefore a good source of information.

One of several pubs near Plaistow station was The British Lion, just over a mile away on West Ham Lane, where landlord James Nevill lived with his wife Sarah and their children Julia, James, William and Ada.[41]

The British Lion was used on many occasions as the venue for coroners' inquests, and Swanson would no doubt have attended to give evidence. Over the autumn of 1874, the 20-year-old Julia Ann Nevill caught the young Scotsman's eye. Blue-eyed with reddish-brown hair, Julia had been born at 30 Buttesland Street, Hoxton, on 10th January 1854.[42] She had been sent to a genteel boarding school,[43] and perhaps the combination of education and the family's brewing background struck a chord with Donald.

Father James Nevill had been born in West Hanningfield, a small village south of Chelmsford in Essex, and mother Sarah Ann Turney in Slapton, a Buckinghamshire village near Dunstable. The couple had been married on 20th October 1852 at Edlesborough, near the bride's home.[44] While Julia had been born in London's East End, her siblings had been born at Chelmsford, between 1857 and 1861, with James working as an innkeeper there.

The family moved to London at some point before the 1871 census, when they are recorded at The Marsh Gate public house, 66 High Street, West Ham.[45]

The happy family life of the Nevills was in stark contrast to that of a family some 3,500 miles away in Philadelphia whose youngest child, a four-year-old boy, was taken from outside his home in the well-to-do suburb of Germantown by two strangers on 1st July 1874.

Charley Brewster Ross was playing in the front yard of the family's house with five-year-old brother Walter when two men pulled up alongside the three-foot high wall of the yard in a horse-drawn black wagon. The passenger, a tall, dark man with a deformed nose, climbed down from the wagon and leapt over the wall. He asked the boys whether they would like some of the candy he held in his outstretched hand, which they were only too pleased to help themselves to.[46] Charley asked the man if he could take them to buy firecrackers, at which point the trio left the yard and climbed into the wagon, Walter sitting between the men and Charley on the passenger's lap.

Some minutes later the wagon stopped at a tobacco store on Richmond Street and the passenger gave Walter 25 cents to buy toys and candy.

When Walter came out of the store five minutes later the wagon, both men and Charley had disappeared. It was the first instance of kidnapping a child for ransom in America, and it shocked the world.[47]

When 36 hours had passed and the boy still missing, the family placed a notice in the *Philadelphia Public Ledger*:

> Lost – A SMALL BOY, ABOUT FOUR YEARS OF AGE, light complexion and light curly hair. A suitable reward will be given by returning him to E.L. JOYCE, Central Police Station.

Twenty-four hours later a second notice offered more information:

> 300$ REWARD WILL BE PAID to the person returned to No. 5 North

Sixth Street, a small Boy, having long, curly, flaxen hair, hazel eyes, clear, light-skinned round face, dressed in a brown linen suit with a short skirt, broad buttoned straw hat and laced shoes. This child was lost from Germantown on Wednesday afternoon. 1st lost, between 4 and 5 o'clock.

The following day Charley's father, Christian Ross, spent the morning at the offices of the *Ledger* to see if a reader would turn up with information. When this failed to happen he went to the Central police station, where as soon as he opened the door he was handed a letter, which he read aloud:

July 3 – Mr. Ros: be not uneasy you son charley bruster be all writ we is got him and no powers on earth can deliver him out of our hand. You wil have to pay us before you git him from us, and a big cent to. If you put the cops hunting for him you in only defeetin yu own end. We is got him put so no living power can gets him from us a live. If any approach is maid to his hidin place that is the signil for his instant annihilation. If you regard his lif puts no one to search fo him yu mony can fech him out alive an no other existing powers. Don't deceve yuself an think the detectives can git him from us for that is impossible. You hear from us in few day.

Two days later, on 6th July, he received another letter which spelled out the kidnappers' demands:

PHILADELPHIA, July 6 – Mr. Ros: We supos you got the other leter that ted yu we had yu child all saf an sond.

Yu mite ofer one $100,00 it would avale yu nothing. to be plaen with yu yu mite invoke al the powers of the universe and that cold not get yu child from us. we set god-man and devel at defiance to rest him ot of our hands. This is the lever that moved the rock that hides him from yu $20,000. not one doler les – impossible – impossible – you cannot get him without it. If yu love money more than child yu be its murderer not us for the money we will have if we don't from yu we be sure ti git it from some on els for we wil mak examples of yure child that others may be wiser. We give yu al the time yu want to consider wel wat yu be duing. Yu money or his lif we wil hav – don't flater yu self yu wil trap us under pretens of paying the ransom that be imposible – d'ont let the detectives mislede yu thay can git him and arrest us to – if yu set the detectives in search for him as we told yu befor they only serch for his lif. you wil see yu child dead or alive if we get yu mony yu get him live if no money yu get him ded. wen you get ready to bisnes with us advertise the folering in Ledger personals (Ros. we be ready to negociate). we look for yu answer

Charley Ross
from *The Father's Story of Charley Ross, the Kidnapped Child*

in Ledger.

When details of the demands emerged, City Officials realised the difficult position they were in. $20,000 was an enormous sum,[48] with the President of the United States being paid an annual salary just $5,000 more. Furthermore, Philadelphia had been selected to host the forthcoming Centennial celebrations, with City planners hoping visitors to the event would pour money into the coffers. Who would visit if they feared kidnappers might snatch their children?

In fact, Christian Ross was worried by this potential outcome. As much as he wanted the safe return of his son, he feared being the catalyst for future copycat abductions. Despite his concerns, he agreed to negotiate with the kidnappers.

Over the following weeks and months the family exchanged letters and notices in various newspapers while the Police Department tried to trace the kidnappers, along with the Pinkerton Detective Agency, who had been hired. In the meantime, sightings of Charley came from all over America and as far overseas as Scotland, Germany and Cuba.

A reward of $5,000 was offered to anyone giving information which lead to the discovery of the boy. Unsurprisingly, the unscrupulous attempted to claim the money with clearly fabricated information and presenting children disguised as Charley Ross.[49]

On 14th December 1874, six months after Charley had been taken, two men were shot during an attempted burglary in Philadelphia. One, who said his name was Joseph Douglas, was close to death when he confessed to bystanders that he had helped to steal Charley Ross. The mastermind behind the kidnapping, he claimed, was the other burglar, a man with a distinctively-shaped nose named Bill Mosher. It was Mosher, said Douglas, who knew where the boy was kept. But Mosher had died of his wounds.

With the kidnappers unable to reveal the location of his son, Christian Ross was forced to endure the uncertainty of not knowing whether his son was dead or alive, and if the latter, where he may be.

Over the years which followed, people around the world continued to claim to have seen Charley. Amidst this frenzy of sightings, a strange woman arrived in Loughton, in the Metropolitan Police's K Division, with a young boy whom she never let far from her side. Her bearing showed she was of superior character but she kept herself away from the community, and her face had not been seen by anybody at Loughton due to the thick veils and a headscarf she always wore, both outside and indoors, carefully arranged so as to completely conceal her face.

The curiosity of the local gossips was naturally excited and all sorts of rumours were passed on. When the young boy told a neighbour his name was Ross, the news spread that he was the missing Charley. A letter giving an exaggerated account was sent to Commissioner Henderson, who put the matter in the hands of K Division's Sergeant Swanson.

After several enquiries, Swanson discovered that the woman's father was a retired clergyman living in Margaret Street, off London's Oxford Street, and after befriending her a painful story was revealed.

Known in Loughton as Mrs. Ross, her name was actually Miss Rhodes, a highly educated young lady aged 24 from a well-respected family of Lewes, near Brighton.

She had been seduced at seventeen by a young clergyman, which resulted in the birth out of wedlock of the boy, named George. The young clergyman subsequently married a close friend of Miss Rhodes, who was completely unaware of the illicit liaison.

At this point Miss Rhodes retired from society and led a secluded life, staying at any one place only until the community became too inquisitive and she moved on, forming no new friendships and excluding herself from her old life.

When asked by Swanson why she lived this lonely existence, she replied:

> I do it for two reasons – first that my dear friend, the wife of the father of my child, may not know of my sin; secondly to expiate any sin and nothing possible can ever induce me to re-enter society. I feel as if a brand were on my face marking me as a sinner.[50]

While feeling great pity for the young woman, the detective was concerned for her mental wellbeing:

> She appeared to be perfectly rational and was certainly well informed but I am of the opinion she suffers from a hallucination in supposing that the veils hide her from the world, and that she has many enemies around her.[51]

The mystery of the Veiled Lady of Loughton might have been solved, but Charley Ross was never seen again.[52]

FIVE

The Lady Vanishes

All was well as a porter named Brewer carried out his duties cleaning the exhibition rooms at Thomas Agnew and Sons, an art gallery at 39 Old Bond Street in London's Mayfair. It was just after closing on the evening of Thursday, 25th May 1876.

Brewer visited each room, sweeping the floors and checking the contents were secure.

Hanging in an upstairs room of its own was *The Duchess of Devonshire* by Thomas Gainsborough. It was, at that moment in time, the most famous painting in the world. Measuring 59 inches by 45 inches, the portrait was considered Gainsborough's finest. It showed a young woman of extraordinary beauty turned three-quarters towards the artist, holding a pink rose in one hand and a bud in the other. Her expression was one of mischievous coyness, with a half-smile playing on her lips. She wore an ivory dress with a blue silk petticoat and sash, with an enormous black broad-brimmed hat on her head.

Around eight o'clock two men arrived at the gallery to deliver a large table. Brewer instructed his young daughter to watch the shop door while he helped to move the table to an upstairs room. With the job done, the porter locked and bolted the door, putting the key into his pocket before settling into his quarters at the rear of the building for the night.

Shortly before seven o'clock the following morning Brewer rose to begin reopening the gallery, when he noticed that one of the front door locks had been sprung, and the bolt, while still in position, had been raised. Initially thinking that he had made a mistake the previous evening and failed to lock the door properly, Brewer continued on his rounds of the gallery.

As he entered the Gainsborough room he immediately saw that *The Duchess of Devonshire* was gone, its empty frame hanging in its customary position but the canvas cut out. Its stretcher was resting against the wall, beneath the frame.[1] The single window in the room, opposite the painting and overlooking Old Bond Street, was half-open.

Brewer went to fetch the gallery's owner, William Agnew, while his wife sent an errand boy to Scotland Yard. The police arrived shortly before eight o'clock in the form of Inspector John Meiklejohn of Scotland Yard's Detective Department and officers from nearby Vine Street station. Taking statements from every employee, Meiklejohn initially came to the conclusion that the thief had entered the premises during opening hours, or while the table was being delivered, and secreted himself until Brewer and his family were asleep. The Inspector suggested that the thief's plan had been to leave through the street door, but, being unable to open the mortice lock with the key still in Brewer's pocket, he had been compelled to exit via the window in the Gainsborough room.

A closer examination, however, revealed chisel marks on the window frame outside the premises, indicating that the thief had entered the same way he exited.[2]

The missing portrait had been painted by Gainsborough between 1785 and 1787. Its subject was Georgiana Spencer, the 32-year-old wife of William Cavendish, the 5th Duke of Devonshire. Considered a great beauty of the day, Georgiana was equally as famous for her lifestyle as for her looks, much like her great-great-great-great niece Diana, Princess of Wales. Married to Cavendish on her seventeenth birthday, Georgiana went on to give birth to four children (three by her husband in addition to an illegitimate daughter by Earl Grey, later Prime Minister). She indulged in numerous affairs and introduced her husband to her closest friend, Lady Elizabeth Foster, whereupon the three lived together openly for 25 years in a *ménage-a-trois* before Georgiana died of an abscess of the liver in 1805, aged 48, at which point Cavendish married Elizabeth Foster.[3] Throughout her short life Georgiana was internationally famous, adored and reviled in equal measure.

Upon completion, Gainsborough's portrait had been exhibited at the Royal Academy before being hung at the family seat, Chatsworth House. It was subsequently lost for several years before being discovered in the 1830s in the home of Anne Maginnis, an elderly schoolmistress, who had cut it down from the original full length portrait to a half-portrait in order to fit above her fireplace.[4] The painting was sold to art dealer John Bentley for £56, who gifted it to his friend the collector Wynn Ellis, to be added to his magnificent collection.

The extent of the Ellis collection only became apparent after his death several years later, when it was sold in 1876 in three portions. The first, at the King Street, St. James's Square, premises of Christie, Manson and Woods[5] on Saturday 6th May, saw a total of 135 paintings disposed of, including seventeen by Reynolds, thirteen by Turner and twelve by Gainsborough. When *The Duchess of Devonshire* was placed gently on the easel a burst of applause broke out, with the auctioneer Thomas J. Woods remarking that it was the finest portrait ever seen in that room. Bidding rose through hundreds and thousands of pounds, until the hammer came down on a winning bid of £10,605[6] from William Agnew. It was an incredible sum for the period, the highest ever paid for a picture at auction, and represented a third of the auction's total sales of £32,300.[7]

The painting was put on display in Agnew's gallery a few days later, where from ten in the morning to six in the evening the public could view it, provided they paid the admission fee of one shilling. It was reported that between 200 and 300 people had visited every day.[8]

It was soon announced that Samuel Cousins R.A. had been appointed to produce an engraving of the picture, with proofs issued to subscribers at ten guineas each, and more than £1,000 had already been received.[9] Whether Cousins got a chance to begin work before the painting was stolen is unknown, but almost immediately printers produced a *carte-de-visite* bearing an engraved likeness of *The Duchess of Devonshire*, which could be "hand-coloured after the original" if required. Not missing a trick, the caption was swiftly changed to "the Stolen Duchess of Devonshire" after the theft.

Accusations and excuses soon followed. A resident of New Bond Street wrote to *The Times*, complaining

> On Saturday evening about three weeks ago I wanted to see the policeman on duty, and for that purpose waited at my door from 11.37 until 12.29, a period of 52 minutes, before I saw a constable, and it is impossible for me to say when he did pass prior to this time, but even 52 minutes is quite sufficient time for any amount of booty to be disposed of by well-trained robbers.[10]

The usual watchman at Agnew's gallery, Charles Langham, shifted blame from himself to an unnamed deputy by claiming to have been off duty on the night in question. A retired policeman, Langham pointed out that he was employed as a private watchman by subscribers to a fund, and expressed little sympathy for Agnew, who was not a member of the fund and therefore

> could not feel aggrieved at the loss of his property through the negligence (if there had been any) of the private watchman.[11]

Carte-de-visite of the "Stolen Duchess"
Author's collection

In desperation, Agnew offered a reward of £1,000[12] for the recovery of the painting and the conviction of the thieves. Unsurprisingly, this led to a spate of false sightings, including one as far away as Vienna and what proved to be a copy of the painting in nearby Bedford Square.[13]

A rag-and-bone man almost landed the Leeds-based artist Wells Smith in hot water after going through his rubbish and finding a scrap of paper bearing the words "What a nerve you must have had to collar the Gainsborough. What are you going to do with it?" After lengthy questioning, Smith managed to convince the Leeds detectives that the note had been sent by a friend as a joke, which he had thrown away and forgotten about.[14]

Music hall performers embraced the public's interest in the painting, putting on acts such as Fred Foster's *The Great Impersonation of the "Missing Duchess of Devonshire; or, Another Good Picture Gone Wrong"*, written by Walter Burnot and featuring a facsimile costume by Madame Dolman,[15] and 'Brooklyn', the so-called Leading Female Impersonator, appearing as *The Duchess of Devonshire* every evening at the Northumberland Theatre.[16]

Scotland Yard had reached a complete dead end, but for the officer placed in charge of the investigation, Inspector Meiklejohn, far worse was to come in the months that followed.

Despite frequent rumours of its whereabouts, *The Duchess of Devonshire* was not to be seen again in public for a quarter of a century.

While Donald Swanson would be instrumental in the painting's eventual recovery, as we shall see, at the time it was stolen he was still in K Division and on a beat which took him across a bridge on the River Lea where a blind man regularly stood soliciting alms. Swanson got into the habit of chatting with the man, and one day lent him half a crown towards paying his rent.

This act of kindness was to be repaid, for the blind man told Swanson that a gang of men, two of whom had already served time and were known to the police, were meeting the following evening at a nearby public house to finalise plans of a robbery.

Swanson reported this information to his superior at Plaistow station and was instructed to visit the pub in plain clothes and monitor events. This led to his being taken off ordinary duty and over several weeks he uncovered a larger network of criminals, who were eventually arrested on a number of charges.[17]

Perhaps this different style of policing appealed to him, or maybe his superior officers recognised his talent, but either way Swanson applied to join the Detective Department. He had just turned 28-years-old and had served nine years as a uniformed officer.

The Detective Department had been formed in 1842, although Commissioner Richard Mayne had recognised some years earlier that detection was a specialised skill and not something which every police constable could undertake.

These methods of detection had been displayed in cases such as the murder of Eliza Davis in May 1837, investigated by Inspector Aggs and P.C. Pegler, and the investigation by Inspector Field and P.C. Charles Goff into the May 1838 murder of prostitute Eliza Grimwood,[18] on whom it has been claimed Dickens based the character of Nancy in *Oliver Twist*.[19]

Two years later, Inspector Nicholas Pearce and Sergeant Frederick Shaw, investigating the high-profile murder of Lord Russell in his bed on 5th May 1840, used detective methods to discover silver and jewellery hidden by the murderer, François Courvoisier, leading to his arrest.

It was the search for a murderer on the run in April 1842, however, which finally confirmed the need for a specially-trained detective force.

Around 8.30pm on Wednesday, 6th April, a middle-aged Irishman named Daniel Good drove up to the door of Mr. Collingbourn, a pawnbroker of High Street, Wandsworth, in a four-wheeled pony chaise belonging to his master, Quelez Shiell of Granard Lodge, Putney Heath.

He asked to look at a pair of black knee-breeches and, being known to the pawnbroker, was allowed to take them and pay at a later date. As he left the shop Good was spotted taking a second pair of black trousers from the counter and concealing them under his greatcoat by a boy employed by Collingbourn named Dagnell,[20] and on leaving the shop place them under the cushion of a seat on the chaise on which a young boy was sitting.

Dagnell told Collingbourn, who ran to the door and calmly asked Good if he had "made a mistake", to which Good replied not and drove off.

Collingbourn immediately reported the theft to the police and P.C. William Gardner, accompanied by Dagnell and a young man named Robert Speed who was employed by Mr. Cooper, a neighbouring grocer, went to Granard Lodge, where Good had been employed for at least two years as coachman.

On reaching the lodge they were directed to the stables, where P.C. Gardner told Good he was under arrest for the theft of the trousers, which the Irishman still disputed. Gardner failed to locate the stolen garment anywhere on the chaise, so began searching the stables. As the policeman approached a stable on the south eastern side, Good suddenly stood between the policeman and the door, exclaiming that they had better return at once to Wandsworth to settle the matter. Hearing the commotion, John Houghton, Mr. Shiell's bailiff and gardener who had a residence near the stables, appeared and asked what was going on; the group went into the stable and began searching the stalls and hay-racks.

On searching the fourth stall at the far end of the stable Gardner uncovered what he at first took to be a dead pig, shouting 'Good God! What's this?" At that moment Good ran from the stable and locked the group inside.

Unable to break open the door with a pitchfork, Gardner began to examine the object. Clearing the straw with which it had been hidden, they discovered it to be the trunk of a woman, lying on its front, with the abdomen cut open and entrails removed and missing. The stable door was eventually forced open and Dagnell was dispatched to the police station, returning with P.C.s Hayter and Tye. While Hayter searched the immediate vicinity for Good, Tye rode to Wandsworth station to inform them of the murder. Superintendent Bicknell and Inspector Busain both attended the scene along with Divisional Surgeon Mr. Shillito and his assistant Alfred Allen.

In the harness room they discovered a number of human bones in the fireplace, which proved to be a skull, thigh bone, an arm and fingers. Given the only light was from P.C. Gardner's lamp, it was decided to return to the scene to search in daylight.

The following morning Sergeant Samuel Palmer examined the scene in greater detail and discovered a large quantity of blood and a mattress, sheets and a blanket in one of the stalls. Inspector Busain discovered a large carpenter's axe and a nine-inch long knife.

Sergeant Palmer, examining the area outside the stables, discovered a broken paling on a high wooden fence and footprints in the field beyond which were heading in the direction of Putney.

At Good's lodgings they discovered a 10-year-old boy, who said he was Good's son and also named Daniel. He had for some time been living at 18 South Street, Manchester Square, until nine days previously when his father had taken him to Putney. The boy described a young woman who had lived with him at South Street and who had been very friendly with Good. His father came to the house to fetch the woman the day before returning for his son.[21]

So began the search for Good, and also the identity of the victim.

A wanted poster was quickly produced by the police, outlining the murder and providing a description of Good:

ONE HUNDRED POUNDS
REWARD
WILFUL MURDER

DANIEL GOOD

Stands charged with the Wilful Murder of a Female at Putney (whose Name is at present unknown). He is an Irishman, about 46 Years of Age, 5 Feet 6 Inches high, very dark sallow complexion, long thin features, and dark piercing Eyes: he is bald at the top of his Head, and combs his

Daniel Good
from Illustrated London News, 21st May 1842

Hair from each side over the bald part. He walks upright, and when he absconded was dressed in a Dark Great Coat, Drab Breeches and Gaiters, and Black Hat, but is supposed since to have changed his Dress.[22]

Enquiries soon revealed that Good had been seen with several women not only in Putney, but also in nearby Roehampton and Wimbledon. More recently, he had been seen with one particular woman, and less than a week before the supposed murder the couple had been seen showing off an engagement ring at the Spotted Horse in Roehampton.[23]

Mrs. Jane Brown, who owned the house at 18 South Street at which Daniel Good Jr. lived, said the woman who also lived there was known to her as Jane Jones. She was a "neat" woman about 5 feet 2 inches tall. She and the boy had lodged in the house for two years, and after six months Jane had told her that she had married the boy's father, Daniel Good Snr, who would visit the house three or four times a week. Jane left the house alone on Sunday, 3rd April, and when Good arrived the following morning he informed Mrs. Brown that his 'wife' had been offered a position keeping rooms at a gentleman's house and would not be returning. He was there to collect her things.[24]

Investigations revealed that Good had been courting 16-year-old Susan Butcher,[25] and it was she who had been seen with the missing Irishman in the weeks preceding the discovery of the body. Susan was visited by Good at her home at 13 Charlotte Place, Woolwich, on 6th April and given bags and other items, and told that they had belonged to Good's deceased wife.[26]

Good was besotted with Susan, proposing marriage on more than one occasion. A week before the murder she spent the night at the stables, with Good providing the mattress and blankets but himself sleeping in his quarters.

The motive was clear: Good had murdered Jane in order to be with Susan. Discovering his whereabouts, however, was not proving so easy to ascertain. The police were inundated almost hourly with letters and visitors to numerous stations around London, all offering information and leads on false sightings which wasted valuable time. The newspapers gleefully reported the inability of the police to find the Irishman, while the public became unnecessarily frightened the longer the fugitive remained at large.

Good was finally arrested on 16th April when Thomas Rose, a former police officer from Roehampton, recognised him working as a bricklayer's mate. Good had first fled to the home of his first wife Mary Good, known as 'Old Molly", at 4 Flower and Dean Street, Spitalfields,[27] and then to a niece at Rotherhithe, before ending up on a building site in Tunbridge Wells working for George Steers.[28] He was tried at Bow Street court and hanged outside Newgate Gaol on 23rd May 1842 in front of one of the largest crowds seen at an execution, many arriving the evening before and spending the night sleeping on the pavements and in nearby alleys in order to obtain a good view. The *Morning Advertiser* recorded Good's final moments:

> The tolling of the chapel bell, the reading of the selected portions of the funeral service, and the indistinctly heard shouting of the mob without, altogether combined to produce a most solemn and impressive effect. He bore up against all the circumstances with extraordinary fortitude.
>
> On mounting the scaffold, however, he looked more dead than alive, and quailed before the execrations of the populace. While the rope was being adjusted, his nether jaw actually fell as that of a dead man; but when the cap was being drawn over his face, he with an effort closed his mouth. The signal was then given that all was ready, and the executioner stepped down and raised the lever, the floor fell from under the culprit's feet, and

the next minute he had ceased to exist.²⁹

The bungled search for the murderer during his ten days on the run, with nine police divisions acting almost independently on the case, highlighted the need for a specialised body of officers who could catch criminals as opposed to simply preventing crime, as the Metropolitan Police was at that time trained to do.³⁰

On 14th June 1842, just three weeks after the execution of Daniel Good, the Commissioners wrote a memorandum to the Home Office suggesting the formation of a Detective Department. Three days later followed a list of the men they wished to appoint.

The two inspectors were Nicholas Pearce, a former Bow Street Runner³¹ but now of A Division who had shown a detective's instinct when investigating the murder of Robert Westwood in Princes Street, Soho, on 4th June 1839³² and that of Lord Russell a year later,³³ and John Haynes of P Division, a specialist in horse-theft who had successful tracked twelve stolen 180lb boxes of silk handkerchiefs from Canterbury to London in December 1840 by analysing the capabilities of horses.

Six sergeants were appointed: Sergeant Braddick of F Division; Sergeant William Gerrett of A Division, who had assisted Inspector Pearce in the hunt for Daniel Good; and P.C. Charles Goff, L Division, who had shown promise during the investigation into the murder of Eliza Grimwood in May 1838.³⁴ Joining these were Sergeant Frederick Shaw of E Division, who had worked with Pearce in the Lord Russell case; Sergeant Stephen Thornton, who in July 1841 arrested three London-based thieves in Liverpool armed with a minimum of information and a liberal use of detective instinct; and finally P.C. Jonathan Whicher, perhaps the most famous of the early detectives, who had only joined the Metropolitan Police in 1837 but had already shown great detective skills in identifying a young woman who had stolen a number of items from her former employer, a respectable lady in the West End. Whicher, investigating a crime in a brothel near Gray's Inn, recognised a feather boa around the neck of Sophia Westwood as one described in the list of stolen items circulated two days earlier and arrested Miss Westwood on an instinct which proved correct; the thief was found guilty and transported.³⁵

With this small number of officers, the Detective Department came into being on 15th August 1842.³⁶

The personnel would change over the years as these detectives retired and others appointed. Over the next 20 years, Shaw and

Frederick Adolphus Williamson in 1876
Courtesy Metropolitan and City Police Orphans Fund

Whicher became Inspectors, and important detectives such as George Clarke, William Palmer and Richard Tanner had joined the Department, along with a young constable named Frederick Adolphus Williamson. It was Sergeant "Dolly" Williamson who accompanied Whicher to Road, Wiltshire, in 1860 to investigate the murder of four-year-old Francis Kent. Whicher, by now known as the Prince of Detectives, believed the child to have been murdered by his 16-year-old sister Constance, but saw his reputation severely damaged when he had her arrested and charged only for the case to be thrown out over his lack of evidence.[37]

Whicher became increasingly depressed and retired in 1864, but his protégé, Dolly Williamson survived and ironically was the inspector who heard Constance Kent's confession to the murder the following year.[38]

Williamson was popular with senior officers and lower ranks alike. Despite becoming increasingly serious natured following the fall of his mentor Whicher, Williamson was kind and approachable, and would rise to the position of Superintendent of the Detective Department by the time Donald Swanson applied to join.

He had been born in Hammersmith in 1830, the son of a Superintendent of T Division, and joined the Metropolitan Police in 1850. His ambition extended beyond his working life, spending his evenings learning French from a tutor near Leicester Square,[39] and later learning German.[40]

One of Williamson's Chief Inspectors, John Littlechild, remembered his superior with affection:

> Strangers, when they entered his office, were apt to form the impression that he was heavy and unimpressionable; but they soon changed their opinion, for, no matter the intricacy of the case submitted to him, he immediately gripped its points, and required but ten words of explanation when others asked for fifty. He was always most courteous, and he had the faculty of inspiring confidence in the most timid – a rare qualification in a police-officer in these days.
>
> Williamson was full of dry humour, which frequently came out in the anecdotes he enjoyed telling. One day, he used to say, he was in Brompton Cemetery, attending the funeral of one of the old officers. Having seen his subordinate placed in his final resting place, the day being fine, he walked among the graves almost aimlessly, noting the inscriptions on the tombstones and in a reflective mood generally, when he came upon a labourer doing up a grave. The man, though advanced in years, was tall and well set up, and Mr. Williamson, fancying that he recognised him as an old pensioner, said to him as their eyes met:
>
> "Halloa! Don't I know you? Weren't you in the police force once?"
>
> "No," said the man. "Thank God I have never sunk so low as that yet."[41]

On 12th September 1876, Donald Swanson successfully completed his entrance examinations to the Detective Department, by this time comprising 30 detectives, and was appointed Detective Sergeant. Three days he later he was transferred back to A Division, based at Scotland Yard.[42] His uniformed days were behind him.

Just two weeks after Swanson joined the Department a solicitor from the firm Abrahams and Roffey visited Superintendent Williamson at Scotland Yard.[43] Michael Abrahams expressed complaints from his client, a rich French widow named Comtesse Marie Cecile de Goncourt, that she had been the victim of a gang of London-based fraudsters who had swindled her out of the not-inconsiderable sum of £10,000.[44] It was the first of a chain of events which would bring disgrace to the Detective Branch and many who worked within it.

SIX

Fall of the Detectives

Frauds connected to horseracing were common, and had been throughout the 1870s. Where people were gambling money in the hope of winning more, they often became gullible and therefore easy targets for swindlers. A common scam was to set up a company called "The Systematic Insurance Company" or similar, advertising a system guaranteeing that a person couldn't lose. Circulars would be sent inviting people to send a small amount of money to a particular address, for which they received a receipt. After a few weeks and nothing more being heard, the complainant would find that the offices of the Systematic Insurance Company had closed and the fraudsters vanished, along with the victim's money.

The scam with which the Comtesse de Goncourt had been fooled was more complex. She had received by post a copy of a sporting newspaper called *The Sport and Racing Chronicle*, which carried an article describing how a commission agent named Montgomery had become so successful at backing horses at British race tracks that bookmakers had joined forces to limit their losses. The article claimed that Montgomery's only available option was to seek agents on the Continent who could place bets on his behalf. A covering letter in French explained that should the Comtesse agree to become one of Montgomery's agents, she would be paid 5% commission on all winning bets, expected to be 5,000-6,000 francs per week. She would also have the opportunity to place some of her own money on Montgomery's selections. The Comtesse replied to say she was interested, and happy with the arrangements.[1]

A few days later she received a letter from Montgomery personally, enclosing a selection for a forthcoming race and a cheque for £200 drawn against the Royal Bank of London, pre-signed by a George Simpson. Also included was the name and address of a bookmaker, Charles Jackson, to whom the cheque should be sent and the bet made. The Comtesse duly sent these to the bookmakers.

A few days later she received correspondence from Charles Jackson telling her that the selection had won, and enclosed a sizeable cheque which she forwarded to Montgomery, who duly replied with a cheque representing the Comtesse's commission. He explained that the cheque, again drawn on the Royal Bank of London, could not be presented for a certain time period due to English banking laws.

Soon Montgomery wrote with another selection, sending a cheque for £1,000 and instructions to send it to a different bookmaker named Jacob Francis. Once again the horse won, and again the Comtesse received a commission cheque drawn on the Royal Bank of London.

Encouraged by Montgomery's seemingly foolproof system, the Comtesse decided to bet some of her own money on his selections. First she sent a cheque for £1,000, and was delighted when the horse won and she received her winnings in the form of a cheque drawn on the Royal Bank of London. On the next occasion she sent a cheque for £9,000, which again resulted in a winning selection. She wrote to Montgomery to inform him of her good fortune, and he replied to congratulate her before confiding that he had a tip on a forthcoming race on which he suggested she placed a bet of £20,000. The Comtesse, eager to continue her winning streak, approached her bankers to release the money.

It was at this moment that the penny dropped. The Comtesse's bank, suspicious the scheme was fraudulent, told her to contact her lawyer Monsieur Chavances, who in turn contacted Abrahams and Roffey in London. It was no surprise to learn there was no such institution as the Royal Bank of London, and the cheques held by the Comtesse – for which she had parted with £10,000 – were worthless.

Following the meeting with Michael Abrahams in September, Dolly Williamson put the case in the hands of Chief Inspector Nathaniel Druscovich, who visited 8 Northumberland Street, the address given in correspondence with the Comtesse de Goncourt. The rented offices were deserted, but the landlord was able to give physical descriptions of four tenants. Warrants were issued for the arrest of 'Andrew Montgomery', 'Jacob Francis' and 'Charles Jackson', plus two others known as 'Thomas Ellerton' and 'Richard Gregory'.

Progress in catching the swindlers was inexplicably slow, given the experience of Chief Inspector Druscovich and his colleagues Chief Inspector William Palmer and Inspector John Meiklejohn, who only a few months earlier had failed to find any clue as to the theft of Gainsborough's *Duchess of Devonshire*.

Eventually, almost in spite of the detective's efforts rather than because of them, the identities of the Turf Fraud gang were slowly revealed. First, in mid-November, 'Jacob Francis' was identified as

Henry Benson, a criminal well known to the police.[2]

Then on 27th November another member, Edwin Murray,[3] was arrested by Det. Sergeant Littlechild and Det. Sergeant George Robson on the Strand.

Five days later Benson, Frederick Kurr[4] and Charles Bale[5] were arrested by the Rotterdam police, who telegraphed Scotland Yard. Only William Kurr[6] remained at liberty, and he almost used his freedom to help his colleagues by sending a telegram to the Rotterdam police pretending to be Superintendent Williamson. The request that the three prisoners be released was not heeded.

There had been several unaccountable delays, the reasons for which would soon become apparent, but the majority of the Turf Fraud gang were now captured.

Det. Sergeant Donald Swanson, not involved in the hunt, was at that time investigating a brutal attack on a woman in the early hours of 23rd December. P.C. David Pankhurst of N Division had discovered her slumped in the doorway of The Duke of Cambridge public house on Essex Street, City Road. The woman, though bleeding profusely, was alive and Pankhurst asked her what had happened, to which she replied "Someone has stabbed me in the back." On closer examination the constable saw that the woman also had a wound to her throat and was bleeding from an injury to her wrist.

She was admitted to hospital at 2.30am by Frederick Eve, the house surgeon, who ascertained that the deep incised wound to her throat had been made from right to left, and that she had also suffered six stab wounds between her shoulder blades caused by a knife with a blade an inch wide. Further stab wounds were found on her left hand.

Detectives Swanson and Low were sent to assist local Inspector Thomas Brady of Islington station. They discovered that the woman was a 40-year-old prostitute named Hannah Thompson, widow of a corkcutter and presently living at a lodging house on Golden Lane in the City.

She had been seen walking along City Road at ten to one in the morning by P.C. Thomas Johnson, who then noticed a man walking towards him across the bridge. When the man reached the corner of Macklesbury Street he approached Johnson and asked for a light, which the policeman refused. The man then crossed the road and spoke to Hannah Thompson, the two walking off arm in arm.

Johnson described the man as 5 feet 6 or 7 inches tall with a ruddy complexion, a moustache and tuft, and wearing dark clothes with a soft billycock hat. He had the air of a seafaring man.

When Swanson, Low and Brady arrived at the hospital around midday, Thompson was in a very poor state. Swanson bent down to her bed and said "You are very bad; don't you believe you are dying?" to which she weakly replied "Yes".

Swanson then took her statement, which gave an alternate version of how she came to be with the man, probably to avoid admitting she was a prostitute:

> I, Hannah Thompson, believing myself to be dying, make the following statement: That this is the truth, and nothing but the truth: I was walking along the City Road, when I noticed a man following me; he overtook and addressed me. I would not have anything to say to him; he then knocked me down with his fist, making my nose bleed. When I became conscious again, I found the blood trickling from the wound in my back. I did not feel the knife. I never saw the man before. He was about 5ft 5in, in dark clothes. I thought he had a 'cheese-cutter' hat. I cannot tell if he was dark or fair, or had any hair on his face.

Swanson then made her mark for her, with Hannah Thompson weakly holding the pen. Within hours an arrest was made, but Thompson failed to recognise the man. She died shortly afterwards.[7]

It would not be the last time in Swanson's career that the brutal murder of a prostitute would remain unsolved.

William Kurr, the last of the Turf Fraud gang at liberty, was finally captured a week after Hannah Thompson's death, on 31st December, by Det. Sergeant John Littlechild, who gave a thrilling description:

> About seven pm our man left his house with two of his pals. It was then quite dark, and the three men walked at a quick pace. We had to make after them at a lively rate, and, hearing us in pursuit, the trio turned into a very dark road and quickened their speed, improving their lead.
>
> Owing to the darkness we were not absolutely sure of our man, but we recognised his form and build.
>
> "Now then, run," presently cried one of the men with him.
>
> At this signal off started our man, and I ran after him; but I was suddenly seized round the body by a big fellow – the man who had given the warning – and he put his foot behind me to give me a nasty fall, but I

skipped over his foot and freed myself with a great effort from his grasp.

I held in my hand a heavy blackthorn, and without waiting I brought it down heavily upon his head. The blow caught the brim of his hat and sent it flying like a shuttlecock, and its owner reeled on one side and I dashed ahead.

Away my colleague and I pelted after the other men, who had profited by these few moments' delay, and in chase of a few hundred yards we overtook the man for whose arrest I held a warrant.

He turned at bay, and his right hand moved towards his hip pocket for his revolver, which he whipped out.

I seized the weapon and shouted "For Heaven's sake, don't make a fool of yourself; it means murder!"

"I won't," said he, and released his hold of the revolver.[8]

The following day, New Year's Day 1877, Kurr appeared at Marlborough Street police court. Sitting in the court's public gallery was Harry Stenning, the man who had assaulted Littlechild; when the detective related the incident he was ordered to arrest Stenning, who on being searched was revealed to have prepared a plan of the cells at the court, with an escape route. Stenning was later tried for obstructing a constable and plotting an escape, and was sentenced to a year's imprisonment.

On 12th January, Benson, Bale and Frederick Kurr returned to London from Rotterdam by steamer, accompanied by Chief Inspector Druscovich.

Det. Sergeant Swanson's investigations also saw him travelling. On 29th January he sailed to Dublin to track boxes stolen from two sisters, the Misses Thompson, by Kate O'Brien in London in 1875, and found they had been pledged to a pawnbroker. Swanson communicated with solicitors Seymour Scott & Co. of Dawson Street, but due to the 'awkwardness' of the lawyer in his dealings with the pawnbroker the detective was unable to reclaim the property itself, having to settle for recovering £80 of the £100 value in monies. He returned to London on 2nd February[9] to receive a reward of £2 from the Commissioner.[10]

Six days later Swanson arrested the spiritualist Dr. Monck,[11] and then immediately began investigating a case of fraud against the Pharmaceutical Society, who had received an anonymous letter stating that candidates were using fraudulent means to pass their stringent entrance examinations.

The Society contacted Scotland Yard, who assigned Swanson to the case. He quickly ascertained that a recent candidate, John Colegrove, of College Street, Liverpool, had applied to sit the Society's preliminary examination at Cambridge but in fact his place was taken by a young clerk of the Post Office Savings Bank at St. Paul's named Andrew Ritchie Hunter.[12]

Colegrove, a chemist's assistant, was concerned about the preliminary examination, which tested a candidate's knowledge of English, Latin and Grammar, and approached a colleague named Hinks[13] who put him in touch with Ritchie Hunter, who agreed to sit the examination in return for £10. The highly educated Ritchie Hunter was well known to falsely sit examinations. He wrote to the Society as Colegrove asking to be examined, and on 2nd October 1876 travelled to Cambridge from London for the test after sending a letter to his employers to say he was too ill to work. He arrived late and out of breath, complaining that the train from Liverpool had been running behind schedule.[14]

He was allowed to sit the examination and a few days later wrote asking for his results; he had passed, and Colegrove himself sat the second examination, on medicine, in London in December.[15]

At a result of the anonymous tip off, the Pharmaceutical Society passed the letters written by Ritchie Hunter to Det. Sergeant Swanson, who at once saw that the handwriting matched the sickness letter sent to the Post Office Savings Bank by Ritchie Hunter, and arrested him there on 16th February 1877. Ritchie Hunter and Colegrove, arrested the following day, were taken before the Secretary of the Pharmaceutical Society, Mr. Brembridge, who recognised Ritchie Hunter but not Colegrove.[16] They were both sentenced to six months imprisonment.[17]

The following month, Swanson was called to the premises of James Greenwood, a leather merchant of 44 Packington Street, Islington. Greenwood had been burgled during the night by a gang who had stolen property worth £150 and removed it by means of a horse and cart. Having been informed that the gang intended to return, Swanson persuaded Greenwood to hire a nightwatchman, and left instructions that the merchant was to contact Swanson and the Islington police the moment the gang were spotted.

At one o'clock in the morning of 29th March, the newly-appointed nightwatchman, Stephen Helier, heard a noise as though someone was attempting to break open the side door. Instead of calling for the police as directed, Helier called for Greenwood and the merchant pulled open the door, thrusting out a handsaw. The terrified burglar, George Mitchell, dropped his jemmy and the rest of the gang sped off in the horse and cart, leaving Mitchell to be arrested by a passing constable.

The following day Swanson attended Mitchell's court appearance. He saw a woman at the back listening very anxiously and at intervals stepping quietly out of the court. Feeling sure that the rest of the gang were nearby, Swanson took Greenwood and a uniformed constable with him as they followed the woman through a few streets to a quiet public house.

Swanson followed the woman inside and spotted Edward Lowe and Frederick Anderson, two expert burglars known to the detective. Directing Greenwood to go to the opposite end of the bar, Swanson stood between him and the thieves, with the constable guarding the door. Conversing as though nothing was wrong, he persuaded them to take a drink and in doing so moved out of the way, exposing them to the view of Greenwood, who at once jumped up and shouted "these are two of the scoundrels who broke into my house!"

Swanson succeeded in taking Lowe and Anderson quietly into custody, and they stood trial with Mitchell for the burglary. On receiving 18 months' hard labour they jumped up and began fighting in the dock, loudly blaming each other and Mitchell, while swearing at each other and the Judge, who remarked: "Gentlemen of the jury, these men pretended they knew nothing of the burglary before they were found guilty but now they know all, which justifies your verdict and the sentence of the court. During the many years I have sat here I have never witnessed such an occurrence."

Another of the gang, a burglar named Watson, escaped to Bristol and returned to London three months after the trial, only to be apprehended two hours after arriving at Paddington station. He too was sentenced to 18 months.[18]

A fortnight later the Turf Fraud trial began at the Old Bailey, running for eleven days. Montagu Williams Q.C., representing Murray, described them:

> Benson, who was unmistakably a Jew, was of a very different stamp from his associates. He was a short, dapper, well-made little man. In the calendar he was described as being twenty-six years of age, but he had the appearance of being somewhat older. It was clear that he was a man of good education. His hands and feet were remarkably small, and he was dressed well, and in perfectly good taste, which is more than can be said of the majority of those who make their appearance in the dock at the Central Criminal Court. Benson has charming manners and it transpired in the course of the trial that, during his sojourn in the Isle of Wight, and other places, he had moved in the very best society. There could be no

doubt whatever that Benson's had been the master-mind in a long series of frauds.

William Kurr, the culprit next in importance, was described as being twenty-three years of age. In appearance he was more like a well-to-do farmer than anything else. I am under the impression that, before he became acquainted with Benson, he had been a publican. His face wore an honest expression; but it does not always do to judge by appearances. I think that both in ability and craft he ran Benson very close.

My client Murray, whose age was stated to be thirty-two, was described as a clerk, and looked that part exactly. He, too, was scrupulously well-dressed, and I could not help feeling that, if he had really been a clerk, and an honest one, his services would have commanded a handsome salary. It was he who had conducted the correspondence, or the principal part of it, and done most of the draftsman's work.

The other two prisoners, Bale and Frederick Kurr, were mere nonentities, having been tools in the hands of their more astute confederates.[19]

The Comtesse de Goncourt travelled from Paris to give evidence, and the majority of the press were unsympathetic:

We feel quite humbled in spirit just now, for we have discovered that if a prize for gullibility should be offered for competition it will not be won by the English after all. We had always thought that is the one quality we surpassed our French neighbours, whatever their superiority in other things might be. But it was left to Madame la Marquese de Goncourt of the Chateau de Goncourt, in the Department of the Marne, to exhibit our deficiency in this respect.[20]

Others attending court appreciated the Comtesse's other attributes:

I am deeply touched by Mr. Knox's gallantry to Madame de Goncourt, the victim of the Great Turf Swindle. When the Bible was put into Madame de Goncourt's hands to kiss, after the usual form and procedure in English courts of law, she could not be persuaded to take off her glove or lift up her veil. Mr. Knox chivalrously waived this objection, and to the intense horror of the officials, permitted Madame de Goncourt to perform her osculations on the book after her own fashion. Madame is a pretty woman, and was so elegantly dressed that I do not wonder that Mr. Knox should have shown her so much consideration. I have before pointed out what an effect a becoming *toilette* has upon police magistrates, and if madame had been ten years younger, I firmly believe Mr. Knox would have dispensed with the oath altogether. As one looked at this pretty and fashionably dressed Parisiênne one wondered what could ever have induced her to go in for the bookmaking business.[21]

On 23rd April all five defendants were found guilty and awarded custodial sentences: Benson fifteen years; William Kurr, Frederick Kurr and Charles Bale ten years each; and Edwin Murray, found guilty of being an accessory after the fact, eighteen months.

The following day Benson wrote to Treasury Solicitor Sir Augustus Stephenson from his cell in Pentonville Prison. Although suspected for several months, the reasons the gang had evaded capture for so long would soon become clear.

On 9th May Stephenson's assistant, William Pollard, visited Benson at Pentonville in the first of six meetings; William Kurr was also questioned. It transpired that the two swindlers had hatched a plan to seek remission in their sentences by revealing that several officers of Scotland Yard's Detective Department had been in their pay.

The information given by Benson and Kurr, added to the evidence uncovered by Dolly Williamson, was enough for Treasury Solicitor Sir Augustus Stephenson to write a confidential memorandum to the Home Secretary stating there was "no doubt of the complicity of Meiklejohn and Palmer", but was unsure whether the detectives had committed an indictable offence or should simply be dismissed from the force without trial.[22]

Further investigation soon uncovered the extent of the corruption.

Detective Inspector John Meiklejohn had been receiving money from William Kurr since 1873 in return for information which allowed the latter to continue running fraudulent schemes and avoid arrest. On the first occasion, Meiklejohn was paid £100 to close enquiries on a bogus betting company called Philip Gardner & Co., which was run by Kurr. The following year the detective warned Kurr that a swindle being operated in Glasgow was about to investigated, and received £500 for his trouble. Meiklejohn purchased a house on the South Lambeth Road, which his colleagues no doubt wondered how he could afford on a salary of £225.[23]

In April 1876 Nathaniel Druscovich found himself in serious financial difficulties. His rise to Detective Chief Inspector had been swift not only because of his knowledge of languages, but also because of his intelligence and energy in his work. His downfall came after guaranteeing a bill for his brother, and finding himself confronted with a demand for £60 began to panic. He confided in Meiklejohn, who introduced him to William Kurr. Druscovich received the £60 with no conditions, but he was now in Kurr's pocket. A few months later the criminal asked the detective to let him know should any warrants be applied for in relation to a new betting office; in return he would receive £25. Initially Druscovich refused to take the money, saying he was already in Kurr's debt for the £60, but the notes were thrust into the detective's hand.

When Superintendent Williamson went on holiday following his meeting with Michael Abrahams he had placed the case in the hands of Chief Inspector Druscovich, who almost immediately warned Kurr. Over the coming months Druscovich, Meiklejohn and Palmer leaked details of the investigation to Kurr, who thus managed to stay at least one step ahead. Chief Inspector William Palmer informed Kurr that Williamson was away, and Chief Inspector George Clarke was in charge of the Department. The fraudsters stepped up their efforts to corrupt Clarke.

It was only when Dolly Williamson returned from his holiday to find very little progress that he became suspicious. Druscovich was told to visit The Queen's Hotel in The Bridge of Allan, near Edinburgh, where some of the gang were believed to have stayed. In fact Benson and Kurr were there, and had dined with Meiklejohn. Warning letters were sent, but the gang had already fled.

Druscovich, with no choice but to carry out the work expected of him, collected the letters and returned on 17th November. On reading them, Williamson exclaimed: "This is Palmer's writing!"

His subsequent investigations were conducted in private, instructing Det. Sergeant Littlechild to trace and arrest Kurr, but to carry out his enquiries in the utmost secrecy, from even his colleagues.

On 11th July warrants were issued for the arrests of Chief Inspector Druscovich, Chief Inspector Palmer, Inspector Meiklejohn and a corrupt solicitor named Edward Froggatt, who had been engaged by Kurr. The following day Dolly Williamson arrested the detectives, while Chief Inspector George Clarke arrested the solicitor. The quartet were charged with conspiring to defeat the ends of justice, and on 19th July appeared at Bow Street police court for the committal hearings. It was a complete reversal of the usual state of affairs: the defendants were senior police officers, and the key witnesses convicted criminals. The hearing lasted for two months, with the name of Chief Inspector George Clarke coming up several times in evidence, seemingly implicating him in the corruption scandal. By the beginning of September it was decided to include Clarke in the charges, and he was arrested on 8th

September by his old friend Dolly Williamson. Also under suspicion, but not charged, was Det. Sergeant Charles von Tornow.

It was clear that whatever the outcome of the trial, the Detective Department could no longer exist in its present form, but needed completely restructuring. On 18th October 1877 Commissioner Henderson published an Order announcing the creation of a Department of Crime, to be directed by a civilian, James Davis, a former magistrate from Sheffield who had been appointed legal advisor to the Commissioner in December 1873.[24]

The move was announced in the newspapers shortly afterwards:

> The Press Association states that Mr. [Home] Secretary Cross has given instructions for a thorough re-construction of the Scotland Yard department. It is understood that in future the title of "detective" shall be abandoned, and that the London officers of that ilk shall be known as "Officers of the Department of Crime". Mr. J. E. Davis, who for a considerable time was stipendiary magistrate of Sheffield, and who was afterwards promoted to the office of consulting advisor to the London police magistrates, is to be the head of this Crime Department. To him all undetected cases are to be reported, and with him ulterior proceedings will rest.[25]

Despite the furore over the scandal, police work still had to continue. The day after Henderson's announcement Swanson finally managed to arrest a notorious forger and robber known by the name 'Captain George', long wanted both in England and on the Continent.

After a long criminal career which included stealing railway bonds from Russia, Treasury bonds from Austria and France, and also escaping prison while awaiting execution for the murder of a policeman, on 1st June 1877 the 43-year-old Frenchman had pulled off his most daring crime to date.

Captain George, working with two English criminals named Charles Martin and John Carr, boarded an express train travelling between Calais and Paris and carrying several thousand pounds worth of bonds. Carr pretended to be an invalid and the trio were placed in the carriage next to the bullion van, the lights of which the 'carers' requested be extinguished as the 'invalid' could not bear the brightness.[26] On arrival at Paris the guard discovered that the locks on the bullion van had been substituted for dummies, and that the three men, 'invalid' included, had absconded with £70,000[27] worth of bonds belonging to Messrs H. L. Raphael and Sons and Messrs Louis Cohen and Co., brokers of

Throgmorton Street.

It was quickly ascertained that the gang were in London. Swanson had reason to believe that Captain George would visit a fence named Jacobson in Oxford Street and watched the property. Presently the Frenchman appeared and Swanson followed him to New Bond Street, accompanied by Det. Sergeant Frederick Shaw, where he arrested him. Captain George struggled violently, but the detectives managed to overcome him and place him in a nearby cab, whereupon

> he became violent and attempted to strike Shaw. I seized his right hand and Shaw his left. He then said "I'll show you my name," and while I still had hold of the sleeve of his greatcoat he pulled a small envelope from his breast coat-pocket [which probably contained the address where the bonds could be found]. He bent his head down and put it in his mouth. We tried to get it out of his mouth. We got two pieces; the remainder he swallowed. He was very violent, and when in Regent Street he became so violent that we had to appeal to a plain-clothes policeman. The prisoner was taken to Scotland Yard.[28]

At the committal hearing at Mansion House the next day, 20th October, Captain George gave his name as Charles Hibbert, staying at the Norfolk Hotel, Paddington. Alderman Sir Robert Carden heard that the prisoner was wanted on the Continent for a string of crimes under various names in addition to 'Captain George', including John Henry Frere, George Noble, Muller, Giraud and 'The Admiral'.

Leopold Jocus, Chief of the Detective Department in Paris, appeared to state that the prisoner had previously been arrested in the name of Captain George for producing forged bonds. Another detective of the Paris police, Malen M. Nichols, stated that he had arrested the prisoner in February 1873 under the name of George Noble.

Despite there being no doubt that Captain George had committed the robbery, he was acquitted because the offence had been committed outside the jurisdiction of the Central Criminal Court.[29]

The so-called Trial of the Detectives opened a few days later on 24th October and continued for three weeks. On Tuesday, 20th November, the jury return guilty verdicts on Meiklejohn, Druscovich, Palmer and Froggatt. Each was sentenced to two years' imprisonment with hard labour.

George Clarke was found not guilty, but had become a political embarrassment and would be forced to take early retirement by the Home Secretary.[30]

*William Kurr takes the stand during the Trial of the Detectives
from The Illustrated London News, 3rd November 1877*

They had disgraced the Metropolitan Police force, and Dolly Williamson was crushed. In his annual report at the end of the year he wrote hopefully:

> The conviction of two Chief Inspectors and an Inspector at the Central Criminal Court... was a most deplorable event, but as it occurred under very exceptional circumstances, I trust that such an occurrence will never again take place.[31]

Steps had already been taken to ensure that Williamson would be correct. By the time the shamed detectives finished their sentences, the detective branch was very different.[32]

SEVEN

Mrs. Swanson and the C.I.D.

Commissioner Edmund Henderson was under no illusion that he needed to act quickly and decisively to restore confidence in the detective branch. His report for the year 1877 was stark:

> The reorganisation of the Detective Department was rendered necessary during the year, consequent on the conviction of three of the principal officers for more or less complicity in an extensive case of turf fraud and, subsequent to the period for which this report is compiled, a committee appointed by the Secretary of State for the Home Department has made a careful investigation into the whole question of crime. In accordance with their recommendations, the Detective Department has been entirely reorganised.[1]

The first small step in this reorganisation did not get off to a good start. The new head, James Davis, took up his duties in November 1877 and immediately annoyed the Home Office by submitting an estimate for £119 for the furnishing of his office with mahogany bookcases and a pair of curtains. The Home Office responded that it was of the opinion that "neat bookshelves in grained wood with leather edgings to the shelves will be amply sufficient... it is unusual to provide curtains for rooms used for official purposes."[2]

The Department of Crime was announced as provisional, and Davis' appointment was in the first instance to ensure that offences reported were correctly designated, thereby streamlining the process.[3]

Davis' legal expertise may have helped shape the new detective branch, but when an independent report suggesting a completely different structure was submitted to the Home Secretary, his days were numbered.

Davis' replacement was announced on 6th March 1878:

> Department of Crime: Appointment. The Secretary of State for the Home Department has appointed Mr. C. E. Howard Vincent to be Director of

Criminal Investigations in the Metropolitan Police.[4]

Approaching his 29th birthday, Charles Edward Howard Vincent was a barrister who had been called to the Bar in 1876 after being educated at Westminster School and then the Royal Military College at Sandhurst, and serving a total of eight years in the military. During this time he became war correspondent for the *Daily Telegraph*, travelling through France, Germany, Austria and Russia.

When Home Secretary Richard Cross had appointed a committee to investigate the reorganisation of the Detective Department, Vincent saw an opportunity for himself. Having knowledge of police methods on the Continent, he travelled to Paris and drafted an exhaustive report on the organisation of the Sûreté – the French detective system – with the assistance of the Préfet and his officers, eventually producing eighteen drafts before submitting his report to the committee together with testimonials from numerous legal acquaintances including Attorney-General Sir John Holker, Sir J. Marle Q.C. and Mr. Overend Q.C., the latter two actually sitting on the Departmental Committee.

Vincent was invited to the Home Office, where he met Under-Secretary Sir Henry Selwyn Ibbetson. He was appointed on a salary of £1,000 a year.

The new Director of Criminal Investigations was responsible to the Home Office, but his officers were ruled by the Commissioner.[5]

The interim name "Department of Crime" was not to last long; its permanent successor was announced on Saturday, 6th April 1878:

> Criminal Investigation Department: From Monday next, April 8th, the whole of the detective establishment will form one body under the Director of Criminal Investigation. With the exception of the undermentioned officers, promoted or appointed to responsible posts, the present staff will be placed on probation for three months.[6]

Of the officers remaining from the old Detective Department, only Dolly Williamson (appointed Chief Superintendent) and John Shore (appointed Chief Inspector) were not placed on probation; everyone else had to show they could be trusted following the scandal of the previous year.

Whereas the old Detective Department had consisted of 30 detectives of various ranks all based at Scotland Yard, the new structure meant a Central Office at Scotland Yard consisting of one Chief Superintendent, three Chief Inspectors, three First Class Inspectors and 17 Second Class Inspectors, with a clerical staff of four Sergeants and two Constables.

Charles Edward Howard Vincent
from The Illustrated London News, 13th October 1881

Across the divisions, there would also be 14 local Detective Inspectors, one in each division, and a combined force of 159 Detective Sergeants. Local Inspectors promoted at this time included Abberline (H Division), O'Callaghan (N Division) and Hagen (X Division).[7]

In Central Office, 13 of the 20 Inspectors were promoted almost immediately, but the remaining three positions, and those of the two vacant Chief Inspector roles, took some time to fill as suitable, trustworthy men had to be located and examined. In fact, Det. Chief Inspector Shore shouldered the work of his rank alone for three years.

Shore, who had joined the Metropolitan Police in 1859, was a policeman of the old school. His copper's instincts were described by a future head of the C.I.D.:

> ...when any important crime of a certain kind occurred, and I set myself to investigate it *a la* Sherlock Holmes, [Chief Inspector Shore] used to

listen to me in the way that so many people listen to sermons in church; and when I was done he would stolidly announce that the crime was the work of A, B, C, or D, naming some of his stock heroes. Though a keen and shrewd officer, the man was unimaginative, and I thus accounted for the facts that his list was always brief, and that the same names came up repeatedly. It was "Old Carr," or "Wirth," or "Sausage," or "Shrimps," or "Quiet Joe," or "Red Bob," etc, one name or another being put forward according to the kind of crime I was investigating.

It was easy to test my subordinate's statements... and I soon found that he was generally right. Great crimes are the work of great criminals, and great criminals are very few.[8]

Detective work did not simply stop while these changes were being implemented, and the week in which the creation of the C.I.D. was announced Swanson was actively investigating a case of three cheques stolen from the Cutlers' Company. He was called in by the Company's secretary, a solicitor named William Beaumont of Messrs Beaumont and Son, 23 Lincoln's Inn Fields, and on 1st April interviewed Charles Wang, whose name was on the cheques when cashed. The detective ascertained that these had originally been stolen by an associate of Wang's named Clement Allen, a clerk employed by Beaumont for the previous four years and who had since disappeared. Wang and Allen had been in partnership relating to the invention of a toy called 'the Wheel of Beauty'. Beaumont had never met Wang, but with Swanson went to another solicitor specialising in criminal law and it was decided to charge him with simply larceny,[9] with the trial set for the following month.

The year 1878 marked Swanson serving ten years with the Metropolitan Police, and it was proving to be a period of almost unbroken joy in the Scotsman's personal life.

On 23rd May he and Julia were married at her Parish Church in West Ham after four years of courtship. He was 29-years-old, the bride 24. The ceremony was conducted by Thomas Scott, Vicar of West Ham, and witnessed by Julia's parents James and Sarah Ann Nevill, along with her sister Ada, cousin Tryphena Gadsden and friend Sarah Brittain.[10]

The happy couple were presented with gifts including a silver tea service, kitchenware and a baby's crib. Donald presented his new wife with a pair of gold earrings.[11]

It may seem remarkable that, judging by the marriage certificate and gift list, none of Swanson's own family attended the wedding, although perhaps the distance from Caithness was prohibitive.

There was no time for a honeymoon; four days later Swanson was required at court to give evidence in the Charles Wang case. The court heard that William Beaumont had countersigned cheques on behalf of the Cutlers' Company and handed these to his clerk, the missing Clement Allen, for payment to three suppliers: one made out to a Frederick Sawyer for £206 15s 2d, the second to Messrs Ring and Brymer for £260 4s 6d, and finally a cheque made out to Messrs Thomas and Sons to the value of £37 19s 6d. None of these cheques were paid to the contractors; instead, Allen gave them to Wang, with instructions to cash them. This he did, approaching a friend named David Samuels (to whom Wang owed £8) and bankers William Young and Frederick Orchard, who duly cashed them. Mr. Beaumont had since settled the outstanding debts with the three suppliers from his own account. The judge was unsure as to whether Wang had been aware that what he was doing on Allen's behalf was illegal, and directed the jury to find the defendant not guilty.[12]

Swanson was furious. His investigation had revealed that Wang had a long history of theft, having stolen goods from his father and absconded to America, becoming a sailor for four years and returning to London once his father had died. Swanson firmly believed that Clement Allen had been induced by Wang to commit embezzlement, the latter taking less of a risk but enjoying more than half the proceeds, and commented in his private memoranda:

> Clement Allen: There is nothing particular in this man's career, except that he fell into the hands of a confirmed vagabond named Charles Wang at whose instigation he obtained upwards of £2,000 by means of forging his master's name.

> However absurd it may seem the judge directed the jury to find Wang not guilty in face of the evidence, that he knew that Allen was only a clerk, that he got a friend to cash the forged cheques, that portion of the proceeds went for his own use. These facts were not denied and could not be.[13]

While Swanson may have felt that Clement Allen had been used by Wang, there was still a warrant out for his arrest, and the investigation had to continue.

The happy times continued in Swanson's personal life. Previously living at the section house connected to King Street police station, as a married man Swanson was now able to take private accommodation and the couple move to a rented home at 1 Grove Cottages, Trigon Road in Kennington, where they would remain for the next four years.[14] The couple wasted no time starting a family: within three months Julia discovered she was pregnant.

Around the same time, on 6th July, Swanson was promoted Second Class Detective Inspector on a salary of £150 per annum along with contemporaries including Walter Andrews, Henry Marshall and Thomas Roots.[15]

It was part of the raft of appointments to the new Criminal Investigation Department; these men, handpicked for their ability and integrity, were tasked with restoring the reputation of the detective branch.

The following month, several of his new colleagues presented Swanson with a large photograph album to mark his marriage, with an illustrated plate reading:

> Presented to Donald S. Swanson on his marriage by the undernamed of his Brother Officers as a token of their esteem and desire for his happiness. August 5th 1878.[16]

Later that month Swanson appeared at Bow Street Magistrates' Court at the committal hearing of William Virtue, a writer at the Treasury who had made a foolhardy attempt at forging receipts for witness expense payments using the initials of William Pollard, the Assistant Treasury Solicitor who had been instrumental in bringing to trial Meiklejohn, Druscovich, Palmer and Clarke. Virtue, who had been employed at the Treasury for a year, had taken the forged receipts to Walter Greenway Rider, Clerk of the Department of the Solicitor of the Treasury, whose job it was to cash witness expense claims. William Pollard confirmed that the initials 'W. H. P.' on eight receipts relating to the Regina v King case were not in his hand, and that these witnesses did not even exist. Another receipt had been presented for Regina v Couch, a fictitious case. Swanson described how he arrested Virtue and told him he would be charged with forging and presenting a receipt for £2 10s in the name of one Thomas Gill. On 17th September Virtue was sentenced to six months' imprisonment.[17]

Swanson ended the year in court as witness to a different case of illegal activity relating to horse racing, when he appeared to give evidence at the trial of Mrs. Bannell, landlady of the Blue Posts Tavern on Rupert Street. She had been accused of wilfully permitting the pub to be used for the purposes of betting, and a customer named Elkins summoned for using the house for the purpose of betting. Swanson stated that as a result of complaints he had visited the Blue Posts from time to time and often heard conversations about betting and horse racing, but he had not witnessed any bets being made. On 16th October, P.C. Owen entered the tavern at three o'clock in the afternoon in plain clothes and saw several people talking about betting. He asked a man the price of a horse named Greenback and was told he could have "one point below the newspaper quotation." The landlady's daughter read out the prices from the newspaper, and the man offered P.C. Owen 10/1, at which point the constable put 5s on the counter, which the man took up and put in his pocket. The following week Owen went to the Blue Posts and made another bet, this time with Elkins on a horse called Macbeth. Mr. Abrahams, defending, said that Mrs. Bannell did all she could to conduct the Blue Posts properly but it was an impossible to prevent betting men entering for refreshment, given its close proximity to the Haymarket. Magistrate Mr. Flowers dismissed both summonses, stating that he believed the police to be correct but warned Mrs. Bannell to be cautious.[18]

It would prove to be a mixed start to the New Year. On 25th February 1879, Julia gave birth at home to the Swansons' first child, a son, whom they named Donald Nevill Swanson. Blue-eyed like his mother, the boy was registered by his father on 4th April,[19] the delay caused by the detective being abroad in March apprehending Clement Allen, the forger who had been named in the 'Wheel of Beauty' fraud case a year earlier.

Missing since Charles Wang had been arrested, Swanson had ascertained that the 34-year-old Allen had fled to the safety of Tangier, which had no extradition agreement, and was staying there at the Alhambra Hotel under the name of Louis Dearden.[20]

Keeping watch on Allen from London with the help of local police, Swanson learned that he had gone to Gibraltar on a day trip and at once telegraphed the Gibraltar force, who arrested the forger and held him until Swanson arrived to return him to London.

Tragically, during this voyage his father died at the family home in Durness Street, Thurso. John Swanson had been suffering from dropsy for two months, and succumbed to heart disease on 31st March. The death was reported by daughter Margaret on 5th April, the day after Donald Nevill's birth was registered.[21]

The loss of his father, just three years after the death of his mother, would have hit Swanson hard. He had been raised in a loving family environment, and in many ways his upbringing in Caithness had shaped his character. Not for the first nor last time, Swanson's work would help with his grieving.

Clement Allen's committal hearing took place just days later at Bow Street.[22] He was charged with embezzling the Cutlers' Company of a total of £2,500. He pleaded guilty and was committed for trial on 31st April. Allen, described as "gentlemanly-looking", had been trusted completely by his employers and it had proved a shock to them that he had appropriated not only the three cheques described at the trial of Charles Wang twelve months earlier, but another from the Midland Railway Company. This cheque, to the value of £493 15s representing rent due from the Midland Railway to the Cutlers' Company, was never accounted for by Allen, who forged the signature of his employer William Beaumont and paid it into his own account with the London and County Bank, Southwark branch. Swanson appeared at court to confirm how he had traced Allen to Tangier. Having pleaded guilty to the charges, the only question was as to the length of sentence. Mr. Gerald Geoghegan Q.C., representing Allen, pleaded that his client had resorted to forgery after a series of disastrous investments on the Stock Exchange and that he had a wife and children who depended upon him. Given the nature of the offence, and the fact that Allen had seen fit to abscond to Africa for a year, the judge was in no mood for leniency and sentenced him to seven years' penal servitude.[23]

Months later Swanson was sent to Toronto to trace a criminal which ultimately came to nothing, but while there he was instrumental in the apprehension of the notorious bank robber Charles Bullard, known to criminals and detectives alike as 'Piano Charley' due to his prodigious musical ability.[24] Ironically, but unknown to Swanson, Piano Charley had for many years been a close confidante of the man who had stolen the Gainsborough painting, but at the time of its theft was serving 20 years in Concord State Penitentiary, Massachusetts, for a robbery at Boylston Bank in 1869. Orchestrating a riot on 12th September 1878, Charley had been placed in a holding cell to which he had previously fitted keys and the next morning it was discovered he had escaped. By 1879 making his way to Toronto, Charley resorted to petty crime and was spotted by Swanson on King Street West with an English travelling thief named Logan. The Scottish detective pointed out the crooks to the Toronto police and after two days' surveillance they were arrested when Piano Charley attempted to rob a jeweller's shop. The pair were sentenced to five years at the Canadian Penitentiary.[25]

The year ended with another overseas trip for Swanson. It began when James Bishop, a 20-year-old watchmaker, attended the offices of Bell and Company at 18 Ironmaker Lane in order to claim money owing to him after several cheques paid by the owners had proved to be forgeries. On arrival, Bishop found a notice on the door saying "Will return at five p.m." When this hour passed with no sign of the owners, the office doors were forced open to reveal a room with every last stick of furniture removed, completely bare except for a few cigars left on a window sill.

Bishop went to the police. He said he had been dealing with a man named Henry Pollard and his partner named Ford. Between July and September the pair had obtained goods to the value of £3,000 by false pretences.

Pollard had written to Bishop claiming to be detained in Southampton on business and would meet the creditor on the following Wednesday, an appointment which was not kept, resulting in Bishop's visit to the Ironmaker Lane offices. Swanson and Det. Inspector Thomas Roots ascertained that Pollard had instead absconded to Buenos Aires, knowing that no extradition treaty was in place between England and Argentina.

This wasn't the end of the matter; happy to seek co-operation from other authorities, Swanson asked the Home Office to intervene and they contacted the Argentine government with the result that Pollard was removed to Lisbon, where an extradition agreement with Britain *did* exist. He was there apprehended by English detectives. Swanson then travelled to Bordeaux, where he took the prisoner into custody aboard the SS *Sorata*. Pollard was returned to London and remanded for trial.[26]

EIGHT

The Duchess and the Showgirl

The decade which saw Donald Swanson's reputation established began on an odd note, with the Detective Inspector spending nine days off work over February 1880 with a sprained ankle.[1]

Hobbling back on duty, he was called upon to investigate what would prove to be one of the most frustrating, but most humorous cases of his career. It was not recorded in any newspaper, for reasons which will become apparent.

The episode began when Rev. John James Coxhead, vicar of St. John the Evangelist on London's Charlotte Street,[2] noticed that pages had been torn from the baptismal register and, believing it to be an act of malice from a member of his congregation, contacted Scotland Yard, who put the case in the hands of Det. Inspector Swanson.

Realising that the leaves had not been stolen for their intrinsic value, nor for the sake of an entry upon them because copies could be easily obtained, Swanson immediately suspected that the crime was a forgery, believing the leaves had been stolen to prevent proof of the crime being discovered.

Learning that a copy of an entry relating to an aristocratic name had been recently sent to Messrs Feasdale, solicitors to the Duke of Somerset,[3] Swanson went to the lawyers' offices and demanded to see the page supplied.[4]

The detective learned that Mr. Edward St. Maur, the 30-year-old nephew of the Duke, had married a few months earlier. The bride had said her name was Lillian Stanhope, daughter of Thomas Stanhope, a deceased General, and claimed to have been born in Gibraltar.[5] The family, sensing she was not who she pretended to be, politely informed her that if she could provide proof of her identity from someone they knew they would accept her, but not otherwise.

Unable to do so, a few days later the new Mrs. St. Maur had presented

Feasdale with a copy of a baptism record, with the words:

> Sir, you refused to believe my word as a lady, surely you will not refuse to believe the copy of my baptismal register.[6]

On examining the copy closely some time later, Feasdale noticed that, according to the dates upon it, Mrs. St. Maur had been baptised three months before she had been born. They contacted St. John's and obtained a correct copy, which revealed that the record had in fact been for the baptism of a three-year-old girl. When accused of the forgery, Mrs. St. Maur indignantly denied it; two days later the leaves were removed from the register at St. John's.

Swanson began to investigate Mrs. St. Maur. What he discovered was an incredible story.

Described as a "young woman of pre-possessing appearance",[7] she had been born Florence Bessie Marshall Higgins at Northampton on 21st December 1853, illegitimate daughter of Elizabeth Higgins,[8] whose husband John had been a soldier of the 49th Regiment of Foot but at the time of the birth was an In Pensioner of Chelsea Hospital.[9] One William Higgins, wine merchant, was named on the birth certificate.

Florence gravitated to London, where she remained until early 1871,[10] and then went north to Liverpool where she found work performing as a showgirl. On leaving the Alexandra Theatre one evening in late April[11] she met Edward Goddard, an 18-year-old cotton broker's apprentice to Messrs Buchanan, Wignall and Co. She introduced herself as Lydia Foote, the well-known actress. Within a few weeks of the meeting the naïve Goddard was told that he had made 'Lydia' pregnant, with only one course of action open to him.[12]

The couple were married on 9th July 1871 at the Holy Trinity Church, Liverpool. The 17-year-old bride now called herself Lillian Eleanora Higgins, and stated that her father was an Inspector of Police. The groom was recorded as living at Norton Street, and by a nice coincidence the bride gave her address as Seymour Street. Witnesses included Millicent Mary Jeanette Litton,[13] known in Liverpool as one of the worst of prostitutes and thieves, and a Mrs. Morton, whose arrest was sought for theft.[14]

The newlyweds moved to rooms at 20 Harbord Street,[15] but when Goddard's father Henry, a respected architect and magistrate, learned of the marriage he stopped his son's £100 allowance and there was little choice for Edward but to return to the family home at 122 High Street, Lincoln.[16]

Lillian followed a week later, and was found lying on the doorstep apparently senseless, with a small stream of black liquid issuing from both corners of her mouth. Henry Goddard called the Chief Constable of Lincoln and she was taken into custody for attempted suicide.[17]

Appearing in front of the magistrates on 9th September, she defended herself, stating:

> Gentlemen, I have been taught the definition of suicide is to take away one's own life. I have never even attempted it. My husband was taken away from me and kept away by his father, and with the view of exciting my husband's sympathy I bought a penny bottle of ink, took some in my mouth, allowed it to ooze out at the sides and pretend to have a fit. Had I drank the whole of the contents of the bottle it would not have infused me, therefore I claim to be discharged and at once.[18]

She was discharged on the condition that she left Lincoln immediately. She did so having agreed to a weekly allowance from Goddard of £1.

Arriving back in Liverpool, Lillian resumed her previous life as a prostitute, working with her mother Mrs. Higgins and Milly Litton. The three were known locally as the 'Mother and two daughters'.[19]

Keen to rid himself of the weekly allowance supplied to Lillian, Henry Goddard hired a private detective based in Liverpool named Maguire. Following her to a well-known brothel on 17th October 1871, Maguire found her in bed with a man.[20] On entering the bedroom Maguire addressed her: "Well Mrs. Goddard, you seem very comfortable in bed with another man other than your husband." She immediately jumped out of bed and put out the gas lamp, challenging Maguire that he had no evidence. At this the private detective lit a match and asked the man for his name, receiving the reply: "No English, no co-respondent for me."[21]

At the subsequent divorce hearing the Bench heard that Lillian had tried to enlist the help of a friend, Jessie Gascar, who she asked to go to a pawnbroker's and fetch a dress which had been pledged. Returning with the dress, Jessie was told to try it on, with Lillian remarking to her mother: "Does not Jessie look like me?" She told Jessie that if she would wear the dress in court and say that she was the woman found in bed with the man, she could keep it and would also receive a sovereign. While initially willing to do so, Jessie lost her nerve and did not go through with the charade.[22] Unsurprisingly, a *decree nisi* was granted, and the marriage was finally dissolved on 29th July 1873.[23]

Lillian moved back to London and adopted the name Chesterfield. She became the kept mistress of a solicitor, who gave her up after a year because of her wayward lifestyle, and she then became pregnant by an Army Officer named Currie, rumoured to be her cousin, who abandoned her.

The child, a girl, was born on 16th May 1877 at 41 Windmill Street. She was registered on 4th July as Ambrosezina Lilian Chesterfield, with the father's name left blank on the certificate.[24] Three weeks later the child was baptised under the name Ambrosine Lilian Frances Chesterfield, her father "Ambrose William Chesterfield, a professor of music of 88 Euston Street"[25] created for the ceremony.

Returning to the stage two years later, in May 1879, Lillian was appearing as 'Nellie Armroyd' in a performance of *Lost in London* at King's Cross Theatre[26] and on her way to a rehearsal when she noticed she was being followed by a gentleman of obvious wealth. She led him along Piccadilly and down to Westminster Bridge, where she ran down the steps as if to commit suicide by throwing herself into the Thames. Her plan worked perfectly. The man, Edward St. Maur,[27] ran to stop her and lead her away. Telling him that she was Lillian Stanhope, daughter of General Thomas Stanhope, deceased, the young woman claimed to be penniless and wished to end her life.

St. Maur, infatuated with the good-looking young girl, provided lodgings for her and three months later, on 20th August 1879, married her at Marylebone Church. She was given away by John Joseph Worswick,[28] who was paid 10s for performing the duty. Soon afterwards Worswick was arrested for forgery on a bank and sentenced to 18 months imprisonment.[29]

Given that Edward St. Maur's family had refused to accept Lillian as the lady she claimed to be, it was with incredible cheek that she appeared on stage once more just weeks before Swanson was called in to investigate (in fact while he was off work with his sprained ankle), playing 'Lucy Tregaroon' in a provincial performance of the romantic drama *Nobody's Child*, the title of which could hardly be more appropriate.[30]

Lillian's desperate plan had been to take her daughter Ambrosezina to St. John's Church and have her baptised for a second time, this time under the name 'Lillian Stanhope" and with a father named General Thomas Stanhope, exactly as she described herself. On ordering a copy she altered the age of the person baptised, and then presented the document to Messrs Feasdale.

Having obtained the full story and facts of the crimes committed, Swanson applied to the Public Prosecutor for the necessary arrest warrants. Lillian had one more trick up her sleeve.

Swanson was told the warrants would be issued – as soon as Mrs. St.

Maur had given birth to the child she was carrying. It would be a wait of ten months before it was discovered that she had bribed a doctor to declare she was pregnant, and in the meantime the Duchess of Somerset, protecting the family name, used her considerable influence to ensure that no prosecution would take place.

Swanson was again furious:

> Thus one of the clearest and most disgraceful cases of stealing and forgery was compromised. Mr. and Mrs. St. Maur are now abroad supported by Lord Algernon. There is a probability that this woman will one day become the Duchess of Somerset.[31]

Lillian Stanhope might have escaped arrest, but she and her husband would be punished in another way.

The following year, Lord Algernon St. Maur, Edward's father and heir presumptive to the Dukedom, took the unusual step of publicly renouncing all responsibility for his son's debts.[32] Lord Algernon became the 14th Duke of Somerset in 1891 and when he died three years later, on 2nd October 1894, bequeathed just £7,500[33] to Edward, a relatively small amount compared to the bequests in favour of his brothers Algernon, Ernest and Percy.[34] Edward and Lillian St. Maur remained childless and moved to Wales.[35] Lillian would remain an outcast, conspicuous by her absence on the guest list at the wedding of Edward's brother Percy in 1899[36] and also his funeral eight years later.[37]

Her death in 1910 at Bryn Celyn Hall, Pwllheli,[38] was reported in several newspapers, including *The Times*:

> ### LADY EDWARD ST. MAUR
>
> Lady Edward St. Maur died suddenly, of heart failure, on September 21. She was a daughter of the late Mr. John Stanhope, and married Lord Edward St. Maur, formerly a lieutenant in the 60th Rifles, the youngest son of the 14th Duke of Somerset, and a brother of the present Duke.[39]

It wasn't a bad final review for a Liverpool showgirl, and no doubt the former Florence Higgins would have smiled.

Donald Swanson's next dealings with the aristocracy, just a few weeks later, would be under very different circumstances.

Before then, however, he was called to investigate the puzzling murder of a woman whose body had been found in strange circumstances at 139 Harley Street, in D Division.

Local Inspectors King and Lucas, having hit a brick wall with their own investigations, contacted Scotland Yard for assistance, who sent the experienced Detective Inspectors George Greenham and Donald Swanson. On their first visit to the scene they were joined by Howard Vincent, Director of the C.I.D.[40]

Known facts were few. The butler at the house, a man named Spindlove,[41] had found a cask in the corner of the middle cellar at the house, positioned immediately below a cistern. Inside were discovered the decomposed remains of a woman dressed in the remnants of a coarse linen chemise, placed head-first into the barrel. She was estimated to be between 40 and 50 years of age, with dark brown hair and unusually short front teeth, described "as if sawn". A plaster of Paris cast was taken.[42]

Dr. Spurgin, Divisional Surgeon of D Division, noted a curvature of the spine, which in his opinion had been caused by the body being forced into the barrel. He discovered that the whole of the body had been sprinkled with chloride of lime to speed up the decomposition process. With no residue on the cask, this must have been done prior to placing the body inside.

On examining the body Dr. Spurgin found bloodstains on the ribcage on the left side, indicating stab wounds between the fourth and fifth ribs. The heart, not yet fully decomposed, showed no signs of injury, but the lung had completely dissolved and therefore he could not say for sure whether this had been the cause of death.

Bloodstains found within the cask could have come from either the wound to the chest or from the victim's nose or mouth after death.

Immediately beside the cask were found a quantity of rope, two old pokers and a table knife.

The detectives ascertained that the cask had been first noticed some two years earlier, in the autumn of 1878, by a Mr. Woodroffee, caretaker of the house. He said he went into the cellar to catch a rat and noticed the barrel, which had bottles on top of it. Woodroffee knocked the barrel with a stick to scare the rodent but examined it no further. In July, a plumber named Henry Goatley had undertaken work on the cistern and had pushed the cask into the corner. It was subsequently hidden from view by the packing cases upon which Goatley had stood to reach the cistern.

They spoke with George Campbell, a servant at nearby 134 Harley Street, who for five months over 1876/77 had been employed at no. 139 by the owner, Jacob Henriques. Campbell told them that there had been no cask in the cellar during his time in the house.

Progress finally seemed to be made when German-born William Tinapp said that he had been employed by Mr. Henriques as a footman in August 1878. On his first visit to the cellar he had seen the cask and also noticed a bad smell. Tinapp had also noticed that a quantity of bricks had been replaced on the cellar floor, and was told by the odd-job man, John Green, that he had laid them at the request of butler Henry Smith.

When the 73-year-old Green was interviewed by the detectives, he informed them that on entering the cellar he saw the bricks had been taken up and that there was a hole in the ground about a yard across. Green relaid the bricks without asking Smith why they had been removed, or why the hole had been dug.

It was clear that the police had to find Henry Smith. He had been butler to Mr. Henriques for 18 months before leaving his position in November 1878 for being drunk on duty, and was now a soldier of the 3rd East Surrey Regiment.

Smith claimed that he had never seen the cask, and that he had dug the hole in order to bury a large amount of stale bread for which he thought he would get in trouble. Denying this, John Green said he had seen no bread, and the cook, Mrs. Jewry, said there had never been such an accumulation of waste bread in her five years in the house.

Things looked ominous for Henry Smith, but with no evidence no charges could be brought.

The Illustrated Police News, 26th June 1880

The Duchess and the Showgirl

The Illustrated Police News, 19th June 1880

At the inquest on 14th June, coroner Dr. Hardwicke asked the jury whether they wanted to hear the medical evidence of Dr. Thomas Bond of Westminster Hospital, who had also examined the body. Considering Bond's testimony given in future cases, which we shall learn of later, it is a disappointment that the jury declined. The inquest was then closed with the verdict of "the body of a woman, name unknown, found in the cellar at 139 Harley Street, was the body of a murdered woman, the criminal also unknown."[43]

Two days later it was announced that the Government were offering a reward of £100 for information which would lead to the conviction of the murderer: none came.[44]

For his part in the investigation Swanson was given a reward of 25s,[45] which, although welcome, would be dwarfed by his next award.

His celebrations continued when it was discovered that Julia was pregnant for the second time.

NINE

The Case of the Quarter-Million Pound Pearl

London's Fitzrovia, the capital's aristocratic quarter, was as quiet as usual in the early hours of 24th July 1880. Certainly, no-one noticed the shadowy figure stepping through the open gate of 8 Portland Place at 01.00am.

Slipping inside the house, the man found a suitably quiet spot and secreted himself away for two hours until he was sure that the occupants were asleep.[1]

Emerging from his hiding place around 03.00am, the man crept into the dressing room of the lady of the house and removed a large quantity of jewellery before leaving as quietly as he had entered.[2]

The owners, the Earl and Countess of Bective, were away and the robbery would not be reported for several days.

By the time Scotland Yard were called in the thief had already parted company with much of the jewellery. Det. Inspector Swanson was assigned to the case and met the Earl and Countess, obtaining a list of the missing items.

The 38-year-old Countess of Bective had been born Lady Alice Maria Hill at Hanover Square to Arthur Wills Hill, 4th Marquess of Downshire, and Hon. Caroline Stapleton-Cotton. She was considered one of the great English beauties of the day, but was equally known for her kind, generous nature.[3]

Her husband, Thomas Taylour, was an Anglo-Irish Peer who had become Earl of Bective in 1870 having formerly been styled Lord Kenlis. He had been born in 1844 to Thomas Taylour, the 3rd Marquess of Headfort, whose uncle Lord George Taylour Quin had married the niece of the Duchess of Devonshire. The Earl had been educated at Eton and Christ Church, Oxford, and had been the Member of Parliament for Westmorland since 1871.[4]

The Countess of Bective pictured twenty years after the robbery
from The King, 2nd June 1900

He married Lady Alice Hill at Banbridge, County Down, on 9th October 1867[5] and the couple had two children: Lady Olivia Taylour, born on 22nd January 1869,[6] and Lady Evelyn Taylour, born on 10th February 1873 but who sadly died aged two on 16th September 1875.

Recognising the uniqueness of many of the items, Swanson decided that the best course of action would be to circulate a list of the stolen jewellery around the pawnbroking network, so had a notice placed in the *Pawnbroker's Gazette*.[7] This had the desired effect; Charles Parnacott, a jeweller of 28 New Bond Street, contacted the detective and said he had been approached by a man who wanted to pawn two rings and three pearls. He recognised a diamond and ruby ring worth £200[8] as one which he had remounted for the Countess of Bective some three months earlier.[9]

Swanson then visited several other pawnbrokers in the area. James Moore, an assistant to Thomas Richardson at 11&12 Upper George Street, told the detective that a man named Robinson had pledged 12 loose brilliants (brilliant cut diamonds) and a single pearl. 'Robinson' told Richardson that the jewels belonged to his sister, who lived in Ireland.

A similar story was told to Edward Melhuish, a pawnbroker of Duke Street, by 'George Turner', who pledged three loose brilliants while saying that his sister needed money to settle an account.[10]

Swanson went to the Earl of Bective armed with descriptions of 'George Turner' and 'Robinson', who he suspected of being the same man. The Earl said that it sounded like a former butler named Robert Cumming.

At 12.30am on 24th September Swanson encountered Cumming on nearby Charlotte Street. When asked how he had come into the possession of a single pearl which was found on his person, and which it was known he had shown to several jewellers, the 39-year-old Cumming mumbled something about buying it from a man he didn't know and selling it to another man he didn't know. Unsurprisingly, Swanson replied that these answers were very unsatisfactory. Cumming then said he would tell the truth: he had pledged the pearl and had the duplicate of the ticket in his rooms.

Along with Det. Sergeant John Dowdell, Swanson accompanied Cumming to his home on Weymouth Place, where the *Scotsman* recorded what happened next:

> He searched a pair of drawers, and said that he could not find it. Observing that there was a drawer which he had not looked into, I opened it and found wrapped in tissue paper four diamond rings, two pieces of a diamond necklace, together with the centre cluster. I asked him where he got the jewellery from, and he replied "It is Lady Bective's jewellery. I committed the offence."[11]

Searching the thief, Swanson found two more pawn tickets, one for a single pearl and three brilliants pledged for £20, and the other for three brilliants pledged for £10.[12] Cumming then removed a further pawn ticket from the lining of his hat. Giving it to Swanson, he explained that it related to a diamond ring pledged for £20.[13]

Cumming claimed that the robbery had not been premeditated; he had simply been passing 8 Portland Place and saw the gate wide open, and the temptation had been too great. He claimed that drink and betting on horse racing had been his downfall, and that guilt had left him determined to redeem all the items as soon as he could afford to.[14]

Cumming had also stolen a gold watch worth £70 and some studs belonging to Andrew Hay, another lodger at 11 Weymouth Place, and had pawned these for a total of £13 10s.

He confirmed to Swanson that he would co-operate in any way possible to assist in the recovery of the stolen items, and gave the detective a list of the various pawnbrokers where the jewellery might be found: a diamond emerald ring pawned at Mr. Altoun at 184 Bishopsgate in the name of "R. Marshall"; a diamond and ruby ring pledged under the same name at Henry Harrison, 41 Aldersgate; and three pearls pledged in the name "G. Taylor" at John Tunsall, 69 Brompton Road.[15]

Cumming also told Swanson of a gold brooch which he had given to Ada Read, a young barmaid at the Prince of Wales public house on Charlotte Street. The detective visited Miss Read at her home in Manchester Square and ascertained that she was completely unaware of how Cumming had obtained the brooch; when told of its origins she gave it up at once.[16]

With all the stolen jewellery recovered except for a bracelet worth £10, it transpired that Cumming had received just £120 for items worth a combined £3,070.[17]

He pleaded guilty at the Old Bailey on 18th October 1880 and was sentenced to five years' penal servitude.[18]

Swanson was given a reward of £200 by the Earl of Bective, who sent a cheque representing

> ...the amount I promise for the recovery of Lady Bective's jewels. I am fully sensible that their recovery was entirely due to the perseverance, energy and professional experience which was brought to bear upon the case by yourself and your assistants, and I thank and congratulate you upon the successful issue of your endeavours.[19]

The detective was also later presented with a revolver by the grateful Countess herself. The pistol, a .23 calibre 7-shot Tranter with a silver escutcheon bearing the Countess's monogram and the words "to Donald Swanson 1882" fixed to the handle, was sold by Holland & Holland of 98 New Bond Street.[20]

No doubt the Swansons spent a very enjoyable Christmas following the massive financial windfall. The detective started 1881 tracking an English criminal who had committed a series of frauds overseas but who had returned home in an attempt to escape justice.

Scotland Yard had been contacted by George Dixon Ballantyne, clerk at Messrs Sanderson, Murray and Co. of Gresham Buildings on Basinghall Street in the City. The firm acted as agents to Goldesborough and Co., a company of wool brokers in Melbourne, Australia.[21] One of the firm's agents, a Yorkshireman named Mr. Horsfall, had been introduced some months earlier to a fellow Englishman wearing a Royal Navy uniform who called himself Captain Egerton Pleydell Bouverie Tempest. The officer claimed to be a member of the Tempest family from Yorkshire, his father a clergyman and his uncle Sir Charles Tempest. He was well-known in Melbourne, moving in the best society circles, and earned the trust of Horsfall by mentioning several Yorkshire families known to him.

Tempest showed a letter to Mr. Horsfall which was supposedly from his brother, Walter Tempest of 2 Hyde Park Place, authorising him to draw £200 or more in order to provide funds for his return to England. Trusting the officer, Horsfall advanced £250 and a letter of exchange was drawn up and signed by both parties.[22]

Tempest then sailed from Melbourne on the *Cotopaxi*,[23] which, unknown to him, carried on the same voyage the letters of exchange sent by Horsfall to Sanderson, Murray and Co.[24] During the voyage Tempest borrowed money from the majority of the crew, promising to meet them at the Tavistock Hotel in Covent Garden once the ship had arrived in London. They went, but Tempest was nowhere to be seen.[25]

The bills of exchange, meanwhile, had been received by Horsfall's agents who contacted Mr. Burr of Keighley in Yorkshire, who had been named as a trustee by Captain Tempest. In due course Mr. Burr confirmed that he had no client by that name, and a clerk from Sanderson, Murray and Co. was sent to 2 Hyde Park Place to speak to Tempest's brother.

The door was answered by a Dr. Walter Cheadle, who said that nobody by the name of Tempest had ever lived at that address. Shown the bills of exchange, the doctor said he had no knowledge of them, but recognised the handwriting as that of his brother, James Cheadle, who had emigrated to Australia some 20 years previously.[26]

The matter was then placed in Det. Inspector Swanson's hands on Friday, 14th January. He very soon ascertained that Tempest had taken rooms at the Holborn Viaduct Hotel. Meeting the Captain, Swanson introduced himself as a "Mr. Sutherland" of Brighton, in London on business, and the pair spent an evening in conversation, during which time Tempest let slip that he knew Mr. Horsfall and Messrs Goldesborough of Melbourne.[27] Swanson bade the Captain a good evening.

The following day he returned with a representative of Sanderson and Co. and showed the Captain the letters of exchange, which he denied all knowledge of, exclaiming: "They are certainly impudent forgeries in my name". Swanson then arrested Tempest and took him to Bow Street Magistrates' Court, where he was searched and found to be carrying forged letters purporting to be from members of the Tempest family asking him to return home, thus establishing his identity beyond doubt.[28]

At the committal hearing, however, it was ruled that as the offence had taken place outside of the magistrates' jurisdiction no charge could be brought. Tempest was accordingly released, and fled the country. It was the latest in a long line of cases where proof had been obtained, but the law did not allow a prosecution. Swanson had done his job as a police officer by arresting the offender, but the legal system was not always geared to secure a conviction.

Swanson's discreet efficiency had been noticed, however. He had been personally chosen to handle delicate investigations involving the Duke of Somerset and the Earl of Bective, and early in February was hand-picked by Dolly Williamson to accompany the Chief Superintendent to Dublin to arrest Michael Davitt, a Fenian arms dealer who was on ticket-of-leave following his release from Dartmoor prison in 1877.

Davitt had been born in County Mayo in 1846, but emigrated to Haslingden in Lancashire following his family's eviction from their smallholding. At the age of eleven he lost an arm in an accident at the cotton mill where he was working, later commenting that as a result, in the years which followed he gained a good education. At fifteen Davitt became interested in Irish history and the current social situation in his native country, and in 1865 joined the Irish Republican Brotherhood. Two years later he became a full-time organising secretary for the North East and Scotland region, organising arms smuggling to Ireland, and took over from the still-imprisoned Ricard O'Sullivan Burke as chief arms agent in England in 1868.[29]

On 14th May 1870 Davitt was arrested at Paddington station by Chief Inspector George Clarke, who would later become embroiled in the Turf Frauds scandal. The arms dealer had been waiting to meet John Wilson, an Englishman from Birmingham who was travelling into Paddington with two packages. After both Davitt and Wilson were arrested, the parcels were opened to reveal a total of fifty pistols. Davitt was searched by Clarke and some £152 (£7,000) was found secreted on his person.[30]

Charged with treason, on 11th July 1870 Davitt was sentenced to fifteen years' imprisonment and Wilson seven.

Davitt served his sentence at Clerkenwell, Newgate and Millbank Gaols, and finally Dartmoor prison.[31] His exemplary behaviour worked in his favour:

> ...his good conduct as a prisoner, and his evident desire to use any opportunities allowed him of self-improvement, attracted the notice of Mr. William Fagan, the Visiting Director, who encouraged and helped him in many ways. His influence with the convict was all the greater because he was a fellow-countryman of his and a co-religionist. And as the result the Davitt of the Land League was a very different man from the ignorant fellow who was sent to penal servitude in 1870.[32]

Davitt served just over seven years of his sentence, and was released on 19th December 1877. He returned to Ireland with other freed political prisoners to a hero's welcome, and began a lecturing tour of London, Liverpool, Manchester and Glasgow, before heading to America to speak on the newly-formed Land League, which had Charles Parnell as its President and Davitt as one of the Secretaries.

On 3rd February 1881 Davitt was in Dublin, busy with plans for a forthcoming Land League Convention. Around 2.00pm he left the League's offices and was walking across Carlisle Bridge with two colleagues when he was met by Detective Sheridan of the Dublin Police, who said that Det. Inspector John Mallon[33] wished to see him at his office at the Dublin Castle police headquarters. On arrival at the office, Davitt was met by Dolly Williamson and Donald Swanson, who produced a warrant and arrested the Irishman for breaking his ticket-of-leave conditions. Davitt immediately handed his revolver to Mallon. He was allowed a meal before being taken by Swanson and Williamson by cab to Kingstown, where the trio took the mail steamer *Connaught* to Holyhead, from where they boarded a train to London. A considerable crowd had gathered at Euston station anticipating Davitt's arrival,

The Case of the Quarter-Million Pound Pearl

*The arrest of Michael Davitt
from The Illustrated Police News, 12th February 1881*

so preferring to avoid a potential situation the detectives alighted at Willesden Junction and changed to a train taking them with the prisoner to Broad Street, and finally a cab to Bow Street, where they arrived in the early hours of 4th February.[34] By this time the police presence was bolstered by Det. Chief Inspector Shore and Det. Inspector Butcher, along with Howard Vincent. Davitt's case was immediately heard by Sir James Ingham,[35] and he was removed to Millbank prison to complete his original sentence.[36]

It was a small victory for the police in the ongoing fight against the Fenian threat, but much worse was to follow in the years ahead.

A month after the arrest of Davitt, Julia gave birth to the couple's second son, James John Swanson, at home at Grove Cottages on 5th March 1881. The boy, dark like his father, was named after his grandfathers, James Nevill and John Swanson. He was registered by his father on 16th April 1881,[37] but not before the detective had again been called away from London to trace a forger and thief well known to the Metropolitan Police by the name of Walter Selwyn.

Selywn, whose real name was Walter Bailey, was the son of a schoolmaster at Brighton. In 1876 he set up a company called Walters, Read & Co. Permanent Fire and Life Assurance Co., which invited young men to apply for a position of secretary by enclosing a £50 deposit.

When his manager was arrested and sentenced to nine months' hard labour, Selwyn absconded.

He then appeared at an office on Vigo Street running an agency offering seaside apartments for sale. The scam was a simple one: applicants would view available apartments on a map and, on making their selection, would be asked for a small fee to 'reserve' the property; again, after a number of weeks Selwyn would disappear with the money.

He next set up the Phoenix Banking Company at Queen Victoria Street, again advertising for a secretary and seeking deposits. Over subsequent months Selwyn set up fraudulent companies around the City and closed them just as quickly, until in 1880 he became acquainted with a gang of professional thieves who used him to negotiate stolen bonds, thus transferring the risk from themselves to Selwyn. The first transaction was concerning £3,000[38] worth of bonds which had been stolen between Calais and Paris in 1878. The gang had previously used a German named Oscar Reuman to launder their stolen bonds; finding himself cut out of the deal, the bitter Reuman informed the City of London police, who arrested Selwyn and took him to the Guildhall.

Two days after he was released on bail, £1,400 worth of New Zealand bonds were stolen from a vicarage in Devon. Det. Inspector Donald Swanson was then given the task of capturing Selwyn.

Learning that each time the criminal had disappeared correspondence had been sent to him care of 119 Ditchling Rise, Brighton, the detective began to make enquiries in that neighbourhood. But before leaving for Brighton, Swanson liaised with the City of London Police and made arrangements for them to watch a certain house; as suspected, when Selwyn heard of Swanson's enquiries he fled to the house in question, and was held there by the City Police until Swanson arrived to arrest him.

Selwyn was charged with receiving stolen goods, fraud and forgery. At the Old Bailey on 2nd May he was sentenced to five years' imprisonment on the charge of forgery.[39]

With Selwyn finally behind bars, Swanson was sent to arrest George Drevar, a captain of the merchant navy, who had sent several threatening letters to the Wreck Commissioner Mr. H. C. Rothery. Rothery had been responsible for suspending Drevar's certificate two years earlier after concluding that the stranding and loss of the *Norfolk* in the Cape Verde islands had been the result of negligence on the part of Drevar, its captain.[40]

Drevar held the Commissioner personally responsible for his inability to reclaim his log book, which would show that the accident was not his fault. He claimed that the suspension of his certificate for six months had ruined him.[41]

In one of his letters Drevar called Rothery a "modern Jesuit", and said that "desperate remedies were required for desperate wrongs". He demanded "recompense, employment or an asylum", and said if he did not get what he wanted he would "charge his blood and that of another on the nation that had so cruelly wronged him".

Captain Drevar was well-known to the public, and if Swanson felt a little unsure what to expect when visiting him it would not have been a surprise.

In 1876 Drevar had been Captain of the barque *Pauline* which was carrying coals for H.M. naval stores in Zanzibar, and on 8th July was off Cape San Roque on the north-east coat of Brazil. It was a fine, clear morning when at eleven o'clock Drevar

> observed some black spots on the water, and a whitish pillar, about thirty feet high, above them. At the first glance I took all to be breakers, as the sea was splashing fountain-like about them, and the pillar a pinnacle-rock, bleached with the sun; but the pillar fell with a splash, and a similar one rose. They rose and fell alternately in quick succession, and good glasses showed me it was a monster sea serpent coiled twice round a large sperm whale. The head and tail parts, each about thirty feet long were acting as levers, twisting itself and victim round with great velocity. They sank out of sight about every two minutes, coming to the surface still revolving; and the struggles of the whale and two other whales that were near, frantic with excitement, made the sea in their vicinity like a boiling cauldron; and a loud and confused noise was distinctly heard.
>
> This strange occurrence lasted some fifteen minutes, and finished with the tail portion of the whale being elevated straight in the air, then waving backwards and forwards, and lashing the water furiously in the last death struggle, when the whole body disappeared from our view, going down head foremost to the bottom, where no doubt it was gorged at the serpent's leisure; and that monster of monsters may have been many months in a state of coma, digesting the huge mouthful.
>
> Then two of the largest sperm whales that I have ever seen moved slowly thence towards the vessel, their bodies more than usually elevated out of water, and not spouting or making the least noise, but seeming quite paralysed with fear; indeed, a cold shiver went through my own frame on beholding the last agonising struggle of the poor whale that had seemed

Sketch of the sea serpent battling a sperm whale, drawn by Rev. E L Penny

as helpless in the coils of the vicious monster as a small bird in the talons of a hawk.

Allowing for two coils round the whale, I think the serpent was about 160 or 170 feet long, and seven or eight in girth. It was in colour much like a conger eel; and the head, from the mouth being always open, appeared the largest part of its body.

I wrote thus far, little thinking I would ever see the serpent again, but at 7a.m., July 13th, in the same latitude, and some eighty miles east of San Roque, I was astonished to see the same or a similar monster. It was throwing its head and about 40 feet of its body in a horizontal position out of the water as it passed onwards by the stern of our vessel. I began musing why we were so much favoured with such a strange visitor, and concluded that the band of white paint, two feet wide above the copper, might have looked like a fellow-serpent to it, and, no doubt, attracted its attention. Whilst thus thinking, I was startled by the cry of "There it is again," and a short distance to leeward, elevated some sixty feet in the air, was the great Leviathan, grimly looking towards the vessel. As I was not sure it was only our free board it was viewing, we had all our axes ready, and were fully determined, should the brute embrace the Pauline, to chop away for its backbone with all our might, and the wretch might have found for once in its life that it had caught a Tartar.[42]

No attack came. The *Pauline* continued to Zanzibar, where they told their tale to the crew of the HMS *London*, whose Chaplain, Rev. E. L. Penny, made sketches based on descriptions. These were sent to the

Illustrated London News on 21st October, with Penny's observation that

> Captain Drevar is a singularly able and observant man, and those of the crew and officers with whom I conversed were singularly intelligent; nor did any of their descriptions vary from one another in the last – there were no discrepancies.[43]

The *Pauline* next sailed to Akyab, Burma, and then returned to England, arriving in Liverpool on 8th January 1877 having spent a total of twenty months at sea. Drevar at once went to Liverpool police court, where he told Stipendiary Magistrate Mr. Raffles that he and his crew wished to make a sworn affidavit as to their sightings of the sea serpent. This they did the following day.

Unsurprisingly, the press did not take the claims seriously:

> From the notices which have been recently taking the round of the papers, it is perfectly evident that this animal is tired of being humbugged and having his very existence denied by an incredulous public. The latest contribution to this kind of thing is [Drevar's affidavit], showing quite clearly that business is meant. Until the question of his zoological recognition is settled, he evidently means to make it warm for the whales.[44]

Drevar claimed to have been invited to London by 'several scientific societies' in order to relate what he had seen. Whether he attended such a meeting is unknown, but he subsequently became Captain of the *Norfolk*, a London-based vessel.

When Swanson visited Drevar and told him he was under arrest, the latter said he "might go to court and shoot [the Wreck Commissioner] on the bench". He admitted writing the letters, saying he did so partly because of the 'insults' received from Mr. Rothery, and partly due to the fact that he believed he was "doing the Almighty's work in making his wonders known", referring to the sea serpent. He then showed the detective a smaller serpent which he claimed had been caught by a crew member off South Africa. It was some four or five feet long and of 'peculiar formation', and kept in a glass bottle of spirits.[45]

Swanson would no doubt have been fascinated, having grown up hearing tales of mermaids and sea monsters supposedly spotted in Thurso Bay.[46]

Sea serpents notwithstanding, Drevar had still threatened Mr. Rothery, and at the Old Bailey on 6th May he was sentenced to three months' imprisonment.[47]

After his release Drevar continued to reiterate his story, annoyed at being ridiculed:

> I cannot help, nor do I care much, what people say or think about the "Sea Serpent", but I have been very careful from first to last to confine myself to the strict truth on the subject; and I do not wish anyone to attribute to me things I do not say, for although it is mostly a subject of ridicule to most people in this country, every other nation, as far as I have experienced, treated my information with the respect and interest it deserved.[48]

But Drevar was far from a crazed 'seadog'. He had long been interested in lifeboats and other life-preserving craft, and had invented a 'water-velocipede' which he had patented on 16th January 1877. The machine, a paddle lifeboat which could be constructed within ten minutes, consisted of common items such as a wine packing case and a sawn barrel. The *Evening Telegraph* of 10th October 1882 reported that Drevar was exhibiting this and other inventions at Brighton.

Moving along the coast, in late 1883 it was reported that Captain Drevar had made several attempts to cross the Channel from Dover in his paddle boat, and another invention, a boat made out of a tub affixed to a wooden frame acting as a raft. Both vessels were intended as life-saving equipment, and Drevar's Channel-crossing attempts were merely marketing ploys which each time resulted in him being pulled from the water by various fishing boats. In many of these endeavours he was assisted by a Mr. Ward, whose son Alfred donned another Drevar invention, a waterproof costume.

The Captain's experiments were often met with bemusement:

> Once again the Drevar nuisance has been inflicted upon us. I cannot see that there is anything particularly heroic or meritorious in steadily getting wet through. But Captain Drevar evidently differs from me. I suppose in some way or other he will make it pay. He is probably qualifying for an engagement at the aquarium at 5s a day, where he will lie in the tank when the walrus died, and show how he did not cross the Channel.[49]

While many ridiculed Drevar's actions, others recognised the importance of the development of life-preserving equipment:

> It is not enough to keep people afloat on the sea, if their lives are to be preserved. To place a few half-drowned survivors of a foundered ship

The Case of the Quarter-Million Pound Pearl

*Captain Drevar, Mr. Ward and Alfred Ward conduct their experiments at Dover
from The Graphic, 22nd September 1883*

upon any hastily arranged framework of planks and ropes, where they are exposed to the fury of the winds, aggravated, perhaps, by showers of sleet or snow, and washed by heavy seas, is but to kill them by slow torture. This is the great obstacle to the success of all such contrivances, except as a means of reaching the shore, or of attracting the attention of a passing steamer. There is no doubt that very strong men, accustomed to the sea, might do more wonderful feats than those of Capt. Drevar and [fellow inventor] Mr. Coleman. But such men are rare. What is wanted is some plan by which passengers of both sexes, and children may be protected from the weather in case of a ship going down, as well as from the perils of drowning.[50]

George Drevar eventually emigrated to Australia, where he became a showman at the Royal Aquarium Pleasure Gardens at Tamarama Beach, Sydney, as well as working at the recently-opened Centennial Park, where he offered his cask boats for rent to pleasure-seekers.[51]

He was still selling his story in 1889, publishing a 24-page book titled *The Great Sea Serpent and the Sperm Whale Conflict*.[52]

On New Year's Day 1890, Drevar was on the shoreline of a dam at Centennial Park when he saw a boy in one of his casks capsize and begin to sink. Drevar, some 200 yards away, ran to the water's edge and jumped in. As he reached the boy, a local lad named Edward Hopkins, both sank; a witness dived in and saved Hopkins, but Drevar drowned. It was an ironic way for the master mariner to meet his end.[53]

Captain George Drevar's life story was at times comical, but never dull. As for Donald Swanson, he was about to become involved in a case through which his own name would become known to the nation.

TEN

Lucky Swanson and the Murder of Mr. Gold

It was a quarter to eight in the evening of Friday, 8th July 1881 when Jane Bickers made her way to her home at 32 Smith Street, Stepney. The showers of earlier in the day had cleared and the warm evening sun brightened the smoke-yellow terraced houses along the quiet street.[1]

The family had lived at Smith Street for nine years,[2] but since her two elder sisters, Sarah[3] and Caroline,[4] had left home it had been just Miss Bickers and her widowed mother. They had been forced to take in lodgers since the death of father James Bickers in 1876,[5] and both elder daughters had married men who had lodged with the family. Perhaps the 24-year-old Jane was hoping to follow her sisters' example, and had her eye on one of the young men presently staying at 32 Smith Street: J. W. Goodfellow, a shorthand writer from Merthyr Tydfil, Frederick Evans, a commercial traveller from Chelsea, or Harry Watlings, another traveller, from London.[6] She may have noticed Mr. Clark, the shy new lodger who said he was from Liverpool and had arrived eleven days earlier.

On the other side of the street stood Det. Inspector Swanson. He had arrived at Smith Street minutes earlier with Det. Inspector Frederick Jarvis and P.C. Hopkins,[7] and had positioned the constable at the rear of No. 32, with Jarvis ready to guard the front door.

An hour earlier Swanson had been at Scotland Yard, where he had met two men who said that they had information regarding a murderer who was currently on the run; they wished to see the officer in charge of the C.I.D. to claim the £200 reward which was on offer. Swanson took one of the men to Det. Inspector George Robson, who was on duty in charge of the C.I.D. by night. Having secured a promise that the reward would be paid should his information lead to the arrest of the fugitive, without his own identity being revealed, the informant declined to disclose his source but said that the wanted man could be found in hiding at Smith

from The Illustrated Police News, 16th June 1881

Street, using the name "Clark".[8]

As Miss Bickers opened the front door of No. 32 and went in, Swanson followed and entered at the same time. He was met by her mother, Sarah Bickers, whom the detective took into the parlour and stated the nature of his visit.[9] He was told that the man he was interested in was at that moment in his room on the first floor.

Swanson climbed the staircase, telling Det. Inspector Jarvis to stay downstairs guarding the front door. He quickly opened the door to the first room, and saw a pale, thin man sitting in an armchair.[10]

"Percy Lefroy Mapleton?"

"Yes; I expected you."

"I am a police officer, and I arrest you for the wilful murder of Mr. Gold on the Brighton Railway."

"I am not obliged to make any reply, and I think it better not to make any answer."

Swanson wrote this last comment in his notebook and read it back to the man, who replied: "I will qualify that by saying I am not guilty."

Jarvis then entered the room and was told by Swanson that Lefroy had admitted his identity. Jarvis searched Lefroy, finding a solitary shilling, and the detectives then searched the room. On top of a chest of drawers they saw a pipe, a bottle of arnica oil and a pair of scissors, which the suspect said he had used to cut off his moustache. Inside the drawers were a bloodstained black cloth waistcoat, two caps, three collars, part of a flannel shirt and a false moustache and beard. In a cupboard they found a light coloured scarf and more pieces of material matching the flannel shirt.[11]

Swanson and Jarvis took the suspect downstairs, where Mrs. Bickers was waiting. Addressing Lefroy, she said "I did not know that I had such a man as you in my house, or I would not have had you."[12]

They took him in a cab first to nearby Arbour Square police station and then to Scotland Yard. During the journey Lefroy said:

> I am glad you have found me. I am sick of it. I should have given myself up in a day or two. I have regretted it ever since that I ran away. It put a different complexion on the case, but I could not bear the exposure. I feared certain matters in connexion with my family would be published. I suppose I shall be allowed to see a lawyer? I am glad you did not bring any of my so-called friends from Wallington with you.[13]

On arrival at Scotland Yard, Howard Vincent and Dolly Williamson were waiting. The senior officers had received news of the arrest by telegraph, and after a brief interview with Lefroy ordered that he be taken to King Street police station to be detained overnight. A Central News reporter, at Scotland Yard seeking information on the capture, noticed Swanson and Jarvis descending a staircase with Lefroy between then. They got into a waiting cab and left for nearby King Street, where he was charged with the murder of Mr. Frederick Isaac Gold on 27th

June.[14] After a meal of sandwiches and coffee, the suspected murderer was placed in a cell and watched by no less than three constables.[15] His time on the run had come to an end.

The murder of Mr. Gold was the first on a British railway since that of Thomas Briggs some seventeen years earlier. The 1864 attack by a German tailor named Franz Müller was the first time a murder had occurred on a train, and understandably shocked and alarmed the nation in equal measure.[16]

Prior to this, the railways had often been used by the public as a means of attending public executions, such as the hanging of multiple murderer John Gleeson Wilson at Liverpool in 1849, when it was estimated that almost a quarter of the 100,000 attendees came to the city by train.[17] The previous year, the notorious Swell Mob commissioned a train to take them to Norwich to 'enjoy' the hanging of James Blomfield Rush, only to be turned away by police at Attleborough.[18]

Following the murder of Thomas Briggs, the safety of passengers was widely debated. Railway carriages at the time could be entered via the doors on either side only, with no doors linking compartments or corridors allowing passengers to pass along the train.

In a small measure designed to allay fears and criticism, the South Western Railway installed small portholes in the dividing walls between compartments, supposedly so that passengers would feel more secure. These portholes, quickly christened "Müller's Lights", had female passengers complaining of Peeping Toms.

The Railway Act of 1868 compelled railway companies to install a means of communication between passengers and "servants of the company", resulting in the introduction of a rope equipped with a bell on either end. Unfortunately, these early communication cords failed to work more often than not.

The introduction of American Pullman carriages to Britain in 1874, with their longer interiors and connecting corridors, promised to resolve the problem, but these were initially only used on the Midland Railway and would not be in general use until the 1890s.

The predicament of the lone female traveller was brought into sharp focus on 17th June 1875 when Katherine Dickinson was indecently assaulted by Colonel Valentine Baker on the Vauxhall train.[19] The 22-year-old Miss Dickinson had boarded at Petersfield and entered an empty carriage, when at Liphook the train stopped and in stepped the

50-year-old Baker. Once the train set off Baker began a conversation, declaring that he was an officer in the Army, at which Miss Dickinson relaxed.[20] She had three brothers, one of whom was an officer in the Army, and she understood that an officer was also usually a gentleman. The train called at every stop, with the Colonel and Miss Dickinson conversing amiably, until it reached Woking. After a five minute wait the train set off again, and Baker commented that it did not stop again until reaching its destination at Vauxhall some thirty minutes later.

With this, the Colonel stood up and put up the window. He sat beside Miss Dickinson and put his arm around her waist, kissing her on the cheek. She pushed him away and stood to ring the alarm to alert the guard, only to find that it did not work.

Baker pushed her back into the corner seat in which she had previously been sitting and forcibly leant against her, kissing her firmly on the lips. She felt his hand under her dress, on her stocking above her boot.

Miss Dickinson managed to push away the would-be ravisher and pulled down the window, leaning out backwards to scream for help. With no other means of escape, she took the only option available and, reaching down to the outside door handle, opened the door and stepped out onto the footboard, closing the door behind her.[21] Miss Dickinson travelled this way for some four or five miles, holding onto the door handle and clutching Baker's arm. Her screams alerted several witnesses, who caused the train to stop just outside Esher. At this point Baker was taken to a different carriage, and a Rev. J. B. Brown helped Miss Dickinson down from the footboard. At the Minister's insistence she attended the police office at Waterloo station, where she made her complaint. Colonel Baker was arrested at Guildford station the following day. He told the arresting officer that "if he saw the young lady's brother and arranged it with him, it would be all right".[22]

The trial at Surrey Assizes, Croydon, took place on 2nd August 1875. A packed courtroom heard Baker pronounced guilty of indecent assault, with Mr. Justice Brett sentencing him to twelve months imprisonment and imposing a fine of £500 with costs, a decision which won the applause of those present.[23]

When addressing Baker Mr. Justice Brett paid particular tribute to Miss Dickinson's bravery at reporting the attack:

> It may be suggested that the libertine outrage which you committed has defiled her. I say distinctly that it has not. She walks out of this court pure and innocent and undefiled – nay, more, the courage she has displayed

has added a ray of glory to her youth and innocence and beauty.²⁴

Miss Dickinson had also won the admiration of the Queen. *The Western Daily Press* reported on 25th August that Victoria had written expressing her sympathy, and had requested a photograph of Miss Dickinson be sent to her Majesty.

It is unlikely that Frederick Isaac Gold was worried about being kissed by an intruder as he settled into his seat in the First Class compartment of a composite carriage on the 2.00pm train to Brighton. A regular traveller on that particular service from London Bridge, he had boarded just five minutes earlier, speaking briefly to ticket collector William Franks as he did so.

The 64-year-old Mr. Gold was a big, powerfully-built man, and on that day, Monday, 27th June 1881, was as usual in robust health. As was his custom, he was wearing an eye-glass and a skull cap, with an umbrella hanging from the armhole of his waistcoat, inside his overcoat.

Mr. Gold had previously owned three shops in the capital, but since retiring had let two go and now just retained a baker's shop on East Street, Walworth. Each Monday he visited the manageress, Mrs. Catherine Cross, to collect the takings, and that morning he had received a small bag from her containing £38 in gold, 5s in silver and a penny, the amount written on a slip of pink paper.

Mr. Gold next went to the London and Westminster Bank, Whitechapel, where he paid in £38 in gold, making no withdrawal, before making his way to London Bridge station. Having conducted his weekly business, Mr. Gold was now heading to his home at Preston Park, near Brighton. He checked the time on his newly-adjusted white-faced Griffiths pocket watch, which he had collected that morning from Joseph Boivin, a watchmaker at Market Street, Brighton. It was two o'clock.

Just as the train was about to depart the door burst open and in jumped a pale, thin-faced young man. He sat down opposite Mr. Gold and the train slowly pulled out of the station.²⁵

At Horley, a woman named Ann Brown was looking out of the window of her cottage a hundred yards from the line as the train thundered passed. She saw two men standing up in a carriage, scuffling and waving their arms about as though fighting. The incident was also witnessed by Mrs. Brown's daughter Rhoda.²⁶

William Humphrey Gibson, a chemist at Brighton, was travelling in the Second Class compartment next to the carriage containing Mr. Gold and his fellow passenger. As the train entered Merstham tunnel he heard several loud bangs, which he took to be fog signals. The reports followed one after the other, all in the space of five or six seconds. Twenty-five minutes later the train passed through Balcombe tunnel.

The train's guard, Thomas Watson, heard no such bangs. But when the train stopped at Preston Park station he saw platform ticket collector Joseph Stark talking to the thin man at the window of the composite carriage. The passenger complained of being attacked, and was covered in blood. His face and neck were smeared with blood, and there was a clot beside one ear. There was blood between his fingers, blood upon his clothes, blood in the carriage, and blood upon the train's footboard, which also bore the marks of bloody fingerprints. The carriage was otherwise empty.

The passenger stepped from the carriage, and asked for help. A second ticket collector, Richard Gibson, approached. The stricken man said he had been attacked by two men, one an elderly gentleman and the second a 'countryman', and was desperate for medical attention. Guard Watson left the train and joined them. Scanning the man's clothing, he noticed a length of chain, between four and seven inches long, hanging from one of his shoes. Taking the end between his fingers and giving it a gentle tug, a small gold watch popped out. The blood-soaked man appeared to be as surprised as anyone at the appearance of the watch, but would later claim that he had concealed it there when he entered the carriage and saw his two travelling companions. Richard Gibson was told to accompany the injured man to Brighton, where he attended hospital and was seen by House Surgeon Dr. Benjamin Hall, who commented that some of the marks might have been caused by blows from an umbrella.[27]

At that moment, a platelayer employed by the London, Brighton and South Coast Railway Company named Thomas Jennings was walking through Balcombe tunnel with his nephew William. By the light of their naphtha lamp they saw the body of a large man laying on its back. The face, which had been badly beaten, was covered by part of the coat. The right arm was crossed over the left breast, and the left arm folded underneath the back. One boot remained on the body, the other missing. Jennings thought the body felt slightly warm to the touch.

William Jennings hurried off to telegraph news of the gruesome discovery, and thirty minutes later P.C. George Lewis of the Sussex Constabulary duly arrived. Searching the body and surrounding area, in the pockets of the coat he found a pocket-book, a rail season ticket

The Illustrated Police News, 19th November 1881

and two receipts. The knees of the trousers were torn and bloodied. Six yards from the body Lewis found a broken eye-glass.

The body was removed from the tracks and taken to the Railway Inn at Balcombe, where it was seen by local doctors Byass and Hall, along with Scotland Yard's Divisional Surgeon Dr. Thomas Bond, who had been summoned from London. He recorded the injuries in detail:

> There were excoriations and bruises, and the skull was very badly fractured. The fracture was such as might have been caused by the body coming into violent contact with the ground. The left hand and face were badly cut, as if by some sharp instrument. These cuts must have been made during life, and have bled freely. There was a wound in the corner of the left eye, about half an inch deep, and the mucous membrane of the eye was very much injected with blood. There was a bullet mark under the ear, and a bullet was extracted from the spine, into which it had passed. It was a small bullet such as would fit a small revolver. Such a bullet passing into the neck would cause momentary insensibility. The immediate cause of the death was syncope, coming from the shock and loss of blood. There would be little loss of blood from the shot, but a great deal from the knife wounds, of which there were fourteen on different parts of the body.[28]

Meanwhile, at Brighton Town Hall police station, the thin man was making a statement about the assault. He gave his name as "Arthur Lefroy". Afterwards, he was accompanied back to the railway station, where Superintendent Henry Anscombe asked Lefroy if he was badly injured. "I should think I am, considering I have four or five bullets in my head," replied Lefroy. "Can I have a lawyer? I must offer a reward."

Asked whether he carried a gun, he invited Det. Sergeants George Holmes and William Howland, both Metropolitan Police officers attached to the London, Brighton and South Coast Railway company, to search him. Holmes did so, finding a dozen shillings and a small quantity of Hanoverian medals, along with the blood-smeared white-faced watch and a pocket-book. Holmes was about to examine the notebook when Lefroy exclaimed "I have something private in there." He said he felt ill and wished to return to his home at Wallington, south London.

Holmes and Howland escorted their ward out of the office onto a train, departing at 6.10pm. When stopping at Three Bridges, the Station Master there, Mr. Brown, got in and spoke with Holmes. Brown told the officer that a body had been found on the track, and that murder was suspected. Telling Holmes not to lose sight of the man, the officer complained that he had "no charge against him."[29]

Holmes and his fellow passenger alighted at East Croydon, where the station master passed a telegram to the detective, which read: 'Tell Inspector Holmes to take number of watch on wounded man in 6.10 up train, as man found had no watch.'

Holmes and Lefroy took a cab to a house three miles away at Cathcart Road. There, Holmes took a statement from the man. He gave his name as Percy Lefroy, formerly Mapleton. The owner of the house, Mr. Clayton, said that Lefroy had lodged there since returning from Australia some eighteen months previously. He was a cousin of Clayton's wife Annie, and shared a room with Annie's brother Frank Seale.[30] Holmes asked Lefroy for the serial number of his watch, receiving the confident answer, '56312'. Unfortunately, when the watch found in his shoe was opened, it revealed an entirely different number.

The detective asked Lefroy where he could be reached the following day. He replied that he would be at Cathcart Road until midday, after which he would be at the Union Arts Club, Savoy Street, the Strand.

Courteously holding open the door, Lefroy let Holmes out of the house and the detective went to Wallington railway station. There, he received a telegram telling him to detain Lefroy and immediately returned to the house, having been absent just six minutes. He remained outside awaiting reinforcements, guarding the front door, and an hour later Sergeants Tobutt and Howland arrived. They went inside, with Holmes going to the back door. A few minutes later Tobutt and Howland came out and declared that Lefroy was no longer in the house.[31] In the pocket of a coat he had left they found pawn tickets from Messrs Adams and Hillstead, made out in the name of Lee, Southampton Street, Peckham.[32]

The inquest into Mr. Gold's death was opened at Balcombe on 29th June, two days after the murder. It was presided over by Wynne Baxter,

Lucky Swanson and the Murder of Mr. Gold

*The original sketch of Lefroy made by someone who knew him
from From City to Fleet Street by J. Hall Richardson*

MURDER.
£200 REWARD.

WHEREAS, on Monday, June 27th, ISAAC FREDERICK GOULD was murdered on the London Brighton and South Coast Railway, between Three Bridges and Balcombe, in East Sussex,

AND WHEREAS a Verdict of WILFUL MURDER has been returned by a Coroner's Jury against

PERCY LEFROY MAPLETON,

whose Portrait and Handwriting are given hereon,--

and who is described as being 22 years of age, height 5 ft 8 or 9 in., very thin, hair (cut short) dark, small dark whiskers; dress, dark frock coat, and shoes, and supposed low black hat (worn at back of head), had scratches from fingers on throat, several wounds on head, the dressing of which involved the cutting of hair, recently lodged at 4, Cathcart Road, Wallington, was seen at 9.30 a.m. 28th ult., with his head bandaged, at the Fever Hospital, Liverpool Road, Islington. Had a gold open-faced watch (which he is likely to pledge). "Maker, Griffiths, Mile End Road, No 16261."

One Half of the above Reward will be paid by Her Majesty's Government, and One Half by the Directors of the London Brighton and South Coast Railway to any person (other than a person belonging to a Police Force in the United Kingdom) who shall give such information as shall lead to the discovery and apprehension of the said PERCY LEFROY MAPLETON, or others, the Murderer, or Murderers, upon his or their conviction; and the Secretary of State for the Home Department will advise the grant of Her Majesty's gracious PARDON to any accomplice, not being the person who actually committed the Murder, who shall give such evidence as shall lead to a like result.

Information to be given to the Chief Constable of East Sussex, Lewes, or any Police Station, or to

The Director of Criminal Investigations, Gt. Scotland Yard.

JULY 4th, 1881.

The handbill produced from the sketch
from Masters of Crime by Guy Logan

the Coroner for Sussex Eastern Division.[33] It concluded on Thursday, 7th July, with the jury deliberating for just twenty minutes before returning a verdict of "Wilful Murder against Arthur Lefroy, alias Mapleton", who had still not been located.[34]

Mr. Gold had been buried three days earlier at the Extra-Mural Cemetery just outside Brighton. Four mourning coaches followed the hearse on its sad journey through the streets of Preston Park, and the blinds of many houses and businesses lining the route were drawn as a mark of respect. It was estimated that four or five thousand people witnessed the simple service given by Reverend Allan Freeman at the cemetery,[35] with a large crowd paying their respects, many scattering flowers onto the coffin as it was lowered into the ground.[36]

As the funeral took place, Mr. Gold's murderer was in hiding at the small house on Smith Street some 70 miles away. He had arrived at eleven o'clock in the morning of Thursday, 30th June, telling Mrs. Bickers, the landlady, that he had seen a notice in the window advertising lodgings to let. Giving his name as George Clark,[37] he asked to see the room, which was on the first floor at the front of the house. He said he would take it, and in answer to a question from the landlady said that his baggage would follow the next day. As the room was not ready, Mr. Clark went away and returned at two o'clock in the afternoon, paying advance rent of 3s 6d.[38]

Meanwhile, the search had intensified. A sketch of Lefroy had been produced from a description given by a man who knew the fugitive, and this was turned into a handbill offering a £200 reward (see following pages). The sketch of the wanted man had also been carried by the *Daily Telegraph* of 1st July 1881 – an important event in the history of crime detection, as it was the first time a likeness of a wanted man was circulated in a national newspaper.[39] The newspaper included a detailed description of Lefroy:

> Age 22, middle height, very thin, sickly appearance, scratches on throat, wounds on head, probably clean shaved, low felt hat, black coat, teeth much discoloured... He is very round shouldered, and his thin overcoat hangs in awkward folds about his spare figure. His forehead and chin are both receding. He has a slight moustache, and very small dark whiskers. His jawbones are prominent, his cheeks sunken and sallow, and his teeth fully exposed when laughing. His upper lip is thin and drawn inwards. His eyes are grey and large. His gait is singular; he is inclined to slouch and when not carrying a bag, his left hand is usually in his pocket. He generally carries a crutch stick.

A bookseller and stationer at Wallington named Albert Ellis came forward to say that he had known Lefroy for about 18 months. On the morning of the murder he had received a letter purportedly from Lefroy asking him to visit his cousin Annie Clayton at nearby Cathcart Road, as she wished to order some books. As soon as Ellis arrived he noticed Lefroy hurrying away, next to appear at his shop in Railway Terrace with a sealed envelope which he told the shopboy contained two sovereigns as payment of his account arrears of £1 7s 2d. Asking the boy for the change he was given 13 shillings, all that was in the till. When Mr. Ellis returned and opened the envelope he found two Hanoverian medals, a shilling and a blank piece of paper. It was with this swindled money that Lefroy had purchased his train ticket.[40]

After a few days Mrs. Bickers began to think the behaviour of her new lodger odd; he rarely left the house, and declined to join his fellow lodgers for Sunday lunch as was their custom, preferring to stay alone in his room. He kept the blinds drawn in his room at all times, and when taking breakfast downstairs would draw the blinds in the dining room as well. His luggage, supposedly following from Liverpool, never arrived.

On Thursday, 7th July Clark asked Mrs. Bickers to go to the City to collect his wages; when asked why he did not do so himself, he replied that he had sprained his ankle getting out of bed. He then asked whether she could arrange for a telegram to be sent instead, to which she agreed, and Clark wrote a draft which a neighbour, a greengrocer named Doyle, took to the telegraph office. The message read:

> From G. Clark, 32 Smith Street, Stepney, to S. Seale, J. T. Hutchinson and Co., 56 Gresham Street, London. Please bring my wages this evening, before eight, without fail. Shall have the flour tomorrow. Not 33.[41]

Mrs. Bickers noticed that Clark was wearing a coat belonging to another lodger, and that he must have taken it from the other man's room. Feeling something was not quite right, she went to nearby Arbour Square police station to make a complaint.

The following morning, still harbouring an uneasiness about Mr. Clark, the landlady sent her daughter to see Mr. Hutchinson, the supposed employer. Jane Bickers arrived at the Gresham Street offices and spoke to a young clerk with a "light beard and curly moustache"[42] named Joseph Mugford.[43] He told Miss Bickers that nobody by the name of Clark was employed there, and she then related the suspicions which she and her mother had about the lodger. Having obtained a description of Clark, and the date he arrived at Smith Street, Mugford realised who the man was and at the end of his working hours went to Scotland Yard. It was he who had spoken with Det. Inspector Swanson.⁴⁴

Lefroy was woken early in his cell at King Street on the morning of Saturday, 9th July, and after a breakfast of coffee and sandwiches was put in a cab for Victoria rail station, accompanied by Swanson and Jarvis.

Those at King Street police station who had seen Lefroy commented that he did not have the imbecilic look presented in the circulated portrait, and several officers said that when comparing his appearance with the sketch, while there was a resemblance, they would probably have passed him in the street rather than recognise him as the man they were looking for.⁴⁵

Despite leaving at the early hour of seven o'clock, word had spread of the imminent departure and a large crowd gathered at Victoria station to shout insults at the prisoner. The detectives hurried Lefroy into a first-class carriage and drew down the blinds to screen him from the crowd, which by this time lined the platform. The train set off at 7.35am. Lefroy chatted amiably with Swanson and Jarvis, sharing their cigarettes, and generally seemed relaxed. As Mr. Gold's body had been found within the Cuckfield Petty Sessional Division, and not within the jurisdiction of the East Grinstead magistrates as first supposed, the

Left: Lefroy at Lewes, and right: watched by Det. Inspector Swanson at Cuckfield from The Illustrated Police News, 23rd July 1881

officers' destination had altered.[46] They changed trains at Haywards Heath to travel to Lewes instead of continuing to East Grinstead, and as the party stepped onto the platform Lefroy was immediately recognised and loud roars of disapproval rained down until Swanson, Jarvis and the prisoner boarded another first-class train, where once again the blinds were drawn.

The train left an hour later and arrived at Lewes at 10.32am, where a cab took the detectives and their prisoner to Lewes Gaol. Throughout the journey Lefroy appeared calm, but Swanson and Jarvis noticed that when travelling through Merstham and Balcombe tunnels he looked around and became excited.[47]

On arrival at Lewes Gaol Lefroy was examined by Mr. Justice Molyneux, and then placed in the East Wing, where prisoners awaiting trial were housed.

On Friday, 15th July he was taken to the committal hearing at the Talbot Hotel in the small Sussex village of Cuckfield. His appearance drew a crowd of locals:

> The Cuckfielders gathered around, eyes wide open and mouth agape, for they felt something of surpassing interest to them was about to happen. That "something" was at hand. In another minute a tall, thin, cadaverous young man, tightly held by the left arm by a sturdy policeman, supported, too, on the other side by another constable, and followed by four men in a line, passed through the doorway of the hotel.
>
> It was not "entrancing", yet it was distinctly painful. The wretched appearance of the central figure in that procession as it moved slowly down the principal thoroughfare of that dull village was such as was capable of moving the most careless mind... There was no attempt at mobbing him; there were no shouts uttered; the unhappy prisoner was, if not exactly pitied, at least to a certain extent regarded with a feeling akin to commiseration – his looks were so depressing.[48]

The hotel's function room had been hastily prepared for the hearing, with three long tables arranged for the magistrates, lawyers and members of the press. Lefroy himself sat in an armchair, with the public standing at a cleared space partitioned from proceedings by a barrier constructed of timber. Through the half-open windows drifted the smell of nearby pigsties.[49]

Swanson and Jarvis gave evidence on Thursday, 21st July. Their appearance impressed the reporter from the *Daily Gazette for Middlesbrough*:

Inspector Swanson is one of the keenest and, if the term can be used, most detective-like Scotchmen that it would be possible to find. Lefroy may have received him, as he states, in 32 Smith Street, Stepney, with coolness, but the appearance of such an officer of police was certainly not calculated to inspire a suspected man with confidence. Mr. Swanson's manner of announcing himself as he entered the room was not quite that of the most agreeable visitor. His attitude as he stood opposite Lefroy yesterday did not at any rate suggest that.

There are many people in the world whom a person hiding from general observation would prefer to see than Inspector Swanson. The business-like way in which he proceeded with his evidence suggested what his manner was when he was in the room. He had actually taken down the prisoner's words in a memorandum book at the very moment when Lefroy was in his grasp. No wonder that [Lefroy's solicitor] Mr. Dutton refrained from cross-examining him.

Inspector Jarvis, who had accompanied Mr. Swanson to the house, was a very fit companion indeed. As they stood side by side, while the depositions of Mr. Swanson were being read over, and Mr. Jarvis was waiting to give his evidence, they certainly appeared patterns of what two such men should be. The chances of escape remaining when anyone was in their hands would be very slight.[50]

With all evidence heard, the magistrates had no hesitation in sending the prisoner to trial. Having been held at Lewes Gaol throughout the hearing, Lefroy was transferred to Maidstone on Friday, 28th October, to appear at the Assizes there on 4th November.[51]

The London, Chatham and Dover Railway, recognising an opportunity to benefit from the enormous public interest, announced that they would be running special trains from London to Maidstone for the duration of the trial.[52]

Det. Inspector Swanson was continuing with his inquiries. A revolver had been found in a ditch by the side of the track by a platelayer named Streeter, who took it to the station master at Earlswood. From there it was sent to London Bridge, where Inspector Turpin handed it to the Scotland Yard detective. Swanson took the gun, a six chamber pin-fire revolver, to pawnbrokers Adams and Hillstead of High Street, Borough. Although rusted and the muzzle choked with dirt, the shop manager Henry Creek was able to confirm that the revolver was the one pledged by Lefroy under the guise of "Mr. Lee", and that he had reclaimed it in the early afternoon of the murder.[53]

Having already established that Lefroy's story of being attacked by an unidentified assailant was a fabrication, it was a surprise when on 19th July a letter was received by the magistrates at Cuckfield signed by a " J. Major" of Chapel Street, Penzance, claiming to be the third man in the carriage. The head of the Penzance police force went to the address, finding it occupied by a father and son named M. and J. B. Major. Swanson travelled down to the West Country, his enquiries showing that neither father or son knew anything of the letter, nor recognised the handwriting. It appeared that whoever had written the letter, it had not originated from the supposed source.

Frank Seale, meanwhile, was only too happy to talk to the newspapers. Claiming that he had not been in contact with Lefroy since the murderer had left the house at Cathcart Street, he said that when the telegram arrived at his place of work at Gresham Street he dismissed it as a hoax:

> I had no idea who Clark was, and could not in any way understand why I had a telegram in such a name. My idea was that the telegram was one which came from the police in order to attract me to this house at Stepney. Therefore I took no notice of it. I had no business to call me there. I do not know the locality nor the landlady of the house.
>
> Had I known or had I any inkling that the telegram came from Lefroy I would have gone to Smith Street at all risks and hazards. I have been very fond of him, and we are terribly anxious as to his fate. He has always been a pet of the family.[54]

While awaiting the trial, Det. Inspector Swanson was called upon to investigate a deeply upsetting case, one extremely close to home – the murder of a policeman.

Although fatal shootings of policemen were rare – in fact, since the formation of the Metropolitan Police only two London-based officers had been killed through gunfire up to 1881[55] – the carrying of firearms by burglars was becoming alarmingly more frequent. The notorious criminal Charles Peace had shot and killed P.C. Nicholas Cock at Manchester in 1876, and two years later injured P.C. Edward Robinson when firing five shots at the officer who had disturbed the burglar at Blackheath.

Those constables patrolling remote, outlying locations were becoming increasingly at risk. And so it proved when, in the early hours of Thursday, 22nd September 1881, P.C. Frederick Atkins approached The Knoll, a large house on Kingston Hill in the Met's V Division.

Mr. Short, the butler, was woken by the sound of a pistol firing and got up to search the house, on his rounds meeting the housekeeper, who had also heard the shot. Each door proved to be secure, but as they approached the front entrance they heard a moan coming from outside. On opening the door they found P.C. Atkins, unconscious on the ground and bleeding profusely.

The two members of staff immediately alerted their employer, Mr. Powys-Keck, who telephoned the police station on London Road, Kingston. Several local inspectors, along with Divisional Surgeon Dr. Roots, attended The Knoll, where they found P.C. Atkins in a perilous condition, unable to be taken to hospital. He was, however, moved to Kingston police station, where he was examined by Dr. Roots. It was discovered that the constable had been shot three times, once in the chest, with the bullet entering a lung, and also in the abdomen and left thigh.

The 22-year-old Atkins, who had been transferred to V Division just two months earlier, was gently questioned by Inspector Bond and Dr. Roots as to the attack, and, with great difficulty, was able to make a statement:

> I did not see anybody or hear anything which should cause me to imagine there were burglars at work. I went along the avenue slowly,

The murder and funeral of P.C. Frederick Atkins
from The Penny Illustrated Paper, 8th October 1881

accordingly to my usual custom when on duty there, but there was no-one about. Before I was aware of anything I saw something like the gleam of a lantern, and then whispers, after which there was a report, and then I felt I was struck by something sharp in the chest. I turned to one side quickly, when another shot was fired, and that's all I can remember.

Inspector Bond, with colleagues Crowther and Rushbridge, examined the grounds of The Knoll and a lantern and a jemmy were found underneath some bushes. An iron bar had been removed from the window of a lavatory at the side of the house, and it was here that the officers suspected the burglars were about to enter the house when they were disturbed by P.C. Atkins.[56] With that window sitting in a dark recess, it would have been impossible for the constable to see his assailants.

The young officer survived for another twenty-four hours before succumbing to his wounds. The primary cause had been the bullet which passed through his lung, it still being lodged in his back. A second bullet had been found near the lantern and jemmy, with the third and final dropping from Atkins' clothing as he was undressed at the station.[57]

Reporting his passing, the newspapers commented on a similar case which had also occurred at Kingston Hill, when a P.C. Kerrison was shot by burglars, although thankfully not fatally.[58]

Although the Kingston police diligently searched the grounds of The Knoll and investigated their usual suspects, no clue was found as to the killer or killers, and Scotland Yard was called in. Howard Vincent wasted no time in sending Det. Inspectors Swanson and Andrews to Kingston.[59] A local blacksmith named Brockwell was soon arrested, and interviewed at Kingston police station. His boots were found to match footprints found in the grounds of The Knoll, but, despite being questioned for over five hours, no evidence could be found against him and he was released.[60]

Despite a Government reward of £100, which was added to by a consortium of Kingston businessmen,[61] no clue was found as to those responsible for P.C. Atkins' death. His killer was never identified.[62]

When the funeral of the tragic constable took place a week after his death, nearly two thousand policemen from all divisions attended, most travelling by special train from Waterloo to Walton-on-Thames, where Atkins' family lived.[63]

As the funeral procession made its way to Walton parish church, every shop in Kingston was closed as a mark of respect, with blinds drawn on the windows along the route.[64] As they marched along, the band of the V Division played the 'Dead March' from Handel's *Saul*, with Frederick Atkins' former colleagues acting as pall bearers.[65]

As P.C. Atkins was laid to rest, perhaps inevitably calls came to arm the police:

> A few weeks ago we called attention to the perils of the policeman's vocation, and to the courage which they need to possess while doing the work which nightly devolves them. The soldier has few dangers to encounter in comparison with those which many of our policemen are exposed in their nightly rounds. Soldiers are not always on the field of war or threatened by a sudden attack from ruthless foes; but policemen have very often to face lawless men who seem to set little value upon human life. The question has, therefore, very naturally been raised, can we do nothing by way of enabling policemen to defend themselves against the species of ruffianism which revels in outrage and blood? Ought we not to be able to protect them from the attacks of cowardly wretches who, protected by darkness, will shoot down an unfortunate policemen before he has had a moment's warning?
>
> ...The *Standard* suggests that we should arm the police on night duty. A policeman on dangerous duty, it argues, carries his life in his hand, and we ought to afford him the opportunity of protecting himself. But what would be the effect of such an arrangement as this? Would it tend to the security of human life or the reverse? Would it, in short, be the means of saving the lives of the police, or of endangering the life of everyone who goes out at night? A revolver is an exceedingly dangerous weapon, but nowhere is it so dangerous as in the hands of an easily startled or nervous person.
>
> A policeman deficient in nerve and coolness might fire in hot haste without pausing to consider what he was about. He might suspect where there was no real ground for suspicion. He might mistake for a burglar some stupefied drunken fellow trying to force open the wrong door or to get into his neighbour's house.[66]

While attitudes ran high in the wake of Atkins' murder, it took the fatal shooting of P.C. George Cole by a burglar the following year and the attempted murder of P.C. Patrick Boans in 1883 to force the authorities to seriously consider arming their officers. It was decided to give Superintendents of the outer-lying divisions the opportunity to arm their constables on night duty, an option which received mixed reactions from within the force.

Despite this availability, it wasn't until four years later that the first revolver was fired by a Metropolitan policeman while on duty, when, on 18th February 1887, P.C. Henry Owen fired six shots into the air in an attempt to wake the residents of a burning house after his shouts had failed to rouse them.[67]

The trial of Percy Lefroy Mapleton opened on 4th November. While the result was hardly in doubt, Lefroy's behaviour while in the dock was extraordinary, as recorded by his defence counsel Montagu Williams:

> While the jury were being sworn, Lefroy stood listlessly with his hands behind him. Though self-possessed, it was clear that he was nervous.
>
> Before the Attorney-General commenced his speech, the prisoner placed his hat on a ledge at the side of the dock. He took it up again, and then once more returned it to the ledge. Apparently, he was loth to part with it. It subsequently transpired that Lefroy was a man of considerable conceit. On the first morning of his trial, he actually asked for his dress-coat, in order that he might wear that garment in the dock. He was, in a word, a man steeped in a kind of petty, strutting, theatrical vanity. Nevertheless, it was almost inexplicable that he should devote more attention to his hat than to the proceedings of the trial.
>
> It was curious to note the change that took place in Lefroy's bearing and demeanour whenever he caught sight of an artist from one of the illustrated papers in the act of sketching him. He suddenly brightened up, and, if I am not mistaken, assumed a studied pose for the occasion.
>
> The proceedings apparently made little impression upon Lefroy, for beyond every now and then lifting his eyelids, he made no sign. At times, indeed, he seemed to be dozing.
>
> On the third day of the trial, which was a Monday, the case for the prosecution closed, and, at about eleven o'clock, I rose to address the jury for the defence. My speech lasted for about three hours, and I do not think that I ever saw a jury more attentive than on this occasion. Some of them gave way to tears.
>
> Once during the delivery of my speech, Lefroy shifted his chair a little, and seemed for the moment as though he really intended to wake up and listen. This was a mere spasmodic effort, however, and it soon died away. He either had not any interest in the business in hand, or he took care to disguise it.

Lucky Swanson and the Murder of Mr. Gold

The trial of Lefroy at Maidstone Assizes.
Background: Percy Lefroy Mapleton (2) and the Governor of Lewes Gaol (10).
Foreground: Det. Sergeant Holmes (23); Det. Inspector Jarvis (24);
Det. Inspector Swanson (25) and Sergeant Tobutt (26)
from The Illustrated Police News, 12th November 1881

During the absence of the jury, I noticed that the prisoner, whose life was hanging in the balance, showed symptoms of nervousness for the first time. His hands seemed to come mechanically to his face, his fingers twitched as he tugged at his moustache, and he moved uneasily in his chair, being evidently unable to control his emotion. Once or twice he got up from his seat, leant over the bars of the dock, and addressed a few words to his solicitor, Mr. Dutton; then, as if by a great effort of will, he sat down again, and was comparatively calm.

When the foreman pronounced the word "Guilty", up rose Lefroy, and, placing his hands behind him, advanced to the rails. He seemed to be altogether at ease, though pallid. There was a moment, however, when he grasped convulsively at the rails, and swayed to and fro, as though about to fall. But the weakness was only for a moment. The next minute he was himself again, and, folding his arms, he fixed his eyes intently upon the jury, and said: "Some day you will learn, when too late, that you have murdered me." Then, with a firm step, he retired, and disappeared from the public gaze.[68]

Thomas Dutton, Lefroy's solicitor, acted on the family's wishes and drew up a petition seeking the reprieve by asking for a medical inquiry on the grounds of insanity. He contacted psychiatric doctors Forbes Winslow[69] and Winn, and obtained reports concluding that Lefroy was not, and had not for some time, been responsible for his actions. Dutton's request for Winslow and Winn to visit Lefroy was met with a curt response: "This will be declined of course... There was, I believe, no evidence of insanity at the trial, as the line of defence was that he never did the act. Drs. Winslow and Winn are the last persons to whom such an inquiry should be entrusted."

Dutton attempted to prove that Lefroy came from a background of poor mental health, claiming that his father Henry Mapleton had for 34 years suffered from "mental delusions and fits of insanity", on one occasion attempted to smother his wife and later attempting suicide before dying of cirrhosis and jaundice in 1879. Lefroy's grandfather and uncle, Dutton claimed, had both experienced prolonged bouts of insanity.

Was a history of insanity the "certain matters" in connection with his family which Lefroy told Swanson and Jarvis he feared would be exposed?

As for his client, Dutton wrote:

The accused himself, who has always been of a weak sickly temperament, had a sunstroke whilst standing on the racecourse at Epsom on the Derby Day of 1880, on which occasion he fell down in a fit, and was taken home in a conveyance and confined to his bed for several days, and has never since been the same man, having been subject to long and continued fits of despondency and depression and at the present time and for some years back he has been in consumption.

The Home Office were not impressed:

> I don't think there is anything here to warrant medical enquiry. The father was a drunkard and the mother died of consumption and is said to have been subject to fits of melancholy and frenzy while with child of prisoner. Neither of [these symptoms are] insanity. As to the other relations said to have been insane, there is not a particle of evidence.
>
> This is the oft repeated case of an afterthought defence not set up at the trial or ever suggested and at the last moment fired at the Secretary of State as a forlorn hope.[70]

Forbes Winslow was barred from visiting the prisoner, and would later write:

> Lefroy was cunning, as most lunatics are, and this quality was observed throughout the whole of his transactions. His conduct was very peculiar after the murder, but the fact that it was apparently premeditated strengthened the case for the prosecution. But it might be as well to state that most murders committed by lunatics are premeditated, and that insanity and cunning go hand in hand.
>
> The case from first to last was a very sensational one, and the attention of London was absorbed in it; but under no pretence whatever was the public executioner to be deprived of his victim.
>
> After these years, and reviewing the case calmly and deliberately, and taking into consideration the history of the case and all the concomitant facts, I am very strongly of the opinion that it would have been to the interests of intelligence, humanity, science, civilisation, Christianity, and justice if a deaf ear had not been turned to the prayer of the unhappy man's family and medical petitioners, simply begging that the Home Secretary would grant them an inquiry into the mental condition of the youth standing on the precipice of his fate. We asked no more than this, and were refused.[71]

While awaiting the execution, Lefroy busied himself writing many letters and at least six confessions, each more exaggerated than the last. He also penned a dramatic autobiography, which after his death was sent to the Home Office by the Chaplain at Lewes Gaol, the Rev. Cole. Lefroy had requested that the Chaplain decide what to do with the story after his execution; Home Secretary Sir William Harcourt agreed with Under Secretary Liddell's suggestion that it not be released, commenting "this miserable production should not see the light – keep it locked up."[72]

As one last desperate attempt to delay the inevitable, Dutton wrote to the Home Office to say that Lefroy had confessed to the murder of Lieut. Percy Roper at Chatham Barracks in the February of 1881, which was at that moment in the newspapers alongside the case of Lefroy because a reward of £600 had been offered.

It was too late.

Percy Lefroy Mapleton was executed at Lewes Gaol on Tuesday, 29th November 1881. It was only the fourth hanging to have taken place there in the twenty-five years since the Gaol had opened.

An hour earlier Lefroy had spoken alone with the prison Chaplain, who later informed the Home Office that

> before his death [he] made a full confession to me of the murder of Mr. Gold and acknowledges the justice of his sentence. He also entirely retracted the statement he had made concerning the murder by himself of Lieutenant Roper and expressed regret that, yielding to the pressure of his solicitor and the evidence alleged by him, he had fabricated a confession of a crime of which in reality he knew nothing.[73]

Newspaper reporters were admitted to Lewes Gaol at 8.30am and escorted to a yard where the gallows had been erected in the right-hand corner, a simple crossbeam over a pit into which the prisoner would drop. Forty feet to the left was a grave, already dug in readiness to receive the body. Apart from the press, the only people in the yard were Mr. Bull, the Deputy Governor of the Gaol, and William Marwood, the executioner. At five minutes to nine Marwood went inside to fetch the prisoner:

> In two minutes the procession emerged from the door leading from the corridor in which the condemned cell is situated. First came the Chaplain, the Rev. T. H. Cole, who as he came out began to read the Burial Service in clear and solemn tones, the only other sound being the clang of the "passing bell", which had been tolling some ten minutes. The clergyman was followed by a warder, and then came Lefroy, pinioned

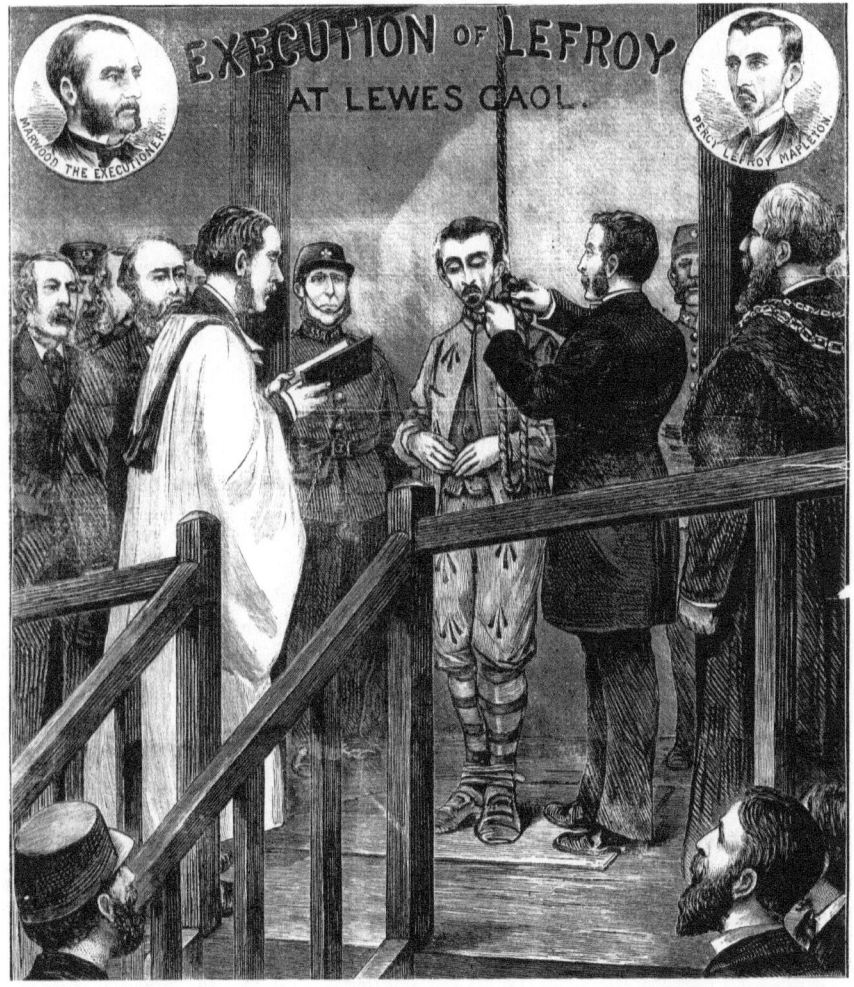

The execution of Percy Lefroy Mapleton
from The Illustrated Police News, 3rd December 1881

and bare-necked, with a warder on either side, and the executioner close in the rear, supporting the convict by a slight touch of the elbow; not that the culprit seemed to require such assistance, as he walked with a set, steadfast face, moving as a man in a dream, his lips tightly closed, looking neither to the right nor left, stepping quietly in time with the remainder of the procession.

Lefroy wore a suit of brown mixture, the same as on the examination at Cuckfield, and not the prison garb in which he has been attired since his conviction. In the rear of him came the Governor, the prison surgeon, one of the visiting justices, and the under sheriff, while the melancholy cortege was brought up by the under governor.

It took but a moment to reach the scaffold, on to which Lefroy stepped without the slightest hesitation, a slight fixing together of the lips alone showing inward agitation. Then Marwood proceeded to his work, first placing Lefroy in proper position under the beam, testing this by laying the rope upon his shoulders, and afterwards fastening his legs with a broad leather strap. He then produced the cap for shrouding the convict's face from his pocket, and instantly placed it in position. As this was being done Lefroy slightly raised his eyes, but not a feature of his face relaxed its rigidity. His lips never moved in response to the clergyman, who all this time, in tones that showed the deep emotion he felt, was reciting the selected portions of the service. As soon as he had drawn the cap over Lefroy's eyes, Marwood put the noose around his neck, and with dexterity and rapidity adjusted the rope.

Marwood stayed a moment to see that all was right, and then with a slight touch of his hand on Lefroy's right shoulder, but without going through the ceremony of shaking hands, he stepped back from the scaffold and stood by the lever that controlled the working of the drop. The next instant the minister recited the words "Lord have mercy upon us"; Marwood pulled the lever, and the doomed man dropped out of sight of the spectators. The surgeon made a short inspection of the body, but did not go into the pit. It was evident that death must have been instantaneous.[74]

Lefroy's body was left hanging for an hour. At 10.15am it was cut down and Richard Turner, surgeon attached to Lewes Gaol, examined the body and pronounced life extinct. An inquest was immediately conducted under Wynne Baxter and the fourteen jury members viewed the body, which by this time had been placed in its coffin, and returned a verdict that the law had been properly carried out. The coffin was then buried in the grave previously prepared.

It is clear that some sympathy was felt for Lefroy, possibly as a result of his perceived mental fragility. But an insight into the murderer's character was later given by Hargrave L. Adam in his book *Police Work From Within*, in a chapter discussing exhibits displayed at Scotland Yard's Black Museum which at that time included the sketch of Lefroy used by the *Daily Telegraph*:

The sketch in question was made by a man who had known Lefroy for some time quite intimately. I was recently discussing the case with a friend of mine who had known both the artist and Lefroy. It was generally supposed, at the time the crime was committed, that this was the only occasion on which the man had "gone wrong," that otherwise he had always been quite a worthy member of society, and had been driven to the commission of the crime from sheer want. In this way a good deal of sympathy was worked up for him. As a matter of fact this was entirely wrong, as he was known generally by his acquaintances to be an inveterate thief and a worthless individual altogether. Everybody who knew him suspected him – nobody trusted him. He would steal from anybody, even his own "chums". He used to play cricket, not so much for the love of the sport as the opportunity it gave him of getting into the tents or pavilion while the players were on the field and rifling their pockets – they having changed into "flannels". He had also been known even to break open their bags, removing anything portable and of value. In fact he was a thoroughly bad lot."[75]

A postscript to the Lefroy case was the matter of the £200 reward. Mrs. Bickers believed that the police had come to suspect that her lodger was Lefroy as a result of her going to Arbour Square station to complain about him wearing another lodger's coat. Swanson and Jarvis had visited 32 Smith Street several times after the arrest to conduct further searches, and had been asked by the landlady whether this was indeed the case. The detectives replied it was not, but declined to tell her from whom they had received the crucial information.

Swanson was also perhaps hopeful of a share of the reward. A newspaper commented on his recent success:

> Inspector Swanson, whose name has been made so prominent in connection with the arrest of Lefroy, bears the soubriquet among his colleagues of "Lucky Swanson". The nephew of a detective also an inspector, he is young, and has done some very clever things. It was he who succeeded in tracing and recovering the Countess of Bective's jewels – a most profitable piece of work, for the Earl gave him as a reward £200. He expects to share in the reward offered for the arrest of Lefroy if the young City clerk, who is already bothering members of Parliament to get him his money down but not to reveal his name, does not anticipate him.[76]

Mrs. Bickers had not wasted any time enquiring about the reward. She had her son-in-law William Farnworth, married to her daughter Caroline, write to the Home Secretary less than a week after Lefroy's arrest. In his letter, Farnworth underlined the fact that it was the suspicions of his mother-in-law which eventually brought about the identification of the wanted man:

> In the *Daily Telegraph* of the 12 inst. a letter appeared from Mr. Hutchinson, who states that his clerk gave information at Scotland Yard solely in consequence of what Miss Bickers told him. As Mrs. Bickers was the cause of her daughter visiting Mr. Hutchinson's office – and but for her action the information could never have reached Scotland Yard – I am induced to make this appeal to you with a consciousness that you will not allow the just claims of a widow lady to escape your notice. Mrs. Bickers does not claim the whole of the reward, feeling certain that some credit is due to the shrewdness of the informer. Considering the expense and annoyance to which she has been subjected before and after the arrest, and the injury her mind appears to have sustained, I must respectfully beg that you will grant her that share of the reward which your sense of justice may dictate as commensurate with the importance of her action which so curiously and promptly resulted in the arrest of Lefroy.[77]

The Home Office forwarded the letter to Scotland Yard for a response. In the national excitement over the hunt for and capture of Lefroy, it had almost been missed that Captain William Harris had retired as Assistant Commissioner (Executive) after 25 years. He was replaced by Lt. Colonel Richard Pearson, who had been educated at Eton and Sandhurst, serving with the Grenadier Guards and had been Aide-de-Campe to General Sir George Brown during the Crimean War.

One of Pearson's first tasks was to send a reply on Mrs. Bickers' claim to Home Secretary Sir William Harcourt. The communication included a report written by Det. Inspector Swanson explaining how he had received the information giving Lefroy's whereabouts from Joseph Mugford.

Swanson clearly felt sorry for Mrs. Bickers, stating in his report: "I have no doubt the matter has caused her considerable trouble and expense, which being a widow she can ill afford to bear."[78]

Following procedure, the Home Office then informed Farnworth and Mrs. Bickers that any claim to the reward would not be considered until a conviction was secured against Lefroy.

On 10th November, two days after the murderer had been found guilty,

Mrs. Bickers wrote seeking an answer to her request for a share of the reward money. She had, by this time, left Smith Street as a consequence of the crowds which continued to congregate outside her home, and moved to nearby Jamaica Street.

It was clear, however, that as the provider of the crucial information, Mugford would receive the full £200 reward: £100 from the Government and £100 from the directors of the London, Brighton and South Coast Railway. This was eventually paid to the clerk on 13th January 1882.

Learning of the payment, the newspapers reported that they "understood" Mrs. Bickers would receive a part. *Lloyd's Weekly Newspaper* was determined to discover whether this was indeed the case:

> We resolved upon a journey to Smith Street, and there found that Lefroy's landlady had removed. After some enquiries her present residence was discovered, but Mrs. Bickers was unfortunately out. Her daughter, however, obligingly answered a few questions. It appears that the whole of the reward has been paid over to the sharp lawyer's clerk, and any "part" for Mrs. or Miss Bickers must come from him. Seeing that the information of which Joseph Mugford so quickly made use was directly afforded by Miss Bickers, it is not unreasonable that something should be expected. The public will, we believe, agree with this; and look forward to hearing that a present has been made to Miss Bickers out of the two hundred pounds obtained by Mr. Mugford for his journey to Scotland Yard, and revelation of the murderer's hiding place.[79]

Sensing that red tape might mean Mrs. Bickers going unrewarded, on 22nd November Howard Vincent personally intervened and suggested to the Home Secretary that she should be awarded a £20 gratuity for her part in bringing the murderer to justice. "Should there not be any fund available at the Home Office out of which to pay such gratuity," he wrote, "I would beg to suggest that the Secretary of State's authority be issued to the Receiver for the Metropolitan Police District for the amount mentioned to be paid out of police funds".

The Home Office relented. A note written on Vincent's letter comments:

> This is unusual but Mrs. Bickers seems to have a claim. The Treasury might perhaps direct their solicitor to pay this gratuity if the [Secretary of State] were to recommend it, but the easiest way would no doubt be to pay it from the Police fund.

Some three months later, the Treasury finally agreed to pay the £20 to

Mrs. Bickers, writing to inform her on 24th February 1882.[80]

Swanson himself was awarded £5 by the Commissioner for "energy and zeal displayed in making numerous enquiries",[81] and also received £5 from the London, Brighton and South Coast Railway.[82] Swanson's nickname of "Lucky" continued to hold. Det. Inspectors Jarvis and Turpin also received £5 each.[83]

As for Joseph Mugford, his windfall did not last long. Just two years later he appeared at the City of London Bankruptcy Court owing creditors £42 11s 9d. He admitted that he was employed as a clerk at the London and Westminster Loan and Discount Company, on a salary of £2 per week, and solicitor Mr. Mason, appearing for the creditors, sought to prove that Mugford could afford to pay considerably more than the 2s in the pound by instalments he had offered.

The clerk was asked whether it was true that his mother had given him her life policy. Mugford replied that it was, but that he had sold it.

Mr. Mason then asked if it was true that the petitioner had received £200 over the capture of Lefroy, asking: "That was the reward you received for being the means of arresting that notorious criminal and bringing him to justice? What did you do with it?" Mugford replied, to laughter from the court, that he had paid £10 of his debts with it, and "made presents" of the rest to his mother, brothers and sisters. He himself had nothing left.[84]

The readers of *Lloyd's Weekly Newspaper* might not have read of Mugford making a present to Mrs. Bickers or her daughter after all, but they would have been permitted a smile when reading of his downfall.

ELEVEN

The Bodysnatchers

Two days after the body of Percy Lefroy Mapleton was buried in an unmarked grave in the grounds of Lewes Gaol, another, very different final resting place some 600 miles away was about to reveal a gruesome secret. A labourer working on the restoration of the mansion house owned by the Earl of Crawford at Dunecht, near Aberdeen, noticed that turf had been disturbed at the entrance to the family tomb. He alerted the overseer of the works, who in turn told the Earl's commissioner. The police were summoned from Aberdeen.

The alterations to Dunecht House, which had been going on for some years, included the building of a chapel under which was a mausoleum where the body of Alexander Lindsay, the 25th Earl of Crawford and 8th Earl of Balcarres, had been entombed.

The late Earl had been notable for his interests in astronomy and theology, and his vast library at the family seat at Haigh Hall, near Wigan, was a testimony to his endeavours in learning. He was a great genealogist, and had published an exhaustive history of his family in *Lives of the Lindsays* over three volumes in 1849.

A great traveller, in 1880 the Earl had visited Egypt despite being in ill health and then Italy, where he died at Florence on 13th December. His body was embalmed by a Florence chemist and placed within three coffins, the inner made of Italian wood, the middle of lead and the outer one of polished oak, elaborately carved and mounted with silver fittings. Once sealed, the three coffins were placed in an enormous walnut shell which bore a carved cross. The resulting half-ton coffin was transported across the Alps and then by steamer to London, where a train took it to Aberdeen, only for the hearse to be stranded by the wayside for several days due to a particularly violent snowstorm before it could complete the final leg of the journey, to Dunecht House.

A week after their return, on 29th December, the remains of the late Earl were finally placed in the newly-built tomb beneath the white-marble chapel, the first tenant of the new family mausoleum built to replace that at Haigh Hall. The steps leading down to the vault were covered by four enormous slabs of Caithness stone, with the interstices of these filled with lime. Six months later the stones were covered by a vast quantity of soil, into which grass and shrubs were sown. Iron railings were then erected in a semi-circular shape to enclose the area.

Now, almost a year after his entombment, it was discovered that the intended final resting place of the Earl had been disturbed. On entering the vault the party saw that the flagstone directly over the steps, some six feet by four feet and weighing 15cwt, had been lifted eighteen inches on one side and propped up by a piece of wood. Descending, they discovered two planks and three iron bars lying on the stairs. The floor of the vault was strewn with further planks and scented sawdust. In the middle of the floor the three coffins lay open side by side.[1]

The body of the 25th Earl of Crawford was missing.

For almost half a century, the feared Resurrection Men had been kept at bay. Commonplace in the eighteenth and early nineteenth centuries, these men were employed by anatomists to secure bodies for dissection. The Murder Act of 1752 gave judges the power to make the bodies of executed criminals currently being put on public display instead available for dissection for medical purposes, in the hope that the thought of being cut open after death would act as a deterrent to wrongdoers.

With the enormous increase in medical schools and hospitals at the turn of the nineteenth century, however, corpses sourced in this way failed to meet demand. This created a market for the Resurrection Men, an undeserved semi-respectable moniker given to graverobbers. Doctors and anatomists would pay for corpses to be supplied, usually with no questions asked, and resurrectionists were prepared to risk attack from nightwatchmen who were often employed at graveyards. Families began to bury their dead in secure coffins and place heavy slabs over the graves to deter bodysnatchers.[2]

In 1828 probably the most infamous bodysnatchers of all came to notoriety. After successfully selling the corpse of an army pensioner who had died of natural causes, William Burke and William Hare decided to create their own supply by murdering sixteen people over the course of ten months in Edinburgh and selling the corpses to eminent anatomist Dr. Robert Knox. Although both were eventually caught and Burke executed – Hare turning King's Evidence – their grim business had

The Penny Illustrated News, 10th December 1881
Courtesy Special Collections Centre, University of Aberdeen

influenced a gang known as the London Burkers to copy their methods. The gang, led by John Bishop, were based in the East End's Nova Scotia Gardens, at the northern end of Brick Lane.[3] On 5th November 1831 Bishop and another gang member attempted to sell a suspiciously fresh body to Guy's Hospital but were turned away. They next took it to the King's College School of Anatomy on the Strand, where they accepted nine guineas in return for the corpse, that of a boy around 14 years of age. An anatomist at the School named Richard Partridge examined the body and, believing it to not have been buried, called the police. The London Burkers were arrested and remanded, and three days later a coroner's court returned a verdict of "Wilful murder against some person or persons unknown".

On 19th November Superintendent Joseph Thomas searched the buildings at Nova Scotia Gardens and discovered several items of clothing in a well in the garden. The police suspected the young body to be that of Carlo Ferrari, an immigrant from Piedmont in Italy who scraped a living by exhibiting caged mice near Smithfield Market, and on 1st December Bishop appeared at the Old Bailey with gang members Thomas Williams and James May charged with his murder.[4] The following day the three Burkers were found guilty and sentenced to death.

In their confessions, Bishop and Williams revealed that the boy was not the missing Italian, but a youth from Lincolnshire whom they had met at The Bell public house in Smithfield. They had lured him to Nova Scotia Gardens where he was drugged with laudanum and then thrown head-first into the well with a cord tied around his ankles. Bishop and Williams went to a local tavern, returning some time later to pull the body from the well before undressing it and placing it in a bag.

While awaiting trial Bishop claimed to have stolen between 500 and 1,000 bodies over a twelve year period, selling them to anatomists from respected institutions including St. Thomas' Hospital and St. Bartholomew's Hospital. Recent murders by the gang included those of Frances Pigburn and a youth named Cunningham, who was murdered in the same manner as the Lincolnshire boy.

The scene of so many horrible crimes was eagerly visited by the public, who showed that collecting criminal mementoes is not a modern phenomenon:

> On Sunday the neighbourhood of Nova Scotia Gardens, Birdcage Walk and Crabtree Walk, and the whole vicinity of the horrible den where so many murders are supposed to have been committed by Bishop and others, presented a scene that will not soon be forgotten by those who witnessed it. Soon after daylight crowds of persons flocked from all parts of the metropolis to Bethnal Green, and by 9 o'clock several thousand persons had assembled. The premises lately occupied by the supposed murderers were besieged by persons anxious to obtain permission, and one gate opened, and ten or a dozen persons were admitted at a time to view the premises, upon the payment of a sum of money, according to

the means or apparent respectability of the parties.

To prove the extraordinary anxiety of the visitors to possess themselves of some memento of the horrid occasion, it may be sufficient to state, that two entire trees, growing in Bishop's garden, were actually cut to pieces, even to the stumps. A portion of the flooring in Bishop's house was torn up, and several trifling articles lying in the house were eagerly seized by the mob and carried off. This scene continued till about half-past 12 o'clock, when the rush of the multitude became so great, that the proprietor of the premises felt it necessary to apply to the police for assistance, in order to disperse the people and close the gates, and, in fact, to prevent the further admission of the public altogether. A body of police of the H division soon arrived, and protected the premises. Subsequently persons of respectability were admitted in small parties, under the protection of the police, to view the premises.[5]

Bishop and Williams were hanged at Newgate on 5th December, while May was spared the death sentence as it was accepted that he was not involved in the murder of the boy. Ironically, their bodies were then sent for dissection: Bishop to the King's College School of Anatomy, where he had sold the body of his victim, and Williams to the Theatre of Anatomy in Windmill Street.

Following the Edinburgh murders by Burke and Hare, a Select Committee had issued a report underlining the importance of anatomical science, and recommended that the corpses of those who had died in the workhouse be used for dissection. After the trial of London Burkers the author of that report, Henry Warburton, submitted a Bill to that end which led to the drawing up of the Anatomy Act 1832, which came into effect in August of that year. The Act ruled that licensed anatomists could use the bodies of paupers for research purposes, and with the vast numbers of workhouse inmates, this put an end to the Resurrection Men.

Since the passing of the Act, no further cases of bodysnatching had been reported in Britain,[6] and the dead could finally rest in peace – until now.

The theft of the Earl of Crawford's remains was soon christened the Dunecht Outrage. The 26th Earl, his son James Lindsay, was informed and returned to Dunecht immediately.[7] Lindsay's mother, the Dowager Countess, had been travelling in Italy for some months and would not

*Swanson's brother John, former Superintendent
of the Aberdeen police force*
Courtesy John Mitchell

learn of the desecration of her husband's tomb for another two days, when she arrived at her villa in Florence.

Officers from the Aberdeen Constabulary conducted a search of the 53,000 acre estate to no avail, and very soon the enormity of the task was realised. Not only was a vast part the estate covered in dense woodland, but the poor weather threatened to hamper investigations. Some focus was required, with a cool head providing direction. An appeal for assistance was issued and four days after the discovery the afternoon train brought two men from London. One was Mr. J. A. Alsop of the Earl of Crawford's London solicitors Alsop, Mann & Co., the other Detective Inspector Swanson of the C.I.D. Their arrival drew a large crowd, with the Scotland Yard man attracting particular attention:

> Inspector Swanson was looked upon with considerable interest, if not with some awe, as the capturer of Lefroy, and the interest was probably heightened by the circumstances that he is a native of the north, and has relatives in Aberdeen.[8]

The fact that his brother John lived in Aberdeen at this time suggests that Swanson perhaps had brought Julia and their two sons with him. Swanson's remit was to act as advisor to the local officers, not supersede them, but his experience and detective insight would be of great value. Although John Swanson had two years earlier retired as Superintendent of the Aberdeen police force, Donald would no doubt have discussed the case with him and gained knowledge not only of the local area, but also its criminal element. By this time, John had been a widower for seven years following the death of wife Elizabeth during childbirth and by 1881 he was living with his five youngest children at Thistle Place.[9] If Julia did travel north, she remained with her brother-in-law as her husband travelled the thirty miles to Dunecht House.

The tomb had been left as discovered until Swanson arrived to inspect it, and the detective began his investigation immediately.[10] The main house itself was inspected in minute detail; tenant cottages, farmhouses and barns on the estate searched. The Dunecht woods were scoured, and old stone walls which might hide a corpse in a recess pulled down. Pits were turned over, and fields probed with iron pikes in the hope of finding an interred box. A pond situated some 500 yards from the house and part hidden by overhanging beech trees was drained. Not a single clue as to the location of the body was discovered.

After a week the local police force was stood down, leaving Swanson as the only detective at Dunecht. Working with the new Earl and his solicitor, Swanson turned his attention to the numerous letters which had been received, many from anonymous authors. Alsop travelled to Florence to investigate a letter sent from a writer there who claimed to know the identity of those behind the theft. Swanson travelled to Aberdeen and Glasgow to conduct inquiries, and it was decided to give no information to the press. Naturally, as a result wild rumours began to appear in the newspapers, some in the form of editorial comment and others from printed letters from the public such as one from a Mr. Hugh Cochrane published in the *Daily News*:

> When returning from the City on the top of an omnibus, which halted at Regent Circus, a man passed down Oxford Street towards the City carrying a parcel which looked like an Egyptian mummy. I was so struck with the appearance that I remarked to a fellow-passenger, a stranger to me, "Is not that for all the world like a body that man is carrying?" and he remarked, "It does look like one." If you think fit to publish this perhaps my fellow-passenger would communicate with me, when we could lay the description before the authorities, and if they thought it of any importance they could perhaps trace this parcel further. It may not be the late Earl of Crawford's body, but if it was not his I feel pretty certain it was the body of someone else, in a state much lighter than during life.[11]

Other accounts claimed that body had been stolen by medical students, or had in fact never been in the vault at all, but had been removed from its coffin before leaving Florence.

Two weeks into the investigation the celebrated sleuth-hound Morgan was called to Dunecht. A bloodhound and retriever cross,[12] it was Morgan who had discovered the arms and partially burned skull of a young girl stuffed up the chimney of a house in Blackburn. The remains were those of Emily Holland, whose limbless torso had been discovered three weeks earlier in a nearby field. The house belonged to barber William Fish, who was arrested and confessed to the murder.[13] Morgan was so popular with the public after his success that he was exhibited on numerous occasions at the Pomona Palace, Manchester,[14] and some 100,000 portraits of him were sold at 6d each.[15] It was reported that he could smell a rabbit buried three feet underground,[16] and would fetch his master's hat, handkerchief or boots when asked to do so, often from a considerable distance away.[17]

Despite Morgan spending two weeks at Dunecht and being allowed into the tomb to smell the coffins and sawdust,[18] the severe frost prevented him from picking up any scent around the grounds and after several abortive attempts he was returned to Blackburn,[19] but would briefly be reunited with Donald Swanson in July 1884 when the detective was sent to Middlesbrough to assist with the investigation into the disturbing murder of 8-year-old Mary Cooper, whose body was found in long grass on the edge of Albert Park. She was lying on her back, her fists grasping tufts of grass. Her throat had been cut, and her light brown hair was saturated with blood, as were her clothes.[20]

When no progress was made by the local police force after a fortnight, an appeal was sent to Scotland Yard, who dispatched Det. Inspector Swanson. The Scot arrived on 5th July[21] and, having heard the known facts, suggested calling in Morgan, who duly arrived two days later. Taken to the home of Mary Cooper, the hound was allowed to smell some of her clothes, and immediately set off following the scent to Albert Park, where he stopped at the spot where the body was found, the blood-soaked earth having been freshly turned over.[22] Encouraged by these initial results, at six o'clock the following morning Morgan was taken out again by his handler, accompanied by Swanson and the local officers. This time he was unable to pick up a scent, perhaps not surprising given that almost three weeks had passed since the murder. While acknowledging Morgan's abilities, the *Shields Daily Gazette* of 9th July 1884 reported the lack of success, at the same time being a little unfair on the sleuth-hound:

Dunecht House and Chapel
Author's collection

> The animal displayed great sagacity and intelligence, but he did not gain any clue which is likely to aid the police. Morgan amply proved that his smell of scent is acute as ever, although he is eighteen years of age, and deaf.

The hound returned to Lancashire, and Det. Inspector Swanson also took his leave of Middlesbrough, returning to Scotland Yard on 8th July. The killer of Mary Cooper was never identified.[23]

The bad weather which hampered Morgan's efforts at Dunecht also interfered with the efforts of a group of spiritualists from London, who arrived at Dunecht House during a fierce snowstorm and proceeded to enter a different sort of cloud. In a trance, the four clairvoyants claimed to see the Earl's body being carried from the tomb by three men and taken to a house on the estate and later buried in a field nearby.[24] Perhaps needless to say, searches based on this supernatural insight proved fruitless.

An advertisement placed in local newspapers which appealed for information relating to any strange occurrences around Dunecht jogged the memories of workmen on the estate, who recalled that a sweet aroma had been noticed issuing from the vault some seven months earlier, on 29th May. The smell, drifting up through the ventilator, had also been detected by the housekeeper at Dunecht. It had been put down to materials used on numerous wreaths left upon the coffin and ignored. Cracks discovered between the flagstones were put down to frost, and were refilled with lime and then cemented. A few days later the stones had been covered with soil and the enclosure erected and

> Sir
>
> The remains of the late Earl of Crawford are not beneath the chapel at Dunecht as you believe but were removed hence last spring and the smell of decaying flowers ascending from the vault since that time will on investigation be found to proceed from another cause than flowers.
>
> —Nabob

Copy of the original 'Nabob' letter
Swanson family archives

the sweet aroma, which had actually radiated from the spilt sawdust in the Earl's upturned coffin, was forgotten about.

Worse was to follow when it was revealed that the Earl's agent in Scotland, a solicitor named William Yeats, had received a strange letter three months before the discovery in which the writer claimed to know something of the body's disappearance:

> Sir,
>
> The remains of the late Earl of Crawford are not beneath the chaple at Dunecht as you beleve, but were removed hence last spring and the smell of decayed flowers asending from the vault since that time will on investigation be found to proceed from another cause than flowers.
>
> Nabob[25]

Yeats contacted the builder who had constructed the vault, who assured him that it had not been tampered with and the letter was dismissed as a hoax. Now, with the Earl's body still missing, the seriousness of the missive became apparent and another advertisement was placed in Aberdeen newspapers asking 'Nabob' to contact Alsop at Dunecht. A further notice was placed on 13th December offering a £50 reward to the writer of the letter on condition that he disclose his identity.

In the meantime, Swanson was satisfied that he could do no more at Dunecht and on 16th December left for London, where he would continue to monitor events and liaise with the Earl.

On 23rd December the mysterious, semi-literate 'Nabob' finally got in touch with James Alsop, but was in no mood to reveal his identity:

> Sir,
>
> The late Earl of Crawford
>
> The body is still in Aberdeenshire, and I can put you in possession of the same as soon as you bring one or more of the desperados who stole it to justice, so that I may know with whom I have to deal. I have no wish to be assinated by rusarectionests, nor suspected by the police for being an accomplice in such dastardly work, which I most assuredly would be unless the gulty party are brought to justice. Had Mr. Yeats acted on the hint I gave him last Sept., he might have found the remains as though by axedand and hunted up the robers at Isure, but that chance is lost, so I hope you will find your men and make it safe and prudent for me to find what you want.
>
> PS – Should they find out that an outsider knows their secret it may be

removed to another place. NABOB.[26]

Despite a printed reply from Alsop promising that 'Nabob' would be safe if he came forward, nothing more was heard in the days that followed. On 30th December a reward notice was published in the Aberdeen newspapers:

£600 Reward

Whereas the body of the late Earl of Crawford and Balcarres has been taken from the Vault at Dunecht House Aberdeenshire

A Reward of £100 will be paid by Her Majesty's Government, and a further Reward of £500 will be paid by Messrs Alsop Mann & Co., Solicitors, 23 Great Marlborough Street, London, to any person, other than a person belonging to a Police Force in the United Kingdom, who shall first give such information as shall lead to the discovery and conviction of the perpetrator or perpetrators of the offence and the Home Secretary will advice the grant of Her Majesty's Gracious

Pardon

to any accomplice, not being the person who actually committed the offence, who shall first give such information as shall lead to a like result.[27]

On the day this reward notice appeared in the newspapers, Donald Swanson appeared at Bow Street Magistrates' Court at the remand hearing of Edwin Hawkins and Edwin Green. Together with Det. Inspector Robson, on 22nd December he had arrested the pair, who worked as clerks at the Ordnance Survey Department in St. Martin's Place. Hawkins had worked at the Department for 20 years, and Green 16 years. They had created a simple scam whereby Green would encourage browsers to buy maps, which would then be sold at trade prices by Hawkins on the cash register. The sales were logged in registers as being made to members of the trade, with the difference divided between the pair. They were remanded for trial, and later sentenced to two months' hard labour each.[28]

Arrests were also being made in Scotland. The offer of a £600 reward[29] had finally brought forth information, and Thomas Kirkwood, a joiner who had been employed for several years by Dunecht House was arrested along with John Philip, a shoemaker. The Earl of Crawford was summoned by telegram, with Det. Inspector Swanson contacted at Scotland Yard and asked to travel north immediately.[30]

After examination both men were released, and John Philip was approached by a local ratcatcher named Charles Soutar, who rather strangely asked whether the shoemaker had mentioned his name while being questioned.

Five months later a breakthrough finally came. A gamekeeper named George Machray came forward to say that Soutar had twice told him that he knew where the Earl of Crawford's body was hidden. Thinking nothing of it, Machray went about his business, but on 14th July 1882 was asked by the ratcatcher to inform a Mr. Cassells, who was acting on behalf of the Crawford family, that Soutar could tell him where the body was. Machray could not find Mr. Cassells, and after being asked by Soutar on three consecutive days decided to go to the police and on 17th July the 42-year-old ratcatcher was apprehended.

Soutar had been born in Brechin, forty miles from Aberdeen, in 1840 and at one point had been married to Ann,[31] but his continued brushes with the law seem to have caused friction in the marriage. He was first arrested in 1861, aged just twenty, for poaching on the Lundie estate at Brechin, and was ordered to pay a total of £4 17s 16d or risk imprisonment of six weeks.[32] Two years later Soutar was arrested for pursing game on land belonging to the Earl of Dalhousie, receiving a £5 fine.[33]

In September 1878 Soutar was one of four men returning from a night's poaching at Stonehaven, Aberdeen, with several bags containing game when they were confronted by Police Sergeant John Gartly and John Moir, the gamekeeper. A scuffle ensured and the gang attacked Gartly and Moir, severely beating them and leaving both badly cut and lying unconscious on the road.[34] Having been in hiding for two months, Soutar was finally captured on 5th November and was sentenced to eighteen months' imprisonment.[35]

Soutar had been employed at Dunecht House as a ratcatcher on and off for a number of years, but had finally been let go as a result of his continued poaching.

Now, before Sheriff Comrie Thomson, he admitted writing the two "Nabob" letters. When asked how he knew the whereabouts of the Earl's body, he claimed to be out poaching in the Dunecht woods when

> As I passed through the wood I heard a stick break on my left-hand side I stood still to hearken. I then heard the rustle of another man crawling on my right-hand side. I thought it was the keepers trying to surround me. I ran as fast as I could for the thickest part of the wood. I had gone about 20 yards when I was tripped up by a third party.
>
> When I looked up, there were two men above me holding me down. They

seemed young and of the middle size. Their faces were blacked and I felt they had on winsey shirts; they had neither caps nor coats on. In about half a minute they were joined by two other men, being those I heard creeping. I was on my back. They were tall, with coats and hats off. Their faces were masked half way down, and I saw their white shirtsleeves.

One of the men pushed a pistol towards my breast, and said to one of the men who had been holding me, "Remove your arm and I will settle him." One of the men who was holding me down took hold of the wrist of the man with the pistol, and said, "Hold on; there's more of them." The man who said so got over me, and led the man with the pistol on one side, and said to him, "It is all right – it's the ratcatcher; he is poaching."

After talking in little whispers, which I could not make out, they called to the other tall man to come to them, which he did. The three conversed for a short time, but I could not hear what they said. They all came back beside me, and told the man who was holding me to let me get up. They then let me go.

I hunted for an hour or two, and when daylight came I went back to the part of the wood where I had been seized. I saw nothing of the men, but on looking at the place where I had first heard them I found a place where they had concealed something. It was a heap of rubbish. I opened it up. I found a blanket, to which I gave a pull. There was the dead body of a man inside it, and after looking at it I covered it up again. I did not observe any smell of putrefaction. There was a strong smell what I thought was benzoline. The smell stuck to my hands for half a day afterwards.

My impression at the time was that the man had been murdered, and that an attempt had been made to destroy the body by burning it with some chemical. The eyes were sunken, but the other features did not seem to be shrunk.[36]

Soutar then claimed to have later been at a tavern where he had a conversation with a plasterer named Cowe who had at one time been employed at Dunecht House. Cowe, he said, had mentioned that the vault had been closed up because a sweet smell was issuing from it, similar to decaying flowers or benzoline, a petroleum spirit. Soutar said it was at this point he realised that this was probably the smell which had been on the body, and had transferred to his hands.

He was remanded in custody while his story was checked, and a renewed search in the part of the wood described by the ratcatcher began. Soutar declined to take the police to the spot himself, claiming it was unsafe for him to do so while the men he had seen were still at

The recovery of the Earl of Crawford's body from The Illustrated London News, 18th July 1882

large.

On 18th July, after eight hours' beating by a party of around twenty men, a keeper's iron stick rebounded when poked into earth near a ditch on farmland leased to a Dr. Copland,[37] just five hundred yards from the house. A spade was obtained and the earth dug up. At the bottom of the old ditch, a foot below the surface, lay the body of the 25th Earl. It was wrapped in a blanket and was undamaged; the original embalming had left his face quite recognisable.

The remains were carried back to the house with all the solemnity of the original entombment, and left to rest in the chapel. When told of the discovery, Soutar remarked "I am very glad to hear it; they did not get it from me, at all events". He was taken to the now-empty grave and asked whether it was the spot he had seen the dead man, but he said he could not recognise it as such. He was taken to view by the corpse and commented that the face bore some resemblance to that of the body he had seen in the wood.

A week after their discovery, the remains of the late Earl left Dunecht in great secrecy at five o'clock in the morning of Tuesday, 26th July. The body was taken to Aberdeen station and from there conveyed to Wigan via the express goods train. The body had been enclosed in three new coffins supplied by Messrs Allan of Aberdeen, with a silver plate affixed to the outer coffin inscribed with the same simple wording as the original. The remains were interred the following day at the family's mausoleum at Haigh Hall, Wigan.[38]

In the meantime, Soutar's background was being looked into. James Collier, a former sawyer at Dunecht, said he knew Soutar by sight. On 27th May 1881, two days before the sweet aroma had been noticed at the Earl's tomb, Collier had been in a coach travelling from Aberdeen towards Echt, two miles from Dunecht House. Also on the coach was Soutar, who had just been released from prison after serving his eighteen-month sentence.

James Cowe, the plasterer whom Soutar claimed had told him about the closing of the Earl's vault and the sweet smell reminiscent of benzoline, was traced and said that while he had known the ratcatcher for three or four years, he had never had a conversation with him about the missing body.

Charles Soutar was taken to Edinburgh's High Court of Justiciary on 23rd October 1882 and indicted, accused of Violating the Sepulchres of the Dead. After hearing all the evidence in a single day, the following morning Lord Craighill began his summing up. He agreed with the belief that more than one person must have been involved in the robbery, but in the eyes of the law the guilt of the prisoner was the same as if he had acted alone. His motive was clearly to obtain a reward, and if Soutar *was* scared for his safety why did he send the two 'Nabob' letters not to the police, but to the solicitors who were offering the reward? The prisoner, it was claimed, had returned to the vault and displaced the turf, hoping that the theft would be discovered. Once the crime had been discovered, and the search being unsuccessful, a reward was finally offered. Realising that it would not be paid to anyone involved in the offence, Soutar supposedly sent the second 'Nabob' letter in a bid to provide the necessary information without implicating himself.

The jury retired for just thirty-five minutes before returning a guilty verdict, and Soutar was sentenced to five years' imprisonment.

Early the following year, a strange story appeared in the *Aberdeen Evening Express* of 12th February 1883 in which it was claimed that a bottle had been found containing the following message:

> This bottle was thrown into the water at Stirling in the River Forth on the 15th July, 1882, by one of the men who was concerned in the lifting of the body of the Earl of Crawford. The body is now, I think, rotted in clay. We lifted it with the intention of selling it, but was published so soon that we buried to get it out of the way.

The *Express* commented that the message in the bottle was probably

Charles Soutar in later life
from the Aberdeen Journal, 6th January 1914

a hoax.

Over the next few months, letters from solicitors representing the three claimants of the reward on offer were received. James Collier and John Philip claimed on the grounds that they had told the police early in the investigation that Soutar was a man who should be looked at. George Machray stated that it was his evidence which had resulted in Soutar's arrest. At an inquiry on 23rd June 1883, Sheriff Guthrie Smith ruled in favour of Machray.[39]

This was not the end of the matter. Alsop, Mann & Co., representing the 26th Earl, had already written to Guthrie Smith stating that they would not be making any payment:

> The Reward was advertised to be paid to any person etc who should first give such information as should lead "to the discovery and conviction of the Perpetrator or Perpetrators of the office". We on behalf of Lord Crawford strongly submit that neither in spirit nor in letter have the terms of the Reward bill been fulfilled by any of the claimants inasmuch as only one man (Soutar) has been convicted and it is clear that he alone could not have been the perpetrator and thus neither "the perpetrators" (ie a sole perpetrator) nor "the perpetrators" within the meaning of the advertisement have been brought to justice and the object of the Reward is by a long way unaccomplished.[40]

The Home Office decided to pay half of their £100 reward, withholding the second £50 until such a time that Soutar's supposed accomplices were brought to justice.[41] Reluctantly, Alsop followed suit.

In February 1886 Machray instructed Alexander Duffus, a solicitor of Aberdeen, to pursue the second half of the reward. The Home Office quickly paid their £50; Alsop once again dragged their heels. It took a threat of legal action to extract the money, and Machray received the second £300 in June 1886.[42]

Despite his windfall, George Machray would continue in his modest profession as gamekeeper until dying suddenly two years later at his home in Broomhill Place, Aberdeen, on the morning of 15th August 1888.[43]

By this time, Charles Soutar had been released from prison. He had served four of his five year sentence, and returned to Aberdeen, where he was visited at his Commerce Street home by a journalist from the *Aberdeen Journal*. The reporter described

> a middle-sized, stoutish man, well dressed in blue pilot cloth and Jenny Lind hat, with roundish face, shaven all but a heavy moustache and imperial, looking more like a well-to-do skipper than a convict capable of serious crime.[44]

Throughout the interview Soutar continued to protest his innocence. He had unsuccessfully petitioned Home Secretary William Harcourt for a pardon, stating that "although there was no evidence to convict... by a judicious display of empty coffins and other such productions, the prosecutions succeeded in gaining their point."[45] He continued to claim that it was his reputation as a poacher which had made it easy to make him a scapegoat. He told the reporter that during his sentence, served

Advertisement for Charles Soutar's verminist service from The Aberdeen Daily Journal, 20th January 1912

*Carte-de-visite of the memorial marking
the spot where the Earl of Crawford's body was found*
Author's collection

at Pentonville and then Dartmoor, he had got on well with everyone despite the nature of his alleged crime until he became ill, when the doctors accused him of faking his symptoms and refused to treat him.[46]

The ratcatcher had returned to his old profession, offering his services as a 'Practical Verminist', with an advertisement informing potential customers that he went about his business "without causing smell or inconvenience".[47] His work did not always go according to plan. In August the following year Soutar had been employed by Hugh Rose Innes to rid his place of business of a large number of rats, and he duly arrived on a Friday and laid poison on consecutive days. Believing all the rats to be dead on the Monday, he left for home. The following morning Mr. Rose Innes found footprints of rats all over the house, and that night heard the rodents in the walls. A week after Soutar's visit Mr. Rose Innes deposited several pheasants from a shoot in a locked room, only to find nothing but feathers in the morning. He refused to pay the verminist, resulting in Soutar taking him to Aberdeen Small Debt Court seeking payment of his fee and railway fare. Sheriff Brown, hearing the case, decided that Soutar had not fulfilled the agreed contract of completely clearing the place of rats, and ruled in favour of Mr. Rose Innes.[48]

Despite his efforts to earn an honest living through vermin extermination, Soutar could not help himself as regards poaching and on 4th October 1889 he was discovered with two other men on the Fetteresso estate of R. W. Duff, M.P. The keepers gave chase but the poachers escaped, dropping their booty of eight pheasants, two bags and a net. A cloth cap also found in the woods led the police to two farm servants named James Burnett and Frederick Cowie, and in turn Charles Soutar.[49] He was sentenced to three months' imprisonment,[50] after which he seems to have retired from a life of petty crime and concentrated on ridding Aberdeen of rodents, cockroaches and other pests, and acquired a second wife, Charlotte. The *Aberdeen Journal* of 14th July 1903 reported that she had given birth to a son. Another son and a daughter completed the family.[51]

Soutar continued to advertise his verminist services in local newspapers, the last notice appearing on 13th December 1913, just three weeks before he died on 5th January 1914 at the age of 73.

As for the 25th Earl, he finally found everlasting peace at Haigh Hall. The spot where the body was discovered was marked by a memorial cross some ten feet high, which amongst others carries the following inscription:

In Memoriam
Under this spot the body of Alexander, Earl of Crawford,
sacrilegiously stolen from the vault under the Dunecht
Chapel, lay hidden during 14 months.[52]

Before Det. Inspector Swanson was called to Dunecht, he had been tracking an enigmatic aristocrat who had a habit of paying his way around the world with forged bills.

In May 1881 a man in his mid-sixties, short in stature and impeccably dressed,[53] arrived at the Cavendish Hotel on London's Jermyn Street.[54] Grey hair neatly parted in the middle and with blue eyes sparkling, he gave his name as Sir Charles Cuffe of Kilkenny House, Ireland. The visitor spoke French and German fluently[55] and charmed staff at the hotel.

During his stay on the street which was, and still is, renowned for gentlemen's clothing, Sir Charles opened several accounts with nearby retailers, ordering four coats, six waistcoats, five pairs of trousers, a dressing gown, two jackets and a pair of pyjamas from tailor John Skinner on 4th May 1881. Three days later he visited shoemaker Robert Dobbie and ordered five pairs of boots, 24 pairs of laces, a pair of boot hooks, two bottles of varnish, one brush, one pair of lace caps, one set of straps, two metal bottles and a large box. Visiting shirtmaker Henry Ludlaw on 9th June, the Baronet ordered seven shirts, two scarves, six handkerchieves and a pair of socks.[56]

All of these items were delivered to Sir Charles at the Cavendish, who stayed for some three months before departing on 13th August. On checking out he owed £22 12s, and wrote a cheque against the Royal Bank of Scotland for £35. The wife of the proprietor, Felipe Santiago Franco, gave him the change in cash.

Sir Charles then disappeared without settling his clothing accounts, and the cheque was returned to M. Franco marked "No account".[57] Complaints were made at Scotland Yard, and Det. Inspector Swanson was assigned to the case.

By supreme irony, Sir Charles, no doubt trying to put as much distance between himself and London, was at this time on his way to Swanson's hometown of Thurso. A few months earlier he had been travelling from Malta to England on board the P&O ship *Australia*, when he had met Sir Robert Sinclair of Caithness.[58]

Amusing and entertaining, Sir Charles made excellent company for the Scottish Baronet during the journey and when the steamer eventually docked in London, Sir Robert insisted that his new friend visit him in Caithness.

Now, intending to go to ground, Sir Charles remembered this invitation. He arrived at Thurso late in August, but not without problems. He told Sir Robert that he had travelled on the wrong train, heading for Skye instead of Thurso, and had been obliged to change at Dingwall where he had spent the night.[59] His luggage, which had gone to Thurso ahead of him, had been allowed to sit on the platform all night and when Sir Charles arrived the next morning was nowhere to be seen.[60] A search discovered nothing, and Sir Charles was obliged to spend his visit dependent on the generosity of his host.

The visitor proved to be very popular in the town with everyone including Sergeant Miller of the Thurso police, and spent a very agreeable time using Sir Robert's guns around his estate.[61]

As he prepared to leave Thurso after ten days, Sir Charles mentioned that as he had no ready money with him, he would have to draw on his account and would be indebted if a letter of introduction could be supplied which he could take to Edinburgh, his next destination. The Baronet was accordingly taken to the Thurso branch of the Royal Bank of Scotland, where he obtained the introductory note he required.

After saying hearty farewells to Sir Robert and his many new friends, Sir Charles travelled the short distance to Wick, where he took a steamer to Edinburgh. On arrival, he wasted no time going to the bank's head office and presented the letter of introduction along with a cheque for £60 against his account with the Royal Bank of Ireland, which was duly cashed. It was at this point that the Baronet's story started to unravel.

The cheque was returned dishonoured, the Royal Bank of Ireland stating that the signature was not that of Sir Charles Cuffe. Attempts to locate the man failed; he had left his hotel without notice, owing £15.[62]

Despite building evidence against the imposter, Swanson was unable to pinpoint his location. It was ascertained that he had passed a cheque for £75 by using Sir Robert Sinclair's name in October at Gibraltar,[63] but had disappeared long before the fraud was discovered. The detective learned that the man had stopped using the name "Sir Charles Cuffe", and was now going under the name of Lieutenant-Colonel Graham. Swanson discovered that he had spent some weeks in Algiers before leaving for Spain, but once again his quarry fled before he could be captured.[64]

Finally, Swanson had some good fortune. Hearing that the missing swindler was in Cairo, the detective travelled to Egypt and on 23rd April 1882 saw the wanted man on board the British ship *Isis* at Alexandria; he was obviously about to leave the country once again, but Swanson apprehended him and told him he was under arrest for forgery and fraud.[65] Immediately on being captured, the prisoner admitted that he was not the Baronet:

> I confess I am not Sir Charles Cuffe, and that I obtained the goods by fraud. I admit uttering the cheque to Mr. Franco. I have felt so very dejected and disgusted with myself that I attempted to take away my own life. I have done wrong, and it is right that I should suffer.[66]

He then claimed to actually be Malcolm Fairfax, and it was under this name that he was tried at the Old Bailey on 26th June 1882, charged with forgery and obtaining goods by false pretences.

Reporters from Thurso could not hide their delight that one of their

*Malcolm Fairfax aka Lochiel Lorimer Graham
from the Police Illustrated Circular No. 12*

own had succeeded in bringing the fraudster to justice:

> The pseudo baronet, whose exploits in the north last autumn will be remembered, has at last been captured at Cairo, and taken to London by Inspector Swanson of the Scotland Yard Detective Department. He denied being Sir Charles Cuffe, but stated that he had some property in Thurso – probably referring to the jewels he reported to have been stolen from him at Thurso railway station. After the London case is disposed of, he will be handed over to the Caithness criminal authorities in connection with the forgery he is said to have committed when leaving his friends in this quarter. Inspector Swanson deserves great credit for his clever capture.[67]

The court heard that in addition to his adventures for which he was arrested, Fairfax had also defrauded various hoteliers in Inverness and Kelso, presumably while making his way from London to Thurso.

A Mr. Norris, secretary to Stuart Villiers M.P., appeared to state that he knew Sir Charles Cuffe; the prisoner was not him, and the signature on the cheque was not that of Sir Charles.[68]

Herbert Dicketts of Schiller and Co., another tailor on Jermyn Street, stated that the prisoner had obtained goods from him to the value of £57 5s in the name of Colonel Graham of the Traveller's Club.[69]

In fact, Swanson had by the time of the trial already ascertained that the prisoner's true name was Lochiel Lorimer Graham.

An American, Graham had been commissioned into the 1st US Dragoons on 9th April 1847, serving as Aide-de-Camp to Emperor

Maximilian in Mexico and being wounded at the Battle of Churubusco before resigning his commission in 1854. He had subsequently enlisted into the 22nd New York Cavalry under the name of John Spreadbury, and served as a Captain in the American Civil War.[70] Since being honourably discharged at Rochester in 1865,[71] however, Graham had drifted into a life of forgery and travelled Europe using his charming personality to pass under names such as Captain Graham, Sir Charles Cuffe and Colonel Hamilton Farquahason.[72]

At the Old Bailey trial on 26th June, he was sentenced to eighteen months' hard labour.

It was not to be his last misdemeanour, nor his last meeting with Donald Swanson.

In May 1886 Graham married Annie Collingwood Shurm. The 71-year-old groom gave his occupation as "retired Lieutenant Colonel". The bride, from Ladbroke Grove, was 32. The couple would have a son, Ronald Douglas Claverhouse Graham, born five years later on 12th January 1891.[73]

The family lived at Littlehampton on the south coast, and it was at nearby Hastings that Donald Swanson arrested Graham in November 1891.[74] The prisoner had obtained £2 10s from a Kensington newsagent by passing a fraudulent cheque and receiving the change in cash. At the London County Sessions Swanson told the court that Graham had committed frauds in all the capitals of Europe, while moving in the best social circles. At one point he had even sat on the Court of Honour which tried an officer of the British Army for cowardice at the Austrian Consulate. Not so easily taken in by Graham's charm, the Judge sentenced him to three years' penal servitude.[75]

Incredibly, this was not to be the increasingly-aged Graham's last offence. Six years later he appeared at the West Sussex Sessions charged with defrauding three businessmen from Horsham.[76] By now 83-years-old and described as being "in a very feeble condition", Graham told the Court that he hoped he would be sent to prison for life, as he "had no object in living, and could not live long". Sentencing the prisoner to twelve months' imprisonment, the Magistrate said he hoped Graham would be properly taken care of in prison.[77]

In fact, Lorimer Graham served his sentence in full and went on to live a further seventeen years. He died on 7th March 1914, aged 98. Two months later his widow Annie, still just 59-years-old, successfully applied for a Widow's Pension, which she continued to receive until her death in 1935.[78]

TWELVE

The Fenians are Coming!

Too long has England proudly stood
Triumphant in her bloody crimes;
But soon the Fenian Brotherhood
Will teach the lying London Times
A lesson that he won't forget,
Which as he reads, he'll puff and pout,
And swear they've come to pay the debt,
And the British Troops to route[1]

An empty preserved meat tin became the unlikely symbol for the beginning of a fresh campaign of Fenian terrorism when, on the afternoon of Friday, 14th January 1881, it was stuffed with dynamite and lowered through a ventilation shaft into a butcher's storeroom at Salford Barracks, Manchester, occupied at the time by the 8th Light Infantry Regiment. Minutes later a great explosion sent bricks, slate and other debris flying 200 yards into the air. The adjoining wall was demolished, and the windows of more than thirty houses in Darley Street opposite were blown out. Passing at the time were a young woman named Mary Ann Nadin, who suffered a fractured arm and leg, and seven-year-old Richard Clarke,[2] who was hit by debris close to his left eye, fracturing his skull;[3] unsurprisingly, he died two days later. A third victim, a young girl whose name was unreported, was hit by debris but not seriously hurt.[4]

It was the first instance of Fenian activity on the British mainland since the Clerkenwell Outrage fourteen years earlier, the very incident which led to Donald Swanson joining the Metropolitan Police.

While Fenianism had abated in Britain in the aftermath of the Clerkenwell Prison bombing, in New York a new organisation seeking Irish independence had been established which would have a major involvement in events of future years. Clan na Gael was formed on 20th

June 1867 by Irish immigrant Jerome Collins, and sought to unite Irish-American Fenian factions by providing a common meeting ground for members of both the Irish Republican Brotherhood and the American-based Fenian Brotherhood. They conducted their plans in secret, rather than with the public displays favoured by the I.R.B. Within a short time more branches had been created, and by 1876 the Clan claimed to have some 11,000 members and had become the dominant faction in America, absorbing most other small societies. Discussions were soon under way to form an alliance with the Irish Republican Brotherhood and an agreement was reached where Clan na Gael began to support the I.R.B. financially and materially.

A 'skirmishing' fund had been created, into which Irish-Americans sympathetic to the Fenian cause made regular donations for the purpose of financing a dedicated group of revolutionaries prepared to wage a 'war in the shadows' on Britain through dynamite attacks. Chief among those behind skirmishing fundraising was Jeremiah O'Donovan Rossa, a prominent member of the I.R.B.

O'Donovan Rossa established a dynamite school at Brooklyn where, for 30 dollars per month, a student could learn about manufacturing explosives. Many students came from Ireland and the British mainland to be trained, and then returned to teach other Fenians. In this way, the skirmishing funds created a band of Dynamitards set on destruction in the name of a free Ireland.

O'Donovan Rossa's increasingly public declarations of the I.R.B.'s intentions, however, caused concern for Clan na Gael, who preferred to conduct their plans under a shroud of secrecy, and he was eventually removed as Secretary of the skirmishing fund, which moved under the control of the Clan. The Clan itself, under a 'New Departure' policy, increasingly saw the presence of Charles Parnell of the Irish Parliamentary Party in the Houses of Parliament as the best way of achieving their objective, and had met with the M.P. several times in the late 1870s.

Frustrated by the idea of relying on the British Parliament in order to achieve independence, O'Donovan Rossa and other Clan members who advocated using violence against Britain set up a convention in Philadelphia in June 1880 to discuss their views, breaking Clan na Gael regulations. They were immediately expelled, leaving O'Donovan Rossa free to form a new Fenian faction called the United Irishmen of America.

It was this faction which produced the Skirmishers – the dynamiters who attacked Salford Barracks in January 1881, the first time in history that an Irishman had exploded a bomb in mainland Britain.[5]

The Skirmishers formed a strategy of targeting institutions of importance. They recognised that instead of choosing heads of state and other notable persons as its victims, by causing damage and disruption to infrastructure and buildings of significance it could create panic and fear among the public.[6]

It was initially thought that the reason for the attack on Salford Barracks was to destroy the armoury, which held approximately 5,000 weapons. If this was the case, the perpetrators had received incorrect information, for the shed in which the armoury was housed was divided into three compartments: one for weapons, the second, where the bomb was deposited, a butcher's storeroom, and the third compartment used as a linen store.[7] Although the shed was destroyed in the blast, the weapons remained unscathed. A more likely reason is that as Salford Gaol where the Manchester Martyrs had been executed in 1867 had since been demolished, the Barracks were a location of strong symbolism to the Fenians.

Concerned that the Salford attack represented a new wave of terrorism, the Home Office requested reports on the current state of American-Irish Fenianism from its diplomats Sir Edward Thornton and Robert Clipperton. Captain Clipperton, based in Philadelphia, wrote to state that Fenians were experimenting with clockwork mechanisms with which to activate their bombs. His informant also supplied a number of targets supposedly on O'Donovan Rossa's list: these included the Houses of Parliament, Whitehall and the Bank of England.[8]

This focus of targeting prominent buildings was underlined two months later when, at around eleven o'clock in the evening of 16th March,[9] City of London Police Constable Samuel Cowell was on his beat which took him along a dark, narrow alley behind the Mansion House, the Lord Major's residence. He had just turned into the alley from Walbrook when he saw fire and smoke issuing from a recess in a window beneath the Egyptian Hall.

P.C. Cowell hurried to the scene to find the smoke billowing from a box measuring 24 inches square by 5 inches deep which was wrapped in brown paper. Smothering the box to extinguish the flames, the constable then took the smouldering object to Bow Lane police station. There, it was discovered just how narrowly P.C. Cowell's prompt action had averted disaster. The box, which was bound tightly with iron hoops, had a round hole in its centre from which a fuse protruded. The outer paper had burned to within an inch of this fuse. When opened, it was revealed that the box contained some 15lb of coarse blasting gunpowder into which the fuse was positioned,[10] a piece of an old carpet bag and a total of four recent newspapers from Ireland, Glasgow and America, indicating the origin of those responsible.[11]

It was thought that the Mansion House had been targeted because the Lord Mayor, Derry-born Alderman William McArthur, had betrayed his Irish roots by supported the recently-passed Coercion Act, which enabled the arrest without trial of persons 'reasonably suspected' of crime and conspiracy.

The Fenians' plans continued. In the early hours of Friday, 10th June a cabman named John Ross was sitting on his trap at the top of Castle Street in Liverpool when he saw two men dressed like sailors approaching the west door of the Town Hall opposite. Between them they were carrying a canvas bag containing something evidently of some weight, which they placed on the steps of the Hall. Thinking they may require his services Ross started towards the men, but paused when he saw two policemen who had also noticed the pair,[12] who promptly ran off. One of the officers dashed to the doorway and picked up the bag. Hearing a 'fizzing' noise coming from within, the constable swung his arm and threw it into the middle of the road, where seconds later it exploded, shooting flames and sending a thick column of smoke billowing into the Liverpool sky. Forty windows of the Town Hall were blown out, along with many belonging to nearby occupiers including Brown's Buildings and the Phoenix Fire Office.[13]

The dynamiters set off along Oldhall Street and into Edmund Street, pursued by the two officers. A third constable, patrolling Oldhall Street, saw the pursuit and captured one of the men, who threw something over a wall. The officers continued their chase of the second man, who by this time had disappeared along Leeds Street towards the canal. It transpired that he had fallen in, for when he was found hiding on a boat his clothes were saturated. A search of his clothing revealed a gun; the object discarded by the first man was discovered to be a loaded revolver.[14]

Both men were taken to the Central Police Office, where their identities were revealed as James McKevitt and Robert Barton.[15] McKevitt claimed to have been born at Warrenpoint, Ireland, and had lived in Liverpool for some years before moving to America; Barton, who spoke with a Scottish accent but who also claimed to have originated in Ireland, had spent six years in New Orleans. The pair had more recently been living in Liverpool's Cottenham Street. Damningly, in Barton's pockets were scraps of paper containing the addresses of O'Donovan Rossa and other heads of the Skirmishing organisation.[16]

Barton and McKevitt told the police all they knew about Rossa's skirmishing cell; Barton had himself been trained in making explosives at the Dynamite School.

As 1881 turned into 1882, yet another Fenian faction was created, this time in Ireland. The Irish National Invincibles were composed mostly of extremist members of the Irish Republican Brotherhood in Dublin and "more determined" Land League members from rural parts of the country, stirred into action by the frustrations of the Coercion Act. Their aim was a simple one: the assassination of anyone preventing Home Rule.[17]

The Coercion Act had been introduced by Chief Secretary for Ireland William Forster in an attempt to deal with the growing Irish National Land League, and had been used to arrest Charles Parnell on 13th October 1881 after his newspaper *United Ireland* had attacked the Land Act. Forster became public enemy no. 1 as far as the Invincibles were concerned and several attempts were made on his life.

An agreement known unofficially as the Kilmainham Treaty saw Prime Minister William Gladstone announce on Tuesday, 2nd May 1882 that Parnell would be released from prison. The agreement acted as a prelude to Gladstone announcing the Arrears of Rent (Ireland) Act 1882, which cancelled £2million of rent arrears; in return, Parnell pledged an attempt to curtail future outrages. This turn of events saw the resignation of Forster, who was replaced by Lord Frederick Cavendish, Financial Secretary to the Treasury.

Denied their intended quarry through Forster's resignation, the Invincibles were determined to still taste blood and switched their attention to Thomas Burke, the Permanent Under Secretary at the Irish Office based at Dublin. Less than a week after Forster's resignation they would fulfil their wish, and Parnell's efforts to prevent outrages proved woefully inadequate.

It was fine and warm as Under-Secretary Burke strolled towards Dublin's Phoenix Park with Lord Frederick Cavendish just after six o'clock on the evening of Saturday, 6th May. Just that morning Cavendish had been sworn in at Dublin Castle as Forster's replacement, and now the two politicians intended to take the evening air in the pleasant surroundings of the Park. A brass band could be faintly heard playing in the distance as a cricket match further up the Park neared its end; a knot of spectators nearby were enjoying a polo match.[18]

Inspector John Mallon of the Dublin Metropolitan Police was also walking through the Park on his way to a meeting with informer John Kenny when he was approached by a plain-clothes detective named Thomas Simons, who appeared highly agitated. Simons expressed concern for Mallon's well-being, asking the inspector his proposed route and whether he was armed. Asked to explain himself, Simons confirmed that he had seen a number of Invincibles in the Park that evening, all names known to Mallon.[19]

The Detective Inspector changed his mind about meeting John Kenny and made his way to his home nearby instead, only to see the informer run full-pelt past his window minutes later with "a state of terror in his eyes of one pursued by a thousand devils." Shortly afterwards a detective called for Mallon with the words "Mr. Burke has been stricken to the heart, and there is another gentlemen lying hard by, literally hacked to pieces."[20]

A Mr. Maguire and a friend were riding tricycles through the Park and had passed Burke and Cavendish when on their way along the main route through the Park. On their return journey they found the bodies of the two men, Cavendish lying on the dusty main road in the middle of the carriageway and Burke on the pathway. Both were lying in a large pool of blood.

The *Western Times* recorded the full horror of the attack:

> The upper part of Mr. Burke's body was perforated in a shocking manner, blows having been rained on it with a sharp instrument in a way too shocking to contemplate. The body of Lord Frederick Cavendish displayed similar dreadful wounds, with the addition that the left arm was broken and torn as if he had put it up to protect his breast... The locale of the outrage is terribly marked with blood, the spot where Lord Frederick Cavendish's body was found being absolutely deluged, while Mr. Burke's body lay in a pool of blood only some ten or twelve feet distant...
>
> The police at once proceeded to the scene of the murder, and conveyed the bodies to Stephen's Hospital.
>
> On examination it was found that Mr. Burke had received several stabs near the region of the heart, and his throat had been almost cut across. His clothes were absolutely saturated with blood, and the haemorrhage must have been tremendous. The clothes were also much torn. His gloves had been torn in many places, and his hands bore marks suggestive of a fierce and lengthened encounter with his assailants. Lord Frederick had not gloves upon his hands. He had been stabbed in several places about the chest. One wound was through the right lung and penetrated deeply.

The Fenians are Coming!

*The Phoenix Park murders
from The Illustrated Police News, 20th May 1882*

At the time of the dreadful occurrence the Park, as might be expected on such a lovely evening, was crowded in many places by citizens, and it a remarkable fact, and one suggesting that the onslaught must have been short, terrible, and decisive, that many persons sitting and walking within a few hundred yards of where the bodies were found heard nothing of the affair.[21]

News of the murders was met with horror and disbelief. Michael

Davitt, released on the day of the attacks, recognised that the episode would undo all the good work recently achieved by Charles Parnell and denounced the murders. A shocked Parnell offered to resign his seat in the House of Commons, a move which was refused but which strengthened the bond between Parnell and Gladstone.

Predictably, the Invincibles reacted triumphantly:

> What unusual midnight cry is that? It is the newsboy shouting the exciting news; his papers are quickly bought up by eager purchasers. For the first time in the recollection of the Dublin press, Saturday night papers are issued.
>
> Let this daring act be placed in its proper place in history. At least by Irishmen; for what the enemy has called "crime" read in golden letters, "patriotism" and "Virtue". God bless and strengthen the arm of every brave patriot who will destroy the fomenters of infamy in his native land! It was an act of daring; by such acts are prostrate nations ennobled.[22]

That the Invincibles slaughtered their intended target, Thomas Burke, and also by sheer luck the new Chief Secretary, it really was a case of being in the wrong place at the wrong time for Lord Frederick Cavendish.

The hunt for the gang of murderers began immediately. Posters were put up detailing a government reward of £10,000 for the capture of the assassins, with a further £5,000 and a pardon offered for information which led to arrests. Inspector Mallon went a step further and had this information relayed to Fenians currently detained at Her Majesty's pleasure. The intention was of course to try to obtain a lead, but the obvious happened and the police were inundated with letters, all worthless, which wasted many hours for those tasked with dealing with them.

A list of likely names had already formed in Mallon's mind, and several of these were confirmed a week after the murders when the detective was informed that the conspirators included Joe Brady, Tim Kelly, Daniel Curley and James Carey.

Carey in particular interested Mallon. He had been told two years earlier that Carey, a supposedly-respectable builder who was also a town councillor, was part of a vigilance committee which exacted revenge killings on suspected informers. Perhaps coincidentally, Mallon's informer John Kenny was murdered by two men on 4th July.

The following day, Mallon, acting on information received from an imprisoned Fenian named James Mullett, arrested Invincibles Daniel

Curley, Joseph Poole and Thomas Caffrey. James Carey followed 24 hours later, the news of which jogged the memory of a former tenant of Carey's at a house in South Cumberland Street. The man had seen Carey enter the attic of the property two days after the murders of Burke and Cavendish; now, nosing around he found two long knives and a rifle, all of which he removed and later took to the police. A few weeks later Carey's wife, brother and son, along with Joe Brady, went up into the attic themselves to retrieve the weapons. Finding them missing, they went to see the tenant and learned that Mallon was now in possession of the knives and rifle.

Although these were most likely not the knives used to murder Cavendish and Burke, the fact that Mallon now had weapons linked to James Carey, who was still in custody, frightened the Invincibles and they decided that the detective had to go the way of Burke, Cavendish and Kenny.[23]

Before they could plan the Inspector's demise, a strange story emerged from Puerto Cabello, Venezuela.

Apparently driven by remorse, an Irishman named William Westgate had confessed to being one of the Phoenix Park murderers, claiming he had had three accomplices. The quartet had supposedly been employed by "several influential persons" and each received £20. He was arrested on 16th July on board the *Gladstone* by Captain George Richards and taken to the British Consulate at Caracas.

Westgate claimed he had escaped from Dublin on the 7.45pm mail train to Waterford, thirty minutes after the murders had taken place. From there he went to Cork and boarded a steamer to Swansea under the name O'Brien, docking on the evening of 7th May.

Lodging at the Museum Hotel, Strand in Swansea for four days, Westgate caught the attention of the landlady who described him as "very dirty, poor, and much mentally depressed, and that he avoided speaking to anyone".

The *Gladstone* left Swansea on 11th May, with Westgate joining the crew as a fireman.[24]

With no announcement of any arrests in connection with the murders at that point, the newspapers jumped on the story. Although the Dublin police believed little of Westgate's story they were duty-bound to investigate.

The first step was to take statements from the crew of the *Gladstone*. The Home Office was approached with a request for a Scotland Yard officer to find the seamen and bring them to Dublin to give their evidence. This request, by Edward Jenkinson, the Legal Assistant Under Secretary at Dublin Castle, resulted in Godfrey Lushington writing to Howard Vincent on 12th October asking him to send Det. Inspector Donald Swanson to Swansea later that day, where the *Gladstone* was presently berthed but due to depart the next day. The letter gave authorisation for Swanson to inform the owners of the barque that they would be compensated by the Treasury for the four days the crew were expected to be absent to offset any loss of earnings. Swanson was requested to telegraph Howard Vincent and Jenkinson informing them of his expected arrival in Dublin.[25]

And so it was that as Charles Soutar languished in a cell at Edinburgh waiting to be tried for his part in the robbery of the Earl of Crawford's body, Det. Inspector Swanson was on his way to Swansea, catching the 5.45pm train from London[26] and arriving at his destination at midnight. He immediately took the statements of Captain Richards of the *Gladstone*, its former steward Frederick Fairchild (who was now steward of the *Ensign*) and David Thomas, the mate, who was now Captain of the *Betsy*. The detective therefore had to negotiate compensation with owners of all three ships, which he did the following morning.

Having achieved the necessary permissions, the quartet travelled by train to Chester where Swanson telegraphed Jenkinson with the news that they would arrive in Dublin early the following morning. On arrival at Dublin Castle Swanson introduced the witnesses to Crown Solicitor Samuel Lee Anderson, elder brother of Robert. Anderson read over the statements taken by Swanson at Swansea and all three witnesses stated they had nothing further to add. They were then taken before a magistrate and the statements sworn to; Inspector Mallon then made arrangements for the D.M.P.'s Det. Inspector Morrow to travel to Jamaica to fetch Westgate. It was agreed that Frederick Fairchild, to whom Westgate had first made his confession, would meet Morrow at Southampton and then travel with the detective in order to identify the prisoner.

The fleeting appearance at Dublin Castle ended as Swanson took the three witnesses back to Chester, where they parted company and the detective headed back to Scotland Yard. It would be far from his last involvement in the fight against Fenian activity.[27]

Det. Inspector Morrow arrived in Plymouth with Westgate in his custody on the morning of 16th December. He had little hesitation in describing his prisoner as an 'imbecile' to the waiting newspaper reporters, revealing that he had remained docile throughout the voyage and had obeyed all orders given.[28]

Ten days later Westgate appeared at Dublin's Northern Divisional police court, but only for a few minutes. He appeared nervous as he listened to the Prosecutor Mr. Murphy Q.C. tell the courtroom that having spoken with the crew of the *Ibex*, it was discovered that Westgate had in fact spent all day of 6th May on board that vessel, anchored at Dublin. The log book confirmed that the *Ibex* cast off her moorings at seven o'clock sharp, and was well clear of the River Liffey long before the Phoenix Park murders took place, then sailed for Swansea where Westgate stayed for a couple of days before boarding the *Gladstone* bound for Caracas.

Murphy finished by telling the Magistrate, Mr. Curran, that given the evidence the Prosecution consented to the prisoner's discharge. Mr. Curran agreed, and William Westgate hurriedly left the dock without uttering a word, never to explain why he had laid claim to the murders.[29]

It had been a long, arduous example of wasting police time, with several thousands of miles travelled with the end result of only a few minutes in court.

Throughout December, Det. Inspector Mallon repeatedly pulled in members of the Invincibles, asking a few questions and then releasing them, only to re-arrest the same individuals a few days later. His plan was to play one off against the others, until they cracked and revealed information.

It worked. By the middle of January, Mallon had enough information with which to request a warrant from Magistrate Curran, who was no doubt happy with this turn of affairs after the debacle of the Westgate case. On the night of 12th January, seventeen Invincibles were arrested, with more in the days which followed.

It had become clear that James Carey was a senior member. It was said that he enrolled members and planned the crimes. Held at Kilmainham Gaol, Carey became convinced that his erstwhile colleagues had informed on him, and that he was doomed. He readily agreed to Mallon's suggestion that he give evidence on behalf of the Prosecution in an attempt to save his own neck.

On Saturday, 17th February 1883 the Invincibles appeared in the dock at Kilmainham courthouse. Fully expecting James Carey to be in alongside them, their reaction when they realised he had turned Queen's Evidence and would be testifying against them was a mixture of fear and loathing:

> ...if the facial expression of the majority of the prisoners can be taken as
> a true index of thought the absence from their midst of their associate in

the Park tragedy appeared to strike terror into them. The names of the prisoners having been called over, and the prisoners having answered to their names, James Carey was brought into court, and mounted the table to the witness chair amid the greatest excitement, some of the prisoners hissing their old companion.[30]

Giving evidence from the dock, James Carey confirmed that he had been at Phoenix Park on the morning of the murders, it being his job to identify Burke. He was sitting in a cab,

> on the front seat next to the horse, left hand side as you go up. I had a white handkerchief in my hands, with which I made signals. Before we stopped we passed two men in constabulary uniform on a seat. We passed Fitzharris's cab before we stopped on the right hand side. There were seven men where we stopped, scattered about in three groups. They were Joseph Brady, Timothy Kelly, Patrick Delaney, Thomas Caffrey, Michael Fagan, Daniel Curley and Joseph Hanlon. Curley had charge of the arrangements. Curley asked me, "Is he [Burke] coming?" I said, "Yes; the man in the grey suit."... Afterwards a consultation was held between Curley, Brady and I. I asked Brady, "What's to do?" "You may go," said he. Before I went he said, "Mind, be sure; the man in the grey suit."
>
> I started then for Island Bridge. [Burke and Cavendish] were 200 yards away. Kavanagh, with his car, was right opposite me as I was going off. Looking back I saw the two gentlemen come up about 160 yards off. I did not see a car then pass down from the Phoenix, but Joe Brady told me afterwards one did. The gentlemen when they came up were allowed to pass this collection. After they had passed about 250 yards from the place where I had left those men I looked round and saw the seven men meet the two. The first three were abreast – Curley, Fagan and Delaney. About 12 ft after them were Kelly and Brady, and 6 ft behind Caffrey and Hanlon. They let the gentlemen pass through. After going a few steps further I looked round, and saw a right-about movement made by the last four. I went on a few steps farther, and looked again, and saw the two men in the rear getting to the front and closing on the two gentlemen. I saw one figure come in collision with the two gentlemen. This man, Joe Brady, raised his left hand and struck the man facing him. That is all I saw.

Carey then testified how he had met Daniel Curley that evening, who told him what had happened next:

> I saw them close up on the two gentlemen, and Joe Brady strike one

gentleman and follow the other out into the road and attack him also. I saw him go back from the gentleman in the road to the other gentleman, and strike him also, and then I saw him wipe the knife in the grass to take the blood off. I next saw them get on the car and drive away. They drove straight to the Gough statue, where they [saw] two men on velocipedes, who they covered with revolvers as long as they were in sight. I met Brady that night. He said after reaching town he went to the *Express* office and put a card into the letterbox stating how the deed was done. It bore the words, "Executed by order of the Irish Invincibles."[31]

Explaining how he came to be involved with the Invincibles, Carey said that a range of weapons had been supplied on two occasions by a woman he believed to be the wife of Frank Byrne, a Fenian Carey knew to be Secretary to the Land Confederation of Great Britain.[32] The weapons were smuggled into Dublin under the woman's cloak.[33]

This was new information to the police; the following afternoon six detectives from Scotland Yard went to Gothic Villas, the Byrne family home on Avondale Road, Peckham, where two of them – one being Det. Inspector Swanson[34] – entered the house and arrested Mary Ann Byrne and her sister, the two being so similar in appearance that they were unable to tell which was Frank Byrne's wife. The remaining officers searched the residence while Swanson and his fellow officer escorted the two women to King Street police station, where they were questioned before the sister was released around six o'clock in the evening. Mary Ann Byrne was detained on suspicion of conspiracy to murder Government officials in Ireland.[35]

At eight o'clock that evening she was driven to Euston railway station and placed on the 8.25 Irish mail train for Holyhead, escorted on her journey by Inspector Straight of A Division and a detective from the Dublin Metropolitan Police named Donoghue.[36] On her eventual arrival at Dublin Castle she was questioned for several hours and then taken to Kilmainham to be identified by James Carey, who at once said she was not the woman who had brought the weapons. Rather embarrassingly for the London and Dublin forces, Mrs. Byrne was immediately discharged with an apology.[37]

Reporting her release, the *Ayr Advertiser* commented how ludicrous the idea that the "quiet, lady-like woman" had been involved with the assassination plot:

> Anyone to look at Mrs. Byrne would never for a moment imagine that she is capable of carrying two thousand rounds of ammunition, a couple of revolvers and a Winchester repeating rifle concealed among her

clothes.[38]

Following her discharge, Mrs. Byrne gave an interview in which she described her treatment by the authorities:

> I was not at all surprised at my arrest, after what I had seen in the papers; but I was not in the least upset, for I was confident that I could thoroughly establish my innocence... Although those who arrested me... were exceedingly kind, the incident created great sensation in the neighbourhood where I live, and notwithstanding that everything was done very quietly, a good many people must have seen the detectives prizing desks and examining papers in the bay windows of our house. I was treated very kindly also while at King Street, Westminster, where I stayed all night. In fact, Mr. Sheridan, of the Dublin police, and the English detectives treated me with every consideration.
>
> ...All my expenses have been paid by the police, and Mr. Mallon gave me £7 in order to defray my expenses back to London. I have received every consideration at the hands of the police, but I have not been in the least degree disturbed by the incident, because I was so conscious of my ability to disprove the calumnies spoken by the informer. I propose to return home tonight, and am anxious with regard to my sister and my children.[39]

In fact, Mrs. Byrne was so keen to let her family know that all was well that she sent the following triumphant telegram to her husband's sister:

> Hurrah! Mrs. Byrne released. She stops with your mother tonight, and will return tomorrow. She is in excellent spirits.[40]

In a more sombre mood were the Invincibles; 26 members were put on trial between 9th April and 17th May, with five sentenced to death for murder as a result of James Carey's testimony and many more convicted as accessories and sentenced to long spells of imprisonment. The actual murderers, Joe Brady and Timothy Kelly, were the first and last to be executed by William Marwood at Dublin's Kilmainham Gaol, on 14th May and 9th June 1883 respectively.

Frederick Moir Bussy, the biographer of Superintendent John Mallon, would later recall the hanging of the 19-year-old Timothy Kelly:

> Not the least saddening sight it has been my lot to behold was provided on the morning of Kelly's execution outside Kilmainham Gaol. Kneeling

in the roadway were his poor father and mother. They had taken up their positions in the very early hours of the morning, and had prayed incessantly and most earnestly for the spirit of the boy they were so soon to lose. As the fatal moment grew nearer and louder they poured forth their words of supplication. When at last the black flag was run up from one of the turrets of the grey, frowning building, to announce the vindication of justice, the father groaned piteously and the mother uttered a piercing shriek as they both fell forward upon their faces, still sobbing vehement prayers.[41]

Carey may have escaped the hangman for his part in the Phoenix Park murders, but his story would have but a very short time left to run.

In mortal danger should he stay in Dublin, he was an enemy of thousands of angry Irishmen. Attempts to burn down his house had already been made; on one occasion turf saturated with oil was placed against his door and ignited, with police extinguishing the flame before much damage was done.[42]

Eventually, it was decided by the authorities that the informer must leave Ireland. Carey had no say in the matter – he would either comply with the demands of the authorities or be left to fend for himself on the streets of Dublin. His passage to London was paid for, and he was accompanied by an Irish detective to Holyhead and the capital, where he was reunited with his wife and children.

Shortly afterwards he was given a new identity, and on 6th July, under the name of Jim Power, boarded the steamer *Kinfauns Castle* bound for Cape Town. During the voyage he became friendly with a fellow Irish passenger named Patrick O'Donnell, who had no idea that his new friend was the notorious informant responsible for the death of the five Invincibles. On arrival at Cape Town, however, O'Donnell saw an old copy of *The Weekly Freeman* which included an illustration of James Carey, who he immediately recognised as 'Jim Power'.

O'Donnell joined Carey in boarding the *Melrose*, bound for Natal. On 29th July the pair were drinking in the ship's bar when O'Donnell confronted his companion and produced a revolver, shooting him in the neck and then twice in the back. James Carey died fifteen minutes later.[43]

News of Carey's assassination was met with jubilation across Ireland. Scores of bonfires were lit in the streets of Dublin, children dancing around them in celebration as their parents placed effigies of Carey upon them and cheered as they burned. As the police put out the bonfires, so the crowds relighted them.[44]

Patrick O'Donnell was taken to London where he was tried for murder. He was executed at Newgate on 17th December 1883, but his actions had afforded him hero status in Ireland and America. A tribute, *The Ballad of Patrick O'Donnell*, was swiftly written, immortalising the assassin of the informer:

> My name is Pat O'Donnell
> And I come from Donegal,
> I am, you know, a dangerous foe
> To traitors one and all;
>
> For the shooting of James Carey
> I've been tried in London town,
> And now upon the gallows high
> My life I must lay down.

Swanson had travelled to Dublin in October 1882 in the knowledge that Julia was once again pregnant, with their third child due the following spring. Back in England, he ended the year on a relatively quiet note, having arrested one John Crunden for sending a threatening letter to the Prime Minister, William Gladstone, a missive with which some could actually have some sympathy:

> Professed Head of Liberalism, what benefit are you to the country – liberal, indeed, to those who are not in want, but under your (liberal) guidance, in what state are the hard-working classes of the country? Hundreds and thousands crowd the streets actually starving, but willing to work for a very small pittance. If I should come across you or the Prince of Wales or any such who are petted with their thousands, wherever it happens to be, they would have a rough time of it, for I would not stand particular what I would do. So take this warning, for I don't care.[45]

Swanson traced the unemployed 47-year-old Crunden to a lodging house on Wilson Street, Gray's Inn Road, and took him into custody.[46]

At the trial at the Old Bailey on 9th January 1883, Crunden was charged with threatening to murder the Prince of Wales and Gladstone; even Mr. Poland, prosecuting, admitted that there were doubts that the letter contained anything which could be construed as a threat to murder, and Mr. Justice Hawkins wasted little time in declaring that he was of the opinion that no such threat had been intended, and Crunden was acquitted.[47]

Just two days later, however, an incident occurred which revealed the true state of Crunden's mental health. Walking past a jewellery shop belonging to Mr. Samuel Reid at 360 Oxford Street, he picked up a stone and threw it at the window, smashing a plate of glass. Crunden calmly walked up to P.C. William Chapman and told him what he had done, and escorted the constable to point out the stone, now lying on the floor inside the shop. He admitted that he didn't know why he had done it.

At Marlborough Street police court the following day, Det. Inspector Swanson told the Bench that, having had a long discussion with the prisoner, he was of the opinion that Crunden was "mentally weak", if not actually insane;[48] his own wife believed him to not be responsible for his actions. Crunden had already served two prison terms for forgery, and for smashing the jeweller's shop window was sentenced to another custodial sentence of six months.[49]

If Swanson and his colleagues at Scotland Yard welcomed the quiet start to the New Year, they were soon to be shaken from their slumbers. A week after John Crunden was taken to prison, three explosions in Glasgow in a little over four hours signalled the return of the Fenian dynamiters.

Just after 10.10pm on Saturday, 20th January a bright glare suddenly lit up the sky, followed seconds later by a terrific blast which caused houses to shake in their foundations and their windows to shatter. The source of the explosion was found to be at the Corporation South Side Gasworks in Lilybank Road, Tradeston; a row of houses in nearby Muirhouse Lane were partly demolished, with nine residents being severely injured through serious burns or otherwise cuts and bruising caused by flying debris.[50] The cause was soon discovered to be not the gas works itself, but a bomb containing a quantity of dynamite attached to a large gas holder some 60 feet tall by 160 feet in diameter, which when detonated ripped a hole in its side and ignited the gas bellowing from within.[51]

The ignition of the supply caused the gas lamps illuminating the majority of the south side of Glasgow to go out, plunging the streets and housing into darkness.

Two hours later, at around 12.30am, a group of men discovered a tin travelling box lying on the parapet of the Keppoch Hill Bridge, which carried the Forth and Clyde Canal across Possil Road.[52] One, a soldier named Adam Barr,[53] cautiously opened a clasp and raised the lid, revealing what he took to be black sand. At that point a loud explosion reported from the tin, sending Barr and his colleagues flying. None were seriously injured, although Barr himself suffered cuts from metal shrapnel and burns from small pellets blasted out from the tin. The contents of the box burned for several minutes before self-extinguishing, causing no further damage.[54] It was later claimed that the object of the bomb had been to destroy the viaduct, which would have resulted in the water filling the canal for a distance of sixteen miles being drained onto Glasgow city centre.[55]

Just 45 minutes later a third loud blast was heard to the north-west of the city, which proved to have occurred on the premises of the Caledonian Railway Company at their Buchanan Street station.[56] A disused brick shed measuring 24 feet long by 20 feet wide was completely destroyed, but no other damage occurred.[57]

Although there had been no loss of life in the Glasgow attacks, the panic which had probably been the dynamiters' aim had well and truly taken hold.

Seven weeks later they struck again, this time in the capital, and very close to home as far as Det. Inspector Swanson was concerned.

On Wednesday, 14th March, William Gladstone made a speech in which he told Parnell that he would decline to reopen the Land question; if the Fenians were angered by the Prime Minister's stance, they were prompt in their reply.[58]

At around 7.45 the following evening, a young man named Coleman had just left his work at the offices of *The Times* in Blackfriars and on his way to Ludgate Hill station when he passed Play House Yard, a small, quiet square which was bordered on three sides by various offices of the newspaper, the square being completed by printers Drake, Driver and Leaver. As Coleman passed, his attention was caught by a sudden flash of light which was followed immediately by an explosion like a rifle. Several workmen from Drake, Driver and Leaver rushed out to find flames shooting from a box under the window of *The Times'* offices. A boy named Dawes, who was employed by the printers, was washing in a pail of water at that moment and he calmly handed the bucket to Alfred Evans, one of the workmen, who promptly threw the contents over the box, extinguishing the fire[59] with no injuries or damage to surrounding buildings.

The smouldering box was taken into the offices of *The Times* and a policeman sent for, who took it to Bridge Street police station,[60] where it was discovered to be an oval-shaped tin bonnet box, some 13 inches by 8 inches and 9 inches deep, with rough slits cut into the lid. The contents were found to be pieces of towel, paper and a quantity of a dark brown substance, later confirmed to be sawdust impregnated with 30% nitroglycerine. The construction of the bomb led investigators to believe that it was the same as that found on Keppoch Hill Bridge in Glasgow seven weeks earlier.[61]

There was little time to celebrate a near escape, however, as a short time later, with Big Ben striking nine o'clock, a huge blast sounded across Westminster. At the House of Commons, where a few members were still in debate, Sir Thomas Brassey's speech on the Navy Estimates was interrupted as the building shook. Members took little persuading to leave the Chamber, and headed to the lobby, where they were joined by the Duke of Edinburgh, who had been observing from the Peer's Gallery with Sir Henry Fletcher.[62]

A whole convoy of fire engines sped to the source of the explosion, in a large block of Government buildings bordered by Whitehall, Downing Street and Charles Street, where they were met by a crowd numbering several hundred. The block housed several departments including the Home Office and the Foreign Office, and the blast had occurred outside the south side, on Charles Street, which housed the Local Government Board.

It was evident that a large bomb had been placed behind an ornamental balustrade, eight feet of which had been destroyed. Masonry debris was blown out in a fan shape, with large lumps of concrete landing with a thud on the roof of King Street police station, 25 yards away opposite the Local Government Board offices. Separating the station from the Board offices was a stretch of wasteland contained within a tall wooden fence; chunks of debris weighing at least 200lbs had been blown through the fence, flattening 13 yards of the structure, and striking the walls of King Street station with great force. The glass of windows as far as 180 yards away were broken by the explosion. It is unknown whether Donald Swanson was at King Street at that moment, but officers from the station and others close by were soon on duty controlling the curious and frightened of the neighbourhood.

It was a miracle that not a single injury was reported. The caretaker of the offices, a Mr. Whittlestone, was sitting with his wife in their quarters in the room adjacent to where the bomb went off, and apart from shock escaped harm.[63]

A Sergeant Rose was walking along King Street when the explosion occurred, which he at first took to be an earthquake. He raised his hands to his helmet to prevent it falling from his head, at which point his hands were cut by a hail of falling glass. Hearing screams from a nearby house, Rose and another officer recorded only as P.C. 95A ran up the stairs to rescue a woman and her two children, both with cut faces, taking the family to the safety of King Street station.[64]

The attempt to blow up Government offices in Westminster. Sgt. Rose is standing in front of King Street police station, where Donald Swanson was based at the time of the incident. Author's collection.

Rumours soon started that the dynamiters' target had been the Prime Minister, as Gladstone had been in Downing Street at the time, or Sir William Vernon Harcourt, who had been in his Home Office apartment. It was far more likely that the bomb had been deposited outside the Local Government Board offices simply as Charles Street was a quiet, seldom used thoroughfare, with no intention of an assassination attempt.

Early the following morning the Local Government Board offices were visited by Howard Vincent and H.M. Chief Inspector of Explosives, Colonel Vivian Dering Majendie.[65]

Majendie had been born in 1836, the son of Major J. R. Majendie. He was educated at Leamington College and entered the Royal Military Academy in 1851, earning a commission in the Royal Artillery at the age of eighteen. He served in the Crimean War and the Indian Mutiny, taking part in the capture of Lucknow.[66]

On his return to England, Majendie was appointed Captain Instructor and then Assistant-Superintendent of the Royal Laboratory, Royal Arsenal under Major-General Edward Boxer and became an expert in gunpowder and other explosives,[67] investigating accidental and suspicious explosions.

In 1871, following Boxer's retirement, he was appointed Chief Inspector of Explosives on a salary of £1,000, with former Royal Artillery colleague Major Ford paid £800 as his assistant.[68] Majendie next recruited the assistance of Dr. August Dupré, a German-born chemist, who advised on chemical explosives.[69] The trio undertook many experiments to further their knowledge, and eventually drafted the Explosives Act of 1875, which introduced licences governed by strict rules to which explosives had to be manufactured, in the process saving the lives of many who worked in that industry, for not only was it previously common practice to open sealed barrels of gunpowder by striking them with a hammer and chisel, but on one occasion Majendie interviewed a young assistant who, on looking for something in the cellar of his explosive-manufacturing master, had actually wedged a lighted candle into an open barrel of gunpowder without realising the danger in his actions. Before the Explosives Act, such incidents were apparently commonplace.[70]

At the end of the first nine months following the passing of the Explosives Act, some 1,213 licences had been issued across the United Kingdom. Majendie and his team had inspected 457 premises;[71] this had grown to 1,391 in 1883. In addition, they had visited dynamite factories in Hamburg, Prague and Presburg, Hungary, to observe experiments in

Colonel Vivian Dering Majendie, H.M. Chief Inspector of Explosives
Author's collection

blasting gelatine.[72]

Once the dynamiters began using clockwork and other timed mechanisms – so-called 'infernal machines' – Majendie and his team had more experimentation to undertake. When these machines failed to detonate they would be passed to Majendie to examine.

Two such machines were discovered at Liverpool, both packed with 28 lbs of dynamite. Alongside these was a quantity of apparatus which allowed local expert Dr. Campbell Brown to determine how the infernal machines worked: sulphuric acid would enter the top of a length of brass tubing and then flow to the lower section, which was perforated with two holes. Against these holes were folded sheets of paper, with the acid eventually soaking through to seep into a mixture of chlorate of potash and sugar, igniting a detonator fixed to the end of the tube. As simple as it sounds, the number of folds in the paper determined how long it would take to detonate the dynamite.[73]

In a later interview with *The Sketch*, the Chief Inspector explained why he refused to destroy an unexploded bomb which had been sent to him:

> I always like to find out what it's made of. This has often proved useful in pointing to a common source of outrage. I take, too, a certain pride in not being baffled. But in some cases the only plan might be to destroy the thing. Recently, in Paris, they found a machine, and they did not know what to do with it, so they deliberately exploded it and the greater part of a house at the same time.

In the same interview Majendie bemoaned the curse of hoax bomb threats, which had sadly, but predictably, followed the Fenian attacks:

> I have noticed that whenever an outrage or attempted outrage excites attention it is always followed by a kind of reflection or shadow in the shape of hoaxes... One suspicious box, it turned out, contained nothing more dangerous than figs... Another bomb proved to be a case containing peptonised cocoa, which was subsequently eaten by a little friend of mine. I tell him he is the first person who ever ate an infernal machine.
>
> One thing I should like to say, and that is that the evening papers pander to this kind of thing by making so much fuss about each hoax as it occurs. It would be so very easy to send round to me or to the head of the Criminal Investigation Department, and we would tell them at once if there was anything in it or not. They seem determined to give currency to a sensation, whether there is any foundation for it or not. I daresay

they don't ask, because they are afraid of losing their sensation. In any case, they are very negligent, and they help to cause us a great deal of trouble.[74]

The Home Office obviously felt that no amount of hoaxes were worth taking a risk over. Five days after the Whitehall outrage, steps were taken to tackle Fenian activity at its source, by infiltrating their communities and learning their plans.

Since the disbanding of the Counter Revolutionary Secret Service Department in May 1868, no dedicated government department existed in London to tackle terrorism. Robert Anderson had remained attached to the Home Office as Advisor on Political Crime, but with little to do he had been appointed secretary to several government inquiries to justify his salary, such as the Royal Commission on Railway Accidents (1874) and the Royal Observatory of Edinburgh Commission (1876), where the Chairman was Lord Lindsay, later Earl of Crawford, whose father's body had been removed from the tomb at Dunecht. In 1877 Anderson was appointed secretary to the new Prison Commission.[75]

At the time of the Salford Barracks attack, Home Secretary William Vernon Harcourt was understandably concerned with the lack of an intelligence network on Fenian activity, and on 23rd January 1881, nine days after the Salford bombing, instructed the C.I.D.'s Director Howard Vincent to select a number of detectives from within his department to form a team to focus on Irish affairs. The result was the 'Fenian Office', an embryonic political arm which was headed by Howard Vincent, aided by Chief Superintendent Dolly Williamson, and included officers including Det. Inspectors Charles Hagen and Charles von Tornow, the latter having finally shaken off the suspicions hanging over him during the Trial of the Detectives three years earlier. The branch was led by Det. Inspector John Littlechild, who later recalled:

> As years rolled on all those officers who had obtained a knowledge of Fenian conspirators [in the 1860s] had either died or left the service, and in 1880 [sic], when the first rumblings of fresh troubles were heard, I was instructed by Mr. Williamson to take up the matter as a special study, and every point calling for inquiry was referred to me. The lack of previous knowledge concerned me not at all, as the conspiracy business was to a certain extent under new management. Most of the [Fenians] who had taken part in the '67 movement had retired or gone over to the majority.[76]

By 1883, however, the intelligence-gathering efforts of the Fenian

Office frustrated Harcourt; Howard Vincent's plan of relying on cities with strong Irish communities keeping him informed of any Fenian activity seemed pointless when those local constabularies could receive due credit for information if passed directly to the Home Office.

It was clear therefore that a centralised department dedicated to observing Fenian suspects and their activities, and responsible directly to the Home Office was required, and this was quickly assembled in the aftermath of the Local Government Board attack. It was decided that officers recruited were to be Irish Catholics with knowledge of the politics of the day, so that they may infiltrate Fenian groups more easily.

On 19th March 1883 the new department was announced in Police Orders, with Inspectors Pope and Ahern, Sergeant Jenkins, P.C.s O'Sullivan, Walsh, Foy, Thorpe and McIntyre selected from across the divisions being the first eight officers recruited; four detectives from the C.I.D. were temporarily attached to the new branch, which would be based at Central Office, Scotland Yard, under the command of Chief Superintendent Williamson, who was relieved of other duties. The department was responsible to the Home Secretary, and would liaise with Robert Anderson, who had been recalled to the Home Office as Fenian activity increased, Howard Vincent, and London-based members of the Royal Irish Constabulary.

At ten o'clock in the morning of 20th March, five days after the Whitehall bombing, the Special Irish Branch met for the first time.[77]

Patrick McIntyre, formerly known as L Division's P.C. 224, recalled their immediate work:

> My first duty was to make investigations respecting the explosion at the Local Government Board offices. I was told to watch three public houses. All these places were under strict surveillance for some time, but no trace could be found of the perpetrators of the outrage. Mr. Williamson and his chief Littlechild were getting disheartened. They were in the habit of working sixteen and eighteen hours a day. Hundreds of letters which came daily from all classes of people, giving descriptions of supposed Fenians, had to be gone through by the two chiefs, and the reports sent into them were also to be carefully attended to.[78]

Although the new Branch was to shoulder most of the responsibility for detecting terrorist activity, officers throughout the metropolis were told to be extra vigilant for suspicious activity, as remembered by Maurice Moser, then an inspector at the C.I.D.:

> The members of the detective force of Scotland Yard had... an unusual

amount of hard and tedious work thrown upon them, in an almost wholesale manner, by the sudden irruption of the Fenian element, with all its corollary of horrors to this country generally and to London in particular. If I state that every possible resource at the disposal of the Criminal Investigation Department was taxed to its very uttermost, I am putting, even then, the matter very mildly indeed.[79]

It was part of this approach that on 11th April Det. Inspectors Donald Swanson and Henry Marshall of the C.I.D. entered what appeared to be an empty house at 16a High Road, Knightsbridge. The building was directly opposite the Life Guards barracks, which they had reason to believe was a target for a Fenian attack.[80]

As Swanson and Marshall systematically searched the building for dynamite, they discovered three persons living in the basement. The room was filthy, with a couple of old chairs being the only furniture, and rags on the floor acting as bedding. The occupants turned out to be a family: a widow named Mary O'Connor and her children, 27-year-old Edward and Elizabeth, aged 22. Finding no sign of explosives, the detectives left the building but directed Det. Sergeants Arthur Standing and Matthew O'Brien of the local B Division to watch the house.[81]

It transpired that Edward O'Connor had represented himself as a travelling salesman to a Mr. Dolman, a solicitor of Jermyn Street, who owned the Knightsbridge property. O'Connor said he wanted to use the house as a boot shop, and supplied references from Thomas Morgan of 218 Tottenham Court Road and John Andrews of 48 Blackfriars Road.

O'Connor was supposed to make payment for the agreement before taking possession of the property; when this failed to materialise Mr. Dolman sent his cashier, Walter Elms, to the house at Knightsbridge. There he found that O'Connor and his family had already moved in, by virtue of an unlocked back door. Edward O'Connor was nowhere to be found, and his mother told Elms that her son was travelling on business. Unsatisfied with the present state of affairs, Mr. Dolman looked into the references and found both to be false; both addresses were occupied by stationers but neither had heard of the men purported to reside there. Thomas Morgan and John Andrews were, of course, aliases of Edward O'Connor, who in the meantime had written to George Stokes, foreman to boot manufacturer William Hooker of 117 Bethnal Green Road, requesting some samples be taken to his new shop. This he did, and O'Connor subsequently ordered 24 pairs of boots.

A fortnight later, on 11th April, when Hooker and assistant William Hearn arrived to deliver the boots they were stopped by Det. Sergeant

O'Brien and on being told of the suspicion attached to the O'Connor clan left with their stock intact.

Between seven and eight o'clock in the morning on 13th April, Mary and Elizabeth O'Connor were observed in Rutland Yard, the stableyard of the Rose and Crown public house of which 16a was part,[82] both carrying large bundles. Standing and O'Brien demanded to see the contents, which proved to be six pairs of boots, six pairs of half-soles and twelve pairs of heels. The women were also carrying a number of pawn tickets for more boots. They were arrested, with Edward O'Connor finally being captured a week later.

On 28th May he was found guilty at the Old Bailey of obtaining by false pretences and sentenced to twelve months' hard labour; Mary and Elizabeth were found guilty of conspiracy, each receiving two months' hard labour.[83]

Det. Inspector Swanson, meanwhile, was in New York. He had travelled in order to bring a fugitive calling himself Captain Archer to justice; Archer, also known as Major Templer,[84] had absconded to America after being committed to trial at Bristol on a charge of forgery relating to a promissory note for £53 16s.[85] Archer was arrested by the New York police, and taken into custody by Swanson on 26th May 1883 under the Extradition Treaty. The detective and his prisoner arrived back in London on the morning of Saturday, 2nd June and headed straight to Bow Street,[86] where Archer was charged under his real name of Edward Harvey Wadge. As no prosecutor was present the case was adjourned for a week, but on 9th June when again no prosecution appeared, Wadge was awarded bail; a costly mistake, as he promptly disappeared.[87]

If Swanson felt annoyance at his prisoner escaping, this soon evaporated when Julia gave birth to their first daughter, less than a fortnight later on 21st June. Ada Mary was named after Julia's sister, Ada Nevill, and Donald's mother. She was the first addition to the family born at the new family home of 5 Camden Villas, Kennington, and was registered by her father on 20th July 1883.[88]

The summer of 1883 passed without further Fenian activity, and as autumn began Swanson must have felt relief at being handed another relatively mundane case, looking into the possibility that gambling was being undertaken on the card game baccarat at the Park Club at Park Place, St. James's. It was part of a crackdown on illegal gaming, and baccarat, which had only recently made its way across the channel from France, was seen by clubs as an exciting game to offer their members.

The Park Club was run by proprietor Captain Jenks,[89] aided by Secretary Mr. Dalton. Swanson visited the Club with Inspector Turpin on 19th September, primarily to warn Jenks that gaming for money was illegal. The detective was told that the Park Club, in keeping with many other West End establishments, simply could not survive without the baccarat games being played, with Jenks bemoaning the fact that "the kitchen has been a loss, and wine and cigars are sold at almost cost price." A dozen members would play baccarrat at a time, with a game usually starting at 4.30 in the afternoon and sometimes lasting until eight o'clock the following morning, with a bank every twenty minutes of up to £300.[90]

Swanson returned two days later, finding Jenks helpful but defiant. It was clear that the threat of a summons was not acting as a deterrent.

For now, however, the gamblers of the Park Club would have to wait. Swanson was tasked by Howard Vincent with responding to a request for information from the Copenhagen Police with regard to a notorious thief and arsonist, Denmark's most wanted man, Jens Nielsen.[91]

The Director of Criminal Investigations had noted various newspaper reports of Nielsen's confession to starting what had been a disastrous fire at the Royal Victoria Docks on 8th February 1881,[92] for which there was no doubt that it had been started deliberately. The police had determined that the blaze had been started in three places, and near a lit bale of straw three unspent matches were found. Had the straw bale caught fire quickly instead of merely smouldering, it was claimed, the nearby tobacco warehouse would have ignited, causing substantially more damage.[93]

If the confession was true, it would not have been the first time Nielsen had started a blaze. Having been caught stealing a gold watch in Odense, when the young thief was 15-year-old, Nielsen was placed in a reformatory which he set alight, escaping in the process. Soon recaptured, Nielsen was transported to Canada but decided to return to his homeland, homesick, leaving a trail of robberies and custodial sentences throughout America and Europe as he made his way back to Copenhagen. Here he resumed his criminal activities, setting fire to farmhouses and other residences with the intention of stealing valuables while the owners were distracted by the blaze.[94]

He was captured having set fire to five farmhouses near Copenhagen on 1st and 2nd July 1883, and under interrogation confessed to three arson attacks in London. Hoping to fill his pockets with valuables at the Victoria Dock, Nielsen claimed to have found only three dresses and two bonnets.[95] In addition to the Victoria Docks blaze, he had also set fire to a Rope Works at Glengall Road and then Brewers Quay, London Bridge.

Howard Vincent wrote to Copenhagen's Chief of Police on 10th July, asking whether there was any truth in the newspaper reports of Nielsen's confession, and received a reply asking for further information on the London arson attacks.[96]

Vincent wrote again on 9th October, asking that Scotland Yard be informed at once should Nielsen be "set at liberty and return to this country."[97]

On 17th October Donald Swanson prepared a report responding to the Copenhagen police's request, confirming that only buildings were targeted, not ships, and that Mr. Swainton, Chief Officer of the London Salvage Corps, had estimated total damage at £1,500,100. Swanson also reported that no lives were endangered, and that no rewards were offered, probably to the disappointment of the Danish officer who had arrested Nielsen in Copenhagen.[98]

As Jens Nielsen sat in a cell in Copenhagen while the Scotland Yard detectives corresponded with their Danish counterparts, the Fenians returned.

At three minutes past eight on the evening of 30th October 1883, less than a fortnight after Swanson's report to the Danish authorities, passengers on a platform waiting for a train at Charing Cross underground station were thrown to the floor as an explosion blasted out from the tunnel between that station and Westminster, half a mile to the west. Plates of glass in buildings at both stations shattered as lamps were extinguished simultaneously and a large cloud of black smoke mushroomed out of the tunnel into the platform at Charing Cross, causing panic among those in the station at that time. At that moment a train pulled into Charing Cross from Mansion House, and although its passengers heard the explosion, they were thankfully uninjured.[99]

Three minutes later another bomb exploded just fifty yards out of Praed Street underground station,[100] on the opposite side of the capital. A train had just left Praed Street on its way to Edgware Road when the explosion occurred, causing serious damage to six carriages as 62 people were injured,[101] mostly from cuts. Thirty-eight were taken to nearby St. Mary's hospital, four suffering serious injuries.[102]

The carriage which had borne the blast was removed from the track and taken to the railway company's depot at Neasden for inspection the following day.[103]

Colonel Majendie and Major Ford examined the two scenes. In the tunnel at Charing Cross a crater had been formed in the ballast between the line and the wall, while at Praed Street a hole had been blasted in the tunnel wall. The Explosives Inspectors concluded that both bombs had consisted of nitro-compound dynamite and had been dropped from trains a couple of minutes before they exploded.[104]

A search of both stations revealed no clue as to the identity of the dynamiters. A reward of £500 offered by the railway companies was matched by another of £500 by the Home Office.[105]

Det. Inspector Donald Swanson, meanwhile, had been making enquiries into Jens Nielsen's activity in London.

On 30th November he was finally ready to submit his report. While the fire at Victoria Docks had taken place on 8th February 1881, and that at the Glengall Road Rope Works three days later, there was a gap of more than two months before the Brewers Quay blaze.

Swanson discovered that a Jans Nelson, an 18-year-old seaman, had been convicted at Thames Police Court on 18th February that year, a week after the Glengall Road attack. He had been charged with the theft of a coat of a Customs Officer on the day of the Victoria Docks fire, and had been sentenced to two months' imprisonment, confirming the Dane's confession. On being freed he had set fire to Brewers Quay, and a fortnight later had appeared at the Old Bailey,[106] where he pleaded guilty to the theft of a key from the home of one Joseph Cornish. He was sentenced to twelve months' hard labour.[107]

The detective's report was countersigned by Det. Chief Inspector John Shore and sent to Copenhagen.[108]

Jens Nielsen was tried in Copenhagen on 14th March 1884. Found guilty, he was sentenced to penal servitude for life.[109]

Faced with a lifetime behind bars – he was still just 22-years-old – Nielsen chose to die rather than suffer possibly sixty years behind bars. In the years which followed, he made three vicious attacks on staff at Horsens Correctional Institution in an attempt to be awarded the death penalty for attempted murder.[110] Eventually, his wish was granted and he was executed on 8th November 1892,[111] being decapitated by executioner Jens Seistrup.[112] It was Denmark's last execution until new penal laws came into effect in 1945 in response to the Second World War.

Once his work on the Nielsen case was complete, on 19th December Swanson returned to the Park Club in Mayfair, acting on information received from solicitors Lewis & Lewis of nearby Ely Place that despite warnings the Club intended to continue their baccarat sessions and would contest any proceedings.[113] Accordingly, Captain Jenks, Mr. Dalton and the rest of the Club's Committee, along with three members, appeared at Bow Street Police Court on 31st January 1884 charged with acts of gambling on 29th and 30th November and 1st December.[114] On 7th February 1884 Judge Sir James Ingham finally ruled that although baccarat in itself was not illegal, playing for money was and accordingly fined Jenks and the Committee £500 each, and those members playing £100.[115] An appeal saw the judgements against the manager and committee of the Park Club upheld, but those members who had simply been playing the game at the time of the raid were absolved.[116] For his part in the investigation Swanson received a reward of 30 shillings.[117]

A predictable side effect of the ruling was the steady rise in the number of clubs in both the West End and the City closing down. The *Derbyshire Courier* reported that

> In the more fashionable quarters several clubs have been entirely closed, and their furniture and fittings sold by auction, since without baccarat it was impossible to carry them on profitably.[118]

The crackdown on illegal gaming met with widespread disapproval, with *Reynolds's Weekly Newspaper* voicing what many thought:

> Mr. Howard Vincent is a wonderful man. He has actually discovered at last that gambling goes on in some of the clubs of the West. Everybody else has known as much as this any time during the last hundred years or so. Surely, if necessary, action is the business of the public prosecutor and not of the detective police. Where is [Director of Public Prosecutions] Sir J. B. Maule all this time? Can he be looking after the accumulating number of murderers whom Mr. Howard Vincent has not caught?[119]

Whether this and similar reports had a bearing on Howard Vincent's thoughts is difficult to say, but just nine days after *Reynolds's Weekly Newspaper* questioned his actions the *Pall Mall Gazette* reported a rumour that he was contemplating resigning his post, intending to enter Parliament.[120] The following day it stated that Howard Vincent had travelled to Egypt, where he met his brother Edgar, the two staying at Cairo before travelling to Paris in March.[121]

1884 had started with a puzzling case, when on the crisp afternoon of New Year's Day a group of boys playing near a clump of trees on a patch of waste land opposite Queen Elizabeth's Walk in Stoke Newington, north London found a number of unusual items under some elm trees.

Thirteen-year-old[122] William Jobson found a hat, a linen collar and cuff, two fingers of a glove, a necktie in two pieces, several visiting cards, half a keyring and half a sleeve link, along with a portion of an eyeglass; Edmund Long, aged seven,[123] found the bar of a watch-chain and a watch-key, as well as a pearl pin and a woman's earring. He gave them to the brother of his friend 10-year-old[124] David Brace, who himself had found a cigar cutter, five keys, a purse, scarf-pin, a ticket and some money, which he spent while also giving the other items to his brother, Jim Brace.[125] Finally, another boy William Lambert, aged 12[126] discovered a coat lying on the ground with the sleeves turned inside-out. On the same afternoon, an apprentice engineer named William Newton found two shillings between a manure heap and a break in the hedge which ran along the boundary of the land. On the other side of the hedge was the West Reservoir, built in 1833 by the New River Company.[127]

When all the items discovered were handed in to police, concerns were immediately raised that someone had come to harm in the water.

When young William Jobson informed P.C. Frederick Davey of the discovery of the items, the constable went at once to the clump of elm trees with another officer, P.C. Dowty and, observing what appeared to be a disturbance on the grass, went up to the bank of the reservoir and discovered footprints leading from the hedge which edged the waste land. There appeared to be marks made by more than one set of shoes. A boat belonging to the New River Company was procured and the water searched until the light faded, but nothing was found.[128]

At nine o'clock the following morning, 33-year-old labourer George Jaggers[129] of the New River Company was sent to drag the reservoir. A couple of hours later he discovered the body of a man floating in the water by some trees, about ten yards from the bank.

N Division Constable Nicholas Michaelston was alerted, and he went to the reservoir along with local surgeon Dr. White, where they examined the body on the bank. It was by then lying on its back with the legs drawn up towards the stomach and the right arm lying across the chest. It was that of a young, slim man, no more that 5ft 5in in height.[130] There was a small laceration on the tip of the nose and a graze on the left ear, apart from which there appeared no other obvious injury. The man was fully dressed, although missing a collar and tie. Several of his pockets had been turned inside-out. Most disturbingly, a handkerchief was tied around the neck, with three knots tied very tightly at the back. With great difficulty, the doctor assisted Michaelston in untying the knots.

The mysterious death of John Broome Tower
from The Illustrated Police News, 12th January 1884

The body was taken to the mortuary, where it was further examined by Dr. White, assisted by Dr. Thomas Bond, who had been sent from Scotland Yard. They found that the face was red and a frothy, blood-tinged mucous issued from the nose, and the mouth, throat and lungs were filled with the same substance. Where the tightly-bound handkerchief had been was found a mark half-an-inch wide and extending three and a half inches to the right of the front of the throat and four and a half to the left.

There was no water in the lungs or stomach.

It was evident, said Dr. Bond later, that the cause of death was strangulation and not drowning.[131]

But had the young man been murdered and his body dumped in the water, or had he attempted to hang himself from one of the trees where the various articles had been discovered, and then staggered off into the reservoir?

Detective Inspectors Glass and Pope of N Division began their investigations, and were soon joined by Scotland Yard's Det. Inspector Henry Moore and Det. Inspector Swanson,[132] assisted by Det. Sergeants Hearn, Helson and Nutkins.[133] Moore made casts of the footprints discovered at the scene, and confirmed that while two of these matched the narrow, pointed boots worn by the dead man, a third footprint was of a broad boot.[134] This seemed to back up the widely-held belief that the death was a case of murder. However, local newspaper *The Islington Gazette* wisely pointed out that while the "marks of the struggle are plainly to be seen, but it is quite possible that other persons may have subsequently passed over the surface, and thus confused the traces."[135] Found on the brow of the ground leading to the reservoir were two pointed indentations, perfectly matching the deceased's boot-tips, as well as knee prints.[136] This raised the question as to whether the man was forced onto the ground by an assailant, or had himself collapsed through exhaustion when close to death following an attempt at self-strangulation.

It certainly was a puzzle.

Not in doubt was the identity of the unfortunate man. Visiting cards found by the elm trees had provided a name which, on investigation, proved to be that of the dead man. When detectives called at 109 Dynevor Road, just over a mile away from the West Reservoir, they were met by Miss Alice Drage, who identified a large number of the items recovered from the waste land as belonging to a friend of the family who had lodged with them for five or six years. His name was John Broome Tower.

He had been born out of wedlock.[137] His mother, Eliza Tower, was a teacher[138] who had been born in London and had given birth to John on 19th January 1864,[139] when aged 33, the father unrecorded. In late 1878 she married John Broome,[140] a schoolmaster[141] whose wife Mary had died the previous spring.[142]

Eliza relocated north to her new husband's home at Raglan Terrace, Stockton-on-Tees, but although he adopted his stepfather's surname in addition to his own, John Broome Tower, then aged 14, remained in London, living with Mr. and Mrs. William Drage at Dynevor Road, Stoke Newington. They had known him since his birth, and he and his mother had been lodging with them for some time. Broome Tower was still living with the Drages at the time of his death.[143] Alice Drage, who provided the identity of the deceased, had been born Alice Goodwin but had been adopted by the Drages.[144] The young man's mother came down from Stockton-on-Tees on the evening of the discovery and formally identified the body.

Broome Tower had been engaged for six months as a clerk at City underwriters Haycraft and Gilfillan at 3&4 Winchester Buildings, Great Winchester Street. On the morning of his death – Monday 31st December – he had been at his desk as usual, and had that day been instructed to visit the firm's bank in order to cash a cheque for the monthly salaries, which he did, and received his own payment of £8 6s 8d. He was told to meet Mr. Haycraft at Lloyd's of London at 3 o'clock that afternoon in order to collect some cheques for depositing at the bank, which again he carried out perfectly properly, but instead of returning to the office as expected seemed to vanish.

Broome Tower was next seen around 6.30pm at the offices of his friend Ernest Cogden, who worked as a travelling merchant for Julius Beypis and Co. Cogden, two years older than Broome Tower,[145] knew the deceased well outside of work, and had seen him three times already that day; firstly in the Winchester Buildings offices around 10.30am, then 1.15pm in Winchester Street, and in Moorgate about half an hour after Broome Tower had left Lloyd's with the cheques handed to him by Mr. Haycraft. On none of these occasions did he appear troubled.

The two friends left Cogden's office and took a train to the latter's home in Finsbury, leaving at 8 o'clock to visit the home of Mr. and Mrs. Earl at Waltham House, Green Lanes. John Broome Tower was on close terms with one of the Misses Earl[146] – it is not recorded which – and some newspapers reported they were engaged to be married.

After supper, the two men escorted Mrs. Earl and her daughters to St. John's on Highbury Vale to see in the New Year. They left the church at five minutes past twelve and accompanied the ladies home, before heading down Portland Road together and parting just before one o'clock at the end of the street, with Broome Tower walking down Green Lanes in the direction of Highbury. His usual route home, Ernest Cogden would later state, would take him along Green Lanes and then along Lordship Park before turning right into Queen Elizabeth's Walk and the direction of Dynevor Road. However, the fact that Broome Tower's body had been found in the West Reservoir indicated that he had turned left into Queen Elizabeth's Walk instead. By Cogden's admission his friend had taken a glass or two of whisky with supper, but certainly not enough for him to lose his bearings.[147] Had he walked towards the reservoir by himself with a dark purpose in mind, or had he been lured in that direction by something or someone?

This possibility was put forward by a Stoke Newington resident, who complained:

> The neighbourhood of Green Lanes, like many other suburban localities, is pestered to no inconsiderable extent with fallen women, and there is no doubt whatever that the piece of ground on which the hat and great coat were found was used by them for their vicious purposes. The supposition now is that the murdered man was decoyed by a woman to this deserted spot...[148]

John Broome Tower was buried at ten o'clock on the morning of Saturday, 5th January. The early hour was decided upon to deter the ghoulish.[149] The small band of mourners including his mother and stepfather, Mrs. Mary Ann Drage, Alice Drage and Ernest Cogden, along with the murdered man's former schoolmaster and some of his friends from his schooldays, met at Abney Park Cemetery to witness a ceremony conducted by the Rev. Mr. Haslem of Holy Trinity Church, Dalston.[150]

Not only were the morbid sightseers denied an opportunity to observe the interment of the deceased, but the authorities also made sure that the scene of his death held no attraction:

> During yesterday many thousands of people, mostly respectably dressed, visited the neighbourhood of the murder, though there was absolutely nothing to repay them for their trouble, the police preventing sightseers trespassing upon the piece of waste ground where the elm trees stand, and where the hat and other things were picked up. The bank has also been raked over, so that even the footprints are gone.[151]

The inquest into Broome Tower's death concluded on the same day as he was lowered into his final resting place, with Coroner Sir John Humphreys telling the jury that he believed the evidence firmly indicated that the young clerk had been killed. Dr. Thomas Bond's medical testimony was especially compelling, and the surgeon said that he felt the cause of death was "homicidal strangulation", and concluded that because of the absence of water in the lungs or stomach he did not "think it at all possible that the death could have been the result of suicide." After a brief deliberation the jury agreed, and returned a verdict that John Broome Tower was "wilfully and maliciously murdered by some person or persons unknown."[152]

But doubts began to surface. Ernest Cogden's revelation at the inquest that Broome Tower had been courting not only Miss Earl, but for some time had been corresponding with a woman named Maggie Waller from the north of England, whom he had presumably met during a visit to his mother.[153]

Did Broome Tower have a darker side to his personality, not generally known to friends and acquaintances?

Excitement was created when a man with a black eye and an injury to his nose arrived in Watford and attempted to sell a watch chain similar to that missing from the murdered man's effects. The man – later named as H. B. Thompson – had arrived the previous evening, 8th January, and took rooms at The Essex Arms. Having run up a bar tab of 15s over the course of the following 24 hours, the uproariously drunk Thompson claimed to have no money to settle his account and threatened to jump out of a window. However, he took the watch chain to nearby jeweller Mr. Simms in an attempt to raise the necessary funds. The shopman, immediately struck by the resemblance of the chain to circulated descriptions, informed the police and the imbibed Thompson was arrested and searched. Amongst other papers was found a newspaper cutting on the murder of Broome Tower; it looked ominous of the drunken visitor. But by the time he appeared in front of the magistrate the following day it was obvious that he was not connected with the murder, and was convicted on the charge of being drunk and disorderly, being fined 5s or seven days' imprisonment. Being penniless, H. B. Thompson remained at Watford Gaol for the full week.[154]

Police investigations were proving fruitless, even when a reward of £200 was offered for information leading to the capture of the murderer. But two weeks later the *Globe* reported on a startling development:

> The police authorities have so far obtained no clue to the murderers of Mr. Broome Tower, the young man whose body was found in the New River Company's reservoir, but they have just received most important information, which tends to revive in a very great measure the grave doubts which formerly existed as to the circumstances under which the young man came to his death. It appears that in consequence of an examination made by the deceased's employer of the books of which he was formerly in charge, very serious discrepancies are found to exist, of which the deceased must have been cognisant. A cheque book has also been proved to be missing, and it is stated that upon the last day on which he attended his employer's office, Tower terminated his duties for the day some hours earlier than usual, and afterwards obtained cash for a cheque which is said to have been taken from the missing book. The theory of suicide has, therefore, been revived.[155]

The *St. James's Gazette* stated that the missing money amounted to between £50 and £60.[156]

A representative of the Press Association visited the offices of Messrs. Haycraft and Gilfillan on 15th January seeking confirmation, but instead was directed to Scotland Yard. There he was informed that the police had known for some time that Broome Tower had money troubles.[157]

Neither Ernest Cogden nor Mr. Earl accepted that John Broome Tower would take his own life; neither had an inkling of his supposed financial problems, and said that when they last saw him a matter of hours before his death he was in fine spirits.[158]

But a week after the revelations of Broome Tower's apparent dishonesty, Scotland Yard had seemingly arrived at the definitive conclusion that the young man had indeed committed suicide, and no further action would be taken. It was reported that they were in discussion with Coroner Sir John Humphreys to find a way to quash the verdict of murder given by the jury at the inquest.[159]

The feeling that a verdict had been rushed through was unavoidable, and Dr. Thomas Bond was also on the receiving end of a backlash, with the press reporting that he had

> been severely criticised by several prominent members of the medical profession on account of the positive statements made by him as to the cause of death.[160]

There the matter rested for two years until, out of the blue, a man named George Thackray alias King was arrested in Grimsby on a charge of vagrancy. Heavily under the influence of something stronger than tea, he excitedly confessed to the murder of John Broome Tower.[161]

His statement, riddled with inaccuracies, ran as follows:

> On New Year's Eve, 1884, I and a man named Mick Sullivan were drinking in the Three Nags public house, Whitechapel Road, when a clerk came in and began talking about the amount of money in his possession. Sullivan said we would have the money, so we dodged him about until after midnight. He bade a companion goodbye under the trees in St. Mary's Walk, Islington, and then I pounced upon him, put a handkerchief round his neck, and strangled him. We dragged him up the embankment and threw him in the reservoir, after robbing him of £50. We took his watch, but afterwards lost it. After that I went to my lodgings at 72 St. Dunstan's Row, Burdett Road, Islington. I got £20 as my share of the £50. We dragged the body through a hedge before throwing it into the reservoir,

and we left the handkerchief round his neck.¹⁶²

The truth of Thackray's confession was immediately doubted; there was no Three Nags on Whitechapel Road, and in any case it would be unlikely that a City clerk would spend an evening at such a venue, risking his well-being by boasting about how much money he had on his person. The story was at complete odds with the evidence of Ernest Cogden. On hearing of the supposed confession, Thackray's mother wrote to Superintendent Waldron of the Grimsby police, saying: "Poor fellow, he is much to be pitied, as at times he is not accountable for his actions."¹⁶³

Reporting that enquiries would be taken no further by the Metropolitan Police, the newspapers commented:

> It will be remembered that Inspector Swanson, who had the [Broome Tower] inquiry in hand, was of opinion that the case was one of suicide.¹⁶⁴

In fact, just a month after it was reported that the police were attempting to have the verdict of murder quashed, Det. Inspector Swanson and his colleagues had moved on to another, more deadly threat; the Fenians had returned, once again striking on London's transport system.

In the early hours of 26th February 1884 an explosion at Victoria railway station destroyed the cloakroom – where the bomb had been deposited – and the booking office, along with a glass-covered shelter outside, and the entrance to the subway was filled with rubbish. The area of devastation measured some 100 feet by 65 feet, and thirty truck loads of debris would be removed.¹⁶⁵

Concerted police searches revealed that despite the devastation at Victoria, the capital had actually been very fortunate. Infernal machines timed to detonate at the same time as the Victoria bomb were found disguised as baggage left at the cloakrooms of Charing Cross, Paddington and Ludgate Hill railway stations, each containing around 20lb of 'Atlas Powder A', a dynamite manufactured in America.¹⁶⁶ The bombs were constructed with American-made alarm clocks, the backs of which had been removed to allow a pistol to be attached by wires to the winder, so that as the clock mechanism operated, the pistol's trigger was slowly squeezed. The pistol was loaded with a cartridge of fulminate of mercury and pointed at the dynamite, and would fire when the hands of the clock reached a certain time.[167]

While the Victoria bomb had worked correctly, those at the three other stations had failed as the timers ran down harmlessly and the Metropolitan Police were afforded their first clues.

The infernal machine left at Paddington was contained in an old brown portmanteau (leather travel bag), the fastening flap of which had been cut off to accommodate the mechanism. Part of the clock from this bomb was found in the black leather bag containing the bomb found at Ludgate Hill, while the cloakroom records at Charing Cross showed that the valise discovered containing the third bomb had initially been booked in with the brown portmanteau, which had then been removed and taken to Paddington.[168] It seemed certain that the four infernal machines had been made and deposited by the same perpetrators, and possible clues to their identities were discovered in the form of a small tray from a cash box found in the Paddington portmanteau, and a pair of trousers with a 34 inch waist and 31½ inch inside leg stuffed into the Charing Cross valise.[169]

Descriptions of suspected men were published by Commissioner Edmund Henderson, and the reward money increased to £1,000 from both the Home Office and the railway companies.

Almost immediately the police had a lead, when the proprietor of the Waverley Hotel on Great Portland Street came forward to report two men who had rented rooms and acted suspiciously in the days preceding the Victoria outrage and attempted attacks on Paddington, Charing Cross and Ludgate Hill stations.

Det. Inspector Swanson visited the hotel the day after the explosion to take statements. On Wednesday, 20th February, he was told, a man had arrived at the hotel with a single black bag. He was given a room on the third floor, and attended by chambermaid Louisa Sturnham. On the Saturday she was cleaning the room and noticed a second bag, a new black valise. Later that day a second man arrived at the hotel and took a room on the first floor. He had no luggage at that time, but told the maid that he had a case stored at a station and would collect it on the Monday.

Although the two men were at pains to avoid giving the impression they knew each other, when they thought they were out of earshot they spoke with one another continually, ceasing conversation as soon as anyone came into the room. On the morning of Monday, 25th February, both men paid their bills, saying they would be leaving that day. The second man went out for an hour and returned with a brown portmanteau and a black bag, and at around seven o'clock that evening both men left the hotel. The Victoria explosion occurred six hours later.

Cleaning the rooms after the guests had departed, Louisa Sturnham found between four and five pounds of fresh putty and a leather flap which appeared to have been cut from the portmanteau. She gave the putty to the owner of the hotel, Mrs. Ellen Sellick, and threw the flap down the dust chute. Mrs. Sturnham had also found a small wooden box in one of the rooms, which she had kept with the intentions of keeping buttons in.

When Swanson arrived the day after the explosion, he was given the putty by Mrs. Sellick and the wooden box by Mrs. Sturnham. Rooting around in the outside dust heap, the detective unearthed the leather flap. This would prove to match perfectly the portmanteau containing the unexploded bomb at Paddington, and the small tray found in the same case slipped into the wooden box.

Although Mrs. Sellick had not seen either man, Mrs. Sturnham told Swanson that she would recognise them should she see them again.[170] Her descriptions of the men matched those of a suspicious pair who had left Southampton for London on 20th February, the day the first man had arrived at the Waverley Hotel.[171]

Finally, Scotland Yard were beginning to piece together a chain of evidence.

Before they would be able to act on this information, however, fresh attacks took place on 30th May, and at the very heart of the police investigation. The day started with the discovery at around 10.30 in the morning of 16 packets of dynamite bound with a connecting fuse left at the base of Nelson's Column in Trafalgar Square.[172] Had the dynamite been detonated, in addition to the horrendous loss of life there is no doubt that the toppling of the monument to Nelson would have sent a potent message. Their next target, later that same day, would be a greater symbol still – Great Scotland Yard itself. Whether the Fenians intended to destroy the evidence compiled, assassinate the detectives who were engaged in tracking them, or simply to make a major statement, an infernal machine was left by a public urinal situated in one corner of a building standing in the middle of the Yard. Immediately above the urinal was an office occupied by members of the C.I.D.

John Sweeney, in 1884 a junior detective but who would eventually rise to the rank of Detective Inspector of the Special Branch, was in the building at 9.25pm when the bomb exploded:

> By a piece of extraordinary good fortune there was absolutely no one in our offices. A few minutes earlier there were two men in the building,

one of the inspectors and myself. He went out just before me; I was busy making out a report, but on finishing it I also went out, thus escaping death by about a quarter of an hour. A part of the building was blown down and many official documents were destroyed, the bulk of them, curiously enough, containing matter relative to the revolutionary party. The very desk at which I had been working was blown to pieces. The crash was also felt outside the Yard; many people were hurt, and the Rising Sun public-house very much knocked about. We never discovered how the bomb was ignited, though of course the debris was searched with the greatest care; no traces were found that could help us to a conclusion.

...We could not console ourselves in the same way as the proprietor of the Rising Sun. Naturally thousands of people flocked to see the effects of the outrage; he charged threepence per head for admitting spectators, and what with this and the increase of custom that accrued to him at least for the time, he more than recouped himself for the damage done to his premises.[173]

In fact, much of the internal damage to the Scotland Yard building was caused by the falling of a huge iron safe through the floors.[174] P.C. Clark 417A, on duty outside, was blown across the road along with lumps of concrete, brickwork and iron. He suffered serious scalp wounds and concussion, and was deafened in the blast. Others injured included the driver of a cab and his horse passing the building at the time, and drinkers in the Rising Sun opposite were showered with glass fragments as all the windows bar one were shattered in the blast.[175]

Dozens of constables from A and E Divisions controlled excited members of the public, who arrived along with senior officials including Howard Vincent, back from Paris, Dolly Williamson and Superintendent Charles Cutbush. The excitement grew further still as the packets of dynamite found in Trafalgar Square were brought to Scotland Yard and laid on the pavement.[176] Simultaneously, news reached the ears of the senior officers of a minor blast at the Junior Carlton Club at Pall Mall, and another outside the home of Conservative M.P. Sir Watkin Williams-Wynn in St. James's Square. In both cases no serious damage was caused.[177]

Howard Vincent had made up his mind even before the explosion at Scotland Yard. On 13th May, two weeks before the outrage, the Press Association released the news that he had asked the Home Secretary to relieve him of his position as Director of Criminal Investigations from June, and that he intended to undertake a tour of the Colonies before

The bombing of Scotland Yard
Author's collection

entering politics.¹⁷⁸ His last day in his role ironically proved to be the day after the Scotland Yard attack.

The news received a mixed welcome from the *Pall Mall Gazette*:

> General regret will be occasioned by the news that Mr. Howard Vincent is about to forsake the direction of criminal investigation for the more showy but less useful position of a member of Parliament. If, however, Mr. Vincent must exchange Scotland Yard for St. Stephen's, he undoubtedly shows much good sense by resolving to begin his apprenticeship to legislative work by visiting all the English dependencies overseas. It is a thousand pities that such a touch could not be enforced on every member of Parliament as a condition of taking his seat in the House. For most Radical members, whose great weakness is indifference to the English beyond the sea, such a journey would be invaluable.¹⁷⁹

The outgoing Director of Criminal Investigations was, nevertheless, proud of the achievements of his department, stating in his final annual report that

> from the formation of the Criminal Investigation Department on April 6, 1878 to May 31, 1884, 415 officers have passed through it. They

Assistant Commissioner (Crime) James Monro
from The Graphic, 8th December 1888

apprehended 36,187 prisoners, and made 16,898 inquiries not involving the arrest of any person.

Eight hundred and ninety-three criminals were arrested in the Metropolitan Police district for offences committed in the provinces, and 201 were surrendered under the treaties of extradition with foreign countries. The officers of the Department were commended or rewarded 688 times by judicial authorities and juries, and 2,108 times by the Commissioner.[180]

Howard Vincent's departure provided an opportunity to abolish the position of Director of Criminal Investigations, to be replaced with a third Assistant Commissioner, in charge of Crime. Several names had been mentioned in the press as his replacement, including Major Clifford Lloyd,[181] Colonel Dillon, the Chief Constable of Hertfordshire,[182] and Joseph Farndale, Chief Constable of Birmingham.[183]

On 7th July[184] the position was offered to Howard Vincent's friend, James Monro, who had been born in Edinburgh in 1838 and educated at Edinburgh High School then Edinburgh and Berlin Universities before sailing for India at the age of nineteen to join the Bengal Civil Service as Assistant Magistrate. He subsequently held a series of posts including District Judge and Inspector-General of Police. During his time in India Monro suffered an accident which resulted in lifelong lameness:

> As a judge he was desirous of securing the punishment of a thief, and as chief of the executive he himself attempted to arrest him. The thief fled. Mr. Monro, on horseback, pursued; the thief slipped over a garden wall. Mr. Monro, nothing daunted, put his horse to the leap – and that is all Mr. Monro knows. Six weeks afterwards Mr. Monro woke from a state of unconsciousness with a smashed leg and a permanently crippled thigh.[185]

Monro's disability was not to hold him back; his determination and integrity, in addition to his first-rate education and experience of police work, meant he was respected immediately.

Robert Anderson, on the other hand, was not looked on so kindly. Not particularly effective in gathering intelligence on Fenian activities, he was relieved of his duties around the same time as Monro's appointment, to be replaced by Edward Jenkinson from Dublin. Anderson had but one informant, the important Henri Le Caron, who would liaise with nobody else, but otherwise he was seen as a failure. Home Secretary William Harcourt, expecting a resignation, was exasperated when he was told that Anderson could "not do without the money". To get round this, a gift of £2,000 was paid as 'compensation', as Anderson continued his work liaising with Le Caron.

Edward Jenkinson, a former Indian civil servant who was Earl Spencer's private secretary, had replaced Colonel Henry Brackenbury as Under-Secretary to the Lord Lieutenant of Ireland in August 1882 and soon created a network of informers. As Jenkinson was based at Dublin Castle, it was clear that a London-based representative working solely on his direction was necessary. Jenkinson and Harcourt discussed Lieutenant Colonel Charles Warren before deciding on Major Nicholas Gosselin, a magistrate from Ireland who knew the task at hand. Gosselin began work in May, effectively replacing Anderson, and was responsible for gathering intelligence on Fenian activity in Glasgow and cities outside of London with large Irish populations including Manchester, Liverpool and Birmingham.[186]

Gosselin prepared his reports and sent them to Jenkinson, who felt that to be most effective he himself should work from London, initially on a temporary basis. This arrangement started on 8th March 1884, in the wake of the Victoria station bombing.[187]

Further change at Scotland Yard came on 1st December when Assistant Commissioner Douglas Labalmondière retired after 34 years with the Metropolitan Police. By this time, the ill-feeling towards him from the rank-and-file officers seen in his early career under Richard

Mayne had diminished, and he retired on a pension granted by the Secretary of State with "the cordial good wishes of all ranks on his retirement from his onerous duties."[188]

His replacement as the new Assistant Commissioner (Administrative) was announced less than a fortnight later when Alexander Carmichael Bruce was appointed[189] on a salary of £1,500 per annum.[190] He was a 34-year-old barrister who had been educated at Brasenose College, Oxford,[191] and called to the Bar in May 1875.[192]

Carmichael Bruce was welcomed literally with a bang. The same day that newspapers reported his appointment, a large explosion sounded under one of the arches on the south side of London Bridge, startling commuters travelling above. Although a course of masonry on one of the bridge's buttresses suffered a slight crack and some timber beams were destroyed, very little damage was caused.

More of a mystery was the fate of the dynamitards. It was clear that the bomb must have been placed in position from the water, and an empty boat which had only recently been let was found drifting some way along the Thames.[193]

The Special Irish Branch had been watching two prominent members of Clan na Gael, William Mackey Lomasney, a former Captain of the United States army, and John Fleming, but both had disappeared as if into thin air when the London Bridge bomb exploded. As it turned out, that is precisely what had happened. It would take three years, but Det. Sergeant Sweeney of the Special Irish Branch eventually traced Fleming's sister to an address in Southwark, south London, where she burst into tears and showed the detective her brother's coat hanging behind the door and his box of papers in an upstairs room, untouched since he had left the house on 13th December 1884. In the box were documents linking Fleming to the dynamite campaign.

The attack meticulously planned by Lomasney and Fleming had gone horribly wrong for the dynamitards when their bomb exploded sooner than intended, with both being blown to atoms.[194]

A nervy Christmas period passed without incident, but 1885 had barely begun when another attack on the Underground occurred, with a bomb exploding between Gower Street[195] and King's Cross stations on the evening of Friday, 2nd January. A deafening blast rang through the tunnels into the platforms of Gower Street and King's Cross, extinguishing all lamps and, on street level, the ticket collector at Gower Street was blown out of his box[196] and several people crossing Euston Road above were thrown to the ground.[197]

It was suspected that the bomb had been thrown from the window of a third-class carriage at the front of a train bound for Hammersmith, and one of the passengers in this carriage, a Mr. William Smith, later described the moment the bomb went off:

> There were two or three others in the compartment beside myself... and I occupied a corner seat with my face to the engine. We had passed King's Cross without anything unusual happening, and were chatting quietly together when we were terrified by a fearful crash like thunder, accompanied by an immense sheet of flame, which seemed to lick the sides of the carriages, and for the moment it seemed as if the tunnel were on fire. To add to the terror of the situation both our lamps went out and we were left in total darkness. Several of the passengers cried out that they were hurt, and some women who were in the next compartment screamed loudly.
>
> Our first impression was that the compressed gas stowed in tanks under the carriages had by some means or other ignited, and this for the moment seemed all the more probable, as the force of the explosion swayed the carriages, and I could distinctly feel the wheels catch the metals again.
>
> As soon as possible the train was brought to a standstill, and a hasty examination made, when we again went on and slowly steamed into Gower Street station. We had, in the meantime, somewhat reassured ourselves, having by means of lighted matches examined each others' injuries. Several of us cut our hands by incautiously placing them upon the seats of carriages, which were covered with small jagged pieces of glass from the windows.
>
> I should add that the force of the concussion threw us all off our seats, and umbrellas, hats, and papers were mixed up in terrible confusion.[198]

The following morning Colonel Majendie and Major Ford arrived at the scene to survey the wreckage and begin their official inspection, and were joined by Det. Inspector Swanson, representing Scotland Yard, Chief Inspector Dodd of X Division, Inspector Kelly of E Division,[199] Mr. Cropp, Superintendent of the Metropolitan Railway and General Manager of Gower Street station, Mr. Bell.[200]

The group discovered that the exact time of the explosion was preserved by the clock on the signal box some 150 yards from Gower Street, it being stopped at 9.14pm. They then entered the tunnel and walked to the spot where the explosion took place. Majendie surveyed the damage to the tunnel wall and confirmed the cause to be an explosion of dynamite, resulting in a hole some two feet in diameter and six or seven inches deep. The fact there was no sign of an explosion at floor level indicated that the bomb had been thrown from a carriage window rather than being placed on the ground with a timed detonator.[201] Their examination in the tunnel complete, the group went to King's Cross station for a consultation before Majendie left with Swanson for Scotland Yard.

Later that day it was reported that a passenger in a second-class carriage on the train carrying Mr. Smith had noticed a suspicious man carrying a parcel wrapped in cloth enter the adjoining compartment just as the train left Gower Street. The stranger opened a window with a loud slam. After the explosion and the train had resumed its journey, the first passenger noticed the suspicious man alight at Farringdon without his parcel. When he looked at where the man had been standing, he saw that it was not there.[202]

In the months since the Victoria bomb the capital had begun to relax about the possibility of attacks on the Underground system. Now, nearly a year later, the Gower Street incident reawakened panic and nervous anticipation amongst the public.

They would not have long to wait for the next attacks. Three major incidents, all on the same day, would bring terror to the city, but also finally an end to the dynamite campaign.

The Dynamitards chose Saturday, 24th January to perform their most symbolic acts yet, with attacks on the Tower of London and the House of Commons. They realised that the weekend would be the perfect time to strike, with both locations being busy with tourists; at the peak visiting hour, two o'clock in the afternoon, a bright red light suddenly flashed in the Tower of London's Banqueting Room, immediately followed by a terrific explosion[203] which was magnified by hundreds of rifles falling from their racks within the room and crashing to the floor. Fire quickly spread to the first floor of the White Tower, and then to a council chamber on the second.[204] The Grenadier Guards formed a cordon around the inferno, before the Metropolitan Fire Brigade arrived to blast water at the tower.

Hundreds of visitors stumbled through the dust in a panic, trying to find the exit. As they approached, however, they found the gateway shut – closed on the orders of the Lieutenant of the Tower, Lord Chelmsford, and its major, General Milman.

Scotland Yard, the City of London Police and local Metropolitan Police stations were telegraphed, with Assistant Commissioner James Monro arriving along with Superintendent Thomas Arnold and Det. Inspector

Frederick Abberline of the Met's H Division at 2.40pm.[205]

Abberline was instructed to take the names, addresses and occupations of every person inside the Tower gates. One of these was a 22-year-old Irish-American who gave his name as James George Gilbert of Cherbourg Street in Whitechapel. Abberline, who had spent a great many years policing the area, knew there was no 'Cherbourg Street' and asked where it was near, receiving the reply "Great Alie Street". The constable writing down the information piped up "You mean Great Scarborough Street?" The man confirmed that was the name of the street in which he was lodging.

The man's delayed responses and general demeanour made the experienced detective suspicious, and he took 'Gilbert' to the latter's lodgings at Great Scarborough Street where he found a box and a black bag, with papers suggesting his real name was James Gilbert Cunningham.[206] Damningly, also found was a small metal tube containing a white powder, chlorate of potassium and fulminate of mercury: in other words a detonator, and one which resembled those found at Charing Cross and Ludgate Hill the previous year.[207]

He was taken to Leman Street police station pending further enquiries.[208]

While these events were being played out, scenes of greater horror were unfolding across the city at Westminster Hall.

Eight minutes after the explosion at the Tower, a small party of visitors to the Crypt at Westminster noticed smoke and a strange smell emanating from what looked like a quilted petticoat lying on the steps. One of the group, a civil engineer named Edwin Green, recognised the smell as a damp fuse and called for a police officer. P.C. William Cole responded immediately and rushed to pick up the burning package,[209] running up the stairs towards the Hall with it in his arms but, finding hot acid burning his hands,[210] could hold on it no longer and threw it to the ground just outside the gates leading to the Crypt stairs. As it landed, a huge explosion ripped a hole in the pavement some six feet long and three feet across, into which both P.C. Cole and a second officer, P.C. Cox, fell. Glass blew out of the Hall's windows and shattered wood fragments rained over those present.

But the bomb left at the Crypt was merely a diversionary tactic to draw police attention away from the House of Commons, where at that instant a second blast rang out. Thankfully there was nobody in attendance at the time, but the structure of the House was severely damaged. A susbsequent inspection showed all the doors to have been blown off their hinges and the windows shattered. A yawning hole in

*The explosion at Westminster Hall
from The Graphic, 31st January 1885*

the floor revealed the apartments below, with concrete and wooden debris of all description strewn over the exposed rafters. Benches of both the Government and Opposition were torn asunder, with a pile of woodwork, leather and stuffing as far as the eye could see.[211]

It was a shattering blow, and an audacious statement by the Dynamitards. But thanks to the capture of James Cunningham, things were about to come to a sudden end.

The day after the explosion at the House of Commons, Chief Superintendent Williamson and Det. Inspector Swanson visited Constables Coles and Cox at Westminster Hospital to take their statements. Both were in a serious condition, but were able to furnish the detectives with a degree of information.[212]

Investigations over the following fortnight put all the links of the chain together. Cunningham's landlady at his previous address at Great Prescott Street recalled that he had arrived with a large brown trunk, which he claimed belonged to a friend who was lodging nearby. The brown trunk subsequently disappeared and was replaced by a smaller black one. At this time, a City of London P.C. named Thomas Roper who was lodging at 5 Mitre Square had become suspicious of a fellow lodger at the property named Harry Burton, who appeared to have no job. Reporting his suspicions to his superiors, plain clothes detectives were assigned to watch Burton, who was subsequently seen with Cunningham before the Tower of London attack.

Burton's lodgings at Mitre Square were raided and Special Irish Branch officers found Cunningham's brown trunk, along with maps of the Tower and the Westminster area.

The 30-year-old Burton was arrested and, with Cunningham, identified as the mysterious men seen at the Waverley Hotel by chambermaid Louisa Sturnham and reported to Det. Inspector Swanson. A pair of Burton's trousers taken from his lodgings were found to be exactly the same size as those found in the Charing Cross valise.

The trial of Burton and Cunningham took place at the Old Bailey under Sir Henry Hawkins. On 18th May 1885 they were found guilty of Treason Felony, and sentenced to penal servitude for life.

A large number of detectives were rewarded for their work in tackling the Dynamite Outrages. Chief Superintendent Williamson received £200 and Det. Inspector John Littlechild £100.[213] Det. Inspector Swanson was one of several given a reward of £12.[214] Colonel Majendie and Major Ford had to approach the Home Office seeking a reward for their dangerous work inspecting dynamite and deconstructing infernal machines, despite this search for knowledge undoubtedly saving many lives. They finally received £300 and £200 respectively.[215]

For now, the Fenian threat was over. Nineteen bombs had been exploded in Britain, eleven in London, over a period spanning almost exactly four years.

There would be further attacks in years to come, most notably in 1887, but the Metropolitan Police, and the Special Irish Branch in particular, would look back at the Dynamite Outrages with a sense of relief that the toll had not been greater.

Chief Inspector John Littlechild would later recall that

> there was a wide difference between the movement of '67 and the [1880s] dynamite campaign... The former was undoubtedly a Fenian 'rising', popular among all Fenians, and having the avowed object – abortive though it proved – of making a strike for Irish independence. Many of the attempts then made were simply fiascos – the intended raid on

Chester Castle in February 1867, to wit; yet other events demonstrated the determined spirit of some of the leaders, as for instance the attack on the police van in Hyde Road, Manchester on September 18 the same year, made with a view to the rescue of two notorious prisoners – Colonel Kelly and Captain Deasy – accused of treason-felony. On that occasion, it will be remembered, Sergeant Brett lost his life. A more disastrous outrage still was that committed at Clerkenwell House of Detention, when the wall was blown up by means of a barrel of gunpowder, and some of the houses in the neighbourhood deprived of their fronts, leaving them like "so many dolls' houses" – as Williamson used to say – "with the kettles still singing on the hobs." Here, again, the object was the attempted rescue of a prisoner – Colonel Ricard Burke...

But as regards the 1881-89 period... there was no intention of making a blow for independence. Certainly the patriotic element which no doubt animated the '67 rising was absent from the dynamite campaign. I know that many tried and trusted Fenians held entirely aloof from it, and the instigators of the Physical Force Movement took very good care not to risk their freedom and their lives by crossing the Atlantic. They left that portion of their diabolical work to be done by their tools and agents. It makes me shudder to think of the consequences if these emissaries had been successful in all their operations. That more lives were not sacrificed is to me marvellous. The public does not realise the peril in which is was placed. It was indeed fortunate that detection dogged the steps of these desperadoes, and that their arrest followed so surely upon their crimes.

Terrorism was the object of this later movement, in order to compel legislation in a desired direction; but that terrorism reckoned without its host. Evil-doers rarely give Scotland Yard credit for efficient policing; so much the better for the public good.[216]

The work of the detectives, and the Special Branch in particular, had raised the stock of the Metropolitan Police not enjoyed for many years.

But over the course of the following two years, any credit the force had with the public would run out.

THIRTEEN

Blood on the Square

It is an unusual thing in London to have bodies of police loudly hissed by the crowd, as was the case on Lord Mayor's Day in a number of instances. The action of the chief and the conduct of individual members of the force have done much to alienate the good feeling which has hitherto existed between the police and the people. Every allowance being made for irritability brought about by extra and trying work, recent events have given rise to an impression that the people are being used in a manner foreign to their original purpose, and the public are quick to resent even a suspicion of any attack upon their liberties.[1]

Britain in the 1880s was, for many, a time of great struggle, and not just for Irish nationalists seeking Home Rule. A global financial crisis, the so-called 'Panic of 1873', had resulted in a decade-long trade slump and in 1886 the country was still suffering what became known as The Long Depression. Bankruptcies were commonplace, public works were halted and, of course, unemployment escalated massively. As men from rural England moved to urban areas in search of work, so the problem intensified as available jobs decreased, with wages lowered and working conditions worsening due to the availability of demand.[2]

Unemployed workers from all over London, but especially the East End, began to band together to demonstrate against their plight, with myriad official – and unofficial – workers' parties springing up, most peaceful but some more radical and forceful in sharing their opinions.

Trafalgar Square became the geographic symbol of class struggle, where the working class East End met the riches of the West, and it was here that the unemployed would come to feel solidarity, often to listen to speakers, and sometimes as part of organised marches and demonstrations.

It was one such event, initially harmless, which resulted in a sudden change in command at Scotland Yard.

On Sunday, 7th February 1886 the committee of The London United Workmen announced their intention to march on Trafalgar Square the following day in complaint against "a system which is making the rich richer and the poor poorer." They extended an open invitation to their fellow workers:

> English and Irish operatives, come in your thousands from all parts of London to Trafalgar Square on Monday, February 8th, and demand from the Government some means to relieve the now existing distress and starvation amongst multitudes of the wage-earners of London.[3]

The revolutionary Social Democratic Federation also gave notice of their intention to meet at the Square on the same day.

The afternoon of the 8th started peacefully enough, with an estimated 20,000 attendees listening to speeches by the likes of Patrick Kenny of the General Labourers' Amalgamated Union and Captain Thomas Lemon, President of the British Seamen's Society. Anticipating little trouble, a small body of police were on duty with others on reserve.

The Social Democratic Federation's Henry Hyndman, addressing the crowd, called for a physical demonstration of their frustration and encouraged them to ransack symbols of the well-off. Members of the Federation, followed by "half the ragged ruffians, loafers and pickpockets in London",[4] mingled with those gathering peacefully and several fights broke out.

The meeting over, Hyndman intended to continue his colourful address at Hyde Park and pointed the red flags he was brandishing in the direction of Pall Mall; his excited army, led by prominent members John Burns and Henry Hyde Champion, who were also waving flags, marched off hooting and screeching and almost immediately began a trail of destruction, starting with smashing the windows of the Reform Club, followed by the Carlton Club.

Along they went, attacking the clubs of Pall Mall, with the startled police slow to respond. A garbled message was sent to the reserve of 563 officers waiting by Trafalgar Square, who misunderstood the instructions and set off instead for The Mall, one hundred yards to the south. As they arrived to guard Buckingham Palace and Marlborough House the scene was as peaceful as any normal Sunday afternoon, while the rioters continued their way towards Hyde Park Corner, marching along St. James's Street and up into Piccadilly, attacking shops and other businesses with impunity.

The meeting at Hyde Park evidently stoking the fires of rebellion, the mob set off several hours later back down to Oxford Street where they again began looting shops and causing substantial damage.

At that moment, D Division's Inspector James Cuthbert was parading a sergeant and fifteen constables when he heard news of the mob approaching; marching his men to Oxford Street, Cuthbert led a baton charge which sent the looters running for cover, ending the riot.[5]

New Home Secretary Hugh Childers, who had only been in the position for two days following the Liberal Government's election win, immediately had two very different incidents with which to contend with. On the day of the riots, his uncle, the former Member of Parliament for Cambridgeshire and Malton, John Walbanke Childers, passed away.[6] Far from being left alone with his thoughts, Childers had to censure Sir Edmund Henderson for the disastrous actions of the police at Trafalgar Square earlier that day. The Commissioner didn't wait to be pushed – he resigned immediately.

Although Henderson had been a popular Commissioner, in more recent years he had become less and less active, out of touch with the needs of the growing Force and happy to leave the hard work required during the previous year's Fenian campaign to James Monro, Howard Vincent and Robert Anderson. The disorder of 8th February 1886 exposed his inactivity, the farce of The Mall being confused for Pall Mall reminiscent of Sir Richard Mayne's misunderstanding of Fenian plans to blow *up* the walls of Clerkenwell Prison thirty-seven years earlier.

An embarrassed Metropolitan Police began to chase down the rioters. On 13th February, Chief Superintendent Dolly Williamson and Det. Inspector Donald Swanson attended Bow Street to collect summonses from Sir James Ingham, which they later served on the leaders of the mob including Messrs Hyndman, Champion, and Burns. At the same time, at Marlborough Street Police Court, a group of traders met to present a claim for losses incurred during the rioting. A list had been drawn up containing 200 claims amounting to £11,000.[7]

Home Secretary Childers, meanwhile, knew just the man he wanted as his new Commissioner of the Metropolitan Police. When Secretary of State for War at the time of the Egyptian campaign of 1882, Childers had become acquainted with the then Lieutenant Colonel Charles Warren, a highly experienced officer with the Royal Engineers. It was clear that a new broom was required, one which would sweep away the cobwebs of lethargy within the Metropolitan Police and restore public order, and Childers firmly believed that Warren was exactly the right man.

Warren was born in Bangor, Wales, in 1840 and educated at Bridgnorth Grammar School, Wem Grammar School and Cheltenham

College, before entering the Royal Military College at Sandhurst and then the Royal Military Academy at Woolwich.

In 1861 he was sent to survey Gibraltar, spending four years measuring and compiling information on the headland's geography, roads and buildings, eventually creating a finely-detailed scale model some 26 feet in length.[8] In 1865 Warren acted as an assistant instructor in surveying at Chatham's School of Military Engineering, and in 1867 was employed by the Palestine Exploration Fund to undertake archaeological research in the Holy Land, in the process becoming the first to perform excavations of the Temple Mount at Jerusalem. He returned to England three years later, subsequently spending several years in South Africa on both military and archaeological expeditions.[9]

Warren returned to England and the School of Military Engineering in Chatham in 1880 to become Chief Instructor in Surveying, but by early August 1882 volunteered for active service in the forthcoming Egyptian Campaign, only to be told that his services were not required as Professor Edward Palmer was already conducting an expedition in Sinai. As fate would have it, on 23rd August a telegraph from Sir Beauchamp Seymour, Commander of the British Fleet at Alexandria, requested Warren be sent to Egypt to discover the fate of Palmer, from whom no word had been received for some time.

After a frustrating two months tracking the movements of Palmer and his party, with frequent obstruction from his Bedouin guides, Warren and his team learned that they had been robbed and murdered several weeks earlier. His colleague in the search party, Captain A. E. Haynes, gave a harrowing account of the discovery of the remains in his book *Man-Hunting in the Desert*:

> ...Colonel Warren and I were next lowered to the bottom of the gully, which was here forty-seven feet deep, and from ten to twenty wide, with precipitous sides. Below, we found the remains of our unfortunate countrymen – a skull, jaw-bone, numerous ribs and broken bones, much gnawed by wild beasts; a truss of a very small man, supposed to be Professor Palmer; two socks marked W.G., with the feet still in them; and parts of socks and drawers marked H.C. and H. Charrington; also a pair of duck-trousers, with buttons marked with the name of a Bombay tailor; these latter were in such a condition that we burnt them.[10]

Warren quickly caught the attackers, and brought them to justice via the Egyptian courts, where, having confessed, they were executed. The party returned to England where Warren received a knighthood for his efforts, despite the grim conclusion.

During 1884 and '85 he commanded a military expedition to Bechuanaland in South Africa, to assert British sovereignty, with 4,000 troops heading north from Cape Town led by the first war balloons used for observation by the British Army in the field, tested personally at Mafeking by Sir Charles,[11] and watched by the local ruler, 80-year-old Chief Montsioa. The incident was incorporated into a ballad composed by Sergeant O'Harra of the expedition:

> One day the Engineers, who were possessed of a balloon,
> Sent old Chief Montsioa up, a captive, towards the moon:
> And it was a spirit-stirring sound to hear his women swear,
> As they saw their lord and master floating gaily through the air.
>
> For it is the usual belief in Montsioa's town
> That when a Chieftain dies he takes a lengthy journey down;
> While a missionary murmured, as he gazed up in the sky,
> 'How strange that soldiers are the first to waft my flock on high.'[12]

The expedition was a huge success, with Warren making treaties with African chiefs to form the Bechuanaland Protectorate in March 1885, whereby an area measuring some 225,000 square miles was governed by local Tswana rulers with British administrators policing the borders.[13]

Back in England, Sir Charles was unexpectedly approached with an offer to stand as a Liberal candidate in the Sheffield Hallam constituency at the forthcoming General Election, less than a month away in the November. Finding party politics distasteful, he stood as an Independent Liberal and with but a very short amount of time to conduct his campaign succeeded in winning the votes of 3,155 people, only to be defeated by a mere 609 votes by the experienced Conservative C. B. Stuart-Wortley, who would go on to serve as Under-Secretary of State for the Home Department. Sir Howard Vincent, recently-resigned former Director of the Criminal Investigation Department, won the vote at Sheffield Central at the same election to begin his parliamentary career.

In January 1886 Warren received another unexpected appointment, this time returning to the military. He was to serve as Major-General of the Staff of the Army in Egypt, commanding the troops at the Port of Suakin, which was the subject of some debate in parliament as to how anxious the locals were to avoid returning to Egyptian rule.[14]

Sir Charles arrived in Suakin on the very day that Sir Edmund Henderson resigned, and wasted no time in adopting his new

Sir Charles Warren tests the first war balloons used in the field
"From a Sketch by an Officer of the Bechuanaland Field Force"
from The Graphic, 6th June 1885

responsibilities, the press reporting that he had "already begun inspecting the garrison and fortifications."[15]

He would later write of the motley collection of servants found at Suakin, giving an insight into his skill of putting the right man in the right position:

> I found at Government House convicts of the deepest dye told off as our official servants and batmen, and I chose a well-known poisoner to make the coffee which is always served to visitors, and I did this as a precaution against poisoning. The face of the Chief Civil Intelligence Officer may be imagined when he was first served with coffee by the hands of such a convict, but when I gave my reason he quite agreed with me. Of course, as host I had, in accordance with ancient custom, always to drink before my guests, and I may say I was not unmindful of the convict, who always drank the first cup of coffee of each brew![16]

Warren would not have to worry about his coffee for long, for on 13th March he received a telegram from Home Secretary Hugh Childers offering him the position of Chief Commissioner of the Metropolitan Police. He accepted on the same day, on the understanding that he would not permanently abandon his military career but would resign the Commissionership once the duties he was appointed to address were accomplished.[17]

The *Pall Mall Gazette*, long critical of the increasingly ineffectual Henderson, was giddy with delight at the announcement:

> Mr. Childers, we frankly admit, has taken away our breath by his selection of Sir Charles Warren for the Chief Commissionership of the Metropolitan Police. We never believed it possible that any Home Secretary could have taken so bold, so daring a step as this. It is one of the most courageous, and at the same time one of the most venturesome, appointments ever made. There is only one parallel to it in recent times, and that was the despatch of General Gordon to Khartoum. We only hope that having selected as Colonel Henderson's successor the man who of all others left to us is most like General Gordon in conviction, in temper, and in impatience of being meddled with, Mr. Childers will avoid the fatal precedent of the Soudan, allow his Chief Commissioner free hand, and back him up like a man when he sets to work to make a clean sweep of the Augean stable of Scotland Yard. We need hardly say how delighted we are with this appointment. Sir Charles Warren is a man after our own heart. He has not, unfortunately, the gaiety of spirit and genial humour which lit up all the other attributes of the hero of Khartoum. That is to

say, he is a man of deep religious conviction, of intense earnestness, dominated throughout by an overmastering ideal of duty. There is no fear of man before his eyes, and he had as small respect for right honourable imbecilities in high places as any blunt, straightforward soldier who ever wore uniform. He is a stern, just, incorruptible, religious man, a kind of belated Ironside, born in a century which has but scant sympathy with his Puritan ideals. And this is the man who is to succeed the Dodo at Scotland Yard!

...Sir Charles Warren, we may depend upon it, will not allow personal or trivial considerations to stand in the way of the restoration of an efficient constabulary. He is a man of resolute will, with a determination fixed almost to doggedness. He is active, vigilant, energetic, with great gift of organisation and direction. His difficulty will be in getting on with his subordinates and his superiors, especially with the latter. He is certain to give Mr. Childers many a bad quarter or an hour, and before six months are over half of the papers who are now vying with each other in chanting his praises will be cursing him up hill and down dale.[18]

While the *Pall Mall Gazette*'s comments would prove prophetic, some were amused at their excessive praise, although agreeing with the appointment:

The scream of exultation by the *Pall Mall Gazette* on the appointment of Sir Charles Warren to the office of Chief Commissioner of Police is, to say the least, premature... Not that a lifetime spent in pursuits as different as possible from that he is about to enter upon is a drawback to his success in the latter. A man entirely unhampered by tradition, and with no reverence whatsoever for existing rule and custom, is precisely the man required to head the Metropolitan Police. If the broom is to sweep clean, it must be entirely new... It cannot be long before he discovers how much kissing has gone by favour at Scotland Yard, and if he is as keen-eyed as report avows, he must see the necessity of taking the loafing London detective in hand.[19]

Perhaps driven by the excitement of a new Commissioner for the first time in seventeen years, and only the third since Sir Richard Mayne had become sole Commissioner in 1855, the return to England of the hero of the hour was breathlessly reported step-by-step in the press. Warren left Suakin at noon on 15th March,[20] bound for Brindisi. The next leg of his journey was to leave the southern Italian port on the London-bound mail train at eight o'clock in the morning of 27th March,[21] arriving at Dover two days later and heading for Charing Cross on the 9.30am express train.²² Sir Charles formally took over the Commissionership of the Metropolitan Police on Wednesday, 31st March 1886.²³

The support offered to Warren by the 'bold' Hugh Childers was not to last, for within three months the Home Secretary was to become a victim of his own criticism of the First Home Rule Bill, which had been introduced on 8th April by Prime Minister William Gladstone as an attempt to create a devolved assembly for Ireland. Childers threatened to resign over certain financial clauses and these were removed, but the contentious Bill was rejected on 8th June when 311 Members of Parliament voted for it, with 341 against.

Parliament was dissolved on 26th June and a general election called for 25th July. Gladstone's Liberal Party were ousted, with the Conservatives returned to power, Lord Salisbury resuming his position as Prime Minister just seven months after his earlier departure. His new Home Secretary was Henry Matthews, a 60-year-old barrister.

From the first, relations between Matthews and Warren were strained and for the remainder of his stay at Scotland Yard Sir Charles would be unsure whether he would have Matthews' backing from one day to the next.

The Commissioner continued with his duties as best he could. An inquiry into the riots of February concluded that the number of high-ranking officers was insufficient and consequently five new posts were created: three Chief Constables and two Assistant Chief Constables. All were filled by men with military backgrounds. In addition, discipline across the Force was improved, with Warren personally editing the *Field Exercise and Evolution of Infantry: Part 1 – Recruit or Squad Drill* to create a new Drill Instruction manual for the Metropolitan Police.²⁴

The next challenge for the Commissioner was a severe outbreak of rabies among London's dog population in September. Warren complained that the Muzzling Order of December 1885 was insufficient; a dog muzzled but not on a lead may stray, and a led dog not muzzled could still bite. He insisted that stray unmuzzled dogs, or those muzzled which appeared ill, were to be seized and placed in the Dogs' Home or destroyed.

It provided the first opportunity to attack the new Commissioner. Both press and public wasted little time in venting their anger; an anonymous postcard from an apparent dog-lover, addressed to "Charles Warren, Dog Muzzler in Chief", was received at Scotland Yard bearing the message: "Muzzle yourself as the rabies is in yourself not in the dogs."²⁵

While Warren was adjusting to life at Whitehall Place, his detective force, including Det. Inspector Swanson, were continuing with their caseload.

During his annual holiday visit to Thurso, the Scot was advanced Mark Master at St. Peter's Masonic Lodge 284 on 12th August 1886, his 38th birthday. Swanson had been entered an Apprentice on 21st September 1885 at his hometown lodge at St. John's Square.[26]

Now, it was time to return to his work. Captain Henry Gore Langton, a retired officer of the 72nd Foot now residing in Taunton, had received a letter from a former surgeon of the Regiment named John Meane, who recalled the friendliness between the two former comrades, but soon turned to the real reason for his writing. The letter, sent from Crossford, Dunfermline, on 9th October 1886, continued:

> Through the failure of a relative I lost, for me, a considerable sum, and also had to meet some heavy liabilities which I thought that had long been settled. To add to my trouble I am now hard pressed about some private matters that but for my loss I could have easily settled. Although my difficulty is temporary at present, I hardly know how to turn, and venture to ask you kindly to lend me £10 till the end of March.[27]

Gore Langton, happy to help a supposed old friend, sent two £5 notes. These were collected by a middle-aged man claiming to be Meane at Crossford Post Office on 13th October. It soon transpired that the man was not the former surgeon at all, and fraud was suspected.

Det. Inspector Swanson was sent from Scotland Yard to trace the forger, and it didn't take long for him to realise that the man he was looking for was one George Swain, at one time a respectable Assistant Paymaster in the Navy, but who had fallen into a life of crime resulting in a first conviction in September 1872 at the Old Bailey charged with forgery. Three years later, in February 1875, he was charged with obtaining money by false pretences at Monaghan Assizes and then once again charged with forgery at the Old Bailey in June 1880, when he was sentenced to five years' imprisonment. Swain had been released in November 1885 and sought honest work, but after almost a year had returned to his old ways.[28]

Swanson soon found the forger in Fife.

On 29th November at the High Court of Justiciary, Edinburgh, George Swain pleaded guilty. His Council asked for leniency, but Lord Craighill,

SIR CHARLES WARREN,
THE NEWLY-APPOINTED
CHIEF COMMISSIONER OF THE
METROPOLITAN POLICE.

*from The Worcestershire Chronicle, 27th March 1886.
The beard would not last long.*

presiding, looked at Swain's record of a combined thirteen years' imprisonment and reasonably concluded that he had failed to learn his lesson. He was sentenced to eight years' penal servitude.[29] Swanson himself fared better: his 'judgement and discretion' were rewarded when he received £3 from the Commissioner on 11th December.[30]

Twelve days later, on 23rd December, the Swanson family celebrated an early Christmas gift when a third son was born at the family home. Initially named Willie Nevill Swanson, Julia and Donald seemingly had a change of mind by the time of the boy's registration on 2nd February 1887, and he was recorded as Douglas Sutherland Swanson.[31] Douglas joined Donald Jr, known to his parents as 'Donnie', James ('Jamie') and Ada ('Sis') in the growing family.

The first half of 1887 saw Swanson handed a series of fraud cases, with the Scot arresting George Anderson, a 37-year-old solicitor, very early in the New Year, bringing to an end a complex case of fraud covering both sides of the Atlantic.

The story began on 13th October 1885, when a farmer in Susquehanna,

Pennsylvania, received a letter from a Detroit-based lawyer claiming to have news of a claim on some valuable property in London.[32] The farmer, John Deakin, together with his son, William, read that an ancestor named Thomas Deakin had died in London in 1819 leaving an unsigned Will, which indicated that property at 21 Cock Lane was now owned by John Deakin, should he be able to prove his identity. In addition, there were 2,000 dollars belonging to the estate held in a bank account.[33] The writer, George Franklin Anderson, offered to secure the lease and monies for Mr. Deakin.[34]

When the farmers invited Anderson to visit them to discuss their claim, he stated that he had discovered the claim while browsing the library at Doctors' Commons in London,[35] and that it would take him nine months to obtain possession of the $2,000 and a further three months to sort out the paperwork on the property, which was currently held by three trustees. The trustees were being paid $4,000 a year to maintain the estate which, the lawyer said, was highly desirable and would be worth $40,000.[36]

Anderson told the Deakins that his fee to arrange the paperwork would be 10%, with an advance of $500 required for court costs. He furnished them with references which were checked as he stayed at the farm overnight; satisfied, the following day John Deakin gave the lawyer $500, the equivalent of $15,000 today.

It was agreed that Anderson would travel to London to begin work, maintaining communication with the Deakins, who would follow when the paperwork was ready to sign. The next contact was a letter sent from London on 17th December confirming Anderson's suspicions had been correct – the American farmers were indeed entitled to the estate. Pleased with progress, John Deakin was happy to forward a further $1,000 in January 1886, after which they heard no more until July, when Anderson wrote to say a friend had died, causing a delay in his work. The Deakins decided to travel to England.

They arrived in August and met Anderson in the Strand, catching him by surprise. Far from being nervous, the lawyer suggested they retire to the Crown in West Smithfield, where he told the father and son that he had discovered the estate was also entitled to a second property, this time three acres of land on the outskirts of the capital, with the combined value now worth £60,000.[37] Understandably, the Deakins asked to see the property. Anderson agreed, fixing a date for two days later, and helped the farmers locate lodgings at Langham Street, north of Oxford Street.

Later that evening he returned to their lodgings, excitedly telling

William Deakin "this has been the most eventful day of my life; there are parties here who want to buy this claim of yours; they will give you £40,000." John Deakin, who had retired to bed, was woken and told the news; he said he wanted to see the property before agreeing to sell it. They would visit as arranged two days later.

On arrival at Cock Lane they were shown a house and three shops, with William Deakin noticing the name "Solomon" on a sign above the door; Anderson said this was one of the trustees. The trio then went to Regent Street where they had lunch. Asked how far the second property was, they were told "three or four miles". Mr. Deakin Snr. complained of feeling tired and declined to go – he would accept the £40,000. Anderson asked if he was certain, reminding him that the estate was worth £60,000, but the elderly farmer was happy for the business to be concluded. Later than day the lawyer drew up an agreement, which was signed by John Deakin. It stipulated that the monies would be paid in three instalments: £20,000 on 10th November, £10,000 on 2nd April 1887 and the final £10,000 on 1st September 1887. The payments would be made in New York to avoid a counter claim from any other possible relative of Thomas Deakin. As insurance against the possible failure of the deal Anderson asked for $2,500, a sum William Deakin refused to pay. Pleading inability to access his bank account, Anderson asked for 'some help', to which William gave him 200 dollars in American cash and 300 dollars worth of sterling.

The transfer of deeds was set to go through on 25th November, so the Deakins prepared to return to Pennsylvania. Anderson travelled with them as far as Liverpool, where he said he would follow later on account of his wife's ill-health.

Over the course of the following two months Anderson requested further funds from Deakin, explaining they were for taxes and other court costs – unbelievably, a further $3,000 was sent.

Eventually – and not before time – William Deakin began to feel uneasy and travelled from New York to London accompanied by his brother-in-law, Leonard Stanford, who happened to be a Justice of the Peace. Arriving on 14th November, the men went to see Anderson at his rooms at the Hotel Metropole, and were immediately told that the power of attorney they had brought enabling William Deakin to conduct his father's business was invalid.

Leonard Stanford, not at all satisfied with the situation, asked Anderson whether the first instalment of £20,000 would be paid once the second power was received; he was told that the money was deposited in the bank ready to be transferred. Accordingly, a second power was sent for and arrived on 13th December. Anderson reluctantly agreed it was legal, but refused to show the men the three acres of land, telling William Deakin that his "business was to look after the £40,000, not the three acres." He said the £20,000 couldn't be paid at that point, saying: "A remarkable thing, one of the contractors died last night." Matters would have to be put on hold while the man was buried, he continued.

A further delay was presented when Anderson said that the claim had been sold to a Mr. Wright of Liverpool, who would make a payment of £25,000 on 15th February 1887.

Disappointed and frustrated with this state of affairs, Deakin and Stanford went to Scotland Yard, where the matter was placed in the hands of Det. Inspector Swanson.

Swanson wasted no time in visiting the property at Cock Lane, where he was told by Lewis Solomon that he did indeed act as the agent for the owners, who were in fact his wife, her brother and their two sisters. The siblings' father was John King, grandson of the Thomas Deakin whose 1819 Will had bequeathed the property to his daughter, John King's mother. The quartet had legally owned the property for 27 years. Solomon told the detective that George Anderson had visited him in August or September claiming to represent John Deakin, who considered he had a claim on the property and the two had exchanged angry words.

Swanson went to Somerset House where he was shown Thomas Deakin's Will, confirming Solomon's story, and then to the City Bank, where Anderson held an account. He was told by the chief clerk, William Tucker, that more than £2,000 had been paid into the account from American banks over the course of the preceding months, all of which had been withdrawn.

Closing the net, the detective traced the supposed Liverpudlian buyer, Thomas Wright. He had met Anderson in 1883 on board the *Alaska* travelling from America, and had formed a friendship. Anderson had sent a telegram asking Wright to meet with him at the Hotel Metropole, which he did. On arrival he was told that a good investment opportunity had presented itself, and Anderson wished to buy the property for himself. He did not want his name appearing as the purchaser, so asked Wright to act as the buyer while Anderson would find the funds to pay the £40,000 to his friend.

Swanson had all the evidence he required: he obtained a warrant and went to the Hotel Metropole at 7.30 in the evening of 2nd January 1887, and arrested Anderson in his rooms on suspicion of obtaining money by false pretences. Searching the solicitor, the detective found £295 in notes, £4 10s in gold and two American banknotes. In the room, various letters and telegrams from the Deakins were found, along with documents relating the property.

At the trial on 28th February, an address by Anderson to the jury claiming to have acted in the best interests of the Deakins fell on deaf ears; he was found guilty and sentenced to five years' penal servitude.[38]

Swanson's next arrest, on 16th April, was at 332 King's Road, Chelsea. The address had been given in advertisements by The Hotel Keepers' and Wine Growers' Annual Sweepstake for the City and Suburban, an unauthorised lottery which had seen letters of complaint sent directly to Sir Charles Warren by disgruntled buyers of tickets, which offered cash prizes up to £300. No payouts had yet been made – in fact, there was no record of a draw ever having taken place.

Arriving at the address, a stationer's shop, with local Detective Sergeant Bradford, Swanson encountered a man calling himself Arthur Ward, who was leaving the premises carrying a bundle of twenty-five letters addressed to 'Arthur Fuller'. Swanson took the letters, nine of which proved to contain money orders of one pound each and others enclosing purchased tickets.

Ward claimed to know 'Fuller' by sight and was supposedly collecting the mail on his behalf, but when Swanson took the man inside the shop, the owner, Miss Quixley, confirmed that she knew him as Fuller and he paid her to allow him to receive letters at her shop.

At Westminster Magistrates' Court two days later Ward was told by Judge Partridge that he would be allowed to be remanded in custody should he wish to call Mr. Fuller as a witness; unsurprisingly, he said he had no knowledge of Fuller's whereabouts and was fined £20 and given one week's imprisonment, found guilty of selling tickets for an unauthorised lottery.[39]

Continuing with his workload of fraud cases, an arrest early in May saw Swanson finally bring to justice another petty criminal who had conducted his scam for several years while evading the law. The plan was a simple one: advertisements in daily newspapers by the London Educational and General Institute, which claimed to be a charitable organisation formed by an association of graduates, stated that it was seeking applicants to take Indian and other colonial pupils into private homes or schools, with payments ranging from £90 to £300. The Institute was run on a subscription basis, with the Secretary, James Robertson Reid L.L.D., M.A., requesting applicants send one guinea to the offices at 68 High Street, Camden. Correspondents were told not to visit personally, as the graduates were 'too busy' with forthcoming examinations.

Mrs. Mary Harrison of Epsom was just one of dozens who replied to the advertisement, sending £1 1s. Receiving no response, she wrote again and received an abusive letter in return. Mrs. Harrison decided to go to the police.[40]

When Swanson went to the address with Detective Inspector Walter Andrews on the afternoon of 7th May,[41] they found it to be a second-hand clothes shop, with Robertson Reid having lived in rooms above for two years.[42] The would-be tutor proved to be a 70-year-old man, deaf in one ear.[43] He went willingly with the detectives and was immediately taken to Clerkenwell Police Court, where the fraudster was remanded for trial.

At the Middlesex Sessions on 27th May, Swanson told the Bench that he had linked Robertson Reid to more than forty cases of similar fraud over twenty years, and that the victims, mostly poor governesses, received insulting letters in response to their enquiries and thus were intimidated into silence. Robertson Reid pleaded guilty to the present charges of defrauding Mrs. Harrison and also one Sarah Todd Atkinson and was sentenced to 16 months' imprisonment with hard labour, with the Judge commenting that it was "one of the most heartless cases that he had ever had to deal with during the many years he had sat on that bench."[44]

Just days before appearing in court to give evidence against Ward, Swanson had arrested the captain of a ship in a case of mutiny and murder on the high seas.

The three-masted British barque *Lady Douglas*[45] had arrived in Fremantle, Australia, late in 1886 and then sailed north to Champion Bay and finally to Shark's Bay, Gascoigne.[46] While moored they discharged five crew members who refused to work further, and in their place took on two Malay seamen for the return journey. Both the men, named Hassin and Cassein, were employed fetching coal for the iron ship's voyage back to London.[47]

Departing Shark's Bay on 11th January 1887, all was well during 35 days of clear weather until, two days before reaching the Cape of Good Hope, Hassin became excitable and began acting strangely. The following morning he seemingly disappeared, and was not seen for another ten days until Second Mate James Gleaves found him sleeping on the coals in the forepeak. He was brought up on deck and asked by the captain, James Cocks, why he had stowed himself away, to which the Malay replied to the effect that he was sick, and that the captain was stupid. Asked whether he would hide himself away again, Hassin said he would not and was told to wash himself and get back to his work.

The following morning Hassin was again missing; he was again found in the forepeak, this time armed with two knives. Refusing to come back on deck, Captain Cocks ordered ship's carpenter David Thow to batten down the hatch, it not being known what the Malay's intentions were.[48]

Several times Cocks ordered Hassin to come up from the foredeck, and was refused on each occasion, instead the Malay suggesting that the captain "come down here". The prisoner seemed to have murderous intentions – in addition to his own knife, he now had the cook's carving knife and, saying he would not go to London, continually muttered the ominous phrase "Me kill one, me die."[49]

The crew, understandably, enjoyed little sleep, fearing for their safety.

On the next day Hassin continued to refuse to come on deck, so Captain Cocks fired a shot down into the foredeck intending to frighten him. That night Cocks awoke in his bunk to find Hassin standing over him; the captain shouted in surprise and the Malay ran up on deck, and was found hanging onto the outside of the ship. David Thow and First Mate Edwin Evans dragged him up by his arms, and he was put in irons and placed between decks, only for the prisoner to slip out of them during the early hours. He was clapped into leg irons and kept prisoner in the foredeck for some three weeks, the crew lowering a bucket with food and water in return for the Malay loading the bucket with coal.

On 21st April, after Hassin had attempted to break through the hatch during the night, it was decided that he should be killed; he threatened mortal danger to all on board and the vote was taken to shoot him, the decision registered in the ship's log.[50]

Carpenter Thow sawed through three planks between decks so that Hassin could be reached more easily, during which time the Malay rushed at him with a knife, causing Edwin Evans to fire a shot, hitting him in the foot. The following day, James Gleaves pointed his pistol through the gap and shot Hassin in his side.[51]

The wounded Malay lay on his side, singing what was taken to be a death song. A crewman named Hunt was sent down to investigate; he found Hassin bleeding freely, with a knife laying by his side. In the absence of any rope, Hunt hooked the chain connected to the bucket to Hassin's leg irons and the prisoner was hauled up on deck by his ankles.[52]

The helpless Malay, who was just 5ft 4in[53] and weighing only 40 lbs,[54] was then laid out on the deck, and it was agreed to end his suffering;

shipmate John Webster took the captain's pistol and shot him in the side of his head,[55] spilling his brains onto the deck.[56]

Hassin died within five minutes, and half an hour later the leg irons were removed and his body thrown overboard.[57]

Free from perceived danger, The *Lady Douglas* continued on her voyage to London without further incident. She docked briefly at Le Havre,[58] where Captain James Cocks alerted the authorities and when she landed at Shadwell Dock on Saturday, 23rd April the Board of Trade had heard of the incident from the British Consul and alerted the Home Office, who in turn informed Scotland Yard.[59]

Detective Inspector Donald Swanson accordingly went to the offices of the *Lady Douglas*' owners at 110 Fenchurch Street, where he found James Cocks was in attendance. Cautioning Cocks that he was a detective officer, Swanson told the captain that he was taking him into custody "for causing the death of one Hassin on board the British barque *Lady Douglas* in Shark's Bay on April 23rd." Cocks replied that the murder had happened "on the way home; it was done for the safety of all the crew and the ship also."[60]

Swanson took Cocks to Wapping police station, where, while reading the charge to the station Inspector, the prisoner interrupted, saying:

> I did not say I did it with my own hand; under my direction the following fired the shots: Mr. Gleaves chief mate, Evans, second mate, and Webster, an ordinary seaman. I had fired at him myself, but could not hit him, the day previous, when he was trying to knock a hole in the ship with a crowbar.[61]

The Detective Inspector alerted the Thames Police, who sent Det. Sergeant Wright and Sergeant David Francis to the *Lady Douglas*, where they found Evans and Webster. They were read their captain's evidence, which they agreed with, and were willingly taken into custody, where they were joined later that day by James Gleaves, who was arrested at his home on West India Dock Road.[62]

At their subsequent trial at the Old Bailey, on 27th June 1887, the jury recommended mercy, and the sentence of execution was commuted to five years' penal servitude for James Cocks, eighteen month's hard labour for James Gleaves and Edwin Evans, and twelve months' hard labour for Webster.[63]

By the time of the sentencing, Detective Inspector Donald Swanson had already received a reward of £2 for his part in the arrests.[64]

At this time, and for some months past, a recruitment drive had been in operation which saw the number of Metropolitan Police officers increase significantly, partly as a result of Warren's Commissioner's Report for 1886 which pointed out that police numbers had not in recent years risen proportionately with London's population increase, and also because of Queen Victoria's forthcoming Golden Jubilee celebrations, which would require a great amount of policing.

Applications came in their hundreds; many had to be rejected. Warren himself received several directly, including the following letter from a Mr. Handslip:

> Mr. Gen Warren.
>
> Dear Sir i want for to joine the Metropoliton that is the police force there is one in famley and he was 5 years old the 17th of Feb turn I am myself turn 26 the 5 of Dec and I am 5 feet 7 & ¼ in Hight and a good Steady young man tea totle and I Dont smoke or youse Backey of any Sorte and never was a man that went in Bad Compenny and I have had mind for to goim metropoliton now a few years.[65]

Sadly, despite his obvious enthusiasm Mr. Handslip forgot to include a return address.

Warren was right to be concerned in his Commissioner's Report. In the weeks leading up to the Jubilee, James Monro received information on a Fenian plot to assassinate the Queen, blowing up Westminster Abbey and half the Cabinet in the process.

Monro became increasingly convinced that an American Fenian named Frank Millen was at the heart of the plot, and had his movements watched and even suggested that a detective was placed in the Post Office to intercept his correspondence.

What the Assistant Commissioner did not know was that Millen was a British agent, working under Edward Jenkinson from 1885. Millen's information had come from Henri Le Caron, Robert Anderson's informer. Anderson was aware of Millen's role but decided against revealing this to Monro, as did a select group of members of the Foreign Office and the Prime Minister, who also knew who Millen was.

Home Secretary Henry Matthews did *not* know, however, and took Monro's concerns very seriously.

In an attempt to frighten Millen against coming to England, Monro sent Superintendent James Thomson of the Special Irish Branch to initially observe Millen in Boulogne, where the Fenian was staying with his wife. The detective took Mrs. Thomson with him and, posing as a tourist, found reason to talk with Millen as the two women became friendly.

Supt. Thomson, however, was also working for Robert Anderson. He fed Monro the misinformation that Millen was anxious, and gave the appearance of waiting for someone.

While in previous years Jenkinson had advised allowing a dynamite plot to develop so that exact plans could be ascertained and more collaborators captured, Monro was nervous and dispatched Superintendent Dolly Williamson to Boulogne to outright inform Millen that they believed him to be behind a plot to reignite the dynamite campaign and that he would be arrested on sight should he set foot in England. Millen took the hint and moved to Paris, where he was watched by Inspector William Melville, who posed as an Irish expatriate and ended up tutoring the Fenian informer's daughters in French.

The Jubilee plot was financed by Chicago lawyer Alexander Sullivan, with Frank Millen heading it from his base in France. Days earlier Sullivan had brought American dynamitards Thomas Callan and Michael Harkins into the plot, and on 11th June, ten days before the celebrations, they sailed from New York towards Liverpool. They carried more than a thousand dollars, were armed with revolvers and, most significantly, had over 100lbs of dynamite sewn into the lining of their clothes.[66]

On the morning of Jubilee Day, 21st June 1887, James Monro was, understandably, beside himself with worry. He had received information that the dynamiters had hidden a clockwork bomb in the vaults of Westminster Abbey which was timed to explode during the service. He had detectives search every inch of the Abbey, but nothing was found.

As Victoria's procession through the streets of London made its way to Westminster, and the elite of countries across Europe began to take their places in the Abbey, Monro was faced with an impossible dilemma. He later recalled in his unpublished memoirs:

> I was never in a more difficult position in my life. On the one hand, if the information I received was correct, I could do nothing without certainly giving rise to uneasiness and panic amongst those who were in the Abbey, and they were the flower of England's nobility. Panic would certainly have led to the loss of many lives, for the galleries were so crammed

and the means of exit so very insufficient that anything like a crush would have been fatal to many. If on the other hand I did nothing and an explosion was brought off, what would have been said or thought of me, who having received warning did nothing. If on the other hand if the information was untrue, and I caused panic on such an untrustworthy warning, I should have been denounced for causing needless alarm.[67]

As the Assistant Commissioner took his seat, he decided to do nothing.

It turned out to the right choice. No disruption to the service occurred; no explosion took place. The dynamiters had miscalculated the journey time and landed in Liverpool on the morning of Jubilee Day, with the procession in London already underway.

Despite Monro's fears, the work carried out by the Special Irish Branch and others was seen as a great success, and the Assistant Commissioner later singled out the Branch's Littlechild, Melville, McIntyre and Quinn, along with Dolly Williamson, for praise in a report to Sir Charles Warren.[68]

With the procession and Thanksgiving Service itself passing peacefully thanks to excellent organisation and performance of his officers, Jubilee Day was a triumph as far as Sir Charles Warren and the Metropolitan Police were concerned, and the Commissioner enjoyed letters of thanks from Henry Matthews, Sir Francis Knollys, Equerry to the Prince of Wales, the Earl of Carnarvon and many others. Even *Punch* was complimentary – something Warren would not enjoy in future editions – with their cartoon of 2nd July showing Mr. Punch bowing to the Commissioner above four verses of praise which included the following:

> How many lives and limbs they saved, those Peelers,
> And the Ambulance with which they worked so well,
> Unless he rescued all should turn revealers,
> No record will declare, no story tell.
>
> But Mr. Punch's vigilant observation
> Marked their hard toil amidst the mob's wild fun,
> And, filled with genuine pride and admiration,
> He publicly awards his warm "Well done!"

As for these valiant Peelers themselves; each officer employed by the Metropolitan and City of London Police forces on that day received a specially-commissioned bronze commemorative medal, with the recipient's name engraved on its edge and hanging from a blue ribbon.

Along with thousands of his fellow officers, Det. Inspector Donald Swanson received a Jubilee medal bearing his name.[69]

The goodwill shown to Commissioner Sir Charles Warren by Home Secretary Henry Matthews over the former's handling of Jubilee Day did not last long. Warren was becoming increasingly frustrated with the actions – or rather, non-activity – of Receiver Richard Pennefather, who seemed determined to block the Commissioner's demands for police pensions to be better administered and for clarity on other police-related finances.

When Warren complained to the Home Secretary his letters were ignored beyond a formal acknowledgement, and the Commissioner's justified complaints about the quality of the boots issued to his officers – the men who trod thousands of miles each year in ill-fitting footwear – in his first Annual Report was similarly dismissed by the press as a typical fixation on uniform by a military man.

Sir Evelyn Ruggles-Brise, at the time private secretary to Matthews, would later recall:

> Pennefather was a very able man, but disagreeable to deal with; he rubbed everybody up the wrong way. Warren was the finest man we had in Whitehall, but probably the worst appointment, because he *must* be independent, and the Commissioner of Police is held in very tight bonds by the Home Office. Matthews was an exceedingly able lawyer, but quite incapable of dealing with men; he was a regular Gallio in his attitude to Warren's complaints. Later on he quarrelled with [future Commissioner Sir Edward] Bradford, and if you couldn't get on with Bradford you could get on with nobody.[70]

Worse was to follow when Assistant Commissioner James Monro, whose constant complaints about Edward Jenkinson's lack of communication with the Metropolitan Police had finally seen the Fenian spymaster released from his duties in December 1886,[71] began to chip away at Warren. Widely expected to replace Sir Edmund Henderson as Commissioner, Monro was unhappy with Warren's insistence that the Assistant Commissioner report to him rather then enjoy the free reign he had under the former Commissioner, and indeed the direct access to the Home Secretary which Howard Vincent had enjoyed before him in the equivalent position.

Monro created further problems by accepting a request that he head a new, secret Intelligence Department under the control of the Home Office. In his memoirs, written in 1903, he was at pains to claim that he had not complained about Jenkinson's behaviour for his own ends, and did not want this to be an investigation department, "superceding the police in the discharge of their legitimate duties," as it had under Jenkinson:

> I consented to act as Chief of the Secret Department as regards intelligence, and at the same time to retain my office as Asst. Commissioner. For obvious reasons I had no wish to succeed Mr. Jenkinson. I was Asst. Commissioner of Police and quite satisfied with my position. I strongly objected to do anything as if I had worked to supplant Mr. Jenkinson for my own benefit. All this was fully recognised by the Home Office but I was still urged in the public interests to take up Mr. Jenkinson's work, and I did so.[72]

By taking command of 'Section D', as it became known, Monro put himself in the position of being answerable directly to the Home Office, bypassing his superior Charles Warren completely.

The friction between Monro, Warren and Matthews would be an ongoing problem for some eighteen months, and relations between the latter pair were tested to breaking point when a series of public demonstrations were held late in 1887.

Several disturbances had taken place during October in the run up to the Lord Mayor's Show, most notably heated demonstrations in Hyde Park, but the peaceful passing of 9th November itself, thanks in no small measure to the strict policing of the route and Trafalgar Square, led to a build up of pent-up anger and frustration which manifested itself four days later, a day which would become known as Bloody Sunday.

Sensing the mood, Warren announced a ban on access to the demonstrators' meeting place of choice:

MEETINGS
IN
TRAFALGAR SQUARE.

> In consequence of the disorderly scenes which have recently occurred in Trafalgar Square, and of the danger to the peace of the Metropolis from meetings held there, and with a view to prevent such disorderly proceedings, and to preserve the peace:
>
> I, CHARLES WARREN, the Commissioner of Police of the Metropolis, do hereby give notice, with the sanction of the Secretary of State, and the concurrence of the Commissioners of Her Majesty's Works and Public Buildings, that, until further intimation, no Public Meetings will be

allowed to assemble in Trafalgar Square, nor will speeches be allowed to be declared therein; and all well-disposed persons are hereby cautioned and requested to abstain from joining or attending any such Meeting or Assemblage; and Notice is further given that all necessary measures will be adopted to prevent any such Meeting or Assemblage, or the delivery of any speech, and effectually to preserve the Public peace, and to suppress any attempt at the disturbance thereof.

This Notice is not intended to interfere with the use by the Public of Trafalgar Square for all ordinary purposes, or to affect the Regulations issued by me with respect to Lord Mayor's Day.

CHARLES WARREN
The Commissioner of Police of the Metropolis

Warren's proclamation was a red rag to a bull. In addition to the demonstrations by the unemployed, on Sunday, 13th November 1887 thousands descended on the West End to test the resolve of police. One, a 27-year-old Irishman named Francis Connelly, was heard by P.C. Lambert, on plain clothes duty, telling a crowd of 300 people congregated in Hyde Park:

> I was going down Whitehall last Tuesday, when I saw a placard prohibiting public meetings until some day not mentioned. When I saw this I stood amazed. I wondered whether I was in some part of despotic Russia or in England. This proclamation had been issued by Sir Charles Warren. I intend to go down to the square this afternoon, and I intend to take a stick; and I intend to use it. Mind, I don't tell you to use a stick, but if a policeman strikes me, I'll strike him back. I have got a good, sound oak stick that came from Mitchelstown, and it has got a drop of 'Shinnick's' blood upon it. It has helped to kill one policeman, and it may help to kill another.[73]

Defiant speeches such as this were to be heard around Hyde Park, Clerkenwell Green and many other public places.

In Trafalgar Square itself, police preparations had begun early that morning. Some 1,500 officers lined the square, shoulder-to-shoulder in single line on the eastern, western and northern sides, which all enjoyed the support of a concrete balustrade; the southern side, however, with its open access, was lined three deep. Inside this blue line was a reserve of officers, with more in the vicinity of Charing Cross, so that a combined 2,500 officers were ready to assist their colleagues lining the square.[74]

For three hours they stood in this way in an otherwise empty Trafalgar Square, awaiting developments. It was not until one o'clock in the afternoon that crowds began to gather, which over the following hour grew until, at last, as marchers approached from several different directions, some 30,000 people surrounded the square; some protesting, some curious, the vast majority enjoying an opportunity to create a nuisance. Among the marchers were leading members of the Social Democratic Federation including William Morris, Annie Besant, John Burns and Robert Cunninghame Graham M.P. These were joined by members of the Fabian Society including George Bernard Shaw.

Forty mounted police circled the square and its approaches, attempting to break up knots of people by simply charging towards them, but as some members of the crowd moved from jeering and shouting to physical violence using sticks, rocks and lengths of metal, these mounted officers drew their batons, and blows were dealt.

Just before four o'clock, Inspector Hume noticed a crowd of around 400 protesters approaching the police cordon from the Strand entrance, led by a tall man without a hat. Standing in the front line of the police cordon was P.C. Thomas Maitland. He watched the man approach, arm-in-arm with another, then shout "Now for the Square!" and begin to run towards the officers. Maitland and the officer next to him, P.C. William Blunden, pushed the man away, only to be told "We have as much right to the Square as Policemen,"[75] and Blunden was punched in the mouth, drawing blood.[76] In the struggle, the man was himself struck on the head by a baton, suffering a wound which bled freely; it was Robert Cunninghame Graham, the Member of Parliament for North West Lanarkshire. Cunninghame Graham was from a wealthy family but had converted to Socialism and espoused some radical views. He had apparently attempted to enter the square to test Sir Charles Warren's order, and now had a sore head as his answer. He was taken into custody with John Burns, the flag-waving rioter from Pall Mall nearly two years earlier, who put up no resistance.

At quarter-past four the 1st Life Guards suddenly appeared, with a detachment of 200 troopers approaching the square. They fell into formation eight abreast and proceeded to trot around the square to cheers from the crowd, in marked contrast to the reception given to the police. Just before five o'clock the Grenadier Guards marched into the square from St. George's Barracks. They carried rifles on their shoulders, bayonets fixed, and set about driving back the crowd that remained in the vicinity, as reported by a breathless journalist from the *Hull Daily Mail*:

When the troops got in front of the National Gallery they halted, opened up into lines, and drove the crowd back off the roadway on to the pavement, where they came into contact with the police. Thus caught between constables and soldiers, the roughs had many of them to run the gauntlet. A shove from one policeman, a cuff from another, and a kick from the third accelerated their retreat. A few of the crowd showed a disposition for a moment to maintain their ground against the military, but two or three of the soldiers at once brought their rifles and bayonets to the charge position, and the sight of the cold steel within a yard of their stomachs quickly dispelled all thoughts of resistance. The officers and sergeants of the Grenadiers rushed out in front of their men, and ordered them to put up their arms, or they would certainly have hastened the flight of the roughs by a bayonet prod underneath their coat-tails.

From cheering the mob quickly passed to hooting and cursing the soldiers, and in a short time the Guardsmen were dropping their rifle butts on the toes and bringing their fists heavily across the jaws of all who ventured near them, with a vigour which seemed greatly to delight the weary police.

Shortly after five, the mounted police, who had not had an idle moment during the afternoon, began to make a determined effort to clear the southern end of the square. The mob was charged with more violence than hitherto, and batons were used when necessary. The refugees in the middle of the road, which up to this point had remained crowded, were now cleared, as were also the pavements near the Grand Hotel and the opposite side of Northumberland Avenue. In one of the charges a loud crash of glass was heard, and in a moment the whole of the window of a shop devoted to the sale of electrical appliances under the late premises of the National Liberal Club was demolished. A minute later another window was smashed in a refreshment room adjoining, but this was probably the result of over-pressure during an endeavour of the police to clear the pavement...

Fresh bodies of constables now began to arrive in the square, and with their assistance the mounted police were more successful in their efforts to make the crowds disperse, and by six o'clock all danger of further disturbance was at an end, the mob which remained being easily manageable... The rougher element seemed to get tired of the continual movements of the police, and gradually moved away. This enabled the authorities to relieve in sections a number of the constables, who had now been on duty for nearly ten hours, and they gladly made a hurried march to Scotland Yard.[77]

*The Life Guards patrol Trafalgar Square during Bloody Sunday
as the Metropolitan Police attempt to repel the crowd
from The Illustrated London News, 19th November 1887*

More than 300 rioters were taken into custody, with 150 people conveyed to nearby hospitals, including dozens of policemen.

Predictably, the newspapers were horrified by the disorder, and despite the hard work undertaken by the police, it was at this point that they began to turn against the Commissioner; the only surprise was that it had taken far longer than the *Pall Mall Gazette*'s predicted six months.

The following Sunday – 20th November – another demonstration was held in the vicinity of Trafalgar Square, this time against the perceived police violence on the 13th. Further arrests – and injuries – were suffered. One indignant woman called at Scotland Yard demanding to see Warren personally, complaining that she had been kicked by a police horse during the mêlée. On receiving her note the Commissioner sent a junior clerk to hear the woman's story. She said she had been standing innocently on a pavement when the horse backed and kicked her; at this point she suddenly whipped up her petticoats and exposed the injured part of her anatomy. On hearing the horrified clerk's report Warren roared with laughter, saying "Well, that's worth a sovereign!" and handed the clerk money to give to the woman.[78]

Over the second weekend of disturbances, Swanson was transferred from A Division to Central Office at Scotland Yard, joining a select band of detectives working directly under James Monro.[79] His satisfaction at moving to the headquarters of the C.I.D. was to be tainted by personal sadness, however, as on the day he transferred his mother-in-law Sarah Ann Nevill was diagnosed with bronchitis; cared for by daughter Julia at Camden Villas, she died six days later on 25th November, aged 65. Present at the death was Donald Swanson, who registered the sad event on the 28th.[80]

Swanson had little time to grieve, though, as on 1st December he was required at Bow Street court for the committal hearing of John Burns and Robert Cunninghame Graham. Magistrate Mr. Vaughan heard William Myson, a porter at Morley's Hotel opposite Trafalgar Square, testify that he saw Cunninghame Graham approach with a large crowd; Charles Goodman, a valet at the hotel, gave similar evidence. Neither saw the M.P. attack the police; that crucial evidence came from an Australian banker named Charles Buckland, who had been staying at the Grand Hotel on 13th November. He was sitting outside the hotel when he observed a large crowd standing on the fringes of the Square. After a minute or so Cunninghame Graham was pushed forward, and at that moment charged against the police line. When cross-examined by John Burns as to how he had come to the attention of the police,

Buckland replied that he had been visited by Det. Inspector Swanson two nights before the hearing. When the Australian asked how the detective had heard of him, Swanson replied that "to answer such a question would be to disclose [our] system."[81]

The defendants were committed for trial, charged with riot and assault on the police, and released on bail.

The *Pall Mall Gazette*, who had suggested the case would test the legality of holding meetings in Trafalgar Square, complained:

> No case has been raised which will test the right of policemen to charge a procession and smash the banners and rob the bandsmen of their instruments. They acted more like banditti than like policemen, and yet in the mêlée no one seems to have taken the number of the individual constable who assaulted [Mr. Cunninghame Graham] or to have secured witnesses for his identification. To raise this question by the prosecution of a policeman is, however, obviously the first thing to be done, and it should be done at once.[82]

Calls by heavyweight newspapers for policemen to be prosecuted were bad enough; worse was to follow the day after the committal hearing of Burns and Cunninghame Graham when a 41-year-old law clerk named Alfred Linnell, who had been in the vicinity of Trafalgar Square on the day of the 20th November demonstration, died of injuries supposedly caused by a kick by a police horse.[83]

Linnell had been walking along Northumberland Avenue when the mounted police attempted to disperse the crowd on that thoroughfare; he was knocked off his feet and five or six people fell on top of him. Linnell was carried to Charing Cross Hospital, where it was discovered that among his injuries he had a compound fracture of the thighbone. He was attended by Edward Smith, the House Surgeon, and his condition appeared to improve until he developed blood poisoning from the open wound through which his thighbone protruded, and this would cause his eventual death.[84]

The newspapers leapt on Linnell's passing with relish, writing long stories describing alleged police brutality under banners such as "Killed by the Police". The inquest took place on 5th December under Coroner John Troutbeck. Press and public alike packed St. Martin's Vestry Hall, close to Trafalgar Square, to hear Linnell's sister state that to her knowledge her brother had not been a member of any political party or movement. He had apparently been at work on that Sunday morning and then walked to watch the scenes at Trafalgar Square. When visited by his sister at hospital, Linnell said he had been knocked down by the police and left lying on the pavement, unable to stand.

Dr. Smith of Charing Cross Hospital received a grilling by Mr. Thompson, representing the family, who wanted to know whether Linnell had also told him that he had been knocked down by the mounted police. The medical man denied it, saying that the victim had indicated that he had slipped in the surge of the crowd.

Det. Inspector Donald Swanson was in attendance, representing Scotland Yard. He asked Dr. Smith whether there was any bruise on the body which indicated that Linnell had been struck by a horse, receiving the reply "None whatever." Questioned by the detective as to whether Linnell had indicated that he had even been touched by a policeman or a horse, Smith replied "He said the police were turning the crowd back and the crowd fell upon him."[85]

This response by Smith was dismissed with outrage by the *Pall Mall Gazette*, who reported that

> The body being made over to the relatives of the deceased, it was no sooner placed in a shell for burial that a bruise was discovered immediately under the left knee – a bruise about the size of the palm of the hand, apparently resembling in appearance the blow that would be produced by the kick of a horse.[86]

With the inquest adjourned, the body was re-examined, this time by Dr. Charles Hebbert, who testified at the reconvened inquest on 12th December that three bruises were now visible around the left leg of the deceased, one at the back measuring some five inches in length. This time, the *Pall Mall Gazette* calmly reported Hebbert's opinion that the injury was more compatible with being trampled by a human foot than a horse's hoof, which would probably have caused some laceration of the skin, which had not occurred.[87]

Alfred Linnell's body was released to the family and he was afforded a public funeral on Sunday, 18th December, with the law clerk turned into a martyr for the Socialist movement. In an attempt to avoid further riots, the police stopped the funeral procession passing through Northumberland Avenue, where Linnell fell, and Trafalgar Square itself, but wisely both the Metropolitan and City of London forces maintained a discreet distance.

In fact, in the days leading up to the funeral Sir Charles Warren had warned in a confidential letter to the Home Office the possible threat presented by such a public event:

> The case is just this: the exhibition of a corpse for the purpose of a demonstration will severely shock the feelings of the great bulk of the population, while interference with the procession would be equally repugnant to them.
>
> I think then that unless this demonstration can be stopped by some way otherwise than by Police Regulations it would be the safest plan to let the parties go wherever they please with it, police precautions of course being taken to prevent absolute disorder...
>
> In any case with such an unusual occurrence in contemplation it is impossible to foresee what will be the effect on the mind of the masses as regards its being the possible cause of a riot.[88]

The cortège left Dawes undertaker's in Lexington Street, Golden Square,[89] just after two o'clock in the afternoon and made its way along Wellington Street, Strand, Fleet Street and Ludgate Circus. The black coffin was draped in a red flag and placed upon an open hearse pulled by four horses, the hearse decorated with a black shield bearing the words "Killed in Trafalgar Square", with red, green and yellow flags fluttering above representing Radicalism, Irish Nationalism and revolution. The pallbearers included Cunninghame Graham, Annie Besant, William Morris, W. T. Stead and Michael Dowling of the Irish National League.

The large crowd lining the route booed and hissed any policeman who came into view, but the occasion passed peacefully. As the cortège approached St. Paul's Cathedral the band at the head of the procession began to play the *Dead March* from Handel's *Saul*, and at that precise moment the bells of St. Paul's fell silent from their summoning of afternoon worshippers. The enormous crowd gathered at the spot removed their hats in respect, no doubt moved with emotion at the incredible timing.

The procession continued along Cheapside and Leadenhall Street before entering Aldgate High Street, Whitechapel and Mile End Road. By the time it neared its final destination at Bow Cemetery at half-past four, the cortège was a mile-and-a-half long, an estimated one hundred thousand people marching behind the hearse.

As the coffin was carried into the cemetery in the winter darkness the heavens opened and heavy torrents of rain fell on the mourners, who heard Rev. Stewart Headlam conduct the burial service followed by angry graveside speeches against police brutality. The ceremony closed with a rendering of *A Death Song*, specially composed for the occasion by William Morris.[90]

The trial of Cunninghame Graham and Burns opened at the Old Bailey on 16th January 1888. After two days of evidence they were acquitted of assault and riot, but found guilty of unlawful assembly. Both received custodial sentences of six months[91] and were sent to Pentonville.[92]

Swanson received a reward of £3 for his part in the conviction of the pair,[93] but he was soon called in to investigate a strange postscript to the affair. Just two days after Cunninghame Graham had arrived at Pentonville, a man calling himself A. W. Eayres visited him, claiming to be a member of the jury which had found him guilty. He apparently had Home Office papers authorising his attendance. The man made a second visit on 24th January, when he attempted to obtain money from the M.P., and Cunninghame Graham's lawyer Mr. Wright was informed. Having met Det. Chief Inspector Butcher and Det. Inspector Hare, Mr. Wright then gave details to Det. Inspector Swanson with regards to Eayres' stated residence, 25 Dalmeny Road, Tufnell Park. Needless to say, the address proved to be false, with no sign of the imposter.

Swanson interviewed Captain Welby, the Deputy Governor of Pentonville, who told the detective that Cunninghame Graham's wife had written to him asking that Eayres not be allowed to visit her husband, who believed that the imposter was a man he had seen at political meetings in the past.[94]

Some weeks later, Cunninghame Graham's solicitor wrote to the Secretary of State stating that his client had come to the conclusion that a charge against Eayres, should he be found, would not be successful due to lack of evidence. He believed that Eayres was a dangerous person whose career might be stopped by a caution from the police. Swanson's report of 24th April 1888 commented "I think that the man who dared to obtain [a] Home Office order and entered a prison is not likely to be deterred by a police caution."[95] Nevertheless, enquiries into the mysterious Eayres came to nothing and the matter was dropped.

Sir Charles Warren, meanwhile, was still bearing the brunt of the Socialists' fury. On 6th May 1888 he was booked by the Gordon League to give a lecture on his work in Palestine at the Oxford Music Hall, Oxford Street, where a large number of those sympathetic to the unemployed's cause took advantage of the free entry to wreak their 'revenge' on the Commissioner. Warren had scarcely risen to his feet when he was greeted with a volley of abuse, and less than ten minutes into his presentation the Chairman of the Gordon League, Arnold White,[96] had the lights put up and appealed for calm. Warren attempted to continue his lecture with slides, which were met with cries such as "Show us a little of the funeral" and "What about the wives of the men you have killed?" and shouts of support for Cunninghame Graham and

*Robert Cunninghame Graham and John Burns
in the dock at the Old Bailey*
Author's collection

John Burns, until after a short time he gave up and the curtain was drawn. The Socialists cheered and left the building, loudly singing *The Marseillaise*.[97]

It had been a difficult first eighteen months for the new Commissioner, and a period in which the standing of the Metropolitan Police had been greatly reduced in the eyes of the public. Reporting on the convictions of Burns and Cunninghame Graham, the majority of the press, as might be expected, did not side with the force:

The Judge held that the proclamation of the Trafalgar Square meetings by Sir Charles Warren did not render the meetings unlawful; but he declared that the police were, nevertheless, quite justified in preventing them from being held. He laid it down clearly that an "unlawful assembly is one for carrying out any common purpose, whether lawful or unlawful, in such a manner as to cause an apprehension of a breach of the peace."
...The jury thus had really no option but, accepting this as the law, to find the defendants guilty...

The Judge virtually decided that the police were alone able to determine whether or not there were grounds for apprehension; and, as they had decided that there were, and had issued a proclamation in proof of their decision, the meeting became an unlawful assembly, and those who attended broke the law.

The truth, of course, was that the breach of the peace was caused by the police themselves bludgeoning the crowd; but this case has now made it clear that the London police, if they only give notice beforehand, can bludgeon whom, when, how, and where they choose; and if the public don't like it, they can just go to gaol for their pains.[98]

Although 1887 had ended on a sour note for the Metropolitan Police, for Donald Swanson personally it was a period of progression. On 24th January 1888 he was promoted Detective Chief Inspector (Temporary), replacing Charles Hagen, who had retired on the third of that month.[99] A week later, on 31st January, Swanson witnessed the Will of Detective Superintendent John Shore,[100] who had replaced Dolly Williamson in 1886 when the latter became the first Chief Constable of the C.I.D.

By 1888, Detective Chief Constable Williamson was a sick man. Very much Swanson's mentor, the Scot had been selected by the experienced officer to accompany him on several cases of great importance, and a newspaper would later record that "Mr. Williamson... recognising in Mr. Swanson an originality in method quite unusual, gave him every opportunity of exercising his own especial talent."[101]

Although still only 58-years-old, Williamson had for seven years suffered heart problems[102] and after examination by Drs. Thomas Bond and Alexander Mackellar was signed off work for three months on full pay on 10th February.[103] Losing an officer of such enormous experience would undoubtedly be a huge blow to Assistant Commissioner (Crime) James Monro, who subsequently wrote to Charles Warren seeking permission to appoint an Assistant Chief Constable, recommending a friend named Melville Macnaghten. Macnaghten had run his father's tea plantations in Bengal and in 1881 had been attacked by Indian land rioters, resulting in an appearance before the District Judge, Monro. The pair had remained friends since.

After some confusion as to whether Monro was seeking a permanent or temporary appointment, on 29th March it was agreed that Macnaghten would be appointed on a salary of £400 per annum.[104] But it was not to be: Warren, angry that Monro had attempted to push through his own man, observed that the proposed new Assistant Chief Constable was "the only man in India beaten by the Hindoos"; Home Secretary Henry Matthews, for once listening to his Commissioner, decided that Macnaghten was not the right man after all and the appointment was stopped.

This proved to be the final straw for Monro, who resigned in July 1888. His replacement as Assistant Commissioner (Crime) was Robert Anderson, at that moment in time perhaps not the most popular choice, but a man whom Henry Matthews knew would work with Warren.

Williamson returned to work, and Macnaghten would have to wait another year.

On 2nd July Det. Chief Inspector Swanson was at Westminster Police Court, observing proceedings at the remand hearing of Mrs. Gordon Baillie,[105] the well-known philanthropist socialite who was supposedly concerned with the welfare of Scottish crofters, styling herself "the Glendale Martyr",[106] but who in reality had for several months fraudulently obtained various goods and services from companies in London by settling her bills with a total of 38 worthless cheques.[107] Mrs. Gordon Baillie was charged under her real name, Annie Frost, along with her 'husband' Robert Percival Frost and their butler Robert Gigner, described as a miserable-looking man aged about 40, who wore "a reddish wig" with "a few straggling red hairs on his chin."[108]

The trio would stand trial at the Old Bailey in October 1888, with Mrs. Gordon Baillie receiving five years' penal servitude.[109]

As Donald Swanson celebrated his fortieth birthday on 12th August 1888, he no doubt looked back on his career to date with some satisfaction. He had served twenty years with the Metropolitan Police, enjoying a series of promotions so that he was now one of just five Chief Inspectors at the C.I.D.'s Central Office[110] and had earned a reputation as a reliable, discreet officer who could be trusted with investigations of a complex nature.

His personal life, too, was blossoming. He and Julia celebrated their tenth wedding anniversary, the couple proud of their three fine sons and beautiful daughter. Their happiness was intensified when it was discovered that Julia was pregnant with twins.

Yes, 1888 was shaping up to be a very good year.

Unless otherwise stated, all images are courtesy of and copyright the Swanson family

The ruins of the house attached to Geise Distillery, birthplace of Donald Sutherland Swanson

Donald Swanson aged around 10-years-old, fishing with his father John on Thurso River

Swanson family home at Durness Street, Thurso

Donald Sutherland Swanson in schoolmaster's robes, aged approximately 17, with parents John and Mary

Catherine Court, where Swanson worked as a clerk on arrival in London.
His offices at No. 8 were accessed by the steps shown bottom-left
Courtesy London Metropolitan Archives

Rare photograph of Donald Swanson without a moustache, probably from his time working at Catherine Court

8 Catherine Court,
Seething Lane,
London March 20th 1868
E.C.

E.R.
84 Hatton Garden
E.C.

Sir,
I beg respectfully to offer myself for the vacancy in your establishment advertised in the Daily Telegraph of today. I am now and have been for several months past clerk at the above address; but unfortunately for me my employer will give up business in a few weeks and I am thus compelled to look out for another situation. Should you kindly grant me an interview I shall be happy to furnish you with most unexceptionable references as to character, education & ability. I am 19 years of age and do not so much desire a large salary as a good opening at a moderate one.

I remain Sir
yours obediently
Donald S Swanson

Above: Swanson's letter of application to the Metropolitan Police
Below: Swanson's completed examination form, approved by Examining Clerk William Staples
©The National Archives / photographs Adam Wood

Form for Candidates to fill up on Examination.

The Candidate is to state in writing the following particulars in the presence of the Officer appointed for that purpose:—

His Christian Name and Surname in full	Donald Sutherland Swanson
His present Address	39 King Street, Regent Street W
The Name and Address of his last Employer	Jno Meikle Esqr, 8 Catherine Court, Seething Lane E.C.
If he has ever been employed in the Metropolitan Police Force	No

Witnessed 31 day of March 1868.

Examined in Reading.

Wm Staples
Examining Clerk

Donald Sutherland Swanson circa 1871
Courtesy John Mitchell

Julia Nevill and Donald Swanson in their courting days, mid-1870s

Above left: Painting of Julia Nevill, wife of Donald Swanson. Right: Julia's parents James and Sarah Nevill
Below: Marriage certificate of Donald Swanson and Julia Nevill

Presented
— TO —

Donald S. Swanson

— ON HIS MARRIAGE —

By the undernamed of his
Brother Officers.
As a token of their esteem
— And desire for his happiness. —

AUGUST 5th 1878.

George Aubere. Thomas Roots.
Charles von Tornow. Daniel Morgan.
John J. Dowdell. Walter S. Andrews.
William Reimers. George Robson.
Henry Marshall.

Dedication sheet pasted into photograph album presented to Swanson by the detectives of A Division

Children of Donald and Julia Swanson
Left to right: Ada, Douglas, Donald Jr, Alice and James

Tranter pistol presented to Swanson by the Countess of Bective
© Adam Wood

Swanson's arrest book showing capture and sentence of Percy Lefroy Mapleton

Swanson mid-1870s

Swanson in 1882

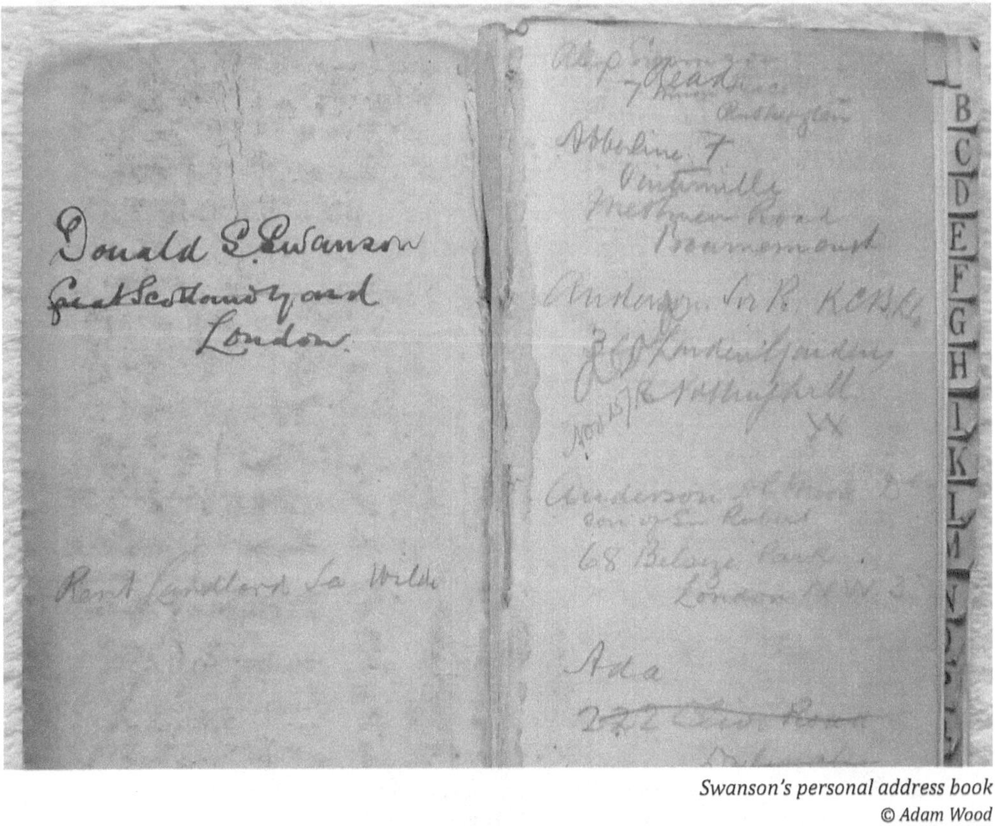

Swanson's personal address book
© Adam Wood

A.C. C.I.D.

Mr Williamson
Supt Shore
&
Ch. Insp. Swanson
to see.
ACW 15.9.88

Seen 15.9.88
[Commissioner's signature]

Seen
AFW
15/9

I am convinced that the Whitechapel Murder case is one which can be successfully grappled with if it is systematically taken in hand. I go so far as to say that I could myself in a few days unravel the mystery provided I could spare the time & give undivided attention to it. I feel therefore the utmost importance to be attached to putting the whole Central Office work in this case in the hands of one man who will have nothing else to concern himself with. Neither you or I or Mr Williamson can do this. I therefore put it in the hands of Chief Inspr Swanson who must be acquainted with every detail. I look upon him for the time being as the eyes & ears of the Commr in this particular case.

He must have a room to himself, & every paper, every document, every report, every telegram must pass through his hands. He must be consulted on every telegram subject. I would not send any directions anywhere on the

First page of a memorandum by Sir Charles Warren appointing Chief Inspector Donald Swanson to act as the Commissioner's 'eyes and ears' in the Whitechapel murders case

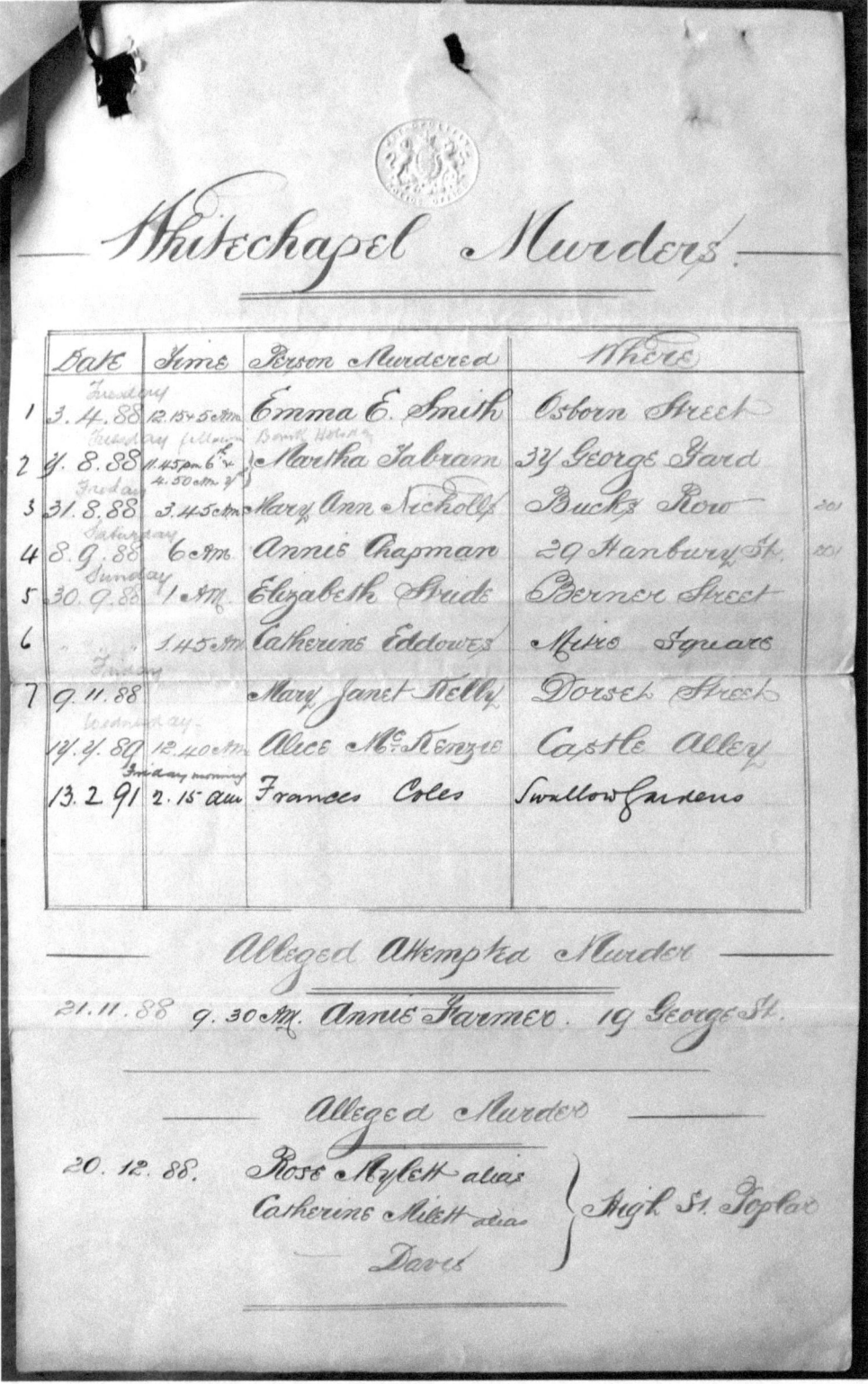

List of Whitechapel murder victims. Only the entry for Frances Coles is written in Swanson's hand, suggesting that the document was prepared for the detective by a secretary

Swanson's list comparing witness descriptions of Jack the Ripper
© The National Archives / photograph Adam Wood

Comparison of the descriptions given of the men who were observed near the scene at the time of the several murders.

	Annie Chapman	Murder of Elizabeth Stride			Eddowes
	Description of man seen by Mrs Long at 5.30	Man seen at 12.35 by Police Constable	First man seen by Schwartz with woman at 12.45.	Man seen on the opposite side of the street by Schwartz.	Man seen with woman at 1.35.
Age.	40	28.	30	35.	30.
Height.		5ft 7 ins	5ft 5 ind	5ft 11 ins	5ft 7 or 8 in
Complexion		dark	fair	fresh	
Hair.			dark	light brown	
Moustache		small dark	small brown	brown	fair
Face.			full		
Figure.			broad shouldered		medium build
Coat.	q. dark	black diagonal	dark jacket	dark with overcoat	pepper and salt colour; loose jacket
Trousers.			dark		
Hat.		Hard felt.	black cap with peak	old black hat; hard felt; wide brim.	grey cloth cap with peak of same color.
Collar.		white collar and tie			
Remarks.	Looked like a foreigner.			clay pipe in his mouth.	Reddish handkerchief tied in a knot round his neck; looked like a sailor.

Left: On duty at Epsom Races; Centre: Rare leisure activities; Right: Taking a well-earned rest

Donald and Julia Swanson circa 1898, their twentieth wedding anniversary

Donald Sutherland Swanson boating in front of Thurso Castle during a holiday visit circa 1900

Sketch believed to be by Swanson's niece Peterishea Alexander

Det. Superintendent Donald Swanson's Pension Certificate

In the back garden of Presburg Road, 1920s

Seated left to right: Julia and her sister Ada Nevill Standing: Douglas, Alice and Donald Swanson

Remembrance book for Donald Swanson

Final resting place of Donald Sutherland Swanson
© *Adam Wood*

Left to right: Ada Mary Swanson ('Sis'), Jim Swanson's wife Peg and Alice Julia Swanson ('Lal') outside Orchard Cottage in the 1970s, where Donald Swanson's papers resided from 1946 to 1981

Left: Donald Swanson's copy of Sir Robert Anderson's autobiography
Right: Jim Swanson, Executor of Alice Swanson's will.
On the left is elder brother Donald William Swanson, who first discovered the Swanson marginalia

My Official Life

people of that class in the East End will not give up one of their number to Gentile justice.

And the result proved that our diagnosis was right on every point. For I may say at once that "undiscovered murders" are rare in London, and the "Jack-the-Ripper" crimes are not within that category. And if the Police here had powers such as the French Police possess, the murderer would have been brought to justice. Scotland Yard can boast that not even the subordinate officers of the department will tell tales out of school, and it would ill become me to violate the unwritten rule of the service. So I will only add here that the "Jack-the-Ripper" letter which is preserved in the Police Museum at New Scotland Yard is the creation of an enterprising London journalist.

Having regard to the interest attaching to this case, I am almost tempted to disclose the identity of the murderer and of the pressman who wrote the letter above referred to. But no public benefit would result from such a course, and the traditions of my old department would suffer. I will merely add that the only person who had ever had a good view of the murderer unhesitatingly identified the suspect the instant he was confronted with him; but he refused to give evidence against him.

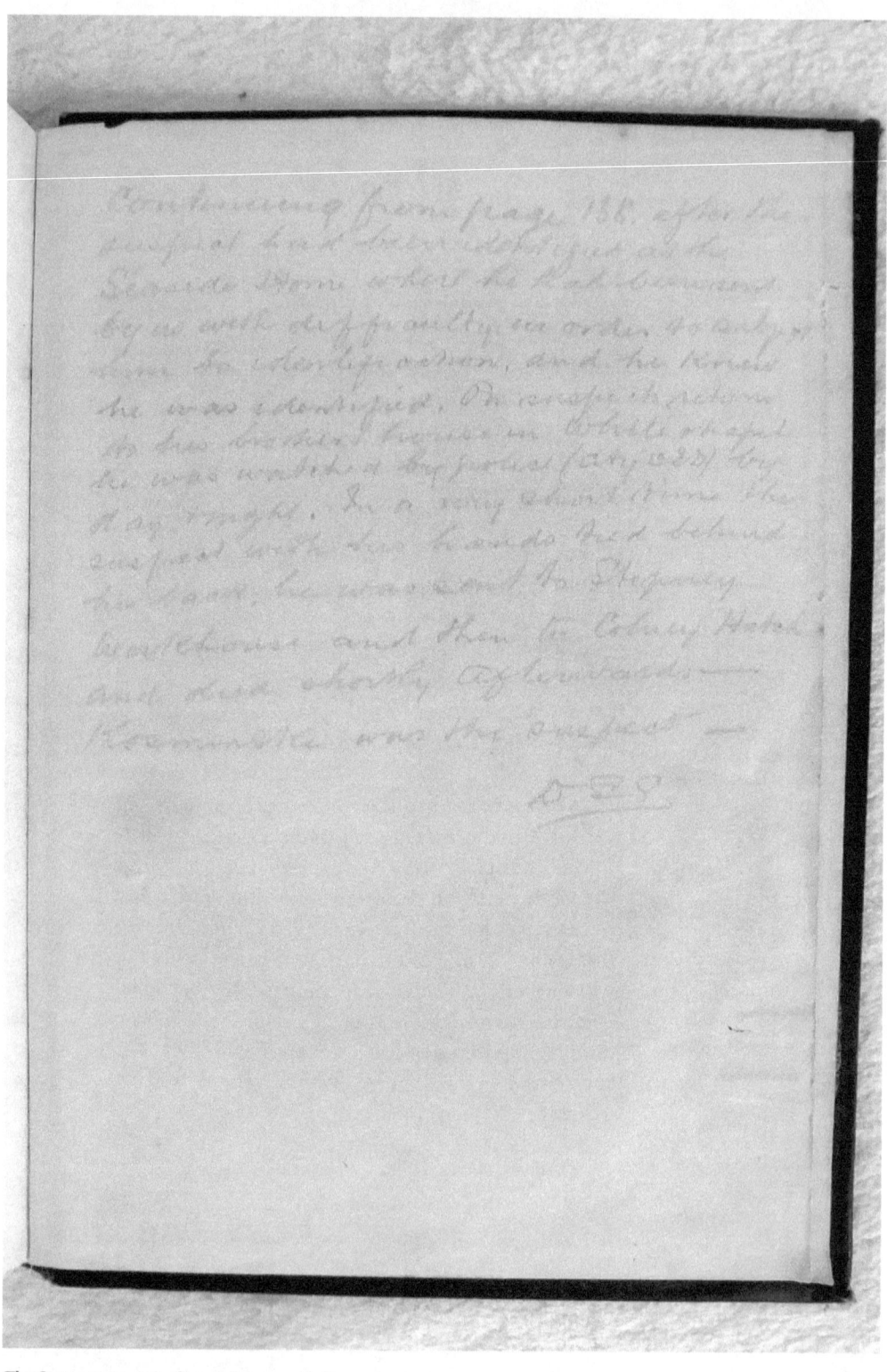

Continuing from page 138, after the suspect had been identified at the Seaside Home where he had been sent by us with difficulty in order to subject him to identification, and he knew he was identified. On suspect's return to his brother's house in Whitechapel he was watched by police (City CID) by day & night. In a very short time the suspect with his hands tied behind his back, he was sent to Stepney Workhouse and then to Colney Hatch and died shortly afterwards — Kosminski was the suspect —

D.S.S.

The Swanson marginalia: endpaper notations
© Adam Wood

FOURTEEN

Eyes and Ears

Dark clouds would begin to gather rapidly for Donald Swanson just a month after his landmark 40th birthday, when on 15th September 1888, a week after the murder of a woman in London's East End, Commissioner Sir Charles Warren issued a memorandum to the newly-appointed Assistant Commissioner (Crime), Robert Anderson, in which he expressed his determination to get to the bottom of the matter:

> I am convinced that the Whitechapel murder case is one which can be successfully grappled with, if it is systematically taken in hand. I go so far as to say that I could myself in a few days unravel the mystery provided I could spare the time & give undivided attention to it. I feel therefore the utmost importance to be attached to putting the whole Central Office work in the hands of Chief Inspr. Swanson who must be acquainted with every detail. I look upon him for the time being as being as the eyes & ears of the Commr. in this particular case.
>
> He must have a room to himself, & every paper, every document, every report every telegram must pass through his hands. He must be consulted on every subject. I would not send any directions anywhere on the subject of the murder without consulting him. I give him the whole responsibility. On the other hand he should consult Mr. Williamson you or myself on every important particular before any action unless there is some extreme urgency.
>
> I find that a most important letter was sent to Divn. yesterday without his seeing it. This is quite in error & should not occur again. All the papers in Central Office on the subject of the murder must be kept in his room & plans of the positions &c.
>
> I must have this matter at once put on a proper footing so as to be a guide for the future in cases of importance.
>
> Everything depends upon a careful compliance with these directions.
>
> Every document, letter received or telegram on the subject should go to

his room before being directed, & he should be responsible for its being directed where necessary. This is [to] avoid the possibility of document being delayed or action retarded.

The memorandum was circulated to Det. Chief Constable Dolly Williamson, Det. Superintendent John Shore and Swanson himself by Assistant Commissioner (Administrative) Alexander Carmichael Bruce, with the two senior officers confirming sight of the order by signing it on the same day.[1]

Anderson had been appointed as James Monro's replacement on 25th August,[2] to take up his new duties on 1st September.[3] Complaining of exhaustion, however, his doctor, Thomas Gilbart-Smith, recommended that he take two months' "complete rest", to be followed by a further two months' sick leave, but with Warren already away on vacation the new Assistant Commissioner would have to wait for his own break.[4]

Warren wrote from his French hotel on 28th August to say that he expected to return to London around 7th September, and suggested that Anderson take his leave then. Referring to the troubles leading up to Bloody Sunday the previous year, the Commissioner hoped that Anderson would be fit to begin his duties sooner than the two months recommended by Dr. Gilbart-Smith, thereby being in place should more disturbances occur, writing: "If a month will be enough to put your throat right I think we can manage it."[5]

Anderson would eventually leave for Switzerland on Saturday, 8th September, completely unaware that in the early hours of that day a woman had been brutally murdered in the back yard of 29 Hanbury Street in Spitalfields, in London's squalid East End.

The troubles of the Home Office and high-ranking police officials were far from the collective mind of those grinding out a living in the poverty-stricken streets ironically just a few minutes' walk from the City of London, the financial centre of the Empire.

As the industrial age had resulted in booming profits and the rapid expansion of the railway network, so these central termini and major thoroughfares needed land on which to be built. As we have seen in Chapter 2, the development of New Oxford Street and Shaftesbury Avenue saw the notorious St Giles rookery demolished, many of its 5,000 impoverished residents relocating to similar accommodation in East London. Further dilapidated housing was cleared to the north and east of the square mile, with the poor displaced also moving to areas such as Whitechapel and Aldgate, straddling the Commercial Road out of the City, with the Docks to the south, and the twin thoroughfares of Commercial Street and Brick Lane snaking northwards to Spitalfields half a mile away, where Hawksmoor's magnificent Christ Church from the early Eighteenth century stood as a reminder of former glories.

The expansion of the railways saw Whitechapel gain its own station in November 1876, when the East London Railway was extended north from Wapping to Liverpool Street. Aldgate station was opened at the same time,[6] reported with admiration:

> The front of the station is in High Street, Aldgate, a door or two from the old church of St. Botolph, and opposite to the Minories. The situation of the terminus is admirable, and will undoubtedly bring the company an enormous amount of business. Within a short distance are the London and the St. Katherine's Docks, Fenchurch and Leadenhall Streets, the Commercial Road, and the densely-populated neighbourhoods of Whitechapel and Tower Hill. Thus the eastern extremity of the City and the best business parts of the East End will be brought within a few minutes' journey of Holborn and the West End of London...[7]

When the underground District Railway (now District line) was extended to Whitechapel from Mansion House in the City in 1884, a new station – Aldgate East – was created, opening in October 1884. The East London Railway service at Whitechapel was withdrawn in 1885.[8]

It seems barely credible that grinding poverty could existing on the magnitude it did in the late Victorian era just minutes from the City, yet when Charles Booth published his *Inquiry into the Life and Labour of the People in London*, a survey into the capital's working class, he found that of nearly half a million people living in the East End, 160,000 – 35% of the local population – were on or below the poverty line.

Social reformer Henrietta Barnett described the living conditions in Whitechapel which she and her husband Canon Samuel Barnett found on moving to the parish in 1873, commenting that the area was

> covered with a network of courts and alleys. None of these courts had roads. In some the houses were three storeys high and hardly six feet apart, the sanitary accommodation being pits in the cellars; in other courts the houses were lower, wooden and dilapidated, a stand pipe at the end providing the only water. Each chamber was the home of a family who sometimes owned their indescribable furniture, but in most cases the rooms were let out furnished for 8d a night. In many instances

broken windows had been repaired with paper and rags, the bannisters had been used for firewood, and the paper hung from the walls which were the residence of countless vermin.[9]

When writer John Mackay visited such a court in 1888 to study the area for his book *The Anarchists: A Picture of Civilization at the Close of the Nineteenth Century*, he and a friend received a startling welcome:

> Sometimes a window was half opened, a bushy head thrust out, and shy, curious eyes followed half in fear, half in hate, the wholly unusual sight of the strangers. A man was hammering at a broken cart which obstructed the whole width of the street. He did not respond to the greeting of the passers-by; stupefied, he stared at them as at an apparition from another world; a woman who had been cowering in a door corner, motionless, rose terrified, pressed her child with both hands against her breast hardly covered with rags, and propped herself, as if to offer resistance, against the wall, not once taking her eye off the two men; only a crowd of children playing in the mud of the street did not look up, — they might have been taken for idiots, so noiselessly did they pursue their joyless games.[10]

Yet despite the dire poverty, the majority of East Enders were hard-working and suffered extreme hardship in order to pay the rent on their scant accommodation, which was collected weekly. Should a tenant lose their employment or fall ill and therefore be unable to work, the landlords were swift to react. The evicted faced an alternative of the casual ward, the dreaded workhouse or, more probably, the common lodging house – the doss house – of which there were nearly 150 registered in the East End, offering a total of over 6,000 beds.[11] In 1888, the most well-known – or most infamous – were on Flower and Dean Street, George Street and Dorset Street in Spitalfields, within a short stone's throw from the splendour of Christ Church.

The cheaper doss houses charged 4d for a single bed for the night, arranged in loose 'dormitories', with a common kitchen area downstairs. Many of those living in the East End spent every night in a doss house, some remaining faithful to their own particular favourite.

The majority of men worked as carmen, labourers, hawkers, cabinet-makers or general dealers,[12] with women and children often working from their meagre rooms undertaking work such as making match boxes or stuffing mattresses. But faced with these circumstances, with the constant pressure of supplying food and a roof over their head, it was no surprise that many women resorted to prostitution on occasion.

As one commentator remarked, "Virtue is easy enough when a woman has plenty to eat, and a character to keep, but it's quite different when a girl is starving."[13]

The East End had long attracted immigrants, many as a result of persecution or poverty. French Protestant Huguenots had fled their homeland in the seventeenth century, many settling in Spitalfields. They were followed by the Irish in the eighteenth and nineteenth centuries.

By the 1880s, living alongside the native poor was a large and rapidly-growing community of Jewish immigrants. Many had fled their homeland as a result of pogroms inflicted upon Russian and Polish Jews by Tsar Alexander III, who blamed them for the assassination in 1881 of his father, Alexander II. They had been confined to an area on the western edge of the Russian Empire some 400 by 600 miles known as the Pale of Settlement since the late 18th century which had seen a steady migration to other parts of Europe.[14]

By 1880 there were approximately 60,000 Jews in Britain, of which 46,000 were in London. Contemporary analyst Joseph Jacobs estimated that half of those in the capital were either working class or deemed 'poor', in receipt of some form of relief.[15]

With vast numbers leaving the Pale as a result of the introduction of the repressive May Laws of 1882 and heading for what they hoped was a different life, the Jewish population rapidly expanded.

When weary immigrants finally arrived on British shores, docking at Gravesend, they were met by an officer from H.M. Customs and a medical inspector from the Port of London Port Sanitary Authority. After the First and Second Class passengers had disembarked, those travelling Third Class – the vast majority – were subjected to a basic medical inspection. Those found to be suffering from diseases such as cholera, yellow fever or smallpox were detained at the floating isolation hospital of the Port Sanitary Authority, while those who appeared in good health were allowed to continue their journey to one of the landing stages at St. Katharine's Dock, Customs Wharf or Irongate Stairs.[16]

As soon as they disembarked they fell victim to 'crimps', conmen who preyed on the new arrivals who were often able to speak in the migrants' native tongue and, offering a helping hand in a strange new country, subsequently tricking them out of their meagre money and possessions.

Some kind-hearted Jewish residents of the area around the docks and the East End offered what help they could, and around 1880 a baker named Simon Cohen offered a disused room in his Whitechapel shop for poor immigrants to sleep in, and provided them with bread. Despite his good intentions conditions were poor, and a writer to the *Jewish Chronicle* was not shy with his opinion:

> At 19 Church Lane Whitechapel there is a refuge for Jewish people who are out of employment... It is obvious that this place of shelter cannot encourage people to be idle, because its abject misery is worse than any workhouse, and it provides less food. There is absolutely no sleeping accommodation except for a wooden floor. The only kind of daily food they get is rice and tea and bread, and this is very irregular. Let us get a 'responsible committee' or... let a few gentlemen see if they cannot get a few cheap mattresses for the older men to lie upon at night and some blankets or rugs. The place, such as it is, is maintained by two co-religionists in very humble circumstances.[17]

Despite these and other negative comments, attention was drawn to Cohen's refuge and he soon found an increasing number of homeless poor Jews at his door. It was not to last. Sanitary inspectors condemned the building as unfit for purpose, forcing him to close.

Despite this setback, the well-intentioned work carried out at Church Lane attracted those with greater means than Simon Cohen and a committee including Samuel Montagu M.P. and banker Hermann Landau, himself a comparatively recent arrival in London, who would later describe the situation at that time for poor Jewish immigrants:

> Many of these people had previously been obliged to sleep in lofts and other miserable places of temporary rest. They were made the easy victims of crimps and of persons who offered to act the part of the Good Samaritan by assisting them to their destination, but were only too eager to take advantage of their ignorance to rob them of all they possessed. In some cases they were made the prey of the sweater, and sometimes the women folk were practically sold to brothels.[18]

A new body was founded, calling itself The Poor Jews' Temporary Shelter. Premises were acquired at 84 Leman Street, and while awaiting for the necessary work adapting the building for use as a shelter to be carried out by architect Lewis Solomon the Committee operated from temporary premises at 12 Great Garden Street,[19] and formally opened at Leman Street on 11th April 1886 with a Consecration Service by the Delegate Chief Rabbi.[20]

A Constitution, drawn up at the end of 1885, outlined the Shelter's aims:

> This Society is formed with a view to prevent new comers from being driven into the Mission House, or lapsing into pauperism, and becoming a burden on the Community. To this end a Refuge is established whereat, after due investigation, newly arrived immigrants can be lodged and fed (in accordance with the strictest Jewish requirements) in cases of utter destitution, or else at as low a charge as possible, until it be determined whether they can permanently support themselves by honest labour here, or must, in their own interest as well as that of the community, be repatriated, or directed to other lands.

The Shelter would provide accommodation for a maximum of 30 at one time; when this number was exceeded, the surplus inmates would be lodged elsewhere at the Shelter's cost. It would be open primarily to adult males who had been in England less that six months, and were out of employment. They would be provided with at least two meals a day, no charge being made either for food or shelter to those absolutely destitute, and a charge of not more than 2d per meal for food and 2d per night for shelter being made to those who can afford to pay.

The Committee made up of 15 members met weekly to review the case of each applicant; each successful applicant was able to remain at the Shelter for a maximum of 14 days, and could not be re-admitted. A Superintendent residing on the premises received applications, and kept registers and accounts.

The running of the Shelter was funded by subscriptions of a minimum of 1d per week, paid either weekly, monthly, quarterly or yearly, along with donations gratefully received from more wealthy benefactors.[21]

By 1888 the Shelter had become an important institution within the Jewish community, not only for offering temporary accommodation to those arriving in the East End, but also actively seeking to dissuade many others from embarking on the voyage to England. In their introduction to the Third Annual Report, published in October 1888, the Committee addressed their critics:

> The persistent opponents of the principle of free immigration have been actively engaged during the past twelve months in drawing the attention of the country to the foreign population in the East End, and attempts have been made to prove that the volume of immigration during the past few years has been abnormally large. It is reassuring, however, to perceive the almost unanimous declaration of 'official' opinion against such an assumption. The Poor Jews' Temporary Shelter claims not only to have diverted a considerable stream of immigration from this country,

but also to have been the direct means of discouraging many from leaving their native land.

The Board gave such an example:

> On September 24th [1888], Joseph Markowitz, aged 20, was admitted as an inmate. He had in his possession 85 Marks (equivalent to £4 4s 0d sterling). He knew no trade, having earned his living in his native country by teaching the Talmud. It being made clear to him that there was no prospect for him in their country, within three days of his admission he was on his way home again with the money he brought with him intact. Illustrations such as this could be multiplied a hundredfold. Had the Shelter not been available for these hapless wanderers to our shores, they would have inevitably got into the toils of those merciless sharks who watch for the arrival of such poor foreign houses, detain them to their dens, misnamed cheap lodging-houses, detain them till their scanty means are exhausted, and then cast them on to the street friendless and penniless. In the face of this state of things, surely the necessity for a temporary refuge like this must be universally admitted.

The positive official opinion welcomed by the Committee of the Shelter had been made before the House of Commons Immigration Committee on 28th April 1888 by Robert Giffen, Assistant Secretary to the Commercial Department of the Board of Trade, and Dr William Ogle, Superintendent of Statistics at the Registrar General's Office.[22]

On 19th March of that year J.B. Lakeman, H.M. Superintending Inspector of Workshops, visited with one of the Shelter's most vocal opponents, anti-Semitic campaigner Arnold White, writing in the Visitors' Book: "A shelter indeed – a boon to the helpless and a place of refuge for the destitute."[23]

On 4th May Maurice Eden Paul paid a visit.[24] A medical student at the nearby London Hospital, Paul was from a privileged background but had assisted Beatrice Webb and Ella Pycroft in the management of the East End Dwelling Company's St Katharine's Buildings, and in 1886 had joined Charles Booth's Board of Statistical Inquiry.[25]

The officers of the Met's local H Division were also interested. On 24th May Sergeant John Greenacre from Arbour Square police station commented "I think you should be registered." Three weeks later, on 14th June, Det. Chief Inspector John West from Leman Street police station, just along from the Shelter, made an inspection and found it "Very clean."[26]

Armed with the findings of his officers, on 27th July Superintendent

Thomas Arnold appeared before the House of Commons Immigration Committee giving the views of the local police force. He stated that many Jewish people arriving in the East End were "in a very destitute condition, their clothes ragged. They were dirty in their habits and persons."[27] He had often seen those arriving with no money "wandering around the streets aimlessly," and acknowledged the work done by the Poor Jews' Temporary Shelter.[28]

The Third Annual Report – covering the period November 1887 to October 1888 – revealed that a total of 1,322 Jewish immigrants had passed through the doors of the Shelter. Almost half of these were aged between 21 and 30. While many stayed for just a few days before heading on to other destinations, almost a quarter remained in the Shelter for the maximum 14 days allowed, before leaving and joining the Jewish population of Whitechapel. Of the 1,322, half either remained in the East End or left the Shelter without specifying their destination; but most likely also remaining in the area.[29]

Those who had enjoyed a few days' respite in the Shelter before being swallowed up in the East End's growing population of Russian and Polish Jewish immigrants joined those families who had arrived at the docks and, crimps notwithstanding, had bypassed the Poor Jews' Temporary Shelter and simply disappeared into the dens of Whitechapel, Goodman's Fields, Aldgate and Spitalfields. Some joined relatives already in London, others with no relations to welcome them arrived armed with the address of someone who had previously arrived who was from the same town or village in the Pale, and who might lend a helping hand.

By 1891, out of a population of 227,849 living in Whitechapel, St George's-in-the-East and Mile End Old Town,[30] almost 22,000 were Russian and Polish Jews – some 82% of that demographic who had settled in London.[31]

A report on immigration into London made in 1894 outlined the reasons why Whitechapel had become the heartbeat of the Jewish community:

> Another powerful influence tending towards concentration [of Jewish immigrants] is the fact that the industries and handicrafts which offer the most likely means of livelihood to the untrained foreigner have become strongly rooted in Whitechapel and the adjacent districts, and hence tend to perpetuate and increase the attraction which these districts exercise on the Jewish poor. If we add to all these influences the proximity of Jewish institutions, both religious and secular, which

are planted in or near Whitechapel – the synagogues and the charities connected therewith, the 'chevras', the great Jews' Free School with its offer of free clothing and partially free board, the Jewish Board of Guardians and the Jewish soup kitchen, not to speak of the proximity of the tradesmen who supply Kosher meat and other special forms of Jewish food – we shall arrive at some idea of the magnitude of the forces which made for local concentration.[32]

According to the same report, there were 180 workshops in Whitechapel and Aldgate, with by far the most common occupation being that of tailor.[33] Unfortunately, that industry was riddled with so-called 'Sweaters'.

A manufacturer, keen to produce a vast number of garments as cheaply as possible, would give his work to a middleman who undertakes to do the work at an agreed rate; sometimes these middlemen would pass on the work to a sub-contractor. Eventually the materials would pass into the hands of the final contractor – the sweater – and it would be he who employed men, women and sometimes children to actually perform the work. As the profit per garment reduced as it was passed down the chain, so the sweater would pay the lowest amount possible to his workers. His workroom would typically be the room in which he and his family lived, or perhaps a basement or wash-house, often not larger than 9 or 10 feet square, into which up to a dozen workers might be crowded.[34]

The workers – often newly-arrived from overseas and unable to find any other work – performed their duties for sixteen to eighteen hours a day. Known as 'greeners', these workers soon learn enough to become employers themselves.[35] A report from a Select Committee on the sweating system dated 18th December 1888 estimated that there were at least 2,000 sweaters in the East End; some streets in Whitechapel had one or more sweating establishment in every house.[36]

The English-Jewish journalist Lucien Wolf offered his thoughts in an article entitled 'The Jews in London' for *The Graphic*:

> Whatever the merits or demerits of the 'sweating system', it is incontestable that the phenomenal industry and thrift of the poor Jewish immigrants from foreign countries (who in nine cases out of ten enter this trade), together with the activity and enterprise of their Jewish employers, have made the trade what it is. But for the Jewish factor in the clothing trade, foreign imports would have long ago taken the place of home-made goods, the prices would be high, and the large export trade in ready-made apparel would hardly exist. The ready-made

boot industry in the East End of London stands somewhat on the same footing, both with regard to its origin and its relations with Jews.

Duke's Place and Spitalfields Market are important centres of the fruit trade, which, together with the cigar industry, is also very largely in Jewish hands. One of the sights in the locality is the Sunday market in Petticoat Lane. Improvements recently carried out by the Board of Works have robbed the market of much of its ancient glory, but it is still a great emporium for secondhand goods of every kind, and offers considerable advantages to purchasers of the small artisan class. The majority of the stall-keepers are Jews, engaged in other businesses during the remainder of the week."[37]

But the constant influx of Jews arriving into the East End obviously created mass overcrowding, and some saw the demand for lodgings as an opportunity to make money by sub-letting. One police officer, tasked with investigating the living conditions of the Jewish population of Whitechapel, recalled:

I have come across a case in which ten people lived in one small room, while a passage in the house was let as a living-room, and the whole house was in a disgustingly filthy condition; while in another house a small front room was used as a shop and also as a bedroom for three men and three women. For families living in one room to take in lodgers is a common occurrence. Even basements and coal-cellars are let.

...when you have one room occupied at night by more than one family (lodgers of both sexes being taken in), with merely a cubicle division of sheets, and the same room crammed by day with people using it as a workshop, it is clear that the conditions do not make for health, cleanliness, or morality.

...The foreign shopkeeper, costermonger, or window salesman sells at lower prices [than the English] because he is satisfied with smaller profits and because the standard of life is low. Thus the ill-feeling is increased, especially as he takes an unfair advantage by keeping his place open in the small hours of the morning.

Contrary to the English practice, the foreign costers will pitch outside a shop and sell the same articles as that shop; they quite obscure the shop fronts. They undersell the English costers... The Jews mostly deal in imperishable goods, and when an English coster goes off his pitch to buy at the market, the Jew coster snaps up his place, and the police have no power to turn him out.[38]

With rents going up as the immigrants were willing to sublet each room to other families, and wages lowered through the cheaper workforce, bitterness began to grow towards the immigrant from the native population. With the Jewish population preferring to deal almost solely with one another, a colony grew so that by 1888 large areas of Whitechapel and Aldgate, spreading north towards Spitalfields, were populated by Jews.

Many immigrants who had stayed in the East End and established roots with both family and business sought to become British subjects. Each application required the support of four British-born referees, who would testify to the good character of the applicant. These were usually someone they knew through business. Each application had to be vetted by the Metropolitan Police, who would send local officers to investigate the details provided and, providing all was as claimed, a Certificate of Naturalisation would be issued by the Home Office.

One such applicant was Samuel Kosminski, a single 29-year-old[39] furrier who had been born in Kalisch, Poland and had arrived in England in 1880, setting up home first at Loraine Road in Holloway and then at 357 City Road, where he was residing at the time of his naturalisation request in June 1887. He had set up business at 146 Aldersgate Street in the City of London some years earlier. Kosminski presented the details of five British-born acquaintances and his application was looked into by Sergeant James Nearn of the local N Division C.I.D. The officer's report, which concluded that the applicant was "in a fair way of business, he appears to be a responsible man and worthy of the certificate he seeks," was approved by Det. Chief Inspector George Greenham at Scotland Yard[40] and forwarded to Commissioner James Monro, who wasted no time submitting the completed application to the Home Office. On 14th June 1887 Home Secretary Henry Matthews issued Samuel Kosminski with his Certificate of Naturalisation.[41]

According to one contemporary of Donald Swanson, not all applications were as they seemed:

> Of course there are certain expenses connected with this process; and some of these people would make extraordinary efforts to raise the money to meet these expenses. Many of them were men engaged in sweating dens, with families including sometimes fourteen members. They would pay in some trifling subscription, perhaps to the amount of about eighteenpence, to some one of certain well-known agents, resident in and about Whitechapel. These agents make a pretty fat living out of it. The usual modus operandi is that the agent forms a club; when there

are members enough for the sum of about seven pounds to be raised in weekly or monthly subscriptions a draw takes place. The winner of the draw then makes his application for naturalisation. The agent defrays all expenses, and pockets the balance of the money raised. Then the process is gone through all over again, and so on.[42]

Aside from applications for naturalisation by Jewish businessmen, perhaps the most efficient instrument in the 'anglicisation' of the immigrant was sending their children to school. A Board of Trade investigation into immigration from eastern Europe found that in 1893 more than 3,500 Jewish children attended the Jews' Free School on Bell Lane in Spitalfields. Coming mostly from households which spoke no English, the adopted-country's language was soon introduced to the immigrant families. Similarly, at the Berner Street School in the same year 925 Jewish children were taught, 864 of whom had been born abroad or had foreign fathers. 719 Jewish children were sent to the Hanbury Street School, just 22 of whom were not born abroad or had an immigrant father.[43]

In the same report it was recorded that while 5,240 people had been admitted to the Whitechapel workhouse during 1893, just 30 were of Polish or Russian nationality. Similarly, while almost 6,000 people were admitted to the Whitechapel Infirmary, only 59 were Russian or Polish. These figures meant that despite forming 18% of the population of Whitechapel at that time, the Poles and Russian Jews contributed less than 1% to the number of paupers in the district.[44] The Jewish community really did keep to their own.

This, then, was the uneasy existence for the population of London's East End at the time of the Whitechapel murders, with friction never far away. In fact, on the very day that Donald Swanson was appointed to head the investigation into the Hanbury Street murder, the *East London Observer* reported that the ill-feeling had begun to simmer over:

> On Saturday in several quarters of East London the crowds who assembled in the streets began to assume a very threatening attitude towards the Hebrew population of the district. It was repeatedly asserted that no Englishman could have perpetrated such a horrible crime as that of Hanbury Street, and that it must have been done by a Jew – and forthwith the crowds began to threaten and abuse such of the unfortunate Hebrews as they found in the streets. Happily, the presence of the large number of police prevented a riot actually taking place.[45]

Early in the morning of Saturday, 8th September 1888, 56-year-old John Davis went downstairs from his room on the third floor of No. 29 Hanbury Street in Spitalfields. As he stepped into the ground-floor hallway he noticed that the front door, which lead out onto Hanbury Street, was wide open. Mr. Davis thought nothing of it, as in the two weeks he and his family had taken lodgings there he had never known the door to be locked.

Davis turned toward the back door and the yard beyond, where the outside privy was situated. It was 6.00am.

As he pushed the door open and started down the few steps, to his left he saw the body of a woman lying between the steps and the fence separating the yard to that of No. 27. She was lying on her back, with her head turned towards the house. Davis turned and ran down the interior passageway and out into Hanbury Street.[46]

He saw a man – Henry Holland – passing on his way to work at Chiswell Street, and implored him to "Come and look in the back yard." Holland went through the passageway and into the yard, where he saw the body but did not touch it. He set off to find a policeman, eventually seeing an officer by Christ Church on Commercial Street. Despite Holland telling him of the murder, the constable was on Fixed Point duty and therefore had to refuse accompanying him back to Hanbury Street; he was unable to leave his post.[47]

By this time Davis had gone to the gate of Bailey's packing-case manufacturers at 23a Hanbury Street, where employees James Kent and James Green were standing. They followed Davis into No. 29 and saw the body as they stood at the back door, without actually going into the yard.[48]

Davis set off for Commercial Street Police Station to report his discovery.[49]

On the way he met H Division's uniformed Divisional Inspector Joseph Chandler, who was on duty in Commercial Street itself,[50] and after being told of the murder the officer made his way to the scene. He later reported how he

> ...found a woman lying on her back, dead, left arm resting on left breast, legs drawn up, abducted, small intestines and flap of the abdomen lying on right side, above right shoulder attached by a cord with the rest of the intestines inside the body; two flaps of skin from the lower part of the

from the Illustrated Police News, 15th September 1888

*Det. Inspector Frederick Abberline
from the Pall Mall Gazette, 28th January 1885*

abdomen lying in a large quantity of blood above the left shoulder; throat cut deeply from left and back in a jagged manner right around the throat.

Chandler immediately sent for the Divisional Surgeon, Dr. George Bagster Phillips of nearby Spital Square, who examined the body *in situ* before it was removed to the Whitechapel mortuary.

Chandler examined the yard, and where the head had lain found half a dozen spots of blood 18 inches up the wall of the house, ranging in size from a sixpence down to a point. On the fence dividing No. 29 from No. 27 he found "smears of blood" about 14 inches from the ground.[51]

29 Hanbury Street consisted of eight rooms, in which seventeen people lived. All were searched and their inhabitants questioned, as were those in the adjacent properties.[52]

In the absence of H Division's Det. Superintendent Thomas Arnold, who was on annual leave, immediate enquiries into the murder were entrusted to Inspector Chandler,[53] and Det. Sergeants Thick and Leach of the local C.I.D. On the day of the murder Acting Superintendent John West submitted a request to Scotland Yard that Det. Inspector Frederick Abberline be deputed from Central Office to assist the investigation,[54] and the senior detective was instructed to do so by Det. Chief Constable Dolly Williamson the same day.[55]

Since working with Donald Swanson on Y Division in 1871, Abberline had been promoted Det. Inspector in 1873, and three days later – on 13th March – transferred to H Division, Whitechapel. In April 1878 he was appointed Local Inspector, head of the C.I.D. – a position he held until February 1887, when he was transferred to A Division and then Central Office, Scotland Yard that November.[56]

Abberline's replacement as head of H Division's C.I.D. was Det. Inspector Edmund Reid, who had seen his own career move in the opposite direction geographically, having been appointed Det. Inspector at Scotland Yard in 1885 and then moving to the East End and J Division, Bethnal Green in 1886 before assuming Abberline's position a year later.[57]

Now, with Reid on holiday as well as Det. Superintendent Arnold, it was decided that Abberline's vast experience of the East End would be invaluable in leading the enquiry into the Hanbury Street murder.

In fact, the experienced detective had already been assisting with the investigation into another brutal killing in Spitalfields just eight days earlier, when in the early hours of Friday, 31st August the body of Mary Ann Nichols was found in Buck's Row. She had turned 43-years-old five days before.

Like the victim found in Hanbury Street, Mary Ann had not only been murdered, but her body terribly mutilated. Her throat had been cut with such severity that she had been almost decapitated, and a large, deep jagged wound had opened up her abdomen from below the ribs to her pelvis, severing internal tissue.[58] She was taken to the mortuary at the Whitechapel Infirmary Workhouse in Eagle Place, Old Montague Street and lay there until the afternoon of 6th September, when her body was placed in a polished elm coffin and transported to undertaker Henry Smith, whose premises were, by sad coincidence, in Hanbury Street,[59] where the body of another murder victim would be discovered two days later. Mary Ann Nichols was buried in the City of London Cemetery at Manor Park. By the time she was lowered into the ground, Det. Inspector Frederick Abberline was assisting local C.I.D. with their investigations.[60]

Following the murder in Hanbury Street the two investigations were merged, and, inevitably, brought fears that the death of Mary Ann Nichols was caused by the same hand which had dispatched two more local women in recent months; Emma Smith,[61] who died of peritonitis at the London Hospital on 4th April 1888 after being horrifically attacked near the Taylor Brothers' Mustard and Cocoa Mill on Osborn Street, a blunt instrument thrust into her vagina with great force,[62] and Martha

Tabram,[63] stabbed 39 times and left to die on the first floor landing of George Yard Buildings on 7th August.[64]

The press soon voiced what many were thinking, with *The Times* commenting that the murder of Mary Ann Nichols

> has so many points of similarity with the murder of two other women in the same neighbourhood – one Martha Turner, as recently as August 7, and the other less that 12 months previously – that the police admit their belief that the three crimes are the work of one individual. All three women were of the class called 'unfortunates', each so very poor, that robbery could have formed no motive for the crime, and each was murdered in such a similar fashion, that doubt as to the crime being the work of one and the same villain almost vanishes, particularly when it is remembered that all three murders were committed within a distance of 300 yards from each other. These facts have led the police to almost abandon the idea of a gang being abroad to wreak vengeance on women of this class for not supplying them with money. Detective Inspector Abberline, of the Criminal Investigation Department, and Detective Inspector Helson, J Division, are both of opinion that only one person, and that a man, had a hand in the latest murder. It is understood that the investigation into the George Yard mystery is proceeding hand-in-hand with that of Buck's Row.[65]

The Metropolitan Police's file on the Whitechapel murders would begin with Emma Smith, who was followed by Martha Tabram and then Mary Ann Nichols. Added to them was the Hanbury Street victim, who was soon to be identified.

As per procedure with unidentified corpses, a photograph was taken of her in the mortuary by Joseph Martin of Cannon Street Road. H Division's photographer of choice of the 'unknown dead', it was Martin who had also photographed Martha Tabram and Mary Ann Nichols.[66]

The following description of the murdered woman was wired around all police stations:

> Age 45, length 5 ft, complexion fair, hair (wavy) dark brown, eyes blue, two teeth deficient in lower jaw, large thick nose; dress black figured jacket, brown bodice, black skirt, lace boots, all old and dirty.

Armed with this, enquiries in the immediate area by H Division officers, which included entering local common lodging houses, soon resulted in an identification of the victim by Timothy Donovan, the Deputy of Crossingham's Lodging House at 35 Dorset Street. He had known the victim for around 16 months; she was a prostitute, and had lodged at Crossingham's for the previous four months. He knew her by the name 'Annie Siffey', and it was under moniker this that Inspector Chandler created his report.[67]

It transpired that this unusual name was a result of Annie living for a while with a man who made iron sieves, and she was at that time widely known locally by the nickname 'Mrs. Sivvey'. This was in 1886, and the couple lived at 30 Dorset Street – another common lodging house – where they had made friends with Amelia Palmer and her husband Henry, an army pensioner who worked as a dock labourer. By early 1887 the sieve maker had left Annie, Mrs. Palmer seeing him in the City and being told that he was now living in Notting Hill, west London.[68]

Mrs. Palmer was able to identify the Hanbury Street victim by her real name – Annie Chapman.

She had been born Annie Eliza Smith in September 1841[69] out of wedlock to 19-year-old George Smith and 22-year-old Ruth Chapman, who subsequently married at Paddington, north-west London five months later, on 22nd February 1842.

Following the marriage George and Ruth would go on to have six further children.[70] George's service with the 2nd Life Guards saw the family constantly relocate as he was stationed at barracks between Knightsbridge and Windsor, west of London.[71]

By the time of the 1861 census 19-year-old Annie had found employment and was working as a housemaid to architect William Lewer at Duke Street in Westminster. But the suicide of her father George Smith in June 1863 saw her mother and younger siblings forced to move to 29 Montpelier Place in lower-middle class Knightsbridge, an area well-populated with those in domestic service. To supplement the family's income Ruth let out rooms, and one such lodger was a gentleman's coachman named John Chapman.[72]

On 1st May 1869 the 25-year-old John Chapman married Annie Smith, by then aged 27, at All Saints Church, Knightsbridge. The couple enjoyed a fairly comfortable lifestyle, with the accommodation provided with John's work seeing the family living in comfort in Bayswater, north west London, and then South Bruton Mews off Berkeley Square in Mayfair, and over the course of the next dozen years they welcomed several children into the family.[73] By 1881 the family had moved to Windsor, where John took a job as a domestic coachman.

It would appear that Annie Chapman had always enjoyed a drink, but the death from meningitis of first born Emily Ruth in 1882 was the catalyst for her descent into heavy drinking. In December that year her sisters Miriam and Emily persuaded Annie to admit herself to the Spelthorne Sanatorium at Feltham to seek treatment, and she would spend a year as a patient before returning home sober on 20th December 1883.

It would not take long for her to return to her old ways. Faced with dismissal from his job if he did not evict his wife from his lodgings, John Chapman realised he needed a regular income to care for the two young children who remained at home and took the latter decision. The couple separated in 1884, Annie probably moving back to Knightsbridge to be with her mother and sisters, supported by a maintenance payment of 10s a week from her husband.[74]

Over the course of the next two years Annie gradually made her way towards the East End, where she met the sieve maker, and soon found herself living in the common lodging houses of Spitalfields, predominantly those on Dorset Street.

Following John Chapman's sudden death on Christmas Day 1886 and the resulting cessation of her maintenance, Annie had sold flowers and undertaken crochet work to support herself, on occasion resorting to casual prostitution.

By September 1888 she had been staying at 35 Dorset Street, Crossingham's Lodging House, for around four months.[75] She had taken up with a bricklayer's labourer named Ted Stanley, who lived in lodgings of his own at 1 Osborn Street but would often visit Annie on a Saturday night, paying for a double bed for the two of them.[76]

On the afternoon of 7th September she was about to ejected from Crossingham's as she did not have the necessary money to pay for her bed. Despite being ill, she went out in search of the few pennies needed and met her friend Amelia Palmer on Dorset Street, telling her: "It's no use my giving way. I must pull myself together and go out and get some money or I shall have no lodgings."[77]

The last definite sighting of Annie Chapman alive was in the early hours of 8th September, when she left Crossingham's for what would be the last time, telling the Deputy "I have not any money now, but don't let the bed; I will be back soon."[78] As she left the lodging house the nightwatchman John Evans saw her enter Little Paternoster Row, walking in the direction of Brushfield Street. It was around 1.45am.[79]

At 5.30am Mrs. Elizabeth Long was walking along Hanbury Street towards Spitalfields Market. As she approached No. 29 she saw a man and woman leaning about the shutters of the house, with the man's back to her. As the woman was facing her, when Mrs. Long passed she clearly saw her face, and later identified the body of the victim lying in the mortuary as the same woman.

The man appeared to be "a foreigner" over 40 years old, a little taller than the woman. They were talking quite loudly, and Mrs. Long heard the man ask "Will you?", and the reply "Yes."[80]

At 5.25am a carpenter named Albert Cadosch living at 27 Hanbury Street went out to the privy in the back yard and heard soft voices on the other side of the fence, coming from the yard of No. 29. The only word he could make out properly was a woman's voice saying "No" as he returned into the house. A few minutes later he went out to the yard again[81] and heard a noise as if something had fallen against the fence.[82] He heard no further voices, nor rustling of clothes, and did not look over the fence, which was about 5ft 6in high. Cadosch then left No. 27 for his work via the front door, onto Hanbury Street. There was nobody in the street, and when he passed Christ Church on Commercial Street it was 32 minutes past 5.[83]

There is obviously some discrepancy here, as Mrs. Long claimed she heard the clock of the nearby Black Eagle Brewery strike the half-hour as she walked along Hanbury Street and saw the couple outside No. 29. According to Albert Cadosch's reckoning, however, the noises he heard coming from the yard of No. 29 took place around 5.28am; he fixed that time because it was 5.32am when he passed Christ Church a few minutes later. If both timings were correct, either the woman Mrs. Long saw was not Annie Chapman, or the noises heard by Cadosch were nothing to do with her murder; more likely is that one of them was out with their timing. A possible explanation is that Mrs. Long heard the clock strike the quarter-hour, and the man and woman she saw outside No. 29 had made their way through the passageway to the rear yard by the time Cadosch first went out to the privy of No. 27 ten minutes later. Alternatively, Cadosch might have been later than he estimated.

Either way, less than thirty minutes later John Davis made his way down to the back yard and his gruesome discovery.

The inquest into Annie Chapman's death opened on 10th September, presided over by the Coroner for East Middlesex, Wynne Edwin Baxter.

A solicitor who had been called to the Bar in early 1867 at the age of 23, Baxter immediately became in demand in his hometown of Lewes,

Sussex, probably through the good name of his grandfather and father, both well-known local businessmen. In addition to offices at Albion Street in Lewes, in 1875 Baxter established a practice at 9 Laurence Pountney Hill, Cannon Street in the City of London.[84]

In July 1879 an opportunity presented itself to Baxter in the most unexpected manner, when Lewis Green Fullagar, the 42-year-old Coroner for East Sussex, absconded when a warrant was issued for his arrest on charges of fraud.[85] It transpired that Fullagar, a solicitor of St. Andrew's Lane in Lewes,[86] had some seven years earlier been entrusted with £2,500[87] from the trustees representing Mrs. Mary Mockett, and had told her that he had invested it in a mortgage, but had in fact misappropriated it for his own use. He attempted to throw her off the scent by sending her what he claimed to be the interest every six months, but his deception was eventually discovered in November 1878.

The coroner fled.

He was finally apprehended on 2nd August 1879 near Preston Park while apparently walking from Brighton to London by P.C. Richard Morris of the East Sussex Constabulary. Despite being heavily disguised, he was recognised by his distinctive walk; a wanted notice in the *Police Gazette* of 9th July 1879 described him as being around 5ft 11in tall, very thin and round shouldered, and walking with a pronounced stoop. He was taken back to Lewes and remanded in custody,[88] and appeared at Maidstone Assizes on 1st November where, despite being defended by heavyweight London-based counsel Edward Clarke and Forrest Fulton, he was found Guilty and sentenced to five years' imprisonment.[89]

Despite his apparent young age, Fullagar had acted as Coroner for East Sussex for almost 15 years, being elected in December 1864 when just 27-years-old following the death of the previous incumbent, Mr. F. H. Gell.[90]

His incarceration left the office of Coroner open, and the astute Wynne Baxter was quick to respond, placing a notice in the press:

EAST SUSSEX CORONERSHIP.

To the Freeholders of the County of Sussex.

My Lords, Ladies, & Gentlemen. The Court of Crown Cases Reserved having upheld the conviction of Mr. Fullagar, the late Coroner, a VACANCY in that office must soon be declared. Under the circumstances, I take the earliest opportunity of informing you that I shall, at the proper time, solicit the honour of Election at your hands. In the meantime, any promises of support will be very highly esteemed by

> Your faithful servant.
> WYNNE E. BAXTER.

Lewes, November, 1879.[91]

The scheme worked. When the Lord Chancellor announced 29th January 1880 as the date set for nominations, only John Fullagar, the younger brother of the disgraced former Coroner who was also a solicitor and who had been his Deputy, subsequently presiding over inquests following the latter's arrest, stood against Wynne Baxter.[92]

But when it was revealed via the newspapers in the days before the nominations that Baxter had secured an enormous 2,300 promises from the freeholders of Sussex, any opposition melted away.

Wynne Edwin Baxter was appointed Coroner for East Sussex unopposed, his acceptance speech underlining the gravitas of the office:

> I trust your confidence will never prove to have been misplaced. I am aware of the importance of the duties of the office I am about to take; I am aware that it has been held to be the safeguard against secret murder and wrong, and I trust I shall perform those duties not only to your satisfaction, but to the satisfaction of the freeholders at large. I assure you that nothing on my part shall be wanting, and I trust that the generous confidence you have reposed in me, time will prove not to have been misplaced.[93]

It had been Baxter, as Coroner for East Sussex, who in 1881 conducted the inquests into the deaths of both Percy Lefroy Mapleton and his victim, Frederick Isaac Gold.

On 9th November that year – in fact, the day after Lefroy had been found Guilty of murder – Baxter was appointed Alderman of Lewes, an office he would hold until 1887. He had been elected Senior High Constable for 1880 and 1881, the only recorded instance since 1544 of a citizen of the Borough of Lewes serving for two years in succession, the reason being the imminent incorporation of the Borough. He conducted the application to the Privy Council for the grant of the Charter of Incorporation in 1880 and 1881, and was named in the Charter as Returning Officer. He was chosen as Mayor for the first year of the Borough (1881-82), subsequently serving as chairman of the Highways and Works Committee in 1882-83.[94]

In April 1884 it was revealed that Baxter was one of several candidates

Coroner Wynne Edwin Baxter
from The Bibliophile, May 1909

who had put themselves forward for the vacant office of Coroner for the City of London following the death of Mr. W. J. Payne;[95] the position went to Payne's Deputy, Samuel Langham, but Baxter's merits were recognised when Langham soon appointed him as his own Deputy.[96]

Baxter's big chance came when Sir John Humphreys, the long-serving Coroner for East Middlesex, passed away in July 1884. As a coroner was paid according to the number of inquests he presided over, the East Middlesex coronership, which covered the East End with its all-too frequent early and unexplained deaths, saw its Coroner handsomely paid; the magistrates for Middlesex later deciding that, given the average number of inquests held in the division over the previous five years, a salary of £2,208 would be paid to the new Coroner.[97]

Although the Justices had announced a review of the East Middlesex district and a probable division, nothing had happened by the time Baxter and the other candidates assembled at the Vestry Hall, Bethnal Green on 10th December 1886 for the nominations. To a backdrop of general disorder – a large unruly crowd somehow having gained access – a show of hands seemed to pronounce solicitor George Hay Young the clear winner, with Wynne Baxter second. But the disturbance inside the Hall was so great that a clear count was impossible, and the losing candidates demanded a poll, which took place on 13th December.[98] This time Baxter prevailed, winning 1,401 votes, beating Dr. Roderick Macdonald into second place with 1,069 votes. George Hay Young, seemingly the clear winner from the nominations, languished in third place with 696.[99]

Although Baxter had been aware on election that the magistrates intended to divide up the East Middlesex district, he surely could not have expected it to take so long. The magistrates' petition was presented to Queen Victoria for assent on 3rd March 1887, yet the Privy Council delayed a decision until May 1888. By this time, Baxter had resigned his office as Coroner for East Sussex. The East Middlesex district was now divided, as was Wynne Baxter's salary. He was now Coroner for South East Middlesex, with the other section being designated North East Middlesex.[100] The coroner for the new district would be Roderick Macdonald, who on 11th June 1888 embarrassed his opponent Dr. G. Eugene Yarrow, Divisional Surgeon for the Met's G Division, by 4,367 votes to 713.[101]

For the East End, the territorial boundary between its two coroners was as important as that between the Metropolitan and City of London Police; Baxter's district included Whitechapel and the south, Macdonald's Spitalfields and northwards. The Coroners' Act 1887 stipulated that jurisdiction for an inquest lay with the coroner in whose district the remains lay, regardless of where death had occurred. In the case of Annie Chapman, as her body had been taken to the mortuary at Old Montague Street in Whitechapel the inquest into her death would be held by Baxter, even though the scene of her murder, Hanbury Street, was in Macdonald's Spitalfields district.

Earlier in the year, on 5th April 1888, he presided over the inquest on Annie Millwood at the Baker's Row Infirmary. Annie has been proposed as a possible victim of an early Ripper attack. On 25th February she was admitted to the Whitechapel Infirmary, in Baker's Row, with multiple stab wounds to her legs and lower torso. She claimed she was attacked at her lodgings at 8 White's Row by a stranger wielding a clasp knife. Annie recovered from her injuries enough to be sent to the South Grove workhouse, but died on 31st March. Richard Sage, a messenger at the workhouse who was the last person to see her alive, told the inquest: "About 11.40am on the 31st ult., I was standing at the door conversing with the deceased, and my attention being called in another direction I turned my back to her, and after a space of three minutes I returned, to find her lying down with her face on the step." The jury returned a verdict of 'Death from natural causes'. [102]

The inquest had taken place the day following the attack on Emma Smith, and it was Baxter's sad duty to hold the inquest into her death at the London Hospital on 7th April. Summing up, he said: "From the medical evidence it was clear that the woman had been barbarously murdered. Such a dastardly assault I have never heard of, and it was impossible to imagine a more brutal case."[103]

With Baxter unavailable, the inquiry into the death of Martha Tabram on 9th and 23rd August was conducted by his Deputy George Collier, who had originally stood as a candidate in the 1886 election but then bowed out to support Baxter's campaign.[104] The inquest was held at the Working Lads' Institute, 285 Whitechapel Road, which would also be the venue for the inquest into Mary Ann Nichols. The move to premises other than a cramped infirmary or workhouse was appreciated by one reporter:

> A word may be said as to the great advantage there is in selecting such a place as the Lads' Institute for coroners' inquiries. The hall is lofty and light, while there is plenty of room for everyone. The improvement upon the custom of hiring a public house room is manifest, and the new departure inaugurated by Mr. Wynne Baxter cannot be regretted.[105]

But the murder of Annie Chapman being committed so soon after that of Mary Ann Nichols, with the inquest of the latter still being conducted, meant that Baxter suddenly found himself conducting inquiries into the deaths of two victims simultaneously. His summing up of the Nichols case on 22nd September provided the coroner with the opportunity to suggest that the murders had been committed by the same hand:

> We cannot altogether leave unnoticed the fact that the death that you have been investigating is one of four presenting many points of similarity, all of which have occurred within the space of about five months, and all within a very short distance of the place where we are sitting.
>
> All four victims were women of middle age, all were married, and had lived apart from their husbands in consequence of intemperate habits, and were at the time of their death leading an irregular life, and eking out a miserable and precarious existence in common lodging-houses.
>
> In each case there were abdominal as well as other injuries. In each case the injuries were inflicted after midnight, and in places of public resort, where it would appear impossible but that almost immediate detection should follow the crime, and in each case the inhuman and dastardly criminals are at large in society.
>
> Emma Elizabeth Smith, who received her injuries in Osborn Street on the early morning of Easter Tuesday, April 3, survived in the London Hospital for upwards of twenty-four hours, and was able to state that she had been followed by some men, robbed and mutilated, and even to describe imperfectly one of them. Martha Tabram was found at three a.m. on Tuesday, August 7, on the first floor landing of George Yard Buildings, Wentworth Street, with thirty-nine punctured wounds on her body. In addition to these, and the case under your consideration, there is the case of Annie Chapman, still in the hands of another jury.
>
> The instruments used in the two earlier cases are dissimilar. In the first it was a blunt instrument, such as a walking-stick; in the second, some of the wounds were thought to have been made by a dagger; but in the two recent cases the instruments suggested by the medical witnesses are not so different. Dr Llewellyn says the injuries on Nichols could have been produced by a strong bladed instrument, moderately sharp. Dr Phillips is of opinion that those on Chapman were by a very sharp knife, probably with a thin, narrow blade, at least six to eight inches in length, probably longer.
>
> The similarity of the injuries in the two cases is considerable. There are bruises about the face in both cases; the head is nearly severed from the body in both cases; there are other dreadful injuries in both

cases; and those injuries, again, have in each case been performed with anatomical knowledge. Dr. Llewellyn seems to incline to the opinion that the abdominal injuries were first, and caused instantaneous death; but, if so, it seems difficult to understand the object of such desperate injuries to the throat, or how it comes about that there was so little bleeding from the several arteries, that the clothing on the upper surface was not stained, and, indeed, very much less bleeding from the abdomen than from the neck. Surely it may well be that, as in the case of Chapman, the dreadful wounds to the throat were inflicted first and the others afterwards...

I suggest to you as a possibility that these two women may have been murdered by the same man with the same object, and that in the case of Nichols the wretch was disturbed before he had accomplished his object, and having failed in the open street he tries again, within a week of his failure, in a more secluded place. If this should be correct, the audacity and daring is equal to its maniacal fanaticism and abhorrent wickedness. But this surmise may or may not be correct, the suggested motive may be the wrong one; but one thing is very clear – that a murder of a most atrocious character has been committed.[106]

When called, Dr. George Bagster Phillips was extremely reluctant to disclose the full nature of the mutilations. Baxter pressed him for details, reminding him that "the object of the inquiry is not only to ascertain the cause of death, but the means by which it occurred. Any mutilation which took place afterwards may suggest the character of the man who did it." A week later, with the room cleared of women and messenger boys, the surgeon finally related the terrible injuries inflicted on Annie Chapman, the majority mercifully after she was already dead.

Dr. Phillips' evidence enabled Baxter, in his summing up, to describe the probable *modus operandi* of the killer. Once in the back yard of Hanbury Street, the murderer took Chapman by the chin, perhaps disguised with an affectionate touch, and squeezed her throat, rendering her unconscious. She was then carefully lowered to the ground – perhaps falling against the fence as she did so, resulting in the noise heard by Albert Cadosch, and laid on her back. Her throat was cut in two places, causing death instantly, and the mutilations were then carried out, including the removal of her uterus.

Baxter then considered the killer's medical abilities:

The body has not been dissected, but the injuries have been made by some one who had considerable anatomical skill and knowledge. There are no meaningless cuts. It was done by one who knew where to find what he wanted, what difficulties he would have to contend against, and how he should use his knife, so as to abstract the organ without injury to it. No unskilled person could have known where to find it, or have recognised it when it was found. For instance, no mere slaughterer of animals could have carried out these operations. It must have been some one accustomed to the post-mortem room.[107]

Annie Chapman was buried on Friday, 14th September. Desperate to keep the arrangements secret in an attempt to prevent a large crowd from congregating, the family and few mourners eschewed the usual practice of following the hearse from the mortuary and instead went straight to the cemetery. Shortly after seven o'clock in the morning a hearse drew up in Old Montague Street and the body was quickly removed, setting off two hours later for Manor Park cemetery. The black-covered elm coffin bore the simple words "Annie Chapman, died September 8, 1888, aged 48 years."[108]

The following day Sir Charles Warren appointed Det. Chief Inspector Donald Swanson as his 'eyes and ears', perhaps having spoken first to his Chief Constable, Dolly Williamson, to find out the officer most suited to the task. Given his work with Williamson on the Fenian investigation and, more recently the Trafalgar Square demonstrations, it's likely that the senior officer had no hesitation in recommending Swanson.

Potential suspects soon became apparent as a result of police enquiries. Among these was a man who entered the Prince Albert public house on Brushfield Street, a mere 400 yards from 29 Hanbury Street, just over an hour after Annie Chapman's body had been discovered and asked for a pint of ale. Landlady Mrs. Fiddymont and a friend in the bar at the time noticed that the man's shirt was torn, and he had spots of blood on his hand. When he noticed he was being observed the man left the pub quickly.[109] When a butcher named Jacob Isenschmid came to the attention of the police his description seemed to tally with that given by Mrs. Fiddymont; he had been confined to an asylum after becoming depressed following the failure of his business, and on his release had taken to wandering the streets, according to his wife with two butcher's knives in his possession.[110] He had since been confined to an asylum, where the Resident Medical Officer, Dr. William Julius Mickle, declined a request to have his patient placed in an identification to confirm he was the same man seen by Mrs. Fiddymont.[111]

Others who came to the attention of the police at this time included Edward McKenna, arrested on suspicion of being a man seen chased by some boys while holding a knife behind his back but subsequently released;[112] William Pigott, arrested at The Pope's Head in Gravesend having apparently walked from Whitechapel and then aroused suspicion by talking of his hatred for women, had a cut to his hand which had been caused, he claimed, when a woman in Whitechapel whose aid he had gone to had bitten him.[113]

A dustman said he had seen a man on the morning of Annie Chapman's murder with blood on his clothing, and Thomas Ede reported seeing a man with a wooden arm and leg carrying a knife.[114]

News of a curious communication received by the police was included in a report on present enquiries sent by Commissioner Sir Charles Warren to the Home Office on 19th September:

> A Brothel Keeper who will not give her address or name writes to say that a man living in her house was seen with blood on him on morning of murder. She described his appearance & said where he might be seen – when the detectives came near him he bolted, got away & there is no clue to the writer of the letter.[115]

Perhaps the most serious suspect was the mysterious 'Leather Apron', who, it was reported, "had more than once attacked unfortunate and defenceless women" after luring them with promises of money only to rob them of what little they had and "half kill" them into the bargain.[116]

The idea of 'Leather Apron' as the murderer began to catch on, possibly because of the lurid name which, as we shall soon see, would be replaced in the public's imagination by another. The moniker had caught on to such a degree that Jacob Isenschmid had told the Medical Superintendent at Bow Infirmary Asylum that the girls at Holloway, where he lived, called him 'Leather Apron', to which he jokingly agreed.[117]

But the fear of the unknown assailant was increased when *The Star* of 5th September 1888 described him as "The strange character who prowls about after midnight; Universal fear among women; Slippered feet and a sharp leather-knife."

Such was the terror the name brought that young Thomas Cox tragically died when his sister told another brother that "Leather Apron was under the bed"; the older boy bent down with a lit candle to look, and set fire to the bed clothes.[118]

Eventually, the clamour for the arrest of 'Leather Apron' became so great that bootmaker John Pizer, who admitted he was known by the nickname, was forced to go into hiding at his brother's house on Mulberry Street, from where he was arrested. Pizer appeared at the inquest into Annie Chapman's death, and was able to provide an alibi.

As the end of September arrived the search for the killer went on, criticism of the Metropolitan Police grew. They were defended in some quarters, however, such as this comment in *The Graphic* of 29th September:

> As regards the action of the police, there is a tendency in some quarters to sneer at the efficiency of our detective arrangements because the person or persons by whom these terrible crimes have been committed are still at large. But surely this is very unreasonable, seeing that the police are men, like ourselves, possessed of no preternatural powers.

The police might well have wished for enhanced powers later that day, as things were about to get much, much worse.

Even as the newspapers of Saturday, 29th September debating the effectiveness of the police were being read and disposed of, the events of that day which would make tomorrow's headlines were already developing.

Elisabeth Stride spent the afternoon cleaning rooms at 32 Flower and Dean Street, a common lodging house where she had stayed on and off for six years, on this occasion since the Thursday just gone, and for her trouble earned sixpence from the Deputy, Elizabeth Tanner.[119]

She was a quiet woman of mostly sober habits,[120] a slender 5ft 2in with blue eyes and brown hair, who had been born Elisabeth Gustafsdotter, second child of four to Gustaf Ericsson and his wife Beata, at the family's farmhouse at Torslanda, some 16 kilometres from Gothenburg, on 27th November 1843. Finding work as a maidservant for Lars Fredrik Olsson and his family in Majorna, in the suburbs of Gothenburg at almost 18 years of age, Elisabeth found herself without a job when her employment was abruptly terminated after three years in February 1864. She was not yet 21.

Over the course of the following year Elisabeth took maid's jobs around various districts of Gothenburg, but in March 1865, when six months pregnant, she was registered by the Gothenburg police as a prostitute. She was treated for syphilis and as a result went into premature labour, on 21st April delivering a stillborn girl.

After further treatment her fortunes finally took a more positive turn and she found employment with a family who intended travelling to London, and so on 7th February 1866 Elisabeth found herself at the dock waiting for passage to England.

In time she would meet carpenter John Stride, 13 years her senior, and the couple married in March 1869. They would remain together for a dozen years, in the process moving to Poplar, in the East End, but by December 1881 John and Elisabeth Stride had parted. He died in 1884, while she found a roof over her head first in Brick Lane, and then at her long-time 'home' at 32 Flower and Dean Street.[121]

Elisabeth met waterside labourer Michael Kidney in 1885 and they had been a couple since, although she had left him on occasion – a total of five months over the three years; "It was drink that made her go away, and she always returned without my going after her."[122] They lived together on nearby Fashion Street, but according to her friend Catherine Lane, a fellow lodger at 32 Flower and Dean Street, she had "had words" with Kidney and as a result had left.[123] Those who knew Elisabeth at No. 32 knew she was from Sweden, and some had heard her speak fluently in Swedish to another at the lodging house in addition to English.[124]

Now, on Saturday 29th September, she had finished her work and was getting ready to go out. She was wearing a long black coat trimmed with fur and a hat, a striped coloured handkerchief around her neck. She asked another lodger, barber Charles Preston, if she could borrow his clothes brush.[125] Shortly afterwards she spoke to Mrs. Lane, and asked her to look after a piece of velvet until she returned. It was not yet 8 o'clock.[126]

Kate Conway, meanwhile, had spent the morning attempting to raise money for herself and her partner John Kelly. The couple had returned to Whitechapel on the Thursday, having been hop-picking in Kent as many East Enders did in the summer months. Although they had lived together for seven years at Cooney's Lodging House at 55 Flower and Dean Street – at the other end of the street from Elisabeth Stride – as they were penniless that night they both slept at the Casual Ward on Shoe Lane.[127] The following day John managed to earn 6d through labouring, so while he spent 4d on a bed at Cooney's – the price of a single bed – Kate took 2d and headed for the Casual Ward at Mile End. They met the following morning at 8 o'clock and Kate pawned John's boots with Mr. Jones at his shop on Church Street[128] in the shadow of Christ Church, fetching 2s 6d, some of which they spent on supplies of tea and sugar to be kept on her person by Kate and the rest on breakfast,[129] which they ate at Cooney's between 10.00 and 11.00 o'clock.[130]

After their welcome meal the couple found themselves once again without any money, so Kate suggested that she go to Bermondsey to see whether she could find her daughter Annie and borrow some. They parted on Houndsditch at 2 o'clock, Kate promising to be back by within a couple of hours.

He never saw her alive again.

Later that evening he heard that Kate had been seen with two policemen on Houndsditch, and subsequently locked up at Bishopsgate Police Station because she had had "a drop to drink".[131] Expecting to see her in the morning, he returned to Cooney's alone and took a single bed for the night.[132]

Wherever Kate had spent the afternoon, she had been drinking heavily. It later transpired that her daughter, Annie Phillips, had moved from Bermondsey some two years earlier, not long after seeing her mother for the last time. She had not left any information as to her new residence in order to stop her Kate from bothering her for money, which she did often.[133] Whether she even attempted to locate her daughter is unknown; she may well have spent the six hours since parting with John Kelly still in the East End, for at 8.30pm, not long after Elisabeth Stride had left 32 Flower and Dean Street for the evening, City of London Police officer P.C. Louis Robinson was on duty in Aldgate High Street when he noticed a number of people gathered around a woman who was lying on the pavement in a drunken slumber; he would later identify her as Kate.

When nobody in the crowd admitted to knowing her, P.C. Robinson picked Kate up from the floor and tried to get her to stand resting against some shutters, only for her to slide down the wall and back onto the ground. She smelled very strongly of alcohol, and was in such a state that she could not have travelled far before collapsing; she must have been drinking in a nearby pub. With the assistance of another constable P.C. Robinson took her to Bishopsgate Police Station,[134] on the way observed by the woman who informed John Kelly.

On arrival fifteen minutes later she had to be supported by the constables while Station Sergeant James Byfield tried to ascertain her details; when asked her name she gave the reply "Nothing". She was taken to a cell and left there to sleep off her afternoon.[135]

Elisabeth Stride's evening had also involved drinking. She was seen in the doorway of The Bricklayer's Arms on Settles Street with a "respectably dressed" man just before eleven o'clock. It was raining heavily and the couple appeared reluctant to venture out onto the street. John Bass,[136] one of the group of men who were entering the pub at the same time, teased the man about how he was cuddling and kissing her despite her being so poorly dressed. Bass said to Elisabeth, "That's Leather Apron getting round you." The couple ran out into the street and out of earshot from the jibes.[137]

Forty-five minutes later, at a quarter to midnight, William Marshall was standing at the door of his home at 64 Berner Street, a five minute walk to the south side of Commercial Road, when he noticed a couple standing together talking. He would later identify the woman as Elisabeth, and once again her respectably-dressed companion was kissing her affectionately. Marshall observed them for ten minutes, during which time he heard the man say "You would say anything but your prayers", before they moved on.[138]

The couple seemingly didn't go far, for at around 12.30am they were seen by P.C. 452H William Smith as he patrolled his beat along Berner Street and the surrounding area. On this occasion Elisabeth's companion – whether it was the same man is uncertain – was carrying something wrapped in newspaper, 18 inches in length and 6-8 inches wide. They were standing on Berner Street outside the London Board School, opposite No. 40, which was home to the International Working Men's Educational Club,[139] a society open to any working man of any nationality who was a supporter of the Socialist movement. It officially had 75 to 80 members, but it was the end of the Jewish holiday and that evening a meeting had taken place at which some 90 to 100 people[140] had heard a lecture entitled 'Judaism and Socialism'. The talk and subsequent discussion ended about 12.30, at which point many attendees headed home, but around 30 members remained to enjoy the festivities.[141]

A man named James Brown left his home to fetch some supper from a shop on the corner of Berner Street and Fairclough Street. He saw a man and a woman standing by another wall of the Board School, this time around the corner on Fairclough Street. She was standing with her back to the wall, with the man leaning over her with his arm up against the wall. As he passed he heard the woman say "No, not tonight, some other night." He returned to his home, estimating the time to be around 12.45.[142]

If this was Elisabeth Stride – and it was widely reported that it was unusual for couples to be seen in the vicinity of Berner Street late at night – then Mr. Brown was slightly out with his reckoning, with 12.45am probably being the time he got back home, for at that time Israel

Schwartz was walking towards his home at Ellen Street, at the southern end of Berner Street, when he saw a woman he would later recognise as Elisabeth standing in the gateway to Dutfield's Yard, between Nos. 40 and 42. The man at first tried to pull Elisabeth into the street, but then turned her round and pushed her to the floor. Alarmed, Schwartz crossed the road and at that point became aware of another man nearby, lighting his pipe. The attacker called out "Lipski',[143] a derogatory term aimed at Jews since the previous year when Israel Lipski had murdered the pregnant Miriam Angel in Batty Street, coincidentally parallel to Berner Street.[144] Schwartz was uncertain whether the insult was aimed at himself or the man lighting his pipe, although the police were later of the opinion that it was meant as a warning to Schwartz, and hurriedly continued on his journey. He noticed that the second man appeared to be following him so started running, but on reaching the railway arch saw that the man was no longer behind him.[145]

The two men had left Elisabeth Stride at the entrance to Dutfield's Yard, its gates open, with her assailant. It was close to 12.50am.

Just under a mile away, in Bishopsgate Police Station, Kate Conway had sobered up. Gaoler P.C. George Hutt had checked on his prisoners several times during the evening, and at five minutes to one found Kate sober enough to be released. As he unlocked the cell and took her to the station desk she asked the time. On being told it was "Just on one" she remarked "I shall get a damned fine hiding when I get home."[146]

When asked by Station Sergeant her name and address, Kate was much more obliging than when she was brought in, responding – albeit untruthfully – with "Mary Ann Kelly, 6 Fashion Street, Spitalfields."[147]

The formalities complete, P.C. Hutt escorted her to the swing door leading to the outer passage and street door, which he asked her to pull to. Kate replied "Alright, Goodnight Old Cock" and, closing the door after herself to within half a foot, turned left down Bishopsgate in the direction of Houndsditch. It was one o'clock.[148]

At almost precisely the same moment Louis Diemschitz, the steward of the International Working Men's Educational Club, returned to 40 Berner Street with his pony and costermonger's barrow, having been out at work since 11 o'clock that morning. His intention was to deposit his goods at the Club before taking his pony to stables half a mile away off Cable Street. As he approached he saw that both gates were open, with the yard itself pitch black. As he drove through the gates the pony shied to the left; Diemschitz peered down into the inky darkness and could just make out a shape on the floor to his right. He prodded it with his whip, then climbed down from his seat and lit a match. The glow, faint as it was, was sufficient to illuminate a women lying near the wall.

The steward went at once into the Club and found his wife, telling her and other members that there was a woman lying in the yard, but he was unsure whether she was drunk or dead. Lighting a candle and returning to the yard, Diemschitz could now see there was blood.[149]

Within a quarter of an hour the yard was filled with Club members and police officers. First to arrive, within five or six minutes of the discovery, was P.C. 252H Henry Lamb, who had been on his beat along Commercial Road when he was approached by two Club members running towards him, calling out "Come on, there has been another murder." Arriving at the scene, P.C. Lamb lit his lamp and saw that the woman's throat was cut. He put his hand upon her face and it felt slightly warm, yet on feeling her wrist could detect no pulse.

About thirty people were already in the yard, and others had followed the officer in. As he examined the body a crowd gathered around him, maintaining a respectful distance of a yard. People had wandered around freely, and given that Louis Diemschitz may well have disturbed the murderer there was a chance he was still in the area. P.C. Lamb had the gates closed, and positioned another officer there to prevent anyone either entering or leaving via the door cut into the gates to allow pedestrian access. He examined the hands and clothing of all Club members, checking for blood, but found none.[150] P.C. Smith arrived back at Berner Street on the next rotation of his beat and found a crowd of people milling around outside the yard; he went to Leman Street Police Station for the hand-wheeled ambulance.[151]

The officer then searched the yard itself and the buildings therein;[152] although known locally as 'Dutfield's Yard' after cart builder Arthur Dutfield, and his name still adorned one of the gates, he had actually relocated two years earlier to nearby Pinchin Street.[153] Opposite the gate were the premises of Messrs. Hindley, sack manufacturers, which were also searched, along with a number of private dwellings. Nothing suspicious was found.[154]

Ten minutes after P.C. Lamb's arrival Dr. Frederick Blackwell attended the scene, having been called from his home minutes away at 100 Commercial Road. Conducting an examination by the light of a policeman's lantern, he pronounced the woman dead, death having occurred between 20 and 30 minutes earlier:

> "The deceased was lying on her left side obliquely across the passage, her face looking towards the right wall. Her legs were drawn up, her feet close against the wall of the right side of the passage. Her head was

The scene in Berner Street following the murder of Elisabeth Stride from the Pictorial News, 6th October 1888

resting beyond the carriage-wheel rut, the neck lying over the rut. Her feet were three yards from the gateway. Her dress was unfastened at the neck. The neck and chest were quite warm, as were also the legs, and the face was slightly warm. The hands were cold. The right hand was open and on the chest, and was smeared with blood. The left hand, lying on the ground, was partially closed, and contained a small packet of cachous wrapped in tissue paper. There were no rings, nor marks of rings, on her hands. The appearance of the face was quite placid. The mouth was slightly open. The deceased had round her neck a check silk scarf, the bow of which was turned to the left and pulled very tight. In the neck there was a long incision which exactly corresponded with the lower border of the scarf. The border was slightly frayed, as if by a sharp knife. The incision in the neck commenced on the left side, 2 inches below the angle of the jaw, and almost in a direct line with it, nearly severing the vessels on that side, cutting the windpipe completely in two, and terminating on the opposite side 1 inch below the angle of the right jaw, but without severing the vessels on that side. I could not ascertain whether the bloody hand had been moved. The blood was running down the gutter into the drain in the opposite direction from the feet. There was about 1lb of clotted blood close by the body, and a stream all the way from there to the back door of the club.[155]

Police officers busied themselves interrogating everyone in the yard as to their movements that evening, searching their clothing and examining any knives, and, with their names and addresses recorded, they were gradually allowed to leave.

While this maelstrom of activity was underway in Berner Street, City of London Police Constable Edward Watkins was patrolling the area to the north-west of Aldgate. He had been on duty since 9.45pm, and had walked his beat which took him on a loop around certain streets in the City territory, starting and ending at Duke Street, without incident since commencing the first circuit at 10.00pm. Calling points included Leadenhall Street, St. James's Place and Mitre Square, a quiet area surrounded by four large warehouses and a row of old dwellings, one of which was occupied by a picture framer and another by a City Police Constable, with the other residences unoccupied.

The beat took 12 or 14 minutes to complete. At 1.30am, as the body of Elisabeth Stride was being examined, P.C. Watkins walked for the umpteenth time along Mitre Street and turned right in the Square, patrolling its perimeter and, with his lantern fixed to his belt, examined the buildings and passageways. Nothing out of the ordinary presented

THE SCENES OF THE RECENT MURDERS.

Dutfield's Yard and Mitre Square
from The People, 14th October 1888

itself, and Watkins turned right out of the square back onto Mitre Street and continued on his beat.[156]

P.C. James Harvey patrolled the adjoining beat to Watkins, which involved walking down Church Passage, a long, narrow passageway leading into Mitre Square from Duke Street, but without entering the square itself. He, too, had walked the beat a number of times that evening after going on duty at the same time as Watkins.[157]

As P.C. Watkins entered Mitre Square at 1.30am, three friends were preparing to leave the Imperial Club, a members' club for local businessmen opened the previous year at 16 & 17 Duke Street.[158] It was on the opposite side of the street to the Great Synagogue, which bordered Church Passage on its right-hand side. Departing the Club three or four minutes later, as the three men walked south towards Aldgate commercial traveller Joseph Lawende was a short distance from his colleagues, butcher Joseph Hyam Levy[159] and furniture dealer Harry Harris. After walking parallel to the Great Synagogue for some 15 feet they approached the turn into Church Passage at 1.35am, and saw a man and a woman standing by the metal pole marking the entrance. She was standing with her back to the trio so they were unable to see her face, but Lawende would later identify her by her clothes.[160] It was, almost certainly, Kate Conway.

Hyam Levy also saw the couple, and commented to Harris: "Here, I'm off. I don't like the look of those people over there. I don't like going home by myself at this hour of the morning. I don't like passing this class of persons."[161] Interestingly, when a reporter sought out Harris and Levy for an interview the latter refused to discuss the matter, leaving the journalist to complain:

> Mr. Joseph Levy is absolutely obstinate and refuses to give us the slightest information. He leaves one to infer that he knows something, but that he is afraid to be called on the inquest. Hence he assumes a knowing air.[162]

Levy *was* called to give evidence at the inquest, where he clarified his comments to Mr. Harris: "There was nothing in what I saw to suggest that the man was doing anything that was dangerous to the woman. Being a little deaf, I could not possibly have heard anything that was said."[163]

The three men walked on towards their respective homes, none of them looking back at the couple.

Five minutes later P.C. Harvey returned on his beat. The couple had left their post at the entrance to Church Passage and Harvey saw nobody about; he went down the passage, checking the doors of premises as he did so. At the end of Church Passage he turned and walked back up the 5ft-wide thoroughfare and back into Duke Street, noticing nothing suspicious.[164]

A scant few minutes later P.C. Watkins returned to Mitre Street. As he had done thirteen times already that evening, he turned right into Mitre Square and lit his bullseye lamp. As he approached the darkest corner, that opposite Church Passage, the light from his lantern suddenly fell on the body of Kate Conway, lying on her back with her feet towards the square. She had been horribly mutilated, and her intestines had been pulled out and now lay around her.[165]

Watkins ran the short distance to the Kearley and Tonge warehouse, where he knew nightwatchman George Morris was on duty. He knocked on the door and Morris, who was just on the other side, pulled it open to be met by a shaken Watkins, who panted "For God's sake mate, come to my assistance." The nightwatchman went outside and asked what was the matter, receiving the reply "Oh dear, there's another woman cut up to pieces."

Morris went over to the corner with Watkins and looked at the body, then immediately blew his whistle and ran up Mitre Street towards Aldgate in search of help,[166] almost immediately finding P.C. Harvey, who was returning on his beat, and P.C. Holland, another City constable. The officers ran with Morris back to Mitre Square, where they found their colleague Watkins with the body. Holland was sent to fetch Dr. George Sequeira,[167] who lived at 34 Jewry Street, Aldgate.

The City of London Police's Dr. Frederick Gordon Brown arrived at 2.18am. The surgeon found the body lying on its back, the head turned to the left shoulder. The arms were lying by the side of the body, with both palms upwards, the fingers slightly bent. A thimble lay on the floor, evidently having fallen off a finger of the right hand.

In addition to the cut throat – the cause of death – Kate had received injuries far in excess of the previous victims, and for the first time the face had been savagely attacked; even her eyelids had been nicked, and the tip of the nose cut off. A kidney had been removed, apparently skilfully, and was now missing, as was part of her womb.

Dr. Brown concluded that it would have taken at least five minutes to carry out the mutilations,[168] which was possible assuming the sighting by Joseph Lawende at 1.35am was of Kate and her killer; they went down Church Passage to the darkest corner of Mitre Square, and almost immediately she was strangled then laid on the floor and her throat cut, as in the case of Annie Chapman. Even if the murderer had fled on hearing P.C. Watkins' approaching footsteps a minute before his discovery of the body, he had more than the suggested five minutes. If this is correct, the murderer must have been carrying out his gruesome work when P.C. Harvey approached down Church Passage; thankfully for him, as Harvey's beat did not include Mitre Square it's probable that he didn't give more than a cursory glance before turning on his heel to continue his inspection of Church Passage.

Inspector Edward Collard arrived from Bishopsgate Police Station and ordered a thorough search of the vicinity; Inspector James McWilliam, head of the City Police Detective Department, joined the growing number of City Police officers and took control.[169]

The murder of Kate Conway in Mitre Square brought the City of London Police in to the Whitechapel murders investigation for the first time, but they had not been sitting on their hands. As early as August, in a response to the horrors committed in neighbouring Whitechapel Colonel Sir James Fraser, Commissioner of the City force since 1863, had added extra men to the Bishopsgate Subdivision which was adjacent to the Met's H Division and ordered the City detectives to keep a close eye on prostitutes walking the City's streets and frequenting its public houses.[170] On the night of 29th October, several City detectives were carrying out this order by patrolling the City all night in plain clothes. Three of these, Detectives Daniel Halse, Robert Outram and Edward Marriott had thus been searching the passageways of houses in the neighbourhood and at 1.50am were by St. Botolph's Church, 100 yards from Mitre Square when they heard news of the murder.[171]

After dashing to Mitre Square to view the body the detectives dispersed and ran off from the scene, with orders to search the neighbourhood and every man to be stopped and questioned. Detective Halse headed up Middlesex Street and then entered the Met's territory at Wentworth Street, where he stopped and questioned two men who gave satisfactory accounts for their movements. He crossed into Goulston Street, where he saw nothing to arouse his suspicions. It was now 2.20am, and Halse headed back to Mitre Square.[172] At around the same time Metropolitan Police Constable Alfred Long – an A Division officer temporarily drafted into H Division to boost police presence – was on his beat which took him along Goulston Street. He passed the spot at which Halse had stood moments before and saw nothing to attract his attention.[173]

By the time Halse arrived back at Mitre Square the doctors had finished their examination and the body had been removed to the City Mortuary at Golden Lane, where it was undressed and her possessions catalogued, including the thimble and other items found on the ground beside the body: three small black buttons and a mustard tin containing two pawn tickets, which would later prove crucial in ascertaining the victim's identity. As the clothing was removed a piece of her right ear dropped to the floor.[174] Photographs of the body were then taken; first in a casket, and then after the post-mortem with the long, jagged wound from her groin to her breastbone stitched up. In the latter, Kate was propped up against a wall with her hair tied to a spike, to allow for a full-body photograph to be taken. As disrespectful as this sounds, as with the Metropolitan Police mortuary photographs were an effective way of obtaining an identification of the 'unknown dead.'

Detective Halse went with Inspector Collard to the mortuary where they saw the undressed body. Looking through her clothing and possessions, Halse noticed that the apron Kate had been wearing had been cut and a portion was missing. He then returned to Mitre Square with the City's Assistant Commissioner Major Henry Smith.[175]

At 2.55am P.C. Long had completed a circuit of his beat and was back in Goulston Street. As he approached the open access to 108-119 Wentworth Model Dwellings he shone his bullseye lamp into the passage and saw a portion of an apron lying on the floor, covered in blood.[176] Above it, written on the black fascia of the wall in white chalk were the words:

> The Juwes are the men that will not be blamed for nothing.[177]

P.C. Long immediately called to P.C. Willie Bettles, on the adjoining beat, to come to his assistance and told his colleague to guard the entranceway[178] while Long himself searched the half-dozen staircases within, but finding no traces of blood or recent footmarks. He took the apron piece to Commercial Street Police Station, instructing P.C. Bettles to keep an observation on anyone entering or leaving the Dwellings,[179] and soon returned with an Inspector who examined the writing before setting off with P.C. Long to Leman Street Police Station, where the piece of apron was handed to Dr. Phillips.[180]

Detectives Halse, Lawley and Hunt were in Mitre Square with Major Henry Smith when they heard that a portion of an apron had been found; Halse, suspecting that this was related to the cut apron belonging to the victim which was at that moment folded neatly at the Golden Lane Mortuary, set off for Leman Street with Detective Hunt.[181] Covered with blood and faecal matter, the portion proved to be a perfect fit to the missing part of the victim's apron.

In exactly the same way, at that moment the fortunes of the Metropolitan and City Police forces were now joined together for the remainder of the investigation. It would not be an easy relationship; minutes later a dispute arose about the chalked message seemingly pointing the finger at the Jewish population.

City Detectives Halse and Hunt arrived at Goulston Street and saw the writing; Halse sent Hunt to Mitre Square to seek instruction from Superintendent McWilliam as to having the message photographed. The senior officer confirmed this must be done, but by the time Detective Hunt returned it was too late.[182]

Superintendent of H Division Thomas Arnold was alarmed that such a message might incite trouble given that there was a strong anti-Semitic feeling in the wake of the Hanbury Street murder, with the fear over 'Leather Apron' crystallising the idea in the minds of many that the murderer was a Jew. Accordingly, he sent an inspector to Goulston Street with a sponge to await the arrival of the Commissioner.[183]

Sir Charles Warren had already been apprised that morning at Commercial Street Police Station the details of the murder of Elisabeth Stride; he then arrived at Leman Street shortly before 5.00am to speak with Superintendent Arnold, who underlined that the most pressing problem was the writing at Goulston Street. Warren went to the scene and viewed the message. It was just beginning to get light and soon the streets would be busy with the usual Sunday morning crowds, a mixture of Jewish vendors and Gentile customers.

With that crowd armed with the knowledge that another murder had been committed, with some 'evidence' that a Jew was responsible, was too much of a risk for Warren. He backed Superintendent Arnold and, after a copy was taken of the exact word, ordered that the message be wiped away.[184] Predictably, the decision was met with outrage.

> *The Times* this morning says that it is "unreasoning petulance" to blame the police for not discovering a murderer who is cunning enough to leave no clue behind him by which he can be traced. But in the case of the murder in Mitre Square the murderer did leave behind him a clue, an invaluable and unmistakable clue, in the shape of an inscription in his own handwriting on a wall immediately above the place where he threw away the piece of his victim's apron on which he had wiped his gory fingers. Here was a clue which, in the absence of all other clues, was of simply incalculable importance. Yet it has been destroyed, and destroyed by the direct act of Sir Charles Warren himself. Strange, almost incredible though it appears, this excellent Major-General, whose first thought it ever how to repress disorder, and to whom the detection of crime is but a secondary consideration, actually persisted in destroying this clue, in the face of protests of the City police and of the suggestion of one of his own men. If we had been called upon to imagine what would afford the public an exact measure of Sir Charles Warren's utter incapacity for the work he has on hand, we could not have conceived anything more cruelly conclusive than this.[185]

It is ironic that the *Pall Mall Gazette* should have been so vocal about Warren's desire to maintain public order above all else; it was the reason he had been offered the Commissionership in 1886 after the ineptitude of Sir Edmund Henderson, when the *Gazette* had applauded the appointment. He had shown the same commitment when banning access to Trafalgar Square in November 1887, with the result being the carnage that was Bloody Sunday. It was clear that Sir Charles Warren was not afraid to make an unpopular decision for what he considered the greater good. In a letter to the Home Office explaining his actions the Commissioner revealed that the Chief Rabbi had personally written thanking him on behalf of the Jewish community for his "humane and vigilant actions at this critical time." Warren plainly felt very strongly about the matter:

> I do not hesitate myself to say that if that writing had been left there it would have been an onslaught against the Jews, property would have been wrecked, and lives would probably have been lost, and I was much gratified with the promptitude with which Superintendent Arnold was

prepared to act in the matter if I had not been there.[186]

In all probability there's little chance that the Goulston Street writing was left by the murderer. While some observers stated that it looked fresh, others said there was no way of knowing how long it had been there. However, on balance it must be probable that the message was recent, because given the residents of Goulston Street and specifically Wentworth Model Dwellings were almost exclusively Jewish such a slur would surely have been cleaned away soon after it was chalked. But how close to a person's normal handwriting would a chalk message be?

The real – and only – obvious clue in the whole of the Whitechapel murders case was the location of the piece of material cut from Kate's apron, which gave an indication of the killer's route out of Mitre Square and therefore an idea of the area in which he resided. The apron portion itself was bloodstained – had he carried the organs taken from Kate wrapped up in the material? If that was the case, why discard it at the entrance to Wentworth Model Dwellings instead of continuing to his home? More likely is that the killer had cut himself while carrying out the mutilations, and had therefore taken the apron piece away to wipe his hands or stem a flow of blood.

As debate over the rights and wrongs of removing the chalk writing in Goulston Street continued, the Mitre Square victim lay in the mortuary at Golden Lane, still officially unidentified. This was soon to change.

When the description was telegraphed around all City stations, P.C.s Hutt and Simmons both felt this tallied with the drunken woman taken to Bishopsgate on the evening of the 29th; Hutt especially recognised the description of her bonnet, and the fact that she was wearing men's boots. He attended the mortuary and confirmed this was the same woman. The name she had given on her release was 'Mary Ann Kelly', and her address as 6 Fashion Street. These were checked, but obviously drew a blank.

Finally, on the morning of 2nd October John Kelly walked into Bishopsgate Police Station and said that as a consequence of reading a description of the Mitre Square victim in that morning's newspaper he was convinced that it was his 'wife'. He was convinced because of the two pawn tickets found in possession of the victim, one in the names of 'Kelly' and 'Birrell', the latter being a women he and Kate had met when hopping. He was escorted to the mortuary by Sergeant Miles, and at Golden Lane he confirmed the deceased was his partner of seven years, Kate Conway. Overcome with emotion, back at Bishopsgate Kelly told Major Henry Smith and Superintendent Alfred Foster of his and Kate's movements in the days leading up to her murder, and what he knew of Kate's past. The initials 'T.C.' tattooed on her arm related to her husband Thomas Conway, he informed the officers, but he was uncertain whether Conway was alive or dead. In addition to the daughter he knew Kate had in Bermondsey, there was a sister much closer, in Thrawl Street, Spitalfields.[187]

The sister, Eliza Gold was soon traced. She also viewed the body at the mortuary and confirmed that it was indeed her sister. Although she had lived for many years with Thomas Conway and they had had children together, Mrs. Gold did not believe they had married; her real name was Catherine Eddowes.[188]

The Midlands girl known as 'Chick' to her family was born on 14th April 1842 at Graiseley Green, near Wolverhampton, to George Eddowes and his wife Catherine Evans. Kate was the sixth of twelve children, half of them born in London following the family's relocation to the capital when she was still a toddler. Settling in Bermondsey, close to father George's work on the other side of the Thames near London Bridge, Kate was fortunate to receive an education when she was enrolled at the charitable Dowgate School which offered places for the poor of the ward. But the death of both parents by the time Kate was 15-years-old broke up the family; the elder children had in the main formed lives for themselves, while the youngest were admitted to Bermondsey Union Workhouse. 'Chick' was found a position back in Wolverhampton and in December 1857 went to live with her uncle and aunt, William and Elizabeth Eddowes, at their home at 50 Bilston Street, and her four young cousins.

In the summer of 1862 she met Thomas Conway, a chap-book seller; a peddler of stories. Quickly falling pregnant, Kate left her life in Wolverhampton behind to join Conway on the road and the couple travelled around the country. By the time her baby was due Kate found herself in Norfolk, and she gave birth to Catherine Ann 'Annie' Conway at the Great Yarmouth workhouse infirmary on 18th April 1863. Sons Thomas and George followed in the next decade, but the relationship between Kate and Thomas had already become destructive, through a combination of her drinking and his violent outbursts. They parted in 1881, with Conway taking the children. Kate gravitated towards the East End and the support of her sister Eliza, who lived at Thrawl Street. When she found herself in possession of the funds, Kate took a bed at Cooney's Lodging House. It was here that she met John Kelly.[189]

Mrs. Annie Phillips, the daughter Kate told John Kelly that she hoped to see in Bermondsey, had last seen her mother just over two years previously and had subsequently moved to Southwark Park Road. She had never seen any papers, but her mother had told her that she and Thomas Conway had been married. Her father had previously lived with her and her husband, lamp black packer Louis Phillips, but father and daughter did not get on and he had left suddenly around 18 months ago. She believed he had gone to live with her two brothers, and had not seen him nor heard from him since.[190]

It would take a fortnight for detectives to interview Thomas Conway, and even then it was purely because he had himself attended the City Police's Old Jewry office with his two sons after learning that the police were keen to speak to him. He confirmed his daughter's story, stating that he left Kate in 1880 as a consequence of her drinking. He knew that she had been living with John Kelly, and had seen her once or twice in the streets, but said he kept out of her way as he wanted nothing to do with her.[191]

By the time he attended Old Jewry his former partner had been in her grave for a week.

Catherine Eddowes was buried on Monday, 8th October. At the Golden Lane Mortuary she was placed in a coffin of polished elm with oak mouldings and a plate with the following simple inscription thereon in gold lettering:

> Catherine Eddowes,
> died Sept. 30, 1888
> aged 43 years.[192]

The coffin was placed on a glass-panelled hearse, and drawn by a pair of horses left the mortuary at half-past one,[193] the cortège being escorted to the City boundary by a strong turnout of the City Police, led by Superintendent Foster. At Old Street it was met by their Metropolitan counterparts, who escorted the sad parade past Whitechapel church along the Mile End road, through Bow and Stratford[194] to the City of London Cemetery at Ilford. The streets were lined by thousands of mourners, who audibly expressed their sympathy to John Kelly and Kate's four sisters and two nieces, who followed the hearse in a mourning coach. At the cemetery itself, crowds of people, some with children in their arms, watched as Rev. Mr. Dunscombe conducted the service as the coffin was lowered into consecrated ground in the Church of England part of the cemetery. The costs were covered by Mr. Hawkes, vestryman at St. Luke's church.[195]

By contrast, Elisabeth Stride had been buried two days earlier with the minimum of fuss at the East London Cemetery on Grange Road,

Plaistow at the expense of the parish.[196] That very evening her spirit was apparently summoned by a group of six people at Cardiff, one of whom – a respectable-looking elderly lady who identified herself as a spiritualist – attended the local police station to report that Elisabeth had told them that her murderer was a middle-aged man who lived on Commercial Street or Road. She apparently mentioned his name, and the fact that he was one of a gang of twelve.[197] It is not recorded whether the Cardiff police wired their London counterparts with this information.

Not least among the worries of the police was the safety of the public; with excitement heightened, it did not take much for crowds to become convinced that any man acting 'strangely' could be the killer, as in the case of Thomas Mills, a 50-year-old cabinet maker who had apparently been arrested for drunkenness more than 100 times. On 27th September he found himself at Worship Street Police Court on the same charge, but on this occasion he had an excuse for his behaviour – he resembled a sketch of 'Leather Apron' which had been published in the *Illustrated Police News*. The previous evening he had been in Wellington Row, Shoreditch, a little the worse for wear, when a crowd spotted and surrounded him, shouting "We'll lynch him; he's Leather Apron!" A constable took him to the police station while he sobered up. Mills complained that he was unable to find work as a result of his remembrance to the likeness, and as a result he took to drink and subsequently became angry.

Magistrate Mr. Saunders fined Mills 2s 6d, telling him it was his own fault if he got drunk. If he stayed sober, the defendant was told, people wouldn't pay any attention of his likeness to the sketch.[198]

Whether Thomas Mills heeded the admonishment or not is unknown, but within days of his appearance in court a new name for the terror would make itself known, banishing 'Leather Apron' to history.

On 29th September Chief Constable Dolly Williamson received communication from Tom Bulling of the Central News Agency at New Bridge Street, London E.C. His covering note said that the enclosed letter had been received by the Central News but treated as a joke;[199] inside an envelope postmarked 27th September and addressed to "The Boss, Central News Office, London City" was a double-sided letter supposedly from the Whitechapel murderer:

Dear Boss,

I keep on hearing the police have caught me but they wont fix me just yet. I have laughed when they look so clever and talk about being on the right track. That joke about Leather Apron gave me real fits. I am down on whores and I shant quit ripping them till I do get buckled. Grand work the last job was. I gave the lady no time to squeal. How can they catch me now. I love my work and want to start again. You will soon hear of me with my funny little games. I saved some of the proper red stuff in a ginger beer bottle over the last job to write with but it went thick like glue and I cant use it. Red ink is fit enough I hope ha. ha. The next job I do I shall clip the ladys ears off and send to the police officers just for jolly wouldn't you. Keep this letter back till I do a bit more work, then give it out straight. My knife's so nice and sharp I want to get to work right away if I get a chance. Good Luck.

Yours truly
Jack the Ripper

    Dont mind me giving the trade name

    PS Wasnt good enough to post this before I got all the red ink off my hands curse it No luck yet. They say I'm a doctor now. ha ha

A follow-up postcard was received by Central News on 1st October, and seemed to have been penned by the same author:

I was not codding dear old Boss when I gave you the tip, you'll hear about Saucy Jacky's work tomorrow double event this time number one squealed a bit couldn't finish straight off. had not the time to get ears for police. thanks for keeping last letter back till I got to work again.

Jack the Ripper[200]

Reaction was swift; perhaps unsurprisingly, as well as sending the letter and postcard to Scotland Yard the Central News Agency had telegraphed their contents around newspaper offices,[201] no doubt in an attempt to make their service seem more valuable. The letter, and the moniker by which it was signed off, were sensational – and sensationalism sold newspapers. Others commented on the 'humorous' phrasing:

Ghastly as these horrors are there is a numerous selection of the populace who see a grimly humorous side to them. The jokist and the caricaturist have made folks laugh, and always – ominous circumstance

– at the expense of the police... Our old friend *Punch* has represented the Investigation Department as playing at Blindman's Buff, whilst a more daring contemporary has pictured the Home Secretary and Sir Charles Warren being drummed out by the members of the force they are supposed to control. But it is 'Jack the Ripper' who has earned the cake as a humorist in this melancholy connection. He has written a really funny epistle to a certain news agency, in which he gloats over the fact that he is the author of the assassinations, and laughs to scorn the efforts of the 'bobbies' to nail him.[202]

One who most certainly didn't see the joke was John Lock, a seaman who was in the Ratcliffe Highway area at six o'clock on the evening of 3rd October[203] when an excited crowd began following him, shouting "Leather Apron! Jack the Ripper!" Thankfully for Mr. Lock, he was saved by police officers who took him to the police station for his own safety; there it was discovered that his light tweed suit was stained red with red paint, which the mob had mistaken for blood. Lock gave a satisfactory account of himself, but it was some time before the crowd dispersed and he was able to go on his way. John Lock bears the distinction of being probably the only person accused of being both 'Leather Apron' and 'Jack the Ripper', with the favoured nickname for the Whitechapel murderer beginning to shift from the former to the latter.

An early mimic of the supposed author of 'Dear Boss' came within hours when it was reported that a postcard from 'Jack the Ripper' had been received at Barrett's Confectionery Factory at Wood Green, threatening six women who worked there.[204]

John Richardson, son of the woman who let rooms at 29 Hanbury Street where Annie Chapman had been murdered and who had appeared at her inquest, received a copy of the *Liverpool Daily Post* of 1st October which included a report of the 'Ripper' letter highlighted in blue pencil. The newspaper had been wrapped and stamped, addressed to "Jack the Ripper, 29 Hanbury Street, London E.C." A note on the reverse read: "Dear Jack, – I send you this paper, and hope you will come to Liverpool as I am an associate of yours. – K.T. Please reply to 39 Pitt Street." Richardson declined to take up the writer's offer, instead handing the correspondence to the police.[205]

It was not long before the wording of the 'Ripper' missives was not enough for some readers; they wanted to view the letter and postcard for themselves. The *St. James's Gazette* was just one title which received contact from its readership commenting on the merits of publishing a facsimile:

> Among the plenitude of suggestions offered by the amateur detectives of crime, it is not common to find one so sensible as that contained in a letter to us from 'H.F.W.':- Since it is, at least, possible that the person signing himself 'Jack the Ripper', who wrote the letter and postcard published yesterday, is really the murderer he claims to be, would it not be well that the press should be enabled and requested by the police to furnish a facsimile of his handwriting? Should he indeed be identical with the assassin, the detection of the latter would be rendered probable, if not certain, by such a course. Should he prove to be but an infamous buffoon, his exposure to universal contempt would surely serve the end of hindering other similar jesters from like diabolical folly.[206]

In fact, the Metropolitan Police had already decided to publish a facsimile of the letter and postcard, and this appeared in the evening edition of the London *Evening News* of 3rd October[207] and then nationally the next day.

The reaction was as massive as it was predictable – and 'Jack the Ripper' was here to stay. Immediately, further correspondence was received by both the Metropolitan and City forces, penned by hoaxers signing themselves 'Jack the Ripper', hundreds of letters and postcards warning of more attacks on women, all of which had to be investigated and eliminated, wasting an enormous number of man hours which detectives could ill afford. Publication of the 'Dear Boss' letter resulted in the exact opposite of 'H.F.W.''s no doubt well-intentioned suggestion that it would prevent "similar jesters from like diabolical folly".[208]

In later years it was revealed that police suspected a newspaper man as having penned the 'Dear Boss' letter and 'Saucy Jacky' postcard in order to fan the flames of panic on the streets, thereby selling more newspapers, and Assistant Commissioner Robert Anderson would accurately write that "one enterprising journalist went so far as to impersonate the cause of all this terror as 'Jack the Ripper,' a name by which he will probably go down in history."[209] Anderson teased readers of his memoirs in 1910 by saying he was "almost tempted" to disclose the writer's identity – a line to which Donald Swanson added "Known to Scotland Yard head officers of C.I.D." in his own copy – but retired Det. Chief Inspector John Littlechild did name the journalist he suspected as having been the writer – Tom Bulling of the Central News Agency, the man who had forwarded the letter to Scotland Yard.[210]

Another letter, this one received on 16th October accompanying a gruesome parcel, appeared much more likely to have been from the killer. It was sent to George Lusk, a builder and decorator who was

Chairman of the Whitechapel Vigilance Committee set up in September by local businessmen concerned that the murders were affecting trade, and as a consequence his name had risen to prominence.

The parcel itself contained what proved to be a human kidney, hinted in the letter as being that removed from Catherine Eddowes:

> From hell
>
> Mr Lusk
> Sir
> I send you half the Kidne I took from one woman prasarved it for you. tother piece I fried and ate it was very nise. I may send you the bloody knif that took it out if you only wate a whil longer
> signed Catch me when you can
> Mishter Lusk

While it was immediately suspected that the kidney could have been obtained by a medial student or indeed anyone employed at a hospital, the episode had to be investigated and it provided an insight into the City and Met officers working together; after taking the kidney and letter to Leman Street Police Station, the organ was sent to the City's Old Jewry for Dr. Gordon Brown to examine. Det. Chief Inspector Swanson allowed Superintendent James McWilliam to borrow the so-called 'From Hell' letter, which he photographed and returned. The senior City detective would comment on the close working relationship: "This department is co-operating with the Metropolitan Police in the matter, and Chief Inspector Swanson and I meet daily and confer on the subject."[211]

This meeting of detectives was the result of a suggestion from Commissioner Warren to his City counterpart Commissioner Colonel Sir James Fraser that the two detective forces be in constant communication to avoid duplicating work; the Met chief asking

> Could you send an officer to Chief Inspector Swanson here every morning to consult or may I send an officer every morning to consult with your officers. We are inundated with suggestions and names of suspects.[212]

Swanson himself commented on the harmonious working relationship, while reporting on the Mitre Square investigation:

> The remaining enquiries of the City Police are merged into those of the Metropolitan Police, each Force cordially communicating to the other daily the nature and subject of their enquiries.[213]

On 3rd October a letter was received from Sir John Whittaker Ellis,

M.P. for Kingston, who suggested to Henry Matthews that a police cordon be placed around Whitechapel and every house entered in a compulsory search.[214] The legality of such an undertaking was debated, with the Commissioner seeking advice from Dolly Williamson. Although the police had previously entered residences illegally, it was on a much smaller scale and even then only when information had been received that a wanted person was concealed in the house. Despite Warren reminding the Home Secretary that the welfare of his officers was at stake: any might be attacked – or worse, hanged – should death occur during a house being entered illegally, the Commissioner confirmed that

> I am quite prepared to take the responsibility of adopting the most drastic or arbitrary measures that the Sec of State can name which would further the securing of the murderer however illegal they may be, provided H.M. Gov. will support me.
>
> ...Three weeks ago I do not think the public would have acquiesced in any illegal action but now I think they would welcome any thing which shews activity & enterprise.[215]

Later that day Whitechapel was flooded by police officers and house-to-house enquiries were carried out without a hitch, and leaflets addressed "To the Occupier" left appealing for any persons with information on the murders to come forward.

Warren later placed a letter in *The Times* thanking the residents of Whitechapel for their "cordial cooperation", commenting that

> ..he is much gratified that the police officers have carried out so delicate a duty with the marked good will of all those with whom they have come in contact.[216]

Understandably, given that six murders had been committed in as many months – and the last five in just eight weeks – the Home Office were keen to be apprised of the ongoing investigation. Commissioner Sir Charles Warren tasked his Assistant, Robert Anderson with supplying this, and the report was subsequently prepared by Det. Chief Inspector Swanson.

Anderson was clearly annoyed at the timing of the request, and wrote in his covering minute:

> At the present stage of the inquiry the best reply that can be made to the Secretary of State's request for a report upon these cases is to send

the accompanying copy of detailed reports prepared by Chief Inspector Swanson, who has special charge of the matter at this office. I wish to guard against its being supposed that the inquiry is now concluded. There is no reason for furnishing these reports at this moment except that they have been called for.[217]

In Swanson's report of 19th October, in which he gave a full account of the murder of Elisabeth Stride, the Scot outlined the police investigation at that moment. In a section regarding a leaflet which had been printed and distributed to the houses within the H Division district appealing for information on any suspicious people, the detective wrote:

...80,000 pamphlets to occupier were issued and a house to house enquiry made not only involving the result of enquiries from the occupiers but also a search by police & with a few exceptions – but not such as to convey suspicion – covered the area bounded by the City Police boundary on the one hand, Lamb St. Commercial St. Great Eastern Railway & Buxton St. then by Albert St. Dunk St. Chicksand St. & Great Garden St to Whitechapel Rd and then to the City boundary, under this head also Common Lodging Houses were visited & over 2000 lodgers were examined.

Enquiry was also made by Thames Police as to sailors on board ships in Docks or river & extended enquiry as to asiatics present in London, about 80 persons have been detained at the different police stations in the Metropolis & their statements taken and verified by police & enquiry has been made into the movements of a number of persons estimated at upwards of 300 respecting whom communications were received by police & such enquiries are being continued.

Seventy six Butchers & Slaughterers have been visited & the characters of the men employed enquired into, this embraces all servants who had been employed for the past six months.

Enquiries have also been made as to the alleged presence in London of Greek Gipsies, but it was found that they had not been in London during the times of the various murders.

Three of the persons calling themselves cowboys who belonged to the American Exhibition were traced & satisfactorily accounted for themselves.

Up to date although the number of letters daily is considerably lessened, the other enquiries respecting alleged suspicious persons continues as numerous.

There are 994 Dockets besides police reports.[218]

It's clear from this that the police were undertaking an extensive and far-reaching investigation.

Thankfully for Swanson and his colleagues, no further murders were committed in October and they were able to concentrate on their enquiries. The press were also running out of inspiration, beyond continuing to lambast the police for their inability to arrest the killer, with one reporter almost wistfully commenting on 3rd November:

> We seldom hear anything about the Whitechapel murderer now. Probably in a short time he will share the proverbial fate of nine days' wonders.[219]

Within a week there would be plenty to report, and 'Jack the Ripper' would prove that he would be far from forgotten.

> Commissioner of Police. Reports that information has just been received that a mutilated dead body of a woman is reported to have been found this morning inside a room in a house (No. 26) in Dorset St., Spitalfields.
>
> The matter has been placed in Mr. Andersons hands.
>
> Pressing.[220]

*

> Anderson says through the telephone that the murder was committed in Spitalfields which is in the Metropolitan Police District. It is believed that the murdered woman is a prostitute named Kelly. The Police Surgeon was when Anderson spoke still examining the body.[221]

*

On the morning Friday, 9th November Thomas Bowyer was as usual serving customers in the chandler's shop at 27 Dorset Street when at 10.45am his employer John McCarthy told him to see whether he could get any rent money from the tenants of 13 Miller's Court,[222] a single ground-floor room which in reality was a partitioned-off part of 26 Dorset Street. In addition to his shop, McCarthy owned No. 26 and also Miller's Court, a cul-de-sac which had once been gardens to the rear of the two Dorset Street properties but by the 1851 census a number of cottages had been built on the land by former owner John Miller; in

1888 there were six, each whitewashed with green shutters.²²³ Nos. 26 and 27 were separated by the arched entrance to the 20ft passageway into Miller's Court, with the door to No. 13 being the second on the right, at the end of the passage.

On leaving the shop Bowyer turned immediately left into the Miller's Court passage and knocked on the door of No. 13. He knew the woman who lived there as 'Mary Jane', and the man was named Joseph Barnett.

Receiving no answer, Bowyer walked around the corner of No. 13 to the side facing into the Court, which had two windows. He saw one pane was broken, so, reaching inside, he pulled the curtain aside and peered into the room.

The first thing he saw were two lumps of flesh on a bedside table. Looking again, he saw a body lying on the bed, with blood on the floor. Bowyer let the curtain drop and returned silently to John McCarthy. Standing in the shop, he reported what he'd seen.²²⁴

They went back to the window and McCarthy looked for himself. Warning Bowyer not to mention the horrors they had seen, the men walked the short distance to Commercial Street Police Station and there saw Inspector Walter Beck, who listened to their story and immediately followed them back to Miller's Court. The body, John McCarthy told the policeman, was that of Mary Jane Kelly, who together with Joseph Barnett had been his tenant for some ten months. He believed they were married. The rent was 4s 6d a week, but Mary was 29s in arrears,²²⁵ probably as a result of Barnett losing his job as a porter at Billingsgate fish market some three or four months earlier. With no money coming in, Mary had resorted to her old ways by working as a prostitute,²²⁶ although landlord McCarthy claimed that he had no idea his property was being used for immoral purposes.²²⁷

John McCarthy might have feigned surprise, but the reality is that he must have been aware, and possibly even have expected it. The street had a notorious reputation, as one newspaper described the day after the murder:

> Dorset Street abounds in women whose features, language and behaviour are such that the smallest vestige of self-respect, if any remained in Mary Jane Kelly, would be sufficient to distinguish her from the more degraded of her associates. This short thoroughfare and the adjoining Paternoster Row, leading direct to the Spitalfields vegetable market, have now been given up to common lodging houses at 4d and 6d a night, or "6d for a single bedded cabin", and to women who have lost every trace of womanliness. The street and the row are places which the police state

*Dorset Street and Miller's Court
from The People, 18th November 1888*

are hardly safe for any respectable person by day and certainly not at night. In such a neighbourhood it was impossible to rise; to sink lower was inevitable.[228]

Likewise, it was almost for certain that McCarthy knew that Mary and Joseph Barnett were not married; he was also probably aware that the couple had parted more than a week earlier. Barnett had left her on 30th October due to her going back to earning a living on the streets. Although he had lost his job at Billingsgate, he found occasional work as a labourer and as a result often visited Mary and gave her money. He went to see her at the Miller's Court room they had previously shared on the evening of 8th November, but as he had not worked that day he had nothing to give her. He departed at 8 o'clock, returning to his new lodgings at Buller's Lodging House on New Street, Bishopsgate.[229]

When he heard the next day that a murder had been committed in Dorset Street he went to the police station, where he was closely questioned and his statement taken.[230] In this way details of Mary Kelly's life were learned; at least, the life as she told it to Joe Barnett.

She was 25-years-old and had been born at Limerick, although her family had moved to Wales when she was very young. Her father's name was John Kelly, a gauger at an ironworks in Carnarvonshire. She had one sister, who travelled from market to market selling materials, and seven brothers; six at home and one in the army. She had been married at the age of 16 to a collier named Davis or Davies, who had tragically died in an explosion two or three years later.

At that point she had left home and gone to Cardiff, where she lived with a cousin and led "a bad life", before making her way to London and quickly finding work at a brothel in the West End. A man whose acquaintance she met there persuaded her to go to France, and she no doubt went full of excitement at the thought of a life on the Continent. But as she told it to Joe Barnett, Mary did not enjoy the experience and returned to London after a fortnight.

She subsequently lived at various locations including the Ratcliffe Highway, Bethnal Green Road and Pennington Street, sharing her life with men such as a 'Morganstone' and then Joseph Fleming, a plasterer of whom she was fond.[231]

This was her life story before she met Joe Barnett. How much was the truth is impossible to tell, as nothing of her past before her return from Paris has ever been confirmed by researchers.

Perhaps the clue lies in the supposed trip to France. This was at the height of the white slave trade, with English girls especially sought after by European procurers. In 1880 Alfred Dyer published a 37-page pamphlet entitled *The European Slave Trade in English Girls: A Narrative of the Facts*, in which he revealed the ongoing traffic in English girls as young as thirteen being transported from London to European brothels, some on their own free will but the vast majority under false pretences, as we shall see in Chapter 16.

With Continental brothels requiring girls to be aged 21 or older, but demand being for those of more tender years, the victim would be tricked into securing a false passport and taken abroad.

Det. Chief Inspector Donald Swanson had himself investigated a similar case in the early 1880s. In this instance, the girl, 23-year-old Hannah Brannan, was aware of the reason for her travelling abroad and had applied for a passport at the Foreign Office, Whitehall, with a medical certificate provided by a Dr. Well of Wandsworth Road: Swanson recorded:

> I ascertained that this girl was about to be sent across to Holland for purposes of prostitution and she knew perfectly well that it was so, but was determined to go, lived by the representation of a designing woman who earned her livelihood by procuring good looking English girls for the Dutch brothels.
>
> The system was carried on as follows:- having gulled her victim into the idea of an idle life of lust & pleasure, [the procurer] then searches the register at Somerset House, getting the certificate of register of birth of another girl over 21, whose name the victim adopts. Some inferior surgeon known to her then medically examines the victim, and gives her an application certificate for the passport in the forged name. On production of this at Foreign Office, the necessary passport is frauded, and then the victim is taken over to Holland by this woman. The fee paid by the Dutch brothel keeper to the procuress is £13 13s.
>
> In the case of Hannah Brannan I prevented her going by advising Foreign Office to keep the passport until I had thoroughly enquired into the matter, the result being as stated. It is no offence against our English law, or in other words, there is no English law to meet the necessity.[232]

It is interesting to consider this system of British girls adopting a false name in order to travel to Continental brothels when trying to unravel the mysteries of Mary Jane Kelly's story. While researcher Neal Shelden located Adrianus Morgenstern and Elizabeth Felix,[233] indicating some truth in her story after arriving in the East End following her spell in France, nothing before this event can be confirmed. Did she in fact adopt the identity 'Mary Jane Kelly' for her visit to Paris, and experience the earlier events in her life under her own, unknown birth name?

When the press caught wind that the victim's identity had become known, Joseph Barnett was a wanted man. So many were the inquiries for him at Buller's Lodging House that by the morning following the murder he had been told to leave, his presence "having become a nuisance".[234] Barnett moved in with his sister at 21 Portpool Lane, Grays Inn Road.[235]

He had first met Mary Jane Kelly on Commercial Street in April 1887, the two going for a drink and agreeing to meeting the following day, when they decided to remain together. Barnett arranged for a room at George Street, Spitalfields, as he was known there. After a while they moved to Little Paternoster Row, but were told to leave for drunkenness and failing to pay the rent. After living for a short time in Brick Lane, the couple moved to the room which was 13 Miller's Court early in 1888.[236]

On several occasions Mary had asked Barnett to read details of the murders to her; she was apparently afraid but never named any particular person.[237] The likelihood is that Mary was aware that by earning a living on the streets she was placing herself in danger.

Although the couple had parted on 30th October, Barnett complaining when Mary had taken Maria Harvey, a fellow prostitute, into the room,[238] they had remained friendly and he would often visit, giving money when he had work. On 9th November when he went to see her a young woman named Lizzie Albrook, who worked at one of the nearby lodging houses, was in the room. Lizzie told reporters of Mary's despair at how working the streets was the only course open to her:

> ...She was heartily sick of the life she was leading, and wished she had enough money to go back to her people in Ireland, where her people lived. I don't believe she would have gone out as she did if she had not been obliged to do so in order to keep herself from starvation.[239]

Lizzie left when Barnett arrived, and he himself departed an hour later.

Mary then went out, no doubt in search of money, and appears to have spent the evening at The Britannia on the corner of Dorset and Commercial Streets, leaving with her drinking companion approaching midnight;[240] Mary Ann Cox, a widow also reduced to earning her living on the streets who resided at 5 Miller's Court and had known Kelly for eight months, entered Dorset Street moments later and saw the couple walk into Miller's Court. The man was around 5ft 5in tall, with a thick carrot-coloured moustache and blotches on his face. He was carrying a quart can of beer. Mrs. Cox said "Goodnight", but Mary was so drunk she could scarcely talk. She managed to slur "Goodnight" in return, and the couple went into No. 13. After warming herself Mrs. Cox went out again, hearing singing coming from within Mary's room as she passed. The drunken chorus was still underway when she returned around 1.00am.[241]

Elizabeth Prater lived at 20 Miller's Court, which was the room above Mary Kelly's and accessed via the first door in the passage when entered from Dorset Street. From around one o'clock until twenty-past she had stood at the entrance near John McCarthy's shop waiting for the man she lived with. When he didn't arrive she went up to her room and, in an indication of what Dorset Street was like, pushed two tables against the door. She went to bed and fell asleep almost immediately, and heard no singing from the room below.²⁴²

At 2.00am George Hutchinson was walking up Commercial Street when as he approached Flower and Dean Street he saw Mary Kelly, who asked him for sixpence.²⁴³ He had known her for three years and had on occasion given her money, but as he had not been working he was unable to give her anything.²⁴⁴ They parted and Kelly went in the direction of Thrawl Street, where a man stopped her. After some discussion the man placed his arm around Kelly's shoulders and they walked up Commercial Street past Hutchinson, who looked closely at the man as they did so. He followed them as they entered Dorset Street, and when Mary and her new paramour entered Miller's Court he stood for some time in Dorset Street, looking up the court to see if they would come out. After 45 minutes he gave up and left.²⁴⁵

Although George Hutchinson would later give a description of the man which was suspiciously detailed, right down to the shape of his tie pin, that he was indeed in Dorset Street watching the court seems to be confirmed by Mrs. Sarah Lewis, who on account of a row with her husband was spending the night with her friends Mr. and Mrs. Keyler at 2 Miller's Court. As she entered the court at 2.30am she noticed a man standing on his own by the lodging house opposite the passage looking up into Miller's Court as if waiting for someone. Mrs. Lewis settled into a chair and dozed for an hour, waking at 3.30. Shortly before 4 o'clock she heard a woman's voice shout "Murder!", seemingly from the direction of Mary Kelly's room.²⁴⁶ Elizabeth Prater, asleep in her bed above No. 13, was woken by her cat walking on her just before 4.00; she too heard a single cry of "Murder". Neither woman thought anything of the cry.

All was then silent, No. 13 Miller's Court undisturbed until Thomas Bowyer knocked on its door.

When Inspector Beck arrived at Miller's Court it was ascertained that the door to Mary Kelly's room was locked. He telegraphed for Det. Inspectors Frederick Abberline and Edmund Reid, and Dr. George Bagster Phillips. The surgeon arrived at 11.15am, followed by Abberline fifteen minutes later. Dr. Phillips looked through the window as Bowyer and McCarthy had done, and concluded there was nothing he could do for the woman. Learning from Beck that bloodhounds were apparently on their way, the consequence of a series of trials held by the police in the weeks before, the doctor suggested that the door to No. 13 not be forced until the dogs had arrived.²⁴⁷

As crowds of officials gathered, it was not until Det. Superintendent Thomas Arnold arrived at 1.30pm with the news that the bloodhounds were not coming that the order was given to break down the only entrance to Mary Kelly's room. John McCarthy complied, and took a pickaxe to the door.

What greeted them was like a scene from an abattoir. Dr. Phillips was the first to enter and noted the position of the body and the myriad of injuries inflicted upon it; Abberline examined the room and its contents. The sheer scale of the horror reflected the seclusion and time that the murderer had with his tragic victim, illuminated, Abberline reported, by the burning of women's clothes resulting in a fire so great as to melt the spout off a kettle.[248]

The police photographer arrived and took shots of the exterior of the building, before entering the room and taking what is undoubtably the most famous crime scene photograph in history.

At four o'clock a covered furniture van arrived and the remains were then placed in a temporary coffin, its straps sealed and put into the van. A large crowd followed it as it made its way to Shoreditch mortuary.

Shortly after four, an officer came out of the room carrying a pail covered in newspaper, reportedly containing body parts. He climbed into a cab and took the short journey to Dr. Phillips' home at Spital Square.[249]

The first doctor to attend the horrific scene at Miller's Court had been Dr. William Dukes, H Division police surgeon residing at 182 Brick Lane, who then deferred to Dr. George Bagster Phillips on the Divisional Surgeon's arrival. Also in attendance were the City Police Divisional Surgeon Frederick Gordon Brown and Scotland Yard's Dr. Thomas Bond. Bond and Phillips returned in the afternoon with Inspectors Abberline, Reid and Moore, along with Bond's assistant Dr. Charles Hebbert.

That Thomas Bond was at the scene would hardly be surprising, given his involvement in a great many cases over more than twenty years, but in fact on New Year's Day, 1888, he had discovered that his medical services were no longer required at Scotland Yard. Seeking an explanation, the following day he wrote to the Commissioner:

> Dear Sir Charles
>
> In the most casual manner I learned yesterday that I had been superseded in my appointment as Surgeon to the Police at Scotland Yard. This has been done without giving me the slightest notice of such intention, nor have I heard of any complaint nor of any reason why my attendance on the men should cease.

*Dr. George Farr, Thomas Bond's replacement
as Divisional Surgeon to New Scotland Yard
Courtesy Rod Farr*

Again, I am informed that the gentleman who has been appointed to supersede me, is Mr. Fredk. William Farre MRCS, a young surgeon, just two years qualified and with no medical qualification.

He may be a very excellent surgeon, I do not know him, but he would not be allowed by the Local Government Board to attend sick paupers till he had passed a medical examination. Why this gentleman has been picked out for such a responsible appointment, of course I have no right to enquire, but, having been intimately acquainted with the secret history of the Metropolitan Police for over twenty years, I know pretty well the wire pulling agencies that manage such appointments but which I am quite sure you would disapprove of.

I think, however, you will agree that I have a right to enquire why I have been superseded without notice & without reason & that it is but natural I should feel aggrieved by such treatment.

I am dear Sir Charles
Yours faithfully
Thos. Bond[250]

Warren's reply was not what Bond had hoped; the Commissioner saw no reason why the surgeon should feel aggrieved. He also corrected

Bond's assumption over his successor as surgeon to Scotland Yard; it was not the young Dr. Frederick Farre, but the experienced Dr. George Frederick Farr, Divisional Surgeon of L Division (Lambeth), at 54 some nine years older than Dr. Bond.[251]

A second letter from Bond to Warren on 4th January acknowledged the mistake, but the surgeon had not finished; on 1st February he wrote to the Under Secretary of State, complaining that the removal from his care of the members of the Executive Branch at Scotland Yard and also the officers of the C.I.D. had been done without the sanction of the Home Secretary. Bond wrote that under Dr. Holmes, the former Chief Surgeon of the Metropolitan Police, it had been the custom that all appointments of Divisional Surgeons were made by the Secretary of State, and as such a Surgeon could only be removed by the same authority. The Commissioner, he argued, had no power to place the men at Scotland Yard under the medical care of another doctor.

The result was the opening of an inquiry into Dr. Bond's complaint, with Sir Charles Warren laying out the facts to the Under Secretary of State as he saw them:

> With reference to your letter of the 11th inst. I have to acquaint you for the information of the Secretary of State, that Dr. Bond is mistaken in saying that he was appointed to the Executive Officers of Scotland Yard and the Detective Force more than 20 years ago; he has no claim to a monopoly of medical charge of the Constables at Scotland Yard. The general rule of the service has always been to place the men as far as practicable in medical charge of the surgeon where they are living which is the natural method of proceeding.
>
> Dr. Bond was appointed on 12th March, 1867, to the 'A' Division which had then only one sub-division, but he was not appointed to have exclusive charge of the 'A' Division, for on the 14th July, 1868, Mr. Butt was appointed to the Hyde Park and Triumphal Arch portion of the 'A' Division; and in 1886 the Rochester Row sub-division was added to the 'A' Division and the surgeon of the 'B' Division continues still in charge.
>
> Dr. Bond on these occasions made no claim to the care of the sick of these sub-divisions, and he is simply Surgeon to the King Street sub-division of the 'A' Division.
>
> Owing to the dimensions to which this sub-division has grown from the large number of men added for protection and other purposes being attached to it for medical care, it appeared evident that Dr. Bond had more constables than he could adequately attend to with the duties he

performs outside the Police.

On the 26th November, 1887, a representation was made to me by the four Heads of Department of the Commissioner's Office, namely the Executive Branch, Criminal Investigation Department, Public Carriage Branch, and Lost Property Office, that it would greatly conduce to the comfort of the men of the Commissioner's Office who are nearly all married men and live on the south side of the river, if the Divisional Surgeon of the 'L' Division were to deal with the sick of the Commissioner's Office. This was recommended by the Assistant Commissioner and was approved by me as desirable, as the 'A' Division is so large and the men of the Commissioner's Office live on the other side of the water.[252]

Dr. Bond can have no grievance in this matter as the 'L' Division is the natural Division to which these men would be attached for sick attendance, and the arrangement thus made was in entire accordance with all precedent, the Commissioner having from time immemorial regulated the number of men attached to any surgeon's district, and this he is continually doing from day to day.

With regard to the 'A' Division itself I may point out that the offices of the Common Lodging House Branch formerly attached to 'A' Division used at that time to be attended by the surgeons of the Divisions in which they were living; and Superintendent Cutbush himself has for many years past been attended by a medical officer on the other side of the river.

It seems to me that Dr. Bond can scarcely have considered the justice of the case to the surgeons in bringing this matter forward, for he has for some time received emoluments for a large number of men attached to 'A' Division for temporary purposes, who might with far greater justice on Dr. Bond's jurisprudence be claimed by the surgeons of surrounding districts, and who would I have no doubt set up a claim if they imagined that Dr. Bond had any right in the principle he enunciates. For example the whole of the Candidates are now actually quartered in 'L' Division, and are on Dr. Bond's principle clearly belonging to the charge of the Surgeon of "L' Division and yet Dr. Bond has not complained of the injustice of allowing him to remain in charge of them.

With reference to the copies of letters which Dr. Bond has forwarded to you there is a remark in that of the 2nd ultimo to which I must make allusion. He talks of the secret history of the Police, and of his knowing pretty well the wire-pulling agencies which manage surgeon's appointments. Dr. Bond has on more than one occasion been to see me upon what he calls his grievances, namely, not having been appointed as Chief Surgeon; and has made similar remarks to these in his letter with regard to other surgeons. I have not found it desirable to encourage Dr. Bond in making such statements, which only appear to me to injure himself.

It has never been the custom for the Commissioner to give notice to surgeons of any change of his nature, which are actually going on every day; for example, 76 men were a few days ago added to the 'A' Division for duty during the session, and no complaint was made by Dr. Bond of this addition without notice being given to him.

I have to remark that I think it would have been more in accordance with ordinary procedure if Dr. Bond has brought this matter to my notice officially through the Chief Surgeon with a request that it should be forwarded to the Secretary of State, his former correspondence with me on the subject, although now submitted by him to the Secretary of State, having been of a private nature. Had I considered his letters official communications I should certainly have considered it my duty to have forwarded them to the Secretary of State as they contained statements of so unfounded a nature.[253]

On 7th March, Dr. Bond, presumably unaware of the Commissioner's lengthy report, once again wrote to the Under Secretary of State, this time drawing attention to a Police Order published on 13th February 1888 which stated:

> In every case where it is proposed to alter the area of the district of a Divisional Surgeon a report is at once to be made by the Superintendent to the Commissioner who will instruct the Chief Constable to enquire into, and after conferring with the Chief Surgeon report on, the proposed arrangement before any alteration is finally made.

The surgeon underlined that neither Chief Constable Adolphus Williamson nor Assistant Commissioner James Monro knew anything about his removal, and that Chief Surgeon Alexander Mackellar had not been involved in the decision either.[254]

Warren's response was to provide evidence of the increasing number of men under Dr. Bond's care, illustrating irrefutably that the surgeon was unable to attend properly to their medical requirements. For six years from 1877, the number of men remained steadily at around 430, but in 1883 had jumped to 535 and had subsequently risen steadily until in 1887 the figure was 746. As the Commissioner pointed out, had he "kept on the Commissioner's Office with [Dr. Bond] he would have had 900". This was, of course, in addition to Bond's consulting practice, his work at Westminster Hospital and the Great Eastern and Great Western Railway Companies.[255]

There could be no argument that Dr. Bond had attempted to take on more work than he was able to cope with. A clue to the reasons for this would appear in his obituary in *The British Medical Journal* of 15th June 1901, where it was noted that there could be no doubt that the married father of six "would have distinguished himself as a surgeon... but the necessity of providing for the needs of a large family compelled him to accept work which interfered with a purely surgical practice."

The Divisional Surgeon must have sensed that he was fighting a losing battle, for on 25th May he wrote to the Receiver claiming a salary for the half-year period to 31st December 1887, the day before he discovered he had been superseded by Dr. Farr. Bond's letter claimed that since 13th November 1887 he had lost the financial reward of treating 5 Superintendents, 38 Inspectors and 124 Constables as these had been transferred to Dr. Farr. Needless to say, payment was not forthcoming.[256]

The end of the drawn-out affair came in late autumn, when Dr. Bond consulted with Alexander Mackellar, Chief Surgeon of the Metropolitan Police. The result was Bond's resignation on 4th October 1888 from his duties as medical officer for the men employed at both the Commissioner's Office and Detective Department at Scotland Yard; he now recognised the advantages of these men having access to medical attention closer to their homes.[257]

Dr. Mackellar later wrote to the Commissioner, confirming the direction which Bond wanted to take:

> Mr. Bond is not only Assistant Surgeon to the Westminster Hospital, but is and has been for many years Lecturer on Medical Jurisprudence in the Medical School. He has had a very large Medico-Legal experience, and he would naturally prefer to be referred to by the Commissioner as a Medico-legal expert, than to retain charge of an extra number of men which would necessitate frequently long journeys to the south of the river, and which would further in many instances disqualify him from being consulted in Police Civil and Criminal business in his higher capacity of Medical Juris.
>
> London, unlike foreign capitals has few medical men possessed of large Medico-legal knowledge and experience, and Mr. Bond has both, is an exceedingly good witness, and has an intimate and extensive acquaintance with the Force. I consider that it would be an advantage to the Service that he should be consulted in Medico-legal difficulties.[258]

Dr Thomas Bond
Courtesy Debra Arif

Although this promotion of the Divisional Surgeon was not put in writing until 1st November, it seems that Bond's decision had reached the ears of the Commissioner's Office sooner, for on 31st October Charles Warren had composed a letter to the Under Secretary of State confirming that Bond now appreciated the difficulties which might arise should he continue to have medical charge of the Scotland Yard men. Importantly, Warren then confirmed that Bond "naturally prefers to be called in by the Commissioner for civil & criminal business in which he is an expert instead of other specialists." The letter was finally sent on 2nd November.[259]

Given his stubborn refusal to back down over Dr. Farr's appointment, Warren's enthusiasm for Bond's medico-legal expertise is interesting. This was referred to in a letter to the doctor dated 25th October, in which Assistant Commissioner Robert Anderson appealed for direction as to the medical abilities of the so-called Jack the Ripper:

> In dealing with the Whitechapel murders the difficulties of conducting the enquiry are largely increased by reason of our having no reliable opinion for our guidance as to the amount of surgical skill and anatomical knowledge probably possessed by the murderer or murderers.
>
> I brought this matter before Sir C. Warren some time since and he has now authorised me to ask if you will be good enough to take up the medical evidence given at the several inquests and favour him with your opinion on the matter.
>
> He feels that your eminence as an expert in such cases – and it is entirely in that capacity that the present case is referred to you, will make your opinion specially valuable.[260]

With the matter settled, Bond began to prepare his response to Anderson's request. Before he could submit his conclusions, Mary Kelly was murdered and the surgeon was able to conduct a post mortem.

His autopsy notes, believed to have been dictated for his assistant Charles Hebbert to write down, were subsequently submitted, appearing with a Registry stamp of 16th November 1888, and reveal the true horror of what had been done to Mary Kelly:

> Notes of examination of body of woman found
> murdered & mutilated in Dorset St.
>
> Position of body.
>
> The body was lying naked in the middle of the bed, the shoulders flat, but the axis of the body inclined to the left side of the bed. The head was

turned on the left cheek. The left arm was close to the body with the forearm flexed at a right angle & lying across the abdomen, the right arm was slightly abducted from the body & rested on the mattress, the elbow bent & the forearm supine with the fingers clenched. The legs were wide apart, the left thigh at right angles to the trunk & the right forming an obtuse angle with the pubes.

The whole of the surface of the abdomen & thighs was removed & the abdominal cavity emptied of its viscera. The breasts were cut off, the arms mutilated by several jagged wounds & the face hacked beyond recognition of the features. The tissues of the neck were severed all round down to the bone.

The viscera were found in various parts viz; the uterus & kidneys with one breast under the head, the other breast by the Rt foot, the Liver between the feet, the intestines by the right side & the spleen by the left side of the body.

The flaps removed from the abdomen & thighs were on a table.

The bed clothing at the right corner was saturated with blood, & on the floor beneath was a pool of blood covering about 2 feet square. The wall by the right side of the bed & in a line with the neck was marked by blood which had struck it in a number of separate splashes.

Postmortem Examination.

The face was gashed in all directions the nose, cheeks, eyebrows & ears being partly removed. The lips were blanched & cut by several incisions running obliquely down to the chin. There were also numerous cuts extending irregularly across all the features.

The neck was cut through the skin & other tissues right down to the vertebrae the 5th & 6th being deeply notched. The skin cuts in the front of the neck showed distinct ecchymosis.

The air passage was cut at the lower part of the larynx through the cricoid cartilage.

Both breasts were removed by more or less circular incisions, the muscles down to the ribs being attached to the breasts. The intercostals between the 4th, 5th and 6th ribs were cut through & the contents of the thorax visible through the openings.

The skin & tissues of the abdomen from the costal arch to the pubes were removed in three large flaps. The right thigh was denuded in front to the bone, the flap of skin, including the external organs of generation & part of the right buttock. The left thigh was stripped of skin, fascia & muscles as far as the knee.

The left calf showed a long gash through skin & tissues to the deep muscles & reaching from the knee to 5 ins above the ankle.

Both arms & forearms had extensive & jagged wounds.

The right thumb showed a small superficial incision about 1 in long, with extravasation of blood in the skin & there were several abrasions on the back of the hand moreover showing the same condition.

On opening the thorax it was found that the right lung was minimally adherent by old firm adhesions. The lower part of the lung was broken & torn away.

The left lung was intact; It was adherent at the apex & there were a few adhesions over the side. In the substances of the lung were several nodules of consolidation.

The Pericardium was open below & the Heart absent.

In the abdominal cavity was some partly digested food of fish & potatoes & similar food was found in the remains of the stomach attached to the intestines.

Bond's profile report, requested by Robert Anderson in late October, was lodged in Home Office file A49301/21, dated-stamped 13th November 1888:

7 The Sanctuary
Westminster Abbey
Nov. 10th 1888

Dear Sir

Whitechapel Murders

I beg to report that I have read the notes of the four Whitechapel Murders, viz:

1. Buck's Row
2. Hanbury Street
3. Berners [sic] Street
4. Mitre Square

I have also made a post mortem examination of the mutilated remains of a woman found yesterday in a small room in Dorset Street.

1. All five murders were no doubt committed by the same hand. In the first four the throats appear to have been cut from left to right. In the last case owing to the extensive mutilation it is impossible to say in what direction the fatal cut was made, but arterial blood was found on the wall in splashes close to where the woman's head must have been lying.

2. All the circumstances surrounding the murders lead me to form the opinion that the women must have been lying down when murdered and in every case the throat was first cut.

3. In the four murders of which I have seen the notes only, I cannot form a very definite opinion as to the time that had elapsed between the murder and the discovering of the body. In one case, that of Berner's [sic] Street, the discovery appears to have been made immediately after the deed – in Buck's Row, Hanbury Street and Mitre Square three or four hours only could have elapsed. In the Dorset Street case the body was lying on the bed at the time of my visit – two o'clock – quite naked and mutilated as in the annexed report. Rigor Mortis had set in, but increased during the progress of the examination. From this it is difficult to say with any degree of certainty the exact time that had elapsed since death as the period varies from 6 to 12 hours before rigidity sets in. The body was comparatively cold at 2 o'clock and the remains of a recently taken meal were found in the stomach and scattered about over the intestines. It is, therefore, pretty certain that the woman must have been dead about twelve hours and the partly digested food would indicate that death took place about 3 or 4 hours after the food was taken, so 1 or 2 o'clock in the morning would be the probable time of the murder.

4. In all the cases there appears to be no evidence of struggling and the attacks were so sudden and made in such a position that the women could neither resist nor cry out. In the Dorset Street case the corner of the sheet to the right of the woman's head was much cut and saturated with blood, indicating that the face may have been covered with the sheet at the time of the attack.

5. In the four first cases the murderer must have attacked from the right side of the victim. In the Dorset Street case, he must have attacked in front or from the left, as there would be no room for him between the wall and the part of the bed on which the woman was lying. Again, the blood had flowed down on the right side of the woman and spurted on to the wall.

6. The murderer would not necessarily be splashed or deluged with blood, but his hands and arms must have been covered and parts of his clothing must certainly have been smeared with blood.

7. The mutilations in each case excepting the Berners [sic] Street one were all of the same character, and showed clearly that in all the murders the object was mutilation.

8. In each case the mutilation was inflicted by a person who had no scientific nor anatomical knowledge. In my opinion he does not even

possess the technical knowledge of a butcher or horse-slaughterer or any person accustomed to cut up dead animals.

8. [sic] The instrument must have been a strong knife at least six inches long very sharp-pointed at the top and about an inch in width. It may have been a clasp knife, a butcher's knife or a surgeon's knife. I think it was no doubt a straight knife.

9. [sic] The murderer must have been a man of physical strength and of great coolness and daring. There is no evidence that he had an accomplice. He must in my opinion be a man subject to periodical attacks of Homicidal and erotic mania. The character of the mutilations indicates that the man may be in a condition sexually, that may be called Satyriasis. It is of course possible that the Homicidal impulse may have developed from a revengeful or brooding condition of the mind, or that religious mania may have been the original disease, but I do not think either hypothesis is likely.

The murderer in external appearance is quite likely to be a quiet inoffensive looking man probably middle aged and neatly and respectably dressed. I think he must be in the habit of wearing a cloak or overcoat or he could hardly have escaped notice in the streets if the blood on his hands or clothes were visible.

10. [sic] Assuming the murderer to be such a person as I have just described, he would probably be solitary and eccentric in his habits; also he is most likely to be a man without regular occupation, but with some small income or pension. He is possibly living among respectable persons who have some knowledge of his character and habits and who may have grounds for suspicion that he is not quite right in his mind at times. Such persons would probably be unwilling to communicate suspicions to the Police for fear of trouble or notoriety, whereas if there were a prospect of reward it might overcome their scruples.

I am,
Dear Sir,
Yours faithfully.
Sd. Thos. Bond[261]

Dr. Thomas Bond's notes on the Whitechapel murderer have, almost from the time they were written, been seen as being among the very first attempts at profiling a serial killer. But had it not been for Sir Charles Warren's obstinacy over the doctor's overloaded practice, it's possible that he may not have been asked to prepare his report in the first place. By the time Dr. Bond's thoughts had been submitted, Warren had resigned his Commissionership.

First to request access to Bond's notes, in September 1892, was Dr. Arthur MacDonald, an official of the US Ministry of the Interior in Washington. Dr. MacDonald approached the Home Office requesting copies of "official reports relating to the condition of the bodies of the victims of 'Jack the Ripper'." He had attended the London and Brussels conferences on Criminal Anthropology held a month earlier. Having already met with Permanent Under Secretary Godfrey Lushington, MacDonald had a second meeting, this time with Assistant Under Secretary William Byrne, where he explained that he hoped to publish the relevant medical reports in *American Blue Books* as well as a French scientific magazine. On 28th September Lushington wrote to decline the request; MacDonald, no doubt disappointed but undeterred, published his *Criminology* the following year, seemingly relying on newspaper reports of Mary Kelly's injuries.[262]

More successful was Dr. Gustave Ollive, a professor at the School of Medicine at Nantes, who, having been instructed by the Juge d'instruction to investigate a case similar in nature to the Whitechapel murders, in the autumn of 1894 wrote to Sir Edward Bradford, by then Commissioner of the Metropolitan Police, requesting a copy of Bond's report. This may well have related to the murder of three young women in Austria six weeks earlier, reported by Reuters as the work of a "Jack the Ripper type."[263]

The body of the first victim, a 21-year-old hotel waitress at Amras, near Innsbruck, was found on Saturday, 22nd September in the countryside with five stab wounds to her neck; a razor-edged knife was found nearby. In her closed fist was a handful of her assailant's hair.[264] The second victim was discovered in a meadow near Castle Ambras on Tuesday, 25th September, stripped naked and extensively mutilated.[265] The body of the third victim was found near the village of Mieders, also hacked to pieces.[266]

Dr. Ollive was told by the Commissioner's office to contact the Home Office, who had to grant permission for Bond's report to be released. The Frenchman subsequently wrote to the Secretary of State on 8th November, who forwarded the request once again to the Commissioner.[267] On 22nd November Bradford wrote again to confirm that the profile sent to the Home Office in 1888 was "the only general report made by Dr. Bond upon the murders in question."[268]

Rather embarrassingly for the Home Office, that original report now appeared to be missing. A note dated 26th November admitted: "This report was with [A49301]/21 but cannot be found. ? Ask Cmmr. To send M. Ollive a copy if he has one unless he sees serious objection."

A response by a perhaps exasperated Robert Anderson on 7th December stated: "This has been done. A copy of the report in question is now attached." The new carbon copy of Dr. Bond's profiling report was stamped 10th December 1894.

By the time Ollive's request was dealt with by the Home Office – a month after his initial request – a bricklayer named Joseph Maier had been arrested and confessed to the murders in the Tyrol, going on to show police where he had buried items stolen from the victims.[269]

The whereabouts of Bond's profiling report in 1894 is interesting; was it a simple case of a civil servant not looking too hard for it, or, perhaps, had then Chief Constable Melville Macnaghten borrowed it from the files some months earlier in order to write his memoranda, in which he echoed Thomas Bond's opinion that the five Whitechapel murder victims were killed by the same hand?[270]

While the original report would find its way back into the official files by the time Ripper researchers were granted access in the 1970s, Bond's autopsy report on Mary Kelly was missing until 1987, when it was sent anonymously from Croydon together with a number of other police papers which almost certainly came from the files of Melville Macnaghten.[271]

Yet the impact of Dr. Bond's report was in the future; more immediate in the thoughts of East Enders following her murder was the capture of her killer and the failure of the Metropolitan Police, with newspapers directing their ire at an obvious target, Commissioner Sir Charles Warren:

> One more unfortunate gone to her death! Not by own suicidal act, by plunging into the black-flowing river, yet perishing gloomily – by the knife of the stealthy assassin, who with mocassined feet unrelentingly traverses the lowest parts of the Metropolis with maniacal, merciless craving in search of his prey, with an Attila-like bloodthirstiness, and who, having effected his ghastly purpose disappears like a shadow, leaving his victim weltering in her gore, mutilated and dismembered... The blood of the miserable mangled victims cries aloud to heaven for vengeance on the crazy vampire, and the name of Sir Charles Warren will stink in the nostrils of the people unless the miscreant be speedily run to earth.[272]

In fact, by the time reports of the Mary Kelly murder had been published the Commissioner had resigned his post.

He had written an article on police administration which had appeared earlier that week in *Murray's Magazine*, and although generally well-received by the newspaper reviewers the piece was not so highly regarded by Home Secretary Henry Matthews, who censured his Commissioner that he had overlooked a rule that prohibited Civil Servants from publicly discussing matters relating to their departments.

Warren responded by tending his resignation on Thursday, 8th November – coincidentally Mary Jane Kelly's final day.

Warren's response was immediate:

> Sir,
>
> I have just received a pressing and confidential letter, stating that a Home Office Circular of May 27, 1879, is intended to apply to the Metropolitan Police Force. I have to point out that, had I been told that such a Circular was to be in force, I should not have accepted the post of Commissioner of Police. I have to point out that my duties and those of the Metropolitan Police are governed by statute, and that the Secretary of State for the Home Department has not the power under the statute of issuing orders for the Police Force. This Circular, if put in force, would practically enable everyone anonymously to attack the Police Force without in any way permitting the Commissioner to correct false statements, which I have been in the habit of doing, whenever I found necessary, for nearly three years past. I desire to say that I entirely decline to accept those instructions with regard to the Commissioner of Police, and I have again to place my resignation in the hands of Her Majesty's Government.
>
> I am, Sir, your most obedient servant,
>   CHARLES WARREN."[273]

With what one can imagine no great reluctance, the same day Matthews replied to accept, and the departure of Warren appeared in the newspapers alongside details of Mary Kelly's demise, many readers merging the two to incorrectly conclude the reason for Warren's resignation.

Over the coming days candidates for his replacement were mentioned, including Malcolm Wood of the Manchester Police[274] and former Director of the C.I.D., Charles Howard Vincent.[275] On 27th November the appointment of the new Commissioner was made – James Monro.

Although the press who had turned against the outgoing Commissioner were jubilant, some support was forthcoming for Warren, with the *St. James's Gazette* commenting on the regulation cited by Matthews: "Advantage was taken of this incident to lead Sir Charles into what looks rather like a trap."²⁷⁶

Rumours of Warren's resignation had first appeared in the papers on the day of the inquest into Mary Kelly's death, which had been conducted in a single day – 12th November, the Monday after her murder – under Roderick Macdonald, Coroner for North East Middlesex. Mirroring the inquest on Annie Chapman which was presided over by Wynne Baxter despite her murder occurring in Macdonald's district, Kelly had been murdered in Baxter's South East London division but her remains taken to Shoreditch, which was under Macdonald's jurisdiction.²⁷⁷

It was time for Mary to be laid unto rest. A week later, on 19th November, hundreds of people crowded around St. Leonard's Church, Shoreditch, watching in silence as its bell was tolled and an oak and elm coffin with metal fittings containing the remains was placed upon an open hearse. On top were placed two crowns and a cross, made of white flowers and heartsease, a purple wild pansy of the 'sweet violet' family. The coffin was adorned with the simple inscription:

> Marie Jeanette Kelly,
> died November 9, 1888,
> aged 25 years

At 12.45pm the hearse set off, followed by two mourning carriages containing Joseph Barnett and several of Mary's friends. Progress was slow as thousands of people lined the route through Whitechapel and, as one reporter described "signs of sympathy were to be seen on every hand, and it was a very tough sight to witness many poor women of the class to which the deceased belonged greatly affected."

The cortège arrived at St. Patrick's Roman Catholic Cemetery in Leytonstone a few minutes before two o'clock.

There, only a small number of mourners were admitted and followed the Rev. Father Colomban, himself preceded by two acolytes and a cross-bearer, to the north-east corner of the burial ground, where the interment took place.²⁷⁸ Further doubt was cast on the past she told to Barnett when it transpired that despite her supposedly coming from a large family, with eight siblings, not one came forward to attend the funeral or even to confirm her story.

The entire cost had been borne by Mr. Henry Wilton, clerk of St. Leonard's for 50 years. It was announced that should anyone wish to offer a contribution these should be sent to Mr. Wilton; should there be a surplus a headstone would be erected. Not surprisingly, given the poverty in the East End this did not come to pass.²⁷⁹

The attack on Annie Farmer
from The Illustrated Police News, 1st December 1888

Emotions in the East End were understandably still running high when word spread of the murder and mutilation of a woman at Satchell's Lodging House on George Street two days after Mary Kelly's funeral.[280]

It very quickly transpired that the victim, Annie Farmer, had not been mutilated; she was not even dead. Instead, she claimed to have had her throat cut by a man with whom she had gone to the lodging house two hours before.

Satchell's had a notorious reputation. It was where Martha Tabram had been staying at the time of her murder, and next door to No. 18 where Emma Smith had lived for 18 months before her own death. Joseph Barnett had frequented at least one of the lodging houses on George Street before meeting Mary Kelly, and it was there that the couple took a room after deciding to live together.[281]

The George Street victim was known locally by the soubriquets 'Dark Sarah' and 'Laughing Liz', although her friend Mary Callaghan knew that her proper name was Annie Farmer. She was said to be a well-educated woman around 30-years-old – although some reports later said she was 34, 38 or 40 – and had been married to a respectable worker in Clerkenwell with whom she had three children before succumbing to drink and resorting to earning a living on the streets.[282] She had been living in the Spitalfields area for nearly four years,[283] and more recently could be seen every night near the railings at Christ Church, sleeping wherever she could if she was unable to persuade anyone to pay her the price of a bed.

In this way she had spent the night of 20th November walking the streets, until finally, in the early hours, meeting a man she had known casually for around twelve months.[284] On being asked why she was out at that early hour, Annie replied that she had no money for lodgings. No doubt sensing an opportunity, the man enquired as to the cost of a double bed and, not being put off by the quoted 8d, took her to several 'early' public houses where she drank so much hot rum that she became intoxicated. They then headed for Satchell's.[285]

The watchman, a mixed-race man nicknamed 'Darkie', saw them enter at around 6.30am. The man paid for a double bed and the couple went up to the first floor, taking possession of one of the partitioned-off boxes. Nothing more was heard of them until around half-past nine when the man suddenly ran downstairs, out through the door and into the street, past two women standing talking and a carman delivering coal next door, exclaiming "Look what she has done!" and, as the carman put it, making use of 'a low expression'. He had blood on his mouth and a scratch, and blood upon his hands.[286]

Waterside labourer William Sullivan[287] had returned to his lodgings at Satchell's ten minutes earlier after failing to find any work. He went first to the kitchen with a colleague named William Kew[288] and then to stand at the front door, where he heard a woman's voice crying out "Darkie, Darkie!" Sullivan pushed open the inner door leading to the stairs and saw Annie Farmer there with blood running down her bare breast from a wound to her throat. She was wearing only a short knitted petticoat, which was torn.[289] She told him that the man who had just gone out had cut her throat; Sullivan ran outside and saw the carman delivering coal, Frank Ruffell, and quickly told him what had happened; the two set off left into Thrawl Street, then on reaching the Frying Pan pub were told that their quarry had turned into Brick Lane, where he was lost. Outside The Bell they passed on information of the attack to two policemen.

The two women who had been chatting with Ruffell minutes earlier had also given chase, but quickly returned to Satchell's. The *Times* of 22nd November described how one, Ellen Marks,

> went to the woman's room, which is on the first flight. The woman was sitting on the bed, dressed in a black body and petticoat. Blood was

trickling down her neck. I said, "What has he done?" and she replied, "He has cut my throat." I asked for a light, and a woman brought a candle, for the room was very dark. I then saw that there were five or six wounds in the neck, which seemed to me to be gaping and at least 3in long. Next I inquired, "Do you know him?" and the woman answered "I knew him about a twelvemonth ago. I drank in his company, and he made himself known to me this morning. He paid 8d for the bed and gave me 6d whilst in the room. I brought him in about 6.30, and when I was half-asleep I felt a knife cross my throat, which woke me up, and I screamed." The woman was very excited. Then the police came, and the constable 256H asked me to hold the light whilst he looked for the knife; he found none.

The deputy of Satchell's wrapped a piece of rag around Annie Farmer's throat and she was dressed by a lodger named Esther Hall, Annie saying she was unable to do so herself.[290] She was then taken to Commercial Street Police Station by ambulance, where the wound to her throat was stitched by Dr. George Bagster Phillips. A detailed description of the man was obtained and telegraphed around all stations.[291]

The fact that Annie had known the man for a year convinced detectives that no matter what the truth was behind the incident, he was not connected with the previous Whitechapel atrocities. Although he had yet to be apprehended, the police expected him to surrender himself for questioning within a matter of days, with *The Times* of 23rd November perhaps accurately giving the truth of the matter:

> It is now believed that the wound to Farmer's throat was not made with a sharp instrument; also, that a quarrel arose between the pair respecting money, as, when the woman was at the station, some coins were found concealed in her mouth.

It was reported that Annie was no stranger to Commercial Street Police Station, having been held in custody there many times for drunkenness. On this occasion she was taken out via the back door to avoid public interest, and conveyed by cab to the Whitechapel Infirmary at Baker's Row, where the medical officer in charge was requested not to allow her any visitors while she recovered.[292]

While the attack on Annie Farmer and the Whitechapel murders were for Sir Charles Warren now a thing of the past, he had not been forgotten by his former subordinates. Superintendents of the majority of the Divisions visited him at his home and paid tribute to the discipline he had brought to the ranks, and how he had taken responsibility for the entire force, always seeking to further their welfare.[293]

Reaction to his departure and the appointment in his place of James Monro continued. While recognising that the new Commissioner would not enjoy an easy start, optimism was high:

> The scape-goat having gone, with all his sins into the wilderness, the new Chief Commissioner of Police enters upon the scene in the person of Mr. Monro, who, having resigned in consequence of differences with Sir Charles Warren, now returns to Scotland Yard in triumph. If he fancies that it is a bed of roses which is spread for him, he will be mistaken. But he probably understands all about that. A gentleman in the front rank of superintendents assures me that Scotland Yard, from the Chief Commissioner down to the lowest grade of policeman, is fully aware that it will never satisfy the public. Of course, if the Whitechapel murderer should be captured between this and Christmas Mr. Monro will begin with flying colours.[294]

A swift capture before Christmas was not forthcoming; instead, another death of a woman in the East End.

In the early hours of 20th December K Division's Sergeant Golding and P.C. Barrett were on their beat along Poplar High Street when they approached the entrance to Clark's Yard, a large area on the south side of the High Street filled with stables and workshops and accessed via a long, narrow passageway between Nos. 186 and 188 Poplar High Street.

Sgt. Golding looked and saw a bundle some 25 feet into the passage; on examination he discovered it was the body of a woman, lying on its left side with the left cheek resting on the ground. The left arm was under the body, and the left leg drawn up. The clothing was undisturbed. Sgt. Golding touched the body and found it was still warm.

Leaving P.C. Barrett at the scene, Golding went to fetch Dr. Brownfield, K Divisional Surgeon, but finding him unavailable was escorted back to Clark's Yard with his assistant, Dr. George Harris. The surgeon examined the body and noted that the lips were livid and the mouth was closed; blood-flecked mucus issued from the nostrils, and the hands were half-clenched. The body was removed to the Bickmore Street mortuary, where Golding searched the clothing and the body was examined.

The body was found to be that of a young woman 5ft 2in tall, with hazel eyes and light-coloured hair which fell in tight curls.

A post mortem was conducted on the still unknown victim by Dr. Brownfield the following morning, and the inquest – presided over by Wynne Baxter – was held immediately afterwards. By this time, 24 hours after the discovery of the body, a mark seemingly made by a cord had appeared on the right side of the neck; alongside this were marks obviously caused by thumbs, index and middle fingers on both sides of the neck. Dr. Brownfield submitted his opinion that death had been caused by strangulation. Baxter closed proceedings, saying that although it seemed that a murder had been committed there was not yet sufficient evidence. The inquest was adjourned to 2nd January 1889.[295]

Dr. Brownfield's comments came as a surprise to the police, who in the absence of any evidence at the scene had believed the death to have been down to natural causes or suicide. Having read a report of the inquest later that day in an evening newspaper, Assistant Commissioner Robert Anderson suggested to Commissioner Monro that he should himself go to Poplar to investigate the case, and requested Dr. Thomas Bond to undertake a second examination alongside Dr. Brownfield. The surgeon was unavailable,[296] however, so Chief Surgeon Alexander Mackellar went and made the examination himself. His findings fully supported Dr. Brownfield's opinion that death was by strangulation.[297] Dr. Bond and his assistant Dr. Hebbert also viewed the body and concurred with the earlier findings. Anderson was certain that the case was not one of murder, and on 24th December Dr. Bond made another examination and reported to Anderson that he had changed his mind; death was due to strangulation, but accidental and not murder.[298]

She would soon be identified; her name was Catherine Mylett, known sometimes as 'Rose', and her mother lived in Pelham Street, near Baker's Row in Whitechapel.[299] A newspaper report of police officers arriving at the house to break the news gives a sad insight into the reaction of those personally affected by this series of murders:

> When the detectives called at the house on Boxing Day they found the inmates indulging in Christmas festivities, and upon stating the object of their visit one of the women in the house had a serious fit.[300]

Investigations were undertaken by Det. Chief Inspector Swanson of Scotland Yard and K Division's Det. Inspector Richard Wildey, and their efforts were soon rewarded, when they visited Charles Ptolomey,[301] the Night Attendant at the Poplar Union:

> They asked me if I could identify the sailors? I told them I could pick the men out of a thousand. How I came to notice them was in this way:- It was about five minutes to eight o'clock on Wednesday night, when I was going to my work. Upon going up England Row (nearly opposite Clark's yard) I noticed two sailors. The shorter one was speaking to the

deceased, and the tall one was walking up and down. So strange did it seem that I stopped and 'took account' of them. Then I heard the woman say several times "No; no! no!" and the short sailor spoke in a low tone. The tall one was about 5ft 11in. He looked like a Yankee. The shorter one was about 5ft 7in. It struck me that they were there for no good purpose, and that was the reason I took so much notice of their movements. I shall always remember their faces, and could, as I say, pick them out of a thousand. I have been to the mortuary, and seen the deceased. She is the same woman, and she was sober when I saw her with the sailors.[302]

Despite conflicting medical evidence, at the conclusion of the inquest the jury returned a verdict of 'Wilful murder against some person or persons unknown'.

In his summing up, Coroner Baxter was afforded the opportunity to vent his frustration at how the Met had sought the opinion of a number of medical men, seemingly in an attempt to prove that the death did not belong in the same class as the previous murders in Whitechapel:

In the course of his remarks, the Coroner said the Assistant Commissioner of Police had, without his knowledge or sanction, sent doctor after doctor down to see the body. He did not wish to say much about that, but he had never before been subjected to such treatment at the hands of the police. All the doctors but one came to the conclusion that death was caused by strangulation... Dr. Bond, however, who disagreed from the other four doctors, was of opinion that death was due to a fall in an awkward position while drunk; and strangulation resulted from a tight collar. At the same time, [the jury] must remember that Dr. Bond did not see the body until several days had elapsed. All the other doctors were of opinion that strangulation was the cause of death. There was no absolute evidence that the deceased came to her death in the place where the body was found.[303]

The Assistant Commissioner himself still had something to say after Baxter's public rebuke, as he wrote in a report to James Monro:

No one is more ready than I am to spare the susceptibilities (or even to humour the vanity) of any official, but my estimate of the position and duty of the Commissioner of Police is wholly inconsistent with the idea that he must obtain the sanction of the Coroner before taking steps imperatively necessary for the investigation of a crime. This question may arise again at any moment, and I submit it to you for prompt and definite solution.[304]

Another death in Christmas week, possibly at the hand of the Whitechapel murderer, meant a fearful end to 1888. The panic was palpable, as one reporter wrote on Boxing Day:

> We watch while we wassail, we keep one eye on Father Xmas and the other on Jack the Ripper. The city beats, especially in the Whitechapel district, have been increased, and the Vigilance Committees are afoot again. The theory is that the miscreant may reckon upon finding victims off their guard owing to the general relaxation and individual indulgence of the time, and that, moreover, he very likely burns to shock the community out of its festival spirit by the fresh horror of some fearful crime. Society, alarmed at the suspicion, has one eye on the look out for the fiend, and the other more congenially bent upon the flowing bowl or its equivalents.[305]

As it turned out, Christmas passed without incident, with no 'gruesome gift' on the part of the murderer.

Clinging obstinately to his view that Catherine Mylett had died from natural causes, Assistant Commissioner Robert Anderson would later write that "but for the 'Jack the Ripper' scare, no one would have thought of suggesting that it was a homicide."[306]

For Donald Swanson, 1888 could not end soon enough. The strain of the past few months was enormous, and no doubt this was felt by wife Julia, who prematurely gave birth to the twins she was carrying on 2nd January 1889. First born was Alice Julia, at 8.30pm, followed by her brother William Alexander twenty minutes later.[307]

If the family hoped that the births were the start of a happier year, they were sadly mistaken. Young William Swanson, born suffering from marasmus – a form of severe malnutrition no doubt caused by his premature birth – died on 10th February, aged just forty days.[308] There seems little doubt that the stresses brought on by the pressure on Donald Swanson to catch the Whitechapel murderer, with Julia obviously deeply worried about her husband's health, exacerbated the condition and caused the premature births. In a sense, William Alexander Swanson could be said to have been an indirect victim of the Ripper.

Although the beginning of 1889 appeared to herald an end of the Whitechapel murders, the police and public alike were still vigilant. As the months passed with no further atrocities, police attention turned inward to matters within the C.I.D. and the health of Chief Constable Dolly Williamson. He was deteriorating fast, but declined to leave his post. With Charles Warren gone, the path was clear for Melville Macnaghten to finally join his friend James Monro within the force, and he was appointed Assistant Chief Constable within the C.I.D. on 1st June 1889, although a caveat was noted that the appointment did not necessarily carry a right of succession to the position of Chief Constable when it fell vacant. Not previously a constable within the Met, Macnaghten had to be attested and this was carried out before Assistant Commissioner (Executive) Richard Pearson on 3rd June.[309]

If the new Assistant Chief Constable was keen to get involved in the hunt for the Ripper, he wouldn't have long to wait. It had been seven months since the last horror; less than seven weeks after Macnaghten's appointment Whitechapel was reeling again at the news of another murder.

On Monday, 16th July labourer John McCormack arrived back at his lodgings at 52 Gun Street, Spitalfields from his job at a Jewish tailors on Hanbury Street. It was four o'clock, and after giving some money to his common-law wife Alice McKenzie he retired to bed for a few hours. The couple had been together for seven years, living in various lodging houses around Spitalfields but for the past year at Gun Street,[310] which was nicknamed 'Tenpenny's' after the owner, Mr. Thomas Tempany.

Before meeting John McCormack, Alice McKenzie had lived for some time with a blind man who made a living playing a concertina in the streets, but he had died around 1878. McCormack would later say that as far as he knew Alice had no relatives in London, but believed she had one son who was in America. Both her parents were dead, and she often spoke about her father, who had been a postman in Peterborough.[311]

When McCormack woke around 11.00 o'clock Alice had gone out. Deputy Betsy Ryder had seen her walk through the kitchen and out the front door onto Gun Street at around 8.30pm.[312]

The next definite sighting of Alice McKenzie alive came at 11.40pm. Margaret Franklin, who had known her for 14 or 15 years, was sitting with two friends on the step of a barber's shop at the Brick Lane end of Flower and Dean Street[313] when she walked past, heading in the direction of Whitechapel. She paused briefly to talk but said she couldn't stop, then continued on her way.[314]

At 12.20am, 40 minutes later, P.C. Walter Andrews was walking his beat and passed through Castle Alley, which ran parallel to Goulston Street. He saw nothing to attract his attention. At 12.30am P.C. Allen entered the street and stopped for five minutes under the lamp[315] outside the offices of Messrs. David S. King and Sons[316] to enjoy some supper. He too noticed nothing suspicious, and on finishing his food went back to his duty. At 12.48am P.C. Andrews turned into Castle Alley on another circuit, when Sergeant Badham approached on his check of the patrols. On receiving the "Alright" he left Andrews, but had gone no further than 150 yards when he heard the shrill blast of the constable's whistle. He rushed back to Castle Alley and found P.C. Andrews standing over the body of a woman, a pool of blood around her head and her skirts pushed up to expose her abdomen. She was lying under the very lamp at which P.C. Allen had enjoyed his supper.[317]

Allen was alerted by Sgt. Badham and went to fetch Dr. Bagster Phillips; P.C. Andrews remained with the body. He touched the body, and felt that it was quite warm.[318]

Dr. Phillips arrived at 1.10am and conducted an examination; the victim was lying on her back, with her face turned to the right. Her eyelids were open, her pupils dilated. There were two deep wounds in the left side of the neck from which a large amount of blood had flowed into the gutter.

The body was removed to the mortuary and at two o'clock that same afternoon Dr. Phillips conducted a post mortem on the body,[319] who had by now been identified by Mrs. Ryder as being that of Alice McKenzie.[320] Doctors Gordon Brown and Mackellar were in attendance as Phillips carried out his work. Death had been caused by the wounds to the throat, and seven or eight superficial wounds on the stomach and pubic area indicated an attempt at mutilation.[321] Had the close proximity of two beat constables frightened the killer into abandoning his plans of evisceration? There were just fifteen minutes between P.C. Allen finishing his supper and departing, and P.C. Andrews returning to that spot at 12.50am. Did Andrews disturb the killer? If so, was the culprit saved from capture by the intervention of Sergeant Badham spending a minute or two with Andrews?

Wynne Baxter presided over the inquest, which opened at five o'clock that day and concluded on 14th August 1889. It returned a verdict of 'Murder against a person or persons unknown'. Alice McKenzie had by this time been buried at the East London Cemetery on 24th July, a quiet affair attended by only a handful of her friends.[322]

Interestingly, Assistant Commissioner Robert Anderson had asked Dr. Thomas Bond to conduct his own examination, which he did assisted by Dr. Bagster Phillips on 18th July, the day after the murder. Anderson was obviously keen for Scotland Yard's new 'medico-legal expert' to compare the murder of Alice McKenzie with the 1888 crimes, and the doctor did not disappoint, writing:

> I see in this murder evidence of similar design to the former Whitechapel murders viz. sudden onslaught on the prostrate woman, the throat skilfully & resolutely cut with subsequent mutilation, each mutilation indicating sexual thoughts & a desire to mutilate the abdomen & sexual organs.
>
> I am of the opinion that the murder was performed by the same person who committed the former series of Whitechapel murders.[323]

Given that Thomas Bond's report profiling the murderer in November 1888 has shaped the way we think about the victims in the series of Ripper killings, it seems probable that had Robert Anderson asked him to write his profile following the murder of Alice McKenzie we would now, all these years later, be debating a Canonical Six.

With it appearing that the Ripper had returned, the pressure increased once again on the police. Swanson had a secretary prepare a table listing the victims, starting with Emma Smith and including the dates, times and locations of the murders, to which the detective added the days of the week. Ominously, the framed table had three blank rows – were more murders expected?

The dates of the attack on Annie Farmer and death of Catherine Mylett were written below. Could Swanson spot a link?[324]

Two months later he would have another case to include in his investigations, when in the early hours of 10th September the body of a woman minus the head and legs was discovered by a constable on his beat along Pinchin Street, a quiet road alongside railway arches a few minutes south of Berner Street. There was no blood within the arch in which the trunk was discovered, indicating that the victim had been killed elsewhere and dismemberment – whether death had been through murder or not – took place not where the body was found.

Medical examination suggested that death had occurred at least twenty-four hours before the discovery, so the trunk must have been kept in some place for a day or two before a decision was made where to dispose of it.[325]

The police seemed to be presented with a lead when the next day's *New York Herald* published a story claiming that a man who had called at their offices with information about a murder supposedly committed in Backchurch Lane, which terminated at its southern end into Pinchin Street.

The story claimed that the informant, a John Cleary of White Horse

Yard off Drury Lane, had told reporters that he had been told about a terrible murder and mutilation by an acquaintance, who happened to be an inspector of police. The two journalists rushed to a cab in order to visit the scene, but Cleary refused to join them. On arrival they walked the length of Backchurch Lane and the surrounding area, but all was quiet. They reportedly met two police officers who knew nothing of the supposed murder, so the reporters returned to their office.[326]

The rumoured murder might otherwise have been forgotten had it not been for the discovery of the trunk in Pinchin Street two days later; Dr. George Bagster Phillip's assistant Percy Clark had estimated death to have occurred 48 hours before discovery. Had the murder taken place as claimed by the informant?

Enquiries by Det. Chief Inspector Donald Swanson found that the reporters had indeed spoken with an officer on Backchurch Lane, H Division's Inspector Pattenden. They had also visited Commercial Street Police Station to find out whether a murder had been reported.[327]

Swanson went to the *New York Herald* offices and saw Mr. Cowen, the night editor, and Mr. Fletcher, one of the reporters who had seen the informant. Neither could provide further information than that which had appeared in the article, so the detective went to the address given by Cleary, 21 White Horse Yard. There he found that nobody by that name was known at the address, but a 'Leary' had been evicted weeks earlier due to non-payment of rent. After some further investigation and confusion over the correct name, he appeared to hit a dead end.[328]

On his return to Scotland Yard it appears that Swanson was given some good news by Sergeant Frank Froest, who told the senior officer that he had been approached at Charing Cross by a newsvendor who admitted that it had been he who had gone to the *New York Herald* offices with some information; he sold copies of the Sunday edition of the newspaper, and expected they would pay for a news story of potentially such magnitude.

Swanson knew the man, whose name was John Arnold. He said he had actually given the name 'John Kemp' in an attempt to stop his estranged wife finding out about any reward. Arnold had taken a drink in the King Lud public house on Ludgate Circus on Saturday night and had crossed Fleet Street heading in the direction of The Strand when a man he described as wearing a black soldier's uniform came up behind him and said "Hurry up with your papers, another horrible murder." Arnold asked where, and was told "Backchurch Lane". At this he ran off to the *New York Herald* offices.[329]

Swanson said that Arnold was well known to the police, having served twenty-one days in prison for deserting his wife. He gambled and drank in equally small measures, but the detective said he had never known him to be dishonest, and believed that if Arnold did know any details of the Pinchin Street crime he would have been one of the first to inform the police.[330] Although the newsvendor claimed he would be unable to recognise the soldier, he might recognise his voice should he be able to speak with him for ten minutes or so.[331]

Swanson reported that the uniform described by Arnold was most like that of the Commissionaires, and suggested that

> ...I submit that a trial might be given him in Strand, where the head quarters of the Commissioners [sic] are, for a few days to see at least whether the uniform is like what he saw.[332]

That Swanson suggested a 'trial' observation be set up is interesting, given his description when in his retirement of another, far more important identification.

Another piece in the *New York Herald*, appearing a week later, would cause another distraction for Swanson, when our old friend Dr. L. Forbes Winslow was interviewed by a *Herald* reporter in which he claimed to have been informed of the identity of the Whitechapel murderer by a man who was convinced he had been a lodger in his house. Furthermore, the informant's wife had supposedly seen the man in the yard at 4.00am on the morning of Alice McKenzie's murder, washing his hands with a 'peculiar look' on his face.

Forbes Winslow told the reporter that although the lodger was supposed to have travelled overseas, he had in fact been seen near Pinchin Street in the days before the body had been discovered, and claimed to know the reason for the murderer's periodic attacks:

> I know for a fact that this man is suffering from a violent form of religious mania, which attacks him and passes off at intervals. I am certain that there is another man in it besides the one I am after, but my reasons for that I cannot state. The police will have nothing to do with the capture. I am making arrangements to station six men round the spot were I know my man is, and he will be trapped.[333]

Perhaps needless to say, on 23rd September the doctor was paid a visit by Det. Chief Inspector Donald Swanson. Back-peddling furiously, the doctor claimed that the reporter from the *New York Herald* had promised him that his comments on the Whitechapel murders would not be published, and he had been surprised and annoyed to see the

Dr. L. Forbes Winslow

resulting article, especially as it supposedly misrepresented what he had actually said.

He told Swanson that the information given in the article had come from a statement he had taken on 9th September 1889 from a Mr. E. Callaghan, who during August 1888 had let rooms to a Canadian named G. Wentworth Bell Smith, who said he was fundraising on behalf of the Toronto Trust Society. The man kept late hours and had been heard saying that "women of the streets" ought to be drowned, especially those of the East End. He owned a pair of India rubber boots, which allowed him to walk without making a sound. When he left Mr. and Mrs. Callaghan in early August, supposedly to return to Toronto, the boots were left behind. Forbes Winslow claimed he had been given the footwear by the Callaghans and showed them to the detective, who later reported: "He produced a pair of felt galoshed boots such as are in common use in Canada, and an old coat. The felt boots were motheaten, and the slough of the moth worm remained on one of them."[334]

Forbes Winslow claimed that Mr. Callaghan had been to the police around 9th August 1888 to report his suspicions. On returning to Scotland Yard, Swanson looked into the matter, reporting:

> I am unable to find any such information given by Callaghan. It would be after the murder in George Yard, and before the 31st of Augt. The matter was then in the hands of H Divn. Insp Abberline has no record of the information.[335]

The London correspondent of the *Western Mail* was forthright in his opinion:

> Dr. Forbes Winslow, the mad doctor, has evidently mistaken his vocation in life. He should have enrolled himself in the police force years ago. It seems that Dr. Winslow keeps up a lively and regular correspondence with "Jack the Ripper." Let me hasten to add, however, that the said correspondence is as yet a one-sided one, although "Jack the Ripper" has this last time of writing given his address as Poste Restante, Charing Cross, so that London's great amateur detective has at length an opportunity of acknowledging the latest communication of his correspondent. Dr. Winslow told a reporter yesterday that "Jack the Ripper" was a lunatic; indeed, he has been telling reporters precisely the same thing for the last twelve months or so. On the whole, it is a pity the doctor cannot attend to his own business. The London police have long since ceased to attach any importance to his investigations and correspondence, whilst his fussy obtrusiveness and his willingness to be "interviewed" only serve to make the detection of these crimes the more difficult.[336]

Despite this censure, Forbes Winslow was not a man to let a self-promoting opportunity go to waste. He replied to the *Western Mail*, saying that contrary to the newspaper's claim of 'fussy obtrusiveness', the Met had always shown him "the utmost courtesy and respect", and in fact a recent letter from Det. Chief Inspector Swanson returning documents relating to his theory apparently showed the greatest respect, stating: "I beg to return with thanks the papers you were good enough to lend me."³³⁷

Donald Swanson's reaction to this twisting of his own politeness was not recorded.

Further boastfulness would come in 1910, when Forbes Winslow published his memoirs, *Recollections of Forty Years*. Claiming that the Ripper ceased his rampage as a direct result of his publishing his theory, the doctor recounted a tale of travelling on a train some time later:

> There were two strangers engaged in conversation. The topic of the Whitechapel murders cropped up. One said, not knowing who I was, to his friend, "At all events, if Dr Forbes Winslow did not actually catch Jack the Ripper, he stopped the murders by publishing his clue." I felt I had done this myself, and I should like to have said, "Hear, hear"; but my companions alighted at the next station. I felt that what they said was the general opinion in England expressed by everyone except the Scotland Yard authorities, who would have deemed such an expression of gratitude towards me as unworthy of the great dignity of their office.

A facsimile of the 'Poste Restante' letter was included, and showed that the date of 'Oct 19th 88' had been clumsily altered from '89'.³³⁸

The end to the Pinchin Street saga came on 5th October 1889, when the remains were laid to rest at the East London Cemetery. Preserved in spirits in order to assist in the possibility of matching it with the missing body parts should they be discovered, Det. Inspector Henry Moore sought the opinion of Dr. Bagster Phillips and was informed that, as long as the trunk was sealed in a tin box filled with spirits, the interment could go ahead.³³⁹

In the event, the tin box intended for the burial could not be sealed without the fluid leaking, so local tin plate worker John Allers was commissioned to construct a specially-made metal box to hold the remains. Once the body had been transferred, the box was filled with preserving spirits and soldered shut, then placed into a wooden box painted black. On top was fixed a metal plate inscribed as follows:

> This case contains the
> body of a woman (unknown)
> found in Pinchin Street
> St. Georges-in-the-East
> 10th Sept./89.

In front of just a handful of witnesses to the sad event, the unusual coffin was lowered into the ground.³⁴⁰

If the police were investigating the crimes at full capacity, there was one area in which they felt things could be improved.

Three days after the discovery of the torso in Pinchin Street Commissioner James Monro, frustrated at the delay currently being experienced, wrote to Chief Surgeon Alexander Mackellar requesting him to direct Divisional Surgeons engaged in all cases of murder and manslaughter to send their post-mortem reports and subsequent conclusions as to the cause of death as quickly as possible.

In response, on 19th September Mackellar prepared a standard letter to be sent to all Divisional Surgeons, requesting they submit their findings to the Commissioner at the earliest opportunity.[341]

No doubt the question of payment for this expedited work was raised by one or more doctors, for on 20th January 1890 Monro was obliged to write to the Under Secretary of State seeking approval on the scale of a fee for these special reports. Having discussed the matter with Dr. Mackellar, the Commissioner suggested that there be no specific amount offered, but rather the work carried out in each case be judged on their own merits.

After two months of internal debate – so much for Monro's wish to speed up the process – Under Secretary Godfrey Lushington replied on 25th March informing the Commissioner that he was granted the authority to request a report "from any Divisional Surgeon who has made a post-mortem examination in any case where a Coroner's jury has returned a verdict of wilful murder, and also in any case where the verdict is one of manslaughter, if you should consider such a report necessary."

This, of course, was completely missing the point of Monro's purpose, and he did not hold back in his reply of 3rd April:

> ...the sanction given does not altogether meet the requirements of the case, inasmuch as it does not approve of my getting a report till the verdict has been given, whereas it is of the greatest importance for Police purposes to have the report before the inquest is finished. For example, in some of the Whitechapel cases, and the Poplar (so-called) murder, I felt the greatest difficulty in directing Police enquiries owing to the absence of a medical report; and to have waited for the verdict of the Coroner's jury had rendered such report practically of no use for Police purposes, as the inquest was not finished for weeks after the crime was committed.[342]

Finally grasping what was being asked of him, Lushington wrote on 12th April to inform Monro that he was authorised, "whenever you think proper, to obtain a report from any Divisional Surgeon who has been directed by a Coroner to make a post-mortem examination of the body of anyone dying within the Metropolitan Police District."

Typically, the question of expenditure was raised, with Lushington asking the Commissioner to exercise "very great care". The maximum amount which could be paid to a Surgeon without the permission of the Secretary of State was to be £3 3s 0d.[343]

The closing of 1889 finally saw the passing, at 58-years-old, of the great Dolly Williamson following seven years of heart trouble, on 9th December. His death was certified by Dr. Thomas Bond at the family home in Smith Square, Westminster.[344] It was reported that his last task was to assist Howard Vincent in the preparation of the Sixth Edition of the *Police Code*, which appeared just a few weeks later.[345]

The loss was keenly felt by all, both within the Metropolitan Police, the Home Office and beyond. The high regard in which Williamson was held by the press was perhaps best recorded by *Reynolds's Weekly Newspaper*, who commented that

> he had been ailing for years past, but resolutely stuck to his duties, as the department could scarcely do without him. He had all the ramifications of the criminal investigation organisation at his fingers' end, and his advice was invaluable, both to the Commissioners and to the Home Office.
>
> ...A man of keen literary taste, it is said that he was engaged shortly before his death in putting his diaries into autobiographical form. Should these diaries ever obtain publication, the work would be one of considerable interest.[346]

Some sections of the press became a little carried away with their tributes to the great man, as wryly pointed out by the *Evening Post* of 11th December:

> It is a little surprising to read in the *Times* obituary notice of the late Chief Constable Williamson that he had charge of the investigation into the murder of Lord William Russell. Courvoisier was hanged for that crime on the 6th of July, 1840, when Mr. Williamson was exactly nine years old.

The funeral took place three days after the death, with a morning service at St. John's the Evangelist in Smith Square, Westminster, attended by more than 300 officers of all ranks from both the Metropolitan and City Police forces. Joining James Monro, Robert Anderson and Alexander Carmichael Bruce were members of the C.I.D. including Donald Swanson, John Littlechild, George Greenham, John Shore, Henry Moore and Frederick Jarvis.

Following a service read by Rev. Canon Furse the coffin was conveyed to the Necropolis station on Westminster Bridge Road and taken by train to Woking, where the coffin, covered in a purple cloth and a multitude of wreaths, was wheeled towards the cemetery with around fifty officers walking two-abreast behind the hearse before being interred.[347]

Sadly, as Williamson had died 'in harness' his wife was not entitled to any pension despite his long service, but to prevent the family suffering financial hardship a grant of £300 was made from the Royal Bounty Fund, arranged by the Treasury.[348]

The passing of Dolly Williamson very much marked the end of an era, and this was underlined early in 1890 as the Metropolitan Police prepared to leave Great Scotland Yard, its home since 1829, and relocate to their new premises on the Embankment, the works having finally been completed.

It hadn't been a straightforward construction project. Designed by Mr. Francis Fowler for James Mapleson, the site was originally earmarked in 1875 for a new National Opera House,[349] but ran into problems almost immediately when it was discovered that the earth was not solid enough to lay foundations. Digging to a depth of 40-50ft revealed nothing but running springs, with water seeping into the excavations as they proceeded below the depth of the Thames and then that of the District Line of the Underground. Eventually clay was reached, and 40ft of concrete was hastily poured into the shuttered excavations. The cost at this stage had already spiralled from the budgeted £5,000 to £33,000, the first of the financial troubles to blight James Mapleson.[350]

The first brick was eventually laid on 7th September 1875 by operatic singer Theresa Titiens and work progressed steadily until July 1876, by which time the building had reached the grand tier boxes. It was then realised that there were not enough funds to complete the project. Despite an appeal for a further cash injection from subscribers, the new Opera House stalled.[351] Mapleson sold the unfinished building to Messrs. Quilter, Morris and Tod-Healey in November 1882, and he eventually filed for bankruptcy in April 1888 having lost an estimated £30,000 on the project. The new owners' intention of building a hotel also fell through, and the site was purchased to house the new headquarters of the Metropolitan Police. James Mapleson would later comment: "With such solid foundations, the cells, if not comfortable, will at least be dry."[352]

Work was well underway on the new building when on the afternoon of 2nd October 1888 – two days after the murders of Elisabeth Stride and Catherine Eddowes – the assistant foreman of the works, Charles Brown, was told by one of the carpenters that he had seen a parcel in one of the recesses of a vault at the western end. The men went to investigate and the carpenter, a man named Wildbore, lit a match. In the dim light Mr. Brown saw what he took to be a ham wrapped in an old coat and took no further notice, but a couple of hours later instructed the foreman bricklayer to send one of his labourers to fetch the parcel. Just before three o'clock a bricklayer named George Budgen went to the recess to remove the object:[353]

> I struck a light and saw the top bare, and the rest wrapped up in some old cloth. I thought it was old bacon, or something like that, and I could not make anything of it, so I took hold of the string around it – it being tied up – and dragged it across a trench into a part of the vault where there was light. I cut the strings there and opened the wrapper. The strings – a lot of old strings of different sorts – were tied up all round it several times across each way. There was only the wrapping I saw, no paper, and when the parcel was opened I saw the body of a woman.[354]

In fact, what Budgen saw was the decomposing trunk of a woman, minus the arms and legs; she had also been decapitated. Dr. Thomas Bond, sent to view the body, was able to confirm that an arm and shoulder found on 11th September were from the same victim; on 17th October a leg was unearthed by a dog brought to the site of the trunk's discovery. It, too, matched. Despite this partial re-assembling of the victim, the head and missing limbs were never recovered and so her identity remains unknown. Given the fact that she had been killed in the midst of the Whitechapel crimes, and her remains hidden at what would be the new headquarters of the Metropolitan Police, some newspapers asked whether the Ripper was responsible and the dumping of the body a deliberate taunting of the authorities. It is a theory which still attracts some today.

But Det. Chief Inspector Swanson, in a report on the discovery of the Pinchin Street remains, felt that the so-called Whitehall Mystery was more aligned to a series of torso murders which at that point had taken place between May 1887 and June 1889:

Postcard showing Westminster Bridge and New Scotland Yard (right of centre)
Author's collection

What becomes apparent is the absence of the attack upon the genitals as in the series of Whitechapel murders beginning at Buck's Row and ending in Miller's Court. Certainly if it be a murder there was enough time for the murderer to cut off the head and limbs there was enough time to mutilate as in the series mentioned. It appears rather to go side by side with the Rainham, Whitehall and Chelsea murders.[355]

But by 1890, construction was now complete. With the Receiver's Office liaising with London County Council over the naming of the new building and its access roads, Commissioner James Monro, on being asked for his approval by Receiver Richard Pennefather, completely misunderstood what was being asked of him and on 14th February fired off a bewildered response:

> I hardly understand what this means. I have made no proposal to call the new police office 'Scotland Yard Avenue', which would be absurd, as our Head Quarters are not an avenue. Can you tell me anything about the proposal?

When Pennefather wrote to patiently explain that it was the access road – the continuation of the existing Derby Street beyond the gates to the new Met offices – which might be named Scotland Yard Avenue, Monro rather sniffily replied:

> I have no objection to the street being designated as proposed, but it seems to me that before any proposal was made to the CC on the subject, the Comr. of Police might have been consulted on the matter.

The new headquarters were to be known as New Scotland Yard, the name being formally approved on 11th April 1890.[356]

For Monro, however, the naming of the new offices was among the last of his worries. He had long been fighting for improved pay and conditions for his men, including a fair pension, as had Sir Charles Warren and Sir Edmund Henderson before him.

A superannuation fund formed in 1839 into which monies deducted from policemen's wages were paid, supposedly to supply a pension for retiring officers, had been invested in Government stocks so badly that within ten years the fund was insolvent. From 1857, payments made by officers was spent not on their pensions, but on improving and building new police stations; pensions were paid through rates received from public taxes.

Despite then Secretary of State Sir William Harcourt promising, at a large gathering of officers at the Metropolitan and City Police Orphanage at Twickenham in June 1881, to place "on a fixed and satisfactory footing... the superannuation and pension of those who have spent the best days of their lives in the service of their countrymen," it would take a further nine years before any firm action was taken.[357]

A Committee of Enquiry into Police Superannuation held in August 1889 saw several serving officers give evidence as to why twenty-five years was the maximum amount of service which an officer could give efficiently, including the likes of Det. Chief Inspectors Littlechild and Butcher, Superintendents Thomas Arnold and Charles Cutbush, and Chief Surgeon Dr. Alexander Mackellar, along with Divisional Surgeon Dr. Thomas Bond.[358]

Also giving evidence to the Committee was Det. Chief Inspector Donald Swanson, who told them:

> I put it on the ground that a man is thoroughly worn out after twenty-five years' service; he is not worth his pay. A man may not be, physically or mentally, apparently unfit, but after twenty-five years a man gets so excessively nervous that, if I were to entrust him, as I would have to entrust him, with an important matter, I should feel altogether lost, and prefer to do the thing myself, and therefore I feel sure that, by the time a man had served twenty-five years, he would be so exhausted that he would not be worth his money.[359]

The Government continued to avoid making any agreement to Monro's proposal and, exasperated by Henry Matthews' refusals, the Commissioner resigned on 21st June 1890.[360]

Although there was obvious friction between the two men, some reports erroneously claimed that Monro was leaving as a result of an inability to work with the Home Secretary.

Several years later, in April 1903, a report in *The Times* which mentioned his resignation appears to have inspired Monro to write his reminiscences of his time at Scotland Yard. Writing to eldest son Charles that "I think it is right that you and my children should know something more than you already know of the life which I led while in the Met. Police," he went on to explain at length the reasons for his departure as Commissioner:

> It is gratifying to note that the *Times* recognizes that the reason for my resignation was not as often believed, a quarrel between the Home Secy & myself – that is was a sacrifice of my interests in behalf of those of the Police. This is absolutely true. There was no absolutely necessity for my resigning my post had I chosen to remain. All that I had to do was to tell my men that I had done all I could for them in the way of getting their pension, but that Govt. would not comply with their demands. This would have been perhaps what the *Times* calls discreet, but to my mind it would not have been honest.
>
> When the recruits attended in my room every Monday I made a point of telling them that they were no longer Thomas Smith or Robert Jones – they were P.C. no 300, or P.C. no 301 – that their private life was gone, and that they were now members of a great force, and servants of the public – that they had to sacrifice themselves for this position – and that in everything they had to put away private consideration in the first instance, and give up themselves.
>
> When this teaching came home to me personally, what was my duty? Surely to practice what I had been preaching to my men every week. To my mind the men were being unjustly treated – it was a matter of right or wrong, not of mere expediency – and under such circumstances I was asked to be a party to wrongdoing towards men, whose interests I was bound to protect, and whom I was under an obligation to shield to the utmost of my power. And that utmost meant that if protecting their interests and shielding them involved giving up my own interests, & sacrificing myself, I was bound as an honest man to make this sacrifice. And this I did. Had I not done so I should have felt myself to be a coward.

And I could never have looked any recruit in the face, and preached to him the duty of self sacrifice, without condemning myself as one who had been called on to make such a sacrifice of self, and had refused to do so.

Every effort was made from all quarters to induce me to withdraw my resignation – the highest in the land, our present King, who was then Prince of Wales used his personal influence to get me kept in my post – but for me, so far as I could judge, there was but one course open which was consistent with right and honour. And that was the path of self sacrifice for my men. Had I not resigned, I have no hesitation whatever in saying that the men would not have got their pensions – when I did resign, and when it was known why I did so, the feelings in Parliament was so strong that the unjust proposals of the Home Secy as to pension were swept away in indignation, and in the end the men got almost what they had asked, and what I had fought for as fair & moderate. They asked pension of 2/3rds of their pay = £1 per week – after 25 years service. The Home Secy scouted this proposal as extravagant, saying that all the men wd. be young men when they retired. I showed him that the average life of a policeman in London was 22½ years! but he would listen to nothing, and proposed that they should get full pension after 28 years, although I showed him that only 2 per cent of the men lived to take pension after 28 years service! This was the proposal of the Home Secy which Parliament, on my resignation, swept away with indignation. Then Govt. tried to get Parliament to sanction full pension at 27 years: this also was rejected. Then 26 years was suggested: this also was considered insufficient. And then Parliament, instead of giving pension at 25 years, gave the men an increased pension on retirement at that time, and full pension at 26 years! As a matter of fact the difference between what the men had asked, and what Parliament sanctioned amounted to sixpence a week on each man who retired!

Nothing I think need be said to show, in the face of these facts, that what the men had asked was fair, and that what the Home Secy had proposed to give was unfair. And this pension was obtained, I unhesitatingly say, because I refused to be a party to the wrong contemplated by the Home Secy and because sooner than be a party to any such injustice, I sent in my papers.

My children will therefore know and believe their father did not resign on account of any quarrel with the Home Secy, but because he refused to do what he considered to be wrong, and because, by God's grace, he was enabled to sacrifice his own worldly interests on behalf of those of the men, which as their Commissioner he was bound in honour to uphold, even at the sacrifice of his own.[361]

Back in the summer of 1890, the departure of Monro was lamented by the press, many laying the blame at Home Secretary Henry Matthews' door:

> [Sir Henry] seems to have been the victim of two excellent Chief Commissioners, Sir Charles Warren and Mr. Monro, both of whom wanted to be master of the Home Office. At least this is his account of it. An old friend of the Home Secretary the other day – an eminent judge who belongs to the same club and has known him for years – said to me, "Matthews always does the right thing, but sometimes he does it in the wrong way." This really sums up the situation. The Home Secretary has evidently been pretty right in the dispute with Mr. Monro, but, at the same time, there seems to have been needless friction according to the Chief Commissioner's account. The dispute ought to have been settled amicably, considering the enormous importance of preserving the discipline of the Metropolitan Police force, and the knowledge that we may yet be face to face with the dangers of a police strike – an event that would put London at the mercy of thousands of ruffians and thieves.[362]

Monro's final parting shot was to write an article for *The New Review* titled 'The Story of Police Pensions', detailing his and his predecessors' struggles. It appeared in September 1890,[363] by which time his replacement had his feet firmly under his desk. To this day, James Monro remains the only Commissioner of the Metropolitan Police not to have been knighted, although it should be remembered that Charles Warren was made a 'Sir' for his work in Egypt years before his appointment to the Met, and it is doubtful that he would have been knighted for his tenure as Commissioner given his constant friction with the Home Office.[364]

The new man had, in fact, been announced at the very sitting of the House of Commons at which Monro's departure was debated.

Asked by Liberal M.P. Octavius Morgan whether there was any truth in the statement published by the *Standard* that morning that there was a likelihood of Monro returning to his post,

> Mr. Matthews rose, and, without further noticing the question, announced that her Majesty had approved of – and here he shuffled among his papers, everyone listening, and some expecting the announcement that Mr. Monro had been restored – the appointment of Sir Edward Bradford.

In response to cries of "Who is he?" Mr. Matthews, indulging in some of his finest mincing mannerisms, and gazing at the ceiling as usual for inspiration, gave a brief sketch of he new Commissioner's career.[365]

In fact, the 54-year-old Bradford had enjoyed an impressive career in India. The son of Rev. William Kirkwall Bradford, he had been educated at Marlborough and entered the Madras Army in 1853, rising through the ranks of captain, major and lieutenant-colonel, before becoming Colonel in 1884. He had served in the Persian campaign of 1857 and the North-West Provinces during 1858/59, for which he had been decorated. Bradford had subsequently acted as General Superintendent of Operation in suppressing Thuggee and Dacoity, and in 1887 had been appointed Secretary of the Political and Secret Department of the India Office.[366]

Like his predecessor who bore lifelong injuries as a result of an incident while in India, Bradford also suffered from a disability inflicted on the sub-continent. In 1863, returning to headquarters following a hunting expedition, Bradford and a colleague named Captain Curtis were passing through a village when they were asked to rid the locals of a tigress that was causing problems. After picking up the scent and tracking the beast, the men were forced to climb trees as the tiger attempted to attack. As it made a rush at Bradford's tree he pulled the trigger, only to see the gun misfire and find himself helpless.

There are several newspaper reports of what happened next, but perhaps the most thrilling account appears in a letter published in the self-published book *Truly A Great Victorian* by the wife of Bradford's grandson:

> After poor dear Bradford vainly pulled the trigger, the beast, after glaring at him for an instant, commenced climbing up to him like a cat, whereupon Bradford dropped off into the water below. The tiger followed him, nearly drowning him, took the arm and crunched. Curtis of the Dragoons was in the tree about 15 yards off and saw part of the scene but he scarcely dared shoot for the animal and its victim were so close together that he feared he would hit Bradford. The tiger now dragged Bradford out on to a bank and lying by its side, whisking its great tail about, began to play and pat with my old friend – just as a cat does with a mouse – occasionally taking his arm into its mouth and giving him a crunch. Poor Bradford had his wits about him all the time and kept quiet, merely sparring with his arm at the beast as it showed inclinations to catch at his neck and the jugular. At this the tiger would take his arm into its mouth and chew it but during this the relative positions of man and

Sir Edward Bradford
from The Illustrated London News, 28th June 1890

beast had changed so Curtis, a very cool and brave fellow, let drive three or four shells into the tiger though, as he said afterwards, "I was awfully afraid once that I had shot Bradford." These shells wounded the animal, which left Bradford after fetching him a crack over the head with his paw, and lay bleeding profusely in a neighbouring bush.

Captain Curtis climbed down from the tree, and with help from the villagers strapped Bradford to a bedstead and sent for a doctor from headquarters at Agar, some 35 miles away. Although Bradford had remained conscious throughout his ordeal, Dr. Beaumont found the arm to be so badly damaged that it had to be amputated at the shoulder without anaesthetic – the normally teetotal Bradford being plied with alcohol. He would, in time, make a full recovery.[367]

Given his ordeal and subsequent determination to continue his career, it was something of a surprise when the *Pall Mall Gazette* greeted news of his appointment with the headline "Is Sir Edward Bradford weak enough?"

The newspaper was referring, of course, to what they saw as the reason for the departure of James Monro – that he had been 'too strong' for Henry Matthews. The commentary included a frank appraisal of relations between Scotland Yard and the Home Office:

Mr. Monro, following in the line of Sir Charles Warren, thought that Scotland Yard should be independent and supreme. Mr. Matthews knew that Scotland Yard must be subordinate and subject to the Home Office. The autocratic spirit infused into Scotland Yard by Sir Charles Warren has been the curse of the place ever since. When Mr. Monro was appointed, both he and Mr. Matthews believed that a new era would begin. But both were wrong. The spirit prevailing at Scotland Yard was too strong for Mr. Monro's virtuous resolve. Sir Edward Bradford, if he is to survive longer than his predecessors, must recognise frankly that he is only the servant of the Home Office, and must administer the Force on that understanding. Men of "adamant" brook no superiors. That is what we mean by asking whether the new Commissioner is weak enough for the post.[368]

In fact, in the years ahead Edward Bradford would prove to be an excellent Commissioner, and the perfect man to soothe the troubled waters of the previous four years.

The new Metropolitan chief would have early experience of the work of his officers, when several of his top detectives worked together on a high-profile case of robbery from the Duke of Edinburgh, Queen Victoria's second son Alfred.

The Duke and Duchess, along with their servants, had been in Edinburgh to open the Edinburgh International Exhibition on 1st May 1890,[369] staying at the city's Balmoral Hotel. The Royal party had arrived two days earlier, on Tuesday, 29th April.

The Balmoral had previously received a telegram from a "T. Leslie" asking for an apartment to be reserved, but on the day the Duke arrived a second telegram was received saying he had missed his train. The guest finally arrived on Wednesday, 30th April and was installed in "H" room.

The following morning the man was twice spotted looking over a balustrade from which the Duke's rooms could be observed. Just after three o'clock that afternoon, the Balmoral's waiter Frederick Burgdorf took two telegrams to the Duke's rooms. The interconnecting apartments were empty – the Royal party being at the opening ceremony of the Exhibition – and Burgdorf left the telegrams in the drawing room. As he made his way to leave, he noticed that the door to Room 11 was slightly ajar, and a man was peering through the gap. When asked what he was doing in the Royal rooms, the intruder claimed he had "made a mistake" and quickly walked down the central staircase. He was seen heading into the restaurant, but by the time Burgdorf got there the man had disappeared.

Returning to the Duke's apartments, the waiter met the hotel's manager, Mr. Umbrecht, and it was discovered that several items of gold and jewellery had been stolen.[370]

As soon as Scotland Yard heard of the theft, and armed with a description of the supposed perpetrator, they suspected an American gentleman thief known to the C.I.D. as Stephen Smith, or Holmes. He had served twelve months' imprisonment on the Continent following an attempted larceny in Aachen, Germany in June 1888.[371] Det. Superintendent John Shore, famous for putting a known name to a crime, was particularly convinced as to the crook's identity and tasked Det. Inspector Abberline with tracking down the American. It would not be an easy job, given the fugitive's frequent changes of address across the Continent.

While Abberline did the ground work, building the case at Scotland Yard were Det. Chief Inspector Swanson and Det. Inspectors Leach and White.

Eventually, after two months, information was received that Smith would be travelling through London's Paddington Station and at noon on 1st July Abberline finally arrested his man and escorted him to King Street police station, where he was identified using an American passport issued in London in June 1888.

Smith was described as being of slim build and small stature, very well dressed and having impeccable manners. He described himself as a barber from Maryland. The studs he wore were made of pearls, and the rings on his fingers were diamonds, rubies and garnets.[372]

While the thief was being held at King Street his lodgings were searched, with detectives discovering several items of interest, including an ingenious folding jemmy and a type of fine saw often used by expert thieves for opening bags and furniture.[373]

As luck would have it, Chief Constable Henderson of the Edinburgh Police was at that time in London, giving evidence before the Select Committee on the Infant Life Protection Bill. He was informed of the arrest,[374] and together with Edinburgh Detective Inspector William McEwan[375] took the prisoner back to Edinburgh to face justice, departing London on the 10.40pm Great Northern train. Smith appeared in front of magistrates at Edinburgh police court the very next morning and was remanded to trial.

On 20th October, before the Lord Chief Justice, Smith appeared at Edinburgh's High Court of Justiciary. The jury heard Det. Inspector Abberline relate how the prisoner had been arrested. John Grieve, proprietor of the Balmoral Hotel, stated that as soon as the accused had arrived there, under the name "T. Lewis", he had been suspicious, as "he had not the usual aroma of people who came to the Balmoral Hotel." He could not identify Smith at the Police Court, but was certain that he was the man seen on the morning of the theft. Manager Mr. Umbrecht and various other members of staff also felt that the prisoner was the man seen at the hotel in Room H, although none were certain. It was only on being told of the theft later that they remembered the unusual visitor, and that the accused bore some resemblance.

Captain John Baxter of the *Windsor* said he had left Leith late in the evening on the day of the robbery bound for Antwerp; he had just two passengers, who gave their names as Holmes and Wilson. He commented that the prisoner resembled "Holmes" but was "changed", saying that he could identify the passenger by his false teeth – going as far as to leaving the witness box to approach the accused and look into his mouth. Other witnesses pointed out that the prisoner, who now had a full beard, had sported only a moustache in May.

Det. Inspector William McEwan told how, on arrival at Scotland Yard, he had been shown a number of photographs of hotel thieves and had selected nine, mixing these with around 60 of his own. When this album of photographs was shown to Miss Amelia Newton, a cashier at the Balmoral Hotel, she selected one – Stephen Smith. McEwan admitted that his sole suspect for the crime had been the man seen on the morning of the robbery, and had not searched the rooms or luggage of the hotel's servants, they being "people of character and standing."[376]

The Duke and Duchess of Edinburgh were not called to give evidence.[377] The jury retired at 4.40pm after hearing the evidence of some 26 witnesses, returning 25 minutes later with a verdict of Not Proven, and Stephen Smith was discharged,[378] escaping into history even before Frederick Abberline had arrived back at Scotland Yard. None of the stolen jewellery was ever recovered.[379]

Although no doubt keeping an eye on developments north of the border, Det. Chief Inspector Swanson had his own welfare to worry about. A bizarre, barely legible letter had been received at Scotland Yard on 16th July which complained of the actions of the Scottish detective:

Scotch Store
Whitefriars
Street
Fleet St

Sir How Dare Swanson
in precense of Moore
anothe tec I suppose
tell me he woud
kick me with
his foot I

─────

Want and

───────

Demand

───────

A Immed

────────

Answer

────────

or Else the

──────────

the same

──────────

Scene Every Day

Yours
Respectably

William
Billings
c/o Mr Jones
Scotch Store
Whitefriars
Street Fleet St

The letter no doubt caused much mirth when received by Central Office, and a cover note created for the file gives the description as "Complains of Swanson for threatening to kick writer."

A note in the file helpfully explains that "Billings is the inebriate informant in the "Pigeon man: case at "L" 82."

The complaint was sent through the Executive Branch and then back to Assistant Commissioner Robert Anderson, who advised the best course of action would be to make no reply.[380]

Whether Mr. Billings complained of not receiving an answer is unknown, but he would no doubt have been livid to learn that Swanson's next public appearance, two weeks later, was at the Goodwood Races. While Det. Chief Superintendent Fisher of A Division and his officers kept the peace around the track and grounds, Swanson and Det. Inspector Frederick Jarvis enjoyed the meeting from the Grand Stand, where they watched a programme of six races including the prestigious Chesterfield Cup, which was won by Father Confessor,[381] who had also triumphed in the Spring and Summer Cups at Aintree that year.[382]

Swanson's next engagement would be far less enjoyable.

Just after seven o'clock on the evening of Friday, 24th October – four days after the discharge of Stephen Smith in Edinburgh – 19-year-old Somerled Macdonald discovered the body of a woman lying on a pile of bricks in Crossfield Road, Hampstead in north-west London. Setting off to find a policeman and returning shortly afterwards with P.C. Arthur Gardiner, it was discovered that the woman's throat had been cut from ear to ear, and her face was smothered with blood. Gardiner blew his whistle and was soon joined by fellow constables John Stalker and Frederick Algar. Medical assistance arrived in the form of Dr. Arthur Wells, and a brief inspection was conducted before S Division's Inspector Thomas Wright arrived with an ambulance to convey the body to Hampstead Hill police station. Here, a more detailed examination was carried out by Dr. Wells and Divisional Surgeon Dr. Herbert Cooper, along with a Mr. Fox.

The woman's head had been almost separated from her body, with the windpipe and spinal column divided. Her skull had suffered a compound comminuted fracture, with several deep cuts and scratches found across her body.[383]

It did not take long for the press to wonder if the Whitechapel murderer had returned, this time away from his East End haunts; in fact, the very next day the *Pall Mall Gazette* was one of several newspapers reporting a Central News release which highlighted the similarities:

Inspector Swanson and several detectives who had been engaged from time to time in the Whitechapel inquiries started for Hampstead and took charge of the case. All the ground in the vicinity has been thoroughly searched, but no weapon nor anything else likely to serve as a clue has been found. The first doctor who saw the body noticed blood flowing from the side, which fact led at first to the belief that the woman had been stabbed, and perhaps mutilated, but a cursory examination did not result in anything to support this theory. People who have seen the body and the scene of the murder are strongly of [the] opinion that the unfortunate victim was seized from behind and was at once rendered speechless by one large, clean cut of a knife, as in the case of the women murdered in Whitechapel.

...As in some points the murder seems to resemble Jack the Ripper's handiwork – the terrible gash which almost beheaded the body having evidently been inflicted from behind – it is thought advisable to have Dr. Bond present at the post-mortem examination. Dr. Bond, it will be remembered, had a great experience of the Whitechapel murders.

...A Press Association reporter who visited the scene at an early hour this morning found that the police discredit the theory that it has the remotest connection with the East-end tragedies. They are of the opinion that the murder was not committed in Hampstead at all, but that the body was conveyed to the spot where it was found and deposited there by the murderer or murderers.[384]

In fact, it hadn't taken Swanson long to realise that this murder – horrible as it was – was not connected with the East End cases. An abandoned pram had been found at Hamilton Terrace, some two-and-a-half miles away; it was soaked with blood. A brass nut found at the murder site by Sergeant William Brown fitted the carriage perfectly, proving that this was how the victim's body had been transported to Crossfield Road and there dumped.

With no clue as to the identity of the victim, S Division's Det. Inspector Thomas Bannister – taking control of the case once Swanson had returned to Scotland Yard – issued a description of the murdered woman and her clothing to the gathered journalists, in the hope that their news reports would be read by someone who recognised the details. And so it was that a Mrs. Barraud of Prince of Wales Road read of the murder and exclaimed to her lodger, Clara Hogg: "What a terrible murder this is at Hampstead! They say Jack the Ripper has been about here."[385] Clara had just returned to her home with a family friend, Mary Pearcey, after the pair had spent the morning looking for Clara's sister-in-law, Phoebe Hogg, who had been missing since the previous afternoon. The physical description of the body made Clara uneasy, and when she read reports that the victim had been wearing petticoats embroidered with the initials "P.H." she was convinced.

Clara and Mary Pearcey set off for Hampstead police station and there met Sergeant Edward Nursey. On being told that they were there to identify the body of the murdered woman, the officers fetched Det. Inspector Bannister and the party headed to Hampstead mortuary, where the remains had been taken.

On viewing the body Mrs. Pearcey became hysterical, and her behaviour seemed strange to the officers present. Their suspicions were later raised still further when, as the police questioned Phoebe Hogg's husband Frank, he was discovered to possess a key to the house on Priory Street where Mrs. Pearcey lived.

Detectives arrived at her lodgings at 2 Priory Street around three o'clock that afternoon, and found the kitchen in darkness. On raising a green shade from the window, Sergeant Nursey saw that two of its panes were smashed – caused, claimed Mrs. Pearcey, by her trying to catch some mice.

Looking around the kitchen, Nursey saw blood everywhere – splashes up the walls, splatters across the ceiling – which Mrs. Pearcey tried to explain away as her suffering a violent nose bleed on the Thursday evening. A poker was found to have hair and blood on the join where the handle was fixed, and a large carving knife in a drawer in the kitchen dresser was stained with blood. Copies of love letters sent to Frank Hogg were found in a box in the bedroom.

While this search was being conducted, Mary Pearcey alternately sat down at her piano and played, and reclined into an armchair and whistled softly to herself.

Inspector Bannister felt he'd seen enough; he took Mrs. Pearcey into custody and by cab to Kentish Town police station, where she was charged with the "wilful murder of Phoebe Hogg" and her infant daughter, also named Phoebe but known as Tiggie, even though the baby had not been found.

However, almost as soon as a description of the infant appeared in the Sunday newspapers, her body was found lying under a clump of nettles by a hawker named Oliver Smith as he walked along the edge of a vacant lot on one side of Finchley Road at half past six in the morning.

There was no doubt that Mary Pearcey was guilty of the murders, and, despite some doubt as to her mental well-being, she was hanged by executioner James Berry on 23rd December 1890.

The brutality of her attack on Phoebe Hogg shocked Victorian society; Arthur Conan Doyle, and, later, Donald McCormick and William Stewart, contemplated a 'Jill the Ripper', citing Mary Pearcey's ferocity as evidence that a woman was capable of such horrific acts.[386]

With 1890 drawing to a close, more changes in the Criminal Investigation Department were coming. Det. Inspector Thomas Roots, whom Donald Swanson had known since 1876 when he had joined the Detective Department, passed away on 3rd November, ten days after the murder of Phoebe Hogg, aged just 41. He had been suffering for some time with tuberculosis, and according to the *St. James's Gazette*, although "the ravages of the disease had reduced him almost to a skeleton, the inspector... remained indefatigable in the pursuit of his duties, and he had only abandoned work for a week when he died."[387]

The funeral of the popular Roots took place at Brompton Cemetery on 7th November and was attended by a large number of officers including Superintendents Shore and Cutbush, and Det. Chief Inspectors Swanson, Littlechild and Greenham.[388]

Thomas Roots's position as Det. Inspector at Central Office was filled by Henry Moore. Announced in Police Orders on the same day, 22nd December 1890, was the permanent appointment of Donald Swanson as Det. Chief Inspector, with Frederick Abberline being advanced Det. Chief Inspector (Temporary).

Another change of role had already occurred by the time of this Order. Since Dolly Williamson's death the previous year, the position of Chief Constable had remained vacant. Now, Commissioner James Monro had written a memorandum supporting the promotion of his friend Melville Macnaghten to the position from Assistant Chief Constable, commenting:

> I always had a high opinion of his qualifications and abilities; but he has shown an aptitude for dealing with criminal administration and a power of managing and dealing with men for which I was not prepared. He has been doing Mr. Williamson's work for months, and he has done it with remarkable efficiency and success.[389]

The result was a foregone conclusion: Melville Macnaghten was appointed Det. Chief Constable of the C.I.D. on 16th December 1890.[390]

At 2.15am on 13th February 1891 P.C. Ernest Thompson, who had only joined the Met three months earlier, was walking his beat along Chamber Street when he heard the sound of a man's footsteps retreating. Seconds later he was at Swallow Gardens and turning on his lamp, discovered Frances Coles lying on the ground, surrounded by a pool of blood. Despite her throat having been cut she was still alive – just – and as P.C. Thompson looked he saw the faint movement of one eyelid.[391]

As Police Orders dictated an officer remain with a victim should they be alive, Thompson was unable to pursue the footsteps and the probable killer of Frances Coles – and possibly Jack the Ripper. She soon died from her wounds.

The victim was known to police as a prostitute; she was in her mid-20s, 5ft tall with dark brown hair and eyes. On the night of her death she was wearing old, dark clothes.[392]

Very soon the archway of Swallow Gardens was filled with police officers and medical men, closed to the public. H Division's Superintendent Arnold and Det. Inspector Reid were joined shortly before 5.00am by Det. Chief Inspector Swanson, and the detectives under their command carried out a thorough examination of the area.[393] In a space between a waterpipe and some brickwork two shillings wrapped in a sheet of newspaper were discovered; whether these had been put there by the victim was impossible to prove.[394] With their investigations completed, and the body removed to the mortuary, Swanson ordered that a small amount of the blood on the ground be collected for analysis and the rest washed away. The archway was then opened to traffic.[395]

The victim had spent two days drinking with a ship's fireman named James Thomas Sadler – known as 'Tom' – who had been discharged from SS *Fez* as she berthed in the East End docks and made his way the short distance to Whitechapel to begin spending his pay. He met Frances Coles, of whom he had been a former client, at the Princess Alice and she certainly helped with his spending, the pair touring the pubs of Spitalfields and Whitechapel over the next couple of days.

Late in the evening of 12th February Coles and Sadler had a drunken argument after she refused to go to his aid when he was attacked and robbed and went their separate ways.

Frances returned to their lodgings at Spitalfields Chambers. Drunk,

James Sadler and Frances Coles, with the arch in Chamber Street where her body was found from Reynolds's Weekly Newspaper, 22nd February 1891

she sat at a bench in the kitchen and fell asleep with her head on her arms. Sadler also soon returned, face bloodied and bruised, but after bathing his wounds was forced to leave as he had no money for a bed. Half an hour later Frances woke up and was also ejected.[396]

At 1.30am she bumped into fellow prostitute Ellen Callana by the Princess Alice on Commercial Street. As they walked together in the direction of the Minories, "a very short man with a dark moustache, shiny boots and blue trousers" approached Callana and solicited her; she refused his offer, at which the man punched her in the face and tore her jacket. He then walked over to Frances who, ignoring her friend's warning, walked away with the stranger in the direction of the Minories and Swallow Gardens.[397]

Around the same time Tom Sadler had made his way to St. Katherine Dock and attempted to force his way onto the SS *Fez*, despite being discharged two days earlier. For his troubles he got into another fight, this time with dockworkers, which left him with a wound to his head. He wandered around Whitechapel until the early hours, when he at last gave in to his injuries and a constable on duty in Whitechapel Road helped him to the London Hospital across the road to seek medical attention.[398]

When the body of Frances Coles was discovered Sadler found himself in trouble; he had been seen in her company for a prolonged period of time and was the obvious suspect for her murder. Around midday on the 14th he was apprehended by Sergeant John Don of R Division and, escorted by H Division's P.C. Gill, taken to Leman Street Police Station, where Det. Chief Inspector Swanson was waiting.[399] The Scot took a statement, with Sadler appearing to be completely open with the detective. Given the number of public houses mentioned, it was a surprise that he would recall any events of his time with Frances.

With a likely murder suspect in custody for the first time, the police stepped up efforts to link Sadler with the atrocities of 1888. It was reported that they had confronted one of the three men who had seen Catherine Eddowes at the entrance to Church Passage with the prisoner, but the attempted identification proved unsuccessful.[400]

Frances Coles was buried on 25th February. An estimated 2,000 people gathered as her polished elm coffin studded with white nails was placed on an open hearse which at 1.15pm set off for the East London Cemetery, Plaistow. The cortège was followed by hundreds of mourners on foot with, as one reporter vividly described, "many of them women with nothing on their heads and with babies in their arms, laboriously running in the wake of the coaches." Taking advantage of the emotional crowd were a number of men passing through the throng hawking memorial cards of the deceased.[401]

At the inquest into Coles' death, evidence was heard that Sadler was so drunk by the time of her murder that it was extremely unlikely that he would have been capable of the deed, a fact commented on by Coroner Wynne Baxter in his summing up. On 27th February the jury returned a verdict of "Willful Murder against some person or persons unknown",[402] and, thanks to legal representation paid for by the Seamen's Union, at a hearing at Thames Magistrates' Court four days later all charges were dropped against him. As he left the court, crowds of people cheered his release.[403]

The press were straightforward in their opinion:

NOT "JACK THE RIPPER"

> The unkempt fireman Sadler, who was arrested for the murder of Frances Coles, has disappointed the London police who hoped he would turn out to be the mysterious fiend responsible for the Whitechapel horrors. There is nothing for it but for the police to begin de novo, and it is, no doubt, heartbreaking work to be foiled time after time, and to feel powerless to mend matters.[404]

Although they didn't know it at the time, the murder of Frances Coles would be the last to be added to the Whitechapel file. The police would continue with their efforts to locate the killer; Det. Chief Inspector Swanson returned to his prepared list of Whitechapel murders and added a new line: "13.2.91 – Friday morning – 2.15am – Frances Coles – Swallow Gardens."

FIFTEEN

The Philosopher's Stone

It had been a hectic – and traumatic – eighteen months for Donald Swanson. When James Sadler was driven away from the Thames Police Court and, thanks to money won from libel proceedings against the *Daily Telegraph* and the *Standard,* into a new life running a chandler's shop,[1] it was the end of the Detective Chief Inspector's involvement with the Jack the Ripper case, at least publicly.

Four years later, the *Pall Mall Gazette*, in a piece on the murders, commented:

> The theory entitled to most respect, because it was presumably based upon the best knowledge, was that of Chief Inspector Swanson, the officer who was associated with the investigation of all the murders, and Mr. Swanson believed the crimes to have been the work of a man who is now dead.[2]

It would take more than 80 years to discover the identity of Swanson's suspect.

But in 1891, it was no doubt something of a relief when, two weeks after charges were dropped against Sadler, Swanson found himself assigned to a case of forgery, the relative mundane nature of the crime probably welcome.

On Friday, 20th March, a young man went into the City Bank on Great Eastern Street and presented a cheque to the cashier, Edgar Childe. It was made out for £30, "Pay F. Shipp or order", and endorsed by Mr. Shipp himself.[3]

Mr. Frederick Shipp,[4] a boxmaker of Myrtle Street, Hoxton, was a long-standing customer of the City Bank and a glance at the cheque told Mr. Childe that the signature was wrong. Asking when the young man was given the cheque, he received the reply that Mr. Shipp's representative was waiting outside; Mr. Childe said he would just fetch his hat and then join them outside to discuss the matter. Less than a minute later he walked out onto Great Eastern Street, but neither the young man nor his supposed companion were to be seen.

Mr. Childe went to Frederick Shipp's premises.

Predictably, Shipp knew nothing of the £30 cheque, and was subsequently to learn that a further nine cheques bearing his signature had been submitted over a five-month period, on these occasions successfully as the cashier had been satisfied with the quality of the signature. Mr. Childe said that under a magnifying glass pencil lines could be seen over which the signatures had been traced, explaining the good quality.[5] The monies paid out totalled £159.[6]

Shipp called the police, who arrived in the form of Det. Chief Inspector Swanson and local Det. Inspector Alfred Leach. Mr. Shipp told the officers that he had discovered the four cheques missing when, upon entering the office one morning, he had found the safe broken open, with some blood on his desk,[7] and sent an employee named John Agombar to the bank to cancel the missing cheques.

Agombar,[8] despite being just 20-years-old, had worked for Mr. Shipp for eight years as a box-cutter. One of his duties was to fill in the counterfoils in the book once Mr. Shipp had completed the cheques. He told the detectives that on 28th February he had been on his way to the City Bank when William Gray, a 24-year-old box-cutter who had previously been employed by Mr. Shipp, stopped him and asked where he was going, being told that Agombar was about to cancel four cheques.

He further revealed that two days before the incident with Mr. Childe at the City Bank, Agombar had been again approached by Gray, who this time asked whether the young clerk could obtain one of the cancelled cheques, saying he wanted to use it as a template for a new, forged cheque, telling Agombar that he would receive a cut if he did so. The young box-cutter declined, saying he "Didn't want to lose his character or be locked up."[9]

Swanson and Leach began their enquiries. Asking Edgar Childe whether any other companies in the Hoxton area were customers of the City Bank, they were told of Mr. Frederick Dredge, another box-maker in nearby Pitfield Street. Mr. Dredge looked in his cheque-book and found two missing; one of these proved to have been used as the false £30 cheque presented in Mr. Shipp's name.

Suspicion immediately fell on Henry Batten, a 21-year-old carman employed for the previous two months by Mr. Dredge.[10] Although Batten knew that Mr. Dredge habitually kept his cheque-book in the pocket of an old coat he wore in the workshop, he claimed to know

The Philosopher's Stone

nothing about the missing cheques.[11]

On 23rd March, John Agombar again saw Gray, and told him about the £30 cheque which had been identified as a forgery by Edgar Childe. Gray said: "If I had had a copy it would have been all right; if you or Jack Eaton [another employee of Mr. Shipp's] say anything about it I will swear you were in it."[12]

On 3rd April Det. Inspector Leach returned to Mr. Shipp's workshop and called for William Gray. As soon as he set eyes on the police officer, Gray assumed he had been informed on, saying that "if Agombar has rounded on me I shall round also," and volunteered the following statement:

> For over twelve months Agombar has been in the habit of falsifying his accounts and stealing money from Mr. Shipp. Agombar first suggested that if I could get anyone to write a cheque we could get a big shilling. He gave me several cheques from time to time, also Batten, who used to get them from the safe. I used to hand them to Harry Passmore to copy. It was a stranger who passed the first £10 cheque, and me and Harry Passmore passed the others. It was Harry who attempted to utter the cheque stolen by Batten from Dredge. The second cheque of Dredge's has been destroyed. I saw it destroyed at 63 Fanshaw Street; Harry Passmore did it because the forgery of the other had been discovered.[13]

Gray was obviously not going to go down alone. He and Batten were taken to Hoxton police station; Harry Passmore – Gray's brother-in-law – was arrested by Sergeant John Scott and also taken to the station, where he was picked out at an identity parade by Mr. Childe as the young man who had attempted to pass the £30 cheque. Passmore also attempted to implicate John Agombar,[14] but the police were confident that he was not part of the gang.

Gray, Passmore and Batten appeared at Worship Street Magistrates' Court on 4th May and remanded.[15] At their trial at the Old Bailey on 25th May 1891, Henry Passmore and William Gray were found guilty and sentenced to eighteen and twelve months' hard labour respectively; Henry Batten was found not guilty.[16]

While doubt may have been cast by some on the innocence of John Agombar, it seems Frederick Shipp was completely satisfied that his young employee was guilt-free, as in 1892 Agombar married Charlotte Shipp, Shipp's niece, going on to raise a family.[17]

On the day that William Gray, Henry Passmore and Henry Batten appeared at Worship Street Magistrates' Court, Det. Chief Inspector Swanson was hiding in the workshop of a jeweller at Tysoe Street, Clerkenwell, with young Detective Inspector Frank Froest, the officers on surveillance.[18]

As the detectives watched, a man named Edward Pinter placed twenty gold sovereigns into a crucible along with some mysterious powders and then, once the contents were mixed, the crucible was placed into a smelting furnace.

Suddenly a dense vapour filled the air and Pinter, along with the small group of people with him, left the room to escape the strong smell, which was reminiscent of ammonia. The three men with Pinter had been warned of the stench, which was caused, he said, by the fusing process of the gold. He was attempting, through the ancient science of alchemy, to turn the twenty sovereigns into a quantity of gold worth much more in value.

The detectives, still concealed, saw Pinter return to the workshop two or three times alone, until at last, some thirty minutes later, an assistant removed the crucible from the furnace and Swanson and Froest entered the room, Swanson arresting Edward Pinter on suspicion of attempting to obtain some monies by false pretences.

Froest searched the prisoner and found two large pill boxes, one empty and the second full of a dark grey powder. In a black bag brought to the workshop by Pinter, the detective discovered a pair of gloves, which were slightly burnt, along with five glass jars, some containing unknown powders.

Ascertaining that Pinter had rooms at Dover Street, Piccadilly, Froest took the prisoner's keys and went to search his lodgings. In a large trunk in the bedroom he found a smelting stove, rubber tubing and fittings, and some bellows. Wrapped in brown paper were a quantity of gold powder, some dark grey powder and, in a glass bottle, some unknown white powder.

Froest took these items, along with the materials from the Tysoe Street workshop, and gave them to Dr. August Dupré, the chemical expert at Westminster Hospital whose expertise had been so valuable to Colonel Vivian Majendie during the Fenian Dynamite campaign six years earlier.

That morning Froest had been at New Scotland Yard when Edward Streeter, a jeweller of New Bond Street, attended saying he believed he was about to become a victim of a fraud.

Mr. Streeter had been at Storey's Hotel on Dover Street on 29th April where he had met a Count Kearney and Edward Pinter. During the conversation Pinter told Streeter, in a conspiratorial whisper, that he had discovered the fabled Philosopher's Stone, and as a consequence knew the secrets of alchemy by which he could manufacture gold from natural ingredients. All he needed to do, Pinter claimed, was to add certain powders to an existing quantity of gold and the amount of precious metal would significantly increase.

To demonstrate, he placed a single sovereign into a crucible and mixed it with powder shaken from a twist of brown paper, and melted the contents over a gas stove. Once the process was complete, a nugget weighing as much as three sovereigns was produced.[19]

Pinter suggested a second experiment to be conducted a week later at Mr. Streeter's workshop, whereby he would attempt to double the volume of gold contained within twenty sovereigns. If this experiment was successful, the supposed alchemist suggested, Mr. Streeter should find £40,000 worth of gold, which would be placed in a tank and covered in a secret acid for eighteen days, after which time the £40,000[20] would be increased to £100,000. The process would only work, Pinter claimed, if the tank remained completely untouched for the duration; the fumes would apparently be strong enough to kill anyone who opened the tank.

The alchemist, seemingly getting carried away by his own words, said that they should discontinue production once £10million[21] worth of gold had been produced.

Mr. Streeter agreed to the second demonstration at his Clerkenwell workshop on 4th May, then went to New Scotland Yard.

Following his apprehension, Swanson and Froest took the 56-year-old Edward Pinter into custody and he appeared at Marlborough Street Magistrates' Court on 19th May 1891.

Although described in the newspapers as 'the Modern Alchemist', Pinter was registered in court as the dull-by-comparison occupation of merchant. He was charged with attempting to obtain the sum of £40,000 by means of a trick, with intent to defraud. Prosecutors Horace Avory and Henry Pollard claimed that Pinter's plan had been to place the £40,000 in the tank, and once the noxious fumes had driven those assembled away, return to remove the gold and coolly disappear. He had, it was claimed, already been successful with a similar plan in Liverpool several years previously, where he had obtained £300, and possibly also in locations overseas.

Dr. Dupré had, by this time, concluded his examination of the materials

*Edward Pinter, 'The Modern Alchemist'
from Lloyd's Weekly Newspaper, 17th May 1891*

found on Pinter and at his lodgings. Mr. Avory Q.C. said he was sorry to report that the Philosopher's Stone had still to be discovered; Dr. Dupré had found that one of the powders was granulated gold, while the grey powder was a mixture of calomel and charcoal. The bottles contained silver nitrate and calcium sulphate.

In Dr. Dupré's opinion, the addition of the grey powder to the gold and silver nitrate would create the reaction seen at Storey's Hotel, and the burnt gloves had traces of nitrate of silver upon the fingers.

It seemed clear that Pinter had a strong knowledge of chemistry, and was using it in the opposite way to Dr. Dupré.

The Modern Alchemist had one more trick up his sleeve; his counsel, Mr. Bernard Abrahams, announced that his client was anxious to show that he could indeed make gold, by performing the process in open court.

Magistrate Mr. Hannay declined the opportunity of such a demonstration, commenting to laughter in the court: "Yes; but I am told that such a stench would be created that we should all have to leave the place."[22]

Pinter was remanded in custody and appeared at the Old Bailey on 27th July, pleading guilty. He was sentenced to three months' penal servitude at Pentonville prison.[23]

His appearance at Marlborough Street Magistrate's Court had alerted the Judicial Authority of Switzerland to Pinter's location, and they were soon in touch with New Scotland Yard seeking an extradition agreement which would see the prisoner surrendered to face charges of fraud in that country, committed under the alias of Schaefer.[24]

Receiving news of the impending extradition, Pinter's solicitor Arthur Newton drew up a petition pleading for the process to be quashed on the grounds of the prisoner's supposed epilepsy. It was sent to Henry Matthews on 10th August 1891, but to no avail.

Upon his release from Pentonville on 26th October, Pinter was arrested by Det. Sergeant Wagner and taken to Bow Street, where he was charged with obtaining money by false pretences within the jurisdiction of the Swiss Government. He was remanded, this time at Holloway.[25]

A desperate appeal lodged against the extradition by Newton bought some time but was ultimately rejected; Assistant Commissioner Robert Anderson formally requested the extradition warrant to be drawn up on 29th December 1891.

The matter was still not resolved, however, as the Swiss authorities wanted the British detectives to investigate further cases of fraud, and authorities as far afield as Dublin were contacted with Pinter's photograph, asking whether he could be recognised as a man responsible for a string of local frauds.[26]

Henry Reynolds, Principal Clerk of Baring Brothers bank, came forward to say that in November 1883 a block of bonds worth £200 each belonging to the Alabama North & South Railway had been taken out of the safe and left on a desk; several hours later it was noticed they were missing – all 105 of them.[27] In all, the stolen bonds were worth £21,000.[28] Whether the Modern Alchemist was responsible was never ascertained; certainly no evidence was produced. But much time was taken in investigating this enormous theft, and Det. Chief Inspector Swanson was assigned to the case.

As 1891 turned into 1892, Edward Pinter remained in Holloway Prison.[29]

For Donald Swanson, the end of the year saw the detective join eight of his colleagues at a dinner hosted by Chief Constable Melville Macnaghten in honour of his friend, the former Commissioner James Monro, who was shortly to return to India on missionary work. Around the table with Monro and Macnaghten sat Frederick Abberline, James Butcher, Frederick Jarvis, John Littlechild, Henry Moore, Billy Peel, John Shore and John Tunbridge, the "varied galaxy of detective talent" completed by Donald Swanson, who was later described by Macnaghten as having "a synthetical turn of mind".[30] It is unlikely that such a glittering group representing the best of Scotland Yard had broken bread together before or since.

While the red tape of Pinter's extradition was being untangled, Det. Chief Inspector Swanson was involved in an extraordinary case played out as a three-act drama, with a cast comprising some of society's most well-known names.

The first part of the story opened when Mrs. Florence Osborne sued her second cousin, Mrs. Hargreaves, for slander over the theft of some jewellery. The Great Pearl Case, as it became known, kept Londoners enthralled for months.

Mrs. Osborne, the 26-year-old wife of the dashing Captain Clarence A. Osborne of the Caribiners (the 6th Dragoon Guards), was born Florence Ethel Elliot, daughter of barrister John Elliot and his wife Charlotte,[31] both of whom died when she was young. Florence lived in South Kensington with her brother and younger sister, the house purchased for them by their wealthy grandfather, who was a partner in a successful brewing company.[32]

In January 1890, an elderly lady named Mrs. Martin died in Collingwood, near Torquay. She was the great aunt of Florence Elliot, and grandmother to Mrs. Hargreaves, to whom she left a sizeable amount of valuable jewellery.

Mrs. Hargreaves and her husband, retired Major George Hargreaves, visited Miss Elliot, as she was at that time, in June 1890, spending several days with her at South Kensington. Mrs. Hargreaves invited Florence several times to visit them in Torquay; this she eventually did on 9th February 1891.

The following day, Mrs. Hargreaves showed Florence the inherited jewellery. It was kept in a secret compartment of a writing desk, the existence of which was known, said Mrs. Hargreaves, to "only five persons... myself, my husband, [family friend] Mr. Englehart, yourself, and the cabinet-maker."[33]

Florence Elliot left Torquay on 18th February. She was now engaged to Captain Osborne, and said she had to return to London that day in order to attend to dressmakers and others involved in the wedding arrangements.

At some point over the next two days Mrs. Hargreaves noticed a number of jewels worth £800 were missing from the hidden compartment.

Major Hargreaves issued an advertisement asking for information on the stolen items, and this was seen by a City-based firm of goldsmiths named Messrs Spink and Son, who reported that on 19th February, the day after Florence Elliot had left Torquay, a young woman had visited their premises at 2 Gracechurch Street wanting to sell two large pearls. She gave her name as Mrs. Price, of 14 Hyde Park Gardens. When the shopkeeper pointed out that there was no 'Mrs. Price' registered at that address in the directory, the woman said she was only a visitor at that moment and her permanent address was Redcliffe House, Bradford. Satisfied, Mr. Spink gave the lady a crossed cheque for £550.

Four days later, however, she returned, saying that the crossed cheque was no good; it was replaced by an open one.

Mr. Englehart, the friend of the Hargreaves', visited Spink and showed them a photograph of Miss Elliot. They recognised her as the woman who had sold the pearls.

This was all the confirmation Major Hargreaves needed. On 12th March he spoke with Captain Osborne, saying that while he was anxious to avoid a scandal, the matter had to be looked into fully, adding that should he receive a written confession from Florence and the stolen jewels returned, no further action would be taken.

Unfortunately, Mrs. Hargreaves was not so discreet. She mentioned the "sad business" to friends Beatrix Goldney and Eva Templar, mentioning Florence Elliot by name.[34]

Subsequently, a short piece on the story appeared in a provincial newspaper called the *Dwarf*, which in their 'Whispers' column stated that residents of Torquay were enjoying the salacious gossip with regard to the case. It named Miss Elliot, but horribly bungled the information it had received and claimed Mrs. Hargreaves was actually behind the theft, and had blackmailed Miss Elliot.

At the initial slander hearing on 26th November, Mr. Ames, the publisher of *Dwarf*, was forced into a complete climbdown, but resolved the situation with Mrs. Hargreaves by offering to pay her costs and to publish a full apology in a future edition. Mrs. Hargreaves gladly accepted.[35]

Less willing to put an end to matters was Florence Osborne, by now married to Captain Osborne. She wanted her name cleared, and the trial began on 15th December 1891.[36] Captain Osborne, who believed implicitly in his wife's innocence, supported her accusation of slander.

Over the following five days, the court heard evidence from various parties attesting to the good character of Mrs. Osborne, underlining

Mrs. Florence Osborne
from the Aberdeen Evening Express, 9th March 1892

how ludicrous the idea was that such a young woman, from a privileged background and newly-married to a dashing Army Captain, would steal from her long-time friends.

Then, on 19th December, the case suddenly collapsed.

A letter was received by the court, sent by an employee of a City Bank who had read newspaper reports of the scandalous case. He remembered a visit from a young lady who had asked for £550 in gold to be exchanged for banknotes, which they had been happy to undertake.

An adjournment of one day was called, so that the City of London Police could investigate this new lead. They discovered that after receiving the £550 open cheque from Messrs Spink, the woman had gone to a bank and had it exchanged for gold. With this subsequently turned into banknotes, she went on a spending spree. Sadly for the thief, the notes were traceable and one of these, paid to a shopkeeper named Maple for a quantity of household linen, was signed by Florence Elliot.

Mrs. Osborne had been found out. She did not wait to hear the facts read out in public; the following day she left her home at South Kensington and fled to the Continent. Some days later, Captain Osborne and Hugh Elliot, her brother, wrote a letter to Major Hargreaves admitting her guilt. Despite his earlier private demand for such a note, it gave the Major no pleasure to now receive one after the affair had been played out so publicly, and he and Mrs. Hargreaves were united in their sorrow at Mrs. Osborne's position.[37]

After a month abroad, where she travelled under the name Ogilvy,[38] Mrs. Osborne decided the best course of action would be for her to surrender herself to justice. Her husband had offered to sacrifice his military career and take her to Buenos Aires, but she would not hear of it and was determined that he should return to London to continue his career, and she to face trial. Hugh Elliot had repaid the £550 to Messrs Spink and also settled Major Hargreaves' legal costs, and Florence hoped that this, added to the fact that she was now pregnant, would result in leniency. On 4th February 1892, the Osbornes left the hotel in Spain where they had been staying and travelled by train to Paris.

And so began the second act.

Det. Inspectors Davidson and Malone of the City of London Police, who had been in France for more than a month searching for Mrs. Osborne, were telegraphed with the information that she had made contact and immediately went to Gare du Nord station in Paris where they met Captain and Mrs. Osborne, who were about to buy tickets for the 3.15pm train to London's Cannon Street.

Davidson decided not to formally arrest Mrs. Osborne, but to accompany the couple on their journey to London. They arrived at Calais shortly before 7.30pm and boarded the steamship *Foam*, operated by the London, Chatham and Dover Company. The short journey was beset by bad weather and both Captain and Mrs. Osborne suffered terrible sea-sickness.

On arrival at Dover two hours later, Det. Inspector Davidson waited for the other passengers to disembark before escorting Mrs. Osborne and her husband across the gangway and onto the pier. Waiting for them was Lieutenant-Colonel Henry Smith, Commissioner of the City of London Police, with Det. Inspector Taylor. Smith saluted Captain Osborne, and bowed to Mrs. Osborne. At that moment she swayed and it appeared she might fall, so Smith offered his arm and, with the help of a member of the *Foam*'s crew, escorted Mrs. Osborne along the platform to a waiting train, with her husband following.

The party moved to a reserved compartment, away from prying eyes. On the journey Captain Osborne asked Commissioner Smith what fate awaited his wife, who spent her time weeping into a handkerchief.

The train stopped at London Bridge station, where Detective Inspector James McWilliam was waiting with officers from the City of

London Police.³⁹ The party was conveyed by cab to Cloak Lane police station, where the warrant was read by Det. Inspector Sagar,⁴⁰ and Mrs. Osborne was formally arrested by Acting Night Inspector Hosking on a charge of fraud, "that she did on February 19th, 1891, obtain a cheque of the value of 550 pounds from Messrs Spink and Son." She was refused bail and spent the night in McWilliam's room, in the custody of one of the female attendants.⁴¹

The following morning – Friday, 5th February 1892 – Mrs. Osborne was taken to the Guildhall, where fewer than a hundred people were gathered outside the historic building thanks to the efforts of the City of London Police.

The socialite, dressed in black with a heavy crepe mourning veil, was ushered into the Council Chamber and, in the absence of any form of dock, was seated at a table between her husband and Det. Inspector Taylor, hiding her face in her hands. It was remarked upon by several present, including members of the press, how pale and worn Mrs. Osborne looked, and how thin she was compared to her appearance at the slander case the previous December.⁴²

Eventually, at half-past ten, the Lord Mayor, Mr. Alderman David Evans, entered the Chamber and the hearing began. Mrs. Osborne began to sob, and Captain Osborne used a sheet of blotting paper to fan his wife's face before handing her a glass of water.⁴³ In attendance were several high-ranking members of the City of London Police force, along with Det. Chief Inspector Donald Swanson of the Metropolitan Police, who, on entering the court, entered into a whispered conversation with Det. Superintendent Alfred Foster of the City Police.

The Chief Clerk, Mr. Douglas, asked whether anyone appeared for the Treasury. Swanson replied that the Treasury had been communicated with, and that in their absence he represented both the Metropolitan Police *and* the Treasury.

The Lord Mayor, dissatisfied with these arrangements, commented that until someone from the Treasury was present to conduct the case it could not proceed, and therefore a recess would be held until the representative appeared. Sympathetic to her condition, he suggested that Mrs. Osborne retire to Committee Room No. 1. As she rose to leave the courtroom, she began to sob hysterically and as she was being led towards the door suddenly cried out "I can't see!," and staggered. She was saved from actually falling by her husband and Commissioner Smith, and was half-led, half-carried into the Committee Room, where she was soon attended by a doctor.⁴⁴

She was still there when Mr. Cuffe of the Treasury Solicitor's office

Captain Osborne helps his wife from the Bow Street dock
from The Graphic, 13th February 1892

arrived at 11.30.

Cuffe apologised for his being late attending Court, and then told Mr. Alderman Evans that the Treasury formally withdrew the warrant issued by the City of London Police on which Mrs. Osborne had been arrested. As he therefore offered no evidence against the prisoner, the Lord Mayor announced that the case was dismissed, which met with applause within the courtroom.

No sooner had the applause died down than Det. Chief Inspector Swanson went to Committee Room No. 1 and arrested Mrs. Osborne on a charge of perjury, "committed in the action tried in the Queen's Bench Division from the 17th to 22nd December of Osborne v Hargreaves".[45] Swanson led her and Captain Osborne outside, where a cab was waiting to take them to Bow Street Magistrates' Court. It appeared that until Swanson whispered to Superintendent Foster, the City of London Police were oblivious to the intentions of their Metropolitan counterparts and the Treasury.[46]

The third and final act was about to commence.

At one o'clock, less than two hours after Mrs. Osborne had appeared in front of the Lord Mayor at the Guildhall, she was sitting in the Bow Street dock, her right hand tightly clenching that of her husband while in her left she held a handkerchief and a bottle of smelling salts.[47] Tears rolled down her face in waves. It was a mercifully brief hearing, with the only witnesses called being Det. Inspector Taylor of the City of London Police, who spoke to confirm that he had escorted the prisoner from Dover, and Det. Chief Inspector Donald Swanson, who confirmed he had arrested Mrs. Osborne at the Guildhall.

She was refused bail and held on remand, and transported to Holloway Prison to await trial at the Old Bailey. The devoted Captain Osborne was allowed to visit daily. Her health was a constant cause for concern, and she was attended at the prison infirmary by Doctor Gilbert.

While awaiting the trial, Major Hargreaves went to the Continent for the sake of his heath. The excitement generated by the Great Pearl Case inspired an enterprising tradesman to exhibit the cabinet from which the jewels were stolen in his Torquay shop.[48]

On 7th March 1892, a large crowd squeezed into one of the smaller courtrooms of the Old Bailey to hear Mrs. Osborne plead guilty. Mrs. Hargreaves pleaded for leniency in the sentencing, probably a combination of her feelings for her cousin, and sympathy at the alarming deterioration in her health.

Addressing Florence Osborne, Mr. Justice Denman said:

> ...If you had succeeded by your wilful and corrupt perjury in obtaining a verdict in your favour your old friends would have left that court with a stain of indelible infamy upon them. These are serious matters. I am aware of your condition and I am aware of your frail health. I am aware that all the jewellery has been returned, that the money which you misappropriated has also been restored, and as [Prosecutor] Sir Charles Russell tells me today, all the costs have been paid to the person who necessarily entered into litigation. Now you have been some time in prison, and you have, I notice, surrendered yourself to justice and confessed your guilt, and all these matters I am willing to take into consideration, and also that which Mrs. Hargreaves had said to me today – a strong recommendation to mercy by her of all others who might have been most injured.
>
> The maximum punishment is seven years' penal servitude for this offence. I am not about to pass any such sentence on you, but I know that the sentence I am about to pass to a person in your position and education is one of great severity. The punishment I am about to inflict is that you be imprisoned with such hard labour as your condition and frail state of health will permit you to perform. During that imprisonment you will be attended by the prison doctors and other medical men.
>
> The sentence is that you be imprisoned and kept to hard labour for nine calendar months.[49]

Mrs. Osborne, who had been convulsed with sobs during the judge's address, was led half-fainting out of the dock and down the steps to the cells underneath the court.

The newspapers reported it was likely that her child would be born in jail.

In the event, Florence Edith Osborne was released from Holloway at half-past eight on the evening of Saturday, 30th April 1892, having served just seven weeks of her sentence due to her continued poor health, which was worsening with each passing day. She was accompanied by a female warder in a cab to her husband's parents home in Ulster Terrace, Regent's Park.[50]

Her daughter Phyllis Evelyn was born a month later on 31st May at Cilwendeg Park, Boncath.[51] A brother, Bryan, and two sisters, Betty and Margaret, would be born in the years that followed.[52]

Mrs. Osborne may have served but a short spell of her sentence, but the shame brought upon herself and her husband was penance enough. Captain Clarence Osborne resigned his army commission days before

Phyllis's birth[53] and became a stockbroker.[54]

In the weeks following Mrs. Osborne's release, Det. Chief Inspector Swanson was called upon to investigate Edward Pinter's involvement in the theft of the bonds from Baring Brothers and others, and to collect evidence to send to the Swiss authorities. His report was submitted on 28th May, three days before the birth of Phyllis Osborne, and was forwarded by Chief Magistrate Sir John Bridge at Bow Street, who made special mention of Swanson's "intelligence and zeal".[55]

As a result, the Modern Alchemist was finally extradited to face Swiss justice in June 1892, and on 10th June Swanson was commended by Commissioner Bradford for his "zeal and intelligence displayed" in the case.[56]

The spectre of Jack the Ripper would loom large again before the end of the year, when on 19th November 18-year-old[57] Emily Smith made her way to New Scotland Yard and made a statement to Det. Inspector Froest and Det. Sergeant Freeman that she had been attacked in Whitechapel, narrowly escaping being murdered. After three hours of questions and examination, a statement, reported to have run to ten foolscap pages, was drawn up and signed, and presented the following day to Commissioner Edward Bradford and the case put in the hands of Det. Chief Inspector Swanson, still the man entrusted with incidents potentially related to the Ripper crimes, however remotely.[58]

It was an extraordinary story.

Emily Edith Smith had packed a lot into her eighteen years. Described by a smitten newspaper reporter as "pre-possessing", she was a petite 5ft 3in with light-brown hair, "soft blue eyes, a small mouth, and a rather short nose." She apparently began work as a dressmaker, but then posed as an artist's model and in 1891 began living with a German who she called Norton, but didn't know his real name. They had parted a few months before the attack, and she had returned to live with her father and stepmother at the family home of 3 Bingfield Street, Caledonian Road. By her own admission, she lived "a gay life".[59]

Wearing a cheap dark blue alpaca dress[60] and an old black hat, Miss Smith was walking down Cheapside towards St. Paul's Churchyard on the early evening of Saturday, 5th November, a wet and foggy day. As she passed Lockhart's Coffee House at No. 41, a tall man called out "Goodnight Nellie," which she ignored. However, he was at her side again soon afterwards, this time inviting her to go for a cup of tea. After some hesitation she accepted, and the couple walked some distance past the Mansion House along Lombard Street, and then into Fenchurch Street, from where a narrow alleyway was taken to a dimly-lit coffee house whose character, one newspaper said, could be judged "by the fact that the tea was served in thick cups without spoons."[61]

The man suggested they finish their refreshments and go to his office at Upton Park, and again the young woman agreed, and the pair made their way along a maze of alleyways before finding themselves back on Fenchurch Street, this time at the Aldgate end. From here they took an omnibus along Whitechapel High Street to the corner of Commercial Road. Not knowing the area, Miss Smith felt quite lost and asked her companion where they were, and the answer she received no doubt caused her no little concern:

> "This is Whitechapel."
>
> "Oh! Then this is where the girls were murdered."
>
> "Pshaw, not girls, old women, you mean. They were better out of the way."

The man then pointed towards Leman Street, saying "That is where Jack the Ripper is known."[62]

Bizarrely, she stayed in the man's company, taking a tram along Commercial Road as he pointed out various shops and told her of his acquaintance with the various owners. They alighted at the George IV tavern[63] on the corner of Commercial Street and Jubilee Street, and walked south along Sutton Street just a few yards before entering a beer house. Although the man ordered a small soda for himself – stating he never drank anything stronger[64] – Emily Smith had a small whisky.[65]

It was here that, for the first time, the light was fully upon him and Miss Smith was able to furnish a detailed description for the Scotland Yard detectives:

> He was tall and thin, looking like a consumptive, with high cheek bones, his face being pale. He stood over 5ft. 9in., wore a hard bowler hat, had very dark hair, though his moustache, which was curled at either ends, was of a sandy tint. He had very peculiar eyebrows, meeting over the nose and the ends turning up towards the temples. She would seem to have taken particular notice of his eyes. These she described as odd and light, almost to squinting, one being a lightish brown and the other a bluey grey. He had a strange habit of blinking them, but they sparkled and were piercing. His face, excepting the upper lip, was closely shaven. Both the "dog" teeth showed decay cavities, but only when he laughed.

The attack on Emily Smith
from the Illustrated Police News, 3rd December 1892

His forehead seemed rather square, and, though speaking English well, he struck her as being a foreigner. She did not notice either his collar or necktie, but took a close look at his clothes. He wore a short, single-breasted jacket coat, of a black, roughish material, and great trousers with a stripe pattern in blue running through them. He had a very uncommon sort of watch-chain, consisting of a number of small squares strung on to a centre connecting plain chain; but she did not see his watch. She has since seen in a jeweller's shop window a chain of the same pattern exactly, and can point it out. He wore no rings, and the girl observed no peculiarity about either his hands or boots. He walked with a military gait, spoke like an educated person, and carried neither cane nor umbrella. His cuffs were white.[66]

Having finished their drinks, the couple left the beer house and continued walking south along Sutton Street. Although the street was nearly always dark and deserted, because of the fog they approached a railway bridge 100 yards further along in almost complete darkness. Almost immediately after the arch they turned right into a narrow passage to the right of The Railway Arms[67] known as Station Place,[68] which, because of a hoarding erected around construction works of a new platform to the railway, was almost pitch black despite the presence of a lamp on a wall a few feet away.

Miss Smith refused to continue any further, despite her companion claiming that his office was at the end of the alley. When she declined once more, he replied quietly, "Then I'll settle you now," and grabbed her by her neck and collar of her dress, dragging her into the darkness.

The man twisted her round so that her back was to him, and as he did so she caught a glimpse of a knife in his hand. Screaming loudly, and managing to partly break his hold, she brought her knee up sharply, striking her assailant in what one newspaper euphemistically called "the lowest part of the abdomen". He shouted "Oh! My God!" in agony and released his grip, allowing Miss Smith to escape to the relative brightness of Sutton Street and the comfort of two women who were passing. Her attacker was nowhere to be seen.

After reading the statement and meeting Miss Smith, Det. Chief Inspector Swanson instructed Sergeant Bradshaw to accompany her over the complete route from where she met the man in Cheapside to the attempted murder spot.[69]

The press reported that the police held reservations about the truth behind the story, with a representative of the *Pall Mall Gazette* visiting New Scotland Yard to be told that the police

...received literally hundreds of similar statements, and that they did not attach any more importance to [Miss Smith's story] with so much circumstantial details than to others sent to Scotland Yard from time to time.⁷⁰

A reporter visited Shadwell police station, less than 100 yards from the scene of the supposed attack, and was told by an inspector that he knew nothing about it; the station had not even been communicated with by the authorities from Scotland Yard.⁷¹

Despite this apparent disinterest from official quarters, it was of great interest to the press that the description of the attacker tallied with that of the man supposedly seen by fruit stall holder Matthew Packer.⁷² The newspapers also commented on the fact that "as in all of the Whitechapel outrages, the passage into which the woman was lured has both an entrance and an exit."⁷³

The fact that the Whitechapel murderer might have returned, despite there being nothing in the way of evidence other than Emily Smith's version of events, particularly impressed one reporter from the *Western Mail,* who hinted at what many believed had happened to the killer:

> The theory that the "Ripper" had been handed over by his friends to the police as a dangerous lunatic, and was now safely under their charge, had begun to be generally credited as a fact. Today that theory has been shattered.
>
> The circumstantial narrative of the woman bore the impress of truth upon it, and every inquiry made today has but confirmed the details of her narrative. The great surprise of every person to whom I have spoken has been about the woman's great power of observation. It certainly was remarkable, but this seems to be a peculiarity of hers. In telling her story to Inspector Froest she was most minute, even drawing the man's features and moustache curl on paper, for the better illustration of her statements.
>
> "I did not," she said, "notice his boots, nor yet his hands, or the colour of his tie."
>
> I am surprised that she did not observe the last article of attire, as after I had interviewed her on Saturday night, she commenced her description of me to the police with the remark that I was "a young gentleman with a red tie." On that occasion she was very neatly dressed, and her appearance did not at all suggest the horrible profession which she follows.
>
> One observation of her attempted murderer – whom every person now

believes to be the dreaded "Ripper" – not recorded by the *Morning*, is particularly significant. Whilst the two were walking along Commercial Road, he said, "There are not many guys about this year. It was entirely different two years ago." "Indeed?" she replied. "Yes, two years ago Jack the Ripper was famous, and he was 'guyed' everywhere here," and as he spoke he laughed quietly to himself. It was this incident which first made Edith Smith suspicious of her companion.[74]

After news of the attack broke, her parents sent for her to return to the family home at Bingfield Street. There, she received visits from numerous reporters, leaving her increasingly weary:

> I was tired to death in talking to them, and some of them were certainly not courteous, insinuating that I had made up a lot of lies. I slammed the door in their faces. I am sorry if I was rude, but I really cannot help it.[75]

If Donald Swanson and his colleagues believed that Emily Smith had fabricated the incident, they at least took their investigations into the story seriously. Asked by one reporter whether she had seen much of Sergeant Bradshaw, tasked by Swanson with looking into the supposed victim's movements, Miss Smith replied:

> "Quite enough. He simply haunts me, and no later than today I went into a restaurant in the Tottenham Court Road to have something to eat, and he also came in and sat beside me."
>
> "Yes," she replied to a further question, "it was he who accompanied me in my tour over the ground in Whitechapel yesterday, but he has nothing to say for himself, and he is particularly dull."[76]

Finally fed up with increasing opinion in the face of not a single lead being uncovered by the police, on 26th November Emily Smith went to the offices of Holborn solicitors Peacock and Goddard to make a sworn declaration that the incident happened exactly as she described it.

In the declaration, she revealed that she and two friends had attempted to retrace her steps on the day in question, and how, remarkably, they had seen the man again, attempting to accost another young women. First, she related having failed completely in attempts to locate the coffee shop off Fenchurch Street which had so disgusted her by serving their tea in cups without spoons. Undeterred, the group went to The Railway Arms and asked landlord John Thorlby about the visit on the night of the attack:

I told [my friends] the landlord of the public house in Sutton Street, when I was in there with my assailant on November 5, tended bar in his shirt sleeves, and that the material of the garment was coloured flannel. When we went there the landlord had on a brown cardigan jacket. One of my friends asked him did he remember, on Guy Fawkes' night, seeing me with a gentleman at about the hour we were there, 5.45 p.m. He looked at me very closely, and said he could not remember. I then asked him could he not recall the incident of my having asked for a small whisky, and his saying that he had only a beer and wine licence, at the same time recommending his sherry... One of my friends then asked did he wear flannel shirts in the bar, to which he replied, 'Nothing but white.' The same friend, almost before he had time to say this, quickly turned up the cuff of the cardigan jacket, and, disclosing a fawn coloured flannel shirt, said, 'You would not call that white?' I then remarked that that was exactly the style of shirt he wore on the night I speak of.

Some of the newspapers try to make a point out of the absence of any statement as to what I did after I ran down Sutton Street, and caught the Commercial Road tramcar. Well, I will tell it now for the public, as I did for the private ears of Inspector Froest and Sergeant Freeman in Scotland Yard. I booked at Aldgate for King's Cross, and there a man whom I thought I knew came up and spoke to me. He asked me why I was so frightened, and what was up with me. I had some tea with him, and went on to my home, where I met a girl of about my own age, from whom I had been estranged for some time through a girl's quarrel. I begged her to stay with me as I was so frightened, which she did. I told her, and mother later that night, but not father, fearing it would upset him. He has been an invalid for a long time.

Now touching my last Sunday night experience referred to in one of the evening papers, I wish to state that on the evening mentioned I was in the King Lud public house, Ludgate Circus, at about ten o'clock, and whilst having a sandwich and something to drink, two gentlemen were there seen by me, and one of them had a most wonderful resemblance to my would be murderer. I was immediately struck by the likeness, but whilst he had the odd eyes I have described, I could not see the decayed cavities in his 'dog' teeth mentioned in my statement in Scotland Yard. I asked the barmaid, did she notice anything peculiar about his eyes. She said, "Yes, they are odd, and I have seen him stare very hard at you.' I then asked her had she ever seen either of them in the King Lud bar before, and she answered not. She thought they were complete strangers. I followed them out, and they went down into the gentlemen's retiring

The Railway Arms, on the corner of Sutton Street and Station Place
© www.eastlondonpostcard.co.uk

place at Ludgate Hill. They then went up towards St Paul's, where they picked up two girls, and walked with them up Cheapside, beyond the Bank of England, until they reached a point right opposite a building with an archway, in which the German Bank has offices, and there they stopped. A dense fog was then quickly setting in, and I determined to stay as close as I could to them. They turned back, and after following them I had to go ahead of them, and the man I suspected was one of the first pair. I stood in a doorway for the purpose, if possible, of hearing his voice; there was a laneway or passage nearby, and I heard him distinctly say, "Let us get up this way." The girl said, "I'll do nothing of the kind," or words to that effect. In a second or two the other pair came up, and on the girl mentioned the matter to her girl companion, she heard her say, "No, no, no." They then all proceeded back towards Cheapside, and I followed them; but just before the Bank the fog became that thick that you could scarcely see your hand before you. I lost them in that fog.

I told this to Chief Inspector Swanson next day, and he wondered why I did not give the man into custody. I told him I could never see his teeth, but that he was a man with the same eyes, same height, same style of dress, and same walking street, and I honestly now swear that I am all but convinced he was the man who took me from Cheapside to Station Place.

I am positive I would be able to identify the man again. To end this statement I will say that throughout the whole of the occurrences above detailed I was perfectly sober. I have never been drunk in my life, and have never been in a court either as a prisoner, a witness, or in any other capacity.[77]

Det. Chief Inspector Donald Swanson must have been exasperated with Emily Smith's story. Privately, he no doubt had his own beliefs on her and her background, probably mirroring those being suggested openly in the press.

Despite her protestations in her declaration that she was "not an unfortunate," the reporter from the *Western Mail*'s comment that during their interview she was "very neatly dressed, and her appearance did not at all suggest the horrible profession which she follows" indicates the opposite.[78] The *Hampshire Telegraph and Sussex Chronicle* described her as "a young girl of the unfortunate class."[79] She herself admitted to having led "a gay life."[80]

Was this a case of a young woman earning money the only way she could, subsequently weaving a tale of being attacked by Jack the Ripper in order to gain some sympathy, or save face?

Emily Smith seems to have disappeared into the mists of time. Nothing more was heard of her following her sworn declaration, and no arrests were made.

Whatever the truth of her story, such incidents had to be investigated and as the Scotland Yard detective with the greatest knowledge of the Ripper crimes, it was Swanson who had to first decide whether a crime was the work of the Whitechapel killer, as he had with the murder of Phoebe Hogg, and would in the future with similar cases.

Jack the Ripper was not done with Det. Chief Inspector Donald Swanson just yet.

SIXTEEN
City of the Plain

Perhaps more has been written about the Victorian's attitude to sex than any other aspect of that era. It was a time of stark contradiction, with the lasting impression of the mid to late 19th century being one of an almost prim nature.

Possessing a strong sexual appetite was seen as being incompatible with mental and artistic endeavour, and male masturbation was believed to cause a wide range of physical and mental disorders.

With this kind of repression, the vast majority of Victorians were uneducated on sex, and such ignorance resulted in embarrassment and even fear.[1] Important issues such as birth control were not discussed in public, as shown in 1877 when Annie Besant, the prominent socialist and women's rights activist, was put on trial along with Charles Bradlaugh for publishing Charles Knowlton's *Fruits of Philosophy*, which advocated birth control.[2]

As displaying an interest in sexual activity and related matters was increasingly frowned upon in public, so the enjoyment of pleasures of the flesh became more private and secretive. Scratch the surface of supposed Victorian respectability and a vast range of depravity was exposed.

At the lower end of the scale was the interest in pornographic literature and prints, with titles such as the sado-masochistic *Venus in Furs* (1870), *The Autobiography of a Flea* (1887), *The Lustful Turk, or Lascivious Scenes from a Harem* (written in 1828 but relatively unknown until an edition published in 1893) and the notorious magazine *The Pearl* (1879) being incredibly popular. The Victorian pornographic publication probably best known today is the memoir *My Secret Life* by 'Walter', first published between 1888-1894,[3] and Jack Saul's semi-autobiographical *The Sins of the Cities of the Plain*.

Since the Obscene Publications Act of 1857 had made the sale of such material illegal, a rampant underground market existed, with buyers more often than not purchasing through covertly-circulated catalogues rather than risking an appearance in person at a specialist book store.

In 1880, two arrests by Donald Swanson in quick succession demonstrated how seriously the police took such activity, and offer an insight into the methods employed to secure an arrest in such cases.

On 15th September, Swanson walked into a bookshop on Green Street, off Leicester Square, and read a warrant to the young man behind the counter, Charles Newbold, before arresting him for selling obscene photographs. Standing on the other side of the counter, looking through a selection of images, was Det. Sergeant Maurice Moser. Working under cover, Moser had visited the shop on numerous occasions since 6th August on the pretext of purchasing 'art photographs', slowly gaining Newbold's trust, until the detective was able to secure a reluctant agreement to sell something racier. A suitable photograph, entitled 'The Dairy Show', was purchased for a shilling. This was enough to allow Swanson to request a warrant, and a search of the property after Newbold's apprehension unearthed more than 1,400 photographs and 30 books, all of an obscene nature. Newbold was able to prove that the shop belonged to his brother, and that he was merely working there, escaping with three months' imprisonment without hard labour.[4]

But the entrapment operation had worked to perfection, and would soon be employed again.

A few weeks later, on 18th October, Swanson went to 19 Leicester Square, a bookshop run by Caroline Thoriste, a Frenchwoman who had worked in London as a governess, and arrested her for selling indecent pictures. Once again, Det. Sergeant Moser had visited the shop on eight consecutive days, on each occasion purchasing obscene material without any difficulty. The shop was searched, and some 500 indecent pictures were found.

At the Middlesex Sessions a month later she pleaded guilty to selling the images, but not publicly selling them. Recognising that the prisoner was completely ignorant to the fact that the sale of such material was illegal in England, the judge declined to imprison her, instead fining the Frenchwoman £50 and binding her with a surety of £100 for twelve months.[5]

Det. Sergeant Moser would later give details of his role in the operation, when describing a visit to one of "at least a hundred shops in London… [each] dealing in exactly the same sort of goods, the originals or negatives of which are invariably imported from abroad":

> When I got into the shop I spoke to a seedy, dirty-looking individual behind the counter, and I asked him if he could sell me some photographs,

indicating the kind I wanted... the next day I bought a few more, and so on every day for nearly a week; then, as I thought, having disarmed any suspicion which might arise, I proffered a request to purchase some other photos of a more improper character, so on the sixth day I boldly asked for what I had really intended trying to secure at the first, and the man was proceeding, on the strength of our short acquaintance, to deal with me confidentially and let me have what I wanted, when, out of an inner room, his wife, a woman equally seedy, equally dirty, with a child at her breast which was, if anything, even seedier and dirtier that either of both the father and mother, suddenly appeared and screamed out, "Don't sell him any, dear, you know the trouble you had last time." (The wretch had served six months' imprisonment previously.)

"Oh," said the man, "I think this gentleman means square, don't you, sir?"
"Well," said I, "do I look like an informer?"
"But you might be a detective, sir, which is worse."

...At last, after considerable conversation, I prevailed upon the man to let me have some of his more valuable wares, and followed him upstairs to a dirty little place, which was part bedroom, part workshop, part storeroom, part anything – as filthy a hole as I have ever been into. I sat on a rickety chair before an equally rickety table, my face looking towards the window, whilst the man was picking out the photographs from a tin box he had pulled out from under the bed, and placing them on the table, his wife watching the proceedings over my shoulder.

The following day, Moser returned with half-a-dozen fellow officers and raided the premises, seizing stock consisting of over 5,000 photographs and prints. The seller was sentenced to the maximum of two years' imprisonment.[6]

The trade in pornographic material continued outside of a formal shop setting. In October 1883, it was to the home of a suspected seller of obscene literature that Det. Inspector Swanson was sent, with Det. Sergeant Froest,[7] to investigate claims that the owner was unlawfully selling illegal material.

The man, 58-year-old Benjamin Judge, had managed to evade arrest for some time despite being known to the police. According to a newspaper report following his eventual arrest,

> from certain information received by Inspector Swanson and Sergeant Froest a plan was laid, and a few days back the Prisoner fell into the trap, and was arrested.[8]

The detectives had been informed by a member of a West End club that Judge was offering offensive material, but exactly what the plan was is not reported. It is possible that, in a plot similar to the inducement method employed by Det. Sergeant Moser, the detectives had replied to one of Judge's advertisements and obtained his address in that way.

They went to the house at Lower Park Road, Peckham, and kept watch. Eventually, their patience was rewarded when they were able to obtain entry. On Judge's person they found letters from subscribers, and a list of names and addresses along with a catalogue of erotic literature.[9]

As Froest took Judge into custody, Swanson went to the prisoner's offices in Johnson's Court, Fleet Street, where he found many of the books listed on Judge's catalogue.[10] These were taken back to Scotland Yard as evidence, and then to Lambeth Magistrates' Court on 31st October, where Judge pleaded guilty to two charges of selling obscene books and was remanded.

At his trial on 5th December, the court heard that Judge had three previous convictions for similar offences, the last being some eleven years earlier.[11] Swanson said that the police had visited some of the prisoner's customers and many were terror-stricken at the possibility of being exposed; one had threatened suicide should his name be published in connection with the case.

Magistrate Mr. Hardman, passing a sentence of four years' imprisonment with hard labour, told the prisoner that the Bench had seen some of the books produced, and, in the case of one of them, he

> could not imagine that anything so horrible could ever have been devised by human depravity.[12]

Mr. Hardman ordered the offending books themselves to be burnt.

But the story of Benjamin Judge didn't end there. Three years later, in February 1886, Swanson was contacted by a John Kendrick, whom he had interviewed during the 1883 case. Kendrick had received a letter from Judge inviting him to purchase some publications of a supposed humorous nature; the enclosed catalogue, however, showed books and photographs of an indecent nature. Kendrick was a Justice of the Peace at Barrow Court, Birmingham, and was determined to take steps to secure the prosecution of Benjamin Judge with the assistance of the Society for the Suppression of Vice, and accordingly ordered more material, sending a cheque for £40.[13]

When the ordered literature arrived, Kendrick was horrified. He immediately destroyed all of the books with the exception of one, *The*

Pearl,[14] which he gave to Swanson after calling the detective to report the incident.

Now, three years later, Kendrick had received a letter from Judge saying that he intended to publish an exposé of the traffic in obscene literature, and that Kendrick and others in "high stations in life would be shown up". The source material for the intended publication was Judge's correspondence with his customers in 1883. Kendrick could, the letter offered, buy back the letters, asking "What do you say to £500?"[15]

Kendrick's answer was to seek out Det. Inspector Swanson, who arrested Judge for the second time on Saturday, 27th March 1886. He appeared first at Clerkenwell Magistrates' Court,[16] and then at the Old Bailey, where on 8th April he was convicted of sending letters demanding money with menaces. Sentencing Judge to life imprisonment, Justice Wills remarked that it was "one of the vilest offences known."[17]

Judge was detained at Portland Prison,[18] Weymouth, where he died in April 1894.[19]

In between his arrests of Benjamin Judge, Swanson was required to investigate another case of obscene literature being sold.

In what appears to be another carefully-laid plan by the Scotland Yard detectives, William Campbell of the Hull Docks Police responded to an advertisement offering French novels. Writing under the *nom de plume* of 'Lecteur', Campbell received the first batch of books ordered, which turned out to be harmless novels as advertised, and then entered into a correspondence with the seller, John Ashley, of South Street, South Kensington.

Eventually, a letter arrived which informed 'Lecteur' that should he return the catalogue and include a certain fee, he would receive a 'suitable parcel'. Doing as he was told, the 'suitable parcel' turned out to be two new catalogues, one containing obscene titles.

The obliging customer ordered a book in English from the 'clean' catalogue, sending four guineas, and a few days later received a sealed parcel containing "a work of an abominably filthy character".[20]

His job done, Inspector Campbell sent all his correspondence to Scotland Yard, with Det. Inspectors Swanson and Marshall visiting Ashley's home address at Thurloe Cottages, South Kensington, where a servant girl told them that no gentleman of that name lived there, but a man named Arthur Grey Tindall did. Being introduced, Swanson asked Tindall whether he used the name 'John Ashley', receiving the reply that he had, on occasion.

The officers had a warrant for the arrest of Tindall, and to search the address at South Street, but not his home at Thurloe Cottages. Despite this, Tindall invited them to inspect the property. The few items found of an offensive nature were his own property, he said, and not for sale. When the South Street address was searched later, nothing was found.

At the remand hearing on 30th December at Clerkenwell, several witnesses appeared to testify to Tindall's good character.[21] It was to no avail. He may have been described by many as a 'Gentleman', but the nature of the material sent to Campbell was enough to persuade Assistant Judge Fletcher to sentence Tindall to six months' hard labour on 11th January 1886.[22]

A postscript to the Arthur Grey Tindall case occurred several years later, confirming that his reputation as a Gentleman was a sham. On 2nd May 1895, Frances Miriam Clements appeared at the Probate, Divorce and Admiralty Division appealing for her marriage to be annulled. She claimed that her husband – Grey Tindall – was a bigamist. They had been married on 2nd October 1892 at Petersham, Surrey, with Tindall informing her that he was a widower.

Since the wedding, Miss Clements told the court, Tindall had treated her cruelly, to the point where she had confided in Sir George Lewis, the famed lawyer, who discovered that Tindall's wife Caroline Giles had not died, but was in fact alive and well. She had left Tindall some years earlier because of the way he treated her.

It took just minutes for a decree nisi to be granted, with Tindall saddled with the costs.[23]

Six months prior to Arthur Grey Tindall's sentencing for possessing obscene literature, influential newspaper editor W. T. Stead[24] published a series of articles in his *Pall Mall Gazette* which exposed a very different, and much darker, side to Victorian sexual tastes.

On 4th July 1885, in an editorial titled "Notice to our Readers: A Frank Warning", Stead told readers that as the Criminal Law Amendment Bill – "An Act to make further provision for the Protection of Women and Girls, the suppression of brothels, and other purposes" – seemed certain to be abandoned for the third time, he felt it right to "open the eyes of the public" by publishing a report prepared by a 'Special and Secret Commission of Inquiry' which he had appointed. Stead's "frank warning" outlined what was to come:

> But although we are thus compelled, in the public interest, to publish the case for the bill, or rather for those portions of it which are universally admitted to be necessary, we have no desire to inflict upon unwilling eyes the ghastly story of the criminal developments of modern vice. Therefore we say quite frankly today that all those who are squeamish, and all those who are prudish, and all those who prefer to live in a fool's paradise of imaginary innocence and purity, selfishly oblivious to the horrible realities which torment those whose lives are passed in the London Inferno, will do well not to read the *Pall Mall Gazette* of Monday and the three following days. The story of an actual pilgrimage into a real hell is not pleasant reading, and is not meant to be. It is, however, an authentic record of unimpeachable facts, "abominable, unutterable, and worse than fables yet have feigned or fear conceived." But it is true, and its publication is necessary.[25]

The opening instalment of the Report, which was titled "The Maiden Tribute of Modern Babylon", was published in the *Pall Mall Gazette* of Monday, 6th July, and featured an explanation from Stead that the purpose of his investigation was "not to secure the punishment of criminals but to lay bare the working of a great organisation of crime."

Stead listed what he considered 'sexual criminality':

I. The sale and purchase and violation of children
II. The procuration of virgins
III. The entrapping and ruin of women
IV. The international slave trade in girls
V. Atrocities, brutalities, and unnatural crimes

He explained how

> For four weeks, aided by two or three coadjutors of whose devotion and self-sacrifice, combined with a rare instinct for investigation and a singular personal fearlessness, I cannot speak too highly, I have been exploring the London Inferno. It has been a strange and unexampled experience. For a month I have oscillated between the noblest and the meanest of mankind, the saviours and the destroyers of their race, spending hours alternately in brothels and hospitals, in the streets and in refuges, in the company of procuresses and of bishops.

> London beneath the gas glare of its innumerable lamps became… a resurrected and magnified City of the Plain, with all the vices of Gomorrah, daring the vengeance of long-suffering Heaven.

Despite withholding details such as the names and other information of those involved for fear of exposure or criminal prosecution, the editor was prepared to present full information of his findings to just six people: the Archbishop of Canterbury, the Archbishop of Westminster, the Earl of Dalhousie (author of the Criminal Law Amendment Bill), the Earl of Shaftesbury, Howard Vincent, and Samuel Morley M.P.[26]

Then, over the next four days, the Report itself was laid bare. And it was horrific.

Stead revealed how there was enormous demand from customers for virginal girls, termed 'maids', the majority too young to understand what was about to happen to them. Some were simply snared and taken to locked rooms, where they were defiled while under the influence of drugs or alcohol, or overcome by the greater strength of the attacker. Many were lured to brothels by 'procurers' with promises of comfortable, respectable lives, only to be gradually introduced to the true purpose of their being befriended and finally taken by a client willing to pay to take advantage of a virgin.

Some were daughters of prostitutes, raised at a brothel and trained until they became twelve or thirteen-years-old, when their virginity was sold for up to £40.[27]

Many of the girls at the brothels had been sold at a young age by drunken parents.

Wealthier brothel-keepers employed agents to seek out 'fresh' girls, and these might be found at servants' registries, at homes for fallen women, or even the workhouse.

Stead interviewed a former brothel-keeper in the Mile End Road, who said he had sent his own daughter out onto the street once she had been deflowered. Sometimes, the man said, there was demand for young girls who had been seduced, but not for virgins; on these occasions, a man was paid to "make them fit for service".

The brothel-keeper proudly told how he once lured a young girl from Horsham to London, pretending to her parents that he was in a respectable line of business; once at the brothel, the girl was sold to a man for £15 and taken away to be seduced. Another girl, aged just twelve, was sold to a clergyman for £20.

Wanting to test the accuracy of the brothel-keeper's claims, Stead had an agent approach him asking for two 'maids' whose virginity could be attested to by a doctor's certificate to be supplied within three days. Two days later a telegram was received, which stated:

> I will undertake to deliver at your rooms within two days two children at your chambers. Both are the daughters of brothel keepers whom I have known and dealt with, and the parents are willing to sell in both cases. I represented that they were intended for a rich old gentleman who had led a life of debauchery for years... after champagne and liquors, my old friend G‑‑, M‑‑lane, Hackney, agreed to hand over her own child, a pretty girl of eleven, for £5, if she could get no more. The child was virgo intacta, so far as her mother knew. I then went to Mrs. N‑‑, of B‑‑street, Dalston, (B‑‑ street is a street of brothels from end to end). Mrs. N‑‑ required little persuasion, but her price was higher. She would not part with her daughter under £5 or £10, as she was pretty and attractive, and a virgin, aged thirteen, who would probably fetch more in the open market. These two children I could deliver up within two days if the money was right. I would, on the same conditions, undertake to deliver half a dozen girls, ages varying from ten to thirteen, within a week or ten days.

Stead ended negotiations at this point, but enquired as to how these attacks on such young girls could possibly remain undiscovered. He was told that some brothels have underground rooms, from which no sound could be heard; one supposedly respectable woman who kept a brothel in the West End said that "In my house, you can enjoy the screams of the girl with the certainty that no one else hears them but yourself." Another reported that a four-poster bed in her establishment was equipped with straps with which to harness the unwilling victim by hand and foot.

Once seduced, the girls were overcome with embarrassment and very often went freely, if reluctantly, into prostitution, too ashamed to return home, and no other way of earning a living open to them.

Over the course of the week, the *Pall Mall Gazette* published interviews with ruined girls, former procurers, brothel-keepers and policemen, exposing the whole underground industry. On 10th July, the newspaper printed a lengthy feature on the import of foreign girls to London, and the export of British girls to the Continent.

As we saw in chapter 14, reform agitation against child prostitution began in 1880 with Alfred Dyer's pamphlet *The European Slave Trade in English Girls: A Narrative of the Facts.*

Dyer later gave an account of how, in 1879, he was approached one Sunday after worship by a man who claimed to have patronised a Belgian brothel where English girls were taken by fraud and held captive.

Travelling to Belgium, Dyer saw for himself the brothel dormitories where doors could only be opened from the outside. Once in the clutches of the brothel-keepers the girls were prisoners, afraid to escape to the authorities on account of their part in a fraud.[28]

Alfred Dyer's report caused an outcry, and gained support from feminist and social reformer Josephine Butler. Home Officer barrister Thomas Snagge was appointed to investigate the claims, discovering that in one year, 1879, twenty-four English girls had been registered in the brothels of Brussels alone.[29] A Home Office Committee was formed, their findings forcing the initial framing of the Criminal Law Amendment Bill.[30]

By 1885, four years later, the Bill had still not been passed and newspapers were vocal in their dissatisfaction at the current state of affairs:

> The papers are full at the present time of articles on the foreign traffic in English girls, a traffic that, either in spite of, or through the neglect of, the authorities, both here and abroad, is carried on in an infamously wholesale manner without any check. Let anyone attempt to smuggle a few cigars or a pint of spirits, and he will be instantly detected and lodged in the cells. But what are paltry things of this kind to the virtue of our innocent females? The Custom House officers will overhaul your portmanteau and boxes until further orders, but they shut their eyes to a cargo of novitiates in immorality. Girls are decoyed hence to Belgium, France, Germany, Italy, and even the United States by thousands yearly, and for the vilest of purposes, whilst the imports are nearly equal in number to those exported. Heaven knows, the African slave trade was bad enough, and British Christianity howls with horror at a Turkish harem, but it sits still with piety whilst a trade in white women is being carried on under its very eyes.[31]

Benjamin Scott, Chairman of the imaginatively-titled London Committee for the Suppression of Traffic in English Girls for the Purposes of Continental Prostitution approached W. T. Stead seeking support and laid bare the true situation of girls being forced into a life of vice, often literally whisked off of the street, while the authorities turned a blind eye. The result was Stead's "Maiden Tribute of Modern Babylon".[32]

Stead's final report included an interview with a former slave trader, who told the editor that some twenty girls left British shores for Continental brothels each month, two-thirds of them believing they were heading for a respectable situation. Once in the hands of the brothel-keepers, they were passed from house to house in the network.

Understandably, the week-long series caused uproar. Stead reported that Samuel Morley had accepted his offer to examine the evidence gathered, and had also proposed to Chair a Committee for that purpose.

On 3rd August 1885, Morley addressed the House of Commons debate on the Criminal Law Amendment:

> No doubt, as a matter of taste, most serious objections might be raised to the modus operandi of the newspaper in question; but [I am] prepared to say distinctly, having been engaged for four days with three or four distinguished men in making an investigation, that the truth of the statements made by the *Pall Mall Gazette* was substantially proved to the satisfaction of the Committee. [I] would even go so far as to say that the half had not been told of the condition of things in London. Although [I] could not approve of the phraseology adopted by the writer of the articles, [I] believe the *Pall Mall Gazette* had done an enormous service to the moral life of London.[33]

Four days later, the Bill passed its third reading, and became law on 14th August 1885. Provisions included raising the age of consent from thirteen to sixteen years of age, punishing those who allowed under-age sex on their premises, and making it a criminal offence to procure girls for prostitution through fraud, the administration of drugs, or intimidation.

Stead had achieved his aim via the pages of the *Pall Mall Gazette*. But for the editor personally, things took a dramatic turn when rival newspapers, jealous of the *Gazette*'s publicity, began to look into the truth behind the story of 'Lily' which had appeared in the pages of the *Gazette* on 6th July as part of the series under the banner "A Child of Thirteen Bought for £5".

Stead wanted to demonstrate how easy it was to purchase a young girl, and described how 'Lily' had been readily sold by her mother after an 'agent' acting on behalf of the newspaper, experienced in the methods of procuring young girls, went to a brothel to negotiate the purchase of a maid with the brothel-keeper, who knew of a suitable child. As the bargain was struck, Stead wrote,

> a drunken neighbour came into the house, and so little concealment was then used, that she speedily became aware of the nature of the transaction. So far from being horrified at the proposed sale of the girl, she whispered eagerly to the seller, "Don't you think she would take

our Lily? I think she would suit." Lily was her own daughter, a bright, fresh-looking little girl, who was thirteen-years-old last Christmas. The bargain, however, was made for the other child, and Lily's mother felt she had lost her market.

The next day, Derby Day as it happened, was fixed for the delivery of this human chattel. But as luck would have it, another sister of the child who was to be made over to the procuress heard of the proposed sale. She was living respectably in a situation, and on hearing of the fate reserved for the little one she lost no time in persuading her dissolute sister to break off the bargain. When the woman came for her prey the bird had flown. Then came the chance of Lily's mother. The brothel-keeper sent for her, and offered her a sovereign for her daughter. The woman was poor, dissolute, and indifferent to everything but drink. The father, who was also a drunken man, was told his daughter was going to a situation. He received the news with indifference, without even inquiring where she was going to. The brothel-keeper having thus secured possession of the child, then sold her to the procuress in place of the child whose sister had rescued her from her destined doom for £5 – £3 paid down and the remaining £2 after her virginity had been professionally certified. The little girl, all unsuspecting the purpose for which she was destined, was told that she must go with this strange woman to a situation. The procuress, who was well up to her work, took her away, washed her, dressed her up neatly, and sent her to bid her parents goodbye. The mother was so drunk she hardly recognised her daughter. The father was hardly less indifferent. The child left her home, and was taken to the woman's lodging in A--street.

...Lily was a little cockney child, one of those who by the thousand annually develop into the servants of the poorer middle-class. She had been at school, could read and write, and although her spelling was extraordinary, she was able to express herself with much force and decision. Her experience of the world was limited to the London quarter in which she had been born. With the exception of two school trips to Richmond and one to Epping Forest, she had never been in the country in her life, nor had she ever even seen the Thames excepting at Richmond. She was an industrious, warm-hearted little thing, a hardy English child, slightly coarse in texture, with dark black eyes, and short, sturdy figure. Her education was slight. She spelled write "right," for instance, and her grammar was very shaky. But she was a loving, affectionate child, whose kindly feeling for the drunken mother who sold her into nameless infamy was very touching to behold."[34]

The article continued, describing how 'Lily' was taken to the house of a midwife and intimately examined to confirm that she was a virgin. A small quantity of chloroform was purchased from the woman, and the girl was taken to a brothel near Regent Street. What happened next is best described as it appeared within the article:

> She was taken upstairs, undressed, and put to bed, the woman who bought her putting her to sleep. She was rather restless, but under the influence of chloroform she soon went over. Then the woman withdrew. All was quiet and still. A few moments later the door opened, and the purchaser entered the bedroom. He closed and locked the door. There was a brief silence. And then there rose a wild and piteous cry – not a loud shriek, but a helpless, startled scream like the bleat of a frightened lamb. And the child's voice was heard crying, in accents of terror, "There's a man in the room! Take me home; oh, take me home!"
>
> And then all once more was still.[35]

It did not take long for Stead's rivals to begin digging into 'Lily's' true identity.

On Charles Street, Lisson Grove, near Marylebone, the child's mother was shown a copy of the *Pall Mall Gazette* three days after the story of 'Lily' appeared and immediately recognised certain descriptions of the child's background as matching those of her daughter, Eliza Armstrong. The woman, Elizabeth Armstrong, went to Marylebone magistrate Mr. Cooke on Friday, 10th July and reported her suspicions that the girl described in the *Pall Mall Gazette* was in fact her daughter, who she had allowed to go off with a woman a month earlier to begin what she believed was a respectable position in service.

Mrs. Armstrong was then befriended by a Mr. Hailes, a reporter from *Lloyd's Weekly Newspaper*, who took her to various houses related to Eliza's movements as the story was unravelled.[36]

It transpired that the procurer had been a reformed prostitute named Rebecca Jarrett, acting on behalf of W. T. Stead himself, who was the purchaser. Although Eliza Armstrong had come to no harm, and in fact had spent several weeks in France at a Salvation Army house, Stead and Jarrett were arrested on suspicion of kidnapping, along with others involved in the plot including Salvationist William Bramwell Booth, Elizabeth Combe and Sampson Jacques of the *Pall Mall Gazette*.

The quintet appeared at Bow Street Magistrates' Court at a committal hearing on 2nd September, and on 30th October 1885 William Stead and Rebecca Jarrett were convicted and sentenced, Jarrett to six months'

The committal hearing of W T Stead, Rebecca Jarrett, Sampson Jacques, William Bramwell-Booth and Elizabeth Combe from the Illustrated Police News, 19th September 1885

imprisonment and Stead three, the majority of which he served at Holloway Prison.

The editor accepted his fate with good grace, later writing "Never had I a happier lot than the two months I spent in happy Holloway."[37]

It is not immediately clear what happened to Eliza Armstrong once the trial concluded. It has been claimed that she later wrote to Stead, saying that she had married and had six children.[38] More recent research identifies an Eliza Armstrong of the right age in the 1891 census, recorded as being 19-years-old and born in London. She was a nursemaid in the household of architect Charles Clement Hodges in Hexham, Northumberland. Two years later Eliza married Henry West, a plumber and gas fitter, the couple living in South Shields, where three children were born. Following Henry's death in 1906, Eliza married Samuel O'Donnell, to whom she bore at five children. Samuel died in 1917 aged 48, with the death of Eliza O'Donnell recorded in County Durham in 1938.[39]

While the Criminal Law Amendment Act had been principally to protect young girls, a clause introduced by MP Henry Labouchère on 6th August 1885, the day before the Act finally passed, made enormous changes to the lives of the country's homosexual men.

Since 1861, when the Offences Against the Person Act was passed, sodomy was deemed an offence punishable by life imprisonment. Before this date, the punishment was death. Despite this extreme penalty for sodomy, other sexual activity between men such as fellatio and masturbation remained legal, and there was therefore great difficulty in securing a conviction unless actual anal intercourse could be proved.

The Labouchère Amendment (Section 11 of the Criminal Law Amendment Act) gave police the power to arrest men for any kind of homosexual behaviour short of sodomy under the loose term 'gross indecency':

> Any male person who, in public or private, commits, or is party to the commissions of, or procures the commission by any male person of, any act of gross indecency with another male person, shall be guilty of a misdemeanour, and being convicted thereof shall be liable at the discretion of the court to be imprisoned for any term not exceeding two years, with or without hard labour.[40]

The effect of this Amendment, much more enforceable than the crime of sodomy itself, was soon apparent in arrest and conviction figures. In the five years immediately prior to the passing of the Act, of 37 men arrested in London on a charge of sodomy or intent to commit sodomy, just sixteen were convicted. Yet from 1885 to 1890, while numbers for sodomy-related arrests remained similar, some 76 men were arrested in the capital for gross indecency, with 30 convicted.[41]

The West End of London had long been the hub of homosexual meetings, with several notorious 'Molly Houses' (homosexual brothels) being set up in the Holborn and Oxford Street areas in the eighteenth century, while in 1781 George Parker, in his *A View of Society and Manners in High and Low Life*, reported the way in which men would use a system of coded signals in public places to signify their intentions:

> If one of them sits on a bench, he pats the backs of his hands; if you follow them, they put a white handkerchief thro' the skirts of their coat, and wave it to and fro; but if they are met by you, their thumbs are stuck in the arm-pits of their waistcoats, and they play their fingers upon their breasts. By means of these signals they retire to satisfy a passion too

horrible for description, too detestable for language.[42]

More common meeting places were the various restaurants, hotels and theatres around the West End, especially around Piccadilly Circus.[43]

It was in the Strand Theatre on 28th April 1870 that a chain of events began which perfectly illustrated the difficulty in securing a conviction for sodomy before the Labouchère Amendment was inserted into the Criminal Law Amendment. At the heart of events were the notorious Fanny and Stella, two young men who revelled in dressing in women's clothing and parading at the West End's nightspots.

Mrs. Fanny Graham, apparently the elder of the two, was described as having 'stern features', with too large a nose, small eyes set too closely together, and a square face given to jowls. She was not as pretty as her companion, Miss Stella Boulton, who was tall and slim with porcelain skin and large blue eyes.

In a box at the Strand Theatre, the resplendently-dressed Fanny and Stella behaved lasciviously toward any man who caught their eye. They had clearly consumed several drinks and seemed not to care what their fellow theatre-goers thought.

One attendee, however, was watching them very closely, and when the pair left the theatre and entered a waiting carriage he took the opportunity to jump inside and introduce himself. He was Det. Sergeant Frederick Kerley of E Division, who, on the orders of Inspector James Thompson, arrested Fanny and Stella on suspicion of being "men in female attire" and took them to Bow Street station.

'Fanny' was discovered to be Frederick Park, a law student lodging in Bruton Street; 'Stella' was Ernest Boulton, a 21-year-old stockbroker's son from Maida Vale. The young men had met a few years earlier and formed a touring act, appearing as their feminine alter egos, but in more recent years had acquired a reputation for lewd behaviour and had been removed from several West End theatres.

After a night in the Bow Street cells they appeared in front of Magistrate Mr. Flowers and heard a string of charges against them:

> That they did with each and one another feloniously commit the abominable crime of buggery;
>
> further that they did unlawfully conspire together, and with divers other persons, feloniously, to commit the said crimes
>
> further that they did unlawfully conspire together, and with divers other persons to induce and incite other persons feloniously with them to commit the said crime

and further that they being men, did unlawfully conspire together, and with divers others, to disguise themselves as women and to frequent places of public resort, so disguised, and to thereby openly and scandalously outrage public decency and corrupt public morals.

With such a list, it was no surprise that Fanny and Stella were remanded for trial. As they were standing in the dock still dressed in their petticoats and dresses, the final charge was easily provable. Now, it was time to obtain evidence of sodomy.

Ten minutes after their appearance before the magistrate, Fanny and Stella were taken to a room at the rear of the building where Dr. James Paul, Divisional Surgeon for E Division, was waiting.

Telling them to step behind a screen and remove their clothes, Dr. Paul told Stella to bend over a stool and performed an intimate examination, afterwards repeating the procedure with Fanny.

His findings, reported to a horrified court, appeared to provide indisputable evidence of the charge of buggery:

> I have been in practice sixteen years, seven years out of that at the St. Pancras General Dispensary, and I have on many occasions examined the anuses of persons. I do not in my practice ever remember to have seen such an appearance of the anus, as those of the prisoners presented.
>
> I examined Boulton, and found him to be a man. The anus was dilated, and more dilatable, and the muscles surrounding the anus easily opened.
>
> Boulton was then removed, and the prisoner Park came behind the screen. I said to him the same I had said to Boulton. The anus was very much dilated, and dilatable to a very great extent. The rectum was large, and there was some discoloration around the edge of the anus, caused probably by sores.
>
> The insertion of a foreign body numerous times would account for those appearances.

When asked exactly what he meant, Dr. Paul replied "The insertion of a man's person would cause the appearances I have described." In his opinion, Fanny and Stella had been sodomised so many times that the anus had lost much of its natural elasticity. More was to come: Dr. Paul revealed how Stella's penis and scrotum were "of an inordinate length", and Fanny's was "elongated". When pressed for a cause of such elongation, the surgeon replied "Traction might produce elongation of the penis and the testicles."

While such evidence could potentially prove damning, Fanny and Stella walked away from their trial in July 1871 free men. Dr. Paul had acted on his own curiosity, with no magistrate's authorisation, when intimately examining the pair; subsequent medical examinations at Newgate Gaol had revealed that Stella had been treated some time before for a painful anal fistula; the jury accepted Mr. Digby Seymour's claims that the act of sodomy would have been physically impossible. No witnesses were produced to say they had actually seen Fanny and Stella in the act, and no semen was found in either orifice.

Despite their obvious enjoyment indulging in such activity, once again no evidence could be presented to secure a conviction against Fanny and Stella.

One aspect of the pair's past which was revealed during investigations leading up to the trial was the presence in their lives of various high ranking gentlemen, including Lord Arthur Pelham-Clinton, son of the Duke of Newcastle, who had actually been living with Stella. Others, who invariably held letters and photographs lovingly presented by Fanny or Stella, and sometimes both, were a high ranking Post Official named Louis Hurt and the American consul in Edinburgh, John Safford Fiske.

When police discovered this circle, further warrants were issued. Within days Lord Clinton had disappeared in the most final way possible, by dying suddenly of scarlet fever. Even before he was supposedly buried, in three coffins, there were whispers that he had not really died at all, but had staged his death and fled abroad.[44]

That certain members of the aristocracy were often involved in such illicit arrangements was no great surprise, and this was certainly the case with perhaps the most infamous homosexual scandal of the late nineteenth century, at Cleveland Street, Fitzrovia.[45]

The events which would eventually expose the affair began during the height of the Whitechapel murders. In fact, on the very day coroner Wynne Edwin Baxter opened the inquest into the murder of Elisabeth Stride at the Vestry Hall on Cable Street,[46] two 17-year-old telegraph messenger boys named Henry Newlove and George Alma Wright slipped unnoticed into a basement lavatory of the Central Telegraph Office at St. Martin's-Le-Grand. Wright would later state that Newlove, a year older, "put his person into me, that is to say behind, only a little way and something came from him."

It was not the first time that the youths had enjoyed encounters in the quiet toilets, and on another occasion Wright attempted but failed to penetrate Newlove.[47]

The latter would also go on to persuade another boy, 15-year-old Charles Swinscow, to visit the lavatories with him.[48]

The promiscuous Henry Newlove would soon reveal a seamier side, telling Wright:

> I know a gentleman I go with sometimes and if you [would] like to come I will show him to you. He wants to have a game at spooning about with you.[49]

Wright agreed, and on 20th December 1888 the two boys went to a house in Cleveland Street.[50] He was introduced to a man "of middling size, [with] rather black hair, bald on the top of his head, black eyebrows and a full moustache." This proved to be Charles Hammond, the landlord of the property. Shortly afterwards another man, "a short foreign looking chap", came in and went with Wright to a bedroom on the same floor:

> We both undressed and got into the bed quite naked. He told me to suck him. I did so. He then had a go between my legs and that was all. He gave me half a sovereign which I gave to the landlord, who gave me four shillings. I treated Newlove to a drop of beer.[51]

It was the only time that George Wright went to the house, but Newlove asked whether he knew another boy, preferably younger and shorter than Wright, who might go to meet gentlemen at Cleveland Street.[52] He introduced Newlove to another messenger named Charles Thickbroom who, although being the same age as Wright, was smaller. He was asked rather directly by Newlove whether he would "go to bed with a man." Thickbroom declined, but quickly changed his mind when he was told he would receive four shillings.[53]

Dressed in his telegraph messenger boy's uniform, on 3rd January 1889[54] Thickbroom went with Newlove to the house at Cleveland Street – No. 19 – and, after meeting landlord Charles Hammond, was taken to a bedroom and told to wash his hands and face. Presently another gentleman entered, and both undressed before getting into bed, where they "played with each other" without any penetration taking place. Handing Thickbroom his four shillings, Hammond said he hoped the boy would come again; he did, on just one other occasion, when he went to bed with a different, unidentified man.[55]

Henry Newlove was encouraged; he next approached the young Charles Swinscow and asked him to visit 19 Cleveland Street. On 10th January he agreed,[56] and received four shillings for spending half an hour with a gentleman who sodomised him. Swinscow went to the house a second time, being told by his gentleman – but not until after he had again been sodomised – that he ought not to visit again.[57] Swinscow heeded the advice, but would shortly afterwards be the catalyst for the whole affair being exposed. In the meantime, Newlove persuaded fellow messenger boys William Meech Perkins, George Barber and Algernon Allies to visit Cleveland Street for the purposes of entertaining gentlemen.[58]

The entertainment would come to an abrupt end early in the summer of 1889. On Thursday, 4th July, P.C. Luke Hanks, a 35-year-old Irishman[59] attached to the General Post Office, was sent to investigate the petty theft of monies from the office of the Receiver and Accountant General. Hanks was told that one of the messenger boys was under suspicion as he had been seen leaving the room from which the thefts had occurred, and that he had been seen with a large amount of money, some eighteen shillings. The boy in question was Charles Swinscow.

When P.C. Hanks told Swinscow of the suspicions against him, the boy replied that it was fourteen, not eighteen shillings. The officer's next question, naturally, was how he had come by such a large amount of money, to which Swinscow replied "I got it for doing some private work away from the office."

> P.C. Hanks: "For whom?"
> Swinscow: "For a gentleman named Hammond."
> "Where does he live?"
> "At 19 Cleveland Street, Middlesex Hospital."
> "What kind of work did you do for him?"
> "Will I get into any trouble if I tell you?"
> "I cannot say."
> "Must I tell you?"
> "Certainly."
> "I will tell you the truth – I got the money from Mr. Hammond for going to bed with gentlemen at his house."[60]

And, just like that, the whole sordid tale began to emerge. What had begun for P.C. Hanks as a case of petty larceny was now unfolding into something much more sinister. The officer made a verbal report to John Phillips, the Assistant Director of the Confidential Enquiry Branch, who told him to take a formal statement from Swinscow, and then, as the

Charles Hammond
from La Lanterne, 20th January 1890

The messenger boys
from the Illustrated Police News, 18 January 1890

boy named names, from Charles Thickbroom and George Alma Wright. The officer sent for Henry Newlove, at that point the villain of the piece, to whom he read the trio's statements. Newlove admitted these were correct.[61]

The boys were suspended and sent home. The Postmaster General, Henry Cecil Raikes, was informed and he contacted Commissioner James Monro, forwarding copies of the three statements on 6th July. The case was immediately placed in the hands of Det. Inspector Abberline, who by this time had been replaced by Det. Inspector Henry Moore as the officer leading on-the-ground investigations into the Whitechapel murders.[62]

On the same day, Abberline attended Marlborough Street Police Court and applied to Magistrate Mr. Newton for a warrant for the arrest of Newlove and the proprietor of 19 Cleveland Street, Charles Hammond,

> that they did unlawfully, wickedly, and corruptly conspire, combine, confederate and agree to incite and procure George Alma Wright and divers other persons to commit the abominable crime of buggery, against the peace of Her Majesty the Queen.[63]

Armed with this, the detective went to Cleveland Street, only to find the house empty, with Hammond absconded.

The following afternoon, Sunday, 7th July, Abberline arrested Henry Newlove at his mother's home on Bayham Street, Camden Town. The messenger told the detective that following his suspension on the Thursday he had spoken with another boy named Hewitt, who said he should warn Charles Hammond that the police were looking into the activity at Cleveland Street. It was Hewitt who had introduced Newlove to Hammond, back in March 1887. As a consequence, Hammond told Newlove to deny everything, and that he himself was going into hiding.[64]

If Newlove was in hot water, he wasn't going down alone. On the way to the police station he told P.C. Hanks: "I think [it] is very hard that I should get into trouble while men in high positions are allowed to walk free." When asked what he meant, Newlove went on: "Why, Lord Arthur Somerset goes regularly to the house at Cleveland Street, so does the Earl of Euston and Colonel Jervois," explaining that the latter resided at Winchester Barracks.[65]

The following day, while waiting to be appear before the Magistrate, Newlove repeated his accusation to Abberline:

> Hammond ought to be locked up. A gentleman used to come to his house whom I knew first as Mr. Brown, but afterwards I knew it was Lord Arthur Somerset. He had to do with me on several occasions there.[66]

As a result of this information, Newlove was remanded while the police investigated his story.

On Tuesday, 9th July, P.C. Hanks visited Henry Newlove's mother at her home at Bayham Street, at the request of Newlove's brother. While the officer was speaking with the family, someone knocked on the door. Mrs. Newlove exclaimed "That's Mr. Veck – I know his knock." At once, Hanks left the room and stepped into a passage, where he could listen to the conversation without the visitor being aware of his presence. After asking Mrs. Newlove whether she had heard anything further, and receiving a reply in the negative, Veck commented:

> Dear me, how very strange. I saw Hammond at Gravesend yesterday and I have been down there today, but he has flown. I cannot say where he is. I will see Henry is right and I will see you alright as well. Do you want any money? If so, let me know. I will instruct a solicitor to defend Henry in the morning.[67]

Understandably, Hanks looked into George Veck's background. He discovered that he had formerly been employed as a telegraphist at the Eastern District Post Office, but had been dismissed for "improper conduct with telegraph messengers", after which he had been residing with Charles Hammond at 19 Cleveland Street, passing himself off as the Reverend G. D. Veck and dressing as a clergyman.[68] In reality, the 40-year-old Veck[69] had acted as an assistant to Hammond, and since the telegraph boys had been interviewed by police had taken rooms at

2 Howland Street, off Tottenham Court Road, where he lived with a boy aged seventeen. Veck was still wanted in connection with non-payment of rates relating to a coffee house he had kept at Gravesend.[70]

Abberline instructed that 19 Cleveland Street be put under surveillance, with P.C. Richard Sladden of D Division tasked with the job, beginning his observation at 5.30pm on the same day that P.C. Hanks visited Mrs. Newlove. Over the next three days, Sladden, accompanied by P.C. Plowman, logged the comings and goings of visitors to the house, until eventually at 8.25am on Friday, 12th July, a van arrived at the house. Over the course of five hours all the furniture was removed from No. 19, and the loaded van departed at 1.20pm. Although the house was now empty, P.C. Sladden continued his watch, alone, for a further six days, making a note whenever someone approached the house, creating a list of various unnamed gentlemen, telegraph messengers and other visitors.[71]

Det. Inspector Abberline had, in the meantime, ascertained that Charles Hammond was in Paris, staying at an address on Passage des Abbesses. In his covering report submitting Sladden's record of observation, he confirmed that for a considerable time Charles Hammond had made his living through the procurement of boys to meet with various gentlemen who visited his house on Cleveland Street. Although the Detective Inspector had no doubt that many more boys from the General Post Office had been involved, he had felt it best not to interview them until Hammond had been arrested.[72] But, having been tipped off by Newlove, the Cleveland Street landlord had fled to France.

While Scotland Yard was attempting to persuade the reluctant French authorities to expel Hammond, despite the offence for which he was sought not being part of the Extradition Treaty between Britain and France, they had more luck with apprehending George Veck. When officers visited the Howland Street lodgings armed with a warrant they found Veck vanished, but the boy still there, sleeping in Veck's bed. He told the police that the wanted man had gone to Portsmouth but was returning shortly, allowing detectives to meet the fraudulent Father Veck off the train at Waterloo station and take him into custody.[73]

Henry Horace Newlove and George Daniel Veck appeared at the Old Bailey on Monday, 16th September 1889. Their defence had been taken by Arthur Newton, Lord Somerset's solicitor, who appointed Charles Gill to appear for Veck and Willie Mathews for Newlove. Having heard the evidence at the committal hearing, both prisoners were advised to plead guilty.[74] Accordingly, Sir Thomas Chambers sentenced George Veck to nine months' hard labour, and Henry Newlove to four months.[75]

If the authorities had hoped that the prosecution of Newlove and Veck would see the Cleveland Street affair slip quietly into the background, they were mistaken.

The strangely fleeting nature of the trial was remarked upon by the *North London Press*, whose comments were widely reported in other newspapers:

> ...a scandal of so horrible and repulsive a character that it would be better un-mentioned if it were not necessary to expose the shameless audacity with which officials have contrived to shield the principal criminals.

Commenting on the sentences awarded to Veck and Newlove, the report continued:

> Their 'trial' practically took place in secret. At the close of the day thy were hastily placed in the dock, their pleas of 'Guilty' taken, and sentence pronounced, all in a few minutes.
>
> Their case was not entered on the list for the day, and the whole circumstances of the hearing justified the inference that counsel and judge desired the case settled with as little opportunity for publicity as possible.
>
> ...When taken, Newlove made a clean breast of the whole horrible business. He gave the names of men highly placed in the nobility who patronised the house, whose money passed through the hands of Newlove, and was used to corrupt the boys.
>
> Amongst them were the heir of a Duke, the younger son of another Duke, and an officer holding command in the southern district. Their names are, says our contemporary [the *North London Press*], in our possession, and we are prepared to produce them if necessary. Week after week the wretched youth Newlove, and the more infamous Veck, were remanded by the Marlborough Street magistrate, ostensibly to allow the ramifications of this unspeakable iniquity to be traced out, but really to give the rich and influential patrons of Hammond's hell time to secure their immunity by flight or otherwise. Then, when the time was ripe, came the committal to the Old Bailey, a few moments in the dock in an empty court, and the farcical sentences of nine and four months' imprisonment.
>
> To properly appreciate the peculiar character of the Recorder's decision one has only to the recall the fact that the Hackney minister who some twelve months ago was convicted of an isolated offence of this kind... had a life sentence, from which hope of release was expressly eliminated.

We of course have no comment to offer on this case. We only want to know (1) why Hammond was permitted to escape; (2) why his high-born patrons, who have been identified to the police by witnesses in the case, were not in the dock with their wretched panders Veck and Newlove.[76]

The "younger son of another Duke" alluded to was Major Lord Henry Arthur Somerset, third son of the Duke of Beaufort, head of the Prince of Wales's stables and a Major in the Royal Horse Guards. Following Newlove's naming him as a client of Charles Hammond, Somerset's movements had been monitored and he was interviewed by two policemen on 7th August at Hyde Park Barracks. After another officer returned on 22nd August to question him for a second time, Somerset obtained permission from the Guards to take four months' immediate leave, and fled abroad to Bad Homburg, Germany, where Prince Edward was taking his summer holiday. A month later he returned to attend a horse sale at Newmarket, but departed suddenly on 26th September for Dieppe, returning to England again, this time to Badminton, four days later. His grandmother, the Duchess of Beautfort, died less than a week later and Somerset travelled to London for the funeral on 8th October.[77]

The freedom seemingly afforded to Somerset infuriated James Monro, who wrote to Assistant Treasury Solicitor the Hon. Hamilton Cuffe stating that he had ascertained that the nobleman was at Badminton, and, unable to do anything, the Commissioner could "only deplore the delay which is being made in high quarters about this horrible case."[78]

Eleven days later, Monro penned another letter, this time to the Director of Public Prosecutions, complaining that while he had reported a 'conspiracy on the part of certain persons to defeat the ends of justice' by attempting to persuade a possible witness against Lord Somerset to abscond, some four weeks later he had still received no reply. Since writing the letter, the Commissioner had ascertained that these 'persons' included Arthur Newton, Lord Somerset's solicitor, and his clerk.

Monro also took the opportunity to complain that newspaper comments accusing the Metropolitan Police of dragging their heels was unfair, given that they were unable to proceed on any level until they were authorised to do so. Noting that proceedings had been pending since July, three months previously, Monro argued:

> Inaction has been publicly attributed to the Metropolitan Police in connection with the case, and this assertion is absolutely groundless, as it has now been magnified into an accusation against the police for

from the Illustrated Police News, 4 December 1889

having brought an unfounded charge against the nobleman in question. It is obvious that I cannot allow the reputation of the police to be thus unfairly assailed, and I must press for definite information as to the action which is to be taken by you in the case referred to.

The Commissioner then asked to be informed of the Government's decision as to whether to proceed or not with the charge against Somerset, and whether a charge should be brought against Arthur Newton.[79]

It could not be argued that Monro was exaggerating the bad press his officers were receiving. On 6th December 1889, *Reynolds's Weekly Newspaper* was blatant in pointing the finger of blame:

> The police have been deliberately employed in attempting to hush up the whole matter. If they had displayed as much activity in their endeavours to discover the Whitechapel murder, "Jack the Ripper", in all probability he would now have met with his desserts. But in the latter case it was merely the lives of unfortunate women that were at stake, whilst in the former the reputations of several of the nobility and others moving in the highest spheres of society that were endangered. Hence Mr. Monro, the chief of the police, in all likelihood with the sanction and approval of Mr. Matthews, the Home Secretary, did his uttermost to keep the hideous doings at Cleveland Street from the knowledge of the public.[80]

By this time, Lord Arthur Somerset had left the country again, this time travelling to France, but not before consulting with his solicitor Arthur Newton. Commissioner James Monro and the Assistant Treasury Solicitor, Hon. Hamilton Cuffe, continued to press for an arrest, with the Lord Chancellor refusing to take action. The Prince of Wales wrote to Prime Minister Lord Salisbury expressing satisfaction that Somerset had been allowed to leave the country, and by the time a warrant was eventually issued for Somerset's arrest, on 12th November, it was too late, and police activity began to be scaled down.[81]

Det. Inspector Frederick Abberline's involvement in the case was over, and on 6th December he submitted a claim for £58 17s 11d for expenses incurred.[82]

The *North London Press*, learning of Somerset's abscondment, decided it was safe to publish a follow-up story, in which it named certain guilty parties:

> In an issue of the 28th September we stated that among the number of aristocrats who were mixed up in an indescribably loathsome scandal in Cleveland Street, Tottenham Court Road, were the heir to a duke and the younger son of a duke. The men to whom we thus referred were the Earl of Euston, eldest son of the Duke of Grafton, and Lord H. Arthur G. Somerset, a younger son of the Duke of Beaufort. The former, we believe, has departed for Peru. The latter, having resigned his commission and his office of Assistant Equerry to the Prince of Wales, has gone too.
>
> These men have been allowed to leave the country, and thus defeat the ends of justice, because their prosecution would disclose the fact that a far more distinguished and more highly placed personage than themselves was inculpated in these disgusting crimes. The criminals in this case are to be numbered by the score. They include two or three Members of Parliament, one of them a popular Liberal."[83]

The Earl of Euston, however, was not in Peru. Still in London, he immediately instructed his solicitors, Lewis & Lewis, to sue for libel against the *North London Press*' editor, Ernest Parke. An application was made to Mr. Justice Field on 23rd November, and on the same day Parke confirmed, in the pages of the *North London Press*, that he stood by his claims. In the same report was a defence of the police:

> Now we hasten to say that we acquit Mr. Monro of any part of the lot in what we solemnly declare to be a deliberate attempt to shield high-placed offenders. On the contrary, all our information is that Mr. Monro has spared neither himself nor his staff in his efforts to detect and punish... During his tenure of Scotland Yard, the Chief Commissioner has won universal esteem as an incorruptible servant of the public, and he has fully maintained his reputation during the preliminaries of this disgraceful case.[84]

The application was granted and Ernest Parke's committal hearing for the libel of the Earl of Euston opened at Bow Street on Tuesday, 26th

November, bringing knowledge of the affair to the public's attention at last, leaving the newspapers finally free to comment, having previously avoided making any allusion

> to a hideous subject which has been discussed in private for weeks, and even months, with a familiarity and a fullness that make London conversation almost as horrible a thing as London vice. It was not, of course, because these things had not been heard of. Everybody who has ever been inside a newspaper office knows that it is as a whispering gallery, in which may be heard every sound that falls from human lips, however faint or remote, and especially when the filthy tongue of scandal wags. Notwithstanding all this, and though some respected contemporaries have written on the subject, *The Star* has hitherto been silent. Silence is no longer possible. The trial has been begun, which must bring to the knowledge of the whole world the terrible scandal of which everybody is talking. Concealment, if desirable, is no longer possible."[85]

Whether *The Star* and the rest of the press really desired concealment is debatable, as details soon to be revealed would no doubt see copies of their newspapers sell in great numbers.

The Old Bailey trial for the alleged libel of the Earl of Euston was fixed for 15th January 1890. Before then, Lord Arthur Somerset's solicitor Arthur Newton discovered that his actions over previous months, referred to by James Monro in his exasperated letter, had caught up with him and he was arrested on suspicion of perverting the course of justice along with his clerk, Frederick Taylorson, and a court interpreter named Adolphe de Gallo.

At the trio's preliminary hearing, the court heard that when George Veck had been arrested at Waterloo station letters were discovered in his pockets by police from Algernon Allies, a 20-year-old youth who had previously been employed at the Marlborough Club, but who had returned to his family's home in Sudbury, Suffolk, after being caught stealing and subsequently fired from his job.

The letters to Veck mentioned a Mr. Brown, whom Allies said was helping supporting him financially. It appeared that Allies had once lived with Charles Hammond at 19 Cleveland Street. Det. Inspector Abberline had sent P.C. Hanks to Sudbury, where he learned that 'Mr. Brown' was in reality Lord Arthur Somerset, and that Allies had received money for services rendered during a three-month spell working for Hammond.

Allies' information promised problems for Somerset and, no doubt trying to protect his aristocratic client, Arthur Newton and his colleagues Taylorson and de Gallo attempted to prevent Algernon Allies and the telegraph messenger boys testifying in any possible trial by offering them money to go abroad. Allies was, by this time, in police protection, and the messenger boys had also been reporting to Det. Inspector Abberline almost daily.

The case against de Gallo was dropped and Frederick Taylorson was found not guilty, but on 20th May 1890 Arthur Newton was sentenced to six weeks' imprisonment.[86] He would serve the full term, but perhaps his biggest involvement in the Cleveland Street scandal was a thinly-veiled threat to involve the 'far more distinguished and more highly placed personage' hinted at in the *North London Press*' exposé of 23rd November.

On 16th September 1889 Assistant Public Prosecutor Hon. Hamilton Cuffe wrote to his superior, Sir Augustus Stephenson, warning:

> I am told that Newton has boasted that if we go on a very distinguished person will be involved (P.A.V.). I don't mean to say that I for one instant credit it – but in such circumstances as this one never knows what may be said, be concocted or true.[87]

The involvement of 'P.A.V.' – the 24-year-old Prince Albert Victor, eldest son of the Prince of Wales and heir presumptive to the throne – was almost certainly a casual invention of Arthur Newton as a scaremongering tactic, but the rumour soon spread through the West End clubs and to the ears of the exiled Lord Arthur Somerset, who later wrote to his friend Lord Esher that he could "quite understand the Prince of Wales being much annoyed about his son's name being coupled with this thing," before wondering whether it was "really a fact or only an invention."

Whatever the truth, the whispers were enough for Prince Edward to step in and request intervention from Prime Minister Lord Salisbury to quietly drop proceedings against his friend Lord Arthur Somerset, at which point the whole affair would, presumably, fade away into memory. In the years that followed, although not a shred of evidence was presented of Prince Albert Victor's attendance at 19 Cleveland Street, or even his being homosexual, rumours of his involvement continued to circulate, and do so to this day. He was created Duke of Clarence and Avondale in his grandmother's birthday honours list on 24th May 1890, but died of pneumonia on 14th November 1892.[88]

The final major episode in the affair was the Ernest Parke libel trial, which opened at the Old Bailey on Wednesday, 15th January 1890. During the committal hearing, the court had heard that Henry Fitzroy, the Earl of Euston, had been walking along Piccadilly when he was handed a card by a tout, which read "Poses plastiques. Hammond, 19 Cleveland Street." The Earl told the Bench that he took this to mean a display of female nudes, and went to the house about a week later to investigate. A man opened the door and asked for a sovereign, which the Earl handed over. On entering, he shortly discovered the true nature of activities at the house. Euston claimed he said to the man at the door: "You infernal scoundrel! If you don't let me out I will knock you down!"

Having returned home and disposed of the card, he apparently put the incident out of his mind. The first he had heard of his name in conjunction with the scandal was when a friend, a solicitor named Edward Bedford, had read the *North London Press* article and shown it to the Earl.[89]

Unfortunately for Ernest Parke, the witnesses for the defence proved to be less than reliable. None were able to conclusively prove they had seen Euston at Cleveland Street at any time. Only the final witness, a male prostitute named John Saul – known as 'Jack' – was to provide evidence of any use. He had known Charles Hammond for some ten years, living together firstly at Oxendon Street, Haymarket, and then Frith Street in Soho. According to Saul, both earned their living as sodomites. Hammond eventually moved to 19 Cleveland Street in 1885, and Saul lived there for five weeks. Although he was a notorious prostitute himself, Jack Saul was just one of many at Hammond's brothel, with the messenger boys employed as temporary 'entertainers'.[90]

Jack Saul had given a statement to Det. Inspector Abberline as far back as August 1889, describing how he met Charles Hammond and describing some of the goings-on at Cleveland Street, including how the Earl of Euston was "not an actual sodomite. He likes to play with you and then 'spend' on your belly."[91]

When his turn in the witness box came, Jack Saul revelled in telling the court how he had met Euston for the first time, in Piccadilly:

> The Duke, as we called him, came near me, and asked me where I was going. I said "Home" and he said "What sort is your place?" "Very comfortable", I replied. He said "Is it very quiet there?" I said yes it was, and then we took a hansom cab there. We got out by the Middlesex Hospital, and I took the gentleman to 19 Cleveland Street, letting him in with my latchkey. I was not long in there, in the back parlour or reception room, before Hammond came and knocked and asked if we wanted any champagne or drinks of any sort, which he was in the habit of doing.[92]

Ernest Parke
from La Lanterne, 19th January 1890

The details of what actually happened between Jack Saul and the Earl of Euston were not published in the newspapers, beyond Judge Hawkins commenting that "It was necessary to have the shocking story from one of the person concerned, but it was filthy, brutal and disgusting."[93]

Despite this testimony, once Euston took his place in the witness box to give evidence for the prosecution, the verdict was a foregone conclusion. Flatly denying ever knowing Jack Saul, or having been at Cleveland Street beyond that single visit to mistakenly view *poses Plastiques*, the Earl's bearing was impressive and Justice Hawkins invited the jury to compare his testimony with that of Saul, a man who had admitted to earning his living by leading an "immoral life" and "practising criminality". Ernest Parke was found guilty of libel and sentenced to twelve months' imprisonment.

By the time of Arthur Newton's release from prison in November 1890, public interest in the Cleveland Street scandal had faded. He recommenced his work as a solicitor, becoming much in demand and gaining a sort of 'celebrity status'. The following year he defended Edward Pinter, the Modern Alchemist, against extradition to Switzerland,[94] and in 1895 acted for Alfred Taylor, Oscar Wilde's co-defendant in their trial for gross indecency. In 1910 Newton was appointed as Dr. Hawley Harvey Crippen's solicitor, the following year being suspended for twelve months by the Law Society for professional misconduct after a falsifying a letter which he had supplied to the newspaper *John Bull*, purportedly written by Crippen. He was shortly afterwards permanently struck off and jailed for three years after fraudulently obtaining more than £13,000 in a land deal.[95]

Charles Hammond never returned to England. The French authorities refused to extradite him despite repeated requests from Scotland Yard; the most they would do was to inform Hammond that he had to leave the country. On 12th September 1889 he left Paris for Halanzy, Belgium with his 19-year-old 'secretary', Herbert John Ames, staying for a fortnight before moving on to Antwerp. On 6th October he set sail for New York aboard the Red Star Line's SS *Pennland*, travelling on First Class tickets bought by Arthur Newton's clerk, arriving a week or so later. The fugitive then headed for Seattle, where he settled on Front Street,[96] where he opened a bar called The Haymarket.[97] Despite being watched by the authorities, on the advice of Prime Minister Lord Salisbury no extradition was attempted and the case against the former landlord of 19 Cleveland Street was dropped.

The *Omaha Daily Bee* of 27th November 1890 reported that Hammond had been arrested for the theft on 1st October of a gold watch and a sealskin *sacque* belonging to Mrs. Augusta Simmons. He was sentenced to two years' imprisonment at Walla Walla, during which time his young companion Ames took the opportunity to speak to the American newspapers about his experiences at Cleveland Street. He had worked there for a year, he said, although Hammond had been running the house for three or four years. In the twelve months before he and Hammond had absconded, Ames estimated around twenty different men visited on a regular basis, and in addition to Lord Arthur Somerset, the Earl of Euston and Captain Jervois, others included Captain Barbey, a banker named Hugh Waglin and Percy Stafford, a capitalist.[98]

Hammond served fifteen months of his sentence. It was reported that he was suffering from pneumonia with complications, supposedly on his death bed,[99] and a petition got up in his favour saw him released in February 1892 and returned to Front Street to run his saloon.[100] The Assistant Director of Public Prosecutions, Hon. Hamilton Cuffe, would later exonerate the Metropolitan Police for Hammond's escape, writing: "If there was any *laches*, it was certainly with the Post Office Police, not Scotland Yard, in not giving notice or preventing Newlove from communication with Hammond."[101]

After fleeing to Boulogne and Monaco, Lord Arthur Somerset travelled to Turkey but was forced to leave on pain of arrest; he went to Budapest seeking employment but, unsuccessful, left and went to Vienna and Paris before settling in the French Riviera resort of Hyeres, where he lived in comfortable exile until his death in May 1926.

What happened to the telegraph boys themselves? In the majority of cases, they went on to enjoy full, normal lives.

Following his release from prison, Henry Horace Newlove returned to live with his mother in St. Pancras, where he worked as a shop assistant, and was still there ten years later, now employed as an election clerk. Following the death of his mother, the 40-year-old Newlove, still single, lived with his brother William and his wife Eliza at their home in Holloway. He attended the St. Pancras Workhouse infirmary in April 1923, but lived to 74 before passing away in September 1945.[102]

Charles Thomas Swinscow married Evelina Mabel Joy on 13th April 1900, and was employed in a variety of jobs including a trader in wines and spirits, a clerk and a pattern card maker. The couple had two daughters, Pearl and Ethel. Swinscow died in 1945 aged 71.[103]

Charles Ernest Thickbroom took a job as a draper's porter, and later married Charlotte Pearce on 31st July 1897, at which point he worked as a packer. The couple moved to the Hampshire village of West End, near Southampton, where Thickbroom worked as a cowman. He died there on 2nd August 1953, aged 83.[104]

Algernon Edward Allies emigrated to America in 1892. Settling in Chicago, he married Louise Wagener on 31st January 1900 and opened a bar, first on East Chicago Avenue and then Dole Avenue. He died on 28th October 1925.[105]

Despite their names being in every newspaper in the land during their youth, it seems that by the time they reached adulthood the telegram messenger boys retired to probably well-received anonymity.

Another 'gay house' was uncovered five years after the Cleveland Street scandal, when twenty men were arrested at 46 Fitzroy Square at what Det. Chief Inspector Donald Swanson called a "Sods Ball" in his private memoranda.

On Sunday, 12th August 1894 Superintendent Shepherd of D Division received information that certain illicit activity was about to occur at the house, less than a minute's walk from Cleveland Street. Shepherd went with Det. Sergeant Kane to the address and discretely kept watch between eleven o'clock and midnight, observing several men at intervals approach the house and enter.

Finally, just before midnight, a hansom cab pulled up and the detectives saw two men sitting inside wearing women's clothing, with a third man sitting on their laps.[106]

As the hansom came to a stop, the man dressed in ordinary attire stepped out and approached the row of Georgian houses, looking at the numbers. Det. Sergeant Kane stepped onto the footboard of the cab and closely examined the occupants, who immediately covered their faces with their fans. One, who later proved to be 21-year-old John Severs, a tobacconist's assistant of Pimlico, pulled up the silk Japanese dressing gown he was wearing, telling the detective: "You see I am not in female attire; I have got a pair of trousers on."

Ignoring this, Superintendent Shepherd instructed Kane to arrest Severs and his companion, 25-year-old Arthur Marley, with being idle and disorderly persons.

It was ascertained that Marley earned a living as a music hall female impersonator, and had been booked by the owner of the house, John Preston, to entertain his guests at a party.

Suspecting the 'party' to be of an illegal nature, the detectives entered the premises. In the basement were five men, one of whom, a 31-year-old clerk named John Hands, complained that they were "only having a bit of a lark"; they were taken upstairs to a room on the first floor, where a further thirteen men had already been apprehended. Preston repeated that it was an innocent party; he had invited the men and had charged 2s 6d for admission, to include refreshments.

The twenty prisoners were taken to Tottenham Court Road police station, giving the detectives a chance to search the parts of the house occupied by John Preston.

All of the windows were draped with heavy curtains. A mattress was found in the kitchen, along with beers and spirits. In other rooms were dresses, corsets and female undergarments. On a makeshift washstand in the kitchen Det. Sergeant Albert Weatherhead found a hare's foot with rouge and powder on it, a powder puff, a box of powder, vaseline and a pair of curling tongs.[107]

Arthur Leverett, who rented the third floor at 46 Fitzroy Square, complained that he had been disturbed by noises from the party below, which he said had begun at eight o'clock that evening.[108]

At Marlborough Street Magistrates' Court the following morning, Magistrate Mr. Hannay heard first the charge against Severs and Marley – who was still dressed in a "fantastic female garb of black and gold" – and then the other eighteen men were brought up, charged with "jointly and severally assembling and associating together at Fitzroy Square for felonious purposes."

Mr. Hannay said that while he recognised the intentions of the five men found in the basement seemed suspicious, he hoped that "something more definite" against the rest would be presented at the next hearing, a week later. In reply, Superintendent Shepherd said that most of them were known to the police.[109]

Despite this, a week later Mr. Hannay said he had no choice but to discharge the eighteen due to lack of evidence supplied by the police. He had received a "number of letters informing him that many of them were of the vilest possible character, but no-one came forward to give evidence to that effect." The five men found in the basement were fined a surety of 40s each and bound over for a month.

He agreed that Arthur Marley and John Severs, this time appearing in normal men's attire, were guilty of disorderly conduct when appearing in the street dressed in women's clothing, but as they had been held in custody all week he was satisfied to bound them over to keep the peace for three months.[110]

There was plenty of suggestion but no actual evidence of wrongdoing in John Preston's rooms at 46 Fitzroy Square, but it was clear that the police were exploring ways of interpreting the Criminal Law Amendment Act in order to prosecute homosexual behaviour.

There is no indication that Swanson was directly involved in this case, and the fact that the names, occupations and addresses of the 20 men as recorded by him appear in exactly the same order as many of the newspapers reporting the raid, it's likely that he copied down the information for data-gathering purposes, part of an ongoing effort to log details of known homosexuals as the Metropolitan Police attempted to find ways of enforcing Section 11.

In fact, for many years after the introduction of the Labouchère Amendment, Swanson recorded the names of any likely homosexuals who entered the Met's radar, from those dressed in women's clothing to literally being caught engaged in sexual activity.

These lists, invariably under the heading 'Sods' – the terminology of the day – were made in notebooks, scraps of paper and even in his personal address book, where on mostly unused pages, such as the space for 'U' names, the detective recorded offenders including Lord Carrington, Lord Bellew and Colonel Johnson.[111] It was in a plain black-covered ledger, previously used to record arrests made following his entry to the Detective Department, where Swanson compiled his largest list of 'sods'.[112]

In addition to the page recording the arrests at Fitzroy Square, Swanson meticulously logged the details of more than 250 men who

City of the Plain

> Names & addresses of persons found at the Sods Ball at 46 Fitzroy Square on 12th August 1894. —
>
> 1. Walter Pilsworth, Gardener, 46 Fitzroy Square, age 32
> 2. Henry Augustus Roberts, Scullery man, 135 Whitfield St " 39
> 3. Charles Smith, butler " " " 43
> 4. William Wright, Valet " " " 33
> 5. Arthur Ovens, Clerk, 6 Egbert St, 17
> 6. George Huckle, butler, 1 Hyde Park Gardens, 43
> 7. George Clement, Costumier, 78 Finborough Road, 32
> 8. John Danback, Valet, 20 Gower Place, 18
> 9. Harold Brown, tobacconist, 48 Hmdon St, 28
> 10. Henry Jas Stevens, Valet, 33 Fernshaw Rd Fulham, 39
> 11. Thomas Coombes, laundaster, 78 Finborough Road, 38
> 12. Samuel Lee, fishmonger, 8 Bury St Fulham, 23
> 13. Herbert Coulton, fruiterer, 3 Buckingham St Benn St, 32
> 14. John Watson Preston, General dealer, 46 Fitzroy Square, 34
> 15. Joseph Skinner, no occupation, 155 Maypole Rd Battersea, 44
> 16. John Hands, Clerk, 83 Newman St, 31
> 17. Charles Parker, no occupation, 7 Regent St, 19
> 18. Alfred Taylor, " , 7 Camera St Chelsea, 32
> 19. Arthur Marling, " , 8 Crawford St, 26
> 20. John Severs, tobacconist assist, 48 Hmdon St Paddn, 21

Donald Swanson's record of those found at the 'Sods Ball' at Fitzroy Square
Courtesy the Swanson family

had come to the attention of the police for being involved in homosexual activity of all kinds, including the following:

> Edward Williams, correct name Eustace William O'Connor, of 170 Earls Court Road. Age 34 height 8½. Compl & hair fair. Eyes blue. Long moustache. Professor of music. Gentlemanly appearance. Was caught in the act of S----y with William Michael Casey age 19, compl & hair dark. Eyes brown. WC & CB left forearm. W inside left elbow joint in blue ink. Labourer. By P.C. 386 F Arthur Healy in Victoria Grove Mews, Ossington St. Paddington at 11.55pm 22.1.99. Tried before Common Sergt. at CCC on 8.2.99 & acquitted. O'Connor's correct address 50 Gordon Place, Kensington.
>
> John Melachrino, tobacconist corner of Albemarle & Grafton St SW1 who assaulted indecently Thos. Hall age 14 residing with his parents at 12 Eccleston Place Pimlico. An Italian of gentlemanly bearing. P.S. Martin C.I.D. in case.
>
> Thos. Newell Mayow age 45 height 5ft 7 or 8in, stiff build. Hair dark & thin on top. High forehead, eyes brown, compl fresh. Full face clean shaven. of good appearance. Resided at 15 Catherine St Strand, describes himself as a lecturer for the Liberal Party & Secty of National Trade Defence Union – a suspected sodomite said to live on means supplied by his family in Dorset.
>
> William Flowedean alias Flowerdew, age 32 ht 5ft 9 stiff build, hair dark brown, eyes hazel pointed nose. Compl sallow, dk brown moustaches. Secty to Mayow & sleeps with him at 15 Catherine St. Strand.
>
> Arthur John Compton alias Arthur Previtt alias Dolly Compton, a sodomite. clerk. address in 1899 15 Catherine Street, Strand. Age 37. Ht 5ft 9. C. Fresh h. Brown e. Grey. Scars on left side of forehead, in front of right ear, 3 mos H.L. at West. P. Court 11.4.93 for embezzlement.
>
> Fitch, a solicitor of 29 Bedford Rd said to be guilty of filthy practices with boys but no sufficient evidence.
>
> William Geok alias Jules Thiel, a German masquerades as a woman. Sentd to 3 mos for masquerading as above and 3 mos for assault on police at Clerkenwell Police Court on 16th Oct 1899. P.C. Garratt on case.
>
> Montague Lind, artist living with his sister at No. 2 Spencer Mansions, West Kensington. Sod. Said sometimes to dress in female attire with his brother Vivian. Age about 36, height 5ft 11. Compl. Very pale, hair & whiskers & moustache black, effeminate appearance and demeanour. Usually dressed in blue serge jacket and black felt hat. Known to Col.

Moffatt of 61 Marlowes Rd Kensington.

Robert Prudhoe or Prudho alias Goggles or 'Carny trouble', no home. Clerk, born 1870 ht 5ft 8½ compl dark. Hair dark brown, eyes blue or brown a cast in right. Pro build, large scar from wound on middle of forehead. Sentd to 6 months at ML. Sessions on 9th Oct 1891 for stealing part of a chain val £2.10. Goods of Fritz Eichlorst said to have taken place in a urinal near the barracks Leicester Square. Committed from Marlboro St. Known to P.C. Thomas Dalby 46 C.

Frank Atkins alias Charles Colley, a music hall artist age in 1898 about 24. Was a witness in the Oscar Wilde case. Arrest with Berner & Abrams in the Meliss case of blackmail. Known to Mr. Littlechild. 16 Hanway St, Tottenham Ct. Road.

These last two entries reveal another pitfall for the homosexual man of the late Victorian period: blackmail and theft. With Section 11 making it easy to be placed under arrest for all manner of activity deemed as gross indecency, if a seemingly willing partner stole money or jewellery, very few would complain to the police for fear of exposure or arrest.

Blackmailers had learned very quickly that large amounts of money could be extracted from frightened men, and set simple traps in order to do so, as shown in this newspaper report covering the trial of 17-year-old Archie Phillips for obtaining goods by menaces from a Mr. George St. Clair, who was

> a stranger in London, and in December [1898] was standing in Regent Street when [Phillips] came across the road and entered into conversation with him about the weather. He was wearing a naval uniform, and in reply to a question said he was in the merchant service. They chatted for some time, and then had a drink together. [Phillips] asked [Mr. St. Clair] where he was going, and he replied that he was not going anywhere particular. Prisoner said he lived down Westminster, and they walked together in that direction. They went into a room, and after two or three minutes, during which he had been examining some music on the piano, two other young men entered and locked the door.
>
> One of them said, "What business have you in my room?" and he replied that he had been invited there by prisoner. The man said, "I know what your game is," and on being told that [Mr. St. Clair] did not understand his meaning, added "If you want to settle this you must give me £40. Unless you give me £40 you will not be allowed to leave the house." [St. Clair] said he did not have £40 on him, only £1 7s and a few coppers.

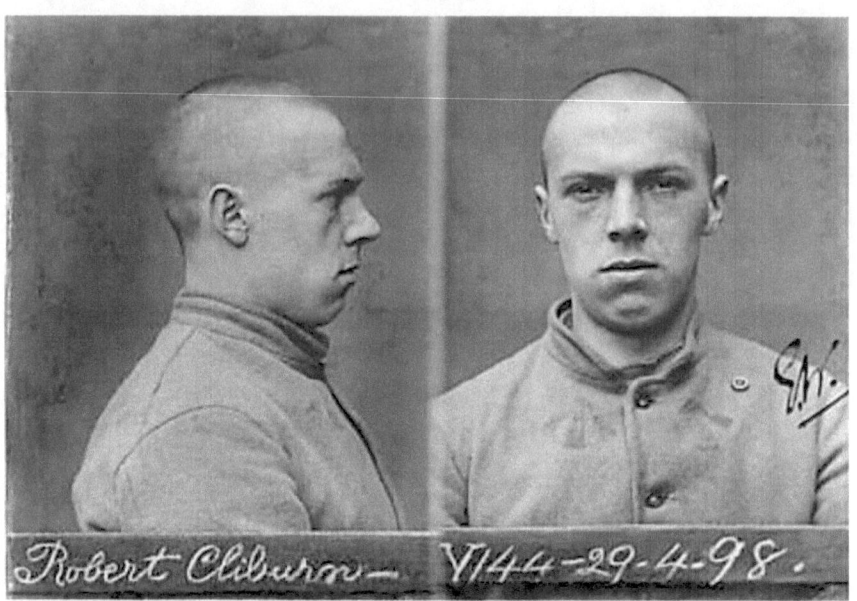

Blackmailer Robert Cliburn
from Dorchester Prison Admission and Discharge Registers, 1782-1901

> He produced a sovereign, and the man took it and threw it on the table, and said he would send for the police. The other man went out but soon returned, stating that he could not find a constable. The spokesman then said, "You do not leave this house until you give your watch and chain." [St. Clair] said he did not wish to part with them, and the man replied, "You can rest contented where you are then." [Mr. St. Clair] realised he was in a difficult predicament and was so frightened after waiting an hour and a half, that his only desire was to leave the house.

George St. Clair eventually surrendered his watch and chain, worth 180 guineas, and was allowed to leave. A few days later he went to the police and the gang was soon arrested, quite probably because of the data compiled by the C.I.D.[113]

Cases such as this were commonplace in the 1890s, with the most notorious blackmailer being Robert Cliburn, who ironically had targeted the Earl of Euston a number of times, making a mockery of the nobleman's claim of a simple interest in "poses plastiques".[114]

Cliburn, born in 1875, was a long-standing blackmailer. He had worked for a short spell as a telegraph messenger,[115] but was first sentenced for blackmailing in December 1890, aged just 15, receiving nine months' hard labour from Justice Henry Hawkins at Lewes Assizes for extorting money from one James Haylock.[116] He appeared at the Old Bailey in March 1898 charged with receiving being an accessory to a theft, and was sentenced to seven year's penal servitude,[117] being sent to Dorchester Prison in Dorset.

It was the culmination of a long, slow period of information gathering by Det. Chief Inspector Swanson and his colleagues at the C.I.D. They had adapted to the Labouchère Amendment and the powers it gave them, and accordingly painstakingly collected a long list of men who could be charged under the Act.

This knowledge allowed detectives to perform their duties both prosecuting and protecting homosexual men. At the turn of the century homosexual blackmailing was largely under control.

By the time Robert Cliburn was released, in 1905, Donald Swanson had retired from the Metropolitan Police force.

SEVENTEEN

The Death is Reported of Detective Swanson

As Herbert Schmalz left his home in west London's artistic community late in the evening of Sunday, 25th November 1894 to post a letter, probably the last thing he expected was to witness a murder. The 37-year-old artist,[1] who had exhibited at the Royal Academy, walked along Holland Park Road towards Melbury Road at 11.30pm when he saw a woman walking towards him accompanied by a tall, well-dressed man.[2]

Schmalz passed the couple and, having walked the short distance to the post box, turned to return to his home. By this time, the couple had reached No. 1 Holland Park Road, owned by eminent Pre-Raphaelite painter Valentine Prinsep, and were standing together, with the woman leaning against the wall and the man facing her, about a foot away. The artist saw the man suddenly fall against his partner, remaining in that position for a second or so, and then both fell to the pavement with a thud. The woman cried out "You brute!"

Schmalz rushed forward and shouted "What the devil are you up to?", at which point the man jumped up and ran off towards Addison Road, slowly at first and then quickening his pace. Chasing the attacker, Schmalz ran past the woman, who by this time was on her knees. As he passed he heard her heard groan "Oh Christ."

The artist followed the man as he turned into Addison Road and then Kensington Road, but lost him in Kensington High Street. He returned to his home and also immediately heard the blast of a police whistle.[3] William Case and Mr. T. G. Foreman, living opposite Mr. Prinsep, both heard the dull thud and the sound of two people running along the street.[4]

While Schmalz had been chasing after the attacker, at about 11.45pm Hermann Lauver had entered Holland Park Road and saw the victim lying across the pavement, her head towards the kerb. When she didn't react to his shouts he went to nearby 8 Holland Park Studios, where his friend Alfred Corbould lived.[5] Corbould, another artist, listened to Lauver's story and went out to look for himself. Seeing the still body he rushed off to find the nearest policeman,[6] meeting P.C. William Patterson 106F on Kensington Crescent. The blast of his whistle attracted another nearby officer, P.C. Gordon 218F,[7] and the three men rushed back to Holland Park Gardens.[8]

Alfred Corbould recalled what happened next:

> There was something dark round the body but I could not see what it was, it was too dark. When the constables came the bullseye was used, and I saw blood on the pavement round the head and it had run into the gutter.[9]

Sending P.C. Gordon to fetch the Divisional Surgeon for F Division, Dr. Meredith Townsend, Patterson investigated the scene. Lying close to the body was a cherrywood walking stick, one end lying in the pool of congealing blood.[10]

Dr. Townsend arrived and quickly found a deep wound to the left side of the woman's neck, from which a large quantity of blood had flowed. The body was taken to Kensington Mortuary for further examination.[11]

Early the following morning a builder's labourer named James Andrews found a knife sticking in a scaffold board in the yard of his employer, Mr. Stanham, at Edwards Terrace, Kensington. The board was lying on the ground, some six or seven feet from the gate, over which the knife had seemingly been thrown. Andrews called the police and Sergeant Thompson arrived to take possession of the weapon, returning it, along with the cherrywood walking stick, to Kensington police station.[12]

Early newspaper reports, perhaps unsurprisingly, voiced a concern that this was another crime by the Whitechapel murderer, some even running headlines such as "A Jack the Ripper Murder in Kensington".[13]

Whether these reports were read by the attacker and inspired him to write to the authorities is uncertain, but on Wednesday, 28th November, three days after the attack, a letter was received by Det. Inspector John Smith, addressed to "Police Station, Kensington, W., London, England":

> Dublin, Nov. 27th
>
> Dear Sir,
>
> The murder that was committed I did it. I did it just to the right of the door of a gentleman. I got her by the throat and tried to choke her, but

without success. I got her on the ground and cut her neck with a sloid knife. It was a very good cut. When I had cut her a fellow was coming along, so I flew for my life, but left the stick, and the knife was thrown away in the back lane in a back street. I did the murder at 12.30.

So good bye. On the job.

From Jack the Ripper.

You will find my name is well known at certain places round there. I am now at ———.[14]

The possibility of another murder by the Ripper, however remote, resulted in Scotland Yard's Det. Chief Inspector Donald Swanson liaising with the local officers, as with the cases of Phoebe Hogg and Emily Smith. Another familiar name from the Whitechapel murders investigations involved with the Kensington case was Dr. Thomas Bond, who on 27th November conducted a post mortem on the victim's body alongside Dr. Meredith Townsend:

> I noticed the blood which had flowed from the wound. It was principally on the right side and had clotted on the hair and face. There were only a few splashes on her dress.
>
> I formed the opinion that the woman was probably on the ground at the time the wound was inflicted with her face turned towards the right side. The cut was made with the sweep of the knife commencing first on the right side of the larynx and extended to the left, first underneath the left ear and 2 inches below it. The cut was caused by a right handed person and was much deeper on the left hand side than on the right and divided all the large vessels and notched the cervical vertebrae.
>
> The blood in my opinion would spurt out at first for a moment. I should expect the sleeve and hand and part of the coat of the assailant to be marked with blood. I should not expect to find so much blood on the assailant if the woman was down as if she was standing up.
>
> The marks of pressure on the throat were caused before the wound. On the left side was a thumb mark.
>
> I have seen the knife produced. It is just the sort of knife which would produce such as sweeping wound. The marks on the knife are those of mammalian blood and are comparatively recent.[15]

By now, the victim had been identified as 27-year-old Augusta Dawes, born in Bristol to a respectable family but in more recent years eking out a living as a prostitute in London.[16] At the time of her death she was living at 26 St. Clements Road, Notting Hill. Also in the house was fellow 'unfortunate' Lillian Creber, who knew Dawes as 'Gus Dudley', and who told detectives that her friend had one child, who lived with her, a young girl.[17] According to *Reynolds's Weekly Newspaper*, the child was just three months old and had been carried in Lillian Creber's arms when she had attended the mortuary to identify her friend's body.[18]

Kate Forsyth, a carpenter's wife, told police that she had known Augusta for two years, she until recently having lodged with the Forsyths at Hammersmith, and at that time she had been receiving a weekly income from the child's father, sometimes £1 and on other occasions 25s. Mrs. Forsyth revealed that Augusta also had a second, older child, whom she believed was in the workhouse.[19] According to the *Ross Gazette* of 6th December, Mrs. Forsyth claimed that Augusta had at one time been a Sunday School teacher near Blythe Road in Kensington.

Lillian Creber had last seen 'Gus' at about 6.00pm on the evening of her death, when she had left the house alone. The next time she saw her was at the Kensington Mortuary, where she identified the body.[20]

Far from taunting the police, the arrival of the Ripper letter proved to be the evidence which they had been looking for. The day after the murder, officials of Eastcote school at Hampton Wick, an establishment for boys from privileged families considered intellectually weak, had reported that one of their older boys had absented himself without permission. It was not the first time this particular pupil, 21-year-old Reginald Saunderson, had taken leave of the school. But on this occasion, also missing were a cherrywood walking stick and a Sloyd knife, a Swedish-style tool which the boys used during carpentry lessons.[21]

Det. Chief Inspector Swanson and Det. Inspector John Smith went to Eastcote, where they saw schoolmaster Francis Rollison.[22]

The detectives showed the Ripper letter and envelope to Mr. Rollison, who immediately recognised the handwriting as Saunderson's, saying: "The spelling in the letter is very bad. [Saunderson] was backward in his education and made mistakes in spelling, but not so bad as in the letter."[23]

Eastcote had been established by Dr. John Langdon Down in 1882 as a private asylum for weak-minded boys and young men from upper class families, following the success of a similar establishment at nearby Teddington called Normansfield.[24]

Dr. Langdon Down operated a medical practice at 81 Harley Street and

from The Illustrated Police News, 15th December 1894

acted as honorary consultant physician to the London Hospital,[25] and continued in these roles while his wife Mary ran the establishments at Eastcote and Normansfield on a day-to-day basis. Mrs. Langdon Down told the detectives that Reginald Saunderson had arrived at Eastcote on 17th December 1888, a month after his fifteenth birthday. He was now the eldest boy at the school, having celebrated his 21st birthday the previous November.[26]

Inmates were not allowed to leave the grounds without being accompanied by a master or the matron, Miss Young, but Saunderson had absconded three or four times between 1888 and 1892 and had often been a source of trouble. To Mrs. Langdon Down's knowledge he had never been violent, but she had heard that he once said that he would "put a knife into Miss Young." Saunderson had last been seen around 6.00pm on the day of the murder, when he was visiting church with the rest of the boys.[27]

Reginald Saunderson was born in Cavan, Ireland, one of ten children to Llewellyn Traherne Bassett Saunderson, formerly of the 11th Hussars and now a Justice of the Peace, and Lady Rachel Scott. His uncle was Colonel Edward J. Saunderson, Conservative M.P. for North Armagh.

Llewellyn Saunderson reported how his son had suffered an injury to his head in early childhood, and had undergone treatment until the age of 11-years-old. For the next two years he attended a school, before being placed under the care of a clergyman. Reginald was kept at home for several months, but due to his increasingly strange behaviour his father took medical advice and decided to enrol him into Eastcote, under the care of Dr. Langdon Down. There was, apparently, no history of mental illness in either family and Reginald's weak-mindedness appeared solely the result of his childhood accident.[28] It was widely reported that in recent months he had taken a deep interest in the trial of James Canham Read, who had murdered his young lover, Florence Dennis, in June 1894 and was found guilty on 15th November, ten days before the murder of Augusta Dawes.[29]

The stamp on the envelope in which the supposed Ripper letter arrived showed that it had been posted at the post office at Monkstown, Dublin; contact was made with the Royal Irish Constabulary, and Sgts. Thompson and Dyson of the Met's F Division were dispatched to Ireland.[30]

Reginald Saunderson had made a meandering journey to Dublin immediately after the attack on Augusta Dawes, along the way carrying out the worst example of covering one's tracks as could be found.

Three hours after the murder, at about 2.00am on Monday, 26th November, he approached Knightsbridge Barracks and spoke to a trooper of the Second Life Guards who was on sentry duty. Asking first for a glass of water, Saunderson remarked how he would like to enlist. He ignored the reply to return to the Barracks in the morning, suddenly exclaiming that he had no money, asking whether the sentry would like to buy a razor; the sentry did, and handed over 3s.[31]

The fugitive's next appearance was at Gower Street railway station, where at 5.20am he approached a porter named Thomas Jefferson saying he needed to use the lavatory. Being told that there was a charge of a penny, the desperate Saunderson complained that he had no money but instead offered a cricket cap from his pocket, which on later inspection was found to have the name 'Saunderson' sewn inside.[32]

A fishmonger's assistant named William Hollier was driving a cart towards Harrow when, at around 8.15am, he saw Saunderson walking along the road. Hollier agreed to the request of a lift, and once settled in his seat the new passenger suddenly said he had witnessed the dreadful murder of a woman in Kensington the previous night. Somewhat bizarrely, Hollier asked no questions about the incident and nothing more was said until he set Saunderson down at High Street, Harrow.[33]

Ten minutes later Saunderson knocked on the door of Henry Davidson, a master at Harrow School who knew his father. The weary traveller told Mr. Davidson that he had cycled all the way from Portsmouth, where he lived with his aunt, but while he had been visiting a friend near Willesden his bicycle had been stolen. He had no means to return, and wondered whether Mr. Davidson could kindly loan him some money. Saunderson went on to claim that there had been a murder the previous night near Westminster Bridge, and as he passed by a policeman had called to him to help lift the body of the woman, who had had her throat cut. Mr. Davidson gave the young man £1, who then left at about 10.30am. Half an hour later he returned, saying the amount lent was not enough for his fare, and could he please have another half a crown. Receiving this, Saunderson went on his way.[34]

With money in his pocket, the murderer was thus able to purchase a train ticket from Harrow to Dublin, a journey requiring several changes which began just after midday on Monday, 26th November.

The following evening, Colour Sergeant Thomas Brien of the Royal Dublin Fusiliers was on duty at the Linenhall Barracks when Reginald Saunderson approached him, accompanied by a private, saying he wanted to enlist in the Army. When asked for his details, Saunderson said his name was "Drake", and that he came from Eton College. As it was too late for him to be interviewed that night, Saunderson was permitted to sleep at the Barracks. That evening, he had written the letter addressed to Kensington police station signed "Jack the Ripper".

He was examined by the army doctor the next day and subsequently rejected, but was allowed to stay at the Barracks another evening.[35]

Saunderson left the next morning, 29th November, but by this time details of the murder had been telegraphed to the Royal Irish Constabulary. Four days later District Inspector William Miller of Killeshandra County Cavan traced the fugitive to the nearby home of a Mrs. Jous. Searching his prisoner, Inspector Miller found copies of *The Star* and *St. James Gazette*, both dated 26th November 1894, and which contained accounts of the Kensington murder, along with an old knife and the blade of another.

Saunderson was taken before a magistrate and remanded at Armagh prison for eight days.[36]

He had been held there for four days when Sergeants Thompson and Dyson of the Metropolitan Police's F Division arrived, on 7th December.[37]

They took Saunderson into their custody and the following day arrived back in London, the *Illustrated Police News* vividly describing the journey from Willesden Junction train station to Kensington police station:

> Saunderson, simultaneously with Sergeant Thompson, stepped on the platform. The young fellow, quite composed, but looking pallid, haggard, and fatigued, turned and watched a collection of the wraps and a large travelling bag taken from the carriage, ignoring everything else in the surroundings. He is tall – about 6ft – and very slim, and his face is almost boyish, with no indication of hair growth. His hair is dark. He wore a hard black felt hat and a long brown ulster cape, which hung open and loosely about his slender form from a pair of broad shoulders. The detectives took the arms of the accused, and thus linked together the trio proceeded to the cab in waiting. The accused was not handcuffed. As they proceeded along the platform it was noticed that prisoner was somewhat taller than his custodians.
>
> Daylight had just dawned when the four-wheeler conveying the prisoner and the detectives arrived at Kensington police station.[38]

Saunderson appeared before Magistrate Mr. Henry Curtis-Bennett at the West London Police Court for the remand hearing, where it was reported that although he appeared respectful to the Bench, on occasion "his eyes vacantly wandering around the court, and gave to his face quite a painful expression of dwarfed mental powers."

Having heard the evidence, Mr. Curtis-Bennett directed that the prisoner be remanded at Holloway Gaol.[39]

The inquest into the death of Augusta Dawes, otherwise Dudley, had opened at Kensington Town Hall on Thursday, 29th November, then adjourned until 4th December. At the later hearing, the coroner for West London, Mr. Drew, heard that the artist Alfred Corbould, who had seen the body in situ, had produced a sketch of the locale in pen and ink for the police, which proved to be extremely accurate:

> From his pencil the coroner was enabled to gauge the precise position of the body of the victim as it lay outside Mr. Val Prinsep's house. Mr. Corbould is not unused to scenes of violence, having been a war correspondent in Turkey and Ashantee. He stands rather over six feet, and is an Apollo in figure and features.[40]

By the time the inquest concluded on 11th December the identity of the assailant had been confirmed, and the jury took but a few minutes to

Reginald Saunderson
from The Graphic, 15th December 1894.
As Alfred Corbould's illustrations regularly appeared in The Graphic,
it it likely that this sketch was his work

return a verdict of "Deceased was murdered by Reginald Saunderson".

The concluding of the inquest allowed the remains of Augusta Dawes to be buried, after a fortnight lying in the Kensington Mortuary. That same afternoon, a large crowd watched as the hearse left for Kensington Cemetery, Hanwell, with a mourning coach containing a sister and a cousin of the deceased following behind and then two more coaches bearing friends.[41] Inscribed on the coffin plate were the simple words: "Augusta Dawes. Died 25th November 1894. Aged 28 years."[42]

Saunderson's committal hearing took place over several weeks, attended by Det. Chief Inspector Swanson with the prisoner's father, Llewellyn Saunderson.[43] Much discussion took place as to Saunderson's mental condition and his suitability to stand trial, with psychiatric specialists Dr. Forbes Winslow, Dr. Edgar Sheppard, Dr. George Fielding Blandford and Dr. Charlton Bastian examining the prisoner and reporting unanimously that he was unable to stand trial.[44] At the Old Bailey on Wednesday, 28th January 1895 Dr. Edward Walker of Holloway Gaol stated that he had kept the prisoner under observation since 28th December, and in that time his mental state had deteriorated, the prisoner betraying an obviously unsound mind and committing sporadic bouts of violence so that he had had to be placed in a padded cell.[45] In the face of such evidence, Saunderson was found unfit to plead.[46]

On 2nd February 1895 Home Secretary Herbert Asquith authorised the removal of Saunderson from Holloway Gaol and to be detained under Her Majesty's Pleasure at Broadmoor Lunatic Asylum.[47] He remained there until his death in 1943, aged 69.[48]

By the time Reginald Saunderson made his final court appearance, Det. Chief Inspector Swanson had succumbed to the severe outbreak of influenza currently ravaging the capital. He had been diagnosed with pharyngitis on 12th January, being off work for a week. It was his first absence from work through illness since spraining his ankle in February 1880. Despite returning to work on 19th January, Swanson then developed tonsillitis and was sent home for another twelve days, returning on 2nd March only to be diagnosed with influenza. He would spend twenty-two days recovering, returning to his duties on 27th March after a total of 41 days absent.[49]

Swanson was not the only sufferer; virtually all officers of the C.I.D. were struck down, along with Hon. Hamilton Cuffe, by now the Director of Public Prosecutions, some 50 workers at the Bank of England, firemen at the Brigade's Southwark headquarters and soldiers at Knightsbridge Barracks.[50]

President of the Local Government Board Arthur Balfour, later Prime Minister, was severely affected, as was Lord Rosebery, also a future Prime Minister. The Rev. Samuel Flood Jones, a Minor Canon and Precentor of Westminster Abbey, died there on 26th February following a week suffering from bronchitis.[51]

On 27th February, the *Birmingham Daily Post* reported that 111 people had died in the previous seven days as a direct result of influenza, compared with just 24 the week before. In total, there were 3,119 deaths from diseases of the respiratory organs that week, against the previous week's 1,840. By way of contrast, 2,156 people would die in London alone as a direct result of influenza during the sixteen-week outbreak of 1895.[52]

In 1892, 2,242 people died in London during an eighteen-week outbreak, including, it was reported, Det. Chief Inspector Swanson. The *Sussex Agricultural Express* of Saturday, 6th February 1892 wrote:

> Over a thousand of the London Police are still down, and the death is reported of Detective Swanson who it may be remembered took a prominent part in the Lefroy murder a case a few years ago.

In fact, reports of Swanson's demise were premature. It had actually been his nephew James Alexander Swanson, fourth son of Donald's eldest brother John, who had passed away. James had served in the Metropolitan Police for several years, and at the time of his death, on

26th January 1892 aged just 28,⁵³ was a Sergeant living at Lewisham.

Once Det. Chief Inspector Donald Swanson had recovered, he was sent to Jersey to take custody of a prisoner arrested there by the local police. Leonard Harper, a 57-year-old lawyer was wanted for fraud by the New Zealand authorities.

Harper had been born in Eton, the son of the Rev. Henry Harper. The family emigrated to New Zealand and Rev. Harper became the first Anglican bishop of Christchurch. In his youth, Leonard Harper was a keen explorer; in 1857, aged 20, he became the first European to cross New Zealand's Southern Alps from Canterbury to the West Coast, when two Maori led him through the pass which today bears his name.⁵⁴

Seven years later he married Joanna Dorothea Dyke Troyte and went on to father a total of nine children. In 1866 he became Member of Parliament for the Cheviot region, resigning in 1878, and later represented the Avon electorate from 1884 to 1887.⁵⁵

Harper soon moved into law, and became a qualified barrister. He formed the firm Harper, Harper and Maude, based at Christchurch,⁵⁶ and operated there for some years before leaving New Zealand for Jersey in November 1892, supposedly to liaise with creditors to his ailing company.⁵⁷ He would later tell police that he stayed on the island as it was cheap to do so, and Mrs. Harper could add to her allowance made by her relatives by taking in lodgers.⁵⁸

By the summer of 1895 some six people from Christchurch had complained to police of being defrauded of their investments, and a further complaint had been received from a man in Wellington. The monies claimed by these cases amounted to £6,275.⁵⁹

A total of seven warrants were issued to Inspector Peter Pender of the Wellington police by the Christchurch Stipendiary Magistrate Mr. Bishop,⁶⁰ and the experienced officer wasted no time in contacting the Jersey authorities, with the result that Leonard Harper was arrested at St. Helier on Tuesday, 14th May.⁶¹

The same day, a telegram was sent to New Scotland Yard by the Minister of Justice of New Zealand, at the time a British colony. Det. Chief Inspector Donald Swanson was tasked with taking Harper into the custody of the Metropolitan Police, and accordingly applied for a warrant at Bow Street Police Court, this being granted immediately by Mr. Vaughan.⁶²

The Death is Reported of Detective Swanson

Leonard Harper
General Assembly Library:
Parliamentary portraits. Ref: 35mm-00109-A-F.
Alexander Turnbull Library, Wellington,
New Zealand. natlib.govt.nz/records/23079477

Inspector Peter Pender
from The Cyclopedia of New Zealand, 1897

Swanson travelled to Jersey, arriving on 16th May. The detective read the warrant, to which Harper replied: "I have not advantaged myself by one penny. I am living upon the charity of my wife's friends, and the furniture which I have in the house is hired." The prisoner said that he had even written to the New Zealand Law Institute expressing his willingness to return to face the accusations against him.[63]

It was reported that on the return journey to London, Swanson "treated [Harper] very courteously, and the twain came to London so that other passengers by boat and train knew nothing of their relative positions."[64]

On arrival in London the detective took his prisoner directly to Bow Street Magistrates' Court, where before Mr. Lushington he was charged under the Fugitives Offenders' Act with fraud as an attorney or agent in New Zealand, a British Colony. Swanson requested a lengthy remand, stating that the necessary papers would not arrive from New Zealand until around 10th July. Leonard Harper was thereby sent to Holloway to await the arrival of Inspector Pender.[65]

The next event in Donald Swanson's diary was the consecration of a new Masonic lodge, Justicia 2563. On 27th May, the Scot was in attendance as a visitor at Freemasons' Hall along with founders including Det. Chief Inspector George Greenham as the new lodge, formed for those involved in the fight for justice, was consecrated by Bro. Edward Letchworth, G. Sec.[66]

Inspector Peter Pender of the Wellington Police arrived in London a few days later. He had enjoyed a formidable career, worthy enough to feature in a biography of Wellington two years later:

> There is no better known or more noticeable figure in and about Wellington than Mr. Peter Pender, Inspector of Police for the Wellington District. He has had a long and distinguished career. He has served in the Royal Irish Constabulary, and afterwards joining the Mounted Staff Corps, as a volunteer, fought under the gallant Raglan in the Crimea, being present at the taking of Sebastopol, and afterwards at Tchernaya, and later on he did good work, under Col. Grant, in organising the Turkish Contingent Cavalry in Asia Minor, and after a return to his Royal Irish Constabulary duties, went out to Melbourne, in 1856, and joined the Victorian police, being greatly esteemed by his superiors for his unfailing diligence and probity. In 1862 he arrived in Canterbury, and since then has been a highly respected member of the New Zealand Police Force. From 1864 to 1892 Mr. Pender was Inspector of Police at Christchurch, where his name is a household word. In 1892, he was transferred to Wellington. He owns the Crimean war medal and clasp for Sebastopol, the Turkish medal and the New Zealand long service medal.[67]

On 29th July, Assistant Commissioner Robert Anderson wrote to Home Office Clerk Charles S. Murdoch requesting that Inspector Pender and Det. Chief Inspector Swanson be named on the Extradition Warrant.[68]

Although Harper's remand was due to expire on 6th August, it was discovered that the planned passage, on the *S.S. Aotea*, was unavailable until the 8th. Swanson wrote a report to Chief Constable Melville Macnaghten explaining the problem; Harper was remanded at Holloway for a further 48 hours,[69] and Inspector Pender sailed for New Zealand with his prisoner on Saturday, 8th August.

Det. Chief Inspector Swanson's involvement in the case ended with his submitting his expenses incurred of £21 1s 1d, to be reimbursed to the Metropolitan Police Receiver by the New Zealand authorities.[70]

Leonard Harper eventually went on trial in Auckland on December 1895. The jury was unable to reach agreement on his guilt, and he was freed on bail pending a second trial at Wellington.[71] It would be three months before this commenced, on 18th March 1896,[72] and the following day he was acquitted of the first charge;[73] three days later, on 23rd March, he was also found not guilty of the second charge.[74]

The Australasian, reporting on this second acquittal, gave details of the final case, which was a sample of all the charges:

> The Rev. Mr. Gillett, of England, asked the Harpers if they could find a good investment for £5,000, and, receiving a reply in the affirmative, the money was paid to Harper and Co.'s credit. It was paid into No. 2 account, which was overdrawn by over £24,000, while the firm was hopelessly insolvent. Although ostensibly advanced on mortgage, the money was never lent out or invested. Harper and Co. paid the interest till the crash came, and then Mr. Gillett merely ranked as an ordinary creditor. The Crown has now abandoned the remainder of the charges, and Harper is free, the only punishment he has received being the striking of his name off the roll.[75]

Following his acquittal Harper returned to Jersey. By the 1911 census he had retired and returned to the mainland, living at Bruton, Somerset. He died there in 1915 aged 78.[76]

EIGHTEEN

The Hero of Bow Street

If you can keep your head when all about you
Are losing theirs and blaming it on you,
If you can trust yourself when all men doubt you,
But make allowance for their doubting too;
If you can wait and not be tired of waiting,
Or being lied about, don't deal in lies,
Or being hated, don't give way to hating,
And yet don't look too good nor talk too wise.

That Rudyard Kipling's inspirational poem *If-* would have its roots in the South African land struggles of the 1890s may come as a surprise, but events of that decade in the British colony could well have been borne from the fertile imagination of a gifted storyteller.

Since Sir Charles Warren had left Bechuanaland in March 1885, the British had taken steps to secure their hold on large tracts of land across the continent. In October 1888, as Warren was fighting the press over the inability of his officers to apprehend the Whitechapel murderer, the British South Africa Company was incorporated, an amalgamation of the previously competitive Central Search Association and the Exploring Company Ltd, financially backed by Baron de Rothschild. These two companies both had an interest in exploiting the mineral wealth of Mashonaland, not yet mined, and joined forces in order to secure government backing, which occurred in December 1889 when the company was granted a Royal Charter.

Owner of the Central Search Association, and subsequent Managing Director of the Chartered Company, was Cecil Rhodes, founder of the De Beers Mining Company and Prime Minister of the Cape Colony. Born in Bishop's Stortford in 1853 and educated at Oxford, Rhodes was sent to South Africa at the age of seventeen in the hope that the climate would improve his poor health. A year later he entered the diamond trade at

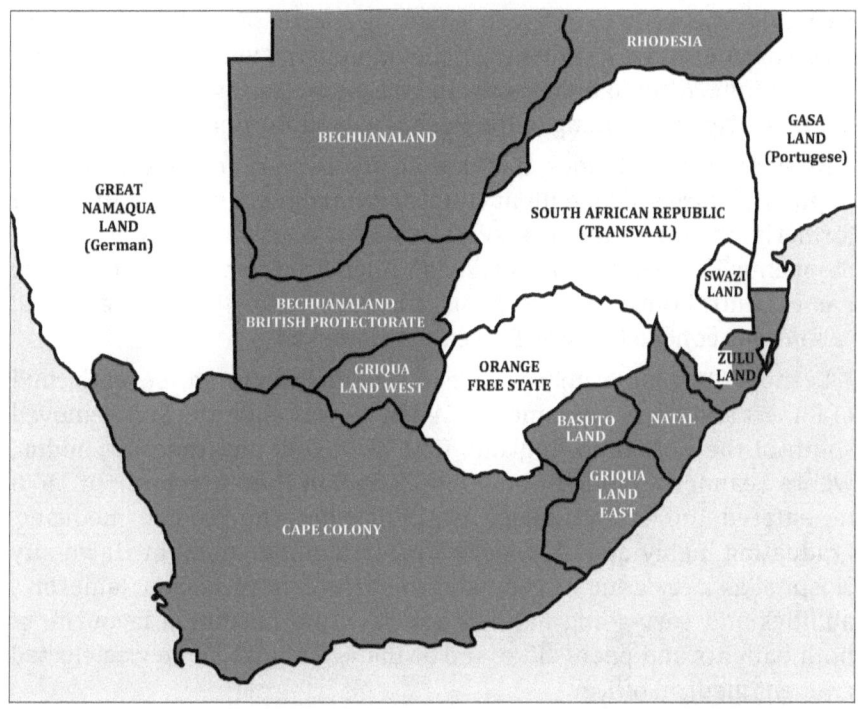

*South Africa in 1895.
Grey shading denotes British territories*

Kimberley, and over the following twenty years came to dominate the world diamond market.

Rhodes' popularity with European settlers was underlined when the area of over one million square feet governed by the British known as 'Zambesia' was officially renamed Rhodesia in 1895.[1] In reality, the territory had been taken by force two years earlier. Rhodes and his business partner Alfred Beit reached agreement with Lobengula, king of Matabeleland, to allow them to dig for minerals in return for securing funds and weaponry for the Matabele. Long negotiations were concluded only when a friend of Rhodes, Dr. Leander Jameson, who had allegedly treated Lobengula's gout and thereby gained his trust, intervened and persuaded the king to sign the treaty.[2] Lobengula soon realised that Beit and Rhodes intended to annexe his territory, and the First Matabele War broke out in October 1893. The native warriors were no match for the guns of the British, and the territory was conquered.[3]

With the grant of a Royal Charter, the British South Africa Company obtained substantial powers of territorial government, which Rhodes in particular was keen to utilise in acquiring control of further territories. Also considered was taking over the administration of Bechuanaland Protectorate. Although this failed to take place, the Chartered Company did take over the running of the Bechuanaland Border Police in 1892.

Now, in 1895, Rhodes had his sights set on the South African Republic, a large independent country immediately south of Rhodesia formerly known as the Transvaal, which was governed by President Stephanus Kruger, known as Paul, an Anglicised version of his middle name. Central once again to plans, and responsible for their eventual calamitous conclusion, was Dr. Leander Jameson.

Leander Starr Jameson was born in 1853 in Edinburgh, eleventh child of Robert and Christian Jameson. When he was eight the family moved south of the border to England, first to Suffolk and then to London, where Leander attended Godolphin School in Hammersmith. In 1870 he entered University College Hospital where he studied medicine, graduating highly qualified, before gaining employment at University Hospital as a resident surgeon and then resident physician. Jameson's abilities and easy-going nature soon saw him become a favourite of both patients and peers alike, and at the age of just 23 he was elected resident medical officer.

Within two years, however, the young doctor had worked himself into a state of nervous exhaustion, and was no doubt relieved when a Dr. Prince of Kimberley, in the Cape Colony, wrote to University College Hospital seeking a partner for his practice. Jameson, like Cecil Rhodes before him, no doubt saw the warmer climes of South Africa as being beneficial to his health, and in 1878 departed aboard the *Drummond Castle*.[4]

Jameson had made a name for himself within three days of starting at Dr. Prince's practice, when he operated on a highly-regarded businessman when other Kimberley doctors were reticent to do so; the operation was a success, and Jameson's reputation was immediately established.

At the time the doctor arrived in Kimberley, the town had taken over as the centre of the diamond diggings from Hopetown, where the 'Eureka' and 'Star of Africa' diamonds had been found in the 1860s, and was now the second largest town in South Africa. Originally named 'New Rush' in reference to the diamond rush of the 1870s, the town was officially renamed Kimberley in 1873.

At the centre of this burgeoning industry was Cecil Rhodes. He and Jameson soon became close friends within weeks of the doctor's arrival.

Dr. Leander Starr Jameson
Author's collection

As Rhodes' fortune grew through his diamond empire, he used his wealth to fund his other plans, namely politics. It was said of him that his overriding passion was to claim the vast tracts of land across the north of South Africa for the Empire, "linking the Cape to Cairo". Having entered parliament as early as 1880, Rhodes began to set the wheels in motion to achieve his aim, entering into various treaties and charters in order to gain a foothold in new territories.

Instilled with a sense of adventure, Dr. Leander Jameson went along with him, abandoning his medical career for positions in the years ahead such as Chief Magistrate of Mashonaland, Administrator of the British South Africa Company, and Resident Commissioner for Territories of Ikaning and Montsioa.[5]

Now, in 1895, Rhodes enviously eyed the Transvaal.

Once part of the British Colony, the Transvaal had been transferred to a population of some 40,000 Boers – those descendants of Dutch settlers who had moved north from the Cape Colony to the Orange Free State, the Transvaal and Natal to escape British rule – under the Sand River Convention. As a result, the South African Republic came into being in 1852, and was fully independent at the signing of the London Convention in February 1884.

The following year, large quantities of gold were discovered in the South African Republic. Crucially, the Boer settlers were farmers, not miners, and the discovery of gold led to an influx of many thousands of mainly British immigrants, called 'Uitlanders' (Outlanders).

Although the South African Republic tolerated the immigrants in no small measure thanks to the taxes they poured into government coffers, the Uitlanders themselves grew increasingly frustrated at a lack of representation.

Cecil Rhodes, sensing an opportunity, took matters into his own hands. In June 1895 he and Alfred Beit devised a plan whereby arms and money would be provided to the Uitlanders in order to fuel this discontent, in the hope of sparking an armed uprising by the settlers with the result of the overthrowing of the South African Republic government, based at Pretoria. An armed force under the control of Dr. Jameson was to be placed on the Transvaal border, ready to assist and support the insurrection.

Over the next few months, Rhodes met with the leaders of the insurrection party at Johannesburg and eventually, in October, agreement was reached. The insurrectionists were to rise, seize the Pretoria Arsenal and ammunition and return to Johannesburg, with

Jameson's help controlling the town while the High Commissioner would travel from Cape Town to mediate the handover of power.

With the plan prepared, Jameson proceeded to create a force of some 750 men, taken from various bodies including the Bechuanaland Border Police and military based at the Cape and Bulawayo.

Rhodes then paid large sums of money for arms to be sent from England to the Chartered Company at Cape Town, supposedly to Rhodesia, but which were diverted to Johannesburg, smuggled into the Transvaal though Rhodes's De Beers Company.

By the end of November, with plans well advanced, a letter signed by all involved was given to Dr. Jameson, to be used as an authority with the Directors of the Charter Company in the hope that they would join in the Raid, which was set for Saturday, 28th December 1895.

Numerous obstacles presented themselves, not least the Uitlanders losing their nerve, and Rhodes telegraphed Jameson to tell him not to take any action until he heard from him again. Jameson and his men, ready at Pitsani, began to get restless, and considered that they could persuade the insurrectionists to still carry out the plan. On the 28th, the planned day of the Raid, Jameson telegraphed Rhodes saying "Unless I hear definitely to the contrary, shall leave tomorrow evening." The following day another message was wired: "Shall leave tonight for Transvaal."

These two telegrams arrived with Rhodes at 11.00am on Sunday, 29th December, who composed the following reply which, due to telegraph wires being down at Mafeking, was never sent: "Things in Johannesburg I yet hope to see amicably settled... On no account whatever must you move. I most strongly object to such a course." By the time the High Commission at Cape Town became aware of the Raid, it was too late to inform Jameson to stop – he and his troops had cut the wires.[6]

The column entered South African Republic territory and marched 39 miles through the night to Malmani, which they reached at 5.15 on the morning of the 30th. After watering their horses and resting for an hour or two, Jameson and his men crossed miles of open country until at midday they were intercepted by a messenger dispatched from Zeerust, who handed Jameson a letter warning him that his action was a contravention of international convention, and therefore illegal. Jameson responded that the letter of invitation he held gave him the authority to proceed. The Troopers marched again though the night.

Three days into the Raid, on New Year's Day, Jameson and his men entered Krugersdorp, where a force of Boer soldiers had blocked the road to Johannesburg and prepared defensive positions. After several hours exchanging fire, during which he lost several men, Jameson regrouped later that evening and attempted to flank the Boer resistance by moving south east. This move proved to be the undoing of the Raiders; the Boers tracked their progress overnight, and as dawn broke on 2nd January 1896 a substantial armed force was waiting for them at Doornkop. Despite initially exchanging fire, in which they lost more men, the tired Raiders eventually surrendered to Commandant Piet Cronjé, at which point they were taken to Pretoria and jailed.[7]

After pondering what to do with his prisoners, President Kruger decided to avoid turning Jameson and his men into martyrs and passed the problem on to the British Government.

On 10th January Major General George Cox, Commanding Troops Natal and Zululand, received orders to proceed to Pretoria, where he was instructed to take military custody of the prisoners. On arrival, he was told that they had been sent to Volksrust, where they would be held until handed over to the British authorities.

Four days later the terms of surrender were agreed between President Kruger and the British authorities, and on 15th January Major General Cox arrived at Volksrust, where he found the prisoners held in three large iron goods sheds alongside the railway.[8] A formal count revealed that a total of 407 men, made up of 34 officers and 373 sergeant majors, sergeants and rank and file men, as well as 41 native transport drivers, were being held under guard.[9] Eighteen of Jameson's troopers had been killed, 40 wounded and 28 were missing.

The 41 native prisoners were taken by train to Charlestown and handed over to the Natal Police, receiving any arrears in pay due to them by the Chartered Company. They were subsequently released and told to go to their homes.

The remaining prisoners were taken by special train to Durban, where two steamships waited. Dr. Leander Jameson and his officers were placed on the *Victoria*, which departed on 21st January.[10]

On board alongside Dr. Jameson were twelve fellow officers deemed equally responsible for the Raid, all of whom would be charged:

> Major Sir John Willoughby of the Royal Horse Guards, seconded for service in the British South Africa Company's Police in May 1890 and again for two years in May 1895.
>
> Major Henry White of the 3rd Battalion, Grenadier Guards, seconded to the British South Africa Company in July 1894, and appointed Magistrate for both the Victoria and Salisbury Districts in 1894.

Captain Rayleigh Grey of the 6th Inniskilling Dragoons, employed with the Bechuanaland Border Police since January 1889, became its Commandant in early 1895.

Captain Hon. Robert White of the Royal Welsh Fusiliers, seconded for service as Staff Officer of the British South Africa Company in March 1895. In October was appointed Magistrate of Territories of Montsioa and Ikaning.

Major John Stracey of the Scots Guards, at the time of the Raid on leave with permission to travel in South Africa.

Captain Charles Lindsell of the 4th Battalion, Durham Light Infantry. Appointed Captain of the Bechuanaland Border Police and later Magistrate of the Victoria District.

Lieutenant Harold Grenfell of the 1st Life Guards, seconded to the British South Africa Company just two weeks before the Raid.

Captain Charles Villiers of the Royal Horse Guards, seconded in March 1895 for two years' special service with the British South Africa Company's Volunteer Forces.

Lieutenant Kenneth Kincaid-Smith of the Royal Artillery, second to the British South Africa Company for two years in April 1895 as an Artillery Officer.

Captain C. L. D. Monro of the 3rd Battalion, Seaforth Highlanders, seconded in 1891 to the Bechuanaland Border Police.

Captain Cyril Foley of the 3rd Battalion, Royal Scots Militia, at the time of the Raid on leave with permission to travel in South Africa.

Captain C. C. Holden of the Derbyshire Yeomanry, treated as if on leave at the time of the Raid.

Also under arrest, but unable to travel aboard the *Victoria* as he was in hospital recovering from injuries sustained in the Raid, was Captain Hon. C. J. Coventry of the 3rd Battalion, Worcester Regiment, seconded in March 1889 to the Bechuanaland Border Police and later appointed Magistrate for the British Protectorate and the Tati District.[11]

A week later, on 28th January, the rest of the men boarded the *Harlech Castle* and departed for England, soon to swap the warm South African sun for the English winter.[12] Also aboard were seven witnesses, including Captain Ellis, Captain Tighe and Lieutenant Williams. They were met by a representative of the Treasury.[13]

Somewhat surprisingly, first to arrive in England was the *Harlech Castle*, which docked at Plymouth on Sunday, 23rd February after a

26-day voyage. They had stopped briefly at Madeira, where they were joined by Det. Inspector Frank Froest of New Scotland Yard and Mr. Angus Lewis from the Treasury. Almost immediately the detective and civil servant distributed a form to each man on board, to be completed that day, which requested information of service details, length of service and payment amounts.[14] Railway tickets for their onward journeys from London were also supplied,[15] and during the remainder of the voyage Froest spoke to each man in turn, attempting to obtain information as to the Raid.

On disembarking at Plymouth, Froest met with Det. Chief Inspector Swanson, who had travelled down from London the previous day. Froest proceeded with a roll call, and the men boarded one of two waiting trains depending on their destination.

With all passengers aboard, Swanson and Froest took their own seats and, as their train slowly pulled out of the station, the cheering of the passengers could be heard as they leaned out of open windows and waved their hats.

At quarter to seven that evening, the first train, containing the detectives and some 200 of Jameson's troops, pulled into Platform 5 at Paddington Station. Waiting were Chief Constable Monsell, Superintendent Ferrett and a body of local F Division constables. An estimated 2,000-strong crowd lined Praed Street outside, as a cordon of officers under the direction of Chief Inspector Belton blocked entry to the station. As the train slowed to a halt, windows on both sides opened and bronzed faces emerged, waving and giving hearty cheers, which were echoed by the throng outside.[16] The troopers hurried off the train and out of the station, eager to reach their destinations. Three hailed a passing cab and caused those within earshot to laugh by ordering the cabman to "drive to the nearest pub."[17]

The arrival of Dr. Jameson and his men themselves three days later was an altogether different affair. Recognising that intense press and public interest would no doubt hinder the smooth transportation of the Raiders to Bow Street Magistrates' Court, the Metropolitan Police decided on a different plan. Rather than have the *Victoria* dock at Plymouth, they had telegraphed orders to delay the voyage, and on entering British waters the steamer was directed to Gravesend, the tactic drawing applause from one newspaper man:

> Inspector Swanson did baffle the reporters and the Press Association, not a very easy matter, since the Press Associate spend money most lavishly. Swanson is a fat, jovial man, like Count Fosco [from Wilkie Collins' *The*

Dr. Jameson and his officers aboard the Victoria
from The Illustrated London News, 7th March 1896

Woman in White]. The crowd took him for Jameson.[18]

This back-handed compliment highlighted the fact that the detective had, perhaps unsurprisingly, seen his waistline increase steadily as the longer hours sitting at his desk coincided with his increased salary and resulting comfortable lifestyle.

The *Victoria* docked at Gravesend on Tuesday, 26th February, where she was boarded by port officials and Inspector Chisholm of the Thames Division. Proceeding slowly to Long Reach, the vessel was finally anchored off Purfleet, and at four o'clock in the afternoon Jameson and his fellow officers were transferred to the tug *Cambria*. Waiting for them was Det. Chief Inspector Swanson, who read the warrant authorising their arrest under the Foreign Enlistment Act. The detective took them into his custody, as the innocent-looking *Cambria* made its way up river, ignored by bystanders, to meet the Thames Police launch *The Watch*, onto which the party was transferred. They subsequently arrived at Waterloo Pier at quarter-past six, in the winter darkness. After a five minute wait for two private omnibuses to arrive from New Scotland

Yard, the party was on its way to the Magistrates' Court.[19]

Ten minutes later the prisoners were finally delivered to Bow Street, the loud cheers heralding their arrival from those outside heard by those already seated within the court, who began applauding and stamping their feet, "as if an impatient audience having paid for their seats at a theatre and being kept waiting unduly long for the commencement of the play thought it high time that the curtain should rise."[20]

A further wait of twenty minutes was required, however, as Jameson and his men were taken directly to the police station where they were formally charged

> That they and certain other persons in the month of December, 1895, in South Africa, within her Majesty's dominions, and without the licence of her Majesty, did unlawfully prepare and fit out a military expedition to proceed against the dominions of a certain friendly State, to wit, the South African Republic.[21]

Finally, as the counsel and clerk of the court took their places, the seating reserved for reporters overcrowded, the thirteen prisoners were brought up by Det. Chief Inspector Swanson to a deafening chorus of cheers, with some of the seventy to eighty people in the public gallery standing on their seats in an effort to see Jameson, who, it was reported, although tanned from his time in South Africa, looked nervous and depressed, his eyes cast to the floor.[22]

Sir John Bridge, Bow Street Magistrate of many years standing, entered and took his seat, immediately having to warn that he would clear the court should the disruption continue. Once preliminary legal introductions were made, the names of the defendants were read by gaoler Sergeant White.

Det. Chief Inspector Donald Swanson was then called to the witness box, where he answered questions put to him by Treasury Solicitor Horace Avory as to how and when the arrests had been made, and confirmed that these had been effected in accordance with the warrant issue by that court.

This was the extent of the first remand hearing. All that remained was the question of bail. Magistrate Bridge left the court in no doubt as to the seriousness of the charge:

> The question as to bail is left in my hands, and I am responsible for the way in which that discretion is used. Before I say what I am going to do I have one observation to make. In my opinion there cannot be a graver

offence than the one these men are accused of committing. I do not mean with regard to the facts of this case. I know nothing as to the facts. All I say is that it is a crime of the highest possible gravity, and must be treated as such when one regards the risk which such an offence creates. First of all, there may be a battle in which many valuable lives are lost, and many a home made desolate. Besides that, there is another danger. An offence of this kind – an offence such as is alleged against the prisoners – might lead to a war between two friendly countries. Therefore, it must be treated as a very grave offence.

In an ordinary way, the gravity of offences guides a Magistrate as to whether he should accept bail; but… the chief consideration is whether the accused persons are likely to appear to their bail. I feel that the circumstances of this case are most peculiar. I feel sure that the defendants will come here on the next occasion, and I shall take their own recognisances in £2,000 each to come here in a fortnight.

I have only one other observation to make, and that is to the defendants. I would beg of them for their own sakes, and for the credit of their country, to keep away from places where their presence might raise excitement. I hope they will not appear before the public more than is needful, and not together more than is necessary.[23]

As the announcement was made, another huge cheer erupted within the court from the public gallery, and the prisoners were taken to the court clerk's offices to sign the bail agreements.

As the crowd made their way out of court, and others outside became aware that the day's proceedings were at an end, a large, excited crowd gathered outside Bow Street hoping for a glimpse of Dr. Jameson.

Suddenly, the door opened and two figures dressed in long overcoats and cloth caps emerged into the throng. It was Det. Chief Inspector Swanson and a fellow officer, but the crowd, not for the first time, mistook the detective for Jameson and immediately surrounded the pair, cheering them loudly. Swanson and his companion walked off in the direction of Covent Garden with the mob at their heels, and Jameson took advantage of the distraction to emerge from the court himself, attempting to slip unnoticed into a waiting cab on Long Acre. A few people still remained outside the court, however, and gave a hearty cheer. Those following Swanson stopped in their tracks and came running back, until Jameson was practically hemmed in and had great difficulty in reaching the cab. Once he did so, the driver set off, being forced to crack his whip at the crowd of men who ran behind.[24]

The immense goodwill shown to Dr. Jameson extended to a large number of female admirers. It was reported that on his arrival some 130 letters were waiting for the dashing doctor, many containing offers of marriage. In one, a lady of a good standing wrote that she was "still considered good looking, but that she also had two marriageable daughters, and the gallant doctor might make his choice of the three."[25]

The defendants returned to Bow Street a fortnight later, and on six subsequent occasions, until finally, on 15th June, nine were discharged, with Jameson, Willoughby, Grey, Henry and Robert White and Captain Hon. Charles Coventry, who had arrived from South Africa after the initial Bow Street hearing, being committed for trial, to be held a month later.

In the midst of the Raiders' numerous committal hearings, a call to New Scotland Yard from New Bond Street jeweller Edward Streeter was about to bring to an end the mystery of the theft in New York five months earlier of a large amount of valuable jewellery. Mr. Streeter was the diamond expert whose prompt actions in 1891 had resulted in the arrest of the Modern Alchemist, Edward Pinter.[26]

On 11th April 1896 two men entered his shop, offering a few precious stones for sale. The assistants realised that the pair had no clue as to the real value of the gems and, their suspicions aroused, ascertained that the men had further valuable jewellery at their lodgings. The shop men encouraged them to bring more of these objects in to be viewed, and an appointment was fixed for the following day. Once the mysterious men had left, Mr. Streeter made contact with the police.[27]

The matter was placed in the hands of Det. Chief Inspector Swanson, who realised that the two men may be connected with an unsolved New York robbery. On that occasion, on 27th December the previous year, the American millionaire I. Townsend Burden of the wealthy Troy, New York, family had gone to the opera with his wife, Evelyn Moale, when their house at 5 East 26th Street was broken into and jewellery valued at £20,000 was stolen.

Swanson instructed Det. Inspectors Froest and Hare to attend the New Bond Street jewellers the following day and observe what transpired. The inspectors took Det. Sergeants Shaddock and Allen.[28]

Arriving punctually, the mysterious sellers showed more items from their collection to the jewellers, who in turn discreetly alerted the watching Froest and Hare to their targets.

After some discussion, the two men left the shop empty handed, but their day hadn't ended without incident, for just a few steps along New Bond Street they were stopped by Det. Inspector Hare, who said "We have reason to believe that you are in possession of some diamonds that have been stolen. We are police officers." The men said nothing in reply, and Froest put his hand into the breast coat pocket of one, retrieving an envelope containing two packets of diamonds. The men were taken to Vine Street police station, where they were searched and several valuable items found in their pockets.

One gave his name as William Turner; he was a footman, formerly employed by a gentleman in New York. He gave as an address the King's Arms public house, in Mayfair's Shepherd's Market, where he and the second man had been staying for five days.

When Det. Sergeants Allen and Shaddock called at the King's Arms, they were shown to a room shared by Turner and his accomplice by landlord Mr. G. W. Lander. Under the dressing table they found a bag containing a mass of diamonds, emeralds and other precious stones, along with bracelets, tiaras and other items, all wrapped in a flannel body belt.[29]

It transpired that the second man was William Dunlop, who had, at the time of the New York robbery, been employed as I. Townsend Burden's valet.

News of the capture was telegraphed to the New York Police Department, who requested that Turner and Dunlop be held by their London counterparts while the necessary extradition paperwork could be arranged.[30] Accordingly, on 16th April the two thieves, both in their early twenties, appeared at Marlborough Street Magistrates' Court and were charged with having in their possession 28 diamonds, believed to be stolen, valued at around £3,000. They were remanded for eight days.

In the meantime, Mr. Burden and his wife travelled to England.[31] It was confirmed that all of the stolen articles had been recovered, and the American millionaire stated that he was "glad to have an opportunity of rewarding the skill and fidelity of Scotland Yard by paying over the reward he had promised." The amount of this reward, £2,000, was to be split between Mr. Streeter, Det. Chief Inspector Swanson and Det. Inspectors Froest and Hare, each receiving £500. The latter two were expected to offer a share of their rewards to Allen and Shaddock.

However, Burden left England without supplying the payment, and as soon as he arrived back in New York his attitude to honouring a reward changed completely. Having already received the recovered jewellery, he refused to pay the £100 costs relating to the shipment and insurance of the returned jewels. Several polite letters from Edward Streeter were ignored.³²

Two months later, the London newspapers reported that Turner and Dunlop had pleaded guilty while on trial in New York, and both were imprisoned to nine years' penal servitude.³³

The matter of the missing reward continued.

Firm letters were sent to Burden, who responded saying that he was being sued by people in New York for the amount of the reward. When one of these cases came to court and the plaintiff failed to appear, talk of a compromise was entered into. Burden offered a total of £1,300, promising to send half of this, £650, in cash on the next steamer to London, with the balance to be forwarded once the imminent case against the American had been concluded.³⁴ This offer was agreed to, but it seems that the payments made under this arrangement were not actually made, for on 2nd April 1897 – almost a year after Dunlop and Turner were arrested – the *Daily Mail* reported:

> ...The reward offered by Mr. Burden for the recovery of his stolen jewellery has not yet been paid. At all events Superintendent Swanson, of Scotland Yard, who is the superior of the English officers who made the arrests which led to the recovery of the jewels, has not had his share...

18 months later, Edward Streeter had obviously had enough of waiting for the second payment from Burden, and authorised Charles Oakes of New York to commence proceedings to recover the balance of the reward.³⁵

The mention of Swanson's rank by the *Daily Mail* hinted at a major change at the C.I.D. which had occurred since the arrest of the thieves.

Det. Superintendent John Shore, who had held that rank since replacing Dolly Williamson in 1886, took the decision to retire from the Metropolitan Police and resigned on 31st March 1896, having completed a combined 37 years service. On 15th April his resignation was formally accepted and he was granted a pension of £283 6s 8d per annum.³⁶

Shore would spend two years working as the London representative of the Pinkerton Detective Agency, but not before his home had embarrassingly been burgled on 22nd July while he was enjoying a seaside holiday following his retirement.³⁷ He would be replaced in his Pinkerton role by Frederick Abberline, who himself had resigned from the Metropolitan Police in 1892 and subsequently worked as a private enquiry agent.

The resignation of Shore left a vacancy in an important position within the Criminal Investigation Department, and very few candidates had the required ability and experience. Shore's plans to retire had been known for some weeks, with the newspapers reporting as early as 9th April that

> It is expected that the vacancy... will be filled by the promotion of either Chief Inspector Greenham, now in attendance upon the Queen at Cimiez, or of Chief Inspector Donald Swanson.[38]

Det. Chief Inspector George Greenham, who had accompanied Swanson to the scene of the Harley Street Mystery in 1880, had joined the Metropolitan Police a year after his colleague and had regularly been selected for special duties in relation to the Royal family. He had been promoted Det. Chief Inspector in 1880, specialising in large-scale forgeries and robberies.[39]

It was Swanson who was selected, on 28th April,[40] three weeks after the arrests of Dunlop and Turner. He was 47-years-old, and had just become the top detective in the country.

The following day the *Pall Mall Gazette* reported the appointment:

> It is understood that Chief Inspector Swanson has been appointed to the position of the Senior Superintendent of the Criminal Investigation Department, Scotland Yard, in the place of Mr. John Shore, who has retired. This is an important position in the department, and no one is more worthy to fill the post than Mr. Swanson.[41]

A Police Order of 30th April 1896 confirmed the changes, with John Shore's pension starting from 1st May. Donald Swanson would begin his new role on the same date, receiving a yearly salary of £400.

Det. Inspector Henry Moore, temporary Chief Inspector since 27th September 1895, was made permanent in Swanson's place. Det. Inspector Henry Marshall was promoted Det. Chief Inspector (temporary), Det. Inspector Alfred Leach was advanced 1st Class and transferred to Central Office,[42] as was Det. Inspector Arthur Hare.[43]

Det. Chief Inspector Greenham returned to his Royal duties but, probably recognising his one chance of promotion had passed, within four months had resigned on a pension.[44]

Almost immediately, the new Detective Superintendent was called upon to look into the mysterious disappearance of two large baskets from the Ostend to Dover mail packet boat. When the *Albert* arrived at Dover on the morning of 11th May, it was noticed that the baskets, containing several registered parcels containing goods believed to be worth in excess of £6,000,[45] were missing.

It was reported that

> How or where the robbery was effected remains for the present a mystery. As soon as the matter became known the Scotland Yard authorities were communicated with, and during the whole of yesterday Superintendent Donald Swanson and his officers were investigating the affair. It is believed that Continental thieves are at the bottom of the affair. Be that as it may, it is certain that this is the most successful mail robbery that has been effected for some years past.[46]

Perhaps as a sign of the new regime, it took less than four hours for the matter to be resolved,[47] when it was discovered that the missing parcels were in fact still at Ostend, having failed to have been placed on the *Albert* with the rest of the post.[48]

This false alarm provided some light relief before the opening of the trial of the Jameson Raiders, on 20th July.

By this time the British public were better educated about the Raid than seven months earlier, when they had cheered Jameson and his men to the rafters, and now recognised the gravity of the situation which Magistrate Sir John Bridge had underlined at the opening of the Bow Street hearing. Both press and public agreed that punishment must be made, although not too severe.

Following a seven day trial at the Royal Courts of Justice, the Raiders were found guilty. Leander Jameson was sentenced to fifteen months' imprisonment, Willoughby to ten, Robert White to seven, and Grey, Henry White and Coventry to five months each. They were sent at first to Wormwood Scrubs, but shortly afterwards transferred to Holloway Gaol where they were treated as 'first class misdemeanants' and allowed to wear their own clothes.[49]

Right from the start of his sentence, concerns were raised over Jameson's health. On arrival at Holloway, it was noted that he was suffering from chronic indigestion and palpitations of the heart, and was severely depressed, supposedly worrying over the welfare of his fellow prisoners. Dr. James Scott, the medical officer at Holloway, noted that the haemorrhoids from which Jameson had been suffering for some years had been aggravated by the inactivity of prison life, and the resultant pain was bad enough for the patient to request an operation, which was performed on 19th November.⁵⁰

Over the following ten days, correspondence between the Prison Commission and the Secretary of State debated Jameson's declining health. On 30th November, a confidential letter to the Chairman of the Prison Commission instructed him to release Dr. Jameson on medical grounds, as soon as it was possible to remove him safely. Three days later, the prisoner was gently lifted from his bed and placed on a stretcher, taken to a waiting ambulance and then transported to a nursing home.⁵¹

While it appeared that Jameson was growing weaker still and in danger of becoming seriously ill, a visit by his old friend Cecil Rhodes immediately lifted his spirits, and he slowly began to recover.

By the time a government inquiry into the Raid began early the following year, Jameson was strong enough to appear, telling a Select Committee comprising fifteen members of the House of Commons⁵² that

> Of course in a thing of this kind, I perfectly recognise that the proper thing would have been to tell the High Commissioner; but then I would never have entertained the subject if I was going to do a proper thing. I know perfectly well that as I have not succeeded, the natural thing has happened; but I also know that if I had succeeded I should have been forgiven.⁵³

The work of Swanson and Froest was recognised by Director of Public Prosecutions the Hon. Hamilton Cuffe, who after the Raiders' imprisonment, wrote to Commissioner Edward Bradford expressing his

> appreciation of the services of Superintendent Swanson and the officers who, under his directions, carried out the duty of arresting and bringing the Defendants to the court. Superintendent Swanson was of the greatest possible assistance to me subsequently in arranging as to meeting the witnesses and providing for their accommodation in London, and arranging for sending those not required to their destinations.
>
> You were good enough to allow Inspector Froest to accompany Mr. Angus Lewis of this Department to Madeira, to meet and come home in the *Harlech Castle* and assist Mr. Lewis in arranging for the Troopers being sent to their homes on arrival at Plymouth and that officer performed the duties entrusted to him with the zeal and discretion which he has always shown in the work he has done for my Department...

> I am extremely indebted to both these officers – to Superintendent Swanson for his services in the earlier part of the proceedings, and throughout to Inspector Froest, and I shall be obliged if you will convey to them my high appreciation of the manner in which they have carried out the duties entrusted to them.[54]

The ramifications of the failed Raid began almost immediately, with the Matabele Rebellion occurring in March 1896, leading to a Mashona uprising three months later. Tensions between Britain and the Dutch resurfaced and simmered for several years, ultimately resulting in the Second Boer War of October 1899 to May 1902. This animosity was exploited by Kaiser Wilhelm II, who, just days after the Raid, sent a telegram to President Kruger in which he wrote:

> I express to you my sincere congratulations that you and your people, without appealing to the help of friendly powers, have succeeded, by your own energetic action against the armed bands which invaded your country as disturbers of the peace, in restoring peace and in maintaining the independence of the country against attack from without.[55]

When the contents of the telegram were reported in British newspapers the reaction was one of outrage. Relations between Germany and Britain deteriorated, and although Wilhelm II later wrote to Queen Victoria, his grandmother, denying that his words were meant to stir ill-feeling against the country, the incident was the beginning of friction between the countries which culminated in the First World War.

Jameson would return to South Africa to a successful political career. In 1903 he was elected as leader of the Progressive (British) Party in the Cape Colony, and served as Prime Minister of the Cape from 1904 to 1908. He was made a Privy Counsellor in 1907, and served as the leader of the Unionist Party (South Africa) from its founding in 1910 until 1912, when he returned to England. Jameson died at his London home in November 1917 and was laid to rest in a vault at Kensal Green cemetery. In 1920 his body was transported to Rhodesia, where it was buried in a grave at Malindidzimu Hill close to that of his great friend Cecil Rhodes, who himself died in 1902.[56]

Leander Starr Jameson would later become immortalised when Rudyard Kipling, who had become a close friend of both Rhodes and Jameson in the last years of the nineteenth century, was inspired by the latter's character to write his much-loved poem, *If-*.[57] Voted in 1995 and 2009 Britain's favourite poem,[58] it is doubtful how many know that the inspiration behind the uplifting work was a man who, through his own recklessness, took his country to the brink of war in the name of imperialism.

Swanson's role as Detective Superintendent was very different to his days as an active inspector. It was his job now to ensure the smooth running of the C.I.D., to oversee the running of cases under investigation by the department and to liaise directly with his superior, Assistant Commissioner (Crime) Robert Anderson.

It also fell upon the Scot to meet and greet visiting dignitaries and reporters, as happened when William Drysdale, the well-known journalist from the *New York Times*, visited London in July 1897 with a travelling companion, a month after arrangements for the proposed payment of the Burden reward had been made.

Far from conducting his various invitations with respect and politeness, Drysdale would later report on his visit under the banner "Sightseeing in London: Glances at things which all who visit the English metropolis are expected to look at". After spending some time viewing "those dreadful things called the sights of London", the American was ushered into the 'private den' of Det. Superintendent Swanson courtesy of a letter of introduction supplied by the New York Police Department.

While Swanson was undoubtedly courteous to the reporter, the only part of their meeting published was the detective's apology that he could not

> ...show you our Rogues' Gallery, for under our system that is never shown to anyone. The theory is that the criminals whose pictures we have may reform and lead respectable lives, and that it is not fair to them to make the public familiar with their faces. When they do reform no hint is given by the police of what their past has been. We punish an officer severely who makes any disclosures about the past life of a reformed criminal.

The sniffy Drysdale responded later in print saying that he hadn't wanted to see the Gallery anyway, it being Swanson's idea in the first place, and that in any case "there is hardly anything in the world that can more easily be dispensed with that the sight of a lot of murderers and burglars."

Swanson put the reporter in the hands of Det. Sergeant Allen, who would show the visitors around Bow Street Magistrates' Court the following day. At this Drysdale brightened up, primarily because of Allen's involvement in the Burden jewels case – a classic example of a reporter being interested only in what is local to them.⁵⁹

Det. Superintendent Swanson's respect for the reformed criminal was mirrored by his concern for his subordinates, even when they had to be disciplined, as recalled by Det. Inspector John Sweeney of Special Branch, who described Swanson as "one of the best class of officers":

> Several times he has had occasion to speak with me shortly after some individual has been reduced in rank or otherwise severely punished, and I have always felt that he was, if possible, feeling more pain than the man punished.⁶⁰

This characteristic – the kindly disposition despite seniority – had been recognised by Swanson's former Headteacher James Waters almost 30 years earlier.

It was a period in which many long-serving officers of the Criminal Investigation Department severed their ties with Scotland Yard. As the positions of Commissioner and Assistant Commissioner were still filled by 'gentlemen' with military or public school backgrounds, there was no prospect of advancement for an officer coming up through the ranks beyond the rank of Detective Superintendent,⁶¹ and many decided to retire on a pension after serving the required 25 years' service, and thus still in the prime of life.

First of these to draw their pension, in October 1897, was Det. Chief Inspector Frederick Jarvis, who had attended 32 Smith Street with Donald Swanson as the latter arrested Percy Lefroy Mapleton. Jarvis had gone on to enjoy a hugely successful career, being involved in investigating the Dynamite campaign of the 1880s, and in July 1892 he had been sent to America and Canada to investigate the background of Lambeth Poisoner Dr. Thomas Neill Cream.⁶² In the years prior to his retirement Jarvis had been involved in the investigation of numerous high level bank forgeries.

Frederick Jarvis was soon followed by Det. Chief Inspector Henry Marshall, who had joined the Detective Department at the same time as Donald Swanson and who had investigated the suspicious house in Knightsbridge with the Scot in 1883, as well as taking charge of the Adelaide Bartlett poisoning case and investigating many other infamous crimes.⁶³

Three months after Marshall's retirement came that of Det. Inspector Charles Nutkins, with whom he had worked closely on the Muswell Hill murder case of 1896.⁶⁴ Before that, in 1882, Nutkins had assisted in the apprehension of Thomas Orrock, killer of P.C. George Cole at Dalston.

Det. Chief Inspector Frederick Jarvis
from the Buckingham Advertiser and Free Press,
2nd October 1892

Det. Inspector Charles Nutkins
from Lloyd's Weekly Newspaper,
23rd November 1890

His steady methods had earned him the nickname of 'Nil Desperandum Nutkins' amongst his colleagues.[65] On 1st October 1898, at New Scotland Yard, Det. Superintendent Swanson made a presentation to Nutkins to mark his retirement from the force, the occasion attended by many prominent detectives.[66]

Before the century was out, Det. Chief Inspector Henry Moore, the senior detective at New Scotland Yard behind Swanson, also decided to leave the force and draw his pension. Moore, who had joined the Metropolitan Police in 1869, had been stationed in W, Y and P Divisions before being transferred to Central Office in 1888. He was seconded to Whitechapel in September of that year, and had replaced Det. Chief Inspector Frederick Abberline as the officer on the ground in charge of the investigation into the Jack the Ripper murders.

At his retirement presentation at New Scotland Yard on 14th November 1899, Moore was presented by Det. Superintendent Swanson with a tea service from the C.I.D.'s inspectors, and a gold hunter and match box from detective sergeants and constables.[67]

The impact which the departure of these senior offices would have was noted in the press, with the *Daily Telegraph* commenting:

One by one, familiar faces are disappearing from the detective branch of

New Scotland Yard... The latest officer to retire on a pension is Mr. Henry Moore, senior chief inspector, who has just completed thirty and a half years' service in the Metropolitan Police. He leaves behind him one or two colleagues only who can recall the early history of the department subsequent to its reorganisation by Mr. Howard Vincent, as he then was, when the late Superintendent Williamson was still the occupant of the little room on the first floor of the isolated brick building in the middle of Great Scotland Yard...

Williamson, the level-headed, was succeeded by the late Superintendent Shore, a man who was credited with an intimate knowledge of the criminal world, but who upon his resignation developed an extraordinary bad memory for faces. Shore was replaced by the present very efficient Superintendent, Mr. Donald Swanson, who was also contemporary with Mr. Williamson.

Chief Inspector Hare remains too, with one or two others who were juniors in the dynamite days; but otherwise the detective work has passed into the hands of a new school of men, and it may be said that they are more strictly under the control of their department chief than was formally the case.[68]

This new school included men such as Frank Froest and Alfred Leach, who would both go on to enjoy highly successful careers, taking the Criminal Investigation Department into the twentieth century.

But their training began under the watchful eye of Donald Swanson, for whom there was still time to be involved in one final celebrated case.

NINETEEN

Return of the Duchess

While many of Donald Swanson's contemporaries were heading into retirement, the Scot's career was being widely celebrated. As the twentieth century dawned, the Detective Superintendent featured in *Some Crime Stories: The Careers of One Hundred Clever and Cunning Criminals* by Charles Windust, the Crime Investigator for the *Weekly Dispatch*.

In a volume in the series featuring 24 of these so-called 'clever and cunning criminals', Windust wrote of Edward Pinter, the Modern Alchemist, and his attempt to defraud Edward Streeter of £40,000 in 1891. In this account Pinter was awarded the nickname 'Gold Dust Teddy', but it is Windust's description of Swanson, whom he called "England's greatest detective", which no doubt drew admiration from his readers:

> Mr. Swanson is a Scotchman – a well-educated and cultured officer who has performed yeoman service in the Department at Scotland Yard to which he was attached, and of which he is now the chief. There is an entire absence about this officer – whose personality cannot be without interest to those who read these pages – of the detective of fiction personified in the wonderful creation of Conan Doyle – Sherlock Holmes, whose tall, attenuated form will ever remain that of the ideal detective of the century. Mr. Swanson is a handsome man of sturdy build, with a quick wit, and a resourceful mind – a thorough man of the world – though not all the criminal experiences of many years have succeeded in altering an iota his kindly disposition.[1]

If the increasingly-frequent changes within the Criminal Investigation Department felt like the end of an era within the Metropolitan Police, that a new dawn was breaking generally was underlined on Tuesday, 22nd January 1901, when Queen Victoria died at Osborne House, Cowes.

The 81-year-old monarch had arrived on the Isle of Wight to spend

Christmas at Osborne House as per her recent custom, but had been ill for several days when, at eight o'clock on the morning of the 22nd, a bulletin was issued which revealed that Victoria showed signs of "diminishing strength"; at noon it was announced that the Queen was sleeping, and that several members of the Royal family had arrived at Cowes. A final bulletin at 4.00pm by physicians James Reid, R. Douglas Powell and Thomas Barlow announced that Victoria was "slowly sinking".

The next news was a formal announcement by Victoria's son and heir:

> Osborne, 6.45 – My beloved Mother has just passed away surrounded by her Children and Grandchildren.
>
> (Signed) Albert Edward.[2]

As the curtain was brought down on the longest reign of any British monarch – 63 years, seven months and two days[3] – an aristocratic lady not seen in public for almost twenty-five years was about to make a reappearance.

Just six days before the old Queen had passed away, a telegram from Det. Superintendent Donald Swanson was wired across the Atlantic to the New York offices of the world-famous Pinkerton Detective Agency. The message informed the recipients that, as a consequence of recent discussions between the American detectives and New Scotland Yard, plans were to be put in place to finally secure the return of a long-missing work of art.

A subsequent cable sent by Swanson in March stated that a representative of a certain London company had left England on board the steamer *Etruria*, bound for New York. On arrival he was met by a representative of the Pinkertons and directed to the Chicago offices of William Pinkerton, where he arrived on 27th March.[4]

The following morning the Englishman met with William Pinkerton at the latter's offices and concluded a pre-agreed financial arrangement. He then returned to his rooms at the Auditorium Hotel, where he waited nervously along with his wife and the American detective:[5]

> As the hour approached... I noticed Mr. Pinkerton become more and more nervous, even more nervous than I was myself. About a quarter of an hour before the time appointed [we] adjourned to the room upstairs, where it had been agreed that the picture would be delivered.

C. Morland Agnew in later life
Courtesy Andy Ramus

The few minutes we spent behind the closed door were just a trifle nerve-shattering. By-and-by there came a knock at the door.

"Come in," said Mr. Pinkerton, and the door opened. An adult messenger was standing in the doorway, carrying a brown paper roll in his arm. "Mr. Agnew?" he queried. "Yes," I replied, and held out my hand. The messenger handed me the roll in silence, as if he had been charged to deliver the most common-place message in the world, at once turned on his heel and left the room, closing the door quietly behind him...

Save for the slightest trace of a scar on the rim of the hat the picture is perfect, the face, hands, and body of the portrait are absolutely untouched."[6]

With these words, Mr. Charles Morland Agnew, second son of William Agnew, confirmed that Gainsborough's *The Duchess of Devonshire* had been safely recovered, a quarter of a century after its theft from the family's gallery on Bond Street.

Wasting no time returning to England, Agnew travelled again on board the *Etruria*, and docked at Liverpool on Monday, 8th April. Apart from his wife, it is unlikely that any of the other 191 passengers knew that on board was a very valuable cargo.[7]

Rumours of the painting's whereabouts had circulated for years, but it wasn't until 1893 – seventeen years after it had been stolen – that a name was given to the thief, at least publicly.

On 24th July 1893 the *Pall Mall Gazette* published a story in which it claimed to have sent an emissary to interview a prisoner at Louvain gaol, Belgium, who claimed to have stolen the *Duchess*. The man's name was Adam Worth.

A week after the story was published, the *Indépendance Belge* poured scorn on the *Gazette*'s claims by reporting that the man who had interviewed Worth, a Mr. Marsend, had been fed a false story about the stolen painting by the prisoner, and the *Pall Mall Gazette* had therefore been 'hoaxed' into believing it. According to the Belgian newspaper, when Worth heard that the *Gazette* had published the story he went into "fits of laughter".[8]

But the suspicion attached to Adam Worth refused to go away. In fact, New Scotland Yard had known for some time that he was responsible, and when a Mr. Frank Bowden, a partner of a company from whom two valuable paintings were stolen in July 1896, visited Det. Superintendent Swanson at his offices he was told that *The Duchess of Devonshire* was "known to be rolled up in a New York mansion, and is subject to return if a sufficient sum is paid for it".[9]

Following Worth's release from Louvain gaol in 1897 Det. Superintendent Swanson sent a cablegram to William Pinkerton confirming this belief:

> I have learned from several sources that Adam Worth alias Raymond on his release from 7 years' penal servitude in Belgium sailed from Antwerp to the United States, and a New York officer named Cuff who is here on an extradition matter corroborated the information and added that they were aware of his presence in New York. I still retain the belief that Worth has control of the Gainsbro' picture which has been a "White Elephant".[10]

Just who was Adam Worth?

In his *Famous Crimes and Criminals* (1924), C. L. McCluer Stevens claimed that Sir Robert Anderson (by then deceased) had once told him that Worth was the cleverest and most resourceful criminal he'd met, supposedly saying "He was the Napoleon of the criminal world. None other could hold a candle to him".

In his *Criminals and Crime: Some Facts and Suggestions* (1907), in which he proposed that they were in reality very few 'criminal masterminds', Anderson certainly stated that Worth's "schemes were

Napoleonic", and said that he was "the most eminent of the criminal fraternity" in his time as Assistant Commissioner.[11]

Adam Worth was born in 1884 in eastern Germany to Jewish parents who emigrated to Cambridge, Massachusetts when their son was just five years old. Acquiring the nickname 'Little Adam' due to his short stature, Worth ran away from home at the age of fourteen and after some years in Boston drifted to New York, where he took a job as a clerk in a fashionable New York store, the only honest employment he would have in his entire life. It lasted one month. When the Civil War broke out Worth enlisted into the Union army with the New York Light Artillery. Despite being just 17-years-old, Worth said that he was twenty. Later wounded at the Second Battle of Bull Run, Worth was mistakenly pronounced dead three weeks later on 25th September 1862.

The mistake provided him with the means to reinvent himself, and he became what was known as a 'bounty jumper', meaning he and countless others would enlist into a regiment under an assumed name, collect the bounty on offer and then promptly desert.

The Declaration of Peace in August 1866 brought an end to this stage of Worth's criminal career. He drifted once more to New York, where he joined the thriving criminal fraternity in the Bowery by becoming a pickpocket. Aged just twenty, Worth established a team of 'pocket-dippers' of varying ages, with himself as the head.

Just as his career seemed to be on the up, he was caught stealing a package from an express delivery truck and sentenced to three years' imprisonment at the notorious Sing Sing prison. He would not serve much of his time, however, managing to escape and slipping back into the anonymity of the Bowery.

Now realising that pickpocketing brought potentially heavy consequences for a relatively small reward, Worth reformed his gang, but with the intention of committing burglaries and other thefts. He soon attempted to step up another level, to bank robberies.

In the late 1860s Worth undertook a number of large-scale robberies, his first success being the theft of $20,000 worth of bonds from an insurance company in Cambridge, Massachusetts. With this and subsequent thefts, Worth took the spoils to notorious New York fence Fredericka 'Marm' Mandelbaum, who could sell on just about anything, in return for 10% to the actual thief. It was estimated that over two decades from 1862 she handled between five and ten million dollars. Through her regular soirees, Marm Mandelbaum would provide Adam Worth's introduction to the criminal big league as he met fellow crooks, including Maximilian Schoenbein alias Max Shinburn, recognised as

Left: Adam Worth, alias Harry Raymond and Right: 'Piano' Charley Bullard from "Adam Worth, Alias 'Little Adam'. Theft and Recovery of Gainsborough's 'Duchess of Devonshire'" Swanson family archive

one of the very best bank burglars, and 'Piano' Charley Bullard, the musically-talented, multi-lingual criminal playboy who would be recognised by Donald Swanson in Toronto and subsequently arrested by local police in 1879.

Bullard and Shinburn had joined forces in 1869 with another professional thief, Ike Marsh, to relieve the Ocean National Bank of more than $100,000 after tunnelling through the basement.

Later the same year Ike Marsh and Piano Charley teamed up once again to rob the Hudson River Railroad Express as it travelled from Buffalo to Grand Central Station, emptying the on-board safe and jumping off as the train went through the Bronx with $100,000 stuffed into carpet bags.

The Pinkerton Detective Agency was called in, and they traced Bullard and Marsh to a high-class hotel in Toronto. They were extradited back to America, and remanded at White Plains, New York. They did not have to languish in their cells for long before they were rescued by Worth and Shinburn, who dug through a wall to release the pair.

It strengthened the bond between Worth and Bullard, who went into partnership.

Over the coming years they robbed several banks, sometimes with the help of Marsh and Shinburn.

When Worth, Bullard and Marsh tunnelled into the Boylston Bank in Boston and made off with almost a million dollars in cash and bearer bonds in November 1869, it didn't take long for the Pinkertons to discover who was responsible. It was time for the thieves to lie low.

Stuffing cash into false-bottomed trunks, Worth and Piano Charley headed for England under new names: Bullard became 'Charles H. Wells', and Worth 'Henry J. Raymond'. Settling in Liverpool, the wealthy Americans were welcomed with no questions asked.

After robbing a pawnshop, Bullard began to tire of life in Liverpool and, with a new wife in tow, he and Worth made their way south to London, and then, in June 1871, to Paris, where they opened The American Bar, which proved incredibly popular, especially with the criminal fraternity in Europe, men such as Max Shinburn, Charles Becker, Joe Chapman and 'Little' Joe Elliott, many of whom joined Worth and Bullard in their schemes.

The Pinkertons continued to keep an eye on The American Bar, largely with the assistance of their European agents. Eventually, in 1873, William Pinkerton himself casually walked into the bar and ordered a drink. Worth joined him and the pair talked over old times, before the private detective announced that he had better be leaving.

It was a simple tactic of letting the criminals know that they were being watched, and it worked. Back home in Chicago, Pinkerton passed on his suspicions that The American Bar was the centre of operations for a foreign criminal enterprise, and recruited overseas police forces including the Met's John Shore in an attempt to force the local French police to close it down, and this happened after a raid, for once not tipped-off. Piano Charley, the legal owner of The American Bar, skipped bail and headed for London, with Adam Worth, Kitty Wells – Charley's wife – and the rest of the gang following on some time later.

Still a wealthy man, Worth rented a mansion close to Clapham Common along with rooms on Piccadilly, and re-established himself as Henry Raymond. Almost immediately he began plotting a series of daring robberies for which he used a network of criminals in the capital. In this way, although he profited from each scheme, he himself was all but immune from prosecution.

It was in this way that, over several years, Adam Worth earned himself the nickname 'the Napoleon of Crime', as one audacious robbery after another was carried out.

Through the vast amounts stolen Worth was able to purchase a 110-

foot yacht, which he named the *Shamrock*. In 1874 the gang sailed to South America and the West Indies, where, at Jamaica, they stole $10,000 from a warehouse safe before heading out again to the open seas. It was another case to be added to the growing list held by the Pinkertons.

Worth now lived the life of a wealthy English gentleman, which infuriated John Shore, who had a file on the criminal equally as large as William Pinkerton's, but who also was unable to find any proof of the American's involvement.

In 1875, however, Worth's idyllic world imploded when a Europe-wide forgery operation involving Charles Becker, Joe Chapman, Little Joe Elliott and another gang member named Carl Sessiovitch collapsed. All four were arrested and convicted to serve seven years' hard labour in a Constantinople prison. It took several months and a large amount of cash in bribes, but eventually Becker, Elliott and Sessiovitch were released to be met by Worth, waiting on board the *Shamrock*. Joe Chapman was not so lucky; held in a different part of the prison, he was to see out his full sentence.

To make matters worse, with Worth engaged in attempting to free the quartet, Piano Charley took himself off to New York and was promptly arrested for the 1869 robbery at Boston's Boylston Bank, being sentenced to twenty years at Concord State Penitentiary, Massachusetts.

This was the state of affairs in April 1876, when a plan was hatched to raise funds by means of a forged cheque. The skilled Charles Becker created the forgery, and Little Joe Elliott cashed the cheque without any problems at the London and Westminster Bank. It was now time to change the bank notes before the forgery was noticed, and for this part of the plan Worth recruited his brother, John, whom he dispatched to Paris with instructions to convert the notes at a busy Bureau de Change on the Grand Boulevard. However, John Worth was not as blessed with intelligence as his brother, and went instead to the offices of Meyer & Co. Having already fallen for one of Becker's forgeries in the past and been warned by Shore to look out for English notes of a large denomination, the bank wasted no time in alerting the French police, who arrested John Worth. He was extradited and held in Newgate gaol.

Adam Worth found himself in a predicament. Unable to implicate himself in the forgery, he could not post the £3,000 bail himself despite being comfortably able to afford to. He needed a plan whereby a seemingly respectable person could post his brother's bail, who would then be spirited back to America.[12]

And this is when Worth saw announcements that Gainsborough's *The*

Duchess of Devonshire, recently won at auction by William Agnew, was to be exhibited at their Bond Street gallery.

Immediately, Worth saw a way of using the world's most famous painting to achieve the release of his brother. By taking control of the Gainsborough, he thought, he could force William Agnew to post John Worth's bail, thus keeping himself and 'Harry Raymond' out of things. He would persuade a crooked solicitor to visit John in Newgate, claiming to represent him, and covertly hand over a slim cutting from the canvas which would serve as 'proof' for the next part of the plan. The solicitor would then contact William Agnew, saying his client currently languishing in Newgate would be able to furnish him with information regarding the stolen painting in return for his help.

Although this legal advisor has never been identified, a snippet of information published in *The Graphic* some years later claimed that a man named Edwin James, a disbarred solicitor who in 1876 had offices in Old Bond Street almost opposite Agnew's Gallery, had been approached by "certain international thieves" who had asked him to undertake exactly the plan outlined above. According to *The Graphic*'s correspondent, James said he had declined the proposal.[13]

Worth enlisted the assistance of two of his gang, the American Little Joe Elliott to act as lookout, and an English thief who would assist in the actual theft.

Late at night on Thursday, 25th May, the gang made their way to Agnew's gallery. It was a foggy night, perfect for the activity which they were about to undertake.

Little Joe stopped on the corner of Old Bond Street and began his watch.

The other two men continued to Agnew's, where the tall, powerfully-built Englishman stood directly outside, below a second floor window. "Little Adam", at just 5ft 4in, was easily able to climb up onto the Englishman's shoulders and then climb up to the top of the awning, waiting for the all-clear before prising open the window with a chisel. Once inside, Worth climbed a stepladder and cut the *Duchess* from its frame, then rolled it up and simply passed it down through the window to his English accomplice.

Then, as silently as they had arrived, the gang slipped into the fog.

There is some confusion as to the identity of the Englishman. In the Pinkertons' booklet telling the story of the theft he is named as John 'Junka' Phillips, a notorious travelling thief who had been responsible for countless robberies across Europe and in America; he had once been transported to Australia but escaped and made his way back to the Continent.

However, in both *Criminals and Crime* (1907) and *The Lighter Side of My Official Life* (1910) Assistant Commissioner Robert Anderson names the accomplice as "an old sinner" named Powell, a claim which had already appeared in newspaper stories published just prior to Worth's release from Louvain gaol in 1897.[14] And in Donald Swanson's personal copy of the Pinkerton booklet, alongside the passage describing Worth climbing up onto Junka's shoulders, the detective noted in pencil "No. It was Old Powell on whose shoulders he climbed."[15]

Sensibly lying low for several days after the theft, Worth waited before putting the next part of the plan into action (although it is possible that they approached Edwin James as described above and, having their approaches rebuffed, spent some time searching for another suitable solicitor to act on their behalf).

In the meantime, the solicitor retained to defend John Worth discovered that his client had been extradited under an incorrect charge, in that he should have been arrested as an accessory after the fact rather than a principal in the forgery. This legal loophole resulted in the prisoner being released and told to leave the country within 30 days – he didn't need telling twice.

This put Adam Worth in a difficult position; he had the Gainsborough hidden away and no longer needed it, but had no way of disposing of it. With no immediate solution presenting itself, this would continue for a great many years.

Yet it would only take a year for the truth behind the theft to reach the ears of both the Pinkerton National Detective Agency and Scotland Yard.

Little Joe Elliott, having received money from Worth for his share of the Gainsborough, returned to New York, where he married Kate Castleton, the well-known comic opera singer, with whom he had lived for several years while in America. Elliott was soon arrested for getting involved in a $64,000 forgery on the Union Trust Co., and was convicted and sentenced to seven years' imprisonment in April 1877. Much like Harry Benson offering to give information on Scotland Yard's corrupt Detective Department in return for his release at almost exactly the same time, Elliott told everything he knew about the painting's theft to Robert Pinkerton, who passed on the information to John Shore. Although this gave the English and American detectives valuable knowledge, for Joe Elliott no help could be given, as he had sold out his share of the painting and therefore had no say on having it returned to its owners. He would serve his full sentence.

With it now known that Adam Worth had masterminded the theft, it was a case of obtaining the evidence. In the meantime he continued with his career, eventually travelling across the Atlantic with the *Duchess* hidden in the false bottom of a trunk. Once in America, the painting was placed in another specially-made trunk for protection, and was held in storage in Brooklyn, then New York, and then finally to Boston, where it lay undisturbed for a number of years while Worth continued to mastermind a number of robberies and forgeries in the United States, South Africa and Europe.

Eventually, in October 1892 he was caught in Belgium after attempting a mail robbery in Liege. He was convicted for the first and only time and sentenced to seven years in penal servitude, which he would spent in Louvain gaol.

It was during this spell that Mr. Marsend visited Worth to enquire about *The Duchess of Devonshire*, as reported in the *Pall Mall Gazette*.

Worth was released four years into his sentence.[16]

As Donald Swanson had learned by the time of his 1897 telegram, upon his release from prison Worth had sailed to America. In early 1899 he was in Chicago, and on 10th January went to the Ashland Boulevard home of William Pinkerton. Finding the detective absent, away at his offices on Fifth Avenue, Worth left a letter with the strict instructions that it was private communication and not to be opened by anyone else.

At 12.28pm Pinkerton received a telegram at his office from 'Roy', simply stating: "Letter awaiting you at house; send for it."

Having called home and arranged for the letter to be forwarded, Pinkerton found himself reading a request for a meeting with Worth, in order to discuss "a matter that might be to our mutual benefit". Writing under the name "H. Raymond", the thief asked the private detective to give a sign that he was willing and able to meet to discuss the matter, by placing an advertisement in the personal notices column of the *Chicago Daily News* stating simply: "Assurance Given. W. A. P." Should such assurance be received, Worth would contact Pinkerton immediately and arrange an appointment.[17]

Pinkerton did as he was asked that afternoon, and at eleven o'clock the following morning received a telephone call from the Napoleon of Crime. Reassured that he could visit the Pinkerton office with impunity, five minutes later Worth was sitting opposite William Pinkerton. He was 55-years-old, physically weak from years spent in prison and financially destitute.

He had come to see whether the Agency could assist in the disposal of *The Duchess of Devonshire*. Worth told Pinkerton that he wanted both himself and the private detective to make some money out of the painting being returned to the Agnews; he was told that under no circumstances could the Agency take any money, and furthermore they would not do anything to jeopardise their good working relationship with New Scotland Yard.[18]

Pinkerton read out the statement of Joe Elliott from the late 1870s regarding the theft of the Gainsborough, with Worth correcting minor errors. He then proceeded to narrate his life story, concluding by telling William Pinkerton that he was free to make use of it how he saw fit, once Worth himself was dead.

Once the criminal had left his offices, William Pinkerton sent the confession to his brother Robert, who in turn wired the information to Det. Superintendent Donald Swanson at New Scotland Yard. The Scottish detective now had the evidence which had been missing for so many years. Swanson handed confirmation of Worth's involvement to Det. Chief Inspector Frank Froest, who had taken charge of the case for several years.

Froest discussed the matter with Agnew's solicitor Sir George Lewis, along with the accompanying demand for a payment for the safe return of the painting. Having been the victim of several hoaxes in the years that the Gainsborough had been missing, Lewis and the Agnews were understandably reluctant to open the purse strings too eagerly, and after drifting for some time the deal was abandoned.

At this stage a mutual acquaintance of Worth and Pinkerton, Patrick Sheedy, intervened. Sheedy, a respected professional gambler, was well-known in both London and America and was therefore able to approach New Scotland Yard with a proposal. On hearing that the Agnews refused to pay the amount asked for, Sheedy suggested to Froest that he could arrange for the painting to be returned for free, on the condition that he would be allowed to exhibit it for four months. This, too, was rejected by Lewis & Lewis, but a second proposal from Sheedy a month later, that he be allowed to make a steel engraving of the picture, seemingly convinced them that he really was able to facilitate its return.

They instructed Donald Swanson to put the wheels in motion, and on 19th January 1901 the Superintendent cabled the Pinkertons telling them to begin plans for a handover. In it, he said that the terms requested by Worth would be agreed to, providing an identifying witness confirmed that this was indeed the missing *Duchess*.

This is how C. Morland Agnew found himself anxiously waiting in his room in the Auditorium Hotel, Chicago, on 28th March.[19]

The painting's arrival back on English shores was eagerly anticipated, but this didn't extend to all aspects of the Duchess's style – a fashion note bemoaned the likely increase in popularity of the large Gainsborough hat, last seen in the 1870s. By the turn of the century small bonnets were being heavily promoted for ladies of a more petite frame, complaining that there was nothing "so unbecoming to the short and stout as a large Gainsborough hat, especially when worn at anything like an extravagant angle, as in the picture."[20]

Another travelling from America to London who would have a huge impact on the future of the painting was J. Pierpont Morgan, the steel magnate, who arrived on board the *Teutonic* and docked at Liverpool on 10th April,[21] two days after Morland Agnew stepped off the *Etruria*.

It was soon reported that Morgan had joined Senator W. A. Clark of Montana in making an offer to Agnew's for the *Duchess*,[22] and eventually Lockett Agnew, Morland Agnew's cousin who had taken over the day-to-day running of the gallery, confirmed that an agreement had been reached with Pierpont Morgan. The amount was reported as either £25,000 or £30,000 – either way, a tidy profit for the gallery.[23]

Reaction to the American purchasing such a 'national treasure' was met with alarm in some quarters, who, while commending the Agnews on their business sense, complained that

> since the picture has been sold to the American millionaire, it is to be supposed that Londoners, who were simply thirsting to pay their shillings for a view of the Duchess, will be baulked of their desire. So far as the British public is concerned, the picture might as well have remained at the bottom of a trunk in Chicago, for it will now probably go to adorn Mr. Morgan's town mansion in New York.
>
> This purchase, indeed, opens up an alarming prospect of what will happen to our English masterpieces when the Yankee millionaires have acquired a taste for them.[24]

In fact, Morgan did allow his acquisition to be displayed at Agnew's gallery for a spell, as part of an exhibition that November in aid of the Artists' General Benevolent Institution.[25] A reviewer commented that "hundreds of connoisseurs" had visited daily, and that the canvas was "a most captivating one", the subject's "sensual beauty" being brought out by a fresh coat of varnish.[26] *The Duchess of Devonshire* stayed on display for some weeks before being retired to Morgan's Kensington mansion, where it would remain for a decade.[27]

Despite agreeing to display the painting, the American steadfastly refused to allow any engraving to be made, much to the disappointment of C. Morland Agnew, who had made a promise to William Pinkerton that he would supply copies of the painting in thanks for the Agency's part in the recovery. Agnew's letter of apology was met with good heart by William Pinkerton, whose reply concluded:

> I hope you will never have the misfortune to lose another picture, or any other valuables, but if you do, I trust that we may be the medium of their return.[28]

Just a few short weeks after Gainsborough's masterpiece was admired once more by London's public, the man who had stolen the painting a quarter of a century before passed away quietly at his home near Regent's Park. In an increasingly poor state of health, Adam Worth had followed the Duchess across the Atlantic and returned to London. The end, on 8th January 1902, was brought about by heart failure and liver disease, no doubt exacerbated by his lifetime of thoroughly enjoying the fruits of his ill-gotten gains.

The Pinkertons wasted no time in taking up Worth's offer of publishing the details of his career and the theft of *The Duchess of Devonshire* after his passing. On 19th August, Robert Pinkerton sent a proof to his brother, explaining:

> We intend to have this history pasted on the back of the Gainsborough pictures which we will give out from time to time to friends of the Agency as an advertisement. I have gone over this story myself and made some corrections; Mr. Dougherty is to read it over and make whatever corrections he can, and then we will have a final proof submitted to us. Meanwhile, I wish you would read this over and see if you have any suggestions to make. If so, mark them right on the proof and return it to me.

William Pinkerton's simple reply was: "I think this article very well gotten up – is very satisfactory."[29]

Details of how the Gainsborough painting had been stolen and subsequently recovered were published by the Pinkertons three months later in a pamphlet simply titled *Adam Worth*, with a second edition quickly appearing in February the following year, with the more descriptive title of *Adam Worth, Alias 'Little Adam'. Theft and Recovery of Gainsborough's 'Duchess of Devonshire'.*[30]

The Preface warned the reader that: "If a fiction writer could conceive such a story, he might well hesitate to write it for fear of being accused of using the wildly improbable."

The British newspapers agreed, commenting that while the credit for the recovery of the painting belonged to the American detectives in conjunction with New Scotland Yard, the Pinkerton booklet gave "an elaborate history of their share in the transaction, which reads like a chapter from Sherlock Holmes".[31]

With Adam Worth described by some as the real-life Moriarty, perhaps that was fitting.

With Gainsborough's masterpiece finally recovered, the press were exuberant with their praise for the Pinkertons and the detectives of New Scotland Yard.

Ironically, at the same time as efforts were underway to recover the painting, one of the most senior of Metropolitan Police officials was the subject of heated debate within the corridors of the Home Office, his reputation diminishing as quickly as that of William Pinkerton was increasing.

Robert Anderson, Assistant Commissioner (Crime), had always been a writer; now, however, his article published in the February 1901 edition of the magazine *The Nineteenth Century and After* had landed him in hot water.

Commenting on what he saw as "Our Absurd System of Punishing Crime", despite reasonably claiming that the major robberies, forgeries and frauds were committed by a select band of professional criminals, Anderson made several criticisms of his own employer:

> ...The fact remains that systematic, organised crime against property is entirely the creature of our present penal system. A single prison would suffice to hold the entire gang of known criminals who now keep the community in a state of siege, and a single wing of any one of our gaols would more than suffice to provide for the band of outlaws who may be described as the aristocracy of crime in England.[32]

It was not the first time that Anderson's indiscreet public comments had been brought to the attention of the Home Office. A decade earlier, Anderson had an article titled "Morality an Act of Parliament" published in the *Contemporary Review* of January 1891. Fortunately for the Assistant Commissioner, no action was taken despite Godfrey

Lushington writing that "Mr Anderson cannot plead ignorance of the rule. He has had experience of it in Sir C. Warren's case & in his own (Le Caron's papers)."

Eventually, the Secretary of State decided that as Anderson's comments were about the Prisons department, where he had not been employed for some years, no action could be taken. But a file was opened on his ongoing breach of Home Office rules, which had been drawn up by Lushington in a Minute dated 27th May 1879:

> The Secretary of State having had his attention called to the question of allowing private publication by officers attached to the Department of books on matters relating to the Department, is of the opinion that the practice may lead to embarrassment, and should in future be discontinued. He desires, therefore, that it should be considered a Rule of the Home Department, that no officer should publish any Work relating to the Department, unless the sanction of the Secretary of State has been previously obtained for the purpose.

Ironically, this very Minute had been circulated as Standing Order No. 63 by Robert Anderson on 22nd July 1879 during his time as Prison Department Secretary.

After some discussion regarding the February 1901 article, it was suggested to Under-Secretary of State Charles Stuart-Wortley that

> a letter should be written either officially – or (better as I think) by yourself to the Commissioner calling attention to the article and expressing regret that it should have been published by a person in Dr. Anderson's position.

A note written below this, dated 11th February, commented "S. of S. has written to the Commr."[33]

What action was taken by Sir Edward Bradford is unknown, but can be guessed at when it was announced on 19th April that Anderson was to retire, with his replacement already lined up.[34]

If the outgoing Assistant Commissioner was perturbed by the situation, he continued to fulfil his duties. The day before the announcement, Anderson was at Exeter Hall on the Strand attending the conference of the International Christian Police Association, which for eighteen years had sought to promote the spiritual welfare of policemen and their families by providing religious and educational classes and other social gatherings. Another of its concerns was the Central Police Institute, which provided convalescent accommodation for officers and their dependents including rooms at Adelphi Terrace, the Convalescent Home at Hove, and orphanages at Redhill and Harrogate.[35]

Whatever the truth behind Anderson leaving his position, he would later claim that he retired simply because he wished for a more peaceful life. In fact, his sole complaint was a mild annoyance at not receiving the full pension to which he believed he was entitled.[36] He would have to 'make do' with £900 per annum.[37]

Anderson's replacement as Assistant Commissioner (Crime), to begin duties at the end of May 1901, was Edward Richard Henry, Inspector-General of Police of Bengal. Aged 50, Henry had been born in Shadwell, east London, and educated at Ware, Hertfordshire, before entering the Indian Civil Service in 1873. He subsequently travelled to Allahabad, where he became Assistant Magistrate Collector with the Bengal Taxation Service. By 1891 he was Inspector-General of Bengal,[38] and a year before Anderson's retirement had been seconded to act as head of the Civil Police Department at Johannesburg.[39] Perhaps most famously, however, it had been Edward Henry who had introduced the Galton system of fingerprinting to the Bengal police department, a development which would soon prove to have great repercussions for the Metropolitan Police force itself.[40]

Despite his less than noble departure, the long service of the former Assistant Commissioner was recognised when King Edward announced his first Birthday Honours List on 8th November, with Anderson receiving a K.C.B.[41] Having already been made a C.B.E. in 1896, he was now *Sir* Robert Anderson. Among the many letters of congratulation was one from his former right-hand man at New Scotland Yard, Det. Superintendent Donald Swanson, who wrote:

> It was with real pleasure that I read this morning that my old master was the recipient of honour from H.M. The King. Everybody I have spoken to here is pleased.[42]

While the two men had worked closely together for thirteen years, Anderson's knighthood was the start of a period of personal communication between them which would continue for several years.

Not for Anderson was a retirement spent fishing or gently relaxing. Instead, he continued his lecturing on criminal and Christian matters. Just three weeks after receiving his knighthood, he appeared at the Mission Hall on Little Wild Street, Drury Lane, to give a talk to the assembled patrons at the annual prize-giving meeting of the St. Giles' Christian Mission, a benevolent organisation created in 1869 to provide care to discharged prisoners. It was reported that since the Mission

Lieutenant-Colonel Henry Smith
from the Leeds Mercury, 7th December 1901

Dr. Robert Anderson
from the Aberdeen Weekly Journal, 1st May 1901

had been founded "401,000 free breakfasts have been provided for discharged prisoners, and 104,000 discharged prisoners have been provided with tools, clothing, or employment."[43]

Over the coming years, Anderson's pen would be increasingly busy. Having already written several religious books, the following year would see his *The Bible and Modern Criticism* released. Free from Home Office red tape, he was now able to turn to his other passions – police work and Irish matters. In 1906 *Sidelights on the Home Rule Movement* was published, followed a year later by *Criminals and Crime*. In 1910 Anderson published his autobiography, *The Lighter Side of My Official Life*. In both these latter books the former Assistant Commissioner revealed that, as far as he was concerned, the identity of the miscreant responsible for the Whitechapel murders was known, and that he had been "safely caged" in an asylum.

The claim drew criticism from a contemporary of Anderson's from the City of London Police, who had also retired in 1901 and released his memoirs in 1910.

Lieutenant-Colonel Sir Henry Smith, for eleven years the Commissioner of the City force, retired in December 1901. His own book, *From Constable to Commissioner: The Story of Sixty Years, Most of Them Misspent*, was published by Chatto & Windus nine years later, shortly after Anderson's *The Lighter Side of My Official Life*, which had initially been serialised in *Blackwood's Magazine* in March of that year. Commenting that he had read Anderson's comments in *Blackwood's* after writing his own chapter on the Whitechapel crimes, Smith angrily dismissed his counterpart's assertion that the murders were the work of a low-class Jew shielded from justice by his people, writing:

> In this article Sir Robert discourses on the Whitechapel, or Jack the Ripper, murders, and states emphatically that he, the criminal, "was living in the immediate vicinity of the scenes of the murders, and that, if he was not living absolutely alone, his people knew of his guilt and refused to give him up to justice. The conclusion," Sir Robert adds, "we came to was that he and his people were low-class Jews, for it is a remarkable fact that people of that class in the East End will not give up one of their number to Gentile justice, and the result proved that our diagnosis was right on every point."
>
> Sir Robert does not tell us how many of "his people" sheltered the murderer, but whether they were two dozen in number, or two hundred, or two thousand, he accuses them of being accessories to these crimes before and after their committal.
>
> Surely Sir Robert cannot believe that while the Jews, as he asserts, were entering into this conspiracy to defeat the ends of justice, there was no one among them with sufficient knowledge of the criminal law to warn them of the risks they were running.
>
> Sir Robert talks of the "Lighter Side" of his Official Life. There is nothing "light" here; a heavier indictment could not be framed against a class whose conduct contrasts most favourably with that of the Gentile population of the Metropolis.

It would be more than seventy years before any light was shed on Sir Robert Anderson's firm assertion that Jack the Ripper was a low-class Jew.

But the problems caused by his incautious writings in *Blackwood's* would not be confined to Henry Smith. His former employer, the Home Office, was perturbed by the former Assistant Commissioner's continued revealing of sensitive information and new Home Secretary Winston Churchill – a month into the role when *Blackwood's* published Anderson's comments about Jack the Ripper – instructed Permanent Under Secretary of State Edward Troup to write to newly-appointed Solicitor General Sir Rufus Isaacs, ironically the son of a Spitalfields Jewish fruit importer, to see whether Anderson's pension could be withdrawn, or at least suspended due to his indiscretions:

> ...it is extremely discreditable for an ex-police officer of high rank and in a

confidential position to earn money by the publication of reminiscences which are full of attacks on those to whom he was opposed politically, and of spiteful, and in many cases, untrue statements with regard to his former chief and colleagues.[44]

The question of Anderson's pension was at that moment being debated in the House of Commons; Churchill confirmed on 13th April that the £900 was awarded in respect of "service at the Home Office before 1877, service from 1877 to 1888 as Secretary to the Prison Commissioners, and service from 1888 to 1901 as Assistant Commissioner of Police."

A week later, on 20th April, the discussion continued, with Hon. Jeremiah MacVeagh, M.P. for South Down, amazed that Anderson had been awarded his £900 while former Commissioner James Monro had left without any pension at all:

> Why is it that Sir Robert Anderson had an increase of salary, a pension and a knighthood, whilst his superior official receives neither a pension nor a knighthood?

Home Secretary Churchill seemed equally bewildered, replying: "I am afraid I cannot give any explanation of the freaks of fortune in the world."[45]

On the same day Solicitor-General Sir Rufus Isaacs wrote to Churchill offering his opinion that although "information of a confidential nature has been published by [Sir Robert], and that at least some of it was obtained in the course of his employment in the police," the likelihood was that should Anderson contest any decision to forfeit his pension, as was his right as stipulated in the Police Act of 1890, it was by no means certain that the Court of Quarter Sessions would uphold the decision.[46]

At the House of Commons the following day, the journalist T.P. O'Connor, now M.P. for Liverpool Scotland, waded into the debate, giving a long history of Anderson drawn on personal knowledge.

Informed by Isaacs, Churchill told the house that two of the three charges levelled against Anderson in relation to his indiscretions were so far in the distant past that proof of any wrongdoing would be difficult to obtain; the third charge, relating to his articles in *Blackwood's*. The Home Secretary then dismissed the minor revelations in Anderson's writings:

> I have looked through these articles and they seem to me to be written in a spirit of gross boastfulness. They are written, if I may say so, in the

style of "How Bill Adams Won the Battle of Waterloo." The writer has been so anxious to show how important he was, how invariably he was right, and how much more he could tell if only his mouth was not what he was pleased to call closed.

There was, Churchill continued, nothing within the articles which had any real bearing on the Home Office at that time. Should Anderson commit any indiscretions in the future, the Home Secretary warned, the power remained to take appropriate action.⁴⁷

As 1901 turned into 1902, there was just one event on the horizon which captured the attention of each and every Londoner: the coronation of Edward VII, due to take place in June of that year, in what would be the first time a new British monarch had been crowned for 64 years.

In fact, so unaccustomed to the ceremony were the Metropolitan Police that it was decided the easiest way to begin planning for the great day was to use the instructions drawn up for Queen Victoria's Coronation on 28th June 1838, with vital entries edited to reflect changes in street names and suchlike.⁴⁸

It was clear from the outset that the current strength of the Force would not be sufficient to cope with policing the expected huge crowds, so on 20th February a notice was issued to recently-retired Metropolitan Police pensioners inviting them to assist, the majority for a period of fourteen days but some for a month. On offer was remuneration of £3 per week, with £2 per week being paid for each subsequent week. Those living more than 50 miles from New Scotland Yard were offered 10s travelling expenses.

Existing officers scheduled to work on Coronation Day itself would receive three days' extra leave, and three days' extra pay, in recognition of the demanding duties which they would be expected to perform, both in preparation for the Coronation and, more likely, keeping order during the post-ceremony celebrations.

As the great day inched closer, various official orders and proclamations were released by the Metropolitan Police. On 2nd June, A Police Caution bearing Commissioner Sir Edward Bradford's name was issued, warning the public that anyone throwing money, printed bills or advertisements onto or near the Royal Procession would be apprehended immediately and fined forty shillings.⁴⁹

No doubt the possibility of an assassination attempt was also at the back of the Commissioner's mind; Edward had been shot at by 15-year-old Jean-Baptiste Sipido while travelling through Belgium two years earlier in protest at the Second Boer War.[50]

Perhaps to ensure the safety of the Royal Party, on 18th July a confidential memorandum from the War Office estimated that some 23,784 troops would be required for the day, with more than 9,000 being massed in Whitehall and the Mall.

While most would have to be content with witnessing the Procession passing through the streets of the capital, some 5,888 people were invited to attend the crowning itself at Westminster Abbey, all issued with one of four coloured tickets, denoting the entrance to be taken, each stamped with the authorisation of Commissioner Bradford.[51]

The Coronation was originally scheduled to have taken place on 26th June, but just two days beforehand had been postponed with Edward suffering an abdominal cyst which required immediate surgery, quite possibly a result of his years of overindulging in eating and drinking. An operation was successfully carried out by Frederick Treves, who had been appointed one of several Honorary Serjeant Surgeons to the new King in March 1901, and the eminent surgical authority Lord Lister.

With Edward all but recovered, the Coronation took place on 9th August. The provincial newspapers travelled to London to report the historical event alongside their metropolitan counterparts, with one, *The Whitby Gazette*, ably capturing the public's anticipation of the transition from Victorian to Edwardian era:

> God Save the King! At last King Edward VII has been crowned, to the delight of his people, and it is pleasant to announce that he bore the ceremony, long as it was even in its cut down form, without the least fatigue. His sudden illness and the postponement of his Coronation from the original date is one of the most dramatic events in the history of England; and it was hard to believe last Saturday that the King – bright, jubilant and in the best of health – was the same man who only seven weeks before had been so near to death. Though undoubtedly the occasion lost much from the awkwardness of the postponement when all was practically ready, and the public loss and inconvenience entailed, nevertheless there is no doubt that his Majesty proportionately gained popularity; and never did even Queen Victoria receive such an enthusiastic and rousing reception as fell to his lot all along the route, both going to the Abbey and returning to the Palace. The scene was a most remarkable one, and will long live in the hearts of those who saw it;

and it may almost be written down without parallel.⁵²

As with Queen Victoria's Golden Jubilee, that the day was a huge success was thanks in no small measure to the actions of the Metropolitan Police. Two days after the Coronation, the Secretary of State wrote to Commissioner Bradford:

> By the King's Command I have the pleasure of signifying to you His Majesty's complete satisfaction with the Police arrangements made for the day of His Coronation. He feels confident that the orderly passage of the procession through the public streets could only have been ensured by great carefulness and discretion in the previous arrangements, and by the exercise of much zeal, tact and good temper on the part of the individual officers responsible for carrying them into effect. His Majesty desires me to congratulate you very heartily on the efficiency of the Force under you which has rendered such a happy result possible.⁵³

The Secretary of State also informed the Commissioner that the King had approved the issue of a commemorative medal for every officer employed by the Metropolitan Police on Coronation Day; a bronze medal with the recipient's name engraved on the edge, each hung from a red ribbon was to be awarded to each serving officer and re-enlisted pensioner, and the same medal in silver to be issued to the Commissioner, the three Assistant Commissioners, the Receiver, the Chief Constables, the Chief Clerks of the Commissioner's and Receiver's Offices, the Private Secretary to the Commissioner and last, but by no means least, the Superintendents.⁵⁴ As one of the latter group of officers, Donald Swanson also received a silver King's Coronation Medal, which doubtless was kept in pride of place with his 1887 Queen's Jubilee Medal.⁵⁵

A week later, on 18th August, another letter of gratitude, to a very different recipient, was sent from New Scotland Yard to the offices of William Pinkerton in New York:

> I have to acknowledge with very many thanks the receipt of your letter of the 14th of June last giving a list of thieves likely to visit this city during the Coronation. I am pleased to say that there was no crime of any consequence and our arrangements to meet and deal with international criminals were a great success.
>
> I enclose you a cutting from *Pearson's Weekly*, a paper published here, in which you will find under your brother's name an article upon the recovery of the Gainsboro' picture.

Trusting that you are well and with kindest regards to yourself and brother.

> I am
> Yours very truly
> Donald S Swanson
> Superintendent[56]

Three weeks after this letter of thanks came the conclusion of a case which, although outwardly a simple burglary, produced a result of such significance that the Metropolitan Police, and forces around the world, would never be the same again.

On 9th September, 42-year-old burglar Harry Jackson appeared at the Old Bailey accused of stealing silver cutlery and medals, along with other items including a set of billiard balls, from the Denmark Hill home of Charles Driscoll Tustin. The court heard Mr. Tustin's parlourmaid Rose Gilder state that on the morning of 27th June she had discovered that the billiard room had been broken into, and that the billiard balls were missing. Crucially, she also noticed a thumbprint on a sash of the freshly-painted windows and pointed this out to the investigating officer, who in turn alerted Det. Sergeant Charles Collins.

Collins's testimony at Jackson's landmark trial is worth repeating in full:

> I am employed specially in connection with finger print identifications – I have been so employed for about six years, and during that time have examined and classified many thousands of finger prints. Each pattern has its name, definition, and numerical value, and we classify them accordingly. All finger prints which are the same must ultimately find their way into the same pigeonhole, and throughout my experience I have never found two persons having identical finger prints – I have never found any variation – the pattern remains the same on each finger from birth till death.
>
> On June 28th in consequence of information I went to 156 Denmark Hill, and took a photograph of a print on the sash of a window in the billiard room. I produce the negative, the enlargement, and some prints from the enlargement.
>
> On August 7th I went to Brixton Prison and obtained a print of the prisoner's hand. I compared it with the impression on the window sash, and with a print of the prisoner's hand, which we had at Scotland Yard, taken on July 24th, 1901, and have no hesitation in saying that they are identical. The print on the window sash is that of the prisoner's left

thumb; the points of resemblance are as follows: in the centre of the thumb there is a line going down and another, an independent line, coming up, terminating on the left side. Those lines are identical in the photograph of the thumb mark on the window sash, and the photograph of the prisoner's thumb taken at Brixton Prison. The line terminating on the left in the photograph of the print on the window sash is not quite perfect, probably owing to the prisoner's thumb being dirty at that particular point. There are also identical in each photograph lines shaped like a tuning fork, with a line at the side, and another line terminating at the point of bifurcation. I have also counted the ridges from the core or delta, and they number eleven in each print.

Another remarkable thing in each print is a line forking off into two, and in my opinion it is impossible for any two persons to have any one of the peculiarities I have selected and described.[57]

The jury agreed, and having had five previous convictions taken into account, Jackson was sentenced to seven years' penal servitude. It was the first conviction in the United Kingdom using fingerprint evidence.

The prosecuting counsel, the thorough Richard Muir, had been hand-picked by Assistant Commissioner Edward Henry to persuade the jury of the reliability of fingerprints; Det. Sergeant Collins had been sent to Muir in advance of the trial to brief him on fingerprinting techniques. Muir would also be the prosecutor in the milestone first conviction for murder using fingerprint evidence, that of the Stratton brothers in 1905, and in the Dr. Crippen trial of 1910.

In 1894 the then-Home Secretary Herbert Asquith had instructed Assistant Commissioner (Crime) Robert Anderson to explore the 'new system' of fingerprinting with scientist Sir Francis Galton to discuss how this might be beneficial in police work; Anderson wrote requesting a appointment on 10th May,[58] but whether the two men met is unknown; the following year the Metropolitan Police created the Anthropometry Department, its system of measurements of criminals based on the work of Alphonse Bertillon sadly proving to be less than reliable.

Edward Henry, meanwhile, upon his appointment as Inspector General of the Bengal Police, discovered that local administrators routinely used finger and palm prints to help prevent corrupt impersonation by native workers, a form of the system pioneered by Sir William Herschel forty years earlier. Henry worked with Francis Galton to develop the system and in 1897 his *Classification and Uses of Fingerprints* was published by the Government of India.

The Fingerprint Bureau had been established by Henry on 1st July

1901, soon after his appointment as Assistant Commissioner. Head of the Bureau was Det. Inspector Charles Steadman, assisted by Det. Sergeant Charles Stockley Collins and Det. Constable Frederick Hunt, all previously employed in the Anthropometry Department but since trained by Henry in his fingerprint system.[59]

Edward Henry's impact on the Metropolitan Police was to be immense. There seems little doubt that he had been appointed as Robert Anderson's replacement with a view to make him Commissioner once Sir Edward Bradford had retired, and this came to pass on Friday, 6th March 1903, when the long-serving Bradford said his goodbyes at New Scotland Yard.[60] Henry's successor as Assistant Commissioner (Crime) was Melville Macnaghten, the Chief Constable.

There was widespread sorrow at the departure of Bradford after thirteen years; he had steadied the ship after the stormy period of 1886 to 1890, when three Commissioners in quick succession resigned their post. Having quelled the threat of strike action by the police, Bradford had subsequently proved himself popular with his men by personally visiting each station to hear what they had to say, something that no commissioner had done previously. During his tenure, crime had continued to fall, and figures were the lowest ever in 1899. He built more police stations, and improved living conditions in the section houses. Under Bradford's watchful eye, the Metropolitan Police gradually came to enjoy more respect from both the press and public alike. His successor would continue his work, firmly taking the Force into the Edwardian era.[61]

For Donald Swanson, the end was also drawing nigh. His father-in-law, James Nevill, died aged 74 on 11th May after slipping into a coma following eight days suffering from influenza.[62] Probate was granted on 16th June to his daughter Ada Nevill and son-in-law Donald Swanson.

Whether this sad passing had any bearing on his decision, or whether his mind had already been made up is unknown, but on Wednesday, 1st July 1903 Det. Superintendent 50282 Swanson resigned his post.[63] It had been 35 years and 102 days since he had written to the Metropolitan Police seeking a "good opening" at a moderate salary, and it must be said that he had most certainly made the most of his opportunity, gaining the highest rank he was able to achieve, unlike many of those above him earning his raft of promotions on merit.

He had joined the Force in the last days of Commissioner Sir Richard Mayne, when officers had been sent for cutlass drill in order to battle the Fenian threat, and he was now retiring under Edward Henry, as fingerprint evidence was about to change the life of a detective forever.

Swanson's Pension Certificate was signed by Henry on 3rd July 1903, his conduct recorded as 'exemplary' – his youthful climbing over the King Street police station railings seemingly forgotten. He was awarded a pension of £280.[64]

His entry in the Records of Police Pensioners describes him as being 54-years-old, having served 35 years and 64 days.[65]

Four days later Swanson received a letter at his New Scotland Yard desk, the envelope bearing a Parliamentary stamp. It was from the former Director of the Criminal Investigation Department, Sir Charles Howard Vincent:

> Dear Mr. Swanson
>
> When I learned at Scotland Yard yesterday that you had retired from the Metropolitan Police on July 1 I felt that the last link almost linking me to the Criminal Investigation Department had gone for with the exception of Supdt. Hare & Chief Inspector Leach there is I fear no-one left of the friends with whom I served.
>
> I must therefore say how truly I wish you well. You were always one of our ablest officers & the high position to which you rose shows the confidence in which you were held by all.
>
> May good health & happiness attend you & yours for many years.[66]

At a farewell dinner hosted by fellow superintendents on 12th August 1903 – his 55th birthday – Swanson was presented with a case of silver-plated serving spoons.[67]

His replacement as Superintendent was to be Arthur Hare, who in turn would later be succeeded by Frank Froest.

But for Donald Sutherland Swanson, his days in the Metropolitan Police were a thing of the past.

TWENTY

At the Going Down of the Sun

For Swanson, retirement meant just that.

Not for him lecturing tours or memoirs, despite the temptation given that several of his contemporaries had already written about their careers, or were about to: Det. Chief Inspector John Littlechild had retired in 1893 and published his autobiography the following year,[1] while in the immediate years ahead Det. Chief Inspector George Greenham[2] and Det. Inspector John Sweeney[3] released their memoirs, with those Sir Robert Anderson and Sir Henry Smith following.

It might well have been the former Det. Superintendent Swanson that Edward Henry had in mind in 1910 when he expressed his fears to Permanent Under Secretary of State Edward Troup regarding Sir Robert Anderson's indiscretions:

> The Commissioner of Police fears that his example may be followed by other ex-officers of the Criminal Investigation Department, whose departments were humbler, but who, in some cases, possess material for even more sensational autobiographies.[4]

Swanson's old colleague from Y Division in the 1870s, Frederick Abberline, also declined to release his memoirs. The retired detective did compile a 100-page scrapbook of newspaper cuttings relating to his career, which he presented to a friend named Walter Green, and towards the end included a note entitled "Why I did not write my Reminiscences when I retired from the Metropolitan Police" explaining:

> At the time I retired from the service the authorities were very much opposed to retired officers writing anything for the press as previously some retired officers had from time to time been very indiscreet in what they had caused to be published and to my knowledge had been called upon to explain their conduct and in fact they had been threatened with

At the Going Down of the Sun

Drawing of Donald Swanson,
believed to be by his niece Peterishea Alexander
Courtesy the Swanson family

actions for libel.

> Apart from that there is no doubt the fact that in describing certain crimes you are putting the criminal classes on their guard and in some cases you may be absolutely telling them how to commit crime.[5]

As for Swanson, his grandson James would later describe him as "that breed of officer who did not seek publicity nor financial gain from his public office, he kept his knowledge to himself."[6]

Many of the books by his former colleagues found their way to Swanson's library, however, and the retired Detective Superintendent was not adverse to writing additional material in their margins where he had knowledge of the events described. In fact, in one instance he confirmed his own view of retired officers publishing their memoirs without saying as much, when he underlined a line in Sir Robert Anderson's *The Lighter Side of My Official Life*; Anderson had rather brazenly written "Scotland Yard can boast that not even the subordinate officers of the department will tell tales out of school, and it would ill become me to violate the unwritten rule of the service" while doing just that – Swanson underlined the final part of that sentence.

The Scot preferred to spend his time fishing, both in England and Thurso, but especially in his hometown.

Although Swanson had regularly visited Thurso on annual holiday trips throughout his working life, now he was retired he was able to spend extended periods visiting friends and family.

Since he had left in 1867, the town had grown. The telegraph was extended to Caithness the year following Swanson's departure and the railway had finally arrived in 1874, linking Thurso with the rest of the country. The improved connections saw visits from the Prince and Princess of Wales in 1876 at the town's Grand Exhibition, and the following year former American President Ulysses S. Grant visited as part of his post-politics world tour.

The town's population had initially crept up to 4,000 by 1881, but by the turn of the twentieth century had fallen back to around 3,500.[7]

In 1883 the Boys' Brigade had been founded in Glasgow by William Smith, a Thurso native and fellow former pupil at the Miller Institution. Six years younger than Donald Swanson, Smith had probably been taught for a spell by the older boy during his time as pupil-teacher. The Miller Institution itself had been extended, firstly in 1892 and then again in 1900, when a new block was built to house two additional classrooms.[8]

The turn of the century also saw the peak of the Caithness flagstone industry, with Castlehill Quarries employing some 500 local men at that time.

For Donald Swanson, his trips to Thurso were more than just a chance to visit childhood haunts.

He still had family living in the town; his sister Jannet – known as 'Jessie' – had remained in Thurso with her husband George Gunn, a successful tailor, and their seven children. It had been George who had provided one of the testimonials on Donald Swanson's application to the Metropolitan Police all those years ago. George had passed away in 1893, but in 1901 Jessie was living on Princes Street with four of her children.[9]

Living nearby was another sister, Margaret, who had married English fireman Peter Alexander in London in 1861 and had four children, only to return to Thurso six years later following the death of her husband. Margaret settled once more on Durness Street, where she operated as an ale and porter dealer.[10]

English-born, but growing up in Thurso, were Margaret's sons William and John, and daughters Mary and Peterishea. The latter, who had been born just days before her father's death, seems to have been very close to her uncle Donald. By the time of the 1891 census she was a teacher in Thurso, and in 1897 had married Andrew Robertson, a Headmaster.

Peterishea was a talented artist and writer, for many years having her Caithness-inspired poetry published on an almost weekly basis in both the *John O'Groat Journal* and the *Caithness Courier* under her married initials of P.A.R. A volume of her work inspired by the Great War was published in 1919 under the title *Until the Dawn and Other Poems*.[11]

Donald and Julia's own children were also successful.

First born Donald Nevill Swanson worked for a short time as a banker's clerk[12] before becoming a civil servant with the Admiralty. Following his marriage to Charlotte Mister in December 1906 the couple moved to Gibraltar, where Donald worked as a Naval Store Officer at H.M. Dockyard. Dividing their time between Gibraltar and their London home at Micheldever Road, Lee in South London, Donald and Charlotte raised a family of three sons and two daughters.[13] He eventually became Superintending Naval Store Officer and was awarded the M.B.E. Seemingly proud of his Scottish heritage, he became proficient on the bagpipes and played with the London Scottish for many years.[14]

Ironically, second son James took the opposite career path to his brother, working first as a clerk at the Admiralty[15] but soon going into

Left to right: Donald Swanson Jr., James Swanson, Ada Swanson ('Sis')
Courtesy the Swanson family

banking. He joined the Standard Bank of South Africa and established branches in several African locations, including Kampala, Mombasa and Cape Town. In 1916 he opened the bank's first branch in Dar es Salaam.[16]

Youngest son Douglas became a Shipping Clerk for the Royal Mail Steam Packet Co. at Custom House.[17] His passion seems to have been clay pigeon shooting, at which he represented the Wimbledon and District Gun Club. Numerous newspaper cuttings held in the Swanson family archives report on his successes, including high placement in the 1923-25 period at both Club meetings and the Clay Target Shooting Championship of Great Britain of 1925.

The family had moved from their long-established home at Stockwell Park Walk to 3 Presburg Road in New Malden in 1911. A tenancy agreement dated 30th August was signed by Donald Swanson and landlord William Wilde, a solicitor of Cliveden Road, Wimbledon, commencing on 29th September 1911 at a rent of £33 per year.[18]

In the event, the family would remain at Presburg Road for more than thirty years, with Ada eventually purchasing the house on 8th February 1927 for £745.[19]

Donald Sutherland Swanson seems to have suffered health problems in his later years. Photographs of the retired detective show him having lost a vast amount of weight, probably on the advice of his doctor. Ongoing problems appear to include hand tremors, as revealed in a letter dated 13th August 1923 sent to son Donald Nevill with thanks for his birthday wishes:

Left to right: Douglas Swanson, Alice Swanson ('Lal'), niece Peterishea Alexander
Courtesy the Swanson family / Wick Society Johnston Collection

My dear Don

Thank you very much for the wishes in your letter of 11th which I got today, and please thank the others for me. You will see my difficulty is in writing as my hand shakes so. No more just now but my love to you all.

Your loving father
Donald S. Swanson

Nine days later a letter to grandson Donald William Swanson confirmed the same ailment:

My dear Donald

Thank you very much for your very kind letter. It was so interesting to me that I have read it several times. I was with you (in thought) at Stonehenge and your thought as to placing those heavy stones has been mine many a time when thinking over the prehistoric. I am sorry for writing in pencil my hand shakes paralytically and causes me to stop. I am glad you are having a good time. I hope you all will have a good time. My love to you my dear Don, and also to your dear father, mother, Jim, Margt. & Graeme.

Your loving grandfather
Donald S. Swanson

Ps I am sorry my hand begins to shake so that I have had to stop.

DSS

Again thank you my dear Don.[20]

At home with Alice, 1920s
Courtesy the Swanson family

The end came a year later, when the retired detective succumbed aged 76 to heart failure on Tuesday, 25th November 1924 at home, wife Julia by his side. The death was registered the following day, with Dr. Kaye Rashell Davison recording the cause as 1) arteriosclerosis, and 2) heart failure asthenia.[21]

The funeral took place at noon on Saturday, 29th November. A crowd of mourners gathered under heavy grey clouds[22] to pay their respects:

> The service and interment at Kingston Cemetery were conducted by the Rev. B. S. W. Green, B.D, curate of New Malden, in the presence of many sympathising friends, who included members of the C.I.D. from Scotland Yard and members of the Malden police. The mourners were Mrs. Swanson (the widow), Mr. Donald Swanson and Mr. Douglas Swanson (sons), Miss Nevill (sister-in-law). Mr. Wood, Mr. F. J. Hawkins and Nurse Lunn. The beautiful floral tributes sent included wreaths from the Superintendents of the Metropolitan Police, and the Malden Police. The funeral arrangements were carried out by Mr. F. W. Paine, of Malden and Kingston.[23]

The coffin was placed in Consecrated grave 4233,[24] planted with a Lawson's Cypress tree[25] and framed by a square stone border adorned with the words:

> IN LOVING MEMORY OF
> DONALD SUTHERLAND SWANSON,
> WHO DIED 25TH NOV. 1924. AGED 76

Alongside was the newly-buried George Wainwright, who had passed away three weeks earlier.

Revealing his own sense of duty, on the day of the death Donald Nevill Swanson wrote to his father's former employers with the sad news, receiving a sobering, official response:

> Sir,
> I am directed by the Receiver for the Metropolitan Police District to acknowledge with regret the receipt of your letter of the 25th instant reporting the death of Mr. D. S. Swanson. His Certificate of Identity has been duly received.[26]

A less formal communication was sent by Donald to the newly-appointed Chief Constable (C.I.D.), Frederick Porter Wensley, after the funeral:

> Dear Mr. Wensley
>
> Will you & your colleagues please accept my sincere thanks for the very beautiful wreath which you sent for the funeral of my father. I think my mother & I recognised all who attended, although we had forgotten names. We were most anxious to have stopped & spoken to most old friends of my father but at the last I think the ceremony was just too much for my mother & I lost no time in getting her back home.
>
> It was indeed very gratifying to see that after all the years he had been away from Scotland Yard, my father was still kindly remembered, & particularly so that some of his old colleagues came such a long way to attend his funeral.[27]

Donald Sutherland Swanson lived his life as he approached his work – in the words of his former headmaster James Waters, "mild but firm".

He was a brewer's son from the far north of Scotland who had gone to London in search of opportunity, which few could argue he found and took full advantage of.

The 35-year period of the late Victorian era in which Swanson served was one of massive development for the Metropolitan Police, culminating in the dawn of fingerprint detection. Perhaps more than anyone, it was he who epitomised the evolving Victorian detective, representing that era in the force's history.

He was by all accounts, firm but fair, but not above bending the rules when required, as William Billings and Charles Newbold would no doubt testify.

Methodical in his manner and praised for his 'synthetical turn of mind', Donald Swanson kept the secrets of his days within the Met, preferring to live by the code of conduct which saw his official life kept to himself.

But he would have plenty to say after his passing.

APPENDIX ONE

Continuing from Page 138

"I thought he deserved a mention – even if long after his death."

Jim Swanson, 27th January 1984

Sadly, the years following Donald Swanson's passing were marked with further deaths in the family.

Youngest son Douglas died at the family home on 4th December 1930 from heart failure brought on by tuberculosis[1] which he had caught from a work colleague with whom he shared an office. He was just 43-years-old, and was buried alongside his father in the same plot at Kingston Cemetery. In the middle of the plot, was placed a stone marker engraved with the following words taken from Laurence Binyon's Great War poem *For the Fallen*:

> AT THE GOING DOWN
> OF THE SUN
> AND IN THE MORNING
> WE WILL REMEMBER THEM

Five years later, on 16th May 1935, Swanson's widow Julia passed away aged 81 at the home of her sister Ada Nevill with her family by her side.[2] She was also buried at Kingston Cemetery, next to her husband and son, but as per her strict instructions no money was spent on a headstone. Her name was added to the border of the plot alongside.[3]

A year later, on 22nd July 1936, Ada herself died, and Probate was awarded to her niece Ada Mary Swanson on 13th November.

With Donald Jnr. raising a family at Micheldever Road, Lee in south east London, and James abroad, Ada and Alice were now the only children of Donald Sutherland Swanson and Julia Nevill remaining at Presburg Road, in this way inheriting various papers, books and other possessions belonging to their father. They would not stay at New Malden long before moving out of London completely.

Swanson's great-grandson Nevill remembers Alice:

> I knew her as my Great Aunt Lal (and her elder sister [Ada] as Sis). Sis and Lal ended up living in an old cottage in Edlesborough, near Dunstable with an orchard and studio (she painted). It has since been knocked down and is now a small development of houses called "Swansons".[4]

The two sisters remained unmarried, living together at Orchard Cottage[5] until Ada died aged 93 in 1976. Donald Swanson's granddaughter Mary Berkin recalled that the detective's papers and possessions were kept in an oak chest in the hallway.[6]

She remembered:

> When [Lal and Sis] moved to Edlesborough circa 1942, [3 Presburg Road] was let. It was damaged by enemy action, and subsequently sold to the tenants at a loss. Lal was the dearest of aunts... she should have been married and had lots of children! Sis was pretty good too, and very intelligent... she taught me how to identify good glass, and judge antique furniture.[7]

Alice, the last surviving child of Donald and Julia Swanson, died aged 91 on 14th November 1980. Her Executor, nephew Jim Swanson,[8] was assisted by elder brother Donald in sorting her papers and effects.

According to Mary, her brothers had little time to inspect the possessions at Orchard Cottage because of the need to empty the property, so simply boxed everything up and removed it to Jim's home at Badgers Walk, Peaslake in Surrey.[9]

It was here that on flicking through a copy of Sir Robert Anderson's *The Lighter Side of My Official Life* Donald noticed handwritten notes on some pages, which he brought to the attention of Jim.[10] They had discovered what is now known as the Swanson marginalia.[11]

Reading in more detail, Jim saw that his grandfather had made handwritten comments on four pages and also the endpaper, either adding to or correcting what was on the printed page. The major discovery, however, was notes written in the margin on page 138, which carried Sir Robert Anderson's comments on the Whitechapel murders and his Polish Jew suspect.

Where Anderson had written:

> I will merely add that the only person who had ever had a good view of the murderer unhesitatingly identified the suspect the instant he was confronted with him; but he refused to give evidence against him.

Swanson wrote underneath in a purple-tinged pencil:

> because the suspect was also a Jew and also because his evidence would convict the suspect, and witness would be the means of murderer being hanged which he did not wish to be left on his mind. D.S.S

At some later date, using a different, grey pencil, Swanson underlined Anderson's "identified the suspect the instant he was confronted with him" as well as his own comment 'also a Jew', and added in the left-hand margin:

> & after this identification which suspect knew, no other murder of this kind took place in London.

Elaborating on this, on the endpaper he wrote:

> Continuing from page 138. After the suspect had been identified at the Seaside Home where he had been sent by us with difficulty, in order to subject him to identification, and he knew he was identified. On suspects return to his brothers house in Whitechapel he was watched by police (City C.I.D.) by day & night. In a very short time the suspect with his hands tied behind his back, he was sent to Stepney Workhouse and then to Colney Hatch and died shortly afterwards – Kosminski was the suspect –
>
> DSS

On page 138, Swanson had also highlighted Anderson's statement

> So I will only add here that the "Jack-the-Ripper" letter which is preserved in the Police Museum at New Scotland Yard is the creation of an enterprising London journalist.

Swanson added:

> Known to Scotland Yard head officers of C.I.D.

Mary Berkin recalled the discovery:

> When the family gathered at Orchard Cottage after Lal's funeral, [Jim] read the Will to us. At that time the passion for antiques was at its height and I, knowing that some pilfering had already taken place, had arranged a transport van and brought large pieces of furniture back to Beverley. Some of these I bought from the estate at Probate value. Other pieces I brought to [Jim's home at] Badgers Walk, where Jim had assembled the

pictures and valuables including the documents and books. Valuation prices had been put on objects (except the documents and criminal memoranda), and we could choose things we desired and their value was debited from each inheritance. [When we were shown the Marginalia it] was the first time that any of us had seen the name of the suspect, written very faintly in pencil! [Jim] must have realised the significance... I don't think DSS would have broken the Police Code to impart it to anyone, but we, in the family, had all been assured that the culprit was known.[12]

These notes made by Donald Sutherland Swanson represent the only written comment he made as to the identity of Jack the Ripper,[13] and were intended for his own private use.

A letter from Jim Swanson to Ripper researcher and author Paul Begg dated 24th November 1988 states that "no-one in the family not even my grandmother... had the slightest inkling that these notes had been made."

At some point over the next few months, Jim Swanson decided to share them with the public, to hopefully obtain some long-overdue recognition of his grandfather's work.[14] Over the next six years, he entered into correspondence with three national newspapers with a view to having the information contained in the marginalia printed. Fortunately, Jim made carbon copies of letters he sent and retained these in a file with correspondence received, giving us invaluable insight into his dealings with the media.[15]

On 26th March 1981 Jim wrote to the Editor of the *News of the World*, a Sunday newspaper with a reputation of printing sensational stories.[16] He mentioned the upcoming trial of Peter Sutcliffe,[17] the Yorkshire Ripper, writing that he felt it would stimulate interest in the Whitechapel murders of 1888, and offered for sale the information provided in Donald Swanson's notations, being careful not to reveal the name of the suspect in his letter.

On the same day he wrote to the *Sunday Express*, whose Deputy Editor (Features) James Kinlay replied on 9th April 1981 expressing interest in Swanson's information.[18] However, by this time negotiations with the *News of the World* were well underway and their Chief Crime Reporter Charles Sandell[19] visited Jim twice, on one occasion taking his daughter Claire,[20] to view the material and also agree a fee.[21] On 16th April 1981 News Editor Robert Warren[22] wrote to Jim confirming the agreement of £750 in return for exclusive rights to the information.[23]

On 20th April 1981 Jim wrote to Sandell, saying that he had discussed the arrangement with his family and they felt it fair to request a further

£250 should a second article be published using the information.[24] Robert Warren wrote again on 22nd April to confirm the new arrangement.[25] Happy that a deal with the *News of the World* was now firmly in place and that an article would shortly be published, Jim wrote to James Kinlay of the *Sunday Express* on 23rd April 1981 to confirm that the story had been sold.[26]

On 14th May 1981 the *News of the World* made the £750 payment to Jim Swanson,[27] which he subsequently split between himself and his four siblings.[28]

For some reason, however, the *News of the World* didn't run the story. In a letter to his accountant dated 27th January 1984, Jim mused:

> I was told by Mr. Charles Sandell, the *NOW* chief crime reporter, that he would write the article and that it would be published to coincide with the trial of the Yorkshire Ripper. In the event no story was published. I do not know what Mr. Sandell wrote, he did say that he would say something nice about my grandfather. I do not know why nothing was published.[29]

At this moment in time we are no clearer as to why the story wasn't published. It is far from uncommon for newspapers to buy the rights to a story and not use it, particularly if there are big news stories going on at the time, or if developing the story proves too time consuming, too expensive, or dries up. It is possible that 'Kosminski' defied identification back in 1981 and otherwise meant nothing, or that the story of a less than glitzy suspect was simply swamped by the big stories of the day, including the trial of the Yorkshire Ripper, the Brixton Riots and shots being fired at the Queen during the Trooping of the Colour, as well as the long succession of stories on the wedding of Prince Charles and Diana Spencer which the newspaper ran from June to late August.

The *News of the World*'s lack of interest didn't surprise Charles Nevin, the journalist at the *Daily Telegraph* which eventually printed the story:

> I've always assumed (almost certainly correctly) that [the *News of the World* didn't publish] because the marginalia raise more questions than answers and because an untraceable unknown wasn't sensational enough for their mass circulation purposes. I was most excited by the discovery, but I failed to find out any more about Kosminski. As a result, the *Telegraph* was nearly as underwhelmed as the *NOTW*, although, of course, the story was printed.[30]

In late January 1982 Charles Sandell suffered a heart attack.[31] While recuperating, on 29th April 1982 he wrote to Jim Swanson from his home in Redhill, returning a 'booklet' and saying he hoped to be back at work shortly after being off for three months. He further commented that he believed Donald Swanson didn't receive the credit for which his "fine work in the Ripper case... richly deserved."[32]

Sandell retired later in 1982 and was replaced as Chief Crime Reporter by Jeff Edwards, who had been at the newspaper for just a year.[33] He died on 19th August 1987. His son-in-law, Brian Hill, was tasked with sorting his papers and in 1989 contacted New Scotland Yard's Crime Museum to donate the reporter's notes on the Ripper, being invited to visit and to pass over the papers personally. Mr. Hill recalls: "It was rather nice as they remembered him as one of the few reporters with integrity and not for sensationalism."[34]

This batch of papers donated by Sandell's family was put into a filing cabinet and forgotten about until researcher Keith Skinner rediscovered them while sorting paperwork at a Crime Museum office reorganisation in July 2011.

Contained in the papers was an internal memo from Charles Sandell to the *News of the World*'s News Editor dated 15th April 1981, which read:

> Re Letter to the Editor about Jack the Ripper
>
> Scotland Yard's files on the original Jack the Ripper case have remained a secret. The name of the man who murdered and mutilated five prostitutes in the late 1880s has been a matter of speculation for decades.
>
> One author named the Duke of Clarence as the Ripper, another said the killer was a homicidal doctor named Pedachenko, while a third said he was a barrister named Montague John Druitt.
>
> Now the grandson of the Scotland Yard detective, who was ordered to investigate the Ripper murders, believes he has stumbled on the true identity of Jack the Ripper.
>
> Mr. James Swanson, a 69-year-old retired Tannery director and general manager, who lives in Peaslake, near Dorking, Surrey, believes he has discovered the Ripper's identity and the reasons why he was not brought to justice.
>
> Before he died in 1924 Detective Supt. Donald Swanson of Scotland Yard wrote details of the Ripper investigation and his views (about 200 words) in the back of a book written by Sir Robert Anderson, former head of the C.I.D. at Scotland Yard.
>
> The Yard detective names the man as Kosminski, a Polish Jew.

Continuing from Page 138

*Charles Sandell,
Chief Crime Reporter for the News of the World*
Courtesy Brian Hill

Mr. James Swanson only recently discovered the book while examining the property of his Aunt who died a few months ago.

He had also discovered the original document ordering the Yard detective to investigate the Ripper case. This in itself is unique. The document shows nine murders and one attempted murder.

I have twice visited Mr. Swanson and I am convinced of his authenticity.

The Yorkshire Ripper trial is bound to stimulate interest in the original Jack the Ripper and it seems an appropriate time to run a story.

Mr. Swanson originally asked for £1,000 but he has come down to £750.

Attached to this memo was a 12-page document numbered 'Jack 1' to 'Jack 12', with Charles Sandell's name appearing on the top right hand corner of the first page.

The document, obviously a draft of the unused *News of the World* article (complete with handwritten revisions to the text), admits that little was known about the suspect named by Donald Swanson and that he was far from an exciting solution to the world's greatest crime mystery:

Somewhere at Scotland Yard there must be a file on Kosminski for his name, and any papers referring to him, have been omitted from the papers available at the Public Records Office.

The known facts about him are sketchy. He had a great hatred of women and according to Macnaghten, he had committed many crimes. He particularly hated prostitutes. Macnaghten's report says: "This man became insane owing to many years indulgence in solitary vices and he was removed to a lunatic asylum in 1889." This substantiates Swanson's comments.

Kosminski lived in Whitechapel and consorted with prostitutes until he caught a venereal disease which may have led to his insanity. He certainly knew all the small alleyways in Whitechapel and he was known to have strong homicidal tendencies.[35]

With the centenary of the Whitechapel murders fast approaching, a rash of Ripper books were being prepared for release in 1987, among them Martin Howells and Keith Skinner's *The Ripper Legacy*, Melvin Harris's *Jack the Ripper: The Bloody Truth* and *Jack the Ripper: Summing Up and Verdict* by Colin Wilson and Robin Odell.

Also on this list was Martin Fido's *The Crimes, Detection and Death of Jack the Ripper*, reviewed by veteran Ripperologist Dan Farson for the *Sunday Telegraph* on 27th September 1987. This stirred Jim, a lifelong *Telegraph* reader, into action. He wrote to its Editor in the hope of getting some much overdue recognition for his grandfather, and also to put an end to "all the fanciful conjecture concerning the killer." The same day as reading Farson's review, Jim wrote to the *News of the World* asking to be released from the 1981 contract and to be given consent to share the information. On 1st October, News Editor Robert Warren replied to confirm.[36]

The following weekend, on Saturday, 3rd October 1987, the *Telegraph* printed a feature on the forthcoming Ripper centenary by Charles Nevin[37] titled 'Jack: The Gripping Tale'. Jim wrote on the same day to the Editor offering sight of his grandfather's annotations and other documentation, suggesting "the truth" could be published "after others have had their speculative fling."[38]

With Charles Nevin tasked to write the story, he made a single visit to Jim's home in Surrey to view the material and borrowed the annotated *The Lighter Side of My Official Life*.[39]

Continuing from Page 138

Researching the background to 'Kosminski' and the Seaside Home, Nevin contacted Ripper author Don Rumbelow, who advised the journalist to get in touch with Martin Fido, who had discovered an Aaron Kosminski who had been confined to Colney Hatch asylum during his own researches.

Martin later recalled:

> I met Don for the first time at Wood Street Police Station, going over the transcript [of the Marginalia which] the *Telegraph* had given him. I can't remember whether it was a photocopy.
>
> Then Charles Nevin met me at the Corporation Archives, and told me he too had gone over the Infirmary records and failed to find Kosminski passing through them – I think (but am far from certain) he'd then been notified of Keith's discovery [that the address of Aaron Kosminski's brother Woolf was 'Sion' rather than 'Lion' Square], and realised the writing was so bad it was not really surprising he and I had both missed it.[40]

On 9th October 1987 Jim wrote again to Charles Nevin, revealing he had found more papers belonging to his grandfather.[41]

These referred to Donald Swanson being placed in overall charge of the Ripper case, and a list containing the names of the victims and alleged victims, as well as the attack on Annie Farmer. Neither documents were 'new' discoveries, as Jim had shown both to Charles Sandell six years earlier.

On Monday, 19th October 1987 the story of Swanson's margin notes was finally revealed to the public when the *Telegraph* printed Charles Nevin's story. In it, Nevin confirmed "there could scarcely be a better source than Donald Swanson" but highlighted the problems with some of Swanson's comments such as the date of Kosminski's death (Aaron Kosminski lived until 1919, while Swanson wrote that the suspect died shortly after being admitted to Colney Hatch asylum) and the venue of the supposed identification. Describing Martin Fido as "intrigued but unconvinced", the article also quoted Don Rumbelow:

> It's fascinating and frustrating at the same time. Remember he must have written this at least 20 years after the murders. We're dealing with old men's memories. The case is not closed.

Printed reaction in the following weeks came in the form of a letter from Martin[42] saying that it was "misleading to say that [I am] 'intrigued but unconvinced' by Chief Inspector Swanson's crucial identification of

Jack the Ripper", and another from prominent criminologist Jonathan Goodman[43] rather sniffily complaining that he found it "peculiar – or rather suspicious – that so much evidence about Jack the Ripper is coming to light just when his centenary year is starting."

Jim Swanson's reaction to these comments went unpublished. But in an undated letter to the Editor of the *Telegraph*, he made his feelings plain:

> Sir
>
> ### JACK THE RIPPER
>
> When I made my Grandfather's notes on the Whitechapel murders of 1888 available to the *Daily Telegraph* it was with the objective of putting an end to all the speculation concerning the identity of Jack the Ripper... However it seems that the Ripperologists don't want to know and that speculation may "Rumblelow on ad in fidotum."
>
> My Grandfather Chief Inspector D. S. Swanson C.I.D. was appointed to be the Eyes and Ears of the Commissioner in this case and everything concerning these murders was to pass through his hands. Surely in these circumstances the one person that would know the identity of the murderer would be my Grandfather.
>
> My Grandfather was a highly intelligent man. He was in complete command of all his faculties at the time of his death in 1924 at the age of 76. My Grandfather's notes were made in 1910 when he was 62. We are hardly dealing with an OLD MAN'S MEMORY as Sergeant Donald Rumbelow suggests. My Grandfather would have been 40 when appointed to this case. Jack the Ripper would have been his main concern for several years. The identity of the murderer would have been indelibly imprinted on his mind.
>
> Jack the Ripper was my Grandfather's main concern until he, the Ripper, was put safely away and the file closed, presumably about 1890. My Grandfather would then have been occupied with other cases. Kosminski would no longer have been his concern so my Grandfather would no longer have kept a tally on him and his demise.
>
> The fact that some one's idea of how a murderer should behave during his stay in Colney Hatch does not coincide with the reported behaviour of the man in question cannot possibly challenge the unequivocal signed statement of the man who knew that Kosminski was the suspect. Surely it is time that poor demented Kosminski and the victims he disembowelled should be allowed to Rest in Peace.[44]

Continuing from Page 138

Over the next few years, the Swanson marginalia appeared in every book on the Ripper, firstly in Paul Begg's *Jack the Ripper: The Uncensored Facts*, the only Ripper book published in the centenary itself.

That year Paul met Jim Swanson during production of London Weekend Television's *Crime Monthly*, for which both were filmed. Also working on the programme was Dr. Richard Totty, Assistant Director of the Home Office Forensic Science Laboratory. Recognising an opportunity to confirm that the notes were definitely written by Donald Swanson, albeit in a non-scientific, casual manner, Paul asked Dr. Totty to look at photocopies of the marginalia and compare them against known writing by Swanson, also in photocopied form – all Paul had available to send.

Initially, Dr. Totty's results were unexpected: in a telephone call to Paul, he said that in his opinion they were not written by the same hand. Paul recalls:

> I was shocked. Martin Fido recalls my phone call to him. What we discovered was that the handwriting [in the sample supplied] was that of a secretary (amanuensis) and only signed by DSS. This was common practice. Anderson said that he often signed blank sheets of paper so that the secretary could send letters when he was himself absent or otherwise engaged and unable to sign them. That Parnell did the same was Anderson's explanation for the Pigott forgery.[45]

A new sample was provided, with Dr. Totty writing to Paul on 5th October 1988:

> The further documents you sent me signed by Donald Swanson (MEPO 3/140 009089) bear handwriting that differs significantly from the handwriting on the first document you sent bearing his signature (HO 144/221/A49301C 009056) and I can only conclude that the first document is a transcript of his notes by some individual.
>
> The handwriting on the further documents matches that in the pencilled footnotes in the copy of Anderson's memoirs – or that part of the footnotes I have seen. All the features I had noted that differ between the footnotes and the first document can be matched in the handwriting on the further documents. I should still be interested in seeing a full version of the footnotes however.

On 29th November 2001, Jim was filmed discussing the marginalia for L.W.T.'s *The Trial of Jack the Ripper*. Sadly, he died three weeks later on 20th December. His grandfather's papers passed to his eldest son, Nevill Swanson.[46]

On 24th April 2006, Keith Skinner was conducting research at the Metropolitan Police Historical Collection at Charlton when, in the absence of Maggie Bird, the Manager of the Collection, he answered a telephone call which was from Nevill Swanson. Nevill was attempting to find information on a gun, allegedly presented to Donald Swanson in 1882, which was being advertised for sale on the Internet.[47] They discussed Keith's past association with the Swanson family, and during the course of the telephone call Keith suggested that *The Lighter Side of My Official Life*, along with other Swanson material, be looked after by the Metropolitan Police Historical Collection.[48]

Nevill wrote on 3rd May 2006 to say that after discussion with the rest of the Swanson family it had been agreed that it would be appropriate to loan the annotated *The Lighter Side of My Official Life* on an open-ended basis to the Crime Museum, as per Keith's later suggestion. In the meantime, the Museum's Curator Alan McCormick had expressed his keenness to tie in the presentation of the book with the relaunch of the Museum.[49] This took place on 13th July 2006, and was attended by several journalists, who mistakenly thought that the Marginalia represented new evidence. As a result, as the only Ripper historian in attendance Keith found himself answering questions which had been discussed some 19 years previously, and was quoted in the following day's newspapers concluding: "The Swanson Marginalia produces as many questions as it does answers."[50]

Keith recalls:

> At that time I was helping Alan McCormick to refurbish the Crime Museum and it subsequently occurred to me that *Lighter Side* might sit neatly as a Ripper exhibit in the Crime Museum, there being absolutely nothing else on display! Alan agreed. I didn't even know it was going to be used as a vehicle to relaunch the Crime Museum. I knew there was going to be a little informal ceremony where the Swanson family officially handed over the book to the Crime Museum as custodians on a loan basis, but I had absolutely no idea that this was to coincide with the relaunch and was staggered when I arrived at Scotland Yard to see it besieged by the press and media!

The book was sent to the Metropolitan Police's Forensic Science Service by Curator Alan McCormick, who wanted it on record that he'd taken this precaution, along with one of Donald Swanson's notebooks which was also supplied by the Swanson family. The examination was conducted by Dr. Christopher Davies, who joined the Metropolitan Police Forensic Science Laboratory in June 1981, since when he had been employed solely as a questioned document examiner. At the time of the 2006 analysis, he was one of the senior document examiners in the London Laboratory of the Forensic Science Service.

On 3rd November 2006 Dr. Davies concluded his report. A press release by the Forensic Science Service dated 11th January 2007 quoted Dr. Davies on his findings:

> What was interesting about analysing the book was that it had been annotated twice in two different pencils at different times, which does raise the question of how reliable the second set of notes were as they were made some years later. There are enough similarities between the writing in the book and that found in the ledger to suggest that it probably was Swanson's writing, although in the second, later set, there are small differences. These could be attributed to the ageing process and either a mental or physical deterioration, but we cannot be completely certain that is the explanation. The added complication is that people in the Victorian era tended to have very similar writing anyway as they were all taught the same copybook, so the kind of small differences I observed may just have been the small differences between different authors. It is most likely to be Swanson, but I'm sure the report will be cause for lively debate amongst those interested in the case.[51]

In his report, Dr. Davies commented on the sample provided of Swanson's known writing, a green hardback ledger, and explained that his comparison had been restricted by the bulk of this known writing being penned around 30 years prior to that of the marginalia, and also that it was written in ink:

> It is also, for the most part, written on previously blank pages and is, therefore, not constrained by the presence of previous material. Where there is evidence of writing being added to pre-existing text there are also signs that features of the writing, such as its size, can be affected. The [marginalia] is written in pencil, some of it around pre-existing printed text. This may have affected the way in which it was written.

Dr. Davies concluded:

I found that the questioned and known writings are in a similar basic style with a similar slope and similar proportions. I also found other similarities between them in the more detailed features of the writing. However, I also found a number of differences. These included such things as:

1) the overall quality of the known writing is superior to that of the questioned writing.
2) the known writing often has strokes connecting words but this is not found in the questioned writing.
3) in a number of characters the majority of the known examples are somewhat different from the questioned examples but a minority of the known examples do match the questioned examples quite closely.

I have not found any direct evidence for copying and I have not seen any indications that questioned writing has been erased and rewritten.

I have considered my findings in the light of the following two propositions:

1) Swanson wrote the questioned annotations in the book *The Lighter Side of My Official Life*.
2) some other person wrote the questioned annotations in the book *The Lighter Side of My Official Life* and many similarities with Swanson's writing are due to chance resemblance or copying.

If the first proposition were correct then I would expect to find a high level of similarity between the known writing and the questioned writing. I would expect some differences, as a consequence of natural variation, but these should not include consistent differences in fundamental features of the writing.

If the second proposition were true I would expect to find some differences between the writing that include consistent differences in fundamental features. In many respects, the writings, and possibly in most respects, may still be similar but I would expect differences that are greater than those normally resulting from natural variation.

...I have not found any differences between the known and questioned writings in features that I consider are clearly fundamental structural features of the writing. However, in certain circumstances my findings might occur if Swanson were not the writer of the questioned writing. Consequently, my findings do not show unequivocally that Swanson is the writer of the questioned writing but they do support this proposition.

Continuing from Page 138

I have, therefore, concluded that there is strong evidence to support the proposition that Swanson wrote the questioned annotations in the book *The Lighter Side of My Official Life*.

With the annotated *The Lighter Side of My Official Life* deposited back in the Crime Museum at New Scotland Yard, then-Curator Alan McCormick arranged for scans to be made of the marginalia as requested by Nevill Swanson as part of the loan agreement.[52] It was at this point that red lines made with a felt-tip pen were noticed to the left of the notes on page 138. Alan McCormick, not having seen the marginalia before, had no reason to think there was anything unusual about these lines so didn't bring them to anyone's attention.

The first time that the red lines were commented on by a Ripperologist was on 21st November 2010, when Paul Begg, John Bennett and Jeff Leahy filmed the marginalia for a segment in the documentary *Jack the Ripper: The Definitive Story*.

As John recalled:

> As the documentary featured the marginalia, it was suggested that we attempt to film the real thing and get an interview with Nevill Swanson. The latter was achieved by Paul and Jeff on 18 November 2010. Nevill gave Paul permission to use the marginalia for the programme – it belongs to him and is effectively on loan to the Black Museum.
>
> On 19 November 2010, Paul and I went to New Scotland Yard to pick up the book. Security was tight and we met Alan McCormick in the foyer. Paperwork was signed and the book was handed over in a protective archival box. It was then taken back to Kent. The book did not leave the box until the 21 November, when it was filmed at the studio. Only Paul and I touched the book during that time (wearing gloves, I might add). The relevant marginalia pages had a sheet of acetate covering them, held in place by a paperclip. Obviously these were removed during filming...
>
> We noticed that there were red lines drawn in felt tip on the relevant pages and Paul mentioned that they were not there when he last saw the book (20 years previously, I think). We could offer no conclusion as to when these lines were added. I believe Paul discussed these with Keith Skinner soon afterwards.[53]

Keith could only confirm that the red lines were not there when he visited Jim Swanson with Stewart Evans in July 2000, as evidenced by photographs taken by Stewart at the time. He commented that when the book was loaned to the Crime Museum in 2006 he realised the anomaly of the date of a letter pasted on to the first page and that it covered an inscription.[54] This had been his focus at the time and meant his attention was not on page 138 and the red lines.

Nevill Swanson, however, *had* noticed the markings prior to 2006 but took no account of them or their possible significance, regarding them as something that his father would have done because "he liked to highlight DSS's achievements."[55]

Further confirmation that Jim drew the red lines came when the author met Nevill on 5th July 2012.

Among a number of items viewed and discussed was a copy of Paul Begg's *Jack the Ripper: The Uncensored Facts*. The book, a 1989 reprint of the first paperback edition, had belonged to Jim and had passed to Nevill on his death. On page 195, on which Paul writes of the discovery of the marginalia, Jim highlighted the relevant paragraphs with red felt-tip pen, and in pencil corrected Paul's assertion that Jim made contact with the *Telegraph* "on reading about Martin Fido's book," with:

> On the 100th anniversary of the Ripper murders – some more rubbish in papers. I got in touch with *D Telegraph*.

It would seem that Jim Swanson made the red pen marks on page 138 of *The Lighter Side of My Official Life* some time between July 2000 and his death in December 2001, probably just prior to filming *The Trial of Jack the Ripper*, in an effort to be helpful by highlighting the relevant passages.

In more recent years Nevill Swanson had begun slowly collating items relating to his great-grandfather Donald Sutherland Swanson from the various branches of the family, and as the process of collating books, materials and memorabilia began, on 29th June 2012 Keith Skinner retrieved *The Lighter Side of My Official Life* from the Crime Museum and returned it to the Swanson family.

With the collection growing, Nevill began sifting through papers and other memorabilia. Among these was Donald Swanson's marriage certificate, an extract of his birth certificate, the undertaker's booklet for his burial, and his police rattle. When the author met Nevill on 5th July 2012 to take possession of these items to photograph them, one particular item caught his eye: Donald Swanson's personal address

Continuing from Page 138

book.

Crammed into this slim, fragile book are hundreds of entries in ink, grey and purple pencil, featuring addresses for names which have appeared elsewhere in this book such as Anderson, Abberline and Littlechild, along with many family members of both Swanson and Nevill clans. On the inside cover, written in black ink, is 'Donald S Swanson, Great Scotland Yard London'. The address has been crossed out in grey pencil, either after the C.I.D.'s move to New Scotland Yard in 1889 or his retirement in 1903.

In many instances Swanson dated when a person changed address or died, and we can thus date his use of this address book from the earliest dated entry of 28th January 1887 to the final date recorded, the change of address of his daughter Ada on 9th January 1924.

There are entries in purple pencil ranging from 1st October 1896 to the 1924 change of address, and on one instance Swanson has signed an entry 'D.S.S', confirming that he would – and did – make his signature in personal items.

Some of the later entries show evidence of the so-called 'shaky hand' commented on by Ripper students with regards to the endpaper notes in *The Lighter Side of My Official Life*.

The use of different pencils in the address book is reminiscent of Stewart Evans's thoughts on viewing the marginalia at his July 2000 meeting with Jim:

> Sitting on the sofa with Keith I then inspected the marginalia with a powerful magnifying glass. I was immediately struck by the fact that the writing in the bottom margin, patently very old in appearance, was in grey pencil but with a sort of purple tinge and was clearly indented. This was in stark contrast with the writing on the rear endpaper which was in a different pencil entirely – a pale hue, larger writing and not impressed on the page as was the other writing. I said, "Take a look at this Keith, the writing at the rear of the book is in a different pencil." Immediately thinking that Mr. Swanson may have interpreted this as a suggestion that it was a later addition in someone else's hand, I added, rather obviously, "Perhaps he used a different pencil when he wrote that." Keith looked at it and agreed with me that I was correct. In fact it was not even necessary to use the glass to see the difference. Mr. Swanson made no comment.[56]

In his 2006 report, Dr. Davies confirmed Stewart's observations, stating that parts of the annotations were done later than others. He also noted that the writing betrayed a slight and occasional shakiness:

> The [endpaper notes] show evidence of occasional tremor which is similar to that sometimes found in the writing of individuals with certain neurological conditions, such as Parkinsonism.

The recently-discovered letters written by Donald Swanson a year before his death, mentioned in the previous chapter, in which he complains of his hands shaking provide impeccable evidence of the 'occasional tremor' as mentioned by Dr. Davies.

At the conclusion of Dr. Davies' 2006 report, he stated:

> I have, therefore, concluded that there is strong evidence to support the proposition that Swanson wrote the questioned annotations in the book *The Lighter Side of My Official Life*.
>
> If I were able to examine known writings by Swanson that were more nearly contemporary with the questioned writing then I might wish to alter this conclusion. Such writings would enable me to determine whether or not the difference that I have attributed to the passage of time between the production of the known and questioned writings are truly caused by this.

Armed with Swanson's address book and the newly-rediscovered letters, the author contacted Dr. Davies on 29th August 2012, asking if he would consider re-examining the marginalia against the 'new' handwriting samples. Happily, Dr. Davies agreed to do so.

On 24th September 2012, Dr. Davies completed his second report on his examinations. He upgraded his 2006 conclusion, stating:

> There is very strong support for the view that the notes towards the bottom of page 138 in Donald Swanson's copy of *The Lighter Side of My Official Life* and the notes on the last leaf in this book were written by Donald Swanson.

Asked about suggestions in certain Ripper circles that the crucial line "Kosminski was the suspect" may have been added more recently, Dr. Davies commented:

> I have concluded that there is no evidence to support the view that the final line on the last leaf of the book was added much later to a pre-existing text.[57]

The marginal notes in *The Lighter Side of My Official Life* relating to the Whitechapel murders of 1888 were, then, as far as can be proved written by Donald Sutherland Swanson, Detective Chief Inspector in

Continuing from Page 138

overall charge of the investigation into the case.

When the marginalia was written is unknown, but it's probable that the first set, in purple pencil, were made on Swanson receiving his copy of the book. His revisiting Anderson's comments, in which he added further details as well as the name of the suspect in a grey pencil, may well have been spurred by the death of his former superior in 1918.

But where was the Seaside Home identification? Who was the witness? And who was 'Kosminski'?

APPENDIX TWO

Kosminski Was the Suspect

The facts alluded to in Donald Swanson's margin notes have, from the time they were first seen outside of the family, proved elusive. Reporter Charles Sandell, writing his aborted story for the *News of the World*, could find nothing of value on 'Kosminski'. Six years later Charles Nevin of the *Daily Telegraph* faced similar problems when he attempted to reconcile the chronology set out by Swanson with the known facts of one Aaron Kosminski, who had at that time been recently discovered by author Martin Fido.

While everything in this book up to this point has been fact backed by evidence, some of what follows is, through necessity, my opinion based on as much evidence as I have been able to gather through my researches. Where I have made an assumption or suggested probability this is clearly stated.

One such issue which has caused much head-scratching among Ripper students is the supposed identification of the suspect.

Why would this be held at a seaside convalescent home, rather than at a London police station? As I'll explain over the following pages, it is my belief that at the time of the identification, the investigation into that particular suspect was in its infancy. He had come to the attention of the police as a potential person of interest, and no doubt any suspect in such a position being paraded in a police station or other official location such as the Tower of London or a workhouse would have drawn considerable interest, as can be seen from newspaper reports of public reaction when various men had been arrested on suspicion of being Jack the Ripper. There seems little doubt that the police were handling this particular suspect with extreme care, for reasons I shall explain later.

Which 'Seaside Home' was Swanson referring to? Generally assumed to be a reference to the Metropolitan Police Convalescent Home at

Clarendon Villas in Hove, this immediately presents a problem because that facility didn't open until March 1890. With Robert Anderson writing that the last Ripper murder was that of Mary Kelly, can we accept that the identification took place at least sixteen months after her murder?

Having read hundreds of documents written by Donald Swanson, I feel confident that had he been referring to the Metropolitan Police Convalescent Home – a reference made by a policeman about a police institution for his own personal use – he would have simply written "after the suspect had been identified at Hove..."

It should be remembered that this was an era when dozens of convalescent homes operated around the country, many along the coast. Further along the south coast from Hove was the Metropolitan Convalescent Institution at Bexhill-on-Sea, which opened in 1881. However, this was a general convalescent home for any poor person over the age of 14, not a venue specifically offering beds for police officers in need. Would Swanson have arranged for a potentially dangerous suspect to be escorted by police officers to a venue where they would have stood out?

Sixty miles further still along the coast, under the auspices of the district of Dover, is the small, picturesque village of St. Margaret's-at-Cliffe.

An entry in the local *Directory for 1889*, prepared in late 1888, describes a building which is, in my opinion, of extreme interest:

> On the road from the village to the Bay is 'Morley House' a Seaside Convalescent Home for Working Men. This institution was opened in 1883 in connection with the London Hospital Saturday Fund, and claims to be the 'property' of working men, 'managed' by working men, for the 'benefit' of working men. There are now 36 beds, which are kept full during the greater part of the year. Each patient pays 5s. per week (five shillings) towards his maintenance, and the balance is made up by voluntary contributions from London workmen or their employers in their various workshops. During the ten months of 1888 (January to October) over five hundred men have received the benefits of the institution. Particulars and conditions of admission can be obtained of the Honorary Secretary, 5 Mitre Court, Temple, London, or of the Secretary of the Hospital Saturday Fund.[1]

The Hospital Saturday Fund was founded in 1873 by the politician and philanthropist Reginald Brabazon, later 12th Earl of Meath. Long before the existence of the National Health Service, and with little government aid, London's hospitals and dispensaries were reliant on donations from the capital's workers, and with most of these receiving their wages on a Saturday, this was the day on which the Fund would receive donations from businesses through collection boxes. In addition, on one day each July an Annual Ladies' Streets Collection would be mounted by female volunteers. In the six years up to 1879 the Fund had collected £30,000 from London's workers, and in 1878 distributed £5,000 among 96 institutions.[2]

President of the Hospital Saturday Fund was Samuel Morley, woollen manufacturer, Liberal Member of Parliament and philanthropist. Youngest son of John Morley and Sarah Poulton, Samuel Morley was born in Homerton in October 1809 and spent his early working life as an accountant at the offices of the family's wholesale hosiery business at Wood Street in the City of London. Uncle Richard Morley managed the manufacturing premises at Nottingham, from where the family hailed, before John Morley went to London. When his father retired in 1840, Samuel took over the management of the London end of the business with his brother John, who himself retired in 1855. Samuel Morley would spend the next 30 years building up the business into the largest of its kind in the world. He became M.P. for Nottingham in 1865, and then for Bristol three years later – a post he would hold for the next 17 years.[3]

Morley became a great philanthropist, distributing large amounts of his wealth to charitable causes. A Nonconformist, he donated £500 each towards the building of 24 new chapels, £5,000 towards preserving Exeter Hall on the Strand for the use of the Young Men's Christian Association, and £6,000 for the building of the Congregational Memorial Hall on Farringdon Street. The amount of money donated or sponsored by Morley to these and many other endeavours was so great that a friend was reported as saying "I should think he spends from £20,000 to £30,000 a year in benevolent works."[4]

The Hospital Saturday Fund had arrangements with a number of convalescent homes, including the Metropolitan Convalescent Institution at Bexhill,[5] but since its inception in 1873 it had been recognised that a seaside home was a necessity for patients leaving hospital who still required recuperation, and the trustees began looking for a suitable location at which to establish a coastal convalescent home.[6]

In 1883 a building was found – Marine House in St. Margaret's-at-Cliffe near Dover. Originally built as a private residence, a country house with a large old-fashioned garden,[7] it was purchased around

Samuel Morley
Author's collection

1840 by Mr. James Temple, who ran the nearby Cliff House School for young gentlemen,[8] and opened as a boarding school for young ladies. The census return for the following year lists 22 pupils ranging from 10 to 18-years-old, taught by three teachers under the auspices of Governess Susanna Eaton.[9]

Numbers steadily rose over the next thirty years, but by the time of the 1881 census just eleven pupils were recorded at Marine House, although of course more could have attended living elsewhere in the village. Sisters Sarah and Isabella Bower ran the school, seemingly teaching the pupils as well as acting as governesses.[10]

The struggles endured by Marine House school at this time were echoed in the ownership of the building, which passed out of the hands of the Temple family in October 1880 to a Mr. F. Bower. Two-and-a-half years later, on 2nd March 1883,[11] the building was sold to the Trustees of the Hospital Saturday Fund, who had selected the property after inspecting several seaside locations. The freehold of the house, along with seven acres of land, was purchased for £2,500.[12]

The location of the new convalescent home was ideal; sitting 100

Martin Mill station, where travellers for St. Margaret's Bay and Morley House would alight
Author's collection

yards away from the cliffs of St. Margaret's Bay, the stimulating sea air was conducive to recuperation. The journey to the Home from London could scarcely be easier; since 1861 the London, Chatham and Dover Railway had operated a service from the capital to Dover, with trains departing from Victoria.[13] A terminus was opened in the City on 2nd March 1874 at Holborn Viaduct, and then at Snow Hill station, which was opened five months later on 1st August opposite the City of London police station of the same name. In June 1881 a branch line from Kearsney, one stop before Dover, was opened, calling at Martin Mill and Walmer stations on its way to Deal.[14]

Martin Mill station, situated less than two miles from St. Margaret's-at-Cliffe, was where visitors to the new convalescent home would alight. Although an omnibus was available to take travellers from the station to the village,[15] many preferred to walk the short distance.

The home was opened on Saturday, 30th June 1883, when a crowd of around 400 people left London in two specially-commissioned trains to arrive at Martin Mill early in the afternoon.[16] Led by Samuel Morley, the Committee of the Hospital Saturday Fund was joined by a large number of those with an interest in the home, in the main working men and their wives.[17]

The occasion saw the building officially renamed Morley House Convalescent Home, and after inspecting the rooms and facilities the party retired to a marquee which had been erected in the grounds. The report of the Committee was read by Mr. Robert Frewer, the Fund's

Secretary, who outlined that while Morley House was connected to the Hospital Saturday Fund, it was to operate as a separate entity funded by its own endeavours. This had been agreed to at a meeting of some 1,200 representative working men held earlier in the year at Exeter Hall; when the previous owner of the property had agreed a price of £2,500, the Hospital Saturday Fund's bankers, Messrs. Hoare, advanced a loan of £2,000. Numerous donations were subsequently received in addition, including £200 from Samuel Morley himself, raising enough to furnish the Home and leave a small fund of £400.[18]

Morley House, therefore, would have to be self-sufficient. This was achieved not only through donations and numerous fundraisers, but by charging the working men of London a small fee in return for bed and board at the Home, in addition to a subscription fund which maintained the institution. This saw dozens of London-based companies and individuals become annual subscribers, with the majority based in the City of London. It was popular with workers from many different industries, as diverse as postmen, printers, railway workers and the London Fire Brigade.

The City of London Police also retained a subscription, and over the years hundreds of officers of that force would enjoy a visit to the Home when recuperation was required, as underlined in December 1888 by the superintendent of the Home, Charles Bray,[19] when he wrote that "the whole of the City Police that have been sent to a Home have come here."[20]

In fact, Morley House would prove so popular with the City of London Police that they would pay for the exclusive use of four beds and a sitting room.[21] In 1892, the *Daily News*, commenting on the forthcoming opening of an extension to Morley House, reported:

> ...the City Police, whose benefit funds enable them to do the thing handsomely, are furnishing their own rooms in the new wing, and are served in almost luxurious style. They pay a pound a week for maintenance and a rent for their rooms in addition, and are treated altogether on a different footing.[22]

The City of London Police Wing was part of the extension, eventually opened on 2nd September 1893 by Sir William Crundall, the Mayor of Dover, which also included the Caxton Wing for members of the printing trade and the Wolverton Wing for London's postmen.[23]

One commentator, writing on the welcome increase in coastal convalescent homes, reserved special praise for Morley House:

Not one of these homes presents upon the whole more that is gratifying than the Morley House Seaside Convalescent Home for Working Men. Everything about the place strikes one as being thoroughly sound and healthy – everything, that is, but the little groups of invalids one finds here and there about stretched on the little sheltered lawn, or snoozing in basket chairs, or patiently plodding their way with shaky limbs or wheezy lungs out towards the blue sea, with its crisp waves and its swirling foam hissing and bubbling over sand and pebbles down below the chalk cliffs.

...the convalescents, of course, get all the benefit of sunshine and sea breezes, and wholesome diet, and the effect of two or three weeks here is something marvellous on most of them. In some cases, indeed, the progress they make is almost alarming. One good man, for instance, was here for a month, and in the thirty days or so he actually put on thirty-two pounds in weight. What he might have attained to if he had settled here permanently one is almost afraid to try and imagine. "I tell 'e what it is," inmates are often heard to say in effect as their time for leaving draws near, "If I stay here much longer I shall want another suit of clothes. These are so tight I can't get into 'em."[24]

The presence of the City of London Police was reinforced by the fact that the honorary medical officer to Morley House was Dr. Frederick Gordon Brown, Divisional Surgeon to the City force, who no doubt agreed that this combination of a healthy environment and solid diet accelerated the recuperation of his patients.

Gordon Brown had volunteered his expertise to the Hospital Saturday Fund in the early 1880s, and had attended the opening of Morley House in 1883.[25] He and practice partner Dr. Stephen Appleford regularly visited the Home to attend patients where required,[26] but in Dr. Gordon Brown's case, his involvement was even greater, as described by a reporter for the *Daily News* when writing of the system by which an inmate would be assessed for suitability for a bed at Morley House:

A convalescent who wants to come here has to obtain a subscriber's letter. Armed with this he presents himself to Dr. Brown, of the City Police, who carefully inquires into his fitness for the Home. Every Friday night the committee sit at the office, at 39 Farringdon Road, to consider applications, and if they are able to comply, the convalescent goes down the following Monday. The London, Chatham and Dover Railway takes him there and back for five shillings, and he has to pay four shillings a week while he stays. The usual period is three weeks, so that a pound

Postcard showing Morley House convalescent home, St. Margaret's Bay – scene of the Ripper's identification?
Author's collection

covers everything. Under exceptional circumstances the stay may be prolonged a little, but as there are always more applicants than beds, this is not conceded if it can be avoided.[27]

While this report dates from August 1892, it must be considered probable that the same system had operated for many years, given that Morley House had been open for almost a decade by that point.

Originally providing beds for 24 inmates, these had been increased thanks to the benevolence of Lord Wolverton to 36 in the summer of 1887.[28] With day visitors taken into account, there were between 70 and 80 patients at Morley House at any one time at the end of 1888.[29] In the three months to September 1888 alone, some 200 admissions had been granted.[30]

With all this activity going on, it would be unlikely that a small group of men comprising a witness, a suspect and a police escort or two would stand out.

The identification almost certainly took the form of a 'confrontation' rather than a formal line up; Robert Anderson stated as much in his memoirs by writing that the witness "unhesitatingly identified the suspect **the instant he was confronted with him**" (author's emphasis).

All the police had to do, therefore, was to engineer a 'chance' meeting

Entrance to Morley House, 1898
Author's collection

of the two men in order to observe the reaction of both, and this could have taken place anywhere within Morley House or the grounds, quite possibly in the City of London Police's sitting room.

The suspect would have been escorted to the Home by City of London officers, perhaps having first been detained at Snow Hill police station, although not formally arrested.

The witness may have been recuperating at Morley House or, more likely, invited there on the pretext of viewing the Home for the purpose of taking out a subscription, attending as a guest of a City Police officer.

With the reaction of the witness confirming immediately that he recognised the suspect, the police would have been confident that they had the right man. As for the suspect, Swanson wrote in the marginalia that "he knew he was identified".

The refusal of the witness to testify was explained by Swanson as being "because the suspect was also a Jew, and witness would be the means of murderer being hanged which he did not wish to be left on his mind", which could simply mean that the witness was not certain *enough* to swear to the fact in court, thereby being the cause of the man's conviction and execution; not to mention a potential riot in

London's East End, given the tension which existed between the native East Enders and the Jewish immigrant population.

But despite not having a witness prepared to testify, the promising result of the identification was not wasted, as the police now had confirmation that this man was indeed a prime suspect.

As Anderson would later write many times, the *moral* proof of guilt existed – at least as far as the police were concerned – but the *legal* evidence to convict did not. He would complain that the Metropolitan Police did not enjoy the same powers as their French counterparts, who were able to detain a suspected person without any reason while evidence was found, or not, as the case may be:

> ...you are walking along the streets of Paris, and are merely suspected as a criminal who has been in the hands of the Police on a previous occasion. The evidence against you may be of the flimsiest possible character – there may be really none at all – but you are seized all the same, and at once subjected to a searching scrutiny at the hands of the Police. Your measurements are taken, your finger prints etc examined, and you are not released until the authorities have satisfied themselves that they have made a mistake. Such a method is repugnant to British law and feeling.
>
> Here we cannot drag you to Scotland Yard and examine you in the summary fashion. If there is good reason to suspect you of being a criminal all that can be done is charge you before a magistrate, and if the charge fails there is no way by which you can be subjected to examination for purposes of identification. We can only use our albums against you if you are remanded.[31]

This was well known to all officers in 1888; since 1881, when former Director of the C.I.D. Howard Vincent had first issued his guide to Metropolitan Police officers, *A Police Code*, it was understood that

> Identification by bringing a suspected person alone into a room, or by showing him to a witness in a cell, is not a fair mode of identification, and is likely to lead to difficulties and mistakes.[32]

The result of the Seaside Home identification, therefore, would not have been of much use on its own; further evidence would have been required, or confirmation from another, independent witness that this was the right man.

The episode was probably carried out simply to test whether the suspect was indeed a person of interest, and with this confirmed he was returned to Whitechapel and placed under continual surveillance.

It was the same technique employed by Swanson back in March 1877, when he had engineered a 'confrontation' meeting between burglars Edward Lowe and Frederick Anderson and their victim James Greenwood,[33] and in 1889 when he suggested that witness John Arnold be taken to The Strand to see whether he would recognise the soldier who had told him of a murder in Whitechapel's Backchurch Lane which pre-dated the discovery of the torso in Pinchin Street a few days later, or at least the uniform he wore.[34]

Modern commentators have said that such an identification would have been illegal, but as Commissioner Sir Charles Warren had confirmed to the Home Office that he was quite prepared to undertake the most drastic measures "which would further the securing of the murderer however illegal they may be," providing the Government would support him, this would not have been an issue to the police.[35]

Sadly, no dedicated records for Morley House appear to have survived, so it is impossible to say for certain that the identification took place there.

But bearing in mind that Donald Swanson wrote in the marginalia that the witness was a Jew, he was seemingly one of the three men who saw Catherine Eddowes with a man on the corner of Church Passage. Her subsequent murder was a City of London Police investigation. Swanson also stated that following the identification and the suspect's return to Whitechapel, he was watched day and night by the City C.I.D.

Here, we have a Seaside Home whose medical officer was the Divisional Surgeon of the City of London Police. The same force paid a subscription to maintain beds and a private sitting room at the Home.

Getting to Morley House was extremely easy, with a direct train running from opposite the City of London Police's Snow Hill station.

It was also part of Dr. Gordon Brown's job to monitor the health of City of London police suspects.

It is interesting to note that Swanson said the suspect had been "sent by us with difficulty" rather than "taken by" – had the trip to St. Margaret's Bay been organised by Swanson, but executed by his City colleagues? I suspect that the problems no doubt encountered in devising such a plan between the two forces, with the logistics of arranging for the suspect and witness at the Home at the same time, was the "difficulty" referred to by Swanson.

In addition to the City of London Police links to Morley House, it is interesting to note that Robert Anderson, who wrote with such certainty that the Ripper had been identified, was a personal friend of Sir William Crundall, who was the Mayor of Dover in 1888.[36] The Assistant Commissioner was a frequent visitor to the Kent coast, both in an official capacity and enjoying holidays there with his family. With Scotland Yard officials regularly visiting the port towns in response to the activities of professional criminals on board the cross-channel ferries, Anderson had been presented with a free pass between London and Calais by the London, Chatham and Dover Railway, who also operated steamers across the channel, and this privilege was continued into his retirement. He would no doubt have known Dover and the surrounding area very well.

Intriguingly, researcher Sean Crundall learned from his father that during the 1960s he had been told by his own father, Harold Crundall, that Jack the Ripper was a "Shylock", and that there was a "Dover connection". Harold's uncle was Sir William Crundall, who, he further claimed, was a friend of the "chief of police".[37]

Although this is family oral history with as yet no evidence to confirm the story, it is interesting to consider the possibility that Robert Anderson may have divulged details of the Seaside Home identification to his friend Sir William, who in turn passed it to family members, and that information similar to the Swanson marginalia may have been known independently some twenty years before those notes were discovered.

In the years after 1888, those occupied in the running of Morley House continued to be involved in the convalescent home.

Dr. Frederick Gordon Brown and his practice partner Stephen Appleford would continue working at Morley House into the 1890s, while also offering their services to the Hospital Saturday Fund by sitting on the Surgical Appliance Committee. They would dispense items ranging from artificial eyes, false legs and crutches to trusses, spectacles and ear trumpets to subscribers at half the cost paid by the general public.[38]

Charles Bray carried out his duties as Superintendent of Morley House until early 1900, when he retired after seventeen years in the role.[39] He was not to enjoy a long retirement, however, dying later that same year of gastroenteritis.[40]

His successor was John Dickenson, previously Chairman of the Morley House Committee.[41] Dickenson was in the position only a matter of weeks before he found himself in court charged with keeping a dog at Morley House without a licence; he explained that the dog belonged to

Charles Bray, but the Committee had decided to keep it at the home.

The 55-year-old Dickenson would not benefit from the healthy environment enjoyed by inmates of Morley House. Suffering for some time from heart disease, just months into his appointment he was confined to bed. On 25th August 1900 he was found dead on his bedroom floor, lying in a pool of blood caused by a large cut to the left side of his neck. When the body was removed, underneath was found the bottom of a broken drinking glass – the rest being discovered in the washstand, presumably smashed by Dickenson. While the Superintendent had been depressed for a spell and suicide suspected, the jury at his inquest decided that there was not enough evidence to confirm this.[42]

A disastrous decision to incorporate Morley House with St. Andrew's Home at Folkestone in 1905 marked the beginning of the end for the St. Margaret's Bay convalescent home.[43] St. Andrew's, a home for working women and children, had large debts, which were transferred to Morley House,[44] and despite struggling on for a few more years, Morley House closed its doors in 1908.[45]

As stated above, after the episode at the Seaside Home the suspect was returned to Whitechapel – Swanson writes "to his brother's house" – and watched by the City's Detective Department, this being a City of London Police investigation.

With little of that force's files surviving bombing during the Second World War, there is no record of a watch being kept on any suspect. However, the *Evening Telegraph and Star* of 17th October 1888 revealed that an observation was indeed underway:

> HAVE THEY GOT HIM?
>
> The police authorities are very quiet about it, but they are quite satisfied in their own minds of the ultimate bringing to justice of the Whitechapel murderer. They have already traced him out, he is never out of their sight, and when one or two missing links in the chain are supplied, which they hope to do in the course of a week or two, this person, who is a foreigner, will be arrested and brought to trial. Meanwhile the police authorities are in a state of feverish anxiety lest any of the facts of the case should leak out, and accordingly do not allow it to be generally known that they think they have a clue.[46]

It was also reported in several newspapers in mid November that, according to information supplied by the Central News Agency, "several houses at which the murderer is believed to call occasionally are under the closest police surveillance."[47]

It would make sense for the suspect to be watched at more than one location, and although no record exists to provide the names of the City officers engaged in the operation, one detective, Det. Constable Henry Cox, would recall his part when writing his memoirs in serial form following his retirement in July 1906 after 25 years' service.[48]

Initially appearing in *Thomson's Weekly News* from 8th September, Cox's articles were repeated in the *Weekly Welcome* magazine in December the same year.[49]

Described as doing his best work as a 'shadower',[50] in an article entitled 'The Truth about the Whitechapel Mysteries' published in the 1st December 1906 edition of *Thomson's* Cox described his involvement in the investigation.

Writing that the final atrocity by the Ripper was that in Miller's Court, Cox explained that while the City detectives had previously been watching several people,

> ...it was not until the discovery of the body of Mary Kelly had been made that we seemed to get upon the trail. Certain investigations by several of our cleverest detectives made it apparent to us that a man living in the East End of London was not unlikely to have been connected with the crimes.

Claiming that the motive for the murders was revenge, with the killer having been "at some time or another wronged by a woman", Cox stated that "the fact that his victims were of the lowest class proves, I think, that he was not, as has been stated, an educated man who had suddenly gone mad. He belonged to their own class."

This echoed Robert Anderson's assertion in his 1907 book *Criminals and Crime: Some Facts and Suggestions*:

> The peril to the community caused by common crimes, as distinguished from crimes of the first magnitude, will be obvious to the thoughtful. For example, a man who murders his own wife is not necessarily a terror to the wives of other men. A man who kill his personal enemy excites no dread in the breast of strangers. Or again, take a notorious case of a different kind, "the Whitechapel murders" of the autumn of 1888. At that time the sensation-mongers of the newspaper press fostered the belief that life in London was no longer safe, and that no woman ought

to venture abroad in the streets after nightfall. And one enterprising journalist went so far as to impersonate the cause of all this terror as "Jack the Ripper," a name by which he will probably go down to history. But no amount of silly hysterics could alter the fact that these crimes were a cause of danger only to a particular section of a small and definite class of the East End; and that the inhabitants of the metropolis generally were just as secure during the weeks the fiend was on the prowl, as they were before the mania seized him, or after he had been safely caged in an asylum.

In the *Thomson's Weekly News* article, Henry Cox went on to describe the suspect and the City force's surveillance of him, which is worth quoting at length:

> The man we suspected was about five feet six inches in height, with short, black, curly hair, and he had a habit of taking late walks abroad. He occupied several shops in the East End, but from time to time he became insane, and was forced to spend a portion of his time in an asylum in Surrey.
>
> While the Whitechapel murderers were being perpetrated his place of businesses was in a certain street, and after the last murder I was on duty in this street for nearly three months.
>
> There were several other officers with me, and I think there can be no harm in stating that the opinion of most of them was that the man they were watching had something to do with the crimes. You can imagine that never once did we allow him to quit our sight. The least slip and another brutal crime might have been perpetrated under our very noses. It was not easy to forget that already one of them had taken place at the very moment when one of our smartest colleagues was passing the top of the dimly lit street.
>
> The Jews in the street soon became aware of our presence. It was impossible for us to hide ourselves. They became suddenly alarmed, panic-stricken, and I can tell you at nights we ran a considerable risk. We carried our lives in our hands so to speak, and at last we had to partly take the alarmed inhabitants into our confidence, and so throw them off the scent. We told them we were factory inspectors looking for tailors and capmakers who employed boys and girls under age, and pointing out the evils accruing from the sweaters' system asked them to co-operate with us in destroying it.
>
> They readily promised so to do, although we knew well that they had no intention of helping us. Every man was as bad as another. Day after

day we used to sit and chat with them, drinking their coffee, smoking their excellent cigarettes, and partaking of Kosher rum. Before many weeks had passed we were quite friendly with them, and knew that we could carry out our observations unmolested. I am sure they never once suspected that we were police detectives on the trail of the mysterious murderer; otherwise they would not have discussed the crimes with us as openly as they did.

We had the use of a house opposite the shop of the man we suspected, and, disguised, of course, we frequently stopped across in the role of customers.

Every newspaper loudly demanded that we should arouse from our slumber, and the public had lashed themselves into a state of fury and fear. The terror soon spread to the provinces too. Whenever a small crime was committed it was asserted that the Ripper had shifted his ground, and warning letters were received by many a terror-stricken woman. The latter were of course the work of cruel practical jokers. The fact, by the way, that the murderer never shifted his ground rather inclines one to the belief that he was a mad, poverty-stricken inhabitant of some slum in the East End.

I shall never forget one occasion when I had to shadow our man during one of his late walks. As I watched him from the house opposite one night, it suddenly struck me that there was a wilder look than usual on his evil countenance, and I felt that something was about to happen. When darkness set in I saw him come forth from the door of his little shop and glance furtively around to see if he were being watched. I allowed him to get right out of the street before I left the house, and then I set off after him. I followed him to Leman Street, and there I saw him enter a shop which I knew to be the abode of a number of criminals well known to the police.

He did not stay long. For about a quarter of an hour I hung about keeping my eye on the door, and at last I was rewarded by seeing him emerging alone.

He made his way down to St. George's in the East End, and there to my astonishment I saw him go and speak to a drunken woman.

I crouched in a doorway and held my breath. Was he going to throw himself into my waiting arms? He passed on after a moment or two, and on I slunk after him.

As I passed the woman she laughed and shouted something after me, which, however, I did not catch.

Det. Constable Henry Cox
from The Dundee Courier, 13th December 1906

Det. Sergeant Robert Sagar
from The City Press, 7th January 1905

My man was evidently of opinion that he might be followed every minute. Now and again he turned his head and glanced over his shoulder, and consequently I had the greatest difficulty in keeping behind him.

I had to work my way along, now with my back to the wall, now pausing and making little runs for a sheltering doorway. Not far from where the model lodging-house stands he met another woman, and for a considerable distance he walked along with her.

Just as I was beginning to prepare myself for a terrible ordeal, however, he pushed her away from him and set off at a rapid pace.

In the end this brought me, tired, weary, and nerve-strung, back to the street he had left where he disappeared into his own house.

Next morning I beheld him busy as usual. It is indeed very strange that as soon as this madman was put under observation the mysterious crimes ceased, and that very soon he removed from his usual haunts and gave up his nightly prowls. He was never arrested for the reason that not the slightest scrap of evidence could be found to connect him with the crimes.

When one takes into account the fact that the suspect knew he had been identified at the Seaside Home, according to Swanson's marginalia, it is not so strange that the crimes ceased once surveillance began. Cox's suspect appears to have realised that he was being watched, and if this was indeed the same man described by Swanson then the suffocating police presence would have prevented him carrying out further attacks.

In his article Cox made a point of dismissing the theory that the Ripper was held at a private asylum, along with other suggestions as to his fate, but by admitting at the conclusion of the article that he did not know whether the murderer was alive or dead, it appears that the former Detective Inspector was unaware of what happened to the man he had trailed along Leman Street and other East End thoroughfares – to Cox, he simply disappeared.

Seemingly more certain was Cox's colleague Det. Sergeant Robert Sagar, who it was claimed in newspaper reports following his retirement had represented the City of London detectives at nightly meetings with the Met's Det. Chief Inspector Swanson at Leman Street station.[51] While it has been seen that Inspector James McWilliam met nightly with Swanson, it is likely that Sagar was also in attendance as one of the leading City detectives.

Known as "The Doctor" because he had initially trained in medicine at Bart's Hospital, Robert Sagar had found lodgings in the nearby house of a City of London detective named Potts,[52] almost certainly the William Potts who lived at nearby 47 Bartholomew Close with his wife Emma and sons William Jr. and Robert.[53]

Sagar became increasingly interested in criminology while studying at Bart's, and apparently assisted with dozens of cases during his five years of medical training until, at last, an accident whereby he fell onto a pickaxe while chasing a burglar, injuring his leg, brought him to the attention of James Fraser, Commissioner of the City of London Police.[54] Fraser invited the amateur detective to join the City force, which he did in 1880. One of his first cases was the arrest of pickpocket Joseph Bignold on 10th December that year.[55] In March the following year he remanded the notorious Walter Selwyn on another charge in connection with the forger's arrest by Donald Swanson in April 1881.[56]

It was reported that during the Whitechapel murders Sagar aroused the suspicion of two policemen while working undercover,[57] and an intriguing newspaper report from late November 1888 described a similar scenario while discussing the excitability of the "Whitechapel mob" when it came to suspicious persons:

> Among others who have had experience of this species of mistaken identity is a police constable of the City. He was parading in the Whitechapel Road in civilian costume, and, ominously enough, wore a

low-crowned felt hat. The hat attracted a crowd, and the poor fellow had ultimately to run for his life. Other constables who wore uniforms explained matters to his persecutors.[58]

As a City officer, Sagar should, of course, have obtained permission from his Metropolitan Police counterparts before embarking on undercover work on their territory.

Following Sagar's retirement on 5th January 1905, a number of newspaper articles discussed the Ripper crimes alongside other memorable cases from his career. *The City Press* of 7th January published stark details of the murderer's fate:

> Much has been said and written – and even more conjectured – upon the subject of the "Jack the Ripper" murders. It has been asserted that the murderer fled to the Continent, where he perpetrated similar hideous crimes; but that is not the case. The police realised, as also did the public, that the crimes were those of a madman, and suspicion fell up on a man, who, without a doubt, was the murderer. Identification being impossible, he could not be charged. He was, however, placed in a lunatic asylum, and the series of atrocities came to an end.[59]

An interview with Sagar conducted by a representative of the *Daily News* on 7th January appeared in their edition of the 9th. When asked what was the most sensational case to which he had been connected during his career, Sagar replied:

> Well, I can hardly say. Possibly that series of tragedies which came to be known as the 'Jack the Ripper' murders. As you know, the perpetrator of these outrages was never brought to justice, but I believe he came the nearest to being captured after the murder of the woman Kelly in Mitre Square.[60] A police officer met a well-known man of Jewish appearance coming out of the court near the square, and a few moments after fell over the body. He blew his whistle, and other officers running up, they set off in pursuit of the man who had just left. The officers were wearing indiarubber boots, and the retreating footsteps of a man could be clearly heard. The sounds were followed to King's Block in the model dwellings in Stoney Lane, but we did not see the man again that night. The apron which had been worn by the unfortunate woman was found under the stairs in a common lodging house in Dorset Street [sic], and on the wall over it were scrawled the words: "The Jewes are not the people who will be blamed for nothing." I feel sure we knew the man, but we could prove nothing. Eventually we got him incarcerated in a lunatic asylum, and the

series of murders came to an end.⁶¹

Confirmation of Sagar's claim that P.C. Edward Watkins met a Jewish-looking man leaving Mitre Square, and a subsequent chase to Stoney Lane, has not been forthcoming, but it is a strange embellishment for the retiring detective to make were there not some truth in it.

On the same day as the *Daily News* report, the *Morning Leader* published their own interview with the detective, which added some more tantalising detail:

> Asked about these mysterious crimes, Mr. Sagar said, despite the many stories which are told, the police never had any proof who committed them.
>
> "We had good reason to suspect a certain man who worked in Butcher's Row, Aldgate," he said, "and we watched him carefully. There was no doubt that this man was insane, and after a time his friends thought it advisable to have him removed to a private asylum. After he was removed there were no more Ripper atrocities."⁶²

Also on 9th January, the *Gloucester Citizen* commented on Sagar's theory in their 'London Letter' column, comparing it to that of the journalist George R. Sims, who had apparently told the writer that "these murders were committed by a medical man who afterwards committed suicide near the Embankment," a reference to Ripper suspect Montague Druitt. Somewhat strangely, The *Citizen* reported it was believed the killer "made his way to Australia and there died".⁶³ Whether this was ever stated by Robert Sagar, or was in fact a misunderstanding on the part of the *Citizen* writer, is unclear.

The 1905 reports of Sagar's retirement not only supply details of the suspect and his fate, but they also confirm that identification was impossible – a full five years before Robert Anderson wrote of the failed attempt in his 1910 memoirs.

The suspect was, claimed Sagar, placed in a lunatic asylum; in one account saying that *"we* got him incarcerated" – presumably meaning the police – and in another by his friends. Either way, once the suspect was under lock and key the Ripper murders came to an end.

But according to the Swanson marginalia, before this happened he was first sent to the Stepney Workhouse.

The facility referred to by Swanson is uncertain. The Stepney Poor Law Union was founded in December 1836, initially representing the parishes of Limehouse, Mile End Old Town, Ratcliffe, Shadwell and Wapping. By the 1880s Wapping and Limehouse had closed; Mile End Old Town separated from Stepney Union in 1857 and soon built its own workhouse. Although geographically in Stepney, it's doubtful that Mile End Old Town Workhouse was ever known colloquially as 'Stepney Workhouse', and it seems unlikely that Swanson would refer to it as such, despite candidate Aaron Kosminski being admitted to the infirmary there first in July 1890 and then in February 1891; more on this later.

A more likely possibility is the workhouse at Bromley-by-Bow, built by the Stepney Union in 1861 and which opened its doors in March 1863.

Although more formally the St. Leonard's Street Workhouse, and later Bromley House, it was known as the 'Stepney Workhouse' from the start.[64] In December 1888 a year-end report counted 194 people in the workhouse, down from 231 the previous year.[65]

Recently removed from that number was 81-year-old Jane Merry, an inmate employed as a bath attendant. An inquest was held at the Workhouse on 9th December 1888, Coroner Wynne Baxter hearing that she had died in extraordinary circumstances on the 6th. Earlier that week Mrs. Merry had enjoyed a day off, seemingly taking advantage of her absence from the Workhouse to seek out some festive cheer. On the morning of her death another inmate named Bridget Davitt went to the bathing room and at first thought it was empty, but then heard a thumping noise. Ms. Davitt went to investigate and was astonished to see a pair of legs sticking up from a hole in the floorboards. A local engineer employed by the workhouse named Edward Sheen came to free the stricken Mrs. Merry and, after no little effort, took her to the infirmary, where she died almost immediately. Mr. Sheen returned to the spot and entered the hole, where under some wood he found a bottle of whisky – "Just where a person, by leaning through the aperture, could reach it," he told the inquest.[66]

Those more fortunate than Mrs. Merry who got to spend their Christmas Day at the Stepney Union Workhouse a fortnight later were treated to roast pork and potatoes followed by plum pudding and ale, with each adult receiving tobacco and snuff and the poor children spending their Christmas in the workhouse being given apples, oranges and nuts.

In contrast to their neighbours at Stepney Union, inmates of the

City of London Union Workhouse and Infirmary a mile away on Bow Road enjoyed roast beef for their Christmas dinner of 1888, along with plum pudding, oranges, apples and beer, with tobacco and snuff again generously handed out.[67]

The City of London Union had been established in the 1830s, one of three covering the City – the others being the East London Union and the West London Union. Initially preferring to give 'outdoor' relief to its paupers rather than building a workhouse of its own, the Union eventually relented and decided to build a workhouse of its own. As was the case with many City of London facilities this was situated outside of the City's boundary, on Bow Road. The premises, which could house up to 800 inmates, opened in 1849.

When the three unions were merged into an enlarged City of London Union twenty years later, the new union took over the former East London Union Workhouse at Homerton and the West London Union Workhouse in Upper Holloway, with the Bow Road site becoming the Union's infirmary.

An example of how easy it would be for a dangerous wandering lunatic to be admitted to a workhouse came with news of an horrific murder at the City of London Workhouse at Homerton in 1880. The incident began when a City of London constable found a man lying unconscious in Aldersgate on the evening of 29th June. He was taken to Moor Lane Police Station and then to the City of London Infirmary, where he was searched and papers including a passport dated February 1880 revealed his identity to be David Saleneskam, a Russian. He was unable to speak more than a few words of English, so the following morning a Polish Jewish inmate named Harris was sent to talk to him in their native Yiddish. Saleneskam seemed pleased to have someone to converse with, and spent the day chatting amiably enough.

That evening he was lying in bed, with Harris sitting reading at a table. Another inmate named Hollingsworth was also in the room, when suddenly the Russian jumped out of bed and swung a chair at the latter, fortunately missing his intended target. Harris was not so lucky and was struck numerous times around the head with the chair, which broke into pieces, and the victim's brains were quite literally knocked out. Saleneskam was overpowered and strapped down to the bed; the police arrived and found him to be in a state of raving madness.[68]

Saleneskam's subsequent court appearance makes chilling reading, with echoes of how 'Kosminski' may have appeared by the time of his admission to the infirmary:

> The Russian who murdered a man named Harris in the infirmary of the City of London Workhouse was brought up at the Thames Police Court, London, on Friday. He appeared to be dangerously insane, stood manacled in the dock, paid no heed to the evidence given, and prayed in a low voice incessantly. The magistrates ordered his removal to an asylum.[69]

Given the suggestion that the identification of the suspect may well have taken place at Morley House, in the City of London Police wing, and detectives of that force afterwards carried out intense surveillance of the man, it's interesting to consider the possibility that the workhouse referred to by Swanson was that of the City of London on Bow Road.

As seen in the above incident, an unknown wandering lunatic was picked up by a City of London constable and taken first to Moor Lane Police Station and then the City of London Union's infirmary on Bow Road.

If 'Kosminski' was treated as a City suspect, could it have been possible that he had been sent to one of that Union's facilities, either Bow Road, Homerton or Upper Holloway? It would have been likely that the City of London Police would refer to their workhouses as Homerton, Holloway and Stepney; is this the 'Stepney Workhouse' written by Donald Swanson?

Yet another possibility is the Whitechapel Workhouse Infirmary, built as the Whitechapel and Spitalfields Union workhouse in 1842 at the corner of Charles Street and Thomas Street. When a new workhouse was opened at South Grove in 1872 the original facility became the Infirmary, with Charles Street renamed Baker's Row.

Again, if this was the workhouse referred to by Swanson he surely would have written "Whitechapel", not Stepney. Yet the Baker's Row infirmary was well used with regards to the Whitechapel murders case; Elisabeth Stride was treated there for bronchitis over a week between 28th December 1881 and 4th January 1882, and Annie Millwood was admitted on 25th February 1888 with stab wounds to her legs and lower torso. At the end of the year Annie Farmer was an inmate at the Infirmary, being admitted with wounds to her throat on 21st November. She would be discharged on 1st December – less than a week before a dangerous wandering lunatic was himself admitted.

But regardless of where the suspect was admitted, Swanson wrote that he was sent with his "hands tied behind his back". Was this for his own safety – or that of others – or did it mean under police restraint? If the latter, and the suspect was not under arrest, was this legal?

An interesting letter on the subject was sent to a newspaper in 1886 by Herman Mozley of Lincoln's Inn regarding a recent case in which a Mr. Yates had complained of being handcuffed and taken to Derby Gaol despite not having been arrested. Mr. Mozley quoted from *Addison on Tests, 5th Edition*:

> A constable or peace officer has no right to handcuff an unconvicted prisoner, unless he has attempted to escape, or except it is necessary in order to prevent his escaping.[70]

If this was indeed the case, would it not be likely that the suspect – especially possibly a dangerous killer – would be placed under restraint?

He almost certainly would have been when being transferred to Colney Hatch Lunatic Asylum.

In 1827 a House of Commons Select Committee revealed the shocking neglect and mistreatment of the insane poor in private asylums and workhouses in the county of Middlesex,[71] the resulting public outcry leading to the building of the first Middlesex County Lunatic Asylum at Hanwell, which opened its doors in 1831.

The institution was a huge success; the specialist skills and care developed by Hanwell's staff won public approval, and the first superintendent, William Ellis, was knighted in 1835. It was at Hanwell that mechanical restraint was abolished in 1839. So popular was the asylum that in its first fifteen years the number of inmates trebled to more than 900, but this still failed to keep up with the demands of Middlesex's constantly-growing population. When it was suggested that the asylum be enlarged in order to double the number of inmates, authorities put their foot down. The result was the decision to build a second asylum, in the eastern side of the county, leaving Hanwell to care for the insane poor of west Middlesex.[72]

While the institution at Hanwell had been built alongside the Grand Junction Canal in order to easily transport goods in bulk, a site comprising 118 acres was purchased for the new asylum adjoining the Great Northern Railway which was at that time under construction, and a new dedicated station – Colney Hatch[73] – would be opened in August 1850.

A competition was launched to find the designer of the building, which would accommodate 1,000 patients, a third in single rooms and the remainder in dormitories of four or five beds. The winner was Samuel Daukes, a pupil of the architect J. P. Pritchett, whose company had been architects of the West Riding County Lunatic Asylum at Wakefield, Yorkshire.

The building contract was awarded to George Myers, whose tender of £138,000[74] was some £61,000 below that of his nearest rival,[75] and the foundation stone was laid during a grand ceremony on 8th May 1849, at which the Chairman of Middlesex Magistrates, Henry Pownall, proudly declared that "No hand or foot would be bound here."

Even while the asylum was being built it was enlarged to take a further 250 patients, with the result that when the keys were handed over on 1st November 1850 the final cost was almost £300,000, or £232 per bed[76] – the most expensive asylum ever built.

More than six miles of corridors provided access to 32 wards, with each containing 30-40 single bedrooms – some padded – and a small dormitory, along with a lavatory, bathroom, scullery, storeroom and two attendant's rooms. Plain tables and benches provided the furniture, and in an attempt to prevent patients injuring themselves corners were rounded. Other measures included locked wire guards for each open fireplace, of which there were three on each ward, and the windows could be locked open or closed by the attendants.[77]

At the time of its opening in July 1851, Colney Hatch was the largest and most modern mental institution in Europe, but within five years flaws in its design had already become apparent. The iron-framed windows, designed with safety in mind, opened just one or two inches at the top and thus admitted little air. The labyrinthine wards were dark and ill-heated, and the long corridor gloomy even in daytime. Handrails on the stairs were not installed until 1887. Serious construction defects were exposed well before 1860, with the bricked arched ceilings cracking and collapsing in Wards 26 and 28; by 1888 all of these arches had been removed and replaced by plastered ceilings reinforced by girders. The roof regularly leaked due to the poor construction of its asphalt covering and required constant repair. Perhaps most seriously, it was discovered that the foundations were insecure, with less than two feet of concrete being used in places instead of the standard four feet; parts of the asylum began to subside. The Committee initiated proceedings against architect Daukes, although these were later dropped.[78]

But with the excitement of the new asylum still fresh upon its completion, the chapel and cemetery were consecrated on 1st July 1851 and the first patients arrived on 17th July, transferred from workhouses and private institutions.

Colney Hatch Asylum
Author's collection

While it might have been expected that patients would be immediately transferred from Hanwell to the new facility, a glitch in the law meant that there was no provision to transfer patients directly between the two institutions; those at Hanwell had to be formally discharged before new medical certificates could be prepared and orders for removal to Colney Hatch then drawn up. For some time the ludicrous position existed of Hanwell being overcrowded while Colney Hatch remained half full.

The medical superintendent of the female side would write of the first arrivals at Colney Hatch:

> The admission during a single week of so many as 135 insane persons, and in another instance, on one day, of even 84 patients, was necessarily not unattended with considerable anxiety; more particularly so, as some of the details of the building and the wards, &c. were not, perhaps, in that state of completeness necessary for the accommodation of their expected inmates... The general inexperience of the attendants... aggravated this anxiety not a little.[79]

The staff soon found their feet. By the end of the first year 515 lunatic men and 729 women resided at the asylum,[80] bringing the institution almost to its capacity of 1,250 patients, within ten years it had been enlarged to accommodate 2,000.

So-called 'Imbecile asylums' were opened in 1870 at Leavesden, 16 miles north of Colney Hatch, and Caterham in Surrey, and although some

491 long-stay patients were sent from Colney Hatch, overcrowding there was not relieved.

A third Middlesex County asylum was built at Banstead in 1877, taking 350 patients from Colney Hatch. A further reduction in numbers was achieved in 1888 when the Committee of Visitors reached an agreement with Lancaster Asylum in the north of England to transfer 150 patients, who "have neither relative not friends to visit them, and therefore to whom locality is of no importance."

In 1888 the weekly cost of keeping a patient at Colney Hatch was 9s 11/4d, worked out by totalling all costs such as salaries, provisions, clothing and medicines and dividing by the number of patients on that given day.

Despite this apparent richness of care, the annual report for 1889 revealed medical neglect of the patients over the preceding twelve months, caused by the limited number of medical staff in the asylum which

> consists of two doctors for 921 male patients, and three for 1,324 female patients; of the former, 101 are actively suicidal, 134 epileptic, 145 are in the infirmaries, 50 are general paralytics; of the latter, 23 are actively suicidal, 122 epileptic, 80 are in the infirmaries, 16 are general paralytics.[81]

A year earlier, in 1887, of the 190 patient deaths at Colney Hatch almost half were as a result of brain disease.[82]

The admission of criminal lunatics – some of whom had done little more than stealing a loaf of bread or breaking and entering – had long been looked upon with regret at Colney Hatch, not only because of the increased propensity for violence but because of the demand for special security measures.

When Broadmoor opened in 1863 an opportunity came to remove the worst of this type of patient, with Colney Hatch's then Female Superintendent Dr. W.G. Marshall writing in that year's annual report:

> The removal of these Patients... to their proper place of detention has considerably relieved the Nurses of a heavy responsibility...

Dr. Sheppard, writing of the male patients, lamented:

> I wish... there was a greater probability than there appears to be of the removal of our Criminal Patients, now numbering 18. The demoralizing effects of... the inter-mixture of this class of men with our ordinary

inmates are... obvious... The difficulty, moreover, of treating these individuals as they require to be treated, is another cogent reason why they should have some other home... than a County Pauper Asylum.[83]

Things had scarcely improved by 1886, when the Committee of Visitors bemoaned the impact of the criminal lunatic element among the Colney Hatch patients on the 'ordinary' patients. They had brought the matter to the attention of the Home Secretary, who had done nothing more than acknowledge their letter.[84]

This, then, was the state of affairs at Colney Hatch Asylum when Det. Chief Inspector Donald Swanson's suspect 'Kosminski' was admitted. Only that year a physical examination on admission had become a requirement after a patient had died from a broken jaw and it was unknown whether it had been sustained prior to his admittance or afterwards; even then, the examination consisted simply of an inspection to ascertain whether the patient had any injuries or bruises on arrival. Subsequently, the parish officer bringing the patient to the asylum had to remain until formalities were completed.[85]

And so to the suspect, 'Kosminski'.

Although the name was supposedly first revealed with the discovery of Swanson's marginalia in 1981, it had actually been included in a report written by Det. Chief Constable Sir Melville Macnaghten in February 1894 to rebut claims made at the time by a national newspaper that one Thomas Cutbush, a 27-year-old clerk who in 1891 had been charged with 'feloniously cutting and wounding' a woman with intent to 'do grievous bodily harm' but declared insane and subsequently detained at Her Majesty's pleasure at Broadmoor Asylum, was in fact the Whitechapel murderer.

A series of articles published in the *Sun* in February 1894 claimed detailed 'proof' that Cutbush was the Ripper,[86] raising the possibility of a public inquiry. Commissioner Sir Edward Bradford would, in all probability, have requested a briefing on the *Sun*'s suspect in order to be prepared for such an eventuality.

Macnaghten's report was written sometime between 17th and 23rd February 1894, first in the form of rough notes and then edited for submission on the latter date.

In the event, no public inquiry was called and the sensational story faded into memory; Macnaghten's memorandum was filed,[87] and would not be viewed by the public until author Robin Odell unearthed it, misfiled, at Scotland Yard in July 1965 during research for the paperback version of his book *Jack the Ripper in Fact and Fiction*.

But before this, another version of the report had been discovered, held by Macnaghten's family and seemingly his draft of the memorandum. The papers were discovered when journalist and presenter Daniel Farson began work on *Farson's Guide to the British*, a two-part television programme scheduled for transmission in November 1959. While staying with a friend, Lady Rose McLaren, he happened to mention his work for the programme, which would include a segment on Jack the Ripper. Lady Rose was amazed at the coincidence, saying she had planned to take him to visit her mother-in-law, Christabel, Lady Aberconway – who happened to be Sir Melville Macnaghten's daughter.

Farson would write of the meeting in the introduction to his 1972 book Jack the Ripper:

> A few hours later at Maenan Hall, I explained my interest to Christabel Aberconway and she was kind enough to give me her father's private notes which she had copied out soon after his death.[88]

Farson was given permission to use these notes, now known as the Aberconway version, on the condition that no names were revealed.

November 1959 proved to be a busy month in the Ripper world. A few days before the first part of *Farson's Guide to the British* aired, the *New Statesman* ran a review of Donald McCormick's *The Identity of Jack the Ripper*. It drew a response from Lady Aberconway, her interest presumably roused by her contact with Farson. Her letter to the *New Statesman* was published on 7th November 1959:

> I possess my father's private notes on Jack the Ripper in which he names three individuals 'against whom police held very reasonable suspicion' and states which of these three, in his judgement, was the killer. None of these three names is mentioned by Mr. McCormick.[89]

This disclosure by Lady Aberconway revealed to the world the existence of Sir Melville Macnaghten's notes; it would beat Farson's 'exclusive' on national television by five days, for it was on 12th November that the second part of *Farson's Guide to the British*, containing his segment on the Whitechapel murders, was screened. In it, Farson discussed the Aberconway notes and Sir Melville's suspects, adhering to Lady Aberconway's wishes by referring to the perceived chief suspect by his initials only: 'M.J.D.'.

The Aberconway version would prove to be more detailed than the official report, and it is this account to which we turn our attention.

After detailing – and dismissing – the case against Thomas Cutbush, Macnaghten established what is now known as the five 'canonical' Ripper victims, echoing Dr. Thomas Bond's 1888 report, and listed three possible suspects whom he felt could be considered more likely to be the murderer:

> The case referred to in the sensational story told in the *Sun* (in its issues of 14 Feb 1894 and following dates) is that of Thomas Cutbush who was arraigned at the London County Sessions in April 1891 on a charge of maliciously wounding Florence Grace Johnson and attempting to wound Isabella Fraser Anderson in Kennington. He was found to be insane and sentenced to be detained during Her Majesties [sic] pleasure.
>
> This Cutbush who lived at 14 Albert Street Kennington Street escaped from the Lambeth Infirmary (after he had been detained there only a few hours) at noon on 5 March 1891. He was re-arrested on 9th idem. Previously to this, – a few weeks before several cases of stabbing girls behind had occurred in the neighbourhood, and a man called Colicott was arrested and charged, but was subsequently discharged owing to doubtful identification. The cuts in the girls' dresses in Colicott's case were quite distinct from those made by Cutbush, who was no doubt influenced in his action by a wild and morbid desire of imitation.
>
> Cutbush's antecedents were enquired into by P.S. McCarthy, (an officer who was specially employed in Whitechapel during the time of the murders there); it was ascertained that he was born, and had lived always, at Kennington. His Father died when he was quite young, and he was a 'spoilt' child. He had been employed as a clerk and traveller in the Tea Trade at the Minories, and subsequently canvassed for a Directory in that part of London – during which time he bore a good character. He, apparently, contracted syphilis about 1888, and after that year led an idle and useless life. His brain seems to have become affected, and he believed that people were endeavouring to poison him. He wrote to Lord Grimthorpe, and others, – and also to the Treasury, complaining of Dr. Brooks, Westminster Bridge Road (whom he threatened to shoot!) for having supplied him with indifferent medicines. He is said to have studied medical books by day, and to have rambled about at night, returning to his home with his clothes covered with mud etc., However, little reliance can be placed on the statements of his Mother, or his aunt, who were both of a very excitable disposition.

I may mention that this Thomas Cutbush was the nephew of the late well-known Supt. of Executive Branch at C.O.[90] The knife found on him was traced, and found to have been bought by him at Houndsditch about a week before he was detained in the Lambeth Infirmary, or just 2 years and 3 months after the last Whitechapel murder was committed! This upsets the statement made in the Sun's issue of 14th Feb. That "the writer has in his possession a facsimile of the knife with which the murders were committed."

The statement, too, that Cutbush "spent a portion of the day in making rough drawings of the bodies of women, and of their mutilation," is wholly based on the fact that two drawings of women in indecent postures were found torn up in his room. The head and body of one had been cut from some old 'fashion plate', and the legs were added and made to represent naked thighs and pink stockings.

The statement in the issue of 15th Feb. that a man in a light overcoat had been seen talking to the woman, who dismembered torso was found in Pinchin St, (and that a light overcoat was among the things discovered in Cutbush's house) is hopelessly incorrect. On 10th Sept. 1889 the naked body, with arms, of a woman was found under a Railway arch in Pinchin Street; the head and legs never came to light, nor was the woman ever identified. She had been killed at least 24 hours before the remains were discovered, and the said remains had evidently been brought from some distance. The head and legs had been severed from the body in a manner identical with that of the women whose remains were discovered, piecemeal, in the Thames, Battersea Park, and on the Chelsea Embankment on 4th June of the same year (1889) and these murders (?) had no connection whatever with the Whitechapel horrors. The Rainham mystery in 1887, and the Whitehall mystery (where the remains of a woman were found under New Scotland Yard in September 1888) were of a similar nature to the mysteries of "The Thames" and Pinchin St.

It is perfectly untrue to say (as the *Sun* asserts) that Cutbush stabbed six girls behind; this is confusing his case with Colicott – already spoken of.

The theory that the Whitechapel murderer was left handed, or, at any rate, 'ambi-dexter' had its origin in the statement of a certain doctor who examined the corpse of one of the earliest victims. Other doctors did not agree with him, and medical evidence, on this point, was (as it not infrequently is!) alike conflicting and confusing.

Now the Whitechapel murderer had 5 victims and 5 only. His murders were, as follows –

31st Aug. '88	Mary Ann Nichols who was found at Bucks Row with her throat cut and slight mutilation of the stomach.
8th Sept. '88	Annie Chapman found in a back yard at Hanbury St. throat cut and bad mutilation as to stomach and private parts.
30th Sept. '88	Elizabeth Stride – throat cut only (no mutilation) in Berners St.
do do	Catherine Eddowes, found in Mitre Square, throat cut, bad mutilation of face, stomach and private parts.
9th Novr. '88	Mary Jeanette Kelly – found in a room in Millers Court, Dorset St. with throat cut and the whole face and body fiendishly mutilated.

The last murder is the only one which took place in a room, and the murderer must have been at least 2 hours over his hellish job. A photograph was taken at the time, – (showing the woman as she was when the officers entered the room) without seeing which it is impossible to understand, or grasp the extent of the awful mutilation.

With regard to the double murder which occurred on 30th September there is no doubt that the 'Ripper' was disturbed by some Jews just after he had cut Elizabeth Stride's throat, and before he had time to commence to mutilate her. He had got the victim behind a kind of stable door through which three Jews drove up to an Anarchist Club in Berners Street. The murderer must have been alarmed and fled away – but, 'nondum satiatus', went off in search of a second victim whom he found in Mitre Square, and on whose body the mutilations far exceeded anything that he had before perpetrated. It will be noted that the fury of the murderer, as evinced in the mode of mutilation, increased every time, and his appetite appears to have become 'sharpened by indulgence.' It seems, then, improbable that he should have suddenly stopped after 9th Novr. 1888 and been content to resume operations by merely prodding a girl lightly from behind some 2 years and 4 months afterwards. A much more rational and workable theory, to my way of thinking, is that the 'rippers' brain gave way altogether after his awful glut in Millers Court and that he then committed suicide, or, as a less likely alternative, was found to be so helplessly insane by his relatives, that they, suspecting the worst, had him confined in some Lunatic Asylum.

No one ever saw the Whitechapel murderer (unless possibly it was the City P.C. who was on a beat near Mitre Square) and no proof could in any way ever be brought against anyone, although very many homicidal maniacs were at one time, or another, suspected. I enumerate the cases of 3 men against whom Police held very reasonable suspicion. Personally, after much careful & deliberate consideration, I am inclined to exonerate the last 2. but I have always held strong opinions regarding no 1., and the more I think the matter over, the stronger do these opinions become. The truth, however, will never be known, and did indeed, at one time lie at the bottom of the Thames, if my conjections be correct.

No.1 Mr M.J. Druitt a doctor of about 41 years of age & of fairly good family, who disappeared at the time of the Miller's Court murder, and whose body was found floating in the Thames on 31st Dec: i.e. 7 weeks after the said murder. The body was said to have been in the water for a month, or more – on it was found a season ticket between Blackheath & London.[91] From private information I have little doubt but that his own family suspected this man of being the Whitechapel murderer;[92] it was alleged that he was sexually insane. no 2. Kosminski, a Polish jew, who lived in the very heart of the district where the murders were committed. He had become insane owing to many years indulgence in solitary vices. He had a great hatred of women, with strong homicidal tendencies. He was (and I believe still is) detained in a lunatic asylum. about March 1889. This man in appearance strongly resembled the individual seen by the City P.C. near Mitre Square. no: 3. Michael Ostrog. a mad Russian doctor & a convict & unquestionably a homicidal maniac. This man was said to have been habitually cruel to women, & for a long time was known to have carried out with him surgical knives & other instruments; his antecedents were of the very worst & his whereabouts at the time of the Whitechapel murders could never be satisfactory accounted for. He is still alive.[93]

And now with regard to the 4 additional murders asertied [sic: ascribed] by the "Sun" writer to the "Ripper".

(1) The body of Martha Tabran [sic], a prostitute, was found on a common staircase in George Yard buildings, Whitechapel, on 7th August, 1888. When last seen she was in company of 2 soldiers and a companion prostitute; her body had received several stabs – apparently with a bayonet. The throat was not cut, and nothing in the way of mutilation was attempted. The two soldiers were arrested, but her companion failed, or rather refused, to identify.[94]

(2) Alice McKenzie was found on 17th July 1889 with her throat stabbed in Castle Alley, Aldgate. No evidence was forthcoming and no arrests were made. The stab in the throat was identically the same as that in the case of

(3) Frances Coles in Swallow Gardens on 13th Feb. 1891 for which

> Thomas Sadler, a Ship's fireman, was arrested, and – after several remands – discharged! It was subsequently ascertained that Sadler had sailed for the Baltic on 19th July '89 and was in Whitechapel on 17th the night when Alice McKenzie was killed. He was a man of ungovernable temper, and entirely addicted to drink and the company of the lowest prostitutes. I have no doubt whatever in my own mind as to his having murdered Frances Coles –
>
> (4) was the case of the unidentified woman who trunk was found in Pinchin Street on 10th Sept. '89 and has already been dealt with in this memorandum.
>
> M. L. Macnaghten.

When eventually discovered in 1965, the official report proved less expansive. While his account of Cutbush's history and the victims remained substantially the same, some of Macnaghten's descriptions of the suspects were diluted, apparently edited down to what seemed to be provable facts. Gone were references to the City P.C. who had seen the suspect near Mitre Square, and Macnaghten's belief that Kosminski was still held in a lunatic asylum at the time of the report.

The report might have been filed away and forgotten about as the *Sun*'s claims receded, but Macnaghten's suspects had their first public airing – albeit unnamed – in his friend Major Arthur Griffiths' *Mysteries of Police and Crime* of 1898:

> The outside public may think that the identity of that later miscreant, "Jack the Ripper," was never revealed. So far as absolute knowledge goes, this is undoubtedly true. But the police, after the last murder, had brought their investigations to the point of strongly suspecting several persons, all of them known to be homicidal lunatics, and against three of these they held very plausible and reasonable grounds of suspicion. Concerning two of them the case was weak, although it was based on certain suggestive facts.
>
> One was a Polish Jew, a known lunatic, who was at large in the district of Whitechapel at the time of the murder, and who, having developed homicidal tendencies, was afterwards confined in an asylum. This man was said to resemble the murderer by the one person who got a glimpse of him the police-constable in Mitre Court [sic].
>
> The second possible criminal was a Russian doctor, also insane, who had been a convict in both England and Siberia. This man was in the habit of carrying about surgical knives and instruments in his pockets; his

antecedents were of the very worst, and at the time of the Whitechapel murders he was in hiding, or, at least, his whereabouts was never exactly known.

The third person was of the same type, but the suspicion in his case was stronger, and there was every reason to believe that his own friends entertained grave doubts about him. He also was a doctor in the prime of life, was believed to be insane or on the borderland of insanity, and he disappeared immediately after the last murder, that in Miller's Court, on the 9th of November, 1888. On the last day of that year, seven weeks later, his body was found floating in the Thames, and was said to have been in the water a month. The theory in this case was that after his last exploit, which was the most fiendish of all, his brain entirely gave way, and he became furiously insane and committed suicide. It is at least a strong presumption that "Jack the Ripper" died or was put under restraint after the Miller's Court affair, which ended this series of crimes. It would be interesting to know whether in this third case the man was left-handed or ambidextrous, both suggestions having been advanced by medical experts after viewing the victims. It is true that other doctors disagreed on this point, which may be said to add another to the many instances in which medical evidence has been conflicting, not to say confusing.

This passage contains details not found in the final, official memorandum, but which do appear in the draft prepared by Macnaghten for that document. It must therefore seem probable that the Chief Constable lent his notes to Griffiths.

When Macnaghten released his memoirs *Days Of My Years* in 1914 he restrained himself considerably in his comments on the Ripper's identity, although by now firmly adhering to his belief that Druitt was the murderer, writing in his Preface: "...I became a detective officer six months after the so-called 'Jack the Ripper' committed suicide, and never had a go at that fascinating individual."

In his chapter on the murders Macnaghten wrote:

Although, as I shall endeavour to show in this chapter, the Whitechapel murderer, in all probability, put an end to himself soon after the Dorset Street affair in November 1888, certain facts, pointing to this conclusion, were not in possession of the police till some years after I became a detective officer.

...There can be no doubt that in the room at Miller's Court the madman found ample scope for the opportunities he had all along been seeking, and the probability is that, after his awful glut on this occasion, his brain gave way altogether and he committed suicide; otherwise the murders would not have ceased. The man, of course, was a sexual maniac, but such madness takes Protean forms, as will be shown later on in other cases. Sexual murders are the most difficult of all for police to bring home to the perpetrators, for "motives" there are none; only a lust for blood, and in many cases a hatred of woman as woman. Not infrequently the maniac possesses a diseased body, and this was probably so in the case of the Whitechapel murderer. Many residents in the East End (and some in the West!) came under suspicion of police, but though several persons were detained, no one was ever charged with these offences.

...I do not think that there was anything of religious mania about the real Simon Pure, nor do I believe that he had ever been detained in an asylum, nor lived in lodgings. I incline to the belief that the individual who held up London in terror resided with his own people; that he absented himself from home at certain times, and that he committed suicide on or about the 10th of November 1888, after he had knocked out a Commissioner of Police and very nearly settled the hash of one of Her Majesty's principal Secretaries of State.

That Macnaghten declined to name his suspect in print is perhaps not surprising, but it is interesting to note that he dismissed Kosminski, against whom he had previously stated "the police held very reasonable suspicion", with a simple "nor do I believe that he had ever been detained in an asylum".

But from where did Macnaghten obtain his information on Kosminski? Perhaps a clue is given in *Days Of My Years*, when he gave mention (and a crass attempt at humour) to the Brighton railway murder by Percy Lefroy Mapleton:

The murder of Mr. Gold, whose body was found in the Balcombe tunnel on the Brighton line, took place in 1881. I was in Bengal at the time, but, even in the Far East, the case caused considerable sensation. I well remember the grim riddle as to why it was expedient to purchase L.B. & B.C. Railway stock; the answer being because "gold" had been found in one of the Company's tunnels!

When I joined the Yard, seven or eight years later, I found that one of the then chief inspectors was the officer who had been deputed to make the various inquiries in London in connection with the case; and he it was, I think, who actually arrested Lefroy at his lodgings in a London suburb. He often told me the salient facts, which afforded an object-lesson to police officers as to the advisability of safe-holding a suspect after they once had laid their hands on him.⁹⁵

That officer was, of course, Donald Sutherland Swanson. Whether the "object-lesson" referred to Swanson and Frederick Jarvis's safe delivery of Lefroy from A Division's King Street Police Station to Lewes Gaol or the bungled observation by Det. Sgt. George Holmes is uncertain.⁹⁶

If Macnaghten had asked the Scot for the 'salient facts' of the Lefroy case following his appointment as Det. Chief Constable, it would be a natural next step for him to ask Swanson for details of some of the Ripper suspects. Note that Macnaghten fails to give a forename for Kosminski, as does Swanson in his endpaper notes in his copy of Anderson's memoirs. And Macnaghten also records that Kosminski had "become insane owing to many years indulgence in solitary vices", a reference to masturbation, a statement repeated by Anderson in *The Lighter Side of My Official Life* when he described his Polish Jew suspect as "a loathsome creature whose utterly unmentionable vices reduced him to a lower level than that of the brute."

It seems obvious that Macnaghten was writing about the same man as Sir Robert Anderson and Donald Swanson. There must have been a file on the suspect at some point, as with any other in the investigation.

But did Macnaghten refer to the full file when preparing his memoranda, or notes taken from conversations with Swanson which he then kept in his office for quick reference?

It's worth remembering that in his *Mysteries of Police and Crime* Macnaghten's friend Arthur Griffiths gave very similar details on the Polish Jew suspect as they appeared in the memoranda; it seems probable that he used Macnaghten's notes.

But who were they all writing about?

*

The man generally accepted today as Swanson's suspect is Aaron Kosminski, whose life and candidacy has been documented in Robert House's excellent *Jack the Ripper and The Case for Scotland Yard's Prime Suspect* (2011), which is a must-read for those seeking to understand the case against 'Kosminski', as is John Malcolm's *The Whitechapel Murders 1888: Another Dead End?* (2018).

Aaron first came to prominence as a result of author Martin Fido's searches in infirmary, asylum and workhouse records for a 'Kosminski' who fitted Robert Anderson's Polish Jew suspect and Melville Macnaghten's description of the man in his memoranda as he completed his book *The Crimes, Detection and Death of Jack the Ripper*.

It was at this time that Jim Swanson approached the *Daily Telegraph* offering his grandfather's notes on the suspect, and reporter Charles Nevin put him in touch with Martin.

Although Aaron Kosminski appeared in *The Crimes, Detection and Death of Jack the Ripper*, which was released in 1987, as a result of how the suspect was described in the marginalia he was almost immediately rejected as the killer by Martin. Despite this, more than thirty years later if someone mentions the name 'Kosminski' most assume they are talking about Aaron.

He was born Aron Mordke Kozminski on 11th September 1865, the youngest of seven children born to Abram Kosminski and Golda Lubnowski in Kłodawa, Poland before the family fled to London with the outbreak of the pogroms.

As we have seen, hundreds of Jews Anglicised their names on arrival in the capital; Aaron settled in Whitechapel with brothers Isaac and Woolf, who adopted the surname Abrahams, and sister Matilda, who married her first cousin Morris Lubnowski. While Aaron must have likewise adopted the name Abrahams, he also continued to use his birth name of Kosminski, as shown in one of the very few mentions of a poor Jewish inhabitant of the East End in the national newspapers.

Aaron appeared in more than one newspaper in their Court appearance columns in December 1889, after he had fallen foul of Commissioner Sir Charles Warren's 1886 edict that dogs being walked in public should be muzzled (see page 239) and appeared at the City Summons Court alongside fellow defendants Henry Rudd, who had muzzled his dog at five o'clock in the morning with the poor animal seen still wearing it three hours later, and Henry Hathaway, who had bought a dog at Leadenhall Market but had left the muzzle in the shop, which had closed by the time he realized and returned.[97] Alongside these gentlemen, Aaron Kosminski appeared after being caught by P.C. Borer[98] walking an unmuzzled dog in Cheapside. There was some disagreement over his correct name – the defendant gave 'Aaron Kosminski', but admitted that "I goes by the name of Abrahams sometimes, because Kosminski is hard to spell," which one of his brothers attending the summons came forward to confirm. His protesting that the dog wasn't his – it belonged to "Jacobs" – and refusal to pay the resultant 10s fine with costs as it was the Sabbath[99] seem to indicate that he was at that time capable of rational, albeit argumentative thought.

It was only in July 1890 that the first cracks in Aaron's mental wellbeing were recorded, when he was admitted to Mile End Old Town recorded as "Qy insane". After a stay of just four days he was discharged into the care of his brother, most likely Woolf, who had brought him in and who lived at 3 Sion Square.

On 4th February 1891 – nine days before the murder of Frances Coles in Swallow Gardens – Aaron was readmitted to Mile End Old Town, this time from the home of his sister Matilda and her husband at 16 Greenfield Street. He was examined two days later by H Division surgeon Dr. Edmund Houchin and declared insane.

Based not only on his own observations but also from facts given by one Jacob Cohen of Carter Lane in the City of London, Houchin's certification concluded that Aaron Kosminski felt himself "controlled by an instinct that informs his mind", and for this reason refused food given to him by others, preferring to eat pieces of bread from the gutter. Jacob Cohen had stated to the doctor that Aaron "took up a knife & threatened the life of his sister", but it is unclear whether this refers to Kosminski's own sister or that of Cohen;[100] there is a suggestion that the informant Jacob Cohen, who in early 1891 was in business at the Carter Lane address with Aaron's brother Woolf Abrahams and a third partner named Thomas Davies, was in fact the brother of Woolf's wife Betsy Kosminski.[101] Crucially, given that Robert Anderson and Melville Macnaghten both mentioned the suspect's "solitary vices", it is important to note that Cohen also told Dr. Houchin that Aaron practiced self-abuse, often blamed by Victorian officials for mental health issues.

With Dr. Houchin declaring Aaron Kosminski insane, the following day he was removed from Mile End Old Town Workhouse and taken to Colney Hatch asylum. He was recorded on discharge from Mile End as being neither suicidal nor dangerous to others, and over the course of the following three years at Colney Hatch he was observed to be in the main apathetic and quiet.

In April 1894 he was transferred to Leavesden Asylum for Imbeciles, where he died on 24th March 1919.[102]

There are many appealing facets to the idea of Aaron Kosminski being the suspect. He is the only inmate of Colney Hatch during the relevant period bearing the name 'Kosminski'. According to informant Jacob Cohen he was a compulsive masturbator, as claimed by Anderson and Macnaghten. He lived in Whitechapel, with easy access to the murder locations, and at one time his brother's family had in fact lived next door to the International Working Men's Educational Club in Berner Street, alongside the yard in which Elisabeth Stride was murdered.[103] Evidence of a murderer's knowledge of a locality, or coincidence?

But there's no record that he "had a great hatred of women", or displayed "strong homicidal tendencies" as claimed by Macnaghten, nor that he entered Stepney Workhouse "with his hands tied behind his back", as recorded by Swanson. And, most damagingly, Aaron Kosminski did not die shortly after his incarceration, as written by Swanson in his marginalia, but in fact lived for a further 28 years.

Taking all this carefully into consideration, I don't believe Aaron Kosminski was the man about whom Donald Swanson wrote, or that Anderson alluded to. The retired Assistant Commissioner wrote that the final Ripper murder was that of Mary Kelly in November 1888; if this is correct, it's simply not believable that the police would undertake surveillance "by day & night" for more than two years; and in fact Swanson wrote that the suspect was sent to the Stepney Workhouse and then Colney Hatch "in a very short time" after the identification attempt.

Equally, I cannot accept that Swanson would make so many serious errors in his account; having read hundreds of documents and personal letters written by him in the family archive I'm convinced that he remained quick-witted to the end of his life, regardless of whether he made his pencil annotations in 1910 when Anderson's book was published or a week before his death in 1924. Accusations of 'old men's memories' ignore the fact that, while he was indeed in his retirement, Donald Swanson was just 55-years-old when he resigned from the Metropolitan Police – the same age as this author as I write this.

Although I hope this book has shown that the Whitechapel murders were just part of a long and important career for the detective, it was the highest profile case of those 35 years and given Swanson held a leading role in the investigation it's inconceivable that he would have forgotten the facts of the case, especially those of the suspect described in print by his former superior – one of the few officers, alongside Swanson himself, who knew the full details.

The fanfare which accompanied the announcement in 2014 that Aaron Kosminski's DNA had been extracted from the so-called 'shawl' which had for many years been claimed to have belonged to Mitre Square victim Catherine Eddowes was soon muted when posters to Ripper message boards Casebook.org and JTRForums.com pointed out the poor provenance of the garment, and – more damagingly – that there were serious flaws in the DNA results as presented in Russell Edwards' *Naming Jack the Ripper* (2014). The evidence was finally published to peer review in *Science* in March 2019, but critics complained that key details of the specific genetic variants compared between DNA samples taken from descendents of Catherine Eddowes and Aaron Kosminski were not disclosed.[104]

No; unless we see future evidence to the contrary, to my mind Aaron Kosminski is an innocent in the ongoing game of 'name the Ripper', a victim in his own way of the honest endeavours of researchers and subsequently becoming entrenched in popular consciousness. By becoming the 'prime suspect' in the minds of the general public over the past thirty years he has, I believe, been unfairly maligned.

*

Another 'Kosminski' long-linked with the marginalia is Martin Kosminski, the brother of Samuel whose naturalisation application we saw as an example of the process on page 278.

Martin, born on 12th July 1845 at Kalisch, Poland, was three years older than Samuel, and had arrived in London several years earlier.

At the time of his application for naturalisation in January 1878 he lived at 36 New North Road, Hoxton with his wife and three children, and was carrying out a business as a furrier at 63 Aldermanbury in the City. On 13th December 1877 Kosminski had attended the Paternoster Row offices of solicitor Mr. H. Wells with referees Robert Ramsay, a collar dresser of East Road, Hoxton who stated that he had known the applicant for six years; Thomas Warrilow, a publican of Cemetery Road, Forest Gate (seven years) and his son Thomas Davis Warrilow of Dove Street, East India Road (eight years). The final referee was Joseph Hyam Levy, butcher of 1 Hutchison Street, Aldgate – the same Joseph Hyam Levy who had seen Catherine Eddowes with a man at the entrance to Church Passage shortly before her death. He stated that he had known Martin Kosminski for six years.[105]

It is unknown how the two men knew each other, but would seem probable that they had met over the six years in a social setting. Did they mix in the same business circles? Was Martin Kosminski a member of the Imperial Club, alongside Levy, Lawende and Harris?

By late 1880 Kosminski had moved to Loraine Road, Holloway,[106] and it was this address that younger brother Samuel gave as his first address on arrival in England in his own application seven years later. That year had been a difficult one for his business, in January being declared bankrupt[107] although this was annulled in the October.[108]

By 1888 Martin appears to have been in a stronger financial position. The Third Annual Report of The Poor Jews' Temporary Shelter, covering the years 1887-88, lists him as a generous subscriber, offering £2 2s.[109]

In July 1888 he was one of fourteen people named in an appeal placed in the *Jewish Standard* asking for donations for a man known personally

*Det. Sergeant James Nearn: the missing link?
from Lloyd's Weekly Newspaper, 29th December 1895*

to all of them whose business had failed, leaving his family destitute.[110]

Intriguingly, a business venture with brother Samuel was ended in March 1889, with the *Morning Post* reporting that the partnership of M. Kosminski and S. Kosminski, wholesale furriers, had been dissolved.[111] The reason is unknown. Further problems followed when the firm M. Kosminski and M. Woolf, trading under the name M. Kosminski and Co., filed for bankruptcy six months later.[112]

Thereafter Martin appears to have followed a successful career, by the time of the 1911 census living in a nine-roomed house in Berners Street in the West End with Augusta and a servant.[113]

The link between Martin Kosminski and Joseph Hyam Levy is still being investigated. Did Levy know Martin's brother Samuel? Was this family in any way related with the Whitechapel murders suspect? This remains to be seen, but it is interesting that the police officer who looked into Samuel Kosminski's naturalisation application, Sergeant James Nearn of N Division, was seconded to Whitechapel to assist with enquiries into the murders following the house to house search in mid October 1888. Was this pure coincidence, or did Nearn have valuable information? A pipe was presented to him on his retirement which, despite scant mention of him in the official files, was inscribed "Souvenir to James Nearn, Whitechapel Murders, 1888, from six brother officers". Who were the six, and what had Nearn done of note in the Ripper investigation which warranted such an inscription?

*

Perhaps the most intriguing candidate put forward as Anderson's Polish Jew is a young Jew brought before magistrates at Thames Police Court just a month after the generally accepted final murder by Jack the Ripper by H Division's P.C. John Patrick, charged with being a 'lunatic wandering at large'.

It was a chain of events which echoed the 1880 case of the insane Russian David Saleneskam; found by a constable on his beat, taken first to the police station and then to the infirmary for a short time before a committal to an asylum.

On Friday, 7th December 1888 the defendant appeared under the name 'Aaron Davis Cohen', with his last-known address recorded as 84 Leman Street. He was clearly mentally imbalanced, and it is therefore not certain whether he provided these details himself, or they were offered to the magistrates by police. If he had been unable to state his name, with no documentation on his person as David Saleneskam had done, how would officials know his identity, or indeed anything about him? Was the Leman Street address where he had been picked up by P.C. Patrick, or perhaps an attempt at providing him with a possible likely address, that of the Poor Jews' Temporary Shelter which was next door at No. 86?

His hearing was minuted with those of Ellen Hickey, Gertrude Smith and Mary Jones; the last two for brothel keeping, which is interesting when considering Charles Warren's report that he had received a letter from a brothel keeper who said there was a man living in her house who had been seen with bloodstains on the morning of Annie Chapman's murder. Despite this, there is no evidence that the cases before the Thames Police Court that day were linked beyond the covering record.

The magistrates wasted no time in committing Aaron Davis Cohen to the Whitechapel Workhouse Infirmary, and he was admitted there later that same day, entry 3983 in the Infirmary ledgers recording:

> Name: Cohen, David
> Age: 23
> Where admitted from: PC 91H Thames Police Ct
> Married or Single: Single
> Calling: Tailor
> Cause of Admission: Insane

Religion: Hebrew
By whose Order Admitted: M.O. [Medical Officer]
Time Admitted: 5.30pm
Ward sent to: B.G.
Settlement:
Date of Discharge: 21.12.88
Remarks: To Colney Hatch Asylum

That his name had now been abbreviated to 'David Cohen' would seem to indicate that it had indeed been given by police. The additional details of his age, occupation and marital status may well have also been supplied by them; an estimate for the patient's age, and 'tailor' being one of the most common occupations for an East End Jew.

In his fortnight at the Whitechapel Infirmary Cohen proved to be very violent; he was considered a danger to others, having threatened other patients, and was suicidal. He tore down a lead pipe and a wire guard from a window in the ward, and was described as "very noisy at night & very difficult to manage."

His behaviour following his transferral to Colney Hatch was recorded in detail:

> A young foreign Jew with dark brown hair, beard and eyes, who is brought to the asylum in restraint, and in a state of great excitement; the first thing he did on admission was to throw himself on the ground with considerable violence, he is exceedingly restless and refused all nourishment; he is pale and exceedingly thin.
> To be fed by tube when necessary.
> 1888 Dec 24 Been restless since admission. Refused food 2nd day after admission and was fed through oesophagal tube twice. Takes his food now with some persuasion. Asks for liquid food and after filling his mouth will spit it out again. Dressed in strong dress and kept under constant watch.
> 26th Takes food better now, but still only in liquid form.
> 28th Kept apart from other patients as patient is restless and agitated. Incoherent and rambling. Chiefly speaks in German.
> 30th Not so restless. Sleeps better at night. No violence recorded.
> 1889 Feb 5. Since last note has several small boils on his arms near wrists which are now cured. Continues in an excited state, but not to such a degree as before. Requires constant supervision. Destructive to clothing. Manner flighty and uncertain. Ordered 2 eggs extra each day. Speech is incoherent. Gesticulates frequently. Habits dirty occasionally.

Takes food well.

April 8th Restless and excited: frequently kicks passers-by; habits uncleanly and destructive, he is gaining strength.

July 7th Mischievous. Takes food well. Destructive to clothing. Requires constant attention. Health fair.

Oct 15th Removed to C5 lately. Becoming feebler lately and unable to walk without help. Examined him. Found him to be excited but incoherent as before. Temperature 108.2 evening. Left infra axillary region dull on percussion also infra mammary and infra scapular left side. Tubular breathing. Friction sound heard interiorly and moist sounds above. Does not speak. Expectorates a mucous, purulent fluid. Confined to bed. Ordered liquid diet. Poultices not retained. Stimulating expectorant mixture ordered.

Oct 20 Died.

David Cohen was located in the Colney Hatch Asylum records by author Martin Fido, who believed that he was by far the best fit for Jack the Ripper; his incarceration soon after the death of Mary Kelly would explain the sudden cessation of the murders, and he was the only violent Jewish inmate admitted. Crucially, he died shortly after being incarcerated at Colney Hatch, as Swanson wrote in his marginalia.

But Martin puzzled as to how 'David Cohen' and Swanson's 'Kosminski' might have become confused, wondering whether the name under which he was admitted to Colney Hatch was the Hebrew version of 'John Doe', a catch-all used when the name of a person was unknown or intentionally concealed. Perhaps, wondered Martin (and others), were the Met and City Forces watching different suspects, the names of whom became mixed up?

As is often the case, there is a much simpler possible alternative. Taking the suggestion above that the wandering lunatic brought up by P.C. Patrick was unable or unwilling to give his name himself, the officials would have supplied one for the purposes of admittance to the infirmary and asylum, unaware of his real name – which was Kosminski.

Allow me to suggest a scenario for which I have no evidence but is, I believe, a plausible chain of events.

As a result of the house-to-house search in mid October several persons of interest become apparent. The police begin observation on a number of suspects, including Kosminski.

On 9th November Mary Kelly was murdered in her room in Miller's Court. By this time detectives had narrowed the search down a handful of suspects, and in mid November Kosminski was sent to Morley House seaside home and identified at the facility's City of London Police wing by one of Lawende, Harris or Hyam Levy, the City witnesses – and for the record I lean towards the last named of the three, whose "knowing air" commented upon by a journalist I believe was exactly that.

Following the refusal of the witness to testify, Kosminski was returned to his brother's house in Whitechapel and placed under surveillance by City of London Police C.I.D. Although the reaction of both witness and suspect confirmed they knew each other, it was not enough to arrest Kosminski but the police now knew he was of extreme interest to the investigation.

City of London detective Henry Cox began his surveillance specifically on Kosminski; his colleague Robert Sagar gives the location as Butcher's Row, Aldgate. Knowing he was under intense observation, after just a few weeks the suspect was tipped over the edge into insanity and at the beginning of December was picked up as a wandering lunatic in Leman Street by the Met's Constable Patrick, who was completely unaware that the man was being watched by Cox and the City detectives.

Unable to get the man's name, or perhaps only part of it, he was recorded at Thames Magistrates' Court as 'Aaron Davis Cohen'. Deemed unable to take care of himself but obviously violent, he was sent to the workhouse infirmary under restraint. He was admitted as 'David Cohen', and a fortnight later transferred to Colney Hatch, where he died ten months later.

Unaware of this accidental intervention, the City police were under the impression that the man they were watching had simply vanished, and informed their Met counterparts to that effect. It was only later that they realised he had been locked up; at the end of December it was reported that detectives had visited a large number of lunatic asylums and made inquiries of those inmates recently admitted, with the *Dublin Express* incorrectly claiming that the Whitechapel murderer had been placed "out of harm's way" by his relatives.[114]

When he was discovered at Colney Hatch, there's no doubt that the police were happy to leave things as they were. If he was not Jack the Ripper, the incarceration of the suspect Kosminski as 'David Cohen' was at the very least a dangerous lunatic removed from the streets.

I would suggest that at this time the police were far from convinced that the Whitechapel murderer's gruesome career was at an end. They went on to investigate several more deaths in Whitechapel up to that of Frances Coles in 1891, and for Donald Swanson himself, the murder of Augusta Dawes by Reginald Saunderson in 1894.

That year Melville Macnaghten prepared his memoranda which included Kosminski, but only as one suspect of three more likely than Thomas Cutbush to be the Ripper.

Two years earlier Robert Anderson, in an interview for *Cassell's Saturday Journal*, despite exclaiming that the murders had been committed by a maniac revelling in blood, had been content to allow the reporter to described the Whitechapel murders as a series of "still undiscovered crimes".[115]

But by 1895 something had changed. Major Arthur Griffiths, writing as 'Alfred Aylmer' in *Windsor Magazine*, revealed that the Assistant Commissioner had come to the conclusion that Kosminski was the murderer:

> Much dissatisfaction was vented upon Mr. Anderson at the utterly abortive efforts to discover the perpetrator of the Whitechapel murders. He has himself a perfectly plausible theory that Jack the Ripper was a homicidal maniac, temporarily at large, whose hideous career was cut short by committal to an asylum.[116]

And, as we have seen, on 7th May 1895, in response to the recent attack on a woman in Spitalfields by William Grant Grainger and a discussion of the Ripper crimes, the *Pall Mall Gazette* reported:

> The theory entitled to most respect, because it was presumably based upon the best knowledge, was that of Chief Inspector Swanson, the officer who was associated with the investigation of all the murders, and Mr. Swanson believes the crimes to have been the work of a man who is now dead.

That Jack the Ripper was a Polish Jew named Kosminski who died in an asylum was now for Anderson, as he would later write, "a definitely ascertained fact."[117]

Other officers did not agree; retired Det. Chief Inspector John Littlechild wrote in a private letter to George R. Sims that "Anderson only thought he knew",[118] and Det. Inspector Frederick Abberline told a reporter from the *Pall Mall Gazette* in a 1903 interview that "it has been stated in several quarters that 'Jack the Ripper' was a man who died in a lunatic asylum a few years ago, but there is nothing at all of a tangible nature to support such a theory."[119] And, of course, he was correct – there *was* no tangible evidence.

As for Donald Swanson, he kept his opinion to himself until the discovery of his marginalia in the 1980s. But his written comment that "after this identification which suspect knew, no other murder of this kind took place in London" seems to confirm that he too believed Kosminski was in fact the murderer, and not just another suspect. And if anyone would know the identity of Jack the Ripper it would be Det. Chief Inspector Donald Sutherland Swanson, the officer in charge of the investigation from Scotland Yard, who read every report, every telegram and therefore knew more than anyone about the case.

None of this brings us closer to learning the identity of 'Kosminski', and if he lived his final months as 'David Cohen' we most likely never will.

But I'm interested by the Kosminski family of which brothers Martin and Samuel were members; it seems a massive coincidence that Martin's naturalisation application was supported by Mitre Square witness Joseph Hyam Levy, and that the Metropolitan Police officer who in 1887 investigated Samuel's background, Sergeant James Nearn, should the following year be seconded to the Whitechapel murders investigation around the time of the house-to-house search, when information came to light which put police on the trail of a Polish Jew. That he was presented with an inscribed pipe to commemorate his involvement in the case – on the surface supposedly minimal – is intriguing.

Both Martin and Samuel lived long lives (Martin died in 1930 and Samuel 1925) and can therefore be discounted, but was there another family member, presently unrecorded or undiscovered in English files, who might shed further light on the suspect – and possibly the identity of Jack the Ripper?

Yours faithfully
Donald S Swanson

APPENDIX THREE

Donald Sutherland Swanson Timeline

12th August 1848	Born at Geise Distillery, youngest child of John and Mary Swanson
1851	Family move to Thurso
c.1858-1863	Educated at the Parish School, Market Place
c.1863-1867	Educated at Miller Institution, Sinclair Street
1866-1867	Employed as Second Master at Miller Institution
July 1867	Moved to London, living with sister Mary and her family
July 1867-March 1868	Employed as a City clerk at offices of John Meikle
20th March 1868	Applied to join Metropolitan Police
31st March 1868	Attended interview at Candidates Department
April 1868	Awarded Warrant No. 50282 Assigned to A Division (Westminster) Sent to King Street station as P.C. 331A
6th October 1868	Fined for being in plain clothes without leave
24th October 1868	Promoted Police Constable 3rd Class
30th April 1869	Cautioned for receiving a shilling from a prisoner for bail the previous day
4th February 1870	Cautioned for being late on roll call and climbing over railings to avoid detection
10th February 1870	Promoted Police Constable 2nd Class
18th February 1870	Promoted Police Constable 1st Class
9th September 1870	Transferred to Y Division (Highgate) Based at Kentish Town station
11th December 1871	Promoted Police Sergeant
12th December 1871	Transferred to K Division (Bow) as P.S. 71K Based at Bow station

8th May 1873	Death of mother Mary Swanson
21st February 1874	Fined for being outside The Lion public house in Carlton Square with armlet off while on duty
3rd October 1874	Appointed Station Sergeant at Plaistow station
12th September 1876	Appointed Det. Sergeant Joined Detective Department Transferred to A Division (Scotland Yard)
23rd May 1878	Married Julia Ann Nevill at West Ham
6th July 1878	Promoted Det. Inspector
25th February 1879	Birth of son Donald Nevill Swanson
31st March 1879	Death of father James Swanson
5th March 1881	Birth of son James John Swanson
21st June 1883	Birth of daughter Ada Mary Swanson
19th November 1887	Transferred to Central Office, Scotland Yard
23rd December 1887	Birth of son Douglas Sutherland Swanson
9th February 1888	Promoted Det. Chief Inspector (Temporary)
2nd January 1889	Births of twins Alice Julia Swanson and William Alexander Swanson
10th February 1889	Death of son William Alexander Swanson
22nd December 1890	Promoted Det. Chief Inspector (Permanent)
30th April 1896	Promoted Det. Superindent C.I.D.
1st July 1903	Resigned on a pension of £280pa
25th November 1924	Died at home, 3 Presburg Road, New Malden
29th November 1924	Buried at Kingston Cemetery
4th December 1930	Death of son Douglas Swanson
16th May 1935	Death of widow Julia Ann Swanson
31st January 1966	Death of son Donald Swanson Jr
14th June 1969	Death of son James Swanson
21st September 1976	Death of daughter Ada Swanson
14th November 1980	Death of daughter Alice Swanson
November 1980	Swanson marginalia discovered
26th March 1981	Jim Swanson writes to the *News of the World* and *The Sunday Express* offering information contained in the Swanson marginalia

Notes and References

A note on money. All present-day monetary equivalents have been made using the National Archives historical currency convertor at www.nationalarchives.gov.uk/currency.

Becoming a Detective through Magnetism

1. H. B. Lodge was a local musician and entertainer who, through his connections with the great Victorian conjuror John Nevil Maskelyne, later became a member of the Magic Circle. Lodge used his conjuring expertise to expose mediums including 'the Davenport Brothers', 'Leontine and Desmond' and 'Herne and Williams'. Information from an obituary of Lodge, *Yorkshire Evening Post*, 5th March 1912.
2. *Leeds Times*, 28th October 1876. For an exposé of the methods used by Monck and other fake mediums of the Victorian period see *The Physical Phenomena of Spiritualism: Fraudulent and Genuine* by Hereward Carrington (1907).
3. *Morning Post*, 15th November 1876.
4. *Huddersfield Chronicle*, 5th January 1877.
5. *Manchester Evening News*, 6th February 1877.
6. The meeting was reported in the spiritualist journal *Medium and Daybreak*.
7. *Sunderland Daily Echo*, 10th February 1877.
8. Address given in a 'review' of *Medium and Daybreak*, in essence an advertisement, placed in *Grantham Journal* of 18th January 1873.
9. For many years the largest circulation weekly journal on spiritualism, *Medium and Daybreak* was founded by James Burns in 1869 as *Medium*, later merging with the provincial newspaper *Daybreak*. The newspaper ceased publication on Burns's death in 1895.
10. Private memoranda of Donald Swanson, a small ledger held in family archives.
11. *Birmingham Daily Post*, 10th February 1877.

Whisky Makers and Booragtooners

1. *John O'Groat Journal*, 22nd September 1886.
2. *Halkirk and its Highland Games*, 1977. The original licence for the Gerston Distillery was awarded to Francis Swanson in 1796 and passed to son George

upon his death, and then, in turn, to George's eldest son James Calder Swanson in 1836. James ran Gerston with his younger brother John under the name "J. & J. Swanson, Distillers". There is, as yet, no known link to the Swanson family at Geise.

3   "Caithness Giant" by Gavin D. Smith, *Whisky Magazine*, January 2010.
4   1851 census.
5   "Caithness Giant" by Gavin D. Smith, *Whisky Magazine*, January 2010. The 1871 census lists Gerston as consisting of 862 acres, of which 342 were arable. The *John O'Groat Journal* of 7th September 1871 carried an advertisement inviting offers for the estate on a 19 year lease, with a deadline of 24th October. Obviously no suitable offers were made, for on 16th May 1872 the same newspaper carried an advertisement for the sale of the estate. Listed alongside the Distillery and various farm buildings were 11 horses, 52 cattle, 639 sheep. The new owners closed the Distillery almost immediately, leaving it to eventually fall into disrepair. Today, just a small retainer wall is visible. Gerston II was built in 1896, being renamed as Ben Morven the following year by the London-based owners, Northern Distilleries Limited. It closed circa 1911. The Lost Distillery Company (*www.lost-distillery.com*) have recreated the Gerston whisky using historical archives and analysing the tools and ingredients available to the distillers of the nineteenth century.
6   The Newlands of Geise was created in the early nineteenth century by Captain John Henderson.
7   The ruins of the Distillery at Geise still stand as part of the Geise Heritage Trail, bearing a plaque with a date of '1851'. This probably relates to when the Distillery last operated, when the Swanson family left for Thurso.
8   1841 census.
9   Swanson Family Register written by John Swanson on 4th May 1871.
10 Swanson Family Register. First born was Alexander on 1st October 1829, followed by John on 8th July 1831. Sadly, Alexander died shortly after his second birthday, on 14th January 1832. A year later, on 16th May 1833, Mary bore John another son, whom they also named Alexander. Three daughters followed: Margaret on 2nd February 1835, Jannet on 3rd April 1837 and Mary on 6th April 1840.
11 Swanson Family Register. Donald Sutherland Swanson was baptised on 2nd October 1848.
12 Record of marriage. The couple had ten children: John (1851-1853), Elizabeth (1853-1911), John (1855-1906), Robert (1857-1857), Mary (1859-1911), Isabella (b1861), James (1863-1892), Donald (1868-1899), Sinclair (1868-1899) and Margaret (1874-1874). Elizabeth Gair Swanson died in childbirth in 1874 while delivering Margaret. John would die on 9th November 1891.
13 1851 census.
14 A booklet entitled 'Testimonials in Favour of Mr. John Swanson, Aberdeen' was put together in June 1884 for what proved to be an unsuccessful application for the position of Chief Constable for the County of Caithness. The testimonials

therein include one from City of London Police Commissioner Daniel Whittle Harvey, which records John Swanson joining the Force as Constable 2152 on 14th October 1852. He resigned on 20th October 1853.

15 Obituary of John Swanson in the *Aberdeen Journal*, 10th November 1891. The obituary mentions that both John Swanson and his son Donald Gair Swanson (1868-1899) served with the Metropolitan Police in London, although no evidence of this has been found. Donald died aged 31 on 3rd July 1899 in Penang Harbour, Malaysia, after falling overboard from the SS *Clive*, of which he was Chief Engineer. A newspaper report of 22nd August 1885 describes a different son, James, arriving in Aberdeen to arrest a German thief and take him back to London, which indicates that it was James Swanson, not Donald Gair, who was a Metropolitan Police officer, and indeed the 1891 census shows James as a Sergeant living in Bermondsey, south London.

16 1851, 1861, 1871, 1881 and 1891 census.

17 *Slater's Directory of Caithness-shire*, 1852.

18 Sir John Sinclair was born at Thurso Castle in 1754 and studied at the University of Edinburgh, University of Glasgow and Trinity College, Oxford. In 1780 he became MP for Caithness and held the position until 1811. He was instrumental in establishing the Board of Agriculture and was its first president, and between 1791 and 1799 compiled the first Statistical Account of Scotland.

19 *Slater's Directory of Caithness-shire*, 1852.

20 Caithness County Officers Default Book.

21 Caithness Constabulary Conviction Book 1858-1880.

22 *Parish of Thurso* by Rev. W. R. Taylor, October 1840.

23 Along with much of the 'Old Town', Durness Street was substantially re-developed between 1919 and 1931.

24 The Meadow Well, which still stands, was in use until the 1920s.

25 £395 today.

26 Caithness County Valuation Rolls 1858-1869.

27 *Slater's Directory of Caithness-shire*, 1852.

28 Caithness County Valuation Rolls 1858-1869.

29 Donald Swanson was born on 2nd February 1812 and joined the Metropolitan Police at Scotland Yard on 17th April 1843. Serving his entire career at A Division (Westminster), he was promoted Sergeant on 4th September 1852 and Inspector on 17th May 1859. He retired on an annual pension of £108 6s 8d on 15th December 1881 after 37 years service, his pension papers stating that he was paralysed and unable to talk, indicating a stroke. He is pictured in a famous photograph taken at Epsom in 1864, which shows Swanson alongside Superintendent Robert Walker and fellow Inspectors Eleazar Denning and David Baldry. He is often mentioned as an uncle to Donald Sutherland Swanson, but I have been unable to find any link between the two families.

30 1861, 1871 and 1881 census. The couple had four children; William (b1858), John (b1860), Annie (b1864) and James (b1870).

31 Marriage register. The union produced four children, William (b1863), John (b1864), Mary (b 19th February 1865) and Peterishea (1867-1957).

32 Marriage register, on which Peter Alexander is listed as a witness. John Bailey and Mary Swanson would have two children, John (1866-1871) and Mary (1873-1896). John Snr. died in service at Clapham Fire Station on 20th December 1882, with a widow's pension of £65 per year being awarded to Mary by the Fire Board. Details from Fire Service records.

33 Jannet, known as 'Jessie', was working as a seamstress at the time of her marriage. The couple remained in Thurso, raising a family of seven children: John (b1861), William (b1866), Mary Anne (b1868), David (b1872), Donald (b1873), Walter (b1875) and Jessie (b1880). George Gunn would be a referee on Donald Swanson's application to join the Metropolitan Police in 1868. Information from marriage register and 1881 census.

34 1871 and 1881 census.

35 *Schools in Thurso Parish from the 17th Century to 1966* by Allan Lannon (2004).

36 *Parish of Thurso* by Rev. W. R. Taylor, October 1840.

37 Robert Meikle's Parish School relocated to Castle Street in 1870. The small building attended by Donald Swanson still stands today as a private residence named "l'Ecole".

38 1861 census.

39 Fees at the Parish School set by the School Board in 1873, were as follows: Reading 2/-, Reading and Arithmetic 2/6, Reading, Writing and Arithmetic 3/-, History, Geography and Grammar 3/6, Latin, French and Mathematics 5/-. Information from *Schools in Thurso Parish from the 17th Century to 1966* by Allan Lannon, 2004.

40 *John O'Groat Journal*, 17th May 1860.

41 *John O'Groat Journal*, 7th June 1860.

42 *Memories of Thurso by an Expatriated Native: Forty Years Ago*, 23rd August 1912.

43 The Miller Institution on Sinclair Street would become popularly known as the Miller Academy and undergo periods of expansion, including the erection of new buildings on the site in 1900 and 1937. In 1958 Thurso High School was opened on Ormlie Road with the Miller Academy becoming a Primary School, at the time the largest in Scotland. The original building continued to be used for lessons until 1960/61, when the Miller Academy moved fully to Princes Street. It continues to be a place of learning, however, becoming Thurso Public Library in 1962.

44 £52,000-£65,000 today.

45 *Miller Academy History and Memories for the Millennium* by Allan Lannon (2000).

46 *Northern Ensign* and *John O'Groat Journal*, 7th June 1860.

47 *Miller Academy History and Memories for the Millennium* by Allan Lannon (2000).
48 *Memories of Thurso by an Expatriated Native: Forty Years Ago*, 23rd August 1912.
49 *Schools in Thurso Parish from the 17th Century to 1966* by Allan Lannon (2004).
50 Ibid.
51 *Memories of Thurso by an Expatriated Native: Forty Years Ago*, 23rd August 1912.
52 Miller Institution Cash Book 1862-1865.
53 *Miller Academy History and Memories for the Millennium* by Allan Lannon (2000).
54 *John O'Groat Journal*, 28th July 1864.
55 Obituary of Swanson in the *John O'Groat Journal*, 12th December 1924.
56 £450 today.
57 *Schools in Thurso Parish from the 17th Century to 1966* by Allan Lannon (2004).
58 Email to author from Allan Lannon, Thurso Schools Historian, 2nd August 2013.
59 *Schools in Thurso Parish from the 17th Century to 1966* by Allan Lannon (2004).
60 Letter of Testimonial by James Waters held in Swanson family archives.
61 Obituary of Swanson in the *John O'Groat Journal*, 12th December 1924.
62 Letter of Testimonial by James Waters held in Swanson family archives.
63 Death certificate, cause given as 'Calculus in ureter'.
64 Peterishea Annie Alexander was baptised on 29th September 1867. By the time of the 1891 census she had followed in her Uncle Donald's footsteps and become a teacher in Thurso. She married Andrew Robertson, a Headmaster, in 1897. As a talented artist and writer, for many years Peterishea had poetry published on an almost weekly basis in both *The John O'Groat Journal* and *The Caithness Courier*, having a volume of work inspired by the Great War published in 1919 under the title *Until the Dawn and Other Poems*. She died on 11th June 1957 age 89.
65 Recorded at Durness Street in 1871 census. Keeping the family brewing gene going, Margaret Alexander is recorded in *Slater's Directory of Caithness-shire* for 1882 as an Ale & Porter Dealer in Durness Street, Thurso.
66 *Northern Times*, 21st August 1964.
67 Ibid.
68 The North Mail coach, the last long-distance stagecoach in the British Isles, was eventually rendered redundant by the arrival of the railway in Thurso and other northern towns. It was reported that on its last journey just weeks after the rail service arrived in Thurso "the villages through which it passed wore black crepe on their doorways and flags at half-mast, for they saw the romance of the road passing with it."

69 North Mail Coach Timebill.
70 Great Northern Railway Programme in *Bradshaw's Guide, Handbook IV*, for 1866. 25s equates to approximately £60 today. Also on offer were Second Class tickets at 53s (£120) and First Class at 67s (£150).
71 The Great Northern Railway Programme in *Bradshaw's Guide, Handbook IV*, for 1866 states overnight breaks could be taken at Newcastle or York. *Bradshaw's Rail Times* for 1895, although being almost 30 years later, gives an indication of Swanson's journey by publishing a timetable showing that the train left Inverness at 6.00am and arrived at King's Cross at 10.45am the following day.

Stench and the City

1 See Stephen Halliday's *The Great Stink of London: Sir Joseph Bazalgette and the Cleansing of the Victorian Metropolis* (1999).
2 Fascinating descriptions of day-to-day life in the Victorian era can be found in Liza Picard's *Victorian London: The Life of a City 1840-1870* (2005) and Judith Flanders' *The Victorian City: Everyday Life in Dickens' London* (2012).
3 Judith Flanders in *The Victorian City* writes that 40,000 horses were employed by omnibus companies, with carthorses, dray horses, carriage horses to be added to that number. Pickford's removal company alone kept 1,500 horses.
4 Henry Mayhew, *London Labour and the London Poor, Vol II* (1861).
5 *Metropolitan Police Reports of Commissioner, 1869-76.*
6 *London Fogs* by The Hon. R. Russell, FMS (1880). Accessed via www.victorianlondon.org/index-2012.htm
7 Henry Mayhew, *London Labour and the London Poor, Vol II* (1861).
8 The pre-1867 assassination attempts on Queen Victoria were by Edward Oxford (1840), John Francis (two consecutive days in 1842), John William Bean (also 1842), William Hamilton (1848) and Robert Pate (1850). Further attempts would be made in 1872 by Arthur O'Connor and 1882 by Roderick Maclean, both helping to improve the monarch's standing in the eyes of the public. The pistol used by Edward Oxford was for some years displayed at Scotland Yard's Crime Museum. For a detailed look at these assassination attempts and their effect on the monarchy, see Paul Thomas Murphy's *Shooting Victoria: Madness, Mayhem and the Modernisation of the Monarchy* (2012).
9 Residential address given by Swanson in his application letter to the Metropolitan Police dated 20th March 1868. (National Archives: MEPO 3/2890).
10 *Kelly's Post Office Directory for London*, 1869. Bailey was stationed at Watling Street Station from 1861-1863, when he was transferred to Baker Street Station. On 3rd January 1865 he moved to King Street Station, being placed in charge of the land steam fire engine in 1866 until 1868 when he was transferred to Westminster Station and then Clapham Station, where he was appointed the officer in charge. Bailey died in service on 20th December 1882. Information

from Fire Service Records. Although the Metropolitan Fire Brigade had been created two years earlier in 1865, King Street station was operated by the Sun Fire Insurance Company.

11 F. H. W. Sheppard, *Survey of London: volumes 33 and 34: St. Anne Soho* (1966). Accessed via www.british-history.ac.uk/report.aspx?compid=41116 &str query=king%20street.

12 Henry Mayhew, *A Visit to the Rookery of St. Giles and its Neighbourhood* (1860).

13 Ibid.

14 F. H. W. Sheppard, *Survey of London: volumes 33 and 34: St. Anne Soho* (1966). Accessed via www.british-history.ac.uk/reportaspx?compid=41116&strquery =king%20street. The site of the Fire Station at 39 King Street became the South Entrance to St. Anne's Church, and as of 2015 is a shop selling London-themed souvenirs. St. Anne's Church was destroyed by a direct hit during the Blitz in 1940.

15 F. H. W. Sheppard, *Survey of London: volumes 31 and 32: St. James Westminster, Part 2* (1963). Accessed via www.british-history.ac.uk/report.aspx?compid = 41455.

16 Company name listed in *Kelly's Post Office Directory for London, 1869*.

17 1841 census (in which Meikle is recorded as being a Clerk) and 1861 census (Commercial Clerk Cotton Trader), in both instances as being born in Scotland.

18 Testimonial letter from John Meikle in Swanson's Metropolitan Police file (National Archives: MEPO 3/2890).

19 *Kelly's Post Office Directory for London, 1869*.

20 The company was at Catherine Court by the time of Swanson's application to join the Metropolitan Police in March 1868.

21 *Kelly's Post Office Directory for London, 1869*.

22 The equivalent of £228,500,000 today.

23 For a comprehensive account of the history of the City of London in the early to mid Victorian era, see David Kynaston's *The City of London: Volume 1, A World of its Own 1815-1890* (1994).

24 Ibid.

25 G. H. Gater and Walter Godfrey, *Survey of London: Volume 15: All Hallows, Barking-by-the-Tower, pt II* (1934). Accessed via www.british-history.ac.uk/ report.aspx?compid=74961. Catherine Court was part of a large area bordered by Seething Lane, Trinity Square and Savage Gardens demolished in 1913 to make way for the new Port of London Authority building, eventually opened in 1922 by Prime Minister David Lloyd George.

26 The closest modern-day underground station to the site of King Street is Leicester Square; the closest to Catherine Court is Tower Hill.

27 A four-mile length of track between Paddington and Farringdon represented the world's first underground line, the Metropolitan Railway. The first journey took place on 10th January 1863. It is estimated that 9,500,000 Londoners

were carried in the first year. For a full account of the London Underground's early days see *London's Underground* by H. F. Howson (1951).

28   *Crutchley's London in 1865: A Handbook for Strangers*, accessed via www.victorianlondon. org/ index-2012.htm.

29   Ludgate Circus, the busy junction where the City of London meets the City of Westminster, was constructed between 1864 and 1875.

30   *Survey of London: volume 15: All Hallows, Barking-by-the-Tower, pt II* by G. H. Gater and Walter Godfrey (1934). Accessed via www.british-history.ac.uk/report.aspx?compid=74961.

31   Accessed via www.victorianlondon.org/publications3/tempted-03.htm.

32   Swanson's application letter to the Metropolitan Police. (National Archives: MEPO 3/2890).

33   Marriage certificate, which stated that Meikle had been born 'in Scotland' in 1812.

34   Birth records of John and Charlotte Meikle's five sons: Thomas (b1835), Michael (b1837) and John (b1841) in London, Frederick (b1847) and Charles (b1849) in Manchester.

35   Meikle died in April 1879 aged 67.

36   Swanson's application letter to the Metropolitan Police (National Archives: MEPO 3/2890).

37   Ibid.

38   *Lloyd's Weekly Newspaper*, 3rd May 1868; *The Leeds Times*, 9th May 1868; and the *Bury & Norwich Post & Suffolk Herald*, 14h July 1868.

A Blue Tunic and Two Pairs of Boots

1   Letter of application in Swanson's Metropolitan Police file (National Archives: MEPO 3/2890).

2   Sir Robert Peel was born on 5th February 1788 at Ramsbottom, Lancashire. As a Tory M.P., he served as Home Secretary from 17th January 1822 to 10th April 1827, and from 26th January 1828 to 22nd November 1830. He was appointed Chancellor of the Exchequer on 2nd December 1834 and Prime Minister eight days later, fulfilling both roles until 8th April 1835 when the Whigs came to power. Peel was Leader of the Opposition for the next six years, becoming Prime Minister for a second time on 30th August 1841. He finally left power on 29th June 1846. He died on 2nd July 1850 following a horse riding accident. See *Robert Peel: A Biography* by the Rt. Hon. Lord Douglas Hurd, 2008.

3   *Police!* by Charles Tempest Clarkson and J. Hall Richardson (1889).

4   Ibid. It should be recognised that many of Peel's ideas were based on the successful principals established from the 1740s at Bow Street Magistrates' Court by Thomas de Veil, Henry Fielding and then John Fielding. See *Policing From Bow Street: Principal Officers, Runners and The Patroles* by Peter Kennison

and Alan Cook (2019).

5   *The Times*, 6th June 1829.

6   *Police!* by Charles Tempest Clarkson and J. Hall Richardson (1889).

7   The 47-year-old Rowan was an Ulsterman of Scottish descent. He had seen continuous active military service from 1806 to 1815, acting as Brigade-Major of the Light Brigade, Assistant Adjutant-General of the Light Division, and second-in-command of the 52nd Regiment at the Battle of Waterloo, at which he was wounded. Rowan applied for the position with the Metropolitan Police but was overlooked in favour of Lieutenant-Colonel James Shaw, who subsequently turned down the position. Reverting to Rowan, Peel sought references from the Duke of Wellington, with whom Rowan had served at Waterloo, and learned that he had brought the 52nd Regiment "to the highest state of discipline", which, by Wellington's standards, was very high indeed. Peel saw that Rowan was the perfect candidate to bring organisation and discipline to the New Police and offered him the role as one of the Joint Commissioners.

8   Peel was seeking as his second Commissioner someone with an in-depth knowledge of criminal law; Mayne, a 32-year-old barrister from Dublin, was recommended by several legal colleagues and was appointed without interview according to a letter dated 2nd July 1829 from William Gregson, Home Office Under-Secretary to Richard Mayne. See *The Official Encyclopedia of Scotland Yard* by Martin Fido and Keith Skinner. Belton Cobb, in *The First Detectives* (1957), claims that Robert Peel approached his cousin Lawrence, a barrister, to ask whether he knew of anyone who might be suitable as Joint Commissioner with experience of criminal law; Lawrence Peel recommended his friend Richard Mayne, and suggested that Sir Robert consult William Gregson for a reference on Mayne.

9   John Wray, a 47-year-old barrister who had been born at Cottingham, Yorkshire, and educated at Trinity College, Cambridge, had been called to the Bar in 1823, and two years later founded the University Life Assurance Society, which benefitted members who had been educated at universities and public schools. The Society had as a Trustee Charles Manners Sutton, the Speaker of the House of Commons, whose father, the Archbishop of Canterbury, became the Society's first President. Vice Presidents included the Bishops of London, Oxford and Bristol, the Attorney-General and the Solicitor-General. Wray's background, connections and financial acumen brought him to the attention of the Chancellor of the Exchequer, who recommended him to the Home Secretary.

10 *From Quills to Computers: The History of the Metropolitan Police Civil Staff 1829-1979* by Norman Fairfax (1979).

11 Later extended to 12 miles and finally 15 miles.

12 *Provisional Instructions for the Different Ranks of the Police Force* (1829).

13 *From Quills to Computers: The History of the Metropolitan Police Civil Staff 1829-1979* by Norman Fairfax (1979).

14 Ibid.
15 *The Official Encyclopedia of Scotland Yard* by Martin Fido and Keith Skinner (2000 revised edition).
16 *Police!* by Charles Tempest Clarkson and J Hall Richardson (1889).
17 Coats, trousers and boots were supplied by Charles Hebbert of 8 Pall Mall, hats by Edward Moore of Piccadilly and rattles and batons by Mr. Parker of Holborn. See *From Quills to Computers: The History of the Metropolitan Police Civil Staff 1829-1979* by Norman Fairfax (1979).
18 The *Morning Post* of 29th September 1829 reported that notices had been affixed to the door of "several of the churches in London" and repeated verbatim that which was pinned to the door of St. Clement Danes: "We, the under-signed Justices of the Peace, appointed under virtue of the Act of Parliament passed in the 10th year of his present Majesty's reign, entitled, 'An Act for improving the Police in and near the Metropolis,' do hereby give you notice, that in pursuance of the said Act of Parliament, a new Police will be ready to undertake the charge of said Parish of St. Clement Danes on the 29th of September instant, upon and after which said 29th day of September, the Night Watch, and the Night Police appointed within the said Parish previously to, or independent of, the said Act of Parliament, will be discontinued. (Signed) C. ROWAN, RICHARD MAYNE."
19 *Metropolitan Police: Its Creation and Records of Service* (National Archives podcast, 20th November 2009).
20 *The First Detectives* by Belton Cobb (1957).
21 *Police!* by Charles Tempest Clarkson and J. Hall Richardson (1889).
22 *The Official Encyclopedia of Scotland Yard* by Martin Fido and Keith Skinner (2000 revised edition).
23 *The Times*, 13th October 1829.
24 *The Times*, 15th October 1829.
25 *The First Detectives* by Belton Cobb (1957).
26 *The Edinburgh Review or Critical Journal for October 1837 to January 1838*.
27 *The Daily News*, 31st December 1849.
28 Rowan died of cancer just two years later on 8th May 1852, aged 69.
29 *The Standard*, 2nd April 1850. Douglas William Parish Labalmondière was born at Bath on 6th March 1815. He was educated at Eton and joined the 83rd of Foot at Sandhurst in 1831 at the age of 16. On 7th October 1856, aged 41, he married Margaret Doveton Paget, at 20-years-old his junior by 21 years. The couple had two children, Margaret Paget de Labalmondière (1858-1945) and Julian Arthur De Labalmondière (1859-1913).
30 *The Aberdeen Journal*, 8th May 1850.
31 *The Leeds Intelligencer*, 20th April 1850.
32 *Reynolds Weekly Newspaper*, 11th August 1850.
33 Letter from "A POLICEMAN", published in *The Daily News* of 30th July 1855.

34 *The Biography of Charles Bradlaugh* by Adolphe S. Hoadingley, 1880. The 'Leave Us Alone Club' were a short-lived group, founded by the author Thomas Lyttleton Holt in response to the Sunday Trading bill proposed by Lord Grosvenor. George Augustus Sala, one of the members, recalled in his autobiography: "[Holt's] ideas were always of a grandiose kind, and his original plan was to acquire the lease of a large mansion in Pall-Mall, at the windows of which on Sunday mornings and afternoons, the members of "The Leave Us Alone Club" could sit in their shirt sleeves, bien entendu handing to each other glistening and foaming tankards of pewter, and smoking the peaceful yard of clay. They were to have nothing to do with licences or licensing laws; they were to sit under their own vines and their own fig trees, and who was to make them afraid? They were to eat and drink what they liked, and play all-fours and bumble-puppy if they chose; and to judges and justices of the peace and inspectors of the police they were simply to say "Leave us Alone."

35 *Daily Telegraph and Courier*, 2nd July 1855.

36 Hansard: Deb 2nd July 1855 vol 139 cc368-71.

37 *Morning Post*, 2nd August 1855.

38 *North Wales Chronicle*, 4th August 1855.

39 *The Daily News*, 30th July 1855.

40 *London Standard*, 30th August 1855.

41 *Morning Post*, 25th July 1855.

42 *Liverpool Mercury*, 8th March 1856.

43 *Scotland Yard Past and Present: Experiences of Thirty-Seven Years* by Chief Inspector Timothy Cavanagh (1893).

44 John Wray died in 1869; his replacement as Receiver, Maurice Drummond, would hold the position until 1883. See *From Quills to Computers: The History of the Metropolitan Police Civil Staff 1829-1979* by Norman Fairfax (1979).

45 *The Kentish Chronicle*, 31st August 1867.

46 *Metropolitan Police Reports of Commissioner, 1869-76*.

47 *The City Press*, 21st March 1868.

48 *The Times*, 14th March 1863.

49 *The Times*, 20th March 1863.

50 *The Globe*, 14th April 1863.

51 *Daily News*, 22nd April 1863.

52 'Proposed amalgamation of Metropolitan and City Police' (National Archives: MEPO 2/24). The file contains numerous newspaper cuttings covering the period 1863-67, including a clipping from the *Morning Herald* of 28th April 1863 in which some 3,000 citizens of the City of London call for a meeting to discuss the proposed amalgamation; on a list of almost 750 names and addresses, someone has taken the trouble to ascertain the occupation of each and record these alongside each name.

53 *Lost London: the Memoirs of an East End Detective* by Benjamin Leeson (1934).

54 Address from Swanson's letter of application. In Dickens's *Oliver Twist*, the Magistrate's Court where Oliver was taken before Mr. Fang following the theft of Mr. Brownlow's handkerchief is based upon Hatton Garden Court, where the Magistrate between 1836 and 1838 was the notoriously harsh Allan Stewart Laing.
55 See *Fenian Fire* by Christy Campbell (2002) and *The Dynamiters: Irish Nationalism and Political Violence in the Wider World, 1867-1900* by Niall Whelehan (2014).
56 'Ireland (Fenians): Safety of Queen Victoria at Balmoral, and Osborne' (National Archives: HO 45/7799).
57 *The Illustrated London News*, 19th October 1867.
58 *The Lighter Side of My Official Life* by Sir Robert Anderson (1910).
59 *Lloyd's Weekly Newspaper*, 15th March 1868.
60 *Dynamite, Treason & Plot* by Simon Webb (2012).
61 *Pall Mall Gazette*, 20th December 1867.
62 *Leaves of a Life, Vol. 1* by Montagu Williams (1890).
63 *The Lighter Side of My Official Life* by Sir Robert Anderson (1910).
64 *Pall Mall Gazette*, 17th January 1868.
65 *Pall Mall Gazette*, 4th February 1868.
66 *The Lighter Side of My Official Life* by Sir Robert Anderson (1910).
67 *Leaves of a Life, Vol. 1* by Montagu Williams (1890).
68 Ibid.
69 For an overview of Robert Anderson's anti-Fenian career see 'Anderson, Monro and Jsfmboe' by Martin Fido, *Ripperologist* issue 80 (June 2007).
70 *Dynamite, Treason & Plot* by Simon Webb (2012).
71 *Police!* by Charles Tempest Clarkson and J. Hall Richardson (1889).
72 William F. Staples served as a Clerk in the Candidates Department from 1864 to 1871, when he was transferred to the Finance/Accounts Department. He was promoted 1st Class in 1874 and ended his service in 1884.
73 An amusing report held at the National Archives (MEPO 2/398) illustrates how inconsistent the measuring was, when candidate G. H. Clarke was told he was ineligible for the Met because he was half-an-inch below the requirement. Undeterred, Clarke went to a different station and was measured to be the exact height required. A third measurement found him to be an eighth-of-an-inch taller still.
74 Swanson's Candidate Form (National Archives: MEPO 3/2890).
75 *Daily Graphic*, 19th August 1907 reporting on Rose's retirement. Rose left Balmoral in October 1860 to join the Metropolitan Police, being one of the last 'Peelers'. It was estimated that in 42 years serving in the Candidates Department, Rose trained some 60,000 new recruits. He became Chief Inspector by 1901, and Superintendent by the time of his retirement in 1907.

Notes and References to pages 41-55

76 Swanson's Form of Recommendation (National Archives: MEPO 3/2890), on which he is incorrectly recorded as being 20 years of age.
77 Ibid.
78 *Law Directory 1869.*
79 *Lost London: the Memoirs of an East End Detective* by Benjamin Leeson (1934).
80 *The Reminiscences of Chief Inspector Littlechild* by J. G. Littlechild (1894).
81 'Metropolitan Police Conditions' (National Archives: MEPO 3/2890).
82 *Lost London: the Memoirs of an East End Detective* by Benjamin Leeson (1934).
83 *Metropolitan Police Reports of Commissioner, 1869-76.*
84 *Law Directory 1869.*
85 *The First Detectives* by Belton Cobb (1957).
86 Swanson's Metropolitan Police file (National Archives: MEPO 3/2890).

Crimes, Fines and the Veiled Lady of Loughton

1 History of Metropolitan Police Stations, Met Heritage Centre.
2 *Kelly's Directory of London, 1869.*
3 History of Metropolitan Police Stations, Met Heritage Centre.
4 'Report on the Condition of the Metropolitan Police Stations, 1881' (National Archives: MEPO 2/898). Although officers were free to find their own accommodation outside of the Section House, it had to be close to the station where they were serving and they had to have not only permission but also the accommodation had to be approved. More often than not, single officers would therefore stay at the section houses as it was cheaper, and many enjoyed the camaraderie of staying with their fellow officers.
5 *Lloyd's Weekly Newspaper*, 7th June 1868; *Glasgow Herald*, 8th June 1868; *Royal Cornwall Gazette*, 11th June 1868; *Nottinghamshire Guardian*, 11th June 1868.
6 *Metropolitan Police Reports of Commissioner, 1869-76.*
7 *Scotland Yard Past and Present: Experiences of Thirty-Seven Years* by Chief Inspector Timothy Cavanagh (1893).
8 Swanson's Metropolitan Police file (National Archives: MEPO 3/2890).
9 Ibid.
10 Death certificate of Katherine Emily Mayne.
11 *Pall Mall Gazette*, 1st October 1868.
12 *Scotland Yard Past and Present: Experiences of Thirty-Seven Years* by Chief Inspector Timothy Cavanagh (1893).
13 Death certificate of Sir Richard Mayne.
14 *Western Daily Press*, 31st December 1868.
15 *The Bury and Norwich Post*, 5th January 1869.

16 *The Morning Post*, 8th January 1869.
17 *Manchester Courier and Lancashire General Advertiser*, 5th February 1869.
18 *Metropolitan Police Reports of Commissioner, 1869-76.*
19 The Lock Hospital was the first specialist hospital founded in London to specifically treat those suffering from venereal disease, with a number of hospitals operating under the name. Founded in 1746, the Hospital treated patients for over 200 years until 1952, when the formation of the National Health Service led officials to wrongly believe that new medicines had conquered the scourge of sexually transmitted diseases. See *The London Lock: A Charitable Hospital for Venereal Disease 1746-1952* by David Innes Williams (1995).
20 Personal memoranda of Donald Swanson.
21 Ibid.
22 Fined for being late for roll call on 4th February 1870; promoted Second Class on 10th February and First Class on 18th February 1870. Swanson's Metropolitan Police file (National Archives: MEPO 3/2890); Police Orders 1870.
23 *Metropolitan Police Reports of Commissioner, 1869-76.* The register was modified by the Prevention of Crimes Act 1871, which inserted the stipulation that every criminal receiving a custodial sentence of one month or more should be recorded in the register. Registers from 1834 (the Bow Street files) to 1959 can be viewed in MEPO 6 at the National Archives.
24 Personal memoranda of Donald Swanson.
25 Personal memoranda of Donald Swanson; *The Standard*, 8th April 1870; *The City Press*, 9th April 1870; and *Reynolds's Weekly Newspaper*, 10th April 1870. Mary Ann Travers is intriguingly similar to Mary Ann Connelly, who would feature as a witness in the Jack the Ripper case some 18 years later. Aged 26 in 1870, Travers would have been 44 in 1888, a similar age to Connelly. Travers is given the nickname "Curly Poll" by Swanson, whereas Connelly was known as "Pearly Poll". Both lived in Whitechapel, with a history of prostitution in that area. Travers' lodgings in 1870 – Star Street – would be the same as Connelly's supposed friend Martha Tabram in 1888.
26 Police Orders 1870 and 1871.
27 I have been unable to establish a familial link between John McDonald and Donald Swanson, although the Caithness Valuation Rolls record a McDonald family near the Geise Distillery. It may be possible that the two had known each other since childhood but were unrelated by blood. John McDonald's career would go from strength to strength, and by 1881 he would be the police officer in charge of the Banqueting Hall at Alexandra Palace.
28 *Pall Mall Gazette*, 23rd October 1871.
29 Ibid.
30 24th October 1871.
31 *Daily Telegraph*, 21st October 1871.

32 *Clerkenwell News*, 21st October 1871.

33 *Daily Telegraph*, 21st October 1871.

34 Abberline was promoted Inspector on 10th March 1873 and transferred to H Division three days later, where he would remain for the next fourteen years.

35 Police Orders 1870.

36 *Reynolds's Weekly Newspaper*, 28th April 1872.

37 Death certificate of Mary Swanson.

38 Retained at his current rank but not to be promoted nor used on any Special Duty. Swanson's Metropolitan Police file (National Archives: MEPO 3/2890); Police Orders 1874.

39 Swanson's Metropolitan Police file (National Archives: MEPO 3/2890); Police Orders 1874.

40 A photograph of Donald Swanson taken at J.J. Larritt's studios in Stepney Green in the mid 1870s bears the handwritten inscription: "To Miss Ruth E. Darby. With compliments. Donald." The fact that the photo is held in a Swanson family album suggests that it was returned by the intended recipient. Family oral tradition maintains that the young policeman was not seen as a suitable match for Miss Darby by her parents. Ruth Ellen Darby was born in 1854 in Chelmsford. In 1878 she married the man deemed more suitable than Donald Swanson, licensed victualler Albert Guntrip, and the couple went on to have seven children. She died in December 1912.

41 *Kelly's Directory of London*, 1874.

42 Birth certificate of Julia Ann Nevill.

43 Email from Mary Berkin, Julia Ann Swanson's granddaughter, to author 9th October 2013.

44 Register of marriage.

45 James Nevill Jnr. (b1857) would also go into the pub trade, initially working for his father at The British Lion before running The Albion on Bridge Road, West Ham. He married Frances and had three children. William Nevill (b1858) also became a licensed victualler, first at St. Pancras then at Penge in Kent; he married Charlotte and the couple had four children. Ada Eliza Nevill (b1861) remained unmarried, living with her father until his death in 1903. Information from Nevill family documents and census returns of 1861, 1871, 1881, 1891, 1901 and 1911.

46 It has been claimed that the warning "Don't take sweets from a stranger", uttered by parents to their children the world over, originates from the Charley Ross abduction.

47 For an emotional telling of the Charley Ross kidnapping read the account written by Christian Ross, *The Father's Story of Charley Ross, the Kidnapped Child* (1876). See *Little Charley Ross* by Norman Zierold (1967) and *We Is Got Him: The Kidnapping That Changed America* by Carrie Hagen (2011) for assessments of the case.

48 Approximately $800,000 today.

49 Over the years, several boys and young men were presented to the Ross family as being the lost Charley, all in search of reward money. In 1931, long after Christian Ross's death, a man in his sixties named Gustave Blair announced that he was Charley, a claim dismissed by the Ross family. In 1934 Blair managed to convince a jury at a civil case that he was indeed the missing boy, and he was allowed to legally change his name to Charley Ross. Walter continually refused to meet 'Charley' and the latter filed a lawsuit against his 'brother', demanding to be recognised as an heir.

50 Personal memoranda of Donald Swanson, in which he notes that Miss Rhodes continued to write for several years until she died at Edmonton in 1896.

51 Ibid. *The Kent & Sussex Courier* of 29th June 1877, writing on the 'Veiled Lady', mentions that her appearance in Loughton corresponds with her departure from Whitstable.

52 Nathan Leopold and Richard Loeb, kidnappers and murderers of Bobby Franks in 1924, stated in court that they had been influenced by Bill Mosher and Joseph Douglas. For a discussion of this and other cases in the context of the Charley Ross kidnapping see Paula S. Fass' *Kidnapped: Child Abduction in America* (1997). In recent years, the Charley Ross case has inspired an online database of over 9,000 missing persons, The Charley Project, with cases dating back to 1910. See www.charleyproject.org.

The Lady Vanishes

1 *The Manchester Evening News*, 27th May 1876.
2 *Pall Mall Gazette*, 26th May 1876.
3 For a full biography of Georgiana Cavendish see Amanda Foreman's *Georgiana, Duchess of Devonshire* (1999). Georgiana was played by Keira Knightley in the 2008 film *The Duchess*.
4 *The Times*, 11th April 1901. For a detailed account of the painting and its history, and a biography of the thief, see *The Napoleon of Crime: The Life and Times of Adam Worth, the Real Moriarty* by Ben Macintyre (2012).
5 The company was formed by James Christie in 1766 and taken over by his son, James Christie II, in 1803. Upon his death in 1831 two sons (James III and George) took on William Manson as a partner and the company was joined in 1859 by Thomas Woods. The business was incorporated as a private limited company in 1940 and listed as a public company in 1973.
6 £525,000 today.
7 *The Bristol Mercury and Western Counties Advertiser*, 13th May 1876.
8 *Pall Mall Gazette*, 16th May 1876.
9 Ibid.
10 *The Sheffield Daily Telegraph*, 1st June 1876.
11 *The Edinburgh Evening News*, 10th June 1876.
12 £50,000 today.

13 *North Devon Journal*, 20th July 1876.
14 *The Northern Warder and Bi-Weekly Courier and Argus*, 30th June 1876.
15 *The Era*, 1st October 1876.
16 *The Era*, 3rd September 1876.
17 Newspaper cutting titled 'Career Founded on Half-a-Crown' kept in Swanson family papers, sadly undated but mentioning his 'recent death' so circa December 1924. The report describes the event occurring "more than 40 years ago".
18 *The First Detectives* by Belton Cobb (1957).
19 See *The Twisted Heart* by Rebecca Gowers (2009).
20 *Morning Advertiser*, 9th April 1842.
21 *The Morning Herald*, 8th April 1842.
22 National Archives: MEPO 3/45.
23 *The Morning Herald*, 8th April 1842.
24 *Morning Advertiser*, 13th April 1842.
25 Named Lydia or Letitia Susan Butcher in some contemporary newspaper reports.
26 *Morning Advertiser*, 14th April 1842.
27 *Morning Advertiser*, 15th April 1842.
28 Ibid.
29 *Morning Advertiser*, 24th May 1842.
30 For a detailed account of the work undertaken by the different Divisions which effectively hindered the hunt for Daniel Good see *The First Detectives* by Belton Cobb (1957).
31 'Bow Street Runners' was the unofficial name given to London's first professional police force, created in 1742 by magistrate Henry Fielding. Attached to Bow Street Magistrates' Court, the Runners did not patrol the streets but arrested offenders on the orders of the magistrate. Their importance dwindled with the formation of the Metropolitan Police in 1829 and the Bow Street Runners were disbanded ten years later in 1839. See *Policing From Bow Street: Principal Officers, Runners and The Patroles* by Peter Kennison and Alan Cook (2018) for a thorough examination of the Bow Street officers and their influence on Sir Robert Peel.
32 The murder of Mr. Westwood by burglars at his home is often cited as an example of police ineptitude, with the killer remaining undetected. However, as part of his investigation Inspector Pearce had realised that the stolen goods, two watches worth £2,000, would be impossible to dispose of in London given that descriptions had been widely circulated. He reasoned that the best market would therefore be overseas, and enquiries confirmed Holland as the likely place to sell stolen items with no questions asked. Realising that the thieves would have to avoid customs, Pearce deduced that there would be an attempt to steal a boat somewhere on the south east coast. Having heard that watches

had been offered for sale at Gravesend the night after the murder, Pearce and Sergeant Otway headed for Kent. They discovered that a boat had been stolen at Ramsgate Harbour and seen heading across the Channel towards France. The officers travelled to Boulogne to no avail, but their actions had shown that detective reasoning could produce new lines of enquiry.

33 Similarly, the Police were lambasted by the press for their inability to identify the murderer of Lord Russell. The breakthrough came when Inspector Pearce examined marks made on a back door to the house in Mayfair; he realised that they had been made from the inside to give the appearance that burglars had forced their way in. Pearce reasoned that if the marks on the door were made to create the impression of a break-in, then all other indications of a burglary such as the ransacked library had also been staged, and it was an inside job. Pearce and his colleague Sergeant Frederick Shaw began looking for the stolen items inside the house rather than a burglar at large in London, and the discovery of these led to the arrest of the murderer, Courvoisier.

34 P.C. Goff, who had assisted Inspector Field in the investigation into the murder of Eliza Grimwood, had displayed a detective's suspicious instinct by being doubtful of the evidence presented by one Catherine Edwin. He pointed out that everything in her description of a possible suspect could have been gleaned from the newspapers reporting on the case, thus saving valuable man hours following up these leads. A year later Goff confirmed his detective instincts when he encountered a sixteen-year-old boy who he knew to keep company with thieves. Seeing that the youth was carrying a bundle, Goff demanded to know the contents. The boy opened the bundle to reveal three shirts, which he claimed his father had told him to carry home. Something about the clean, creased shirts seemed not quite right, and Goff picked them up; they were still damp. The constable arrested the boy and discovered that they had been stolen from the clothesline of a local woman, the shirts having been washed that morning.

35 *The First Detectives* by Belton Cobb (1957). Charles Dickens was particularly impressed with the Detective Department, and requested interviews with them. Two, Stephen Thornton and Jonathan Whicher, agreed and descriptions of them appeared in Dickens's *Household Words* of 1850: "Sergeant Dornton [Thornton], about fifty years of age, with a ruddy face and a high sun-burnt forehead, has the air of one who has been a sergeant in the army. He is famous for steadily pursuing the inductive process, and, from small beginnings, working up from clue to clue until he bags his man. Sergeant Witchem [Whicher], shorter and thicker-set, and marked with the small-pox, has something of a reserved and thoughtful air, as if he were engaged in deep arithmetical calculations."

36 *The Official Encyclopedia of Scotland Yard* by Martin Fido and Keith Skinner (1999).

37 See *The Suspicions of Mr. Whicher* by Kate Summerscale (2008) for a full and enjoyable account of the Constance Kent case.

38 *The Times*, 26th April 1865.

39 *Scotland Yard Past and Present: Experiences of Thirty-Seven Years* by Chief Inspector Timothy Cavanagh (1893).
40 *The Reminiscences of Chief Inspector Littlechild* by J. G. Littlechild (1894).
41 Ibid.
42 Police Orders 1876; Swanson's Metropolitan Police file (National Archives: MEPO 3/2890).
43 Madame de Goncourt contacted Abrahams and Roffey on 23rd September 1876 (trial transcript at Old Bailey Online: t18770409-39) while Williamson left London for a month-long holiday on 28th September (National Archives: MEPO 7/38), so the meeting with Abrahams occurred between these dates.
44 £485,000 today.

Fall of the Detectives

1 For a full account of the Turf Frauds see *The Chieftain: Victorian True Crime through the Eyes of a Scotland Yard Detective* by Chris Payne (2011).
2 Harry Benson is described in Donald Swanson's private memoranda thus: Harry Benson alias Comte de Montague alias Montgomery etc was one of the cleverest and most ingenious of scoundrels. He is the son of a French Jew, was well educated but was obliged to fly his native land and become sub editor in Brussels but he was obliged to leave and went to Switzerland, where he attempted to murder a young lady in a train but did not succeed. He was then obliged to fly and came to England where in 1872 he swindled the Lord Mayor out of £1,000 by pretending that he was the prefet of Chatandeau and that the people were very much in need, but Benson was apprehended, the money recovered and he was sentenced to 18 months hard labour. Whilst in prison he attempted suicide by setting fire to his bed, burning himself in such a manner as he became lame for life. On liberation he went to lodge in Islington where it is said he slowly poisoned his landlord, afterwards inducing the landlady to accompany him to Rosebank, Isle of Wight where he became editor and proprietor of the local paper, which he conducted in such a manner that set all the elite against him. Whilst here he became acquainted with William Kurr and others. This man's career is one long career of swindles the particulars of which are better known on the Continent.
3 Described by Swanson: A notoriously clever swindler, a native of Islington but residing at Leytonstone, Essex, was an accomplice of Kurr, Walters, Benson and others, but Walters and he were more associated together than with the others, and their histories are very nearly similar.
4 Described by Swanson: Brother to William Kurr. Joined his brother from whom he received £2 per week as clerk. It was his duty to receive from Bale all letters delivered to their office and to take them to his brother William at some pre-arranged spot so that if by chance Bale was followed by police Frederick would abscond. Made their plans to prevent being followed so that William Kurr would not be seen to have anything to do with the swindle. It was

Frederick's duty to write letters as well.

5   Described by Swanson: Originally a greengrocer at Islington, there a betting man then a welsher. Joined Kurr and Benson as a runner to look out for police officers if they came near the premises where any swindle was being carried on, also to take all letters to Frederick Kurr.

6   Described by Swanson: William Kurr alias Montgomery etc is the son of a baker at Islington who in early life deserted the baker's barrow for the turf where he became a noted 'welsher'. Welshing became too warm for him and he resorted to all sorts of swindles in connection with the turf and doing at first the same as his companions William Henry Walters and Edwin Murray until Benson appeared on the scene. Whilst with Walters and Murray he performed several small swindles, but had to run to America. He returned again after 'squaring' the prosecutors, and resumed his old games. He committed a larceny at a hotel at Doncaster but was not prosecuted.

7   *The Times*, 11th January 1877.
8   *The Reminiscences of Chief Inspector Littlechild* by J. G. Littlechild (1984).
9   Private memoranda of Donald Swanson.
10 Swanson's Metropolitan Police file (National Archives: MEPO 3/2890).
11 See Introduction.
12 *Reynolds's Weekly Newspaper*, 25th February 1877.
13 Private memoranda of Donald Swanson.
14 *Lloyd's Weekly Newspaper*, 18th February 1877.
15 *Reynolds's Weekly Newspaper*, 25th February 1877.
16 *The Times*, 19th February 1877.
17 Private memoranda of Donald Swanson.
18 *The Standard*, 26th April 1877; Private memoranda of Donald Swanson.
19 *Leaves of a Life, Vol II* by Montagu Williams (1890).
20 *The Freeman's Journal*, 18th December 1878.
21 *The Edinburgh Evening News*, 3rd January 1877. The smitten "Mr. Knox" was the magistrate who had been tipped to replace Sir Richard Mayne as Commissioner following the Clerkenwell Bombing of 1867.
22 See *The Chieftain: Victorian True Crime through the Eyes of a Scotland Yard Detective* by Chris Payne (2011).
23 See *The Trial of the Detectives* by George Dilnot (1928).
24 *From Quills to Computers: The History of the Metropolitan Police Civil Staff 1829-1979* by Norman Fairfax (1979).
25 *Sheffield Daily Telegraph*, 30th October 1877.
26 Private memoranda of Donald Swanson.
27 £3.5million today.
28 Private memoranda of Donald Swanson,

29 *Pall Mall Gazette*, 20th October 1877; *Sheffield and Rotherham Independent*, 22nd October 1877. Captain George was subsequently taken to France and arrested for the forgery for which he was wanted by the Paris Detective Department. He was sentenced to penal servitude for life and sent to French-owned New Caledonia, but in May 1879 escaped and disappeared in the United States.

30 See *The Trial of the Detectives* by George Dilnot (1928) for a transcript of the trial.

31 *Report of the Commissioner of Police of the Metropolis, 1877.*

32 The quartet were released from Coldbath Fields Prison in October 1879. John Meiklejohn set up a private enquiry agency, being engaged in many cases and offering his services in the hunt for Jack the Ripper. He unsuccessfully sued Major Arthur Griffiths for libel in 1903, and wrote his memoirs just prior to his death in 1912. Nathaniel Druscovich also became a private enquiry agent but died of tuberculosis at the young age of 39 in December 1881. William Palmer became manager of The Cock public house in Lambeth before dying in January 1888. Edward Froggatt was immediately arrested on his release from prison for the misappropriation of trust funds and sentenced to seven years' imprisonment. Information from Chris Payne's *The Chieftain*, which I cannot recommended too highly.

Mrs. Swanson and the C.I.D.

1 *Report of the Commissioner of Police of the Metropolis, 1877.*

2 National Archives: MEPO 5/44.

3 Memorandum by Commissioner Edmund Henderson, 6th November 1877 (National Archives: MEPO 2/134).

4 Police Order, 6th March 1878.

5 Charles Edward Howard Vincent was born on 31st May 1849, second son of Reverend Frederick Vincent, Rector of Slinford, Sussex. He was a sickly child and suffered from coughing bouts, sometimes lasting three or four weeks at a time, throughout his life. On 26th October 1882 he married Ethel Moffatt, the 21-year-old daughter of the late George Moffatt MP. The couple had one child, a daughter named Vera born in 1884. *The Illustrated London News*, 13th October 1883; *Nottingham Evening Post*, 27th October 1882; *The Tatler*, 30th March 1904; and *The Life of Sir Howard Vincent* by S. H. Jeyes and F. D. How, (1912).

6 Police Order, 6th April 1878.

7 Ibid. In fact, Dolly Williamson had suggested an "outline of a scheme" for a reorganisation of the Detective Department which was along similar lines as early as July 1870 (National Archives: MEPO 2/134).

8 *Criminals and Crime* by Sir Robert Anderson (1907).

9 Old Bailey Online (t18780527-545).

10   Details from marriage certificate of Donald Swanson and Julia Ann Nevill.
11   Gift list in Julia's handwriting retained in Swanson family papers.
12   Old Bailey Online (t1878 0527-545).
13   Private memoranda of Donald Swanson.
14   Address given on birth certificate of son Donald Nevill Swanson.
15   Police Order, 6th July 1878.
16   Album containing several photographs held in Swanson family archives.
17   *The Times*, 26th August 1878; *Oxford Journal*, 21st September 1878.
18   *The Times*, 4th November 1878.
19   Birth certificate of Donald Nevill Swanson, dated 25th February 1879.
20   *The Times*, 8th April 1879.
21   Death certificate of John Swanson.
22   *The Times*, 8th April 1879.
23   *The Times*, 1st May 1879.
24   Charles Bullard was one of the most romantic characters of the New York underworld, a well-educated heir who had squandered his inheritance and turned to crime. He spoke French and German fluently, and played the piano to a professional level. For a detailed look at Bullard and his career, see *The Napoleon of Crime: The Life and Times of Adam Worth, The Real Moriarty* by Ben Macintyre (2012).
25   Private memoranda of Donald Swanson; *The Napoleon of Crime: The Life and Times of Adam Worth, The Real Moriarty* by Ben Macintyre (2012).
26   *Supplement to The Nottinghamshire Guardian*, 9th January 1880.

The Duchess and the Showgirl

1   Swanson's service medical file (National Archives: MEPO 3/2890), which indicates this was his first absence through illness in over eleven years of service.

2   *Survey of London, Vol 21: The parish of St. Pancras part 3: Tottenham Court Road & neighbourhood* by J. R. Howard Roberts and Walter H. Godfrey, 1949 accessed via www.british-history.ac.uk/report.aspx?compid=65155#s15. The report includes a contemporary description of St. John's from *The Ecclesiologist* of 1846, lamenting the poor design: "It is a most unsatisfactory composition. The style is Romanesque, but whether the Anglo, or Lombardo, or Germano variety, it would probably puzzle the architect himself." St. John's was damaged by a bomb on 25th March 1945 and demolished in the 1960s.

3   The Dukedom of Somerset had been held for centuries by the St. Maur family. The name, corrupted to Seymour, has a strong ancestry, with records dating back to the thirteenth century. Sir John Seymour participated in the French wars with Henry VIII. His eldest daughter, Jane Seymour, married the King and his son Thomas, Lord Seymour of Sudeley, eventually married Henry's

widow Catherine Parr. Another son, Sir Edward Seymour, became Viscount Beauchamp and then Earl of Hertford. After the death of Henry VIII he was constituted Lord Treasurer of England, and council to the young Edward VI, his nephew. Sir Edward was designated the first Duke of Somerset in February 1546.

4   Private memoranda of Donald Swanson.
5   Marriage certificate of Edward St. Maur and Lillian Stanhope, 20th August 1879.
6   Private memoranda of Donald Swanson.
7   *The Liverpool Mercury*, 24th January 1873.
8   Birth certificate and Baptism record of Florence Higgins.
9   Private memoranda of Donald Swanson.
10 Florence B. Higgins recorded on the 1871 census as a visitor at 88 Tower Hill, Aldgate.
11 *The Sheffield Daily Telegraph*, 20th January 1873.
12 *The Liverpool Mercury*, 18th January 1873.
13 Marriage certificate of Edward Goddard and Lillian Higgins, 9th July 1871.
14 Private memoranda of Donald Swanson.
15 Address from divorce papers (National Archives: J 77/119/2188).
16 Ibid. Edward Goddard was the seventh of nine children born to Henry Goddard and Eleanor Baker, who married in 1838.
17 Private memoranda of Donald Swanson.
18 Ibid. This incident is alluded to in the divorce hearing: see *The Liverpool Mercury*, 24th January 1873.
19 Private memoranda of Donald Swanson.
20 *The Liverpool Mercury*, 24th January 1873.
21 Private memoranda of Donald Swanson.
22 *The Liverpool Mercury*, 24th January 1873.
23 Divorce papers, Goddard v Goddard (National Archives: J 77/119/2188). Edward Goddard would relocate to Hull, where he married Catherine Spence in 1877. He died in 1933 aged 80.
24 Birth certificate of Ambrosezina Chesterfield.
25 Baptism record of Ambrosezina Chesterfield.
26 *The Era* of 11th May 1879 features an advertisement by agents Maurice de Frece of Messrs Weatherilt, Parker and Co., stating that "Miss Lillian Chesterfield, King's Cross Theatre. Engaged to play 'Nellie' in *Lost in London*; 'Lady Isabelle Carlyle', 'Madame Vine' in *East Lynne*; and 'Elsie' in *Parted* till further notice."
27 Edward St. Maur was born on 7th February 1849, fourth son of Algernon Percy Banks St. Maur and Horatia Morler. He died in 1920 aged 71 in Marylebone.

28 Marriage certificate of Edward St. Maur and Lillian Stanhope, 20th August 1879.
29 Private memoranda of Donald Swanson.
30 *The Ipswich Journal and Suffolk, Norfolk, Essex and Cambridge Advertiser*, 10th February 1880.
31 Private memoranda of Donald Swanson. In the event, Edward St. Maur did not become Duke of Somerset. When Edward Seymour, the Duke at the time of the investigation, died with no living male heirs in 1885, the title passed to his brother Archibald St. Maur, who remained unmarried. In 1891 younger brother Algernon Percy Banks St. Maur, father of Edward, became the 14th Duke, his eldest son Algernon inheriting the title in 1894. At this point Edward St. Maur was third in line behind elder twin brothers Percy and Ernest, and he moved up a place when Percy died in 1907. This was the closest Lillian St. Maur came to becoming Duchess. Lord Edward St. Maur would die in 1920, still second in line. When Percy died the *Grantham Journal* of 27th July 1907 commented that "only three times in over 350 years has the dukedom of Somerset passed directly from father to son. Scarcely another peerage could show such a broken line of descent."
32 *The Aberdeen Journal*, 4th October 1881.
33 £500,000 today.
34 *The Huddersfield Chronicle*, 20th April 1895.
35 It would seem that Lillian remained an attractive woman. In the 1881 census she gives her age as 23, when in fact she was 27. In 1901 she is listed as being 40-years-old, despite actually being 47. Presumably on neither occasion the census enumerator doubted the information given.
36 *The Nottinghamshire Guardian*, 25th March 1899.
37 *The Grantham Journal*, 27th July 1907.
38 Death caused by valvular disease of heart syncope. Even in death, Lillian is recorded as being six years under her true age.
39 *The Times*, 26th September 1910.
40 *Lancaster Gazette*, 9th June 1880.
41 *The Times*, 15th June 1880.
42 *Hampshire Advertiser*, 9th June 1880. The chemise and other items relating to the Harley Street Mystery, including locks of the victim's hair and the plaster of Paris cast of her teeth, were displayed at the Crime Museum Uncovered exhibition held at the Museum of London between October 2015 and April 2016, and photographs of some of these appear in Jackie Keily and Julia Hoffbrand's *The Crime Museum Uncovered: Inside Scotland Yard's Special Collection* (2015), published to accompany the event.
43 *The Times*, 15th June 1880.
44 *Manchester Courier and Lancashire General Advertiser*, 17th June 1880.
45 Swanson's Metropolitan Police file (National Archives: MEPO 3/2890).

The Case of the Quarter-Million Pound Pearl

1. *The Daily News*, 28th September 1880.
2. *The Standard*, 21st October 1880.
3. Daisy, Princess of Pless writes in her autobiography (1929) on hearing of Lady Bective's death in 1928: "Alas! even as I correct these lines I see that this sweet, gracious, lovable woman has passed away at the age of eighty-six. She had only one child, a girl called Olivia, who has inherited all her mother's goodness and fragrant charm."
4. When the constituency of Westmorland was abolished in 1885 Thomas Taylour became M.P. for Kendal. He was also a Justice of the Peace and Honorary Colonel of the 4th Battalion, Border Regiment. He died aged 49 in 1893, leaving effects to the value of £775,657 (£48million).
5. *Dublin Evening Mail*, 12th October 1867.
6. Lady Olivia Caroline Amelia Taylour married Lieutenant-Colonel Lord Henry Cavendish-Bentinck on 27th January 1892, aged 23. She died on 26th November 1939 aged 70, leaving effects valued at £7,447,882 (£24million).
7. *The Standard*, 5th October 1880.
8. £10,000 today.
9. *Lloyd's Weekly Newspaper*, 3rd October 1880.
10. *The Times*, 28th September 1880.
11. *Supplement to the Manchester Courier and Lancashire General Advertiser*, 25th September 1880.
12. *Lloyd's Weekly Newspaper*, 3rd October 1880.
13. *Supplement to the Manchester Courier and Lancashire General Advertiser*, 25th September 1880.
14. *The Times*, 21st October 1880.
15. *Lloyd's Weekly Newspaper*, 3rd October 1880.
16. *Manchester Times*, 9th October 1880.
17. *The Times*, 21st October 1880. The equivalent of receiving £6,000 against £250,000, the true value of the jewellery recovered by Swanson on the basis of the clue of a single pearl.
18. Old Bailey Online (t18801018-570).
19. £10,000 today – more than a year's salary for the Detective Inspector. Letter of thanks addressed The Carlton Club, sent by the Earl of Bective on 22nd October 1880. Held in Swanson family archives.
20. "H. Holland" is stamped on the chamber of the revolver. Address from an 1883 advertisement for Holland & Holland. The pistol was recently reunited with the Swanson family after some detective work by the author. It had been advertised as being for sale on an American website for some time, with accompanying text unsure of its provenance. I managed to purchase a book formerly in the possession of Lady Bective, the cover of which was embossed with a very

similar personal monogram to that shown on the pistol's escutcheon; both used the same unusual typeface. This was enough to convince the family that the Tranter had indeed been presented to Donald Swanson, and it was purchased through a third party.

21 *The Freeman's Journal*, 22nd January 1881.
22 *The Times*, 20th January 1881.
23 Private memoranda of Donald Swanson.
24 *The Times*, 20th January 1881.
25 Private memoranda of Donald Swanson.
26 *The Times*, 20th January 1881.
27 *The Freeman's Journal*, 22nd January 1881. Swanson's use of his middle name as an alias suggests that detectives would tend to employ names which could be easily remembered.
28 Private memoranda of Donald Swanson.
29 See *Irish Political Prisoners, 1848-1922* by Sean McConville (2003).
30 See *The Chieftain* by Chris Payne for a narrative of the arrests.
31 *The Evening News*, 5th February 1881.
32 *The Lighter Side of My Official Life* by Sir Robert Anderson (1910).
33 Superintendent John Mallon was born on 10th May 1839 at Meigh, County Armagh. Like Swanson, he joined the police at the age of 19. Starting as a Constable with the Dublin Metropolitan Police, Mallon was promoted Sergeant in April 1867, Acting Inspector (September 1867), Inspector (1869), Chief Superintendent (1883) and finally Assistant Commissioner (1892). In 1874 Mallon became head of DMP's detective department, the G Division, specialising in anti-Fenian activities. He retired in 1902. See *Inspector Mallon: Buying Irish Patriotism for a Five-Pound Note* by Donal P. McCracken (2009). Patrick McIntyre, a Detective Sergeant of the Met's Special Branch, named John Mallon as one of five outstanding detectives in his reminiscences published in *Reynolds's Weekly Newspaper* of 17th February 1895. The others were Donald Swanson, John Littlechild, Jerome Caminada of Manchester and James Black of the Birmingham police. The *Illustrated Police News* of 4th September 1897 called Mallon "the Donald Swanson of Ireland's Scotland Yard", presumably as Swanson was, by this time, Superintendent of the C.I.D. and therefore on a par with Mallon's rank.
34 *The Evening News*, 5th February 1881.
35 *Staffordshire Sentinel*, 4th February 1881.
36 Michael Davitt would be released in 1882 and, although again arrested in 1883, would go on to provide staunch support for Charles Parnell's Irish National Land League and Irish National League. He became increasingly humanitarian, supporting an alliance between the Irish Parliamentary Party and the British Liberal Party. In 1898 he founded the United Irish League with William O'Brien. Davitt died in Dublin on 30th May 1906.

37 Birth certificate of James John Swanson.
38 £150,000 today.
39 Walter Selwyn appeared in court on 21st November 1881 dressed in his convict's uniform charged with stealing the New Zealand bonds, for which he received a further six days' imprisonment. In 1892, following his release, he conspired to defraud one George Scears and was arrested by Det. Inspector Frederick Abberline, being sentenced to another five years' imprisonment.
40 Board of Trade Wreck Report for the *Norfolk*, September 1879.
41 *The Times*, 26th April 1881.
42 Extract from a letter sent by Drevar from Chittagong to the *Calcutta Englishman* in 1876, published in *The Graphic* of 27th January 1877.
43 *Illustrated London News*, 20th November 1876.
44 *The Falkirk Herald and Linlithgow Journal*, 18th January 1877.
45 *Edinburgh Evening News*, 26th April 1881.
46 Stories told around the fireplaces of Caithness for generations include tales of silkies (creatures appearing as seals in the sea but who shed their skin to become human on land), witches and water kelpies (shape-shifting spirits). Many strange creatures have been reported, including two sightings of mermaids in the early nineteenth century. The first, by a woman named Mackay, describes a creature floating in the sea with just the head visible: "The face seemed plump and round, the eyes and nose were small, the former were of a light grey colour, and the mouth was large, and from the shape of the jawbone, which seemed straight, the face looked short... The forehead, nose, and chin were white. The head was exceedingly round, the hair thick and long of a green oily cast, and appeared troublesome to it, the waves generally throwing it down over the face: it seemed to feel the annoyance, and as the waves retreated, with both its hands it frequently threw back the hair, and rubbed its throat, as if to remove any soiling it might have received from it. The throat was slender, smooth and white: we did not think of observing whether it had elbows, but from the manner in which it used its arms I must conclude that it had. The arms were very long and slender, as were the hands and fingers, the latter were not webbed. The arms, one of them at least, was frequently extended over its head as if to frighten a bird that hovered over it, and seemed to distress it much: when that had no effect, it sometimes turned quite round several times successively." A year later Rev. William Munro saw a round-faced mermaid sitting on a rock, combing its hair before slipping silently into the water. The *John O'Groat Journal* of 29th March 1860 reported on the discovery some fifty years earlier of the carcass of a giant sea serpent at the Orkneys. The remains of the creature were some forty-five feet long, with a small head resembling a seal at the end of a neck ten feet long. On each side of the body were three fins or paws which resembled a lizard's foot. The skull, one 'paw' and part of the backbone were sent to the University of Edinburgh.
47 *The Pall Mall Gazette*, 6th May 1881.

48 *The Standard*, 14th August 1883. The creatures seen by George Drevar and the crew of the *Pauline* have been documented as among the best sightings of sea serpents, including *The Great Sea-Serpent: An Historical and Critical Treatise*, published in 1892 by A. C. Oudemans, Director of the Royal Zoological and Botanical Society at The Hague. Oudemans concluded that what Drevar saw was the predatory sperm whale attacking the serpent, rather than the other way round. He dismissed giant squids or snakes as possible candidates.
49 *Sheffield Independent*, 3rd November 1883.
50 *The Newcastle Courant*, 2nd November 1883.
51 Centennial Park was opened on 26th January 1888.
52 A copy is held by the National Library of Australia: catalogue.nal.gov/record/588330.
53 *The Brisbane Courier*, 7th January 1890.

Lucky Swanson and the Murder of Mr. Gold

1 Weather forecast for London from the *London Standard*, 8th July 1881. Although the buildings on Smith Street are long gone, it is reasonable to assume that they were constructed of the same material as the majority of houses south of the Whitechapel Road, including surviving adjoining streets such as Jubilee Street and Lindley Street.
2 *The Sheffield Daily Telegraph*, 8th November 1881.
3 Sarah Emma Bickers was born in 1854 at Chigwell, Essex. She married James Anderson, a Brewery Clerk from Berwick-on-Tweed, on 8th June 1878. The marriage register records both bride and groom as residing at 32 Smith Street. At the time of Lefroy's arrest the couple were living nearby at 77 Whitechapel Road.
4 Caroline Bickers was born in 1855, also at Chigwell. She married William Farnworth, a Customs Officer from Liverpool, on 3rd November 1877. Again, both were residing at the family home at the time. The couple moved just a mile away to Antill Road, Mile End.
5 James Philip Bickers was born in 1822 at Millbank. He married Sarah Thompson on 20th August 1848 at St-Martin-in-the-Fields, Westminster, and the couple raised a family at Chigwell before moving to Leinster Street, Paddington by the time of the 1861 census. In 1871 the family are recorded at Exmouth Street, Whitechapel, and around 1872 moved to 1 Providence Place, Bancroft Road, Mile End. James Bickers had a variety of jobs: he was a butler in 1861, a messenger in 1871 and a brewer's messenger at the time of his death on 27th February 1876, at 32 Smith Street. His death certificate records the cause of death as 'asthma exhaustion'.
6 1881 Census, which was taken on 3rd April. These gentlemen may, of course, have left 32 Smith Street before 5th July.
7 *The Times*, 11th July 1881.

8   Ibid.
9   Swanson's report on a letter from Mrs. Bickers claiming the reward, 21st November 1881. (National Archives: HO144/83/A6404).
10 *Portsmouth Evening News*, 9th July 1881.
11 *London Standard*, 9th July 1881; *The Sheffield Daily Telegraph*, 8th November 1881; *Hampshire Telegraph*, 13th July 1881.
12 Swanson's report on a letter from Mrs. Bickers claiming the reward, 21st November 1881. (National Archives: HO144/83/A6404).
13 *The Times*, 11th July 1881.
14 *Sheffield and Rotherham Independent*, 9th July 1881.
15 *Shields Daily Gazette and Shipping Telegraph*, 9th July 1881.
16 See *Mr. Briggs' Hat: A Sensational Account of Britain's First Railway Murder* by Kate Colquhoun (2011) for an excellent examination of the case, and *Trial of Franz Müller*, edited by George Knott (1911) from the Notable British Trials series for a verbatim account of the trial.
17 See *The Victorian Railway Murders* by Arthur and Mary Sellwood (1979), an excellent account of locomotive crimes from 1864 to 1901.
18 *The Norfolk Ancestor*, Vol 7 Part 6, September 1994.
19 Valentine Baker had enjoyed a fine military career, serving in the Crimean War and had later become Major of the 10th Hussars.
20 *The Royal Leamington Spa Courier*, 7th August 1875.
21 *Gloucester Journal*, 7th August 1875.
22 *The Royal Leamington Spa Courier*, 7th August 1875.
23 While serving his sentence the Colonel was dismissed from the Army. Upon his release from prison Baker left the country and joined the Ottoman Army in the war with Russia before becoming head of the Egyptian Police in 1882, a post he held until his death in 1887. It has been suggested that the 1894 Victorian pornographic novel *Raped on the Railway: A True Story of a Lady who was First Ravished and then Flagellated on the Scotch Express* was based on the attack on Miss Dickinson.
24 *Gloucester Journal*, 7th August 1875.
25 This version of events is taken from William Franks' testimony at the trial, but in his autobiography Lefroy states that he sat first in a different carriage, where his intended victim was a man eating strawberries, only to be put off by the man's demeanour and change carriages at East Croydon to that in which Mr Gold was travelling. The strawberry-eating passenger, George Austin, later corroborated Lefroy's claim. See *Trial of Percy Lefroy Mapleton* by Adam Wood (2019).
26 *The Cheshire Observer*, 23rd July 1881.
27 *The Derby Daily Telegraph*, 4th November 1881.
28 *Berrow's Worcester Journal*, 12th November 1881; *The Newcastle Courant*, 11th November 1881.

29 *The Staffordshire Sentinel*, 23rd July 1881.
30 *Berrow's Worcester Journal*, 12th November 1881.
31 *The Huddersfield Chronicle*, 12th November 1881.
32 *The Times*, 22nd July 1881.
33 Wynne Edwin Baxter was born on 1st May 1844 at Lewes, Sussex. In 1868 he married Kate Bliss Parker, the union producing six children. He was called to the Bar in 1867, and in 1875 moved to London where he established a long-running solicitor's practice. He was elected Coroner for East Sussex in January 1880, a post he held for seven years. In 1885 Baxter was elected Deputy Coroner for the City of London and Borough of Southwark, and the following year as Coroner for the County of Middlesex. His title changed in 1892 to Coroner for the City of London (Eastern District) and the Liberty of the Tower of London, a post he held until his death in 1920. He presided over an estimated 40,000 inquests, including well-known cases such as the Elephant Man, Joseph Merrick, Miriam Angel, murdered by Israel Lipski, and ten victims named in the Whitechapel murders files. See 'Inquest, London' by Adam Wood, *Ripperologist* issue 61 (September 2005).
34 *The Alnwick Mercury*, 16th July 1881.
35 *The People's Journal*, 9 July 1881.
36 *Lloyd's Weekly Newspaper*, 10th July 1881.
37 News reports variously spell Lefroy's pseudonym as both "Clark" and "Clarke". I have used the spelling contained in a letter from Mrs. Bickers' son-in-law asking for information on the reward.
38 *The Huddersfield Chronicle*, 12th November 1881.
39 Not everyone applauded the *Daily Telegraph*'s decision to publish the likeness of Lefroy. *The Northern Echo* of 11th July 1881 commented on the number of innocent young men who had found themselves in trouble with both police and public for possessing even a passing resemblance to the sketch: "One of the police officials engaged in the hunt tells me that an incalculable amount of trouble has been given by the publication in the *Daily Telegraph* of an imaginary sketch purporting to be the portrait of Lefroy. This was drawn partly from memory by an acquaintance of Lefroy's and was touched up by a gifted artist. The result was a sketch of a very common criminal type, and it is positively appalling to find how many prototypes it has in real life. It was less like Lefroy than many innocent people to whose arrest it led, and, apart from the actual inconvenience to private individuals and trouble to authorities, it worked in the direction of defeating the ends of justice by withdrawing the public from the right scent."
40 *The Times*, 22nd July 1881.
41 *The Ipswich Journal and Suffolk, Norfolk, Essex and Cambridgeshire Advertiser*, 12th July 1881.
42 *Sheffield and Rotherham Independent*, 9th July 1881.
43 Joseph Mugford was born at Mutley, Plymouth, in 1857 and at the time of

Lefroy arrest was lodging at the home of Mary and Elizabeth Bowen on New Union Street, Moorgate. In 1891 he was an unmarried lodger at Dean Street, working as a General Clerk, and married Annie Bayliss in March 1894. The couple moved to Fulham and had two children, one of whom sadly died at a young age. In 1911 Mugford was working as a Law Clerk, living at Sherbrooke Road, Fulham, with Annie and their son John. He died in 1930 aged 73.

44 Report by Inspector Frederick Jarvis, 7th December 1881. (National Archives: HO144/83/A6404/24).
45 *Lloyd's Weekly Newspaper*, 10th July 1881.
46 *The Times*, 11th July 1881.
47 *Lloyd's Weekly Newspaper*, 10th July 1881.
48 *The North-Eastern Daily Gazette*, 22nd July 1881.
49 *The Northampton Mercury*, 23rd July 1881.
50 *Daily Gazette for Middlesbrough*, 22nd July 1881.
51 *The North Devon Journal*, 3rd November 1881.
52 Ibid.
53 *Surrey Mirror and General County Advertiser*, 26th November 1881.
54 *The Morning Post*, 11th July 1881.
55 P.C. Timothy Daly in 1842 and P.C. William Davey in 1863.
56 *The Penny Illustrated Paper*, 8th October 1881.
57 *Huddersfield Chronicle*, 26th September 1881.
58 *Pall Mall Gazette*, 23rd September 1881.
59 *Huddersfield Chronicle*, 26th September 1881.
60 *The Daily News*, 24th September 1881.
61 *Morning Post*, 27th September 1881.
62 The case of P.C. Frederick Atkins was only the second instance of an unsolved murder of a Metropolitan Police officer, after that of P.C. George Clark in 1846, and the last until 1991. A plaque was erected in Kingston's Police Memorial Garden in Atkins' memory in 1996, and a replica erected in the Watchman public house, on the site of the former New Malden police station.
63 *Gloucester Citizen*, 30th September 1881.
64 Ibid.
65 *Yorkshire Post and Leeds Intelligencer*, 30th September 1881.
66 *South Wales Daily News*, 24th September 1881.
67 *The Official Encyclopedia of Scotland Yard* by Martin Fido and Keith Skinner (2000 revised edition).
68 *Leaves of a Life* Vol II by Montagu Williams (1890). For a verbatim transcript of the trial, see *Trial of Percy Lefroy Mapleton* edited by Adam Wood (Notable British Trials No. 86, 2019).
69 Lyttleton Stewart Forbes Winslow was born in 1844. Raised in lunatic asylums

run by his father, a noted expert on insanity, Winslow himself developed theories on insanity and crime. Prior to the Lefroy case he was involved in a court case in which he attempted to have the celebrated anti-lunacy laws campaigner Mrs. Georgina Weldon committed to an asylum, earning himself a notorious reputation. He was also involved in the Florence Maybrick and Amelia Dyer cases, and claimed to know the identity of Jack the Ripper through detective work carried out on his part in Whitechapel. See *Doctor Forbes Winslow: Defender of the Insane* by Molly Whittington-Egan (2000) and Winslow's autobiography, *Recollections of Forty Years* (1910).

70 National Archives: HO144/83/A6404/24.
71 *Recollections of Forty Years* by L Forbes Winslow (1910).
72 Note from Sir William Harcourt, 12th December 1881. (National Archives: HO144/83/A6404). A full transcript of Lefroy's fanciful autobiography can be read in *Trial of Percy Lefroy Mapleton* edited by Adam Wood (Notable British Trials No. 86, 2019).
73 Letter from Rev. T. H. Cole, 29th November 1881. (National Archives: HO144/83/A6404/24).
74 *Derbyshire Times*, 30th November 1881.
75 *Police Work From Within* by Hargrave L. Adam (1914).
76 *The North-Eastern Daily Gazette*, 18th July 1881. Again, the elder Donald Swanson from Thurso is referred to as an uncle, when in reality they were unrelated.
77 Letter from William Farnworth dated 14th July 1881, sent from 32 Smith Street. (National Archives: HO144/ 83/A6404/24).
78 Report with covering letter from Pearson dated 21st November 1881. (National Archives: HO144/83/A6404/ 24).
79 *Lloyd's Weekly Newspaper*, 15th January 1882.
80 National Archives: HO144/83/A6404.
81 Swanson's Metropolitan Police file (National Archives: MEPO 2/2980).
82 Letter from the General Manager of the London, Brighton and South Coast Railway dated 23rd January 1882, held in Swanson family archives.
83 *The Worcestershire Chronicle*, 10th December 1881.
84 *Trewman's Exeter Flying Post*, 23rd July 1884.

The Bodysnatchers

1 *Twelve Scots Trials* by William Roughead (1913).
2 See *The Bodysnatchers* by Martin Fido (1988).
3 Nova Scotia Gardens was purchased by the philanthropist Angela Burdett-Coutts in the 1840s after it had degenerated into a slum and been razed to the ground. It was here that Columbia Market was established in 1869.
4 See *The Italian Boy: Murder and Grave-Robbery in 1830s London* by Sarah Wise

(2005) for an in-depth account of the case.

5   *Bell's Life in London and Sporting Chronicle*, 4th December 1831.
6   Although no case occurred in Britain, in 1878 the body of American millionaire Alexander Stewart was stolen for ransom from the vaults of St. Mark's Church in New York by a gang of five bodysnatchers. A reward of $25,000 was offered ($450,000 today), but the gang refused to return Mr. Stewart unless a ransom of $200,000 was met ($4.5 million). No payment was made, and neither body nor bodysnatchers were ever located.
7   James Ludovic Lindsay was born on 28th July 1847. He was educated at Eton and Cambridge before joining the Grenadier Guards. He became M.P. for Wigan in 1874 and, sharing the same love of astronomy as his father, President of the Royal Astronomical Society in 1878. Lindsay became 26th Earl of Crawford and 9th Earl of Balcarres following the death of his father in 1880. He would have a minor part to play in the investigation into the Whitechapel murders of 1888.
8   *The Dundee Advertiser*, 6th December 1881.
9   1881 census. In subsequent years, John Swanson moved his family to various addresses around Aberdeen, each smaller and more distant from Aberdeen city centre than the last. In his later years he seems to have endured a battle with the bottle, with his death on 9th November 1891 attributed to cirrhosis of the liver and kidneys.
10 *Supplement to the Sheffield and Rotherham Independent*, 10th December 1881.
11 Reprinted in *Aberdeen Journal*, 7th December 1881.
12 *Sunderland Daily Echo and Shipping Gazette*, 19th April 1876.
13 *The Dundee Courier and Argus*, 29th July 1876.
14 *Edinburgh Evening News*, 24th May 1876.
15 *The Aberdeen Journal*, 15th December 1881.
16 Ibid.
17 *Sunderland Daily Echo and Shipping Gazette*, 19th April 1876.
18 *The Hampshire Advertiser*, 10th December 1881.
19 *Twelve Scots Trials* by William Roughead (1913).
20 *Yorkshire Post and Leeds Intelligencer*, 27th June 1884.
21 *Leeds Mercury*, 7th July 1884.
22 *The York Herald*, 12th July 1884.
23 Two tramps, Thomas Kyne and John McCawley, were briefly linked with the murder of Mary Cooper after they were arrested at the casual ward at Ripon after tearing up their bloodstained clothes during the night (see *Yorkshire Gazette*, 27th June 1884). A former soldier named Thomas Brennan was found wandering around Glossop where, after his arrest, he confessed to the killing. No evidence was found to support this claim (see the *North-Eastern Daily Gazette* of 29th September and 2nd October 1884).
24 *Aberdeen Journal*, 11th March 1882.

25. *The Lancaster Gazette*, 31st December 1881.
26. *Twelve Scots Trials* by William Roughead (1913).
27. Handwritten reward notice (National Archives: HO 45/9615/A11425).
28. *The Morning Post*, 2nd January 1883; private memorandum of Donald Swanson.
29. £30,000 today.
30. *The North Eastern Daily Gazette*, 25th February 1882.
31. 1871 Scotland census lists Charles Soutar as a Vermin Destroyer at George Street, Aberdeen. He is recorded as 30-years-old, with wife Ann Soutar, 29.
32. *Dundee Courier*, 23rd October 1861. The fine was the equivalent of £200 today.
33. *Dundee Advertiser*, 19th December 1863.
34. *The Dundee Courier and Argus*, 23rd December 1880.
35. *Dundee Courier*, 7th November and 17th December 1878,
36. *Evening News*, 4th October 1882.
37. *Southland Times*, 19th September 1882.
38. *Glasgow Herald*, 26th July 1882.
39. *The Aberdeen Journal*, 25th June 1883.
40. Letter from Alsop, Mann & Co., 19th June 1883. (National Archives: HO 45/9615/A11425).
41. National Archives: HO 45/9615/A11425.
42. *Edinburgh Evening News*, 11th June 1886.
43. *Aberdeen Evening Express*, 15th August 1888.
44. *The Aberdeen Journal*, 7th February 1888.
45. *The Aberdeen Journal*, 8th February 1888.
46. *The Aberdeen Journal*, 7th February 1888.
47. *Aberdeen Evening Express*, 18th March 1888.
48. *Aberdeen Evening Express*, 30th October 1890.
49. *Dundee Courier*, 9th October 1889.
50. *Aberdeen Evening Express*, 6th November 1889.
51. The marriage must have occurred between 1901 and 1903, as the 1901 census records Charles Soutar as a 60-year-old Vermin Killer living alone at 107 Commerce Street, Aberdeen. Soutar's obituary in the *Aberdeen Journal* of 6th January 1914 gives details of the verminist's career and claimed that as an expert on the subject his views had been sought in Glasgow during a threatened outbreak of bubonic plague.
52. *The Sketch*, 12th April 1899.
53. Full physical description given in *Illustrated Circular No. 12*, Convict Office, Great Scotland Yard, 12th May 1884: Age 67, height 5ft 6in, complexion fair, hair grey (parted in centre), eyes blue (large), aquiline nose, hands and feet small.

54 The Cavendish Hotel at 83 Jermyn Street was run for fifty years by Rosa Lewis, who started as a kitchen maid and rose to eventually purchase the Cavendish, becoming known as 'The Duchess of Jermyn Street'. Her story was dramatised in the 1970s BBC television series *The Duchess of Duke Street*.
55 *Southern Reporter*, 13th October 1881.
56 Central Criminal Court Indictment (National Archives: CRIM 4/953 31209).
57 *Pall Mall Gazette*, 19th May 1882.
58 *Southern Reporter*, 27th October 1881.
59 *The Southern Reporter*, 13th October 1881.
60 *The Edinburgh Evening News*, 6th October 1881.
61 Ibid.
62 Ibid.
63 *Southern Reporter*, 27th October 1881.
64 *Aberdeen Journal*, 4th February 1882.
65 *Reynolds's Weekly Newspaper*, 14th May 1882.
66 *The Times*, 15th May 1882.
67 *The Aberdeen Journal*, 17th May 1882.
68 *Illustrated Police News*, 3rd June 1882.
69 *Pall Mall Gazette*, 19th May 1882.
70 Applications to United States of America Bureau of Pensions, 14th May 1885; 19th November 1892.
71 Claim for Pension, 20th May 1909.
72 *Illustrated Circular No. 12*, Convict Office, Great Scotland Yard, 12th May 1884.
73 Invalid Application for Pension, 19th November 1892.
74 *Gloucester Citizen*, 26th November 1891.
75 *Yorkshire Post and Leeds Intelligencer*, 19th December 1891.
76 *Dundee Courier*, 22nd October 1897.
77 *Cheshire Observer*, 6th November 1897.
78 Declaration for Widow's Pension, U.S. Pension Agency. Much of the research material on Lochiel Lorimer Graham was collated by the late Norman Fairfax and sent to me in the early stages of writing this book. Norman was intrigued by the possibility that Malcolm Fairfax may have been a distant relation. I am sad that Norman passed away before this book was completed, although wonder if perhaps it may be for the best that he did not learn that 'Malcolm Fairfax' was simply another of Lorimer Graham's pseudonyms.

The Fenians are Coming!

1 *Ah! Who Will Seize* from *The Fenian Songster* (1866).
2 *The Manchester Courier, and Lancashire General Advertiser*, 27th January 1881.

3   *The Times*, 20th January 1881.
4   *Sheffield Daily Telegraph*, 22nd January 1881.
5   This is an extremely simplified description of a complex chain of events. For a detailed study of the politics of the era and those Fenians involved in the Dynamite campaign of 1881-1885 see Shane Kenna's magisterial *War in the Shadows: The Irish-American Fenians Who Bombed Victorian Britain* (2014).
6   In *The Dynamiters: Irish Nationalism and Political Violence in the Wider World, 1867-1900* (2012) Niall Whelehan argues that although Jeremiah O'Donovan Rossa's attitude was the more violent, Clan na Gael's targets represented more danger to the general public.
7   *The Nottingham Evening Post*, 15th January 1881.
8   *War in the Shadows: The Irish-American Fenians Who Bombed Victorian Britain* by Shane Kenna (2014).
9   *The Staffordshire Daily Sentinel*, 17th March 1881.
10 *Inspector of Explosives Annual Report for the Year 1881*. Some newspaper reports incorrectly state 40lb.
11 *Bury and Norwich Post*, 22nd March 1881.
12 *The Manchester Times*, 11th June 1881.
13 *The Nottingham Evening Post*, 10th June 1881.
14 *The Manchester Times*, 11th June 1881.
15 *The Derby Daily Telegraph and Reporter*, 10th June 1881.
16 *The Manchester Times*, 11th June 1881.
17 See *The Irish National Invincibles and Their Times* by P. J. P. Tynan (1894).
18 *Irish Conspiracies: Recollections of John Mallon (The Great Irish Detective) and Other Reminiscences* by Frederick Moir Bussy (1910).
19 See *Inspector Mallon: Buying Irish Patriotism for a Five-Pound Note* by Donal P. McCracken (2009) for a fine account of the Phoenix Park murders and their investigation.
20 Ibid.
21 *The Western Times*, 9th May 1882.
22 *The Irish National Invincibles and Their Times* by Patrick J. P. Tynan (1894).
23 *Inspector Mallon: Buying Irish Patriotism for a Five-Pound Note* by Donal P. McCracken (2009).
24 *The Dundee Courier and Argus*, 27th July 1882.
25 Copy of letter from Godfrey Lushington to Howard Vincent, 12th October 1882, held in 'Ireland: Fenians: Phoenix Park murders' (National Archives: A16380/96).
26 Ibid.
27 Report by Det. Inspector Donald Swanson dated 16th October 1882, held in 'Ireland: Fenians: Phoenix Park murders' (National Archives: A16380/96).

28 *Sunderland Daily Echo and Shipping Gazette*, 16th December 1882.
29 *The Hemel Hempstead Gazette*, 30th December 1882.
30 *The Citizen*, 19th February 1883.
31 *Pall Mall Gazette*, 19th February 1883.
32 Ibid.
33 *The Citizen*, 19th February 1883.
34 Arrest book of Donald Swanson held in family archive.
35 *Aberdeen Evening Express*, 19th February 1883.
36 *Nottingham Evening Post*, 20th February 1883.
37 *Ayr Advertiser or West Country Journal*, 22nd February 1883.
38 Ibid.
39 *The Dundee Courier and Argus*, 22nd February 1883.
40 *Sheffield Independent*, 21st February 1883.
41 *Irish Conspiracies: Recollections of John Mallon (The Great Irish Detective) and Other Reminiscences* by Frederick Moir Bussy (1910).
42 *Portsmouth Evening News*, 16th July 1883.
43 *The Bury and Norwich Post*, 7th August 1883.
44 *Leighton Buzzard Observer and Linslade Gazette*, 7th August 1883.
45 *The Times*, 5th December 1882.
46 *Tamworth Herald*, 9th December 1882.
47 *Morning Post*, 10th January 1883.
48 *Manchester Courier and Lancashire General Advertiser*, 13th January 1883.
49 *The Graphic*, 20th January 1883.
50 *The Northern Warder and Bi-Weekly Courier and Argus*, 23rd January 1883.
51 *Annual Report of Her Majesty's Inspector of Explosives for the Year 1883.*
52 Ibid.
53 *Pall Mall Gazette*, 22nd January 1883.
54 *The Birmingham Daily Post*, 22nd January 1883.
55 *Pall Mall Gazette*, 22nd January 1883.
56 *Annual Report of Her Majesty's Inspector of Explosives for the Year 1883.*
57 *The Birmingham Daily Post*, 22nd January 1883.
58 *Pall Mall Gazette*, 16th March 1883.
59 *Report to the Right Hon. the Secretary of State for the Home Department on the Circumstances attending Two Explosions which occurred in London on the Night of the 15th March 1883, at the Offices of the Local Government Board in Whitehall, and of the "Times" Newspaper in Play House Yard, respectively by Colonel V. D. Majendie, C.B., H.M. Chief Inspector of Explosives.* Author's collection.
60 *The Morning Post*, 16th March 1883.

61 *Report to the Right Hon. the Secretary of State for the Home Department on the Circumstances attending Two Explosions which occurred in London on the Night of the 15th March 1883, at the Offices of the Local Government Board in Whitehall, and of the "Times" Newspaper in Play House Yard, respectively by Colonel V. D. Majendie, C.B., H.M. Chief Inspector of Explosives.* Author's collection.

62 *Sheffield and Rotherham Independent*, 16th March 1883.

63 *Report to the Right Hon. the Secretary of State for the Home Department on the Circumstances attending Two Explosions which occurred in London on the Night of the 15th March 1883, at the Offices of the Local Government Board in Whitehall, and of the "Times" Newspaper in Play House Yard, respectively by Colonel V. D. Majendie, C.B., H.M. Chief Inspector of Explosives.*

64 *Sheffield and Rotherham Independent*, 16th March 1883.

65 *Edinburgh Evening News*, 16th March 1883.

66 On his return to London Majendie wrote *Up Among the Pandies*, an account of his service in India, published in 1859.

67 *The Engineer*, 29th April 1898.

68 'Appointments and Salaries of Inspectors Under 1875 Act' (National Archives: HO 45/938846912).

69 'Home Office: Dr. Dupré, an explosives expert, to be employed in connection with dynamite' (National Archives: T 1/13779).

70 *The Engineer*, 29th April 1898.

71 *Annual Report of Her Majesty's Inspector of Explosives up to 31st December 1875.*

72 *Annual Report of Her Majesty's Inspector of Explosives for the Year 1883.*

73 Ibid.

74 *The Sketch*, 25th April 1894. Vivian Majendie held medals from his Crimean, Turkish and Indian Mutiny Campaigns, and was made C.B. in 1880, then knighted in 1895. He died on 24th April 1896. Majendie was revealed as a cousin by marriage of Ripper suspect M. J. Druitt by J. J. Hainsworth in his *Jack the Ripper – Case Solved, 1891* (2015). A biography of this remarkable man, who put his life on the line many times to further his understanding of explosives, is long overdue.

75 *The Lighter Side of My Official Life* by Sir Robert Anderson (1910).

76 *The Reminiscences of Chief-Inspector Littlechild* by J. G. Littlechild (1894).

77 Police Order, 19th March 1883. See also Bernard Porter's excellent *The Origins of the Vigilant State: The London Metropolitan Police Special Branch before the First World War* (1987).

78 *Reynolds's Weekly Newspaper*, 10th February 1895. After many years service within the Special Branch, Patrick McIntyre was eventually reduced to the rank of a uniformed constable and sent to Y Division for a supposed breach of duty by reporting late to Scotland Yard following a spell of six weeks at Cowes while

Queen Victoria was there. He left the Met in October 1894 and became landlord of the Foresters' Arms, Borough, and was later sued by a former informant named Feargus O'Connor over an alleged debt of 2s 6d. (*Reynolds's Weekly Newspaper*, 21st October 1894; 5th May 1895; 21st June 1896.)

79 *Stories From Scotland Yard* by Inspector Moser with Charles F. Rideal (1890).
80 *London Standard*, 16th May 1883.
81 Old Bailey Online (t18830528).
82 *Survey of London: Volume 45, Knightsbridge*. Originally published by London County Council (2000).
83 Old Bailey Online (t18830528).
84 *The Times*, 11th June 1883.
85 Ibid.
86 *Illustrated Police News*, 2nd June 1883.
87 *Royal Cornwall Gazette*, 15th June 1883.
88 Birth certificate of Ada Mary Swanson.
89 *Pall Mall Gazette*, 24th June 1884.
90 £15,000 today. *The Morning Post*, 1st February 1884.
91 Michael Hviid Jacobsen's *The Poetics of Crime: Understanding and Researching Crime and Deviance* (2014) claims that some 10,000 documents were produced on Nielsen's criminal career.
92 cf *Pall Mall Gazette*, 6th July 1883.
93 *Manchester Courier and Lancashire General Advertiser*, 12th February 1881.
94 See Poul Duedahl's biography of Jens Nielsen, *Silence of the Lambs* (Danish: *Ondskabens øjne*, 2016).
95 *Pall Mall Gazette*, 6th July 1883.
96 'Police documents 1823-1877, 1883-1886' (Provincial Archives of Sjaelland: DC-032).
97 Ibid.
98 Ibid.
99 *The Aberdeen Journal*, 31st October 1883.
100 Today's Paddington tube station. Until 1933, the Underground station was named Praed Street, with access via street level rather than the current concourse entrances of the Paddington station complex.
101 *Annual Report of Her Majesty's Inspector of Explosives for the Year 1883*.
102 *Jackson's Oxford Journal*, 3rd November 1883.
103 *The Aberdeen Journal*, 31st October 1883.
104 *Annual Report of Her Majesty's Inspector of Explosives for the Year 1883*.
105 *Western Times*, 6th November 1883.
106 'Police documents 1823-1877, 1883-1886' (Provincial Archives of Sjaelland: DC-032).

107 Old Bailey Online (18810502).
108 'Police documents 1823-1877, 1883-1886' (Provincial Archives of Sjaelland: DC-032).
109 *Lloyd's Weekly Newspaper*, 16th March 1884.
110 *St. James's Gazette*, 5th March 1886.
111 *Aberdeen Journal*, 9th November 1892.
112 www.danishfamilysearch.com/historier/7.
113 *The Times*, 18th January 1884.
114 *The Morning Post*, 1st February 1884.
115 *Western Daily Press*, 8th February 1884.
116 *Western Daily Press*, 25th June 1884.
117 Awarded 16th February 1884. Swanson's Metropolitan Police file (National Archives: MEPO 3/2890).
118 *Derbyshire Courier*, 5th April 1884. In fact, baccarat continued to gain popularity with the public and was at the centre of the Tranby Croft Affair of 1890, an incident sometimes called the Royal Baccarat Scandal which resulted in Prince Edward giving evidence in court.
119 *Reynold's Newspaper*, 10th February 1884.
120 *Pall Mall Gazette*, 19th February 1884.
121 *Aberdeen Evening Express*, 8th March 1884.
122 Born 5th April 1870 (1939 England and Wales Register; Civil Registration Birth Index 1837-1915; 1871 and 1891 census returns).
123 Born in the fourth quarter of 1876 (Civil Registration Birth Index 1837-1915; 1881, 1901 and 1911 census returns).
124 Born 28th October 1873 (1881, 1901 and 1911 census returns; 1939 England and Wales Register).
125 Presumably James Aveling Brace, aged 15 (1881 census return; Civil Registration Birth Index, 1837-1915).
126 Born in the first quarter of 1872 (1881, 1901 and 1911 census returns).
127 *The Times*, 4th January 1884.
128 *The Islington Gazette*, 4th January 1884.
129 1881, 1891 and 1901 census returns. In the latter Jaggers is specifically listed as an employee of the New River Company.
130 *Reynolds's Weekly Newspaper*, 6th January 1884.
131 Inquest testimony of Dr Thomas Bond, reported in *The Times*, 5th January 1884.
132 *Reynolds's Weekly Newspaper*, 6th January 1884.
133 *The Islington Gazette*, 4th January 1884.
134 Inquest testimony of Det. Inspector Henry Moore, reported in *The Times*, 5th January 1884.

Notes and References to pages 208-217

135 *The Islington Gazette*, 4th January 1884.

136 *Reynolds's Weekly Newspaper*, 6th January 1884.

137 Inquest testimony of Eliza Broome (*The Times*, 5th January 1884).

138 Listed as a governess at an Infant's School in Bird Court, St Alphage in the 1861 census, and as a teacher living at Sandringham Street, Hackney with son John in the 1871 census.

139 Inquest testimony of Eliza Broome (*The Times*, 5th January 1884).

140 Marriage Index.

141 1871 and 1881 census returns. In 1891 he is recorded as a Teacher of Mathematics.

142 Mary Broome *née* Bickerton died in the second quarter of 1877 (Death Index).

143 Inquest testimony of Alice Goodwin, who stated that Broome Tower had lodged at the house "about five or six years." (*The Times*, 5th January 1884).

144 Strangely, in the 1881 census Alice Goodwin is recorded as being 73 years old – 15 years older than her supposed adoptive mother Mary Ann Drage. She is listed as a boarder, an assistant in a confectioner's shop. No other record of her can be found.

145 Ernest Sydney Cogden was born on 6th November 1864 (Baptism record).

146 William and Charlotte Earl had two daughters, Charlotte Jr. (b. 1861) and Jane (b. 1863). Charlotte remained unmarried until her death in 1945. Jane married Edward Pugh in 1890 and had one child. She died in October 1919, leaving her effects to her sister.

147 *Reynolds's Weekly Newspaper*, 6th January 1884.

148 *Manchester Times*, 5th January 1884.

149 *Pall Mall Gazette*, 7th January 1884.

150 *Morning Post*, 7th January 1884.

151 *Pall Mall Gazette*, 7th January 1884.

152 *The Times*, 8th January 1884.

153 Possibly Margaret Waller born in High Coniscliffe, Durham in 1860 (census returns).

154 *The Leeds Mercury*, 11th January 1884.

155 *The Globe*, 15th January 1884.

156 *St. James's Gazette*, 16th January 1884. The amount missing was the equivalent of £3,000-£4,000 today.

157 *Manchester Evening News*, 15th January 1884.

158 *Lloyd's Weekly Newspaper*, 27th January 1884.

159 *St. James's Gazette*, 22nd January 1884.

160 Ibid.

161 *The Globe*, 2nd January 1886.

162 *Reynolds's Weekly Newspaper*, 3rd January 1886.

163 *The Times*, 5th January 1886.
164 *Reynolds's Weekly Newspaper*, 3rd January 1886.
165 *Police!* by Charles Tempest Clarkson and J. Hall Richardson (1889).
166 *Annual Report of Her Majesty's Inspector of Explosives for the Year 1883*.
167 *Police!* by Charles Tempest Clarkson and J Hall Richardson (1889).
168 Ibid.
169 *Lloyd's Weekly Newspaper*, 22nd March 1885.
170 *The Illustrated Police News*, 21st March 1885.
171 *Police!* by Charles Tempest Clarkson and J. Hall Richardson (1889).
172 *Gloucester Citizen*, 31st May 1884.
173 *At Scotland Yard: Being the Experiences During Twenty-Seven Years Service* by John Sweeney (1904).
174 *Police!* by Charles Tempest Clarkson and J. Hall Richardson (1889).
175 *Gloucester Citizen*, 31st May 1884.
176 Ibid.
177 *Annual Report of Her Majesty's Inspector of Explosives for the Year 1883*.
178 *Western Mail*, 13th May 1884. At the General Election of 1885 Howard Vincent successfully stood as M.P. for Sheffield (Central Division) and held his seat through five further elections. He was knighted in 1896. He eventually died in office, suffering a heart failure at Menton, southern France on 7th April 1908. See *Sir Howard Vincent's Police Code, 1889* by Neil R. A. Bell and Adam Wood (2015).
179 *Pall Mall Gazette*, 13th May 1884.
180 Report of the Director of Criminal Investigations for the Year 1883, contained in *Report of the Commissioner of Police of the Metropolis for the Year 1883*.
181 *Northampton Mercury*, 7th June 1884.
182 *Western Times*, 11th June 1884.
183 *Derbyshire Times*, 21st June 1884.
184 *London Evening Standard*, 9th July 1884.
185 *The Yorkshire Evening News*, 14th November 1891.
186 See Bernard Porter's *The Origins of the Vigilant State: The London Metropolitan Police Special Branch before the First World War* (1987).
187 Memorandum written by Edward Jenkinson on 22 June 1885, held in 'Ireland: Fenians: Duties etc of Mr. Jenkinson' (National Archives: HO 144/721/110757).
188 Police Order, reported in *The Morning Post*, 11th December 1884. Douglas Labalmondière died two days after his 78th birthday, on 8th March 1893, at Eaton Place, Belgravia.
189 *Nottingham Evening Post*, 12th December 1884.
190 *London Daily News*, 13th December 1884.
191 *Oxford University and City Herald*, 7th May 1870.

192 *Oxford Journal*, 8th May 1875.
193 *Police!* by Charles Tempest Clarkson and J. Hall Richardson (1889).
194 *At Scotland Yard: Being the Experiences During Twenty-Seven Years Service* by John Sweeney (1904).
195 Gower Street station was renamed Euston Square in 1909.
196 *The Herald*, 10th January 1885.
197 *The North Devon Journal*, 8th January 1885.
198 Ibid.
199 *The Evening News*, 3rd January 1885.
200 *The Standard*, 5th January 1885.
201 Ibid.
202 *The Evening News*, 3rd January 1885.
203 *The Herald*, 31st January 1885.
204 *Police!* by Charles Tempest Clarkson and J. Hall Richardson (1889).
205 *Aberdeen Evening Post*, 26th January 1885.
206 *The Standard*, 27th January 1885.
207 *War in the Shadows: The Irish-American Fenians Who Bombed Victorian Britain* by Shane Kenna (2014).
208 *The Standard*, 27th January 1885.
209 *The Herald*, 31st January 1885.
210 *Police!* by Charles Tempest Clarkson and J Hall Richardson (1889).
211 *The Herald*, 31st January 1885.
212 *The Standard*, 26th January 1885.
213 'Ireland: Fenians: Distribution of Rewards to Police and Others Connected with Dynamite Conspiracies' (National Archives: A26493G).
214 Swanson's Metropolitan Police file (National Archives: MEPO 3/2890).
215 'Appointments and Salaries of Inspectors under 1875 Act' (National Archives: HO 45/9388 46912).
216 *The Reminiscences of Chief-Inspector Littlechild* by J. G. Littlechild (1894).

Blood on the Square

1 *Lloyd's Weekly Newspaper*, reported in the *Pall Mall Gazette* of 12th November 1887.
2 The Long Depression would go on until 1897.
3 *Lloyd's Weekly Newspaper*, 7th February 1886.
4 *Manchester Courier and Lancashire General Advertiser*, 9th February 1886.
5 *The Official Encyclopedia of Scotland Yard* by Martin Fido and Keith Skinner, revised edition (2000).

6   *Pall Mall Gazette*, 9th February 1886.
7   £650,000 today. *The Leeds Mercury*, 15th February 1886.
8   Warren produced two scale models: one, kept at Woolwich, was eventually disposed of but the second is still on display at Gibraltar Museum.
9   See *The Life of General Sir Charles Warren* by Watkin W. Williams (1941) for a full account of Warren's excellent military and archaeological career.
10 *Man-Hunting in the Desert, Being a Narrative of the Palmer Search-Expedition* by Capt. A. E. Haynes (1894). See also an in-depth look at Warren and the search for Palmer in David Sunderland's *These Chivalrous Brothers: The Mysterious Disappearance of the 1882 Palmer Sinai Expedition* (2016).
11 *The Graphic*, 6th June 1885.
12 *A Lost Legionary in South Africa* by George Hamilton-Browne (1912).
13 The Bechuanaland Protectorate became the Republic of Botswana on 30th September 1966.
14 *Hansard*, Deb 4th March 1886 vol 302 cc1891-2.
15 *Pall Mall Gazette*, 9th February 1886.
16 "The Significance of the Geography of Palestine Victoria Institute", paper by General Sir Charles Warren, 1917. Accessed via *The Life of General Sir Charles Warren* by Watkin W. Williams (1941).
17 *The Life of General Sir Charles Warren* by Watkin W. Williams (1941).
18 *Pall Mall Gazette*, 13th March 1886.
19 *Fife Herald*, 17th March 1886.
20 *Aberdeen Evening Express*, 15th March 1886.
21 *Aberdeen Evening Express*, 27th March 1886.
22 *Edinburgh Evening News*, 29th March 1886.
23 *Manchester Courier and Lancashire General Advertiser*, 1st April 1886.
24 The original draft featuring Warren's handwritten annotations is held at the National Archives (MEPO 2/170).
25 *The Life of General Sir Charles Warren* by Watkin W. Williams (1941).
26 Dates from Swanson's masonic certificates. At the time of writing these and other related items including his masonic regalia are held at St. Peter's Lodge, Thurso, on loan from the Swanson family. The Lodge headquarters at the time of Swanson's joining is now a hairdressers.
27 *The Fife Herald*, 1st December 1886.
28 *Edinburgh Evening News*, 29th November 1886.
29 *Aberdeen Journal*, 30th November 1886.
30 Swanson's Metropolitan Police file (National Archives: MEPO 3/2890).
31 Birth certificate of Douglas Sutherland Swanson.
32 *The Times*, 26th January 1887.
33 $50,000 today.

34 Old Bailey Online (t18870228-321).
35 A society of lawyers practising civil law, it had actually been closed in 1865 but the name was still commonly used to describe the resource.
36 $1million today.
37 £2million today.
38 Old Bailey Online (t18870228-321).
39 *The Times*, 18th April 1887.
40 *Reynolds's Weekly Newspaper*, 15th May 1887.
41 *The Times*, 7th May 1887.
42 *The Shields Daily Gazette and Shipping Telegraph*, 14th May 1887.
43 *The Gloucestershire Echo*, 28th May 1887.
44 Ibid.
45 Evidence of Peter King, cook and ship steward (Old Bailey Online: t18870627-718).
46 *Rockingham Morning Bulletin*, 22nd July 1887.
47 Evidence of Cassein (Old Bailey Online: t18870627-718).
48 Evidence of Peter King (Old Bailey Online: t18870627-718).
49 Ibid.
50 *Lloyd's Weekly Newspaper*, 29th May 1887.
51 Evidence of David Thow (Old Bailey Online: t18870627-718).
52 Evidence of Charles Hunt (Old Bailey Online: t18870627-718).
53 Evidence of David Thow (Old Bailey Online: t18870627-718).
54 *The Times*, 1st June 1887.
55 Evidence of Peter King (Old Bailey Online: t18870627-718).
56 *The Times*, 1st June 1887.
57 Evidence of Peter King (Old Bailey Online: t18870627-718).
58 Evidence of David Thow (Old Bailey Online: t18870627-718).
59 *The Times*, 23rd May 1887.
60 Under cross-examination, Swanson accepted that the incident took place on the voyage from West Australia to Le Havre, not in Shark's Bay. The communication he received from the Board of Trade was in error on this point. Old Bailey Online (t18870627-718).
61 Ibid.
62 *Lloyd's Weekly Newspaper*, 29th May 1887.
63 Old Bailey Online (t18870627-718).
64 Swanson's police file (National Archives: MEPO 3/2890).
65 *The Life of General Sir Charles Warren* by Watkin W. Williams (1941).
66 See *War in the Shadows: The Irish-American Fenians Who Bombed Victorian Britain* by Shane Kenna (2014) and *The Origins of the Vigilant State: The

London Metropolitan Police Special Branch before the First World War by Bernard Porter (1987).

67 Accessed via *War in the Shadows: The Irish-American Fenians Who Bombed Victorian Britain* by Shane Kenna (2014).

68 'Rewards granted to Police Officers and others in dynamite cases' (National Archives: HO 144/211/A48482).

69 The medal bore the words "Inspr. D Swanson A Divn.". It was kept by daughters Ada and Alice before mysteriously going missing from their home at some point in the 1970s.

70 Recollections of Sir Evelyn Ruggles-Brise, quoted in *The Life of General Sir Charles Warren* by Watkin W. Williams (1941).

71 "Note of Relations between Mr. Jenkinson and the Metropolitan Police in connection with Fenian Conspiracies etc", a report by Monro which concludes with the paragraph: "I have striven under the greatest difficulties to co-operate loyally with Mr. Jenkinson as required by the Secretary of State, but the attitude which Mr. Jenkinson has all along assumed, and continues to maintain towards the Metropolitan Police, has rendered, I regret to say, trustful co-operation with him practically impossible." (National Archives: HO 144/721/110757).

72 Unpublished memoirs of James Monro; copy in author's collection.

73 *The Standard*, 25th November 1887. The Mitchelstown Massacre occurred on 9th September 1887, two months before Bloody Sunday, when after a series of disturbances on the Mitchelstown Estate the police attempted to break up a protest only to be pelted with sticks and stones. The police retaliated by shooting into the crowd, killing three men including John Shinnick.

74 *Hull Daily Mail*, 14th November 1887.

75 Statement of P.C. Thomas Maitland, Regina v Graham & Burns (National Archives: HO 144/206/A479760).

76 Statement of P.C. William Blunden, Regina v Graham & Burns (National Archives: HO 144/206/A479760).

77 *Hull Daily Mail*, 14th November 1887.

78 *The Life of General Sir Charles Warren* by Watkin W. Williams (1941).

79 Transferred 19th November 1887. Swanson's Metropolitan Police file (National Archives: MEPO 3/2890).

80 Death certificate of Sarah Ann Nevill, which records the fact that she had, at the time of her death, been suffering from bronchitis for six days.

81 *Reynolds' News*, 4th December 1887.

82 *Pall Mall Gazette*, 15th November 1887.

83 *Lloyd's Weekly Newspaper*, 11th December 1887.

84 Ibid.

85 *Reynolds's Weekly Newspaper*, 11th December 1887.

86 *Pall Mall Gazette*, 9th December 1887.

87 *Pall Mall Gazette*, 12th December 1887.
88 Letter from Sir Charles Warren dated 8th December 1887 (National Archives: HO 144206/A47976P).
89 Telegram from Joseph Seddon, Secretary of the Law and Liberty League to the Secretary of State, 17th December 1887. (National Archives: HO 144206/A47976P).
90 *Aberdeen Journal*, 19th December 1887. A pamphlet containing the words to Morris' *A Death Song*, with a cover design by influential artist Walter Crane, was printed and sold, with proceeds being donated to Alfred Linnell's children. A copy is held in the National Archives (HO 144206/A47976P).
91 *Dundee Courier*, 19th January 1888.
92 Following his release, Robert Cunninghame Graham continued to campaign for improved rights of working people and supported them in industrial disputes, such as the Matchgirls' Strike of 1888 and the Dockers' Strike the following year. He had helped establish the Scottish Home Rule Association in 1886 and in 1892 founded the Scottish Labour Party with Keir Hardie. Cunninghame Graham played an active part in the establishment of the National Party of Scotland in 1928, and was elected the first ever president of the Scottish National Party in 1934. He died two years later on 20th March 1936.
93 Awarded by Commissioner Sir Charles Warren on 18th February 1888. Rewards and commendations recorded in Swanson's Metropolitan Police file (National Archives: MEPO 3/2890).
94 Report by Swanson dated 28th March 1888 (National Archives: HO 144/206/A47976O).
95 National Archives: HO 144/206/A47976O.
96 Arnold White went on to become a founding member of the British Brothers League, an anti-immigration group with a particular hostility towards the growing Jewish population of the East End. His *The Problems of a Great City* (1886) stands as a testament to his anti-Semitic views.
97 *The Sheffield Evening Telegraph*, 7th May 1888.
98 *The North-Eastern Daily Gazette*, 19th January 1888.
99 Police Order, 24th January 1888.
100 Shore's address given as 43 Burton Road, Brixton. The second witness was James Wallis, a butcher of 7 Binfield Road, Clapham. John Shore retired from the Metropolitan Police on 1st May 1896 and became the European representative for the Pinkerton Agency. He died just two years later on 12th March 1898.
101 Obituary of Donald Swanson in *John O'Groat Journal*, 12th December 1924.
102 Death certificate of Adolphus Williamson, which states that at the time of his death in 1889 he had suffered "cardiac disease 7 years".
103 'Mr. A. F. Williamson, Chief Constable of Criminal Investigation Department: leave of absence; Mr. Melville Leslie Macnaghten: appointment as Assistant

Chief Constable and then as Chief Constable of the Criminal Investigation Department' (National Archives: MEPO 2/210).
104   Ibid.
105   *Peterhead Sentinel and Buchan Journal*, 6th July 1888.
106   *Pall Mall Gazette*, 3rd March 1888.
107   *Pall Mall Gazette*, 23rd October 1888.
108   *Peterhead Sentinel and Buchan Journal*, 6th July 1888.
109   *The Star* of 19th December 1888 reported that Det. Inspector Henry Marshall, who arrested her, had conducted an investigation into Mrs. Gordon Baillie's criminal career, which spanned more than two decades across several countries including Italy, America and Australia, using her considerable physical charms to persuade wealthy gentlemen to lavish gifts upon her.
110   The others were Det. Chief Inspectors Butcher, Greenham, Neame and Littlechild.

Eyes and Ears

1   Swanson's copy of the two-page memorandum, handwritten on Metropolitan Police Office notepaper, held in family archives.
2   Police Metropolitan: Appointment of Robert Anderson as Assistant Commissioner (National Archives: HO 144/305/B5005A).
3   Home Office Police Entry Books (National Archives: HO 65/62 – Volume 35, 1st September to 20th November 1888).
4   *The Lighter Side of My Official Life* by Sir Robert Anderson (1910).
5   Private letter quoted in *The Ultimate Jack the Ripper Sourcebook: An Illustrated Encyclopedia* by Stewart P. Evans and Keith Skinner (2001 paperback version).
6   *London's Underground* by H. F. Howson (1951).
7   *The Globe*, 11th November 1876.
8   *London's Underground* by H. F. Howson (1951).
9   *Canon Barnett: His Life, Works and Friends* by H. O. Barnett (1918).
10   *The Anarchists: A Picture of Civilization at the Close of the Nineteenth Century* by John Henry Mackay (1891).
11   Letter published in the *Daily Telegraph* of 21st September 1888. See www.jack-the-ripper.org/common-lodging-houses.htm for discussion on the common lodging houses of the East End; *Dottings of a Dosser; being revelations of the inner life of low London Lodging-Houses* by Howard J. Goldsmid (1886) and *Secret World of the Victorian Lodging House* by Joseph O'Neill (2014).
12   London County Council Minutes of Proceedings of the Council, July-December 1890 accessed by Sarah Wise's excellent *The Blackest Streets: The Life and Death of A Victorian Slum* (2008).
13   *Out of Work* by John Law (Margaret Harkness) (1888) accessed via *The Streets of East London* by William J. Fishman (1979).

14 See *Victorian Jews Through British Eyes* by Anne and Roger Cowen (1998) for a description of Jewish emigration and their reception in Britain.
15 *Victorian Jews Through British Eyes* by Anne and Roger Cowen (1998).
16 *Jewish Migration to South Africa: The Records of the Poor Jews' Temporary Shelter, 1885-1914.* Edited by Aubrey N. Newman, Nicholas J. Evans, J. Graham Smith and Saul W. Issroff (2006).
17 *Jewish Chronicle*, 27th March 1885.
18 British Parliamentary Papers: Royal Commission on Alien Immigration (1903).
19 Great Garden Street was renamed Greatorex Street in 1936.
20 *First Annual Report of the Poor Jews' Temporary Shelter, 1885-6* held in 'Records of the Jews' Temporary Shelter, 1896-1998' (London Metropolitan Archives: LMA/4184/2/1/1).
21 *Constitution of the Poor Jews' Temporary Shelter (1885)*, held in 'Records of the Jews' Temporary Shelter, 1896-1998' (London Metropolitan Archives: LMA/4184/02/01/001/02).
22 *Third Annual Report of the Poor Jews' Temporary Shelter, 1887-8* held in 'Records of the Jews' Temporary Shelter, 1896-1998' (London Metropolitan Archives: LMA/4184/02/01/001/01).
23 Visitors' Book for the Poor Jews' Temporary Shelter, 1886-1941, held in 'Records of the Jews' Temporary Shelter, 1896-1998' (London Metropolitan Archives: LMA/4184/1/1/3/1).
24 Ibid.
25 *Mr. Charles Booth's Inquiry: Life and Labour of the People in London Reconsidered* by Rosemary O'Day and David Englander (1993).
26 Visitors' Book for the Poor Jews' Temporary Shelter, 1886-1941, held in 'Records of the Jews' Temporary Shelter, 1896-1998' (London Metropolitan Archives: LMA/4184/1/1/3/1).
27 *Reynolds's Weekly Newspaper*, 29th July 1888.
28 *The People*, 29th July 1888.
29 *Third Annual Report of the Poor Jews' Temporary Shelter, 1887-8* held in 'Records of the Jews' Temporary Shelter, 1896-1998' (London Metropolitan Archives: LMA/4184/02/01/001/01).
30 *The Annual Report of the Sanitary Condition of the Whitechapel District for the year 1893.*
31 *(Alien immigration) Reports on the volume and effects of recent immigration from eastern Europe into the United Kingdom* (Board of Trade, 1894).
32 Ibid.
33 Ibid. Of 7,257 Russian and Russian Poles employed in Whitechapel, 2,476 (34%) were tailors.
34 *Second Report from The Select Committee of the House of Lords on the Sweating System* (Session 1888).

35 *At Scotland Yard: Being the Experiences During Twenty-Seven Years Service* by John Sweeney (1904).
36 *Second Report from The Select Committee of the House of Lords on the Sweating System* (Session 1888).
37 'The Jews in London' by Lucien Wolf, *The Graphic*, 16th November 1889.
38 *At Scotland Yard: Being the Experiences During Twenty-Seven Years Service* by John Sweeney (1904).
39 Samuel Kosminski was born on 10th November 1857.
40 Nationality and Naturalisation: Kosminski, Samuel, from Russia. Resident in London. Certificate A5430 issued 14 June 1887 (National Archives: HO 144/293/B1470).
41 Naturalisation Certificate: Samuel Kosminski. From Russia. Resident in London. Certificate A5430 issued 14 June 1887 (National Archives: HO 334/15/5430).
42 *At Scotland Yard: Being the Experiences During Twenty-Seven Years Service* by John Sweeney (1904).
43 *(Alien immigration) Reports on the volume and effects of recent immigration from eastern Europe into the United Kingdom* (Board of Trade, 1894).
44 Ibid.
45 *East London Observer*, 15th September 1888.
46 Testimony of John Davis at the inquest into Annie Chapman's death, as reported in *The Times*, 11th September 1888.
47 Testimony of Henry John Holland at the inquest into Annie Chapman's death, as reported in *The Times*, 13th September 1888. The reporter quoted Holland as saying the officer was in Spitalfields Market opposite, but *Kelly's Directory of London* for 1888 lists a Fixed Point at 'Spitalfields Church'.
48 Testimonies of James Kent and James Green at the inquest into Annie Chapman's death, as reported in *The Times*, 13th September 1888.
49 Testimony of John Davis at the inquest into Annie Chapman's death, as reported in *The Times*, 11th September 1888.
50 Contrary to their C.I.D. counterparts, Divisional Inspectors were uniformed. For a thorough understanding of police procedures at the time of the Whitechapel murders see Neil R. A. Bell's indispensible *Capturing Jack the Ripper: In the Boots of a Bobby in Victorian London* (2014).
51 Report by Inspector Joseph Chandler, 8th September 1888 (National Archives: MEPO 2/140, ff9-11).
52 Report by Det. Chief Inspector Donald Swanson, 19th October 1888 (National Archives: HO 144/221/A4930C, ff137-45).
53 Now permitted to work in plain clothes, assisting H Division's C.I.D. (Police Orders 20th September 1888).
54 Report by Inspector Joseph Chandler, 8th September 1888 (National Archives: MEPO 2/140, ff9-11).
55 Response to enquiry by Assistant Commissioner (Administrative) Alexander

Carmichael Bruce from Det. Chief Constable Frederick Adolphus Williamson, 8th September 1888 (National Archives: MEPO 2/140, ff11).

56 Police Orders.
57 Police Orders.
58 Testimony of Dr. Rees Ralph Llewellyn at the inquest into Mary Ann Nichols' death, as reported in *The Times*, 3rd September 1888.
59 *Morning Advertiser*, 7th September 1888.
60 A report by Local Inspector Joseph Helson, J Division (Bethnal Green) dated 7th September 1888 states that he and Abberline were heading enquiries into Nichols' murder (National Archives: MEPO 3/140, ff235-38).
61 Little is known of Emma Elizabeth Smith's history before 1888. Newspaper reports of the attack on give her age as 45, and Det. Inspector Edmund Reid describes her in his report as being 5ft 2in tall, with a fair complexion and light brown hair. She had a scar on her right temple. She may be the Emma Smith born Emma Elizabeth Binmore on Christmas Day 1843 in Devon, who grew up in Portsea and married Frederick Wells there in April 1862. On 1st September 1868 Emma Wells married John Smith at Portsea; the couple are recorded as living at 118 Central Street, Finsbury in north London in the 1881 census. Victim Emma Smith told her neighbours in the lodging house that she had formerly lived in Finsbury with her family. See discussion at JTRForums.com/showthread.php?p=380955.
62 Although the attack itself was not witnessed, Emma Smith returned to the lodging house at 18 George Street, where she had lived for 18 months, between 4.00 and 5.00am on the morning of 3rd April with terrible injuries. Such was her condition that the Deputy, Mary Russell, immediately took her to the London Hospital where she was examined by House Surgeon Dr. George Haslip, who noted that her head was bruised and her right ear torn, in addition to a ruptured peritoneum and internal organs. Emma told Dr. Haslip that she had been passing St. Mary's Church on Whitechapel Road at 1.30am when she saw two or three men approaching her, so she crossed the road to avoid them. The men followed her up Osborn Street and robbed and beat her, before inflicting the horrific fatal injury near the cocoa factory on the corner of Wentworth Street. Emma survived for just over 24 hours, dying at 9.00am on 4th April 1888. See *The Ultimate Jack the Ripper Sourcebook* by Stewart P. Evans and Keith Skinner (2000 paperback edition).
63 Born Martha White on 10th May 1849 in Southwark, south London, Martha married widower Henry Samuel Tabram on Christmas Day 1869. The couple had two sons, Frederick (1871-1920) and Charles (1872-1956), before going their separate ways in 1875 due to Martha's heavy drinking. Henry initially gave her an allowance of 12s a week but reduced it to 2s 6d; this was stopped completely when he discovered that she had begun living with another man, Henry Turner. Turner was a carpenter, and he and Martha lived together on and off until July 1888, when they separated for the final time. In his report of 10th August 1888 (MEPO 3/140, f238) Det. Inspector Ellisdon described her as being 37-years-old, 5ft 3in tall, with a dark complexion and dark hair.

At the time of her death she was wearing a green skirt, a brown petticoat and a long black jacket, with brown stockings and a black bonnet.

64 Martha's last known abode was Satchell's Lodging House, 19 George Street. On 6th August 1888 she was seen in various public houses with her friend of four months, a fellow prostitute named Mary Ann Connelly (aka 'Pearly Poll'). The pair were drinking with two guardsmen they had met in the Two Brewers on Brick Lane at around 10.00pm. According to Connelly, the foursome separated about 11.45pm, Martha taking the Private into George Yard and she herself going with the Corporal up the parallel Angel Alley, no doubt both with the intention of having sex. At 2.00am Police Constable Thomas Barrett saw a Grenadier Guardsman in Wentworth Street, at the north end of George Yard, who told him that he was "waiting for a chum who went off with a girl." At about the same time a Mrs. Mahoney and her husband returned to their lodgings at George Yard Buildings and saw nothing suspicious, but when a cab man named Alfred Crow returned to his own rooms in George Yard Buildings at 3.30am he noticed 'something' on the landing. As it was not unusual for people to sleep where they could in the East End, including staircases, Crow thought nothing of it and continued to his bed. The body of Martha Tabram was eventually discovered by John Reeves as he left his lodgings at 37 George Yard Buildings at 4.50am. Returning with P.C. Barrett, still on his beat, it was seen that Martha was lying on her back, legs open, with her arms by her side, fingers tightly clenched. Dr. Timothy Killeen of nearby 68 Brick Lane arrived at 5.30am and examined the body, estimating death to have occurred three hours earlier. She had been stabbed a total of 39 times, at various places including her lungs, heart and stomach. All of the wounds had been inflicted while she had been alive. In Dr. Killeen's opinion, all but one of the wounds could have been made with an 'ordinary penknife', with one wound to Martha's chest seemingly made by a sword, dagger or bayonet. For a detailed examination of the murders of Emma Smith and Martha Tabram, and their place in the list of possible murders by Jack the Ripper, see *The Bank Holiday Murders: The True Story of the First Whitechapel Murders* by Tom Wescott (2013) and *Jack the Ripper: The Forgotten Victims* by Paul Begg and John Bennett (2013).

65 *The Times*, 3rd September 1888. More usually referred to by her earlier married name – Tabram – Martha had lived on and off for more than a decade with Henry Turner, no doubt adopting his surname when necessary. They separated for the final time three weeks before her murder.

66 Joseph Martin had taken over the photography business from Louis Gumprecht in 1886 and many of his photographic cards still bore the contact details of the latter on the reverse, including that of Martha Tabram. See *The First Jack the Ripper Victim Photographs* by Robert McLaughlin (2005).

67 Report by Inspector John Chandler, 8th September 1888 (National Archives: MEPO 3/140 ff9-11).

68 Inquest testimony of Amelia Palmer, reported in the *East London Advertiser*, 15th September 1888.

69 Although the exact date of Annie's birth is unknown, at the inquest into her death youngest brother Fountain Smith said that "her age was 47 this month". Whether this should be read as Annie's birthday being later in September or, like Mary Ann Nichols, it had passed in the days immediately before her murder, is unclear.

70 George (1842-1854), Emily (1844-1931), Eli (1849-1854), Miriam (1851-1854), William (b&d.1854), Georgina (1856-1940), Miriam Ruth (1858-1940) and Fountain (1861-1933). George Jr, Eli, Miriam and William all succumbed to the scarlet fever epidemic of 1854.

71 See *The Five: The Untold Lives of the Women Killed by Jack the Ripper* by Hallie Rubenhold (2019) for a detailed account of Annie Chapman's early years.

72 Although there has long been speculation that John Chapman was in some way related to Ruth Smith, née Chapman, and that he and Annie were cousins, there is in fact no evidence that the families were linked.

73 John and Annie Chapman have generally been believed to have had four children: Emily Ruth Chapman (25th June 1870 – 26th November 1882); Annie Georgina Chapman (5th June 1873 – 16th March 1958); Miriam Lily Chapman (16th July 1879 – 3rd October 1879) and John Alfred Chapman (b. 21st November 1880). However, a letter from Annie's younger sister Miriam Ruth Smith warning of the temptations of alcohol published in the *Manitoba Daily Free Press* of 9th January 1892 claimed that Annie had actually given birth eight times. See *The Victims of Jack the Ripper* by Neal Shelden (2007) and 'Fermat's Last Theorem and Annie Chapman's Missing Children', an article in *Ripperologist* 149 (April 2016) by Team Syphilis, who identify one 'new' child, Georgina Chapman (25th April 1876 – 5th May 1876) and suggest that the others were probably stillborn. In her 2019 book *The Five* Hallie Rubenhold names Ellen Georgina (b&d. 5th March 1872) and George William Harry (November 1877 – January 1878), leaving one accounted for, as suggested most likely stillborn.

74 See *The Five: The Untold Lives of the Women Killed by Jack the Ripper* by Hallie Rubenhold (2019).

75 Inquest testimony of Timothy Donovan, Deputy of Crossingham's Lodging House, as reported in *The Times*, 11th September 1888.

76 Inquest testimony of Edward Stanley, as reported in *The Times*, 20th September 1888.

77 Inquest testimony of Amelia Palmer, reported in *The Times*, 11th September 1888.

78 Inquest testimony of Timothy Donovan, reported in *The Times*, 11th September 1888.

79 Inquest testimony of John Evans, reported in *The Times*, 11th September 1888.

80 Inquest testimony of Elizabeth Long, reported in *The Times*, 20th September 1888.

81 When asked at the inquest why he returned to the yard so quickly, Cadosch revealed that he had recently undergone an operation, presumably urological

in nature.

82 Report by Det. Chief Inspector Donald Swanson, 19th October 1888 (National Archives: HO 144/221/A49301C, ff. 137-45).

83 Inquest testimony of Albert Cadosch, reported in *The Times*, 20th September 1888.

84 In 1880, in an attempt to secure assistance to the practice now that he was busier than ever with his Coroner duties at Sussex, Baxter took on one Henry William Hennicker Rance as partner. The new firm, Wynne-Baxter and Rance, steadily grew in size until 1886 when the firm admitted Edward Meade as a third partner, renaming as Wynne-Baxter, Rance and Meade. This arrangement lasted just two years before the three went their separate ways; Baxter remaining at Laurence Pountney Hill, with both Rance and Meade deciding to form their own companies, Rance at 70 Lincoln's Inn Fields and Meade at 14 Walbrook. In 1888 Baxter employed the newly-qualified Jasper Keeble and renamed the company Wynne-Baxter and Keeble. The company proved extremely successful and continued working under the same name, from the same address, beyond both Keeble's death on 25th November 1912 and Baxter's own passing in 1920, although Wynne had long since retired from the practice. The Lewes practice, run from Albion Street by Baxter's son Reggie until his death, still survives today as Mayo Wynne Baxter. For a detailed biography of Wynne Baxter's life and career see 'Inquest, London: The Life and Career of Wynne Edwin Baxter' by Adam Wood in *Ripperologist* 61, September 2005.

85 *Police Gazette*, 9th July 1979.

86 1878 *Post Office Directory* for Sussex.

87 £165,000 today.

88 *Petersfield Express*, 4th November 1879.

89 *Penny Illustrated Paper*, 8th November 1879. Fullagar served his sentence at Chatham, on release relocating to Hackney in East London where he died in 1896.

90 *Sussex Advertiser*, 7th December 1864.

91 *Hastings and St. Leonards Observer*, 29th November 1879.

92 *West Sussex County Times*, 24th January 1880.

93 *West Sussex Journal*, 3rd February 1880.

94 *East Sussex News*, 8th October 1920. The huge painting of Baxter in his mayoral robes which today hangs in the Assembly Room of Lewes Town Hall was commissioned by the Worshipful Company of Gold and Silver Wyredrawers in 1882 to commemorate Baxter's election as first Mayor. It was painted by Mr Cave Thomas, and presented to the Corporation by Baxter in November 1894.

95 *Lloyd's Weekly Newspaper*, 27th April 1884.

96 *Hackney and Kingsland Gazette*, 2nd July 1884.

97 *The Times*, 25th February 1887.

98 *Hackney and Kingsland Gazette*, 13th December 1886.
99 *The Times*, 24th December 1886.
100 *The Times*, 9th May 1888. For important discussion on the 1886 election and subsequent division of the East Middlesex District, see 'The Green of the Peak Part III: Ruairdh Mac Dhòmhnaill. The Life and Times of Roderick Macdonald, Coroner (1840-1894)' by Robert Linford, John Savage and David O'Flaherty in *Ripperologist* 65, March 2006.
101 *East London Advertiser*, 16th June 1888.
102 *East London Advertiser*, 7th April 1888.
103 *East London Advertiser*, 14th April 1888.
104 *East End Advertiser*, 11th December 1886.
105 *East End Advertiser*, 11th December 1886. The Working Lads' Institute was opened in 1885 by the Princess of Wales, with the Prince also in attendance. The inquests took place in the Alexandra Room, a large reading room overlooking the street, with the Coroner's seat being in front of a painting of the Princess.
106 *Daily Telegraph*, 24th September 1888.
107 Ibid.
108 Various newspaper, cf *Pall Mall Gazette* of 15th September 1888.
109 *Pall Mall Gazette*, 10th September 1888.
110 Report by Det. Inspector Frederick Abberline, 19th September 1888 (National Archives: MEPO 3/140, ff242-56).
111 Report by Inspector John Helson, 19th September 1888 (National Archives: MEPO 3/140 ff29-31).
112 *Daily Telegraph*, 17th September 1888.
113 *The Times*, 12th September 1888.
114 *Gloucester Citizen*, 24th September 1888. For a definitive list of those suspected of being the Whitechapel murderer see Paul Williams' *Jack the Ripper Suspects: The Definitive Guide and Encyclopedia* (2018).
115 Report by Sir Charles Warren, 19th September 1888 (National Archives: HO 144/221/A49301C, ff 90-92).
116 *Sunderland Daily Echo and Shipping Gazette*, 1st September 1888.
117 Report by Sergeant William Thick, 17th September 1888 (National Archives: MEPO 3/140, ff21-23).
118 *Kentish Mercury*, 5th October 1888.
119 Inquest testimony of Elizabeth Tanner, as reported in *The Times*, 4th October 1888.
120 Ibid.
121 See *The Five: The Untold Lives of the Women Killed by Jack the Ripper* by Hallie Rubenhold (2019) for a detailed account of Elisabeth Stride's early years.
122 Inquest testimony of Michael Kidney, as reported in *The Times*, 4th October 1888.

123 Inquest testimony of Catherine Lane, as reported in *The Times*, 4th October 1888.
124 Inquest testimonies of Catherine Lane and Charles Preston, as reported in *The Times*, 4th October 1888.
125 Inquest testimony of Charles Preston, as reported in *The Times*, 4th October 1888.
126 Inquest testimony of Catherine Lane, as reported in *The Times*, 4th October 1888.
127 Statement of John Kelly, Coroner's inquest (L), 1888, No. 135, Catherine Eddowes inquest, 1888.
128 *Morning Post*, 3rd October 1888.
129 Inquest testimony of John Kelly, as reported in *The Times* of 5th October 1888.
130 Inquest testimony of Fred Wilkinson, as reported in *The Times* of 5th October 1888.
131 Inquest testimony of John Kelly, as reported in *The Times* of 5th October 1888.
132 Inquest testimony of Fred Wilkinson, as reported in *The Times* of 5th October 1888. In his testimony Wilkinson said that John Kelly arrived at Cooney's between 7.30 and 8.00pm, but this must be wrong as Kate was found insensible by P.C. Louis Robinson at 8.30pm, meaning that Kelly could not have heard of her arrest until much later. He probably arrived at Cooney's closer to 9.00pm.
133 Inquest testimony of Annie Phillips, as reported in *The Times* of 12th October 1888.
134 Statement of P.C. Louis Robinson, Coroner's inquest (L), 1888, No. 135, Catherine Eddowes inquest, 1888.
135 Statement of Sergeant James Byfield, Coroner's inquest (L), 1888, No. 135, Catherine Eddowes inquest, 1888.
136 Name given as 'J. Best' in newspaper reports, author John Bennett researched the address given by the man in his interview with the *Evening News* and discovered he was actually named John Bass, indicating that the reporter had misheard the name.
137 *Evening News*, 1st October 1888.
138 Inquest testimony of William Marshall, as reported in *The Times* of 6th October 1888.
139 Inquest testimony of P.C. William Smith, as reported in *The Times* of 6th October 1888.
140 Inquest testimony of William West, as reported in *The Times* of 2nd October 1888.
141 *St. James's Gazette*, 1st October 1888.
142 Inquest testimony of James Brown, as reported in *The Times* of 6th October 1888.
143 Report by Det. Chief Inspector Donald Swanson, 19th October 1888 (National Archives: HO 144/221/A49301C, ff. 137-45).

144 See *Trial of Israel Lipski* by M.W. Oldridge (Notable British Trials 84, 2017).
145 Report by Det. Chief Inspector Donald Swanson, 19th October 1888 (National Archives: HO 144/221/A49301C, ff. 137-45).
146 Statement of P.C George Hutt, Coroner's inquest (L), 1888, No. 135, Catherine Eddowes inquest, 1888.
147 Statement of Sergeant James Byfield, Coroner's inquest (L), 1888, No. 135, Catherine Eddowes inquest, 1888.
148 Statement of P.C. George Hutt, Coroner's inquest (L), 1888, No. 135, Catherine Eddowes inquest, 1888.
149 Inquest testimony of Louis Diemschitz, as reported in *The Times* of 2nd October 1888.
150 Inquest testimony of P.C. Henry Lamb, as reported in the *Daily Telegraph* of 3rd October 1888.
151 Inquest testimony of P.C. William Smith, as reported in *The Times* of 6th October 1888.
152 Inquest testimony of P.C. Henry Lamb, as reported in the *Daily Telegraph* of 3rd October 1888.
153 Letter published in the *Daily Chronicle*, 2nd October 1888.
154 Inquest testimony of P.C. Henry Lamb, as reported in the *Daily Telegraph* of 3rd October 1888.
155 Inquest testimony of Dr. Henry Blackwell, as reported in the *Daily Telegraph* of 3rd October 1888.
156 Statement of P.C. Edward Watkins, Coroner's inquest (L), 1888, No. 135, Catherine Eddowes inquest, 1888. See 'City Beat: City PC 881 Edward Watkins' by Neil Bell and Robert Clack in *Ripperologist* 105 (August 2009).
157 See 'City Beat: 964 James Harvey' by Neil Bell and Robert Clack in *Ripperologist* 104 (July 2009).
158 Advertisement for the Imperial Club placed in *The Jewish Chronicle* of 18th March 1887.
159 Statements of Joseph Lawende and Joseph Hyam Levy, Coroner's inquest (L), 1888, No. 135, Catherine Eddowes inquest, 1888.
160 Statement of Joseph Lawende, Coroner's inquest (L), 1888, No. 135, Catherine Eddowes inquest, 1888.
161 *The Scotsman*, 12th October 1888.
162 *Evening News*, 9th October 1888.
163 *The Scotsman*, 12th October 1888.
164 Statement of P.C. James Harvey, Coroner's inquest (L), 1888, No. 135, Catherine Eddowes inquest, 1888. For a detailed examination of Mitre Square and the actions of Constables Watkins and Harvey see 'As Far As Mitre Square' by Neil Bell and Jake Luukanen, *Ripperologist* 71 (September 2006).
165 Statement of P.C. Edward Watkins, Coroner's inquest (L), 1888, No. 135, Catherine Eddowes inquest, 1888.

166 Statement of George Morris, Coroner's inquest (L), 1888, No. 135, Catherine Eddowes inquest, 1888.
167 Statement of P.C. James Harvey, Coroner's inquest (L), 1888, No. 135, Catherine Eddowes inquest, 1888.
168 Statement of Dr. Frederick Gordon Brown, Coroner's inquest (L), 1888, No. 135, Catherine Eddowes inquest, 1888.
169 Statement of Inspector Edward Collard, Coroner's inquest (L), 1888, No. 135, Catherine Eddowes inquest, 1888.
170 Report by Superintendent James McWilliam, 27th October 1888 (National Archives: HO 144/221/A49301C, ff 162-170). See also *Capturing Jack the Ripper: In the Boots of a Bobby in Victorian London* by Neil R.A. Bell (2014).
171 Report by Superintendent James McWilliam, 27th October 1888 (National Archives: HO 144/221/A49301C, ff 162-170).
172 Statement of Detective Daniel Halse, Coroner's inquest (L), 1888, No. 135, Catherine Eddowes inquest, 1888.
173 Report By Det. Chief Inspector Donald Swanson, 6th November 1888 (National Archives: HO 144/221/A49301C, ff. 184-194).
174 Statement of Inspector Edward Collard, Coroner's inquest (L), 1888, No. 135, Catherine Eddowes inquest, 1888.
175 Statement of Detective Daniel Halse, Coroner's inquest (L), 1888, No. 135, Catherine Eddowes inquest, 1888.
176 Report by P.C. Alfred Long, 6th November 1888 (National Archives: HO 144/221/A49301C, ff. 195-196).
177 The exact phrase has been disputed, with varying versions claimed by police officers. The version used here was recorded in a report submitted by Det. Chief Inspector Swanson, and subsequently lodged in Home Office files.
178 Report by P.C. Alfred Long, 6th November 1888 (National Archives: HO 144/221/A49301C, ff. 195-196).
179 Statement of P.C. Alfred Long, Coroner's inquest (L), 1888, No. 135, Catherine Eddowes inquest, 1888.
180 Report by P.C. Alfred Long, 6th November 1888 (National Archives: HO 144/221/A49301C, ff. 195-196).
181 Statement of Detective Daniel Halse, Coroner's inquest (L), 1888, No. 135, Catherine Eddowes inquest, 1888.
182 Statement of Detective Daniel Halse, Coroner's inquest (L), 1888, No. 135, Catherine Eddowes inquest, 1888.
183 Report by Superintendent Thomas Arnold, 6th November 1888 (National Archives: HO 144/221/A49301C, ff. 197-198).
184 Letter from Sir Charles Warren, 6th November 1888 (National Archives: HO 144/221/A49301C, ff. 173-181).
185 *Pall Mall Gazette*, 12th October 1888.
186 Letter from Sir Charles Warren, 6th November 1888 (National Archives: HO

144/221/A49301C, ff. 173-181).
187 *The Times*, 3rd October 1888.
188 Inquest testimony of Eliza Gold, as reported in *The Times* of 5th October 1888.
189 See *The Five: The Untold Lives of the Women Killed by Jack the Ripper* by Hallie Rubenhold (2019) for a detailed account of Catherine Eddowes's early years.
190 Statement of Annie Phillips, Coroner's inquest (L), 1888, No. 135, Catherine Eddowes inquest, 1888.
191 *The Times*, 16th October 1888.
192 *Lloyd's Weekly Newspaper*, 14th October 1888.
193 *Manchester Times*, 13th October 1888.
194 *The People*, 14th October 1888.
195 *Lloyd's Weekly Newspaper*, 14th October 1888.
196 *London Daily News,* 9th October 1888.
197 *Glasgow Herald,* 8th October 1888.
198 *Lloyd's Weekly Newspaper,* 30th September 1888.
199 National Archives: MEPO 3/3153, f 1.
200 National Archives: MEPO 3/3153, ff. 2-4.
201 *Express and Echo*, 1st October 1888.
202 *The Sportsman*, 2nd October 1888.
203 *Sheffield Daily Telegraph*, 4th October 1888.
204 *Eastern Evening News*, 3rd October 1888.
205 *Eastern Morning News*, 3rd October 1888.
206 *St. James's Gazette*, 3rd October 1888.
207 *Dundee Courier*, 4th October 1888.
208 See *Jack the Ripper: Letters From Hell* by Stewart P. Evans and Keith Skinner (1997) and 'Letters to The City Police' by John Bennett, *Ripperologist* magazine issues 112 (March 2019), 113 (April 2010) and 114 (May 2010).
209 *Criminals and Crime: Some Facts and Suggestions* by Robert Anderson (1907).
210 Although see 'Henry Jackson Wells Dam: Part 1. Scandal in California, Murder in London's East End', *Ripperologist* 106, in which Paul Begg and Christopher T. George put forward Harry Dam, an American journalist working for *The Star* 1888 as the creator of 'Dear Boss' and 'Saucy Jacky'.
211 Report by Superintendent James McWilliam, 27th October 1888 (National Archives: HO 144/221/A49301C, ff 162-170).
212 'Metropolitan Police: Office of the Commissioner: Letter Books. Commissioners. Confidential and Private. 31 December 1867 – 6 April 1891' (National Archives: MEPO 1/48).
213 Report by Det. Chief Inspector Donald Swanson, 6th November 1888 (National Archives: HO 144//221/A49301C, ff.184-194).
214 Letter from Sir John Whittaker Ellis, 3rd October 1888 (National Archives: HO

144/221/A49301C, f 87).
215 Letter from Sir Charles Warren, 4th October 1888 (National Archives: HO 144/221/A49301C, ff. 83-85).
216 *The Times*, 18th October 1888.
217 Report by Assistant Commissioner (Crime) Robert Anderson, 23rd October 1888 (National Archives: HO 144/221/A49301C, ff. 116-118).
218 Report by Det. Chief Inspector Donald Swanson, 19th October 1888 (National Archives: HO 144/221/A49301C, ff. 148-159).
219 *The Northern Whig*, 3rd November 1888.
220 'CRIMINAL: Metropolitan Police report the finding of a mutilated dead body of a woman at 26, Dorset Street, Spitalfields' (National Archives: HO 144/221/A49301F).
221 Letter from E.S. Johnson, Private Secretary to Under Secretary of State Charles Stuart-Wortley (National Archives: HO 144/221/A49301C, ff.78-79).
222 Inquest testimony of Thomas Bowyer (London Metropolitan Archives: MJ/SPC, NE1888, Box 3, Case Paper 19).
223 *Daily Telegraph*, 10th November 1888.
224 Inquest testimony of Thomas Bowyer (London Metropolitan Archives: MJ/SPC, NE1888, Box 3, Case Paper 19).
225 Inquest testimony of John McCarthy (London Metropolitan Archives: MJ/SPC, NE1888, Box 3, Case Paper 19).
226 Statement of Joseph Barnett, 9th November 1888 (London Metropolitan Archives: MJ/SPC, NE1888, Box 3, Case Paper 19).
227 *Daily Telegraph*, 10th November 1888.
228 *Daily Telegraph*, 10th November 1888.
229 Statement of Joseph Barnett, 9th November 1888 (London Metropolitan Archives: MJ/SPC, NE1888,Box 3, Case Paper 19).
230 *Sheffield Independent*, 10th November 1888.
231 Statement of Joseph Barnett, 9th November 1888 (London Metropolitan Archives: MJ/SPC, NE1888, Box 3, Case Paper 19).
232 Private memorandum of Donald Swanson. No exact date is given, but the record appears between entries dated 1881 and 1884.
233 *Mary Jane Kelly and the Victims of Jack the Ripper: The 125th Anniversary* by Neal Shelden (2013). Ongoing research by Debra Arif and others on JTRForums appears to be getting closer to Mary's 'beau' Joseph Fleming.
234 *Evening Star*, 10th November 1888.
235 Inquest testimony of Joseph Barnett (London Metropolitan Archives: MJ/SPC, NE1888, Box 3, Case Paper 19).
236 *Penny Illustrated Paper*, 17th November 1888.
237 Inquest testimony of Joseph Barnett (London Metropolitan Archives: MJ/SPC, NE1888, Box 3, Case Paper 19).

238 *Daily News*, 13th November 1888.

239 *Lloyd's Weekly Newspaper*, 11th November 1888. In her statement and subsequent inquest testimony Maria Harvey claims to have been with Mary Kelly when Barnett arrived on 9th November, but in an interview which appeared in the *Daily News* the day following the murder she told the reporter that she had found a room of her own at 3 New Court, off Dorset Street and Kelly had visited her there that evening. If it had been Maria Harvey in the room when Joe Barnett arrived – who was responsible for his leaving Mary – surely he would have said "the woman" rather than "a woman". Lizzie Albrook was not called to give evidence.

240 *Suffolk and Essex Free Press*, 14th November 1888.

241 Statement of Mary Ann Cox, 9th November 1888 (London Metropolitan Archives: MJ/SPC, NE1888, Box 3, Case Paper 19).

242 Statement of Elizabeth Prater, 9th November 1888 (London Metropolitan Archives: MJ/SPC, NE1888, Box 3, Case Paper 19).

243 Statement by George Hutchinson, 12h November 1888 (National Archives: MEPO 3/140, ff. 227-229).

244 Report by Det. Inspector Frederick Abberline, 12th November 1888 (National Archives: MEPO 3/140, ff. 230-232).

245 Statement by George Hutchinson, 12h November 1888 (National Archives: MEPO 3/140, ff. 227-229).

246 Inquest testimony of Sarah Lewis (London Metropolitan Archives: MJ/SPC, NE1888, Box 3, Case Paper 19).

247 Inquest testimony of Det. Inspector Frederick Abberline (London Metropolitan Archives: MJ/SPC, NE1888, Box 3, Case Paper 19). See *Capturing Jack the Ripper: In the Boots of a Victorian Bobby* by Neil R.A. Bell (2014) for a detailed account of the bloodhound trials and usage.

248 Inquest testimony of Det. Inspector Frederick Abberline (London Metropolitan Archives: MJ/SPC, NE1888, Box 3, Case Paper 19).

249 *Daily News*, 10th November 1888.

250 Police – Metropolitan: Appointment of Divisional Surgeons (National Archives: HO 45/9685/A48384/1).

251 George Farr was born on 23rd March 1832 at Baldock, Hertfordshire, moving to London by the time of his marriage to Joanna Lee in 1860. Farr is first recorded as a surgeon in the 1861 census. He died on 11th January 1899. Interestingly, Dr. Farr was called upon to give evidence in the case of Thomas Uberfield, who had attempted to murder his daughter by cutting her throat on 13th September 1888. Uberfield said that the weapon, a razor, had been bought because he "felt something creeping about inside, to cut my bowels open." Dr. Farr testified that he had known Uberfield as a patient of unsound mind for 18 months, his main delusion being that "he had animals crawling around inside him". Two months later, the Divisional Surgeon examined an injury to 19-year-old Ellen Worsfold, who had been stabbed in the abdomen in

the early hours of 15th November in Westminster Bridge Road. Although not life-threatening, the wound bled freely. Her attacker, Collingwood Fenwick, was caught and charged.

252 Dr. Farr, living at 175 Kennington Road (1881 and 1891 census returns), was very much at the centre of L Division and perfectly placed to attend those officers living 'south of the river'.

253 Letter from Sir Charles Warren to the Under Secretary of State dated 18th February 1888. National Archives: Police – Metropolitan: Appointment of Divisional Surgeons (HO 45/9685/A48384/2).

254 Letter from Dr. Thomas Bond to the Under Secretary of State dated 7th March 1888. National Archives: Police – Metropolitan: Appointment of Divisional Surgeons (HO 45/9685/A48384/3).

255 Letter from Sir Charles Warren to the Under Secretary of State dated 3rd April 1888. National Archives: Police – Metropolitan: Appointment of Divisional Surgeons (HO 45/9685/A48384/5).

256 Police – Metropolitan: Appointment of Divisional Surgeons (National Archives: HO 45/9685/A48384/7).

257 Letter from Thomas Bond to Alexander Mackellar dated 4th October 1888. National Archives: Police – Metropolitan: Appointment of Divisional Surgeons (HO 45/9685/A48384).

258 Letter from Dr. Alexander Mackellar to Sir Charles Warren, dated 1st November 1888. National Archives: Police – Metropolitan: Appointment of Divisional Surgeons (HO 45/9685/A48384).

259 Letter from Sir Charles Warren to the Under Secretary of State dated 2nd November 1888. National Archives: Police – Metropolitan: Appointment of Divisional Surgeons (HO 45/9685/A48384/8).

260 National Archives: HO 144/221/A49301/21.

261 Ibid.

262 National Archives: HO 144/221/A49301/219. See post by Stewart P. Evans on 6th August 2011 and subsequent discussion on Casebook: Jack the Ripper: forum.casebook.org/showthread.php?t=5930&page=2.

263 See the *London Standard*, 25th September 1894.

264 *Standard* telegram published in the *Leeds Mercury*, 28th September 1894.

265 *Leeds Mercury*, 28th September 1894; *London Standard*, 25th September 1894.

266 *Leeds Mercury*, 28th September 1894.

267 National Archives: HO 144/221/A49301C/36.

268 National Archives: HO 144/221/A49301C/37.

269 *London Evening Standard*, 17th November 1894.

270 See page 565 for discussion of the so-called Macnaghten Memorandum.

271 The returned autopsy on Mary Kelly was filed in MEPO 3/141. See "Copy be damned, that's the original!: A History of the Macnaghten Memorandum"

by Adam Wood (*Ripperologist* 124, February 2012), in which it is suggested that the sender of the material was a descendant of Melville Macnaghten's grandson Gerald Donner.

272 *Aberdeen Evening Express*, 10th November 1888.
273 Hansard: HC Deb 13 November 1888 vol 330 cc1035-8 1035.
274 *Manchester Courier and Lancashire General Advertiser*, 13th November 1888.
275 *St. James's Gazette*, 13th November 1888. The idea of Howard Vincent as Commissioner is an intriguing one; a long experience of the inner workings of the Metropolitan Police, combined with a later Parliamentary career, he might have been a great success in the position.
276 *St. James's Gazette*, 13th November 1888.
277 See 'The Green of the Peak Part III: Ruairdh Mac Dhòmhnaill. The Life and Times of Roderick Macdonald, Coroner (1840-1894)' by Robert Linford, John Savage and David O'Flahery in *Ripperologist* 65, March 2006. The authors explain that the brevity of the inquest compared to those conducted by Wynne Baxter — often the source of suggestions of incompetence or a cover-up – was due to its jury deciding they had heard all they needed to return their verdict.
278 *Morning Advertiser*, 20th November 1888.
279 *The Times*, 20th November 1888. In 1988. The land containing Mary Jane Kelly's grave and others was reclaimed in the 1950s and she was reinterred elsewhere in St. Patrick's. A large white headstone calling Kelly "The Prima Donna of Spitalfields" was erected by researcher John Morrison in 1986, albeit in the wrong spot, and soon removed. The current simple memorial was placed by the then Superintendent of St. Patrick's in the 1990s.
280 Inquest testimony of Joseph Barnett (London Metropolitan Archives: MJ/SPC, NE1888, Box 3, Case Paper 19).
281 *Daily Telegraph*, 22nd November 1888.
282 *East London Advertiser*, 24th November 1888.
283 *Daily Telegraph*, 22nd November 1888.
284 *Illustrated Police News*, 1st December 1888.
285 *Daily Telegraph*, 22nd November 1888.
286 *Manchester Times*, 24th November 1888.
287 *Daily Telegraph*, 22nd November 1888.
288 *Manchester Times*, 24th November 1888.
289 *Daily Telegraph*, 22nd November 1888.
290 *The Times*, 22nd November 1888.
291 *Bristol Mercury*, 22nd November 1888.
292 *Taunton Courier, and Western Advertiser*, 28th November 1888. On admission the Whitechapel Infirmary recorded Annie Farmer's age as 34. She was discharged on 1st December 1888.
293 *The Times*, 16th November 1888.

294 *The Dover Express*, 7th December 1888.
295 See 'A Rose By Any Other Name? The Death of Catherine Mylett, 20 December 1888' by Debra Arif and Robert Clack in *Ripperologist* 108, November 2009 for an excellent account of the life and death of the Poplar victim.
296 Report by Assistant Commissioner Robert Anderson, 11th January 1889 (National Archives: MEPO 3/143, ff. E-J).
297 Report by Commissioner James Monro, 26th December 1888 (National Archives: HO 144/221/A4930H, ff. 7-14).
298 Report by Assistant Commissioner Robert Anderson, 11th January 1889 (National Archives: MEPO 3/143, ff. E-J).
299 See 'A Rose By Any Other Name? The Death of Catherine Mylett, 20 December 1888' by Debra Arif and Robert Clack in *Ripperologist* 108, November 2009 for a detailed account of Catherine Mylett's life.
300 *Daily Chronicle*, 28th December 1888.
301 Charles Ptolomey was born in Dublin in 1851. Evidently with a long career in caring for the poor, at the time of the 1881 census he was Attendant Domestic Servant at the North Riding of Yorkshire Pauper Lunatic Asylum.
302 *Globe*, 29th December 1888.
303 *Evening Standard*, 10th January 1889.
304 Report by Assistant Commissioner Robert Anderson, 11th January 1889 (National Archives: MEPO 3/143, ff. E-J).
305 *Irish Times*, 26th December 1888.
306 *The Lighter Side of My Official Life* by Sir Robert Anderson (1910).
307 Birth certificates of Alice and William Swanson.
308 Death certificate of William Alexander Swanson.
309 Mr. A.F. Williamson, Chief Constable of Criminal Investigation Department: leave of absence; Mr. Melville Leslie MacNaghten: appointment as Assistant Chief Constable and then as Chief Constable of the Criminal Investigation Department' (National Archives: MEPO 2/210).
310 Report by Det. Inspector Henry Moore, 17th July 1889 (National Archives: MEPO 3/140, ff. 294-297).
311 Interview with John McCormack in *The Standard*, 19th July 1889. At the time of writing research by Debra Arif, Gary Barnett and others is ongoing into one Alice Pitts, born in Peterborough in March 1845. See JTRForums.com.
312 Statement of Elizabeth Ryder, 22nd July 1889 (National Archives: MEPO 3/140, f. 276).
313 *Lloyd's Weekly Newspaper*, 21st July 1889.
314 Statement of Margaret Franklin 22nd July 1889 (National Archives: MEPO 3/140, f. 275).
315 Report by Superintendent Thomas Arnold, 17th July 1889 (National Archives: MEPO 3/140, ff. 7-10).

316 *Lloyd's Weekly Newspaper*, 21st July 1889.
317 Report by Sergeant Badham, 17th July 1889 (National Archives: MEPO 3/140, ff. 272-273).
318 Report by Sergeant Badham, 17th July 1889 (National Archives: MEPO 3/140, ff. 272-273).
319 Report by Dr. George Bagster Phillips, 22nd July 1889 (National Archives: MEPO 3/140, ff. 263-271).
320 Report by Det. Inspector Henry Moore, 17th July 1889 (National Archives: MEPO 3/140, ff. 294-297).
321 Report by Dr. George Bagster Phillips, 22nd July 1889 (National Archives: MEPO 3/140, ff. 263-271).
322 *Nottingham Evening Post*, 24th July 1889.
323 Report by Dr. Thomas Bond to Assistant Commissioner Robert Anderson, undated by bearing a Metropolitan Police 'Received' stamp dated 19th July 1889 (National Archives: MEPO 3/140, ff. 259-262).
324 The list is held in the Swanson family archive, indicating that the detective kept it with him to refer to.
325 Report by Det. Chief Inspector Donald Swanson, 10th September 1889 (National Archives: MEPO 3/140, ff.136-140).
326 Extract from the *New York Herald* of 11th September 1889, held in 'Trunk of a female – Found on 10th September 1889' (National Archives: MEPO 3/140, ff. 134-135).
327 Report by Det, Chief Inspector Donald Swanson, 12th September 1889 (National Archives: MEPO 3/140, ff. 153-157).
328 Report by Det, Chief Inspector Donald Swanson, 12th September 1889 (National Archives: MEPO 3/140, ff. 153-157).
329 Statement of John Arnold, 12th September 1889 (National Archives: MEPO 3/140, ff. 162-164).
330 Report by Det, Chief Inspector Donald Swanson, 12th September 1889 (National Archives: MEPO 3/140, ff. 153-157).
331 Statement of John Arnold, 12th September 1889 (National Archives: MEPO 3/140, ff. 162-164).
332 Report by Det, Chief Inspector Donald Swanson, 12th September 1889 (National Archives: MEPO 3/140, ff. 153-157).
333 The *New York Daily Herald*, September 1889 (precise date unknown). Accessed via *The Ultimate Jack the Ripper Sourcebook* by Stewart P. Evans and Keith Skinner (2000 paperback edition).
334 Report by Det. Chief Inspector Donald Swanson, 23rd September 1889 (Accessed via *The Ultimate Jack the Ripper Sourcebook* by Stewart P. Evans and Keith Skinner (2000)).
335 Ibid.
336 *Western Mail*, 30th October 1889.

337 *Western Mail*, 4th November 1889.

338 *Recollections of Forty Years* by L Forbes Winslow (1910).

339 Report by Det. Inspector Henry Moore, 30th September 1889 (National Archives: MEPO 3/140, ff176-77).

340 Report by Det. Inspector Henry Moore, 5th October 1889 (National Archives: MEPO 3/140, ff178-80).

341 Division Surgeons: Post-mortem examinations fees (National Archives: MEPO 2/229).

342 POLICE – METROPOLITAN: Fees for special medical reports of Division Surgeon (National Archives: HO 45/9711/A51187).

343 METROPOLITAN: Fees for special medical reports of Division Surgeon (National Archives: HO 45/9711/A51187). A drawn-out discussion over the fees paid to the Divisional Surgeons for their duties would rumble on until 1897, when eventually the Commissioner (by then Sir Edward Bradford) was asked to submit a report detailing the work carried out in six cases over the preceding year in which Divisional Surgeons had prepared special reports on post-mortem examinations at the request of the Met. The report was compiled by Donald Swanson, by that time Det. Superintendent of the C.I.D. A draft of the covering letter contained in the file reveals an exasperated Commissioner Edward Bradford echoing James Monro's comments from eight years earlier: "In many cases, the law and practice as regards the Coroner's powers and duties, and medical examination of bodies, could not be more embarrassing to Police work if they were specially designed to thwart it..." See also MEPO 2/229 (Divisional Surgeons post-mortem fees) and MEPO 2/321 (Divisional Surgeons salaries).

344 Death certificate of Adolphus Frederick Williamson.

345 The *Sheffield Daily Telegraph*, 30th December 1889. Howard Vincent's Preface to the Sixth Edition of the *Police Code*, dated October 1889, thanks Williamson for his help in bringing the book up to date. A facsimile of the volume with an extensive introduction by Neil R. A. Bell and Adam Wood is available from www.mangobooks.co.uk.

346 *Reynolds's Weekly Newspaper*, 15th December 1889. The existence of Williamson's diaries is also mentioned in the *Western Morning News* of 10th December1889. To date, no trace of the memoirs has been located.

347 *The Guernsey Star*, 14th December 1889.

348 The amount of the award reported in the *Morning Post* of 31st December 1889; see also discussion in 'A.F. Williamson – Chief Constable: death of' (National Archives: MEPO 2/238).

349 For the story of Mapleson's intended opera house see www.arthurlloyd.co.uk/NationalOperaHouseEmbankment.htm.

350 See *The Mapleson Memoirs, 1848-1888 Vol I* by James Henry Mapleson (1888).

351 www.arthurlloyd.co.uk/NationalOperaHouseEmbankment.htm.

352 *The Mapleson Memoirs, 1848-1888 Vol* I by James Henry Mapleson (1888).

353 See 'In the Ripper's Shadow: The Whitehall Mystery' by Robert Clack in *Ripperologist* 133, August 2013.
354 *The Times*, 9th October 1888.
355 Report by Det. Chief Inspector Donald Swanson, 10th September 1889 (National Archives: MEPO 3/140, ff. 136-140). For an account of the series of torso cases see *The Thames Torso Murders* by M. J. Trow (2011).
356 'New Scotland Yard: naming of' (National Archives: MEPO 2/245). Under Secretary of State Godfrey Lushington wrote to confirm that the names 'New Scotland Yard' and 'Scotland Yard Avenue' had been approved on 11th April 1890. In fact, Scotland Yard Avenue does not appear on any subsequent official documentation and the road seems to have simply continued to be named Derby Street.
357 *The New Review*, No. 16, September 1890. A copy is held in 'The Story of Police Pensions, by J. Monro, late Commissioner' (National Archives: MEPO 2/5809).
358 A list of those giving evidence before the Committee is given in the *South Wales Daily News*, 11th July 1890.
359 *The New Review*, No. 16, September 1890, held in 'The Story of Police Pensions, by J. Monro, late Commissioner' (National Archives: MEPO 2/5809). A copy of the Committee's report is held at the National Archives (HO 45/9698/A50055).
360 Handwritten note on a copy of *The New Review*, No. 16, September 1890, held in 'The Story of Police Pensions, by J. Monro, late Commissioner' (National Archives: MEPO 2/5809).
361 Unpublished memoirs of James Monro; copy in author's collection.
362 *The Nottingham Evening Post*, 21st June 1890.
363 A copy is held in The National Archives (MEPO 2/5809).
364 A so-called 'Monro Fund' set up by his former subordinates raised some £520 for the departing Commissioner. In November 1891, as he was leaving to perform missionary work in India with his daughter, Monro wrote to Sir Edward Bradford thanking his former colleagues and advising them that the money had been given to the trustees of the Police Convalescent Home Fund for the establishment and maintenance of a bed at the Home near Brighton for the exclusive use of Metropolitan Police officers. (*St. James's Gazette*, 16th November 1891). Monro arrived at Calcutta in January 1892, (*Western Daily Press*, 30th January 1892) and he and his daughter established a Medical Mission at Ranaghat some 40 miles away, an area devastated at the time with fever. Monro returned to England in 1903, settling in Cheltenham. He died at Chiswick in January 1920 aged 81 (*Yorkshire Post and Leeds Intelligencer*, 31st January 1920).
365 *Dublin Daily Express*, 21st June 1890.
366 *Nottingham Evening Post*, 20th June 1890.
367 *Truly a Great Victorian: A Quiet Man Before Whom Rogues Trembled* by Constance Bradford (2004). In all official photographs of Bradford the left arm

of his Commissioner's tunic is pinned up. Several items belonging to the Commissioner are on display at the Metropolitan Police Heritage Centre, including his sash and medals – and a set of tiger's claws.

368 *Pall Mall Gazette*, 21st June 1890.
369 *Edinburgh Evening News*, 1st October 1890.
370 *Edinburgh Evening News*, 20th October 1890.
371 *The Dundee Evening Telegraph*, 3rd July 1890.
372 *The Western Daily Press*, 4th July 1890.
373 *Lloyd's Weekly Newspaper*, 6th July 1890.
374 *The Scotsman*, 2nd July 1890.
375 *Edinburgh Evening News*, 20th October 1890.
376 Ibid.
377 *Edinburgh Evening News*, 1st October 1890.
378 *Manchester Courier and Lancashire General Advertiser*, 25th October 1890.
379 *Edinburgh Evening News*, 1st October 1890.
380 The letter – torn in two – is held in Swanson's Metropolitan Police file (National Archives: MEPO 3/2890). No information on the so-called "Pigeon Man" case in L Division can be found. The letter writer could be the same William Billings who attempted suicide in November 1883 at the Commercial Tavern, West India Dock Road, where he was the potman. P.C. Henry Beard was called to the scene, where he found Billings lying on the floor with a rope around his neck. A letter was found among his possessions which blamed his intended death on the unrequited love of a Mrs. Hutchings (*Reynolds's Weekly Newspaper*, 18th November 1883).
381 *Morning Post*, 2nd August 1890.
382 www.galopp-sieger.de/galoppsieger/en/sieger?rennkz=EGoCheC.
383 'CRIMINAL: WHEELER, Mary Eleanor, alias PEARCEY, M.A.' (National Archives: HO 144/237/A52045). See also *Woman at the Devil's Door: The Extraordinary True Story of Mary Pearcey and the Hampstead Murders* by Sarah Beth Hopton (2017).
384 *Pall Mall Gazette*, 25th October 1890.
385 *Lloyd's Weekly Newspaper*, 26th October 1890.
386 For a full, detailed examination of the case see *Woman at the Devil's Door: The Extraordinary True Story of Mary Pearcey and the Hampstead Murders* by Sarah Beth Hopton (2017).
387 *St. James's Gazette*, 5th November 1890.
388 *The Globe*, 7th November 1890.
389 Undated and unsigned draft report recommending Macnaghten for the position of Chief Constable, held in 'Mr. A.F. Williamson, Chief Constable of Criminal Investigation Department: leave of absence; Mr. Melville Leslie MacNaghten: appointment as Assistant Chief Constable and then as Chief

Constable of the Criminal Investigation Department' (National Archives: MEPO 2/210).

390 Letter by Godfrey Lushington dated 16th December 1890, held in 'Mr. A.F. Williamson, Chief Constable of Criminal Investigation Department: leave of absence; Mr. Melville Leslie Macnaghten: appointment as Assistant Chief Constable and then as Chief Constable of the Criminal Investigation Department' (National Archives: MEPO 2/210).

391 Report by Superintendent Thomas Arnold, 13th February 1891 (MEPO 3/140, ff. 112-114).

392 Report by Superintendent Thomas Arnold, 13th February 1891 (MEPO 3/140, ff. 112-114).

393 *Lloyd's Weekly Newspaper*, 22nd February 1891.

394 Report by Superintendent Thomas Arnold, 13th February 1891 (MEPO 3/140, ff. 112-114).

395 *Lloyd's Weekly Newspaper*, 22nd February 1891.

396 Statement of James Sadler, 14th February 1891 (National Archives: MEPO 3/140, 97-108).

397 Inquest testimony of Ellen Callana, as reported in *The Times*, 28th February 1891.

398 Statement of James Sadler, 14th February 1891 (National Archives: MEPO 3/140, 97-108).

399 Report by Sergeant John Don, 16th February 1891 (National Archives: MEPO 3/140, ff. 117-118).

400 *Daily Telegraph*, 18th February 1891.

401 *Lake's Falmouth Packet and Cornwall Advertiser*, 29th February 1891.

402 *The Times*, 28th February 1891.

403 *The Times*, 4th March 1891.

404 *Carlisle Express and Examiner*, 7th March 1891.

The Philosopher's Stone

1 Sadler's shop at 121 Danbrook Road, Lower Streatham, was opened in May 1891 and seems to have been a success at first. After a fortnight he and his wife took in a retired sailor named James Moffatt as a lodger. By December that year things had taken a turn for the worse, and Mrs. Sadler wrote to the police complaining of being assaulted by her husband, a claim backed up by Moffatt (National Archives: MEPO 3/140 ff. 90-90). See *Jack the Ripper: The Forgotten Victims* by Paul Begg and John Bennett (2013) for details of the later activities of James Sadler.

2 *Pall Mall Gazette*, 7th May 1895.

3 Testimony of Edgar Childe (Old Bailey Online: t18910525-475).

4 Usually misspelt as 'Ship' in newspaper reports, correct spelling taken from

census returns and various family baptism records.
5   Testimony of Edgar Childe (Old Bailey Online: t18910525-475).
6   £10,000 today.
7   Testimony of Frederick Shipp Old Bailey Online: (t18910525-475).
8   Usually misspelt as 'Agonbar' in newspaper reports. Correct spelling taken from marriage certificate and 1911 census, written in Agombar's own hand.
9   Testimony of John Agombar (Old Bailey Online: t18910525-475).
10 *Morning Post*, 28th May 1891.
11 Testimony of Henry Batten (Old Bailey Online: t18910525-475).
12 Testimony of John Agombar (Old Bailey Online: t18910525-475).
13 Testimony of Inspector Alfred Leach (Old Bailey Online: t18910525-475).
14 Testimony of Sergeant John Scott (Old Bailey Online: t18910525-475).
15 *London Evening Standard*, 4th May 1891.
16 Old Bailey Online (t18910525-475).
17 Marriage certificate of John Agombar and Charlotte Shipp; 1871, 1891, 1901 and 1911 census.
18 Frank Froest, one of the Metropolitan Police's most celebrated officers, joined the force in 1879 aged 21 and would enjoy rapid promotion, eventually becoming Detective Superintendent of the C.I.D. in 1906.
19 *The Times*, 20th May 1891.
20 £2.5million today.
21 £600million today.
22 *The Times*, 20th May 1891.
23 Old Bailey Online (t18910727-573).
24 'Commissions Rogatoires: Edward Pinter, alias Schaefer. Extradition to Switzerland' (National Archives: HO 144/483/X34262).
25 *Exeter and Plymouth Gazette*, 27th October 1891.
26 Chief Magistrate O'Donel of the Dublin Metropolitan Police wrote to the Home Office returning various papers, but frustratingly the photograph of Pinter mentioned in his letter is not contained in the file at the National Archives.
27 Deposition of Henry Bion Reynolds, held in 'Commissions Rogatoires: Edward Pinter, alias Schaefer. Extradition to Switzerland' (National Archives: HO 144/483/X34262).
28 £1.5million today.
29 'Commissions Rogatoires: Edward Pinter, alias Schaefer. Extradition to Switzerland' (National Archives: HP 144/483/X34262).
30 *Days of My Years* by Melville Macnaghten (1914).
31 Baptismal record of Florence Ethel Elliot, 19th November 1864. Some newspaper reports mistakenly give her name as Ethel or Emma Elliot.

32 *South Australian Register*, 5th February 1892.
33 *Northern Advocate*, 13th February 1892.
34 Ibid.
35 *Manchester Courier and Lancashire General Advertiser*, 27th November 1891.
36 *Nottingham Evening Post*, 15th December 1891.
37 *South Australian Register*, 5th February 1892.
38 *The Morning Post*, 6th February 1892.
39 *The Echo*, 5th February 1892.
40 *The Yorkshire Evening Post*, 5th February 1892.
41 *The Echo*, 5th February 1892.
42 Ibid.
43 *The Liverpool Mercury*, 6th February 1892.
44 *The Echo*, 5th February 1892.
45 *The Herald*, 13th February 1892.
46 *The Times*, 6th February 1892.
47 *Reynolds's Weekly Newspaper*, 7th February 1892.
48 *The Illustrated Police News*, 3rd February 1892.
49 *The Dover Express*, 11th March 1892.
50 *Sevenoaks Chronicle and Kentish Advertiser*, 6th May 1892.
51 Baptism records of Phyllis Evelyn Osborne.
52 1901 census.
53 Resigned 25th May 1892. *South Australian Register*, 26th May 1892.
54 1901 and 1911 census returns.
55 Swanson's actual report is missing from the Home Office file, presumably sent to the Swiss authorities. The covering letter from Sir John Bridge outlines that he believes "the enquiry has been completed so as to satisfy the request of the Swiss Judicial Authority" (National Archives: HO 144/483/X34162).
56 Swanson's Metropolitan Police file (National Archives: MEPO 3/2890).
57 *Hampshire Telegraph and Sussex Chronicle*, 26th November 1892.
58 Ibid.
59 *Evening Express*, 22nd November 1892.
60 Emily Smith's sworn declaration published in the *Western Mail*, 28th November 1892.
61 *The Illustrated Police News*, 3rd December 1892.
62 Ibid.
63 The George IV still stands today, named simply as The George.
64 *The Illustrated Police News*, 3rd December 1892.
65 Emily Smith's sworn declaration published in the *Western Mail*, 28th November

1892.
66 *The Illustrated Police News*, 3rd December 1892.
67 A sketch of the assault printed in *The Illustrated Police News* of 3rd December 1892 gives the landlord of The Railway Arms as one John Thorlby. He is listed in the Post Office Directory as landlord until at least 1894. ClosedPubs.co.uk states that the pub was opened in 1881. It was permanently closed following the fatal stabbing there of John Kennedy on 8th February 1997. His murder is still unsolved.
68 Renamed Shadwell Place in 1912.
69 *The Illustrated Police News*, 3rd December 1892.
70 *Pall Mall Gazette*, 22nd November 1892.
71 *Dundee Evening Telegraph*, 23rd November 1892.
72 *The Illustrated Police News*, 3rd December 1892. Although not mentioned by name, Packer is clearly the man referred to as a "fruit stall keeper" from whom "the murdered woman purchased some grapes a short time before the murder took place... some of the grapes were found in the dead woman's hand."
73 *The Illustrated Police News*, 3rd December 1892.
74 *Western Mail*, 23rd November 1892. The reference to 'guys' means the popular practice of burning effigies of Guy Fawkes on 5th November, Bonfire Night; one can imagine that in the years preceding the supposed attack on Emily Smith, such guys were made to resemble Jack the Ripper. 'Edith' was Emily Smith's middle name.
75 *Western Mail*, 23rd November 1892.
76 Ibid.
77 *Western Mail*, 28th November 1892.
78 *Western Mail*, 23rd November 1892.
79 *Hampshire Telegraph and Sussex Chronicle*, 26th November 1892.
80 Ibid.

City of the Plain

1 See Ronald Pearsall's *The Worm in the Bud: The World of Victorian Sexuality* (1969) for a detailed study of Victorian attitude to sex and morality.
2 Although Besant and Bradlaugh were found guilty of selling an obscene publication and sentenced to six months' imprisonment, the trial raised awareness that information on birth control was available.
3 See *The Other Victorians: A Study of Sexuality and Pornography in Mid-Nineteenth Century England* by Steven Marcus (1974).
4 *Lloyd's Weekly Newspaper*, 3rd October 1880.
5 *London Evening Standard*, 10th November 1880.
6 *Stories From Scotland Yard* by Inspector Moser with Charles F. Rideal (1890).

7   Both Swanson and Froest were at lower ranks at the time of this incident, which took place in 1883, than in the previous chapter.
8   *London Evening Standard*, 31st October 1883.
9   *London Evening Standard*, 25th October 1883.
10 *The Times*, 5th December 1883.
11 Convictions for selling obscene prints in 1862 (12 months imprisonment), 1866 (two years) and 1873 (two years), using various pseudonyms including Adolphus Deplong. Details from *Surrey Calendar of Prisoners 1848-1902*.
12 *The Times*, 5th December 1883.
13 *The Times*, 5th April 1886.
14 *The Pearl: A Magazine of Facetiae and Voluptuous Reading* was a monthly magazine published by William Lazenby in 1879 and 1880, with two Christmas supplements.
15 £30,000 today.
16 *The Times*, 5th April 1886.
17 *Gloucester Citizen*, 8th April 1886.
18 1891 census.
19 *Register of Dorset Deaths and Burials 1813-2010*.
20 *The Times*, 8th December 1885.
21 *The Times*, 30th December 1885.
22 *Western Daily Press*, 11th January 1886.
23 *Morning Post*, 2nd May 1895.
24 William Thomas Stead, born on 5th July 1849, began his journalistic career aged 21 by contributing articles to *The Northern Echo*, the following year being promoted as the newspaper's editor. He travelled to London in 1880 to become Assistant Editor of the *Pall Mall Gazette*, and succeeded John Morley as Editor in 1883. Over subsequent years Stead revolutionised the industry, creating a new contemporary style of newspaper which was the forerunner of tabloid journalism. Prior to his 'Modern Babylon' exposé, in 1883 Stead had created considerable concern with a campaign supporting the claims in Rev. Andrew Mearns's *The Bitter Cry of Outcast London*, which revealed the shocking truth of life in London's slums. Consequently, a Royal Commission recommended that the slums should be cleared and low-cost housing built in their place. Stead resigned from the *Pall Mall Gazette* in 1889 and co-founded the *Review of Reviews*. In 1904 he launched *The Daily Paper*, which proved a spectacular failure, and Stead suffered a nervous breakdown. He died aboard the ill-fated *Titanic*, his body never recovered. Curiously, Stead had twice published stories which featured maritime disasters: *How the Mail Steamer Went Down in Mid Atlantic, by a Survivor* (1886) and *From the Old World to the New* (1892). An excellent resource on W. T. Stead's life and work can be found at www.attackingthedevil.co.uk.
25 *Pall Mall Gazette*, 4th July 1885.

26 *Pall Mall Gazette*, 6th July 1885.
27 £1,500 today.
28 Dyer's report can be accessed at archive.org/details/europeanslavetr01dyergoog.
29 *The Leeds Times*, 4th June 1881.
30 See *Josephine Butler and the Prostitute Campaigns*, edited by Jane Jordan and Ingrid Sharp (2003).
31 *Western Mail*, 31st May 1885.
32 See *London's Shadows: The Dark Side of the Victorian City* by Drew D. Grey (2010).
33 *Hansard*, 3rd August 1885.
34 *Pall Mall Gazette*, 6th July 1885.
35 Ibid.
36 Testimony of Elizabeth Armstrong, 24th October 1885 (Old Bailey Online: t18851019-1031).
37 *My First Imprisonment* by W. T. Stead (1886) accessed via www.attackingthedevil.co.uk/steadworks/imprisonment.php.
38 *The Case of Eliza Armstrong: A Child of 13 Bought for £5* by Alison Plowden (1974).
39 Post by Margaret Makepeace, Lead Curator, East India Company Records at britishlibrary.typepad.co.uk/untoldlives/2012/04/whatever-happened-to-eliza-armstrong.html.
40 The Criminal Law Amendment Act was eventually repealed by the Sexual Offences Act 1967, which decriminalised homosexual acts in private between consenting men over the age of 21.
41 Figures compiled from the annual reports of the Commissioner of Police of the Metropolis, 1880-1890. Accessed via *London and the Culture of Homosexuality, 1885-1914* by Matt Cook (2008).
42 *A View of Society and Manners in High and Low Life, Vol II* by George Parker (1781).
43 See *London and the Culture of Homosexuality, 1885-1914* by Matt Cook (2008) and *Nameless Offences: Homosexual Desire in the 19th Century* by H. G. Cocks (2010) for detailed analysis of activity in the Victorian and Edwardian eras.
44 See Neil McKenna's entertaining *Fanny and Stella: The Young Men Who Shocked Victorian England* (2013) for a complete account of the case as well as biographies of Ernest Boulton and Frederick Park.
45 See H. Montgomery Hyde's *The Cleveland Street Scandal* (1976) and *The Cleveland Street Affair* by Colin Simpson, Lewis Chester and David Leitch (also 1976) for full-length examinations of the scandal focussing on the cover-up of involvement of certain noblemen, and Glenn Chandler's *The Sins of Jack Saul: The True Story of Dublin Jack and the Cleveland Street Scandal* (2016) for a review of the activities of the male prostitutes involved. For analysis of the

affair in the context of attitudes towards homosexuality in the late Victorian period see *London and the Culture of Homosexuality, 1885-1914* by Matt Cook (2008) and *Nameless Offences: Homosexual Desire in the 19th Century* by H. G. Cocks (2010).

46 Indictment of Henry Horace Newlove, in which he gives the date of this offence (National Archives: DPP 1/95/3).

47 Statement of George Alma Wright, given on 6th July 1889 (National Archives: DPP 1/95/3).

48 Statement of Charles Thomas Swinscow, given on 6th July 1889 (National Archives: DPP 1/95/3).

49 Statement of George Alma Wright, given on 6th July 1889 (National Archives: DPP 1/95/3).

50 Indictment of Henry Horace Newlove (National Archives: DPP 1/95/3).

51 Statement of George Alma Wright, given on 6th July 1889 (National Archives: DPP 1/95/3).

52 Ibid.

53 Statement of Charles Ernest Thickbroom, given on 6th July 1889 (National Archives: DPP 1/95/3).

54 Indictment of Henry Horace Newlove (National Archives: DPP 1/95/3).

55 Statement of Charles Ernest Thickbroom, given on 6th July 1889 (National Archives: DPP 1/95/3).

56 Indictment of Henry Horace Newlove (National Archives: DPP 1/95/3).

57 Statement of Charles Thomas Swinscow, given on 6th July 1889 (National Archives: DPP 1/95/3).

58 Perkins visited on 1st February 1889; Allies on 25th March 1889 and Barber on 3rd June 1889. Indictment of Henry Horace Newlove (National Archives: DPP 1/95/3).

59 1881 census, which records P.C. Luke Hanks as living at the Section House attached to Commercial Street police station, Whitechapel.

60 Statement of P.C. Luke Hanks, given on 1st August 1889 (National Archives: DPP 1/95/3).

61 Ibid.

62 In February 1889 Abberline received expenses of £30 0s 1d relating to his work on the Ripper case (approximately £1,900 today), suggesting his involvement had ended by that time. See *The Ultimate Jack the Ripper Sourcebook: An Illustrated Encyclopedia* by Stewart P. Evans and Keith Skinner (2000).

63 Report by Det. Inspector Frederick Abberline dated 18th July 1889 (National Archives: DPP 1/95/3).

64 Report by Det. Inspector Frederick Abberline dated 31st July 1889 (National Archives: DPP 1/95/3).

65 Report by P.C. Luke Hanks, 31st July 1889 (National Archives: DPP 1/95/3).

66 Report by Det. Inspector Frederick Abberline, 31st July 1889 (National Archives: DPP 1/95/3).
67 Report by P.C. Luke Hanks, 31st July 1889 (National Archives: DPP 1/95/3).
68 Additional report by P.C. Luke Hanks, 1st August 1889 (National Archives: DPP 1/95/3).
69 Old Bailey Online (t18890916-696).
70 Report by P.C. Luke Hanks, 31st July 1889 (National Archives: DPP 1/95/3).
71 Observation report by P.C. Richard Sladden 382D, undated but submitted by Det. Inspector Abberline on 18th July 1889 (National Archives: DPP 1/95/3).
72 Report by Det. Inspector Frederick Abberline dated 18th July 1889 (National Archives: DPP 1/95/3).
73 *The Cleveland Street Scandal* by H. Montgomery Hyde (1976).
74 Ibid.
75 Old Bailey Online (t18890916-696).
76 Clipping from *Reynolds's Weekly Newspaper*, hand-dated "22nd or 29th September 1889". Held in 'Cleveland Street: Miscellaneous correspondence (1889)' (National Archives: DPP 1/95/1). As the *North London Press*' report was published on 28th September, the *Reynolds's Weekly Newspaper* clipping must have been of the latter date.
77 *The Cleveland Street Scandal* by H. Montgomery Hyde (1976).
78 Letter from James Monro dated 10th October 1889 held in 'Cleveland Street: Miscellaneous correspondence (1889)' (National Archives: DPP 1/95/1).
79 Letter from James Monro dated 21st October 1889, held in 'Cleveland Street: Miscellaneous correspondence (1889)' (National Archives: DPP 1/95/1).
80 *Reynolds's Weekly Newspaper*, 6th December 1889.
81 *The Cleveland Street Scandal* by H. Montgomery Hyde (1976).
82 Application held in 'Criminal – A residuum of notes: The Cleveland Street Scandal (1889-1891)' (National Archives: HO 144/477/X24427).
83 *The North London Press*, 16th November 1889.
84 *The North London Press*, 23rd November 1889.
85 *The Star*, 25th November 1889.
86 *The Cleveland Street Scandal* by H. Montgomery Hyde (1976).
87 National Archives: DPP 1/95/1-7.
88 Prince Albert Victor has been named several times as a candidate for Jack the Ripper, most notably in the 1970s when the 'Royal conspiracy' theory was at its height. As is the case with his sexual preferences, neither is there any evidence of his involvement in the Whitechapel murders. See *Clarence: Was He Jack the Ripper?* by Michael Harrison (1972), *Jack the Ripper: The Final Solution* by Stephen Knight (1976), *Prince Jack* by Frank Spiering (1978), and *The Prince, His Tutor and the Ripper: The Evidence Linking James Kenneth Stephen to the Whitechapel Murders* by Deborah McDonald (2007).

89 *The Cleveland Street Scandal* by H. Montgomery Hyde (1976).
90 For many years virtually nothing was known about Jack Saul, until the publication of *The Sins of Jack Saul: The True Story of Dublin Jack and the Cleveland Street Scandal* by Glenn Chandler in 2016. With excellent research and an entertaining narrative, it is very much worth a read.
91 'John Saul: Original Statement and Correspondence' (National Archives: DPP 1/95/4/2).
92 *The Cleveland Street Scandal* by H. Montgomery Hyde (1976).
93 *Northampton Mercury*, 18th January 1890.
94 See Chapter Fifteen.
95 See *Doctor Crippen: The Infamous London Cellar Murder of 1910* by Nicholas Connell (2013).
96 *The Cleveland Street Scandal* by H. Montgomery Hyde (1976).
97 *The Sins of Jack Saul: The True Story of Dublin Jack and the Cleveland Street Scandal* by Glenn Chandler (2016).
98 Reported in the *Aberdeen Evening Express*, 3rd January 1891.
99 *Decatur Daily Despatch*, 8th August 1891.
100 *The Sins of Jack Saul: The True Story of Dublin Jack and the Cleveland Street Scandal* by Glenn Chandler (2016).
101 Letter to William Smith, First Lord of the Treasury and Leader of the House of Commons, quoted in *The Cleveland Street Scandal* by H. Montgomery Hyde (1976).
102 1891, 1901 and 1911 census returns; St. Pancras Workhouse Admission and Discharge Register 1922-1924; Death Register.
103 1901 and 1911 census returns; Marriage Banns; Death Register.
104 1891 and 1911 census returns; Marriage Banns; Death Register.
105 Marriages Index 1871-1920, Cook County, Illinois; 1910 and 1920 United States Federal Census returns; Deaths and Stillbirths Index 1916-1947, Illinois.
106 *Reynolds's Weekly Newspaper*, 19th August 1894.
107 *The Liverpool Mercury*, 14th August 1894.
108 *The Birmingham Daily Post*, 14th August 1894.
109 *Reynolds's Weekly Newspaper*, 19th August 1894.
110 *Reynolds's Weekly Newspaper*, 26th August 1894.
111 Personal address book of Donald Sutherland Swanson.
112 This notebook, held in the Swanson family archive, records arrests from October 1876 to October 1883 before being used to list those under suspicion of sodomy and related offences.
113 Newspaper clipping dated 21st January 1899, pasted into Donald Swanson's notebook. *The London Evening Standard* of 9th March 1899 reported that Archie Phillips was discharged after paying a surety of £100.

114 See *The Secret Life of Oscar Wilde* by Neil McKenna (2003) for an entertaining untangling of the events linking Robert Cliburn and his fellow blackmailers with the Earl of Euston, Oscar Wilde and the aristocracy.
115 *Illustrated Police News*, 5th February 1898.
116 Private memorandum of Donald Swanson.
117 Old Bailey Online (t18980307-243).

The Death is Reported of Detective Swanson

1   Age from 1901 and 1911 census returns.
2   Schmalz deposed that the man was 5ft 11 or 6ft with broad shoulders, and wearing a Chesterfield overcoat and a felt billycock hat (National Archives: CRIM 1/41/4).
3   Deposition of Herbert Schmalz (National Archives: CRIM 1/41/4).
4   *The Times*, 11th December 1894.
5   Deposition of Hermann Lauver (National Archives: CRIM 1/41/4).
6   Deposition of Albert Corbould (National Archives: CRIM 1/41/4).
7   *The Times*, 30th November 1894.
8   Deposition of P.C. William Patterson (National Archives: CRIM 1/41/4).
9   Deposition of Albert Corbould (National Archives: CRIM 1/41/4).
10 Deposition of P.C. William Patterson (National Archives: CRIM 1/41/4).
11 Deposition of Dr. Meredith Townsend (National Archives: CRIM 1/41/4).
12 Deposition of James Andrews (National Archives: CRIM 1/41/4).
13 cf *Bury and Norwich Post*, 27th November 1894.
14 *The Times*, 11th December 1894. Some other reports vary the wording of this letter slightly.
15 Deposition of Dr. Thomas Bond (National Archives: CRIM 1/41/4).
16 Augusta Louisa Dawes was born to wine merchant Charles Dawes and his wife Caroline Pritchard, the youngest of five children. She was christened on 9th December 1866 at Holy Trinity Church, Bristol. Information from 1871 and 1881 census returns, christening record, marriage index.
17 Deposition of Lillian Creber (National Archives: CRIM 1/41/4).
18 *Reynolds's Weekly Newspaper*, 2nd December 1894.
19 *Illustrated Police News*, 8th December 1894. This older child could be Frederica Augusta Dudley, born on 21st March 1887 to Frederick and Louisa Augusta Dudley, and baptised at St. John the Baptist, Hoxton, on 1st May 1887. Louisa was Augusta Dawes' middle name. There is no record of a marriage between Frederick and Louisa Dudley.
20 Deposition of Lillian Creber (National Archives: CRIM 1/41/4).
21 Deposition of Francis Rollison (National Archives: CRIM 1/41/4).

22. *The Evening Telegraph and Star*, 8th December 1894.
23. Deposition of Francis Rollison (National Archives: CRIM 1/41/4).
24. www.ezitis.myzen.co.uk/normansfield.html.
25. National Archives: H29/NF/A/1/1-25. Dr. John Langdon Down was the physician who, in 1862, classified the genetic disorder now known as Down syndrome.
26. Reginald Traherne Bassett Saunderson was born on 23rd November 1873. Information from Ireland, Civil Registration Births Index 1864-1958.
27. Deposition of Mary Langdon-Down (National Archives: CRIM 1/41/4).
28. Deposition of Llewellyn Traherne Bassett Saunderson (National Archives: CRIM 1/41/4).
29. cf *St. James's Gazette*, 5th December 1894.
30. *The Evening Telegraph and Star*, 8th December 1894.
31. Deposition of Trooper Frank Barker (National Archives: CRIM 1/41/4).
32. Deposition of Thomas Jefferson (National Archives: CRIM 1/41/4).
33. Deposition of William Hollier (National Archives: CRIM 1/41/4).
34. Deposition of Henry Davidson (National Archives: CRIM 1/41/4).
35. Deposition of Thomas Brien (National Archives: CRIM 1/41/4).
36. Deposition of William Miller (National Archives: CRIM 1/41/4).
37. Deposition of Sgt. Thomas Thompson (National Archives: CRIM 1/41/4).
38. *Illustrated Police News*, 15th December 1894.
39. Ibid.
40. *Cardiff Times and South Wales Weekly News*, 15th December 1894.
41. *Morning Post*, 12th December 1894.
42. *Huddersfield Chronicle*, 15th December 1894.
43. *The Nottingham Evening Post*, 28th December 1894.
44. *Birmingham Daily Post*, 21st January 1895.
45. *Hampshire Telegraph*, 2nd February 1895.
46. Old Bailey Online (t18950128-199).
47. Warrant of Removal for Reginald Treherne Bassett Saunderson. *Criminal Lunacy Warrant and Entry Books, 1882-1898*.
48. Death Index.
49. Swanson's medical records held in his Metropolitan Police file (National Archives: MEPO 3/2890).
50. *The Guernsey Star*, 28th February 1895.
51. *The Birmingham Daily Post*, 27th February 1895.
52. See *A History of the Great Influenza Pandemics: Death, Panic and Hysteria, 1830-1920* by Mark Honigsbaum (2013).
53. Death certificate of James Swanson.

54 'Harper Pass' entry in *Lonely Planet Hiking & Tramping in New Zealand* (2014).
55 New Zealand Parliamentary Record, 1840–1984.
56 *New Zealand Herald*, 18th May 1895.
57 *The Standard*, 27th May 1895.
58 *New Zealand Star*, 6th July 1895.
59 £375,000 today.
60 Deposition of Inspector Peter Pender (National Archives: HO 144/502/X53 193).
61 *The Sydney Morning Herald*, 30th July 1895.
62 Copy of warrant for the arrest of Leonard Harper (National Archives: HO 144/502/X53193).
63 Deposition of Det. Chief Inspector Donald Swanson (National Archives: HO 144/502/X53193).
64 *New Zealand Star*, 6th July 1895.
65 *Otago Witness*, 18th July 1895.
66 *The Freemason*, 8th June 1895.
67 *Past and Present, and Men of the Times* by William Jackson Barry (1897). *The Press* (Canterbury, New Zealand) of 1st April 1902 reported on Pender's retirement the previous day, commenting that of his 73 years, 56 of them had been spent in public service.
68 National Archives: HO 144/502/X53193.
69 Ibid.
70 Ibid.
71 *The West Australian*, 10th December 1895.
72 *National Advocate*, 18th March 1896.
73 *Tasmania Daily Telegraph*, 20th March 1896.
74 *Tasmania Daily Telegraph*, 24th March 1896.
75 *The Australasian*, 11th April 1896.
76 1901 and 1911 census returns; Death Index.

The Hero of Bow Street

1 A natural division in Rhodesia was created by the Zambezi river, and the territory to the north was in time designated Northern Rhodesia before gaining independence as Zambia in 1964. The land south of the Zambezi, which included Mashonaland and Matabeleland, became known as Southern Rhodesia and then Zimbabwe in 1980.
2 There are several biographies on Dr. Jameson, including *Dr. Jameson* by G. Seymour Fort (1908) and *The Life of Jameson* by Ian Colvin (1922). Highly recommended for a full and entertaining version of his life is *The If Man* by Chris Ash (2012).

3   *The Illustrated London News*, 18th January 1896.
4   See *The If Man* by Chris Ash (2012) for a detailed description of Jameson's medical career.
5   Details of Jameson's appointments taken from 'List of officers involved in the Raid' (National Archives: WO 32/7839).
6   *Second Report of the Select Committee on South Africa* (National Archives: WO 32/7845).
7   See *The Jameson Raid* by Hugh Marshall Hole (1930) for a detailed description of the route followed by Jameson and his men.
8   'Report by Major General George Cox, Commanding Troops Natal and Zululand, 31st January 1896' (National Archives: WO 32/7839).
9   'Details of Officers and Men of Dr. Jameson's Force, Confirmed as Prisoners at Volksrust near the Transvaal Border from 11th to 23rd January 1896' (National Archives: WO 32/7839).
10 'Report by Major General George Cox, Commanding Troops Natal and Zululand, 31st January 1896' (National Archives: WO 32/7839).
11 'List of Commissioned Officer of H.M. Regular and Reserve Forces present with Dr. Jameson's Forces' (National Archives: WO 32/7839).
12 'Report by Major General George Cox, Commanding Troops Natal and Zululand, 31st January 1896' (National Archives: WO 32/7839).
13 *The Herald*, 15th February 1896.
14 *Supplement to The Graphic*, 29th February 1896.
15 *The Standard*, 24th February 1896.
16 *The Yorkshire Herald*, 24th February 1896.
17 *The Standard*, 24th February 1896.
18 *The Melbourne Argus*, 4th April 1896.
19 *Lloyd's Weekly Newspaper*, 1st March 1896.
20 *The Yorkshire Herald*, 27th February 1896.
21 *The Herald*, 29th February 1896.
22 *The Yorkshire Herald*, 27th February 1896.
23 *The Standard*, 26th February 1896.
24 Ibid.
25 *Reynolds's Weekly Newspaper*, 1st March 1896.
26 Edward Streeter had been for many years an authority on precious stones and other jewellery, and his views on the subject were often published in newspapers.
27 *The Bury Free Press*, 25th April 1896.
28 *The Standard*, 20th April 1896.
29 *The Bury Free Press*, 25th April 1896.
30 *The Standard*, 20th April 1896.

31 *The Bury Free Press*, 25th April 1896.
32 *Daily Mail*, 23rd March 1897.
33 *London Evening Standard*, 30th June 1896.
34 *Daily Mail*, 23rd March 1897.
35 *The New York Times*, 11th December 1898.
36 John Shore joined the Metropolitan Police on 10th January 1859, having previously spent two years and four months as a constable with the Bristol police force. In August 1868 he submitted an application for the position of Chief Superintendent of Police at Bath, his hometown, but appears to have been unsuccessful, as he remained with the Metropolitan Police and was promoted to Inspector the following year. John Shore's Metropolitan Police file (National Archives: MEPO 3/2833).
37 *Yorkshire Evening Post*, 24th July 1896.
38 *The Aberdeen Journal*, 9th April 1896.
39 *Scotland Yard Experiences From the Diary of G. H. Greenham* by George Greenham (1904).
40 Police Order, 30th April 1896.
41 *Pall Mall Gazette*, 29th April 1896.
42 Police Order, 30th April 1896.
43 *Reynolds's Weekly Newspaper*, 3rd May 1896.
44 *Scotland Yard Experiences From the Diary of G. H. Greenham* by George Greenham (1904).
45 £350,000 today.
46 *The Standard*, 12th May 1896.
47 *Dover Express*, 15th May 1896.
48 *Lincolnshire Chronicle*, 15th May 1896.
49 *The If Man* by Chris Ash (2012).
50 Report of Dr. James Scott to the Governor of Holloway Gaol, 24th November 1896 (National Archives: PCOM 8/177).
51 National Archives: PCOM 8/177.
52 *The Raid on the Transvaal* by P. E. Ashton (1897).
53 Minutes of Evidence, published in *The Life of Jameson* by Ian Colvin (1922).
54 Copy of letter from Hon. Hamilton Cuffe to Commissioner Edward Bradford held in Swanson family archives.
55 *The Jameson Raid* by Jean van der Poel (1951).
56 For a recounting of Jameson's later career, see *The Life of Jameson* by Ian Colvin (1922).
57 *Something of Myself: For My Friends Known and Unknown* by Rudyard Kipling (1937).
58 Viewers of the BBC television programme *Bookworm* voted *If-* the nation's

favourite poem in 1995, as did listeners to Classic FM in 2009.
59   *The New York Times*, 1st August 1897.
60   *At Scotland Yard: Being the Experiences During Twenty-Seven Years Service* by John Sweeney (1904).
61   James Olive, who joined the Metropolitan Police in 1872 as a Police Constable, would become the first uniformed officer to rise through the ranks beyond Detective Superintendent, being promoted Deputy Commissioner in 1922.
62   See *A Prescription for Murder: The Victorian Serial Killings of Dr. Thomas Neill Cream* by Angus McLaren (1993).
63   See *In the Interests of Science: Adelaide Bartlett and the Pimlico Poisoning* by Kate Clarke (2015).
64   *Lloyd's Weekly Newspaper*, 7th August 1888.
65   Ibid.
66   *Leicester Chronicle*, 8th October 1898.
67   *The Daily News*, 15th November 1899.
68   Republished in the *Kalgoorlie Western Argus*, 8th February 1900. The comment about John Shore developing a bad memory for faces seems to suggest possible corruption, hinted at in the next chapter. If Shore was corrupt – and there is no firm evidence that he was – it is ironic that he was one of only two officers, the other being Dolly Williamson, who were safe in their jobs following the Detective Department scandal of 1876.

Return of the Duchess

1   *Some Crime Stories by Charles Windus*, n.d. but circa 1898, held in Swanson family archives.
2   *St. James's Gazette*, 22nd January 1901.
3   Victoria's record reign was surpassed by her great-great-granddaughter Elizabeth II on 9th September 2015.
4   *Adam Worth, Alias 'Little Adam'. Theft and Recovery of Gainsborough's 'Duchess of Devonshire'* (Second Edition, 1903).
5   *Manchester Courier and Lancashire General Advertiser*, 16th November 1906.
6   Interview with Morland Agnew in *The Evening News*, republished in *The Yorkshire Evening Post*, 10th April 1901.
7   Record for the *Etruria*, UK Incoming Passenger Lists, April 1901.
8   Republished in the *Whitstable Times*, 5th August 1893. See *The Napoleon of Crime: The Life and Times of Adam Worth, the Real Moriarty* by Ben Macintyre (1998 revised edition) for a detailed account of Mr. Marsend's involvement.
9   *South Wales Daily News*, 20th July 1896.
10 Cablegram sent 11th March 1897, entered into Pinkerton files 1st April 1897. 'Pinkerton's National Detective Agency: "Duchess of Devonshire," Painting by Thomas Gainsborough, Theft and Recovery, Correspondence, 1897-1902'

(Library of Congress: MSS36301, Box 99 Folder 9).

11   Adam Worth is described as "A Napoleon of Crime" by the *Dundee Evening Post* in their report of his death on 10th February 1902.

12   Biography of Adam Worth from *The Napoleon of Crime: The Life and Times of Adam Worth, the Real Moriarty* by Ben Macintyre (1998 revised edition).

13   *The Graphic*, 29th July 1893.

14   cf *New York Herald*, 18th July 1897. In *Criminals and Crime: Some Facts and Suggestions* (1907), Robert Anderson revealed that when Powell returned to England following a spell in a Continental prison he discovered that his wife had absconded with all his money and another man; the "old rascal" died in Southampton in poverty.

15   Swanson family archives.

16   See *Adam Worth, Alias 'Little Adam'. Theft and Recovery of Gainsborough's 'Duchess of Devonshire'* (Second Edition, 1903) and *The Napoleon of Crime: The Life and Times of Adam Worth, the Real Moriarty* by Ben Macintyre (1998 revised edition).

17   Copy of letter and telegram from 'Roy' held in 'Pinkerton's National Detective Agency: "Duchess of Devonshire," Painting by Thomas Gainsborough, Theft and Recovery, Correspondence, 1897-1902' (Library of Congress: MSS36301, Box 99 Folder 9).

18   Abstract of letter from William Pinkerton to Robert Pinkerton, dated 16th January 1899, held in 'Pinkerton's National Detective Agency: "Duchess of Devonshire," Painting by Thomas Gainsborough, Theft and Recovery, Correspondence, 1897-1902' (Library of Congress: MSS36301, Box 99 Folder 9).

19   *Adam Worth, Alias 'Little Adam'. Theft and Recovery of Gainsborough's 'Duchess of Devonshire'* (Second Edition, 1903).

20   *The Western Times*, 18th April 1901.

21   *Western Daily Press*, 11th April 1901.

22   *St. James's Gazette*, 17th April 1901.

23   *Gloucester Citizen*, 22nd April 1901.

24   *Lichfield Mercury*, 26th April 1901.

25   Interestingly, from the first viewing of the *Duchess* at Agnew's gallery following its return there were whispers that this was not Gainsborough's original painting of Georgiana, but a copy of another portrait by the great artist, that of Lady Elizabeth Foster, the second wife of William Cavendish. In *Let Me Tell You* (1940), the art collector and critic A. C. R. Carter claimed that the painting sold from the Wynn Ellis collection in 1876 was not Gainsborough's Georgiana at all, but a sketched copy of his portrait of Lady Elizabeth Foster, heavily restored and 'painted up' at Christie's by a man named Partington prior to the auction at which the piece was purchased by William Agnew. A story in *The Derby Daily Telegraph* of 12th April 1901 reported that the painting was not referred to as *The Duchess of Devonshire* by the art dealer John Bentley after he

bought it from Mrs. Maginnis, nor when selling it to Wynn Ellis shortly afterwards, although it was recognised as a work by Thomas Gainsborough. Although C. Morland Agnew confirmed that the painting he received in Chicago's Auditorium Hotel was indeed the painting stolen from Bond Street in 1876, whether it was ever Gainsborough's portrait of Georgiana is open to debate.

26   *The Evening Telegraph*, 15th November 1901.
27   *The Duchess of Devonshire* eventually returned to America in 1913, to be kept at J. Pierpont Morgan's New York home at 37 East 36th Street. The millionaire died that same year, and the painting passed to his heirs. When Morgan's last surviving grandchild, Mabel Ingalls, died aged 92 in December 1993, the family decided to sell it. So it happened that *The Duchess of Devonshire* once again went up for auction in London, this time at Sotheby's, just yards from Agnew's Bond Street gallery where it had been stolen almost 120 years earlier. On 13th July 1994 the hammer went down on a winning bid of $408,870 by The Chatsworth House Trust, bidding on behalf of the 11th Duke of Devonshire. After 200 years, Gainsborough's portrait of Georgiana Spencer had returned to the family home.
28   Cablegram sent 11th March 1897, entered into Pinkerton files 1st April 1897. 'Pinkerton's National Detective Agency: "Duchess of Devonshire," Painting by Thomas Gainsborough, Theft and Recovery, Correspondence, 1897-1902' (Library of Congress: MSS36301, Box 99 Folder 9).
29   Copy of letter from Robert Pinkerton dated 19th August 1902. Pinkerton's National Detective Agency: "Duchess of Devonshire," Painting by Thomas Gainsborough, Theft and Recovery, Correspondence, 1897-1902 (Library of Congress: MSS36301, Box 99 Folder 9).
30   'Pinkerton's National Detective Agency: "Duchess of Devonshire," Painting by Thomas Gainsborough, Theft and Recovery, Correspondence, 1897-1902' (Library of Congress: MSS36301, Box 99 Folder 9).
31   *Manchester Courier and Lancashire General Advertiser*, 16th November 1906. Print-on-demand copies of the Pinkerton booklet can be purchased online, but should be read in conjunction with *The Napoleon of Crime: The Life and Times of Adam Worth, the Real Moriarty*, Ben Macintyre's full and entertaining account of Adam Worth's career.
32   *The Nineteenth Century and After*, No. 288, February 1901.
33   Correspondence held in 'Publications: Articles on crime written by Mr. R. Anderson Assistant Commissioner, Metropolitan Police, contrary to policy of Home Office' (National Archives: HO 144/237/A52437).
34   *Yorkshire Evening Post*, 19th April 1901.
35   *London Daily News*, 19th April 1901.
36   See *The Lighter Side of My Official Life* by Sir Robert Anderson (1910).
37   Hansard: Deb 13th April 1910 vol 16.
38   *St. James's Gazette*, 19th April 1901.

39 *The Aberdeen Weekly Journal*, 1st May 1901.
40 *The Cambridge Independent Press*, 26th April 1901.
41 *St. James's Gazette*, 9th November 1901.
42 *Sir Robert Anderson and Lady Agnes Anderson* by A. P. Moore-Anderson (1947).
43 *The Daily News*, 29th November 1901.
44 'Sir Robert Anderson's pension' (National Archives: LO 3/301).
45 Hansard: Deb 13th April 1910 vol 16.
46 'Sir Robert Anderson's pension' (National Archives: LO 3/301).
47 Hansard: Deb 21st April 1910 vol 16.
48 A copy of *Regulations to be Observed on the Day of the Coronation*, hand-annotated to reflect changes from Queen Victorian to King Edward VII, is held at the National Archives (MEPO 2/601).
49 See 'Coronation – King Edward VII' (National Archives: MEPO 2/601).
50 See *Shooting Victoria: Madness, Mayhem and the Modernisation of the Monarchy* by Paul Thomas Murphy (2012). Thankfully, the signing of the Treaty of Vereeniging on 31st May 1902 would bring an end to the Second Boer War.
51 Samples of these passes are held at the National Archives, along with various plans and route maps (MEPO 2/601).
52 *The Whitby Gazette*, 15th August 1902.
53 Police Orders, 12th August 1902.
54 See 'Coronation – King Edward VII' (National Archives: MEPO 2/601).
55 As with the 1887 Jubilee Medal, Donald Swanson's King's Coronation Medal went missing from the home of daughters Ada and Alice at some point in the years just before their deaths.
56 'Pinkerton's National Detective Agency: "Duchess of Devonshire," painting by Thomas Gainsborough, theft and recovery, Correspondence, 1897-1902' (Library of Congress: MSS36301, Box 99 Folder 9).
57 Old Bailey Online (t19020909-686).
58 'Letter from Robert Anderson, Assistant Commissioner of the Metropolitan Police, to Galton requesting a meeting to discuss the use of fingerprints in police work' (Wellcome Library: GALTON/2/9/13/2).
59 See *The Official Encyclopaedia of Scotland Yard* by Martin Fido and Keith Skinner (2002).
60 *The Sheffield Daily Telegraph*, 6th March 1903.
61 Following his retirement Bradford chaired a committee enquiring into the wages of General Post Office employees, and would serve as an equerry to both Edward VII and George V. See *Truly a Great Victorian: A Quiet Man Before Whom Rogues Trembled* by Constance Bradford (2004). He died on 13th May 1911.
62 Death certificate of James Nevill.

63 Police Orders, 1st July 1903.
64 Donald Swanson's pension certificate, Swanson family archives.
65 Records of Police Pensioners (National Archives: MEPO 21/31).
66 Letter dated 4th July 1903 held in Swanson family archives.
67 *Daily Mail*, 13th August 1903. Donald Swanson's great-granddaughter Margaret recalls that the canteen was passed to her father, Donald's grandson Graeme.

At the Going Down of the Sun

1 *Reminiscences of Chief Inspector Littlechild* (1894).
2 *Scotland Yard Experiences: From the Diary of G. H. Greenham, late Chief Inspector, Criminal Investigation Dept.* (1904).
3 *At Scotland Yard: Being the Experiences during Twenty-Seven Years' Service of John Sweeney* (1904).
4 Draft of a letter from Permanent Under Secretary of State Edward Troup to Solicitor General Sir Rufus Isaacs, held in 'Sir Robert Anderson's pension' (National Archives: LO 3/301).
5 Frederick Abberline newspaper cuttings scrapbook held at Metropolitan Police Heritage Centre. Interestingly, Abberline did write two sets of 'Reminiscences', one about his time at Monte Carlo and the other relating to a missing persons case. Both of these, written in longhand, describe cases from his private detective days but remained unpublished.
6 Letter from Jim Swanson to his accountant, 27th January 1984.
7 Census of Scotland.
8 *Schools in Thurso Parish from the 17th Century to 1966* by Allan Lannon (2004).
9 Census of Scotland, 1901. Jannet Swanson Gunn died on 2nd December 1920 (death record).
10 *Slater's Directory of Caithness-shire*, 1882. Margaret Swanson Alexander died on 8th January 1901 (death record).
11 A signed copy of *Until the Dawn and Other Poems* is held at the Imperial War Museum. Peterishea Annie Robertson died on 11th June 1957 age 89 at the Achvarasdal Eventide Home, Reay near Thurso. According to *The Edinburgh Gazette* of 24th March 1959, her estate passed to the Crown, indicating no heirs.
12 1901 census.
13 Donald (b.1909), James (b.1912), Margaret 'Peg' (b.1914), Graeme (b.1916) and Mary (b.1925).
14 Donald Nevill Swanson passed away on 31st January 1966 aged 86.
15 1901 census.
16 Newspaper cutting held in Swanson family archives. James John Swanson remained unmarried. During the Second World War, keen to 'do his bit',

his brother Donald found him an unpaid job at the Admiralty. He spent his retirement years in Cape Town during the winter and with sisters Ada and Alice during the summers, and died in 1969 aged 88.

17 1911 census.
18 Agreement for Tenancy held in Swanson family archives.
19 Receipt for sale of 3 Presburg Road held in Swanson family archives.
20 Letter dated 22nd August 1923. This and the previous mentioned letter held in Swanson family archives.
21 Death certificate of Donald Sutherland Swanson.
22 Weather forecast for London published in *Lincolnshire Echo*, 29th November 1924.
23 Undated newspaper clipping held in Swanson family archives.
24 *Burials in the Burial Ground of Kingston-upon-Thames, in the County of Surrey, Situate at Kingston-upon-Thames.*
25 In 2019 the tree, by now deceased, was removed.
26 Letter from the Secretary to the Receiver for the Metropolitan Police District dated 29th November 1924 held in Swanson family archives.
27 Undated copy of letter to Wensley held in Swanson family archives.

Continuing from Page 138

1 Death certificate of Douglas Sutherland Swanson.
2 Death certificate of Julia Ann Swanson, listing the cause of death as acute pancreatitis.
3 Letter from Julia Swanson to daughter Ada dated September 1934, stressing she was not to "spend any more than is absolutely necessary."
4 Email from Nevill Swanson to author, 26th August 2012.
5 Note sent to Donald Nevill Swanson by sisters Ada and Alice for his 86th birthday in 1965.
6 Email from Mary Berkin to author, 15th May 2016. Mary revealed that she inherited the oak chest following her aunts' deaths and used it to store duvets.
7 Email from Mary Berkin to author, 29th August 2012.
8 James Douglas Swanson was born on 6th May 1912 in Gibraltar, second son of Donald Nevill Swanson. On 29th February 1936 he married Megan Emily Jones ("Peg"). They had three children and also adopted Peg's niece. Jim spent his career in the leather industry and eventually became General Manager of an international group of tanneries. He spent war service in the Royal Navy on the Arctic convoys and in the Pacific theatre, finishing as a Lieutenant in an aircraft carrier where he was fighter direction officer. Jim died on 20th December 2001.
9 Telephone conversation with author on 13th September 2012.

10 Letter from Jim Swanson to Paul Begg, 6th February 1989.

11 For a fuller account of the history of the Swanson marginalia, see 'Red Lines and Purple Pencil' by Adam Wood and Keith Skinner, published in *Ripperologist* 128, October 2012.

12 Email from Mary Berkin to author, 29th August 2012.

13 Although the *Pall Mall Gazette* of 7th May 1895 reported: "The theory entitled to most respect, because it was presumably based upon the best knowledge, was that of Chief Inspector Swanson, the officer who was associated with the investigation of all the murders, and Mr. Swanson believes the crimes to have been the work of a man who is now dead."

14 In a letter to his accountant dated 27th January 1984, Jim wrote: "He was of that breed of officer who did not seek publicity nor financial gain from his public office, he kept his knowledge to himself. I thought he deserved a mention – even if long after his death."

15 Jim Swanson correspondence file.

16 Ibid.

17 Peter Sutcliffe was arrested on 2nd January 1981 and charged with the murders of 13 women between 1975 and 1980. His trial started on 5th May and ended on 22nd May 1981, when he was sentenced to life imprisonment.

18 Jim Swanson correspondence file.

19 Charles Sandell was born on 13th July 1920. During a long career with the *News of the World* he covered crime stories ranging from the Great Train Robbery and the Brixton Riots to the Yorkshire Ripper murders. He retired in 1982 and died on 19th August 1987.

20 Letter from Brian Hill to author, 7th January 2014.

21 Internal memo from Charles Sandell to the News Editor of the *News of the World* dated 15th April 1981.

22 Robert Warren was born in 1935 and worked as a journalist at the *Hampshire Chronicle* and *Coventry Evening Telegraph* before joining the *News of the World* in January 1964. He became News Editor in 1974 and retired in December 2000. He remained at the paper in a part time capacity, becoming Ombudsman and dealing with Press Complaints Commission matters. He died on 6th January 2009.

23 The nature of the agreement was underlined by Jim Swanson in a letter to his accountant dated 27th January 1984: "I did not offer the *NOW* a story, nor provide them with a story. I did not write anything for them. I did not dictate anything for them, I did not even suggest what they might write. I merely allowed them the use of some authentic information in my possession."

24 Jim Swanson correspondence file.

25 Ibid.

26 Handwritten comment by Jim Swanson on Kinlay's original letter of 9th April 1981.

27 Remittance advice slip kindly provided by Nevill Swanson.
28 Carbon copy of letter from Jim Swanson to his accountants dated 31st March 1983.
29 Jim Swanson correspondence file.
30 Email from Charles Nevin to author, 3rd August 2012.
31 The last story by Sandell printed in the *News of the World* is a piece on Ronnie Kray dated 17th January 1982.
32 Jim Swanson correspondence file.
33 Jeff Edwards's statement at the Leveson Inquiry, 28th February 2012. His first printed story for the *News of the World* was a front page piece on Reg Kray moving to Long Lartin prison dated 8th February 1981.
34 Letter from Brian Hill to author, 7th January 2014.
35 Draft article by Charles Sandell held at the Crime Museum, New Scotland Yard.
36 Jim Swanson correspondence file.
37 Charles Nevin (born 1951) read Jurisprudence at University College, Oxford, and was called to the Bar in 1975, but decided instead on a career in journalism. He has worked as a reporter, columnist, foreign correspondent and feature writer for various Fleet Street newspapers, including the *Daily Telegraph* and *The Guardian*. He has written two books, *Lancashire, Where Women Die of Love*, a rediscovery of the romance of his native county, and *The Book of Jacks*, a dictionary of famous bearers of the popular first name, including, of course, the subject of the Swanson Marginalia.
38 Jim Swanson correspondence file.
39 Email from Charles Nevin to author, 3rd August 2012, in which it was confirmed that it was the *Telegraph*'s policy not to pay for stories; payment was neither sought nor offered.
40 Email from Martin Fido to author, 27th August 2012.
41 Jim Swanson correspondence file.
42 "Letters to the Editor", *Daily Telegraph*, 22nd October 1987.
43 "Letters to the Editor", *Daily Telegraph*, 27th October 1987.
44 Jim Swanson correspondence file.
45 Email from Paul Begg to author, 7th July 2012.
46 Nevill Swanson was born on 16th November 1937 and educated at King's School Canterbury and St. Edmund Hall, Oxford. He married on 3rd June 1967 and has three children. Nevill is retired from a career in international sales and marketing of metals and chemicals.
47 The gun, an 1880 brass frame Tranter pistol, bears the inscription "to: Donald Swanson 1882" and is claimed to have been presented by Lady Alice Bective as a reward for the recovery of her jewellery. See pages 113-114. Subsequent research by the author identified a book from the library of Lady Bective which bore the same ducal crest as the escutcheon on the gun, and the pistol has now been reunited with the Swanson family. How it got to the United

States is unknown, but, interestingly, in a letter to Paul Begg dated 28th November 1988, Jim Swanson mentions a revolver which was carried by Donald Swanson after retirement in case of a possible a Fenian 'revenge' attack. Jim wrote that it came to him when he became commander of the local Home Guard early in WWII from his father, and that Jim left the gun with the Home Guard when he joined the Royal Navy.

48 Letter from Keith Skinner to Nevill Swanson, 25th April 2006.
49 Letter from Keith Skinner to Nevill Swanson, 22nd May 2006.
50 *The Independent*, 14th July 2006.
51 web.archive.org/web/20081013075218/http://www.forensic.gov.uk/forensic_t/inside/news/press%20releases%202007.htm#jack_ripper
52 Letter from Nevill Swanson to Keith Skinner, 3rd May 2006.
53 Email from John Bennett to author, 15th August 2012.
54 See 'Red Lines and Purple Pencil' by Adam Wood and Keith Skinner, published in *Ripperologist* 128, October 2012.
55 Email from Nevill Swanson to author, 26th August 2012.
56 'Meeting Jim Swanson', an unpublished article kindly supplied by Stewart Evans.
57 Both reports by Dr. Davies appear in full in the article 'Red Lines and Purple Pencil' by Adam Wood and Keith Skinner, published in *Ripperologist* 128, October 2012.

Kosminski was the Suspect

1   *St. Margaret's Directory 1889*, held in St. Margaret's History Catalogue.
2   Flyer for the Hospital Saturday Fund, held in 'Correspondence and Papers of the Hospital Saturday Fund (Case 2413 or 1/1878)' (LMA: A/FWA/C/D/61/001).
3   See *The Life of Samuel Morley* by Edwin Hodder (1887).
4   £1million – £1.5million today. Information from an obituary of Samuel Morley in *The Graphic*, 11th September 1886.
5   *The Hospital Saturday Fund Journal*, No. 10, Vol. III, June 1895. Held in 'Correspondence and Papers of the Hospital Saturday Fund (Case 2413 or 1/1878)' (LMA: A/FWA/C/D/61/001).
6   *The Daily News*, 2nd July 1883.
7   *The Daily News*, 2nd August 1892.
8   *Canterbury Journal, Kentish Times and Farmers' Gazette*, 25th July 1840.
9   1841 Census.
10 1881 Census.
11 'Schedule of deeds and documents relating to Morley House later Portal House. 1792 to 1919,' held in St Margaret's History catalogue.

12 *The Western Daily Press*, 3rd July 1883.
13 *The London Chatham & Dover Railway* by R. W. Kidner (1952).
14 *The Locomotive History of the London, Chatham & Dover Railway* by D. L. Bradley (Second Edition, 1979). Snow Hill station was renamed Holborn Viaduct (Low Level) in 1912.
15 *The Dover Express*, 27th July 1888, which published an advertisement listing the fee as 6d.
16 *The Western Daily Press*, 3rd July 1883.
17 *The Daily News*, 2nd July 1883.
18 *The Western Daily Press*, 3rd July 1883.
19 Charles Bray, a Lincolnshire-born stonemason, had moved to Lambeth by the time of the 1871 census and raised a family with wife Lucy. He volunteered his time to the Hospital Saturday Fund and also the Hearts of Oak Society, and had been appointed Superintendent of Morley House from its inception, with Lucy Bray acting as Matron. It was Charles Bray who designed and added the ornate fittings to the building's exterior. Information from census returns and *The Dover Express*, 21st July 1899.
20 Letter from Charles Bray published in *Charity: An Unsectarian Record of Benevolence*, No. 31, December 1888.
21 *The Daily News*, 20th October 1891.
22 *The Daily News*, 2nd August 1892.
23 *The Morning Post*, 4th September 1893.
24 *The Daily News*, 2nd August 1892.
25 *The Daily News*, 2nd July 1883.
26 *The Daily News*, 20th October 1891.
27 *The Daily News*, 2nd August 1892.
28 *The Times*, 8th June 1891.
29 Letter from Charles Bray published in *Charity: An Unsectarian Record of Benevolence*, No. 31, December 1888.
30 *Morning Post*, 1st September 1888.
31 'Spotting Criminals: A chat with the Prince of Detectives at Scotland Yard', and interview with Robert Anderson published in the *Evening News* and reprinted in *The Police Review and Parade Gossip*, 28th September 1894.
32 See *Sir Howard Vincent's Police Code, 1889* by Neil R. A. Bell and Adam Wood (2015) for an examination of the version in use by Metropolitan Police officers at the time of the Whitechapel murders.
33 See page 86.
34 See page 355.
35 Letter from Sir Charles Warren to E. J. Ruggles-Brise, Private Secretary to Henry Matthews, 4th October 1888 (National Archives: HO 144/221/A49301C, f. 93).

36 Sir William Crundall had first been elected Mayor of Dover in 1886 and would be re-elected twelve times in the next fourteen years.
37 Emails to author, 28th July 2013 and 26th October 2014. See also www.jtrforums.com/showthread.php?t=24719 for discussion.
38 *The Hospital Saturday Fund Journal*, No. 10, Vol. III, June 1895. Held in 'Correspondence and Papers of the Hospital Saturday Fund (Case 2413 or 1/1878)' (LMA: A/FWA/C/D/61/001).
39 *Dover Express*, 16th March 1900.
40 Death certificate of Charles Bray.
41 *Dover Express*, 18th October 1895.
42 *Dover Express*, 31st August 1900.
43 *The Hospital Saturday Fund Journal*, No. 10, Vol. III, June 1895. Held in 'Correspondence and Papers of the Hospital Saturday Fund (Case 2413 or 1/1878)' (LMA: A/FWA/C/D/61/001).
44 *London Daily News*, 22nd September 1905.
45 *Dover Express*, 25th August 1911. Morley House lay empty until the outbreak of the First World War, when the bedrooms were used by the army for sick and wounded soldiers. In 1920 the National Deposit Friendly Society bought the building and renamed it Portal House, operating it as a convalescent home similar to Morley House. It was closed at the beginning World War Two and came under government control. In 1959 Portal House was re-opened as a Kent County Council home for 66 elderly people, and when this closed in 1975 thought was given to it becoming a hostel for the homeless, but this was rejected on the grounds of cost. It became a school for children with emotional, social and mental health needs in 1977, a function it continues to fulfil at the time of writing. Early in 2016 part of the Victorian building – the 1893 extension - was demolished and replaced with modern, purpose-built school rooms.
46 *Evening News and Star*, 17th October 1888, reporting information which first appeared in the *Nottingham Guardian*, date of edition not stated.
47 cf *Aberdeen Evening Express*, 16th November 1888.
48 Henry Cox was born in Camberwell in 1859. He joined the City of London Police in July 1881 and the following year married Martha Vidler, the couple going on to have thirteen children. Cox went on plain clothes duty in 1884 and was eventually promoted Det. Inspector, before retiring on 26th July 1906. He died on 18th December 1918. See *Jack and Old Jewry: The City of London Policemen Who Hunted The Ripper* by Amanda Harvey Purse (2017).
49 Advertisement in the *Dundee Courier* of 10th December 1906 and subsequent editions.
50 *Derry Journal*, 1st August 1906, which includes a detailed example of Cox's covert surveillance methods when describing the arrest of the notorious bank forger George Johnson.
51 *The Star*, 7th January 1905.
52 *Morning Leader*, 9th January 1905.

53 Robert Sagar gave his address as 47 Bartholomew Close while giving evidence at the Old Bailey on 13th January 1879; William Potts is listed at this address in the 1881 census. Potts gave evidence 21 times at the Old Bailey between 1873 and 1883, and appears in many newspaper reports from the same period. He was born in Wallingford, Berkshire, in 1838.

54 Sagar initially failed the medical examination for entering the City of London Police, the cause often given as varicose veins. The pickaxe injury, the probable reason for this failure, is mentioned in several newspapers reporting Sagar's retirement. cf *Cornish & Devon Post* (14th January 1905), *Totnes Weekly Times* (14th January 1905) and the *Whitby Gazette* (13th January 1905). Sagar passed a second examination.

55 *The Morning Post*, 13th December 1880.

56 *The Exeter and Plymouth Gazette Daily Telegram*, 17th March 1881. See pages 117-118.

57 *Morning Leader*, 9th January 1905.

58 *Enniskillen Chronicle and Erne Packet*, 29th November 1888.

59 *The City Press*, 7th January 1905.

60 Sagar is referring to Catherine Eddowes by the name she gave desk Sergeant James Byfield on her release from Bishopsgate police station: "Mary Ann Kelly" of 6 Fashion Street.

61 *Daily News*, 9th January 1905.

62 *Morning Leader*, 9th January 1905.

63 *The Citizen*, 9th January 1905.

64 See the *Hertford Mercury and Reformer*, 18th October 1862 for a report on tenders for supplying the equipment for the new Stepney Workhouse, and the *London City Press* of 11th April 1863 which mentions the appointment of Mr. Watson as the Master of the facility.

65 *The Standard*, 26th December 1888.

66 *Reynolds's Weekly Newspaper*, 9th December 1888.

67 *The Standard*, 26th December 1888.

68 *The Manchester Courier and Lancashire General Advertiser*, 1st July 1880.

69 *Western Times*, 6th July 1880. The *Graphic* of 10th July 1880 reports that David Saleneskam was sent to Broadmoor.

70 *Derby Daily Telegraph*, 23rd August 1886.

71 *Report of the Select Committee* published in 1828. Accessed via *Psychiatry for the Poor: 1851 Colney Hatch Asylum – Friern Hospital 1973: A Medical and Social History* by Richard Hunter and Ida Macalpine (1974).

72 Although greatly reduced in size, an institution for the mentally ill still exists on the site of Hanwell Asylum under the auspices of the West London Mental Health NHS Trust.

73 Following several name changes, the station gained its current status of New Southgate station in 1971.

74 £8.5million today.

75 *Middlesex: County Lunatic Asylum, Colney Hatch. An Account of Monies Borrowed and Sums Received and of their Expenditure in the Purchase of Land, and in Building, Furnishing and Completing the Asylum* (1852). Accessed via *Psychiatry for the Poor: 1851 Colney Hatch Asylum – Friern Hospital 1973: A Medical and Social History* by Richard Hunter and Ida Macalpine (1974).

76 £18million today (£14,000 per bed).

77 *A Guide Through Colney Hatch Lunatic Asylum* (1852). Accessed via *Psychiatry for the Poor: 1851 Colney Hatch Asylum – Friern Hospital 1973: A Medical and Social History* by Richard Hunter and Ida Macalpine (1974).

78 *Middlesex: The Special Report of the Committee of Visitors of the County Lunatic Asylum at Colney Hatch, as to the Action Brought Against Mr. Daukes* (1859). Accessed via P*sychiatry for the Poor: 1851 Colney Hatch Asylum – Friern Hospital 1973: A Medical and Social History* by Richard Hunter and Ida Macalpine (1974).

79 *Psychiatry for the Poor: 1851 Colney Hatch Asylum – Friern Hospital 1973: A Medical and Social History* by Richard Hunter and Ida Macalpine (1974).

80 *Second Annual Report of the Committee of Visitors of the County Asylum at Colney Hatch* (1853), accessed via *Psychiatry for the Poor: 1851 Colney Hatch Asylum – Friern Hospital 1973: A Medical and Social History* by Richard Hunter and Ida Macalpine (1974).

81 Accessed via *Psychiatry for the Poor: 1851 Colney Hatch Asylum – Friern Hospital 1973: A Medical and Social History* by Richard Hunter and Ida Macalpine (1974).

82 83 patients (44%) died of cerebral diseases such as apoplexy and paralysis, epilepsy and 'maniacal exhaustion'. The next biggest cause of death was through problems of the lungs, such as tuberculosis. Information from *The Thirty-Seventh Annual Report of the Committee of Visitors of the County Asylum at Colney Hatch for the Year 1887*, published in 1888, given in *Psychiatry for the Poor: 1851 Colney Hatch Asylum – Friern Hospital 1973: A Medical and Social History* by Richard Hunter and Ida Macalpine (1974).

83 Annual Report for 1863. Accessed via *Psychiatry for the Poor: 1851 Colney Hatch Asylum – Friern Hospital 1973: A Medical and Social History* by Richard Hunter and Ida Macalpine (1974).

84 Annual Report for 1863. Accessed via *Psychiatry for the Poor: 1851 Colney Hatch Asylum – Friern Hospital 1973: A Medical and Social History* by Richard Hunter and Ida Macalpine (1974).

85 Annual Report for 1889. Accessed via *Psychiatry for the Poor: 1851 Colney Hatch Asylum – Friern Hospital 1973: A Medical and Social History* by Richard Hunter and Ida Macalpine (1974). The death of John Stickley in June 1888 caused controversy when it was debated at the inquest whether the fractured jaw he had suffered which accelerated his death from exhaustion had been caused prior to or after his admission to Colney Hatch, with Coroner George Danford Thomas complaining that a thorough medical examination had not

been conducted. See the *Times*, 23rd June 1888.

86 Transcripts of the *Sun* articles 13th-17th February 1894 can be viewed at www.casebook.org/press_reports/sun.

87 'Memorandum by Leslie Melville McNaghton [sic] concerning details of murdered women and suspected murderers' (National Archives: MEPO 3/141, ff.177-83)s.

88 See '"Copy be damned, that's the original!": A History of the Macnaghten Memorandum' by Adam Wood (*Ripperologist* 124, February 2012) for a full examination of the various versions of Macnaghten's report.

89 A later letter from 1959 written by Lady Aberconway to Ralph Partridge, the *New Statesman*'s reviewer, explained the reason for her insistence that the Ripper was not to be named: "..he might have a nephew or a niece, born about 1890, who would not yet be 70: they in turn might have a child just about to get married. It would not be very pleasant to know that your uncle or great uncle was suspected of being 'Jack the Ripper', would it!"

90 In fact, despite concerted efforts by researchers no link between Thomas Cutbush and Superintendent Charles Cutbush has been found.

91 The body of 31-year-old Montague John Druitt was found floating in the Thames at Chiswick on 31st December 1888, a railway ticket in his pocket indicating that he had been in the water for a month. He came from a prominent Dorset family, and had been extensively educated at Winchester College and the University of Oxford. He was called to the bar in 1885, setting up a practice as a barrister, renting legal chambers at King's Bench Walk in the Inner Temple. To supplement his income Druitt took a job as an assistant schoolmaster at a boarding school in Blackheath, south London, but his dismissal at the end of November 1888 for unknown reasons seems to have caused a mental breakdown. A note addressed to his brother William found in his rooms read "Since Friday I felt that I was going to be like mother, and the best thing for me was to die" – a reference to their mother Ann Druitt, who had long suffered from depression and who had been placed in an asylum in July 1888.

92 In his book *Jack the Ripper—Case Solved, 1891* (2015), Jonathan Hainsworth suggests that Macnaghten's 'private info' came from his friend Colonel Vivian Dering Majendie, H.M. Chief Inspector of Explosives, whose first cousin was Maria Elizabeth Hill. Her daughter Isabel Majendie Hill had married Rev. Charles Druitt on 15th September 1888 – coincidentally the day Donald Swanson was appointed to the Ripper case – and the groom's own first cousin was suspect Montague John Druitt.

93 A thief and scam artist born circa 1833, Michael Ostrog's criminal career was well-documented through his appearances in court for offences committed under a wide range of aliases. There is nothing in his reported misdemeanours to indicate that he was a "homicidal maniac" as described by Macnaghten. Author Richard Jones has commented that given his number of court appearances Ostrog must had been one of the most inept of criminals; hardly the sort of person who could evade the Metropolitan Police in their massive

94   The evidence of Martha Tabram's companion Mary Ann Connelly (aka 'Pearly Poll') proved worthless when she failed to attend the first identification parade organized by the police, then at the second complained that the wrong regiment had been presented for her inspection. At the third parade, on 15th August 1888, she identified a Private George as the man who had been with her and Private Skipper as having gone into George Yard with Tabram. Both soldiers had cast-iron alibis.

95   *Days of My Years* by Sir Melville Macnaghten (1914).

96   See *Trial of Percy Lefroy Mapleton* (Notable British Trials 86) by Adam Wood (2019).

97   *Lloyd's Weekly Newspaper*, 15th December 1889.

98   Ibid.

99   *City Press*, 18th December 1889.

100 *Jack the Ripper and The Case for Scotland Yard's Prime Suspect* by Robert House (2011).

101 See 'New Light on Aaron Kosminski' by Pat Marshall and Chris Phillips in *Ripperologist* 128, October 2012.

102 See *Jack the Ripper and the Case for Scotland Yard's Prime Suspect* by Robert House (2011), and 'Register 9: Kozminski's Missing Leavesden Records' by House in *Ripperologist* 143.

103 See 'New Light on Aaron Kosminski' by Pat Marshall and Chris Phillips in *Ripperologist* 128, October 2012.

104 See www.sciencemag.org/news/2019/03/does-new-genetic-analysis-finally-reveal-identity-jack-ripper

105 Naturalisation papers for Martin Kosminski (National Archives: HO 45/9452/69905). Thomas Warrilow Sr. was born in 1825, and in 1878 was landlord of the Traveller's Rest. His son Thomas Davis Warrilow was born in 1847.

106 *London Standard*, 16th October 1880.

107 *London Standard*, 24th March 1880.

108 *Nottingham Evening Post*, 16th October 1880.

109 *Third Annual Report of the Poor Jews' Temporary Shelter, 1887-8* held in 'Records of the Jews' Temporary Shelter, 1896-1998' (London Metropolitan Archives: LMA/4184/02/01/001/01).

110 *Jewish Standard*, 27th July 1888.

111 *Morning Post*, 9th March 1889.

112 *Morning Post*, 27th November 1889.

113 1911 Census return.

114 See *Gloucester Citizen*, 28th December 1888 and *Bradford Daily Telegraph*, 28th December 1888.

115 See *Cassell's Saturday Journal*, 11th June 1892.
116 *The Windsor Magazine*, Vol.1, January to June 1895.
117 *The Lighter Side of My Official Life* by Sir Robert Anderson (1910).
118 Letter dated 23rd September 1913 in which Littlechild named Tumblety as a possible suspect.
119 *Pall Mall Gazette*, 31st March 1903.

Acknowledgements

The idea of writing a book on Donald Sutherland Swanson came back in 2012, when I was reading through his personal papers in preparation for an article for *Ripperologist* magazine. If Swanson is known at all to the general public, it is for being the officer in overall charge of the investigation into the Whitechapel murders of 1888 and his so-called Marginalia in which he names the suspect 'Kosminski'. But during my researches it became apparent that Swanson had enjoyed a very interesting and successful career, working on other infamous Victorian cases as well as many previously long-forgotten.

I had been very fortunate that not only had the Swanson family retained a large number of original documents, but they also very generously gave me unrestricted access to these. When the article was published and I told the family I would like to write a book on their forebear's life and career they were unhesitatingly supportive, and have been throughout the process. Not only have I enjoyed access to this treasure trove of material, but I have been free to make use of whatever I found without any limitations or caveats.

My deepest appreciation therefore goes to Swanson's great-grandson Nevill, and Mary Berkin, Donald's granddaughter, for their constant enthusiasm, suggestions and answers to my innumerable questions. I am deeply saddened that Mary passed away before the book was completed, but extremely thankful for her unique insight into the family history, without which much of what appears in this book would not have been possible. Thanks, too, to other members of the Swanson family for their support, especially Liz and Bill.

John Mitchell, great-grandson of Donald's eldest brother John, has been equally enthusiastic and supportive and I thank him for the excellent information on his ancestor, and wish I had space to have included more in these pages.

Paul Begg has been a constant source of inspiration and advice, steering me through the uncertain waters of writing my first full-length book. His encouragement, advice and genuine excitement in the project has lifted me in times of uncertainty.

Special mention must be made of the help given by Neil Bell, who not only shared his outstanding knowledge of the Metropolitan Police force in the Victorian era, but also acted as a sounding board when the need arose. Our 'five minute' telephone calls often ended as two-hour discussions which not only enhanced my understanding of police procedures but made the learning enjoyable, and our research trips to the National Archives at Kew often saw us reduced to excited schoolboys when some dusty document or other was unearthed.

I would especially like to thank Alan McIvor, who lifted the mists of Thurso by sharing his unparalleled research into Swanson's childhood home and in the process became a close friend. Allan Lannon, who provided important information on the town's schools and education history, was also incredibly generous in sharing his work. These gentlemen gave me an invaluable understanding of what it meant to grow up in the far north of Scotland in the mid Victorian era.

I'm extremely grateful to David Green not only for his professional input by preparing the book's index, but also for his numerous sage observations and suggestions while reading endless drafts. David, the sea-serpent story is for you!

Several people provided help and support, offering advice and enthusiasm. These include Kate Clarke, Bruce Collie ('The Verminator') for acting as my research assistant in Aberdeen, Sean Crundall, Jeremy Dyer, Kit Havelock-Davies, Robert House, Richard Jones, Loretta Lay, Robert Linford, John Malcolm, Cris Malone, Mark Ripper and Eduardo Zinna.

The following people very kindly provided answers to specific questions or offered additional information: Nathen Amin; Debra Arif; Robert Bain, Library Assistant at Wick Carnegie Public Library; Angela Barclay of Caithness Family History Society; Phillip Barnes-Warden, Metropolitan Police Heritage Centre; Rose Bradley, Headteacher at Portal House School, St. Margaret's-at-Cliffe, Dover; Anna Cunningham, Thomas Agnew & Sons Ltd.; Peter Damgaard; James Darby, Archive Assistant at Highland Archive Centre; Kim Downie and Michelle Gait of the Special Collections Centre, University of Aberdeen; Poul Duedahl; Stewart Evans; the late Norman Fairfax M.B.E., former Senior Executive Officer Metropolitan Police and former Vice Chairman of the Metropolitan Police History Society; Peter Fannon, former Secretary of Lodge St. Peter's No. 284, Thurso; Rod Farr; Harry Gray and Fergus Mather of the Wick Society Johnston Collection; Katy Green, Customer Services Assistant at London Transport Museum; Steve Kentfield of www.EastLondonPostcard.co.uk; Bernd Koschland, Trustee and Council Member of the Jews' Temporary Shelter; Tatiana Laracuente,

Acknowledgements

Library of Congress; David Luck and Jeremy Smith of London Metropolitan Archives; Muriel Murray of Castletown Heritage Society; David O'Flaherty; Jose Oranto; Fiona Platten and Gordon Reid, Archive Assistants at Caithness Archive Centre; Andy Ramus; Jane Rugg, Curator of the London Fire Brigade Museum; Sue Shore; Keith Skinner; Chantalle Smith, Librarian, Research Access, Alexander Turnbull Library, National Library of New Zealand; Steve Stanley; Edward Stow; Simon Wood; and Edward Weech, Deputy Library Manager at Bishopsgate Institute. A special mention for all the wonderful posters on JTRForums.com and Casebook.org for the snippets of information unearthed and selflessly shared.

Thank you all.

Finally, an apology to my father, Derek Wood, who refused to read any of this book while I was writing it, preferring to wait for the final published version. He passed away before it was completed, having not read a single word, for which I will be eternally sorry.

ADAM WOOD
December 2019

Bibliography

Primary Sources

Corporation of London Record Office
Coroner's inquest (L), 1888, No. 135, Catherine Eddowes inquest, 1888

National Archives
A16380/96
A26493G
CRIM 1/41/4
CRIM 4/953 31209
DPP 1/95/1
DPP 1/95/1-7
DPP 1/95/3
DPP 1/95/4/2
H29/NF/A/1/1-25
HO 144/83/A6404
HO 144/206/A479760
HO 144/206/A47976P
HO 144/211/A48482
HO 144/221/A49301
HO 144/221/A49301F
HO 144/221/A4930C
HO 144/221/A4930H
HO 144/237/A52045
HO 144/237/A52437
HO 144/293/B1470
HO 144/305/B5005A
HO 144/477/X24427
HO 144/483/X34262
HO 144/502/X53193

HO 144/721/110757
HO 334/15/5430
HO 45/7799
HO 45/9388 46912
HO 45/9615/A11425
HO 45/9685/A48384
HO 45/9698/A50055
HO 45/9711/A51187
HO 65/62 – Volume 35
J 77/119/2188
LO 3/301
MEPO 1/48
MEPO 2/24
MEPO 2/134
MEPO 2/140
MEPO 2/170
MEPO 2/210
MEPO 2/229
MEPO 2/238
MEPO 2/245
MEPO 2/398
MEPO 2/601
MEPO 2/898
MEPO 2/5809
MEPO 3/2833
MEPO 3/2890
MEPO 3/45
MEPO 3/143
MEPO 3/2890
MEPO 5/44
MEPO 7/38
MEPO 21/31
PCOM 8/177
T 1/13779
WO 32/7839
WO 32/7845

Bilbiography

Hansard
Deb 2nd July 1855 vol 139 cc368-71
Deb 3rd August 1885
Deb 4th March 1886 vol 302 cc1891-2
Deb 13th November 1888 vol 330 cc1035-8 1035
Deb 13th, 20th, 21st April 1910 vol 16

London Metropolitan Archives
A/FWA/C/D/61/001
LMA/4184/02/01/001/01
LMA/4184/02/01/001/02
LMA/4184/1/1/3/1
LMA/4184/1/1/3/1
LMA/4184/2/1/1
MJ/SPC, NE1888, Box 3, Case Paper 19

National Library of Australia
Catalogue.nal.gov/record/588330

Provincial Archives of Sjaelland
DC-032

United States Library of Congress
MSS36301, Box 99 Folder 9

Wellcome Library
GALTON/2/9/13/2

Other Resources
(Alien immigration) Reports on the volume and effects of recent immigration from eastern Europe into the United Kingdom (Board of Trade, 1894)
Annual Report of the Sanitary Condition of the Whitechapel District for the Year 1893
Annual Report of Her Majesty's Inspector of Explosives for the Year 1883
Annual Report of Her Majesty's Inspector of Explosives up to 31st December 1875
Births, Deaths and Marriages database
Bradshaw's Guide, Handbook IV, 1866
Bradshaw's Rail Times for 1895
British Parliamentary Papers: Royal Commission on Alien Immigration (1903)

Caithness Constabulary Conviction Book 1858-1880
Caithness County Officers Default Book
Caithness County Valuation Rolls 1858-1869
Census returns 1841-1911
Criminal Lunacy Warrant and Entry Books, 1882-1898
Fire Service records
Kelly's Post Office Directory for London
Metropolitan Police Reports of Commissioner, 1869-76
New Zealand Parliamentary Record, 1840–1984
Old Bailey Online
Parish of Thurso by Rev. W. R. Taylor, October 1840
Police Orders 1867-1903
Register of Dorset Deaths and Burials 1813-2010
Report of the Commissioner of Police of the Metropolis for the Year 1883
St Margaret's History catalogue
St. Pancras Workhouse Admission and Discharge Register 1922-1924
Second Report from The Select Committee of the House of Lords on the Sweating System (Session 1888)
Slater's Directory of Caithness-shire, 1852
Surrey Calendar of Prisoners 1848-1902
Survey of London
Swanson family archive
United States of America Bureau of Pensions

Secondary Sources

Newspapers, Articles and Journals
Aberdeen Evening Express
Aberdeen Journal
Aberdeen Weekly Journal
Alnwick Mercury
The Australasian
Ayr Advertiser or West Country Journal
Berrow's Worcester Journal
Birmingham Daily Post
The Brisbane Courier
Bristol Mercury and Western Counties Advertiser
Bury and Norwich Post
Bury Free Press
Caithness Courier
Cambridge Independent Press

Bilbiography

Canterbury Journal, Kentish Times and Farmers' Gazette
The Canterbury Press
Cardiff Times and South Wales Weekly News
Charity: An Unsectarian Record of Benevolence
Cheshire Observer
The Citizen
City Press
Clerkenwell News
Daily Gazette for Middlesbrough
Daily Graphic
Daily Mail
Daily News
Daily Telegraph
Daily Telegraph and Courier
Decatur Daily Despatch
Derby Daily Telegraph
Derbyshire Courier
Derbyshire Times
Derry Journal
Dover Express
Dublin Daily Express
Dublin Evening Mail
Dundee Advertiser
Dundee Courier and Argus
East London Advertiser
East London Observer
East Sussex News
Eastern Evening News
Edinburgh Evening News
Edinburgh Review or Critical Journal for October 1837 to January 1838
The Engineer
The Era
Evening News
Evening Star
Evening Telegraph
Exeter and Plymouth Gazette
Falkirk Herald and Linlithgow Journal
Fife Herald
Freeman's Journal
The Freemason
Glasgow Herald
The Globe
Gloucester Citizen
Gloucester Journal

Gloucestershire Echo
Grantham Journal
Guernsey Star
Hackney and Kingsland Gazette
Hampshire Advertiser
Hampshire Telegraph
Hastings and St. Leonards Observer
Hemel Hempstead Gazette
The Herald
Huddersfield Chronicle
Hull Daily Mail
Illustrated London News
Illustrated Police News
The Independent
Ipswich Journal and Suffolk, Norfolk, Essex and Cambridgeshire Advertiser
Irish Times
The Islington Gazette
Jackson's Oxford Journal
Jewish Chronicle
John O'Groat Journal
Kalgoorlie Western Argus
Kent & Sussex Courier
Kentish Chronicle
Kentish Mercury
Lancaster Gazette
Leeds Intelligencer
Leeds Mercury
Leeds Times
Leicester Chronicle
Leighton Buzzard Observer and Linslade Gazette
Lichfield Mercury
Lincolnshire Chronicle
Lincolnshire Echo
Liverpool Mercury
Lloyd's Weekly Newspaper
London Daily News
London Evening Standard
Manchester Courier and Lancashire General Advertiser
Manchester Evening News
Manchester Times
Manitoba Daily Free Press
Medium and Daybreak
Melbourne Argus
Memories of Thurso by an Expatriated Native: Forty Years Ago

Morning Herald
Morning Post
National Advocate
The New Review
New York Herald
New York Times
New Zealand Herald
New Zealand Star
Newcastle Courant
News of the World
Nineteenth Century and After
Norfolk Ancestor
North Devon Journal
North London Press
North Wales Chronicle
North-Eastern Daily Gazette
Northampton Mercury
Northern Advocate
Northern Ensign
Northern Times
Northern Warder and Bi-Weekly Courier and Argus
The Northern Whig
Nottingham Evening Post
Nottinghamshire Guardian
Otago Witness
Oxford Journal
Oxford University and City Herald
Pall Mall Gazette
Penny Illustrated Paper
The People
Petersfield Express
Police Gazette
Police Review and Parade Gossip
Portsmouth Evening News
Post Office Directory for Sussex
Reynolds's Weekly Newspaper
Ripperologist
Rockingham Morning Bulletin
Royal Cornwall Gazette
Royal Leamington Spa Courier
The Scotsman
Sevenoaks Chronicle and Kentish Advertiser
Sheffield and Rotherham Independent
Sheffield Daily Telegraph

Sheffield Evening Telegraph
Sheffield Independent
Shields Daily Gazette and Shipping Telegraph
The Sketch
South Australian Register
South Wales Daily News
Southern Reporter
Southland Times
St. James's Gazette
Staffordshire Sentinel
The Standard
The Star
Suffolk and Essex Free Press
Sunderland Daily Echo and Shipping Gazette
Supplement to The Graphic
Supplement to the Manchester Courier and Lancashire General Advertiser
Supplement to The Nottinghamshire Guardian
Surrey Mirror and General County Advertiser
Sussex Advertiser
Sydney Morning Herald
Tamworth Herald
Tasmania Daily Telegraph
Taunton Courier and Western Advertiser
The Times
Trewman's Exeter Flying Post
West Australian
West Sussex County Times
West Sussex Journal
Western Daily Press
Western Mail
Western Times
Whitby Gazette
Whitstable Times
Worcestershire Chronicle
York Herald
Yorkshire Evening Post
Yorkshire Post and Leeds Intelligencer

Books

Adam Worth, Alias 'Little Adam'. Theft and Recovery of Gainsborough's 'Duchess of Devonshire' (Pinkertons: Second Edition, 1903)

Adam, Hargrave L.: *Police Work From Within* (1914)

Anderson, Sir Robert: *Criminals and Crime: Some Facts and Suggestions*

(1907)
Anderson, Sir Robert: *The Lighter Side of My Official Life* (1910)

Ash, Chris: *The If Man* (2012)

Ashton, P. E.: *The Raid on the Transvaal* (1897)

Barnett, H. O.: *Canon Barnett: His Life, Works and Friends* (1918)

Barry, William Jackson: *Past and Present, and Men of the Times* (1897)

Begg, Paul and Bennett, John: *Jack the Ripper: The Forgotten Victims* (2013)

Bell, Neil R. A.: *Capturing Jack the Ripper: In the Boots of a Bobby in Victorian London* (2014)

Bell, Neil R. A. and Wood, Adam: *Sir Howard Vincent's Police Code, 1889* (2015)

Bradford, Constance: *Truly a Great Victorian: A Quiet Man Before Whom Rogues Trembled* (2004)

Bradley, D. L.: *The Locomotive History of the London, Chatham & Dover Railway* (Second Edition, 1979)

Campbell, Christy: *Fenian Fire* (2002)

Carrington, Hereward: *The Physical Phenomena of Spiritualism: Fraudulent and Genuine* (1907)

Carter, A. C. R.: *Let Me Tell You* (1940)

Cavanagh, Chief Inspector Timothy: *Scotland Yard Past and Present: Experiences of Thirty-Seven Years* (1893)

Chandler, Glenn: *The Sins of Jack Saul: The True Story of Dublin Jack and the Cleveland Street Scandal* (2016)

Clarke, Kate: *In the Interests of Science: Adelaide Bartlett and the Pimlico Poisoning* (2015)

Clarkson, Charles Tempest and Richardson, J. Hall: *Police!* (1889)

Cobb, Belton: *The First Detectives* (1957)

Cocks, H. G.: *Nameless Offences: Homosexual Desire in the 19th Century* (2010)

Colquhoun, Kate: *Mr. Briggs' Hat: A Sensational Account of Britain's First Railway Murder* (2011)

Colvin, Ian: *The Life of Jameson* (1922)

Connell, Nicholas: *Doctor Crippen: The Infamous London Cellar Murder of 1910* (2013)

Cook, Matt: *London and the Culture of Homosexuality, 1885-1914* (2008)

Cowen, Anne and Roger: *Victorian Jews Through British Eyes* (1998)

Crutchley's London in 1865: A Handbook for Strangers

Dilnot, George: *The Trial of the Detectives* (1928)

Duedahl, Poul: *Silence of the Lambs (Danish: Ondskabens øjne)* (2016)

Evans, Stewart P. and Skinner, Keith: *The Ultimate Jack the Ripper*

Sourcebook: An Illustrated Encyclopedia (2000)

Evans, Stewart P. and Skinner, Keith: *Jack the Ripper: Letters From Hell* (1997)

Fairfax, Norman: *From Quills to Computers: The History of the Metropolitan Police Civil Staff 1829-1979* (1979)

Fass, Paula S.: *Kidnapped: Child Abduction in America* (1997)

Fido, Martin and Skinner, Keith: *The Official Encyclopedia of Scotland Yard* (2000 revised edition).

Fido, Martin: *The Bodysnatchers* (1988)

Fishman, William J.: *The Streets of East London* (1979)

Flanders, Judith: *The Victorian City: Everyday Life in Dickens' London* (2012)

Foreman, Amanda: *Georgiana, Duchess of Devonshire* (1999)

Fort, G. Seymour: *Dr. Jameson* (1908)

Goldsmid, Howard J.: *Dottings of a Dosser; being revelations of the inner life of low London Lodging-Houses* (1886)

Gowers, Rebecca: *The Twisted Heart* (2009)

Gray, Drew D.: *London's Shadows: The Dark Side of the Victorian City* (2010)

Greenham, George: *Scotland Yard Experiences From the Diary of G. H. Greenham* (1904)

Griffiths, Arthur: *Mysteries of Police and Crime* (1898)

Hagen, Carrie: *We Is Got Him: The Kidnapping That Changed America* (2011)

Hainsworth, J. J.: *Jack the Ripper – Case Solved, 1891* (2015)

Halliday, Stephen: *The Great Stink of London: Sir Joseph Bazalgette and the Cleansing of the Victorian Metropolis* (1999)

Hamilton-Browne, George: *A Lost Legionary in South Africa* (1912)

Haynes, Capt. A. E.: *Man-Hunting in the Desert, Being a Narrative of the Palmer Search-Expedition* (1894)

Hoadingley, Adolphe S.: *The Biography of Charles Bradlaugh* (1880)

Hodder, Edwin: *The Life of Samuel Morley* (1887)

Honigsbaum, Mark: *A History of the Great Influenza Pandemics: Death, Panic and Hysteria, 1830-1920* (2013)

Hopton, Sarah Beth: *Woman at the Devil's Door: The Extraordinary True Story of Mary Pearcey and the Hampstead Murders* (2017)

Howson, H. F.: *London's Underground* (1951)

Hurd, the Rt. Hon. Lord Douglas: *Robert Peel: A Biography* (2008)

Hyde, H. Montgomery: *The Cleveland Street Scandal* (1976)

Innes Williams, David: *The London Lock: A Charitable Hospital for Venereal Disease 1746-1952* (1995)

Jacobsen, Michael Hviid: *The Poetics of Crime: Understanding and Researching Crime and Deviance* (2014)

Jeyes, S. H. and How, F. D.: *The Life of Sir Howard Vincent* (1912)

Jordan, Jane and Sharp, Ingrid (eds.): *Josephine Butler and the Prostitute Campaigns* (2003)

Kenna, Shane: *War in the Shadows: The Irish-American Fenians Who Bombed Victorian Britain* (2014)

Kidner, R. W.: *The London Chatham & Dover Railway* (1952)

Kipling, Rudyard: *Something of Myself: For My Friends Known and Unknown* (1937)

Knott, George (Ed.): *Trial of Franz Müller* (1911)

Kynaston, David: *The City of London: Volume 1, A World of its Own 1815-1890* (1994)

Lannon, Allan: *Miller Academy History and Memories for the Millenium* (2000)

Lannon, Allan: *Schools in Thurso Parish from the 17th Century to 1966* (2004)

Law, John (Margaret Harkness): *Out of Work* (1888)

Leeson, Benjamin: *Lost London: the Memoirs of an East End Detective* (1934)

Littlechild, J.G.: *The Reminiscences of Chief Inspector Littlechild* (1894)

Macintyre, Ben: *The Napoleon of Crime: The Life and Times of Adam Worth, the Real Moriarty* (2012)

Mackay, John Henry: *The Anarchists: A Picture of Civilization at the Close of the Nineteenth Century* (1891)

Macnaghten, Melville: *Days of My Years* (1914)

Mapleson, James Henry: *The Mapleson Memoirs, 1848-1888 Vol I* (1888)

Marcus, Steven: *The Other Victorians: A Study of Sexuality and Pornography in Mid-Nineteenth Century England* (1974)

Marshall Hole, Hugh: *The Jameson Raid* (1930)

Mayhew, Henry: *A Visit to the Rookery of St. Giles and its Neighbourhood* (1860)

Mayhew, Henry: *London Labour and the London Poor, Vol II* (1861)

McConville, Sean: *Irish Political Prisoners, 1848-1922* (2003)

McCracken, Donal P.: *Inspector Mallon: Buying Irish Patriotism for a Five-Pound Note* (2009)

McKenna, Neil: *Fanny and Stella: The Young Men Who Shocked Victorian England* (2013)

McKenna, Neil: *The Secret Life of Oscar Wilde* (2003)

McLaren, Angus: *A Prescription for Murder: The Victorian Serial Killings of Dr. Thomas Neill Cream* (1993)

McLaughlin, Robert: *The First Jack the Ripper Victim Photographs* (2005)

Moir Bussy, Frederick: *Irish Conspiracies: Recollections of John Mallon (The Great Irish Detective) and Other Reminiscences* (1910)

Moore-Anderson, A. P.: *Sir Robert Anderson and Lady Agnes Anderson* (1947)

Moser, Inspector Maurice with Rideal, Charles F.: *Stories From Scotland Yard* (1890)

Murphy, Paul Thomas: *Shooting Victoria: Madness, Mayhem and the Modernisation of the Monarchy* (2012)

Newman, Aubrey N., Evans, Nicholas J., Smith, Graham and Issroff, Saul W. (Eds.): *Jewish Migration to South Africa: The Records of the Poor Jews' Temporary Shelter, 1885-1914* (2006)

O'Day, Rosemary and Englander, David: *Mr. Charles Booth's Inquiry: Life and Labour of the People in London Reconsidered* (1993)

O'Neill, Joseph: *Secret World of the Victorian Lodging House* (2014)

Oldridge, M.W.: *Trial of Israel Lipski* (Notable British Trials 84, 2017)

Oudemans, A. C.: *The Great Sea-Serpent: An Historical and Critical Treatise* (1892)

Parker, George: *A View of Society and Manners in High and Low Life, Vol II* (1781)

Payne, Chris: *The Chieftain: Victorian True Crime through the Eyes of a Scotland Yard Detective* (2011)

Pearsall, Ronald: *The Worm in the Bud: The World of Victorian Sexuality* (1969)

Picard, Liza: *Victorian London: The Life of a City 1840-1870* (2005)

Plowden, Alison: *The Case of Eliza Armstrong: A Child of 13 Bought for £5* (1974)

Porter, Bernard: *The Origins of the Vigilant State: The London Metropolitan Police Special Branch before the First World War* (1987)

Provisional Instructions for the Different Ranks of the Police Force (1829)

Ross, Christian: *The Father's Story of Charley Ross, the Kidnapped Child* (1876)

Roughead, William: *Twelve Scots Trials* (1913)

Rubenhold, Hallie: *The Five: The Untold Lives of the Women Killed by Jack the Ripper* (2019)

Sellwood, Arthur and Mary: *The Victorian Railway Murders* (1979)

Shelden, Neal: *Mary Jane Kelly and the Victims of Jack the Ripper: The 125th Anniversary* (2013)

Shelden, Neal: *The Victims of Jack the Ripper* (2007)

Simpson, Colin, Chester, Lewis and Leitch, David: *The Cleveland Street Affair* (1976)

Stead, W. T.: *My First Imprisonment* (1886)

Summerscale, Kate: *The Suspicions of Mr. Whicher* (2008)

Sunderland, David: *These Chivalrous Brothers: The Mysterious Disappearance of the 1882 Palmer Sinai Expedition* (2016)

Sweeney, John: *At Scotland Yard: Being the Experiences During Twenty-Seven Years Service* (1904)

Tynan, P. J. P.: *The Irish National Invincibles and Their Times* (1894)

Van der Poel, Jean: *The Jameson Raid* (1951)

Webb, Simon: *Dynamite, Treason & Plot* (2012)

Wescott, Tom: *The Bank Holiday Murders: The True Story of the First Whitechapel Murders* (2013)

Whelehan, Niall: *The Dynamiters: Irish Nationalism and Political Violence in the Wider World, 1867-1900* (2014)

Whittington-Egan, Molly: *Doctor Forbes Winslow: Defender of the Insane* (2000)

Williams, Montagu: *Leaves of a Life, Vol. I* (1890)

Williams, Montagu: *Leaves of a Life, Vol II* (1890)

Williams, Paul: *Jack the Ripper Suspects: The Definitive Guide and Encyclopedia* (2018)

Williams, Watkin W.: *The Life of General Sir Charles Warren* (1941)

Windust, Charles: *Some Crime Stories* (n.d.)

Winslow, L. Forbes: *Recollections of Forty Years* (1910)

Wise, Sarah: *The Blackest Streets: The Life and Death of A Victorian Slum* (2008)

Wise, Sarah: *The Italian Boy: Murder and Grave-Robbery in 1830s London* (2005)

Wood, Adam.: *Trial of Percy Lefroy Mapleton* (Notable British Trials 86, 2019)

Zierold, Norman: *Little Charley Ross* (1967)

Index

NOTE: Ranks are generally the highest mentioned in the text

A Division (Whitehall), 50, 51, 53, 329-33
Abberline, Inspector Frederick: surveillance operation at Winchester Music Hall, 61; promoted Inspector and transferred to Whitechapel, 61, 283, 603; promoted Local Inspector (H Division), 95, 283; and Tower of London bomb attack (1885), 226-7; moves to Scotland Yard, 283; and Buck's Row murder, 283, 284, 639; leads enquiry into Hanbury Street murder, 282, 283; at Miller's Court, 327, 328; expenses for work on Ripper case, 663; and Cleveland Street scandal, 426-7, 428, 433, 435; expenses for work on Cleveland Street case, 432; and Duchess of Edinburgh's jewellery theft, 371, 372; promoted Detective Chief Inspector (Temporary), 377; attends dinner for Monro, 387-8; arrests Walter Selwyn, 615; resigns from Metropolitan police, 474-5; private enquiry agent, 474-5; reminiscences, 510, 675; on memoirs by retired Metropolitan officers, 510-12; on identity of the Ripper, 584
A.B.C. telegraph system, 48
Aberconway, Christabel, Lady, 566, 684
Aberconway version of Macnaghten memorandum, 566-71
Aberdeen Evening Express, 170-1
Aberdeen Journal, 172, 174, 177, 591, 622
Aberdeen Police, 6, 160-1
Abney Park Cemetery, 214
Abrahams, Bernard, 386
Abrahams, Isaac *see* Kosminski, Isaac
Abrahams, Michael, 79, 99, 607
Abrahams, Woolf *see* Kosminski, Woolf

Abrahams and Roffey (solicitors), 79, 81
accidental strangulation, death from, 348, 349
Adam, Hargrave L., *Police Work From Within*, 150-1
Adam Worth (pamphlet), 491-2, 496-7
Adams and Hillstead (pawnbrokers), 132, 139
age of consent legislation, 416
Aggs, Inspector, 72
Agnew, Charles Morland, 484-5, 494-5, 496, 673
Agnew, Lockett, 495
Agnew, William, 69, 70-1, 491, 672
Agnew's art gallery, 68-9, 70-1, 491-2, 495
Agombar, John, 382-3
Albert (mail packet boat), 476
Albert, Prince, 22
Albert Memorial, 22
Albert Victor, Prince: and Cleveland Street scandal, 434; as Jack the Ripper suspect, 664
Albrook, Lizzie, 326, 649
alchemy, 384-5
Aldgate East underground station, 269
Aldgate railway station, 269
Alexander, Peter, 10, 18, 513
Alexander, Peterishea *see* Robertson, Peterishea
Alexander, Sir William, 31
Alexander III, Tsar of Russia, 271
Alexandra, Princess of Wales, 39-40, 512, 643
Alfred, Prince, Duke of Edinburgh, 197, 370, 372
Algar, P.C. Frederick, 374
Allen, Detective Sergeant, 472-3, 479
Allen, Alfred, 74
Allen, Clement, 96, 97, 99, 100

705

Index

Allen, Jeremiah, 44, 46
Allen, P.C. Joseph, 351–2
Allen, William, 43
Allers, John, 358
Allies, Algernon, 425, 433–4, 438
Alsop, James, 160, 161, 165–6
Alsop, Mann & Co. (London solicitors), 160, 166, 171–2
American Bar, Paris, 489
American Civil War, 487
Ames, Mr. (newspaper publisher), 389
Ames, Herbert John, 437
anatomists, 156, 158, 159
Anatomy Act (1832), 159
Anderson, Frederick, 86, 548
Anderson, George, 241–5
Anderson, Isabella Fraser, 567
Anderson, James, 8
Anderson, Sir Robert: Secret Service career, 45–6; as Home Office Advisor on Political Crime, 46, 202; on Michael Davitt, 116; government Commission work, 202; and Special Irish Branch, 203; Fenian intelligence role, 223, 233, 249; replaced by Jenkinson, 223; appointed Assistant Commissioner (Crime), 265, 268; sick leave, 268; frequent visitor to Kent coast, 549; friendship with Sir William Crundall, 549; and Warren's 'Eyes and Ears' memorandum, 267–8; progress report on Ripper manhunt, 319–20; invites Bond's opinion on Ripper murders, 335; and Mary Kelly murder, 321; and Catherine Mylett case, 348, 349, 350; responds to Baxter rebuke, 349; and Alice McKenzie murder, 352–3; at Williamson's funeral, 361; and Billings complaint letter, 374; breaches Home Office rules on disclosure, 497–8; and Edward Pinter extradition, 387; explores new fingerprinting system, 507; interviewed by *Cassell's Saturday Journal*, 584; and Bond's profiling report, 341; and Leonard Harper extradition, 458; censured over crime article, 497, 498; resigns from Scotland Yard, 498–9; knighted, 499; lectures and writes on crime and Christian matters, 499–500; pension, 501–2; memoirs serialised in *Blackwood's Magazine*, 500–2, 502–3; on John Shore, 95–6; on identity of 'Dear Boss' letter-writer, 317; on Adam Worth, 486–7; names Powell as Worth's accomplice, 492, 672; on police powers, 547; on Whitechapel murders, 551–2; Polish Jew suspect, 500–1, 520–1, 576, 584; on Seaside Home identification, 545, 549, 557; as source for Macnaghten's information on 'Kosminski', 574; *Criminals and Crime*, 95–6, 317, 486–7, 492, 500, 551–2, 672; *see also Lighter Side of My Official Life, The* (Anderson)
Anderson, Samuel Lee, 188
Andrews, James, 447
Andrews, Detective Inspector Walter, 98, 142, 246
Andrews, P.C. Walter, 351–2
Angel, Miriam, 301, 618
Anscombe, Superintendent Henry, 131
Anthropometry Department, 507, 508
anti-Semitism, 271, 279, 309–10, 635
Appleford, Dr. Stephen, 544, 549
apron, Catherine Eddowes murder, 308–9, 311, 556
Arbour Square police station, 126, 136, 151
Archer, Captain (Edward Harvey Wadge), 205
Argentina, 101
Armagh prison, 452
Armstrong, Eliza ('Lily'), 416–19
Armstrong, Mrs. Elizabeth (Lily's mother), 418
Arnold, John, 354–5, 548
Arnold, Superintendent Thomas: and Tower of London bomb attack (1885), 226–7; appears before House of Commons Immigration Committee, 274–5; on annual leave (September 1888), 282; and Goulston Street graffiti, 309, 310–11; at Miller's Court, 327–8; evidence to Committee of Enquiry into Police Superannuation (August 1889), 364; and Frances Coles case, 378
Arrears of Rent (Ireland) Act (1882), 183
Ashley, John *see* Tindall, Arthur Grey
Asquith, Herbert, 454–5, 507
Astley's Theatre, Lambeth, 60
Atkins, Frank, 443
Atkins, P.C. Frederick: murdered on duty, 140–2; funeral, 142–3; memorial plaque, 619

Index

Atkinson, Sarah Todd, 246
Atkinson, P.C. William, 31–2
Attenborough, George, 58
Auditorium Hotel, Chicago, 484–5
Aurora Borealis (Northern Lights), 6
Austin, George, 617
Australasian (newspaper), 459
Australia (steamer), 175
Austria: Joseph Maier murder case (1894), 340, 341
Avory, Horace, 385–6, 470
Aymler, Arthur *see* Griffiths, Major Arthur
Ayr Advertiser, 191–2

baccarat, 205–6, 208–9, 628
Backchurch Lane, Whitechapel, 353–4, 548
Badham, Sergeant Edward, 352
Bailey, John, 10, 22, 592, 594
Bailey, Walter ('Walter Selwyn'), 117–18, 555, 615
Baillie, Mrs. Gordon (Annie Frost), 265, 636
Baker, Colonel Valentine, 127–9, 617
Baker's Row Infirmary *see* Whitechapel Infirmary
Balcombe: inquest into Mr. Gold's death, 132–5
Balcombe railway tunnel, 130–1, 138, 573
Baldry, Inspector David, 591
Baldwin, Inspector David, 51
Bale, Charles, 82, 84, 87, 88, 607
Balfour, Arthur, 1st Earl, 455
Ballantyne, George Dixon, 114
balloons: military use, 235
Balmoral, 42
Balmoral Hotel, Edinburgh, 370–1, 372
Bannell, Mrs. (landlady at Blue Posts Tavern), 98–9
Bannister, Detective Inspector Thomas, 375, 376
Banstead Asylum, 564
Barber, George, 425
Barbey, Captain (client at Cleveland Street brothel), 437
Baring Brothers (bank), 387
Barker, Mr. (magistrate), 60, 61
Barker, Frank, 451
Barlow, Thomas, 484
Barnett, Henrietta, 269–70
Barnett, Joseph, 322, 323–4, 325–6, 343, 344, 649
Barr, Adam, 195–6

Barraud, Mrs. (pub landlady), 375
Barrett, P.C. (of K Division), 347
Barrett, Michael, 44, 46
Barrett, P.C. Thomas, 640
Barrett's Confectionery Factory, Wood Green, 316
Bartlett, Adelaide, 480
Barton, Robert, 182–3
Bass, John, 300, 644
Bastian, Dr. Charlton, 454
Batten, Henry, 382–3
Baxter, Captain John, 372
Baxter, Reggie, 642
Baxter, Wynne E.: legal and coronial career, 287–91, 618, 642; civic duties and Mayor of Lewes, 289, 642; Frederick Gold inquest, 132–5; Percy Lefroy inquest, 150; Annie Millwood inquest, 292; Emma Smith inquest, 292; Mary Ann Nichols inquest, 293–4; Annie Chapman inquest, 287, 292, 294–5; links Whitechapel murders, 293–4; on Jack the Ripper's medical abilities, 294–5; Elizabeth Stride inquest, 423; Jane Merry inquest, 558; Catherine Mylett inquest, 347–8, 349; publicly rebukes Met, 349; Alice McKenzie inquest, 352; Frances Coles inquest, 380
Bayliss, Annie (*later* Mugford), 619
Bazalgette, Joseph, 20, 23
Beard, P.C. Henry, 656
beat patrols, 31, 53–4, 304–5, 350
Beauchamp, Emma, 57
Beauchamp, Julia, 57
Beaumont, Dr. (of Agar), 369
Beaumont, William, 96, 97
Bechuanaland (Botswana): Bechuanaland Protectorate, 235, 632; Rhodes urges annexation, 462
Bechuanaland Border Police, 462, 465
Beck, Inspector Walter, 322, 327
Becker, Charles, 489, 490
Bective, Alice, Countess of, 110, 111; presents Swanson with Tranter pistol, 113–14, 613–14, 678
Bective, Thomas Taylour, Earl of, 110–11, 112, 113, 151, 613
Bedford, Edward, 435
Begg, Daniel and James, 16
Begg, Paul, 529, 533, 647; *Jack the Ripper: The Uncensored Facts*, 529, 534
Beit, Alfred, 461, 464
Belgium, 414–15, 437, 504; *see also*

707

Index

Louvain Gaol
Belton, Chief Inspector, 468
Bengal police: use of fingerprinting, 499, 507
Bennett, John, 533, 644
Benson, Henry ('Andrew Montgomery'; 'Jacob Francis'): criminal history, 607; betting fraud, 80-1; arrested in Rotterdam, 82; extradited, 84; on trial, 86-7; convicted and sentenced, 88; implicates Detective Department, 88, 492
Bentley, John, 69, 672-3
Berkin, Mary (Swanson's granddaughter), 520, 521-2, 676
Berner, Street, 300-4, 576
Berner Street School, Whitechapel, 279
Berry, James, 377
Bertillon, Alphonse: anthropometry system, 507
Besant, Annie, 255, 261, 406, 660
Best, J. *see* Bass, John
Bettles, P.C. Willie, 309
Bickers, Caroline, 124, 152, 616
Bickers, James, 124, 616
Bickers, Jane, 124, 125, 136, 153
Bickers, Sarah (Mrs. Bickers): background, 124; rents out room to Lefroy, 135; suspicions, 136; and arrest of Lefroy, 125, 126; leaves Smith Street, 152-3; claims reward, 151-4
Bickers, Sarah Emma, 124, 616
Bickmore Street mortuary, Poplar, 347-8
Bicknell, Superintendent, 74
Bignold, Joseph, 555
Billings, William, 372-4, 518, 656
Birmingham Daily Post, 455
birth control, 406, 660
Bishop, James, 101
Bishop, John, 157-9
Bishopsgate Police Station, 299, 301, 311
Black, James, 614
Black Friday financial crisis (11 May 1866), 24
Black Museum *see* Crime Museum, New Scotland Yard
Blackburn, Lancashire, 162
blackmail of homosexuals, 443-5
Blackwell, Dr. Frederick, 302-4
Blackwood's Magazine: serialises Anderson's memoirs, 500-2, 502-3
Blair, Gustave, 604

Blandford, Dr. George Fielding, 454
bloodhounds, 162-3, 327
Bloody Sunday demonstration (13 November 1887), 253-8, 259, 310
blotchy-faced man, 326
Blue Posts Tavern, Rupert Street: illegal betting at, 98-9
Blunden, P.C. William, 255
Boans, P.C. Patrick, 143
bodysnatching, 156-9, 621; *see also* Dunecht grave robbery case
Boer War (1899-1902), 478, 674
Boers, 464, 465-6
Boivin, Joseph, 129
bombs and bomb-making *see* Brooklyn dynamite school; dynamite campaign (1881-85); 'infernal machines'
Bond, Inspector (of V Division), 141-2
Bond, Dr. Thomas: Harley Street murder case, 109; Frederick Gold case, 131; John Broome Tower case, 211, 214, 216; over-worked, 333; superseded as A Division police surgeon, 328-30, 333; examines Dolly Williamson, 264; dispute with Warren, 329-33; post mortem on Whitehall torso, 362; resignation (4 October 1888), 333; new medico-legal role, 333-5, 352; opinion sought on Ripper murders, 335; at Miller's Court, 328; Kelly autopsy notes, 335-7; profile of Whitechapel Murderer, 337-9; Catherine Mylett case, 348, 349; Alice McKenzie case, 352-3; certifies death of Dolly Williamson, 360; evidence to Committee of Enquiry into Police Superannuation (August 1889), 364; Phoebe Hogg case, 375; documents missing from official files, 340-1, 650-1; Augusta Dawes case, 448
Boness, Sarah, 34
boorag (peat), 9
boot industry, in East End, 277
Booth, Charles: Board of Statistical Inquiry, 274; *Inquiry into the Life and Labour of the People in London*, 269
Booth, William Bramwell, 418
Bordeaux, 101
Borer, P.C., 575
Boulton, Stella (Ernest Boulton) *see* Fanny and Stella
Bovill, Lord Chief Justice, 28
Bow Cemetery, 261
Bow Infirmary Asylum, 296

Index

Bow Lane police station, 181
Bow Street Magistrates' Court, hearings: Rev. Monck, 2; James Smith, 53; Daniel Good, 76; Met detectives, 89; William Virtue, 98; Clement Allen, 100; Captain Tempest, 115; Michael Davitt, 117; Hawkins and Green, 166; Captain Archer, 205; Park Club gambling case, 209; West End rioters, 233; Burns and Cunninghame Graham, 258–9; Edward Pinter, 387; Florence Osborne, 394; abduction of Eliza Armstrong case, 418; Fanny and Stella, 421–3; Earl of Euston libel case, 432–3; Leonard Harper, 456, 457; Jameson and his men, 470–1, 472
Bow Street police station, 58, 421
Bow Street Runners, 605
Bowden, Frank, 486
Bower, Sarah and Isabella, 541
Bowyer, Thomas, 321–2, 327
Boxer, Major-General Edward, 199
Boylston Bank robbery, Boston (1869), 489, 490
Boys' Brigade, 512
Brabazon, Reginald, 539
Brace, David, 210
Brace, Jim, 210
Brackenbury, Colonel Henry, 223
Braddick, Sergeant John, 77
Bradford, Detective Sergeant, 245
Bradford, Sir Edward: education and military career, 368; Indian Civil Service, 368; loses arm to tigress, 368–9, 655–6; appointed Commissioner of Police, 367–8, 369; press reaction to appointment, 369–70; easy-going nature, 252; commends Swanson, 396; requests briefing on Cutbush, 565; and Bond's profiling report, 340; letter from Cuffe appreciating Swanson and Froest, 477–8; on Divisional Surgeons' post mortem fees, 654; and Anderson's retirement, 498; and Coronation, 503–4, 505; retires from police, 508; assessment of tenure, 508; life in retirement and death, 674
Bradlaugh, Charles, 406, 660
Bradshaw, Sergeant, 399, 401
Bradstock, Inspector Daniel, 51–3
Brady, Joe, 186, 187, 190–1, 192

Brady, Inspector Thomas, 82–3
Brannan, Hannah, 324–5
Bray, Charles, 543, 549, 680
Bray, Lucy, 680
Brembridge, Mr. (Secretary of Pharmaceutical Society), 85
Brennan, Thomas, 621
Brett, Mr. Justice, 128–9
Brett, Sergeant Charles, 41–2, 230
Brewer (art gallery porter), 68–9
Brewers Quay, London Bridge: arson attack (1883), 206, 208
Brick Lane, 157, 269, 640
Bricklayer's Arms, Settles Street, 299–300
Bridge, Sir John, 396, 470–1, 476, 659
Bridge Street police station, 196
Brien, Colour Sergeant Thomas, 452
Briggs, Thomas, 127
Brighton railway murder (1881) *see* Mapleton, Percy Lefroy
Britannia (public house), Commercial Street, 326
British Brothers League (anti-immigration group), 635
British Lion (public house), Plaistow, 62
British Medical Journal, 333
British South Africa Company, 460, 461–2, 465
Brittain, Sarah, 96
Broadmoor Asylum, 455, 564, 565, 682
Brockwell (Kingston blacksmith), 142
Brompton Cemetery, 79, 377
Brooklyn (female impersonator), 72
Brooklyn dynamite school, 180, 183
Broome, John, 212, 214
Broome Tower, John: family background, 212; last known movements, 213–14; body and belongings discovered, 209–10; post mortem, 211; murder investigation, 212, 215; burial and inquest, 214; reward offered, 215; money troubles and suicide theory, 215–16, 217; inquest verdict questioned, 216; false murder confession, 216–17
brothels: child, 324, 411–18; Cleveland Street, 424–6, 435–6; Molly Houses, 420; white slave trade, 324–5, 414–16
Brown, Mr. (Three Bridges Station Master), 132
Brown, P.C. Alex, 53
Brown, Ann, 129
Brown, Dr. Campbell, 201

Brown, Charles, 362
Brown, Dr. Frederick Gordon: honorary medical officer to Morley House, 544, 548, 549; Catherine Eddowes case, 307, 318; at Miller's Court, 328; Alice McKenzie case, 352
Brown, Rev. J. B., 128
Brown, James, 300
Brown, Jane, 75–6
Brown, Rhoda, 129
Brown, Sergeant William, 375
Brownfield, Dr. Matthew, 347–8
Bruce, Alexander Carmichael, 224, 268, 361
Buchanan Street railway station, Glasgow: bomb attack (1883), 196
Buckland, Charles, 258–9
Buck's Row, 283
Budgen, George, 362
Buenos Aires, 101
buggery *see* sodomy
Bull, Mr. (Deputy Governor of Lewes Gaol), 148
Bullard, Charles ('Piano Charley'), 100, 488–9, 490, 610
Buller's Lodging House, Bishopsgate, 323, 325
Bulling, Tom, 314, 317
Burden, I. Townsend, 472, 473–4, 479
Burdett-Coutts, Angela, 620
Burgdorf, Frederick, 370–1
Burke, Ricard O'Sullivan, 43, 44, 115–16, 230
Burke, Thomas, 183–6, 190
Burke, William and William Hare, 156–7
Burnett, James, 174
Burns, James, 3, 589
Burns, John: Pall Mall riots, 232, 233; Bloody Sunday, 255; committal hearing, 258–9; convicted of unlawful assembly, 261–2; press reaction, 263–4
Burr, Mr. (of Keighley), 114
Burton, Harry, 229
Busain, Inspector, 74
Bussy, Frederick Moir, 192–3
Butcher, Detective Chief Inspector James, 117, 262, 364, 387–8
Butcher, Susan, 76
Butcher's Row, Aldgate, 557, 583
Butler, Josephine, 415
Butt, Mr. (Divisional Police Surgeon), 330
Byass, Dr. (of Cuckfield), 131

Byfield, Sergeant James, 299
Byrne, Frank, 191
Byrne, Mary Ann, 191–2
Byrne, William, 340

Cadosch, Albert, 287, 294, 641–2
Caffrey, Thomas, 187, 190
Cairo, 176, 209
Caithness Constabulary, 8
Caithness Courier, 513, 593
Calcraft, William, 43, 46
Callaghan, Mr. E. (informant), 356–7
Callaghan, Mary, 344
Callan, Thomas, 250
Callana, Ellen, 379
Cambria (tug), 469
Camden Villas, Kennington, 205, 258
Caminada, Jerome, 614
Campbell, George, 108
Campbell, Inspector William, 410
Campbell Brown, Dr. (of Liverpool), 201
Cape Colony, 462, 478
Captain George (Charles Hibbert), 90–1, 609
Carden, Sir Robert (Judge), 59, 91
Carey, James: nationalism, 186; arrested, 187; turns Queen's Evidence, 189–91, 192; fails to identify Mary Ann Byrne, 191; assassinated, 193–4
Carney, Detective John, 58–9
Carr, John, 90–1
Carter, A. C. R., *Let Me Tell You*, 672
Case, William, 446
Casey, Joseph, 43, 44
Casey, William Michael, 442
Cassein (Malay seaman), 246
Cassell's Saturday Journal, 584
Castle Alley, 351–2
Castlehill Quarries, Thurso, 513
Castleton, Kate, 492
Casual Ward, Shoe Lane, 298
Caterham Asylum, 563–4
Cathcart Road, Wallington, 132, 136
Catherine Court, 24, 26, 595; Mrs. Nunn assaulted in, 27–8
Cavanagh, Timothy, 50; on beat patrols, 53–4
Cavendish, Lord Frederick, 183–6, 190
Cavendish Hotel, Jermyn Street, 174–5, 623
Centennial Park, Sydney, 123
Central Criminal Court *see* Old Bailey trials
Central News Agency, 314, 315, 551

Index

Central Police Institute, 498–9
Central Search Association, 460
cesspits, 19–20
Chambers, Sir Thomas, 428
Champion, Henry Hyde, 232, 233
Chandler, Inspector Joseph, 280–2, 285
Chapman, Annie Elizabeth (*née* Smith): background, 285–6, 641; marriage and children, 285, 641; casual prostitution, 286; movements on night of death, 286–7; possible witness sightings, 286–7; body discovered, 280; wounds, 280–2, 293–4; murder scene, 282; murder investigation, 282, 284; description circulated, 284; body identified, 284–5; inquest, 287, 292, 294–5, 297; funeral and burial, 295; linked to Whitechapel murder series, 293–4; Jews blamed for murder, 279; in Macnaghten memorandum, 569
Chapman, Joe, 489, 490
Chapman, John, 285, 286, 641
Chapman, Ruth *see* Smith, Ruth Chapman
Chapman, P.C. William, 195
Charing Cross Hospital, 259, 260
Charing Cross railway station: failed bombing (1884), 217–18
Charing Cross Road, 23
Charing Cross underground station: bomb explosion (1883), 207–8
Charley Project (missing persons database), 604
Chartered Company *see* British South Africa Company
Chatsworth House, 69, 673
Cheadle, James ('Captain Tempest'), 114–15
Cheadle, Dr. Walter, 114–15
Chesterfield, Ambrosezina Lilian, 105
Chicago Daily News, 493
child kidnapping, 63–6, 604
child prostitution, 324, 411–18
Childe, Edgar, 381–2, 383
Childers, Hugh, 233, 237, 239
Childers, John Walbanke, 233
Chisholm, Inspector (of Thames Division), 469
cholera epidemics, 20
Christ Church, Spitalfields, 269, 287, 345
Christie, Manson and Woods (auction house), 70, 604, 672
Church Passage, 305, 306, 307, 380, 548
Churchill, Winston, 501–3
C.I.D. *see* Criminal Investigation Department
City Bank, Great Eastern Street, 244, 381, 382
City of London, coronership (1884), 289–91
City of London Cemetery at Manor Park, 283, 313
City of London Infirmary, Bow Road, 559–60
City of London Police: assaults on, 39; deployment of officers during Ripper scare, 307; documents lost, 550; letters received from Jack the Ripper, 317; Metropolitan Police, relations and proposed amalgamation with, 30, 33, 39–41, 599; and Morley House, 542, 543, 544, 548; photography, mortuary, 308; riot and crowd control, 39–40; Ripper investigation, liaison with Metropolitan Police, 318, 555; strength, 39; surveillance of 'Kosminski', 550–1, 552–5, 557, 583
City of London Union Workhouse, Homerton, 559
City Police suspect *see* 'Kosminski'
City Press, The (newspaper), 556
City Summons Court, 575
Clan na Gael, 179–80, 224, 624
Clarendon Villas, Hove, 538–9, 655
Clark, P.C. (A Division), 220
Clark, P.C. George, 619
Clark, Percy, 354
Clark, Senator W. A., 495
Clarke, Edward, 288
Clarke, G. H. (police candidate), 600
Clarke, Chief Inspector George: at A Division (Whitehall), 50; joins Detective Department, 78; arrests Davitt, 116; embroiled in Turf Fraud scandal, 89–90, 91
Clarke, Richard, 179
Clark's Yard, Poplar High Street, 347
Clayton, Annie, 132, 136
Clayton, Thomas, 132
Cleary, John, 353–4
Clements, Frances Miriam, 411
Clerkenwell Green, 43, 254
Clerkenwell Police Court, 60–1, 246, 410, 411
Clerkenwell Prison bombing (1867), 43–4, 46, 179, 230

711

Cleveland Street scandal (1889): male brothel, 424–6; police investigation, 425–8, 430–2; prominent aristocrats named, 427, 429, 437; conviction of messenger boys, 428–9; press reactions, 429–30, 431; public revelations, 432–3; aftermath, 433–6; involvement of Prince Albert Victor, 434; Ernest Parke libel trial, 434–6; later revelations from Herbert Ames, 437
Cliburn, Robert, 444–5
Cliff House School, St. Margaret's-at-Cliffe, 541
Clipperton, Captain Robert, 181
Cloak Lane Police Station, 392
Cloud, Thomas, 34
Cochrane, Hugh, 161
Cock, P.C. Nicholas, 140
Cocks, Captain James, 246–8
Coercion Act (1881), 182, 183
Cogden, Ernest, 213, 214, 216
Cohen, Aaron Davis (aka David Cohen), 580–2, 583
Cohen, Jacob, 576
Cohen, Simon: refuge for Jewish immigrants, 271–2
Cole, P.C. George: murdered on duty, 143, 480
Cole, Rev. T. H., 148, 150
Cole, P.C. William, 227, 228
Colegrove, John, 85
Coleman (witness to Play House Yard explosion), 196
Coles, Frances, 378–80, 570–1, 583
Colicott (or Colocott), John Edwin, 567
Collard, Inspector Edward, 307, 308
Collier, George, 292
Collier, James, 170, 171
Collingbourn, Mr. (Wandsworth pawnbroker), 73
Collins, Detective Sergeant Charles, 506–7, 508
Collins, Jerome, 180
Colney Hatch Lunatic Asylum: design and construction, 561–2; building costs, 562; opening, 562; patient admissions, 563; running costs, 564; medical neglect and patient deaths, 564, 683; criminal lunatic patients, 564–5; medical entry examinations, 565, 683–4; 'Kosminski' admitted, 565; Aaron Kosminski at, 576; David Cohen's case notes, 581–2
Colney Hatch railway station, 561, 682

Colomban, Rev. Father, 343
Combe, Elizabeth, 418
Commercial Street, 269, 280, 327, 379
Commercial Street Police Station, 309, 322, 346, 354
Commercial Tavern, West India Dock Road, 656
Commissionaires, Strand, 355
Committee of Enquiry into Police Superannuation (August 1889), 364
common lodging houses *see* lodging houses
Compton, Arthur John, 442
Concord State Penitentiary, Massachusetts, 100, 490
Condon, Edward O'Meagher, 43
confrontation identification, 355, 545–6, 548
Connelly, Francis, 254
Connelly, Mary Ann ('Pearly Poll'), 602, 640, 685
Contemporary Review, 497
convalescent homes, 539; *see also* Morley House Convalescent Home
Conway, Kate *see* Eddowes, Catherine
Conway, Thomas, 312–13
Cooke, Mr. (Marylebone magistrate), 418
Cooney's Lodging House, 298, 299, 312, 644
Cooper, Dr. Herbert, 374
Cooper, Mary: murder of, 162–3, 621
Copenhagen police, 206–7
Corbould, Alfred, 447, 453; sketch of Reginald Saunderson, 454
Cornish, Joseph, 208
Coronation of Edward VII (1902), 503–5
Coroners' Act (1887): local jurisdiction of coroner, 291–2
Cotopaxi (steamer), 114
Counter Revolutionary Secret Service Department *see* Secret Service Department
Countess of Bective jewellery heist (1880), 110–14, 151
Courvoisier, François, 73, 360, 606
Cousins, Samuel, 70
Coventry, Captain C. J., 467, 472, 476
Cowe, James, 168, 170
Cowell, P.C. Samuel, 181
Cowen, Mr. (of *New York Herald*), 354
Cowie, Frederick, 174
Cox, P.C., 227, 228
Cox, Major-General George, 466

Cox, Detective Inspector Henry: life, 681; surveillance of Ripper suspect, 551, 552–5, 583; opinions on Jack the Ripper, 551, 555; shadows George Johnson, 681
Cox, Mary Ann, 326
Cox, Thomas, 296
Coxhead, Rev. John James, 102
Craighill, Lord, 170, 240–1
Crawford, Alexander Lindsay, 25th Earl of Crawford and 8th Earl of Balcarres, 155–6, 174; *see also* Dunecht grave robbery case
Crawford, James Lindsay, 26th Earl of Crawford and 9th Earl of Balcarres, 159, 166, 202, 621
Crawford, Margaret, Countess of, 159–60
Cream, Dr. Thomas Neill, 480
Creber, Lillian, 449
Creek, Henry, 139
Crime Monthly (TV programme), 529
Crime Museum, New Scotland Yard: 'Dear Boss' letter, 521; Edward Oxford's pistol, 594; Harley Street murder mystery memorabilia, 612; *Lighter Side of My Official Life, The* (Swanson's copy), 530, 533, 534; Sandell's papers, 524; sketch of Lefroy, 150; relaunch of Museum (2006), 530; Crime Museum Uncovered exhibition (2015–16), 612
crime statistics, 30, 33, 56–7
Criminal Investigation Department (C.I.D.): created, 93–5; Swanson appointed to, 98; and Fenian Office, 202–3; achievements under Howard Vincent, 221–2; position of Director abolished, 222; Williamson promoted first Chief Constable, 264; Macnaghten promoted Chief Constable, 377; departure of senior officers, 474–5, 480–2; Swanson promoted Superintendent, 475; and upward mobility, 480, 671; *see also* Department of Crime; Detective Department
Criminal Law Amendment Bill (1885): initial framing, 415; lack of progress, 411–12, 415; and Armstrong case, 416–19; Labouchère Amendment (Section 11), 420; becomes Act, 416; repealed, 662
criminal profiling, 337–9

criminal registers, 58, 602
crimps (conmen), 271
Crippen, Dr. Hawley Harvey, 436, 507
Cronjé, Piet, 466
Cross, Catherine, 129
Cross, Richard (Home Secretary), 90, 94
Crossfield Road, Hampstead, 374, 375
Crossingham's Lodging House, Dorset Street, 284–5, 286
Crossness pumping station, 20
Crow, Alfred, 640
Croydon: Surrey Assizes, 128
Crundall, Harold, 549
Crundall, Sean, 549
Crundall, Sir William, 543, 549, 681
Crunden, John, 194–5
Cuckfield, 138
Cuffe, Hamilton: and Cleveland Street scandal, 430, 431, 434, 437; and Florence Osborne case, 392–4; struck down with influenza, 455; praises Swanson and Froest, 477–8
Cuffe, Sir Charles *see* Graham, Lochiel Lorimer
Cumming, Robert, 112–13
Cunningham (murdered youth), 158
Cunningham, James Gilbert, 227, 228–9
Cunninghame Graham, Robert: Bloody Sunday, 255, 259; committal hearing, 258–9; pallbearer at Linnell's funeral, 261; convicted of unlawful assembly, 261–2; press reaction, 263–4; Eayres affair, 262; later political career and death, 635
Curley, Daniel, 186, 190
Curran, Mr. (magistrate), 189
Currie (Army Officer), 105
Curtis, Captain (of the Dragoons), 368–9
Curtis-Bennett, Henry, 453
Cutbush, Superintendent Charles, 220, 331, 364, 377, 568, 684
Cutbush, Thomas: accused of Jack the Ripper murders, 565; rebuttal by Macnaghten, 567–8; not related to Superintendent Cutbush, 684
Cuthbert, Inspector James, 233
cutlass training, 42
Cutlers' Company, 96, 97, 100

Dagnell (shopboy), 73, 74
Daily Gazette for Middlesbrough, 138–9
Daily Mail, 474
Daily News, 36–7, 44, 161, 543–6, 556–7

Index

Daily Telegraph: classified advertisements, 26–7; publishes sketch and description of Lefroy, 135, 137, 150, 618; publishes J. T. Hutchinson letter, 152; settles libel case, 381; on departure of senior officers from C.I.D., 481–2; offered viewing of Swanson marginalia, 526; feature on Ripper centenary, 526; publishes marginalia story, 527; letters from Fido and Goodman, 527–8
Dalhousie, Fox Maule Ramsay, 11th Earl of, 40
Dalhousie, John Ramsay, 13th Earl of, 413
Dalton, Mr. (Park Club secretary), 205, 208–9
Dam, Harry, 647
Darby, Ruth, 62, 603
'Darkie' (lodging house watchman), 345
Daukes, Samuel, 562
Davey, P.C. Frederick, 210
Davidson, Detective Inspector (of City Police), 391
Davidson, Henry, 452
Davies, Dr. Christopher: first report on marginalia, 531–3, 535–6; second report, 536
Davies, Thomas, 576
Davis (or Davies) (supposed husband of Mary Kelly), 324
Davis, Eliza, 72
Davis, James, 90, 93
Davis, John, 280, 287
Davison, Dr. Kaye Rashell, 517
Davitt, Bridget, 558
Davitt, Michael, 115–17, 614; denounces Phoenix Park murders, 185–6
Dawes (workboy), 196
Dawes, Augusta: background, 448–9, 666; murdered, 446–8, 583; as victim of Jack the Ripper, 447; post mortem, 448; inquest, 453–4; funeral and burial, 454
Dawes, Fredericka, 666
De Beers Company, 460, 465
de Gallo, Adolphe, 433, 434
de Goncourt, Comtesse Marie Cecile, 79, 80–1, 87–8, 607
Deakin, John, 242–3
Deakin, William, 242–4
'Dear Boss' letter, 314–17, 521, 647
Deasy, Timothy, 41–2, 230

Debtors Act (1869), 38
Delaney, Patrick, 190
Denman, Mr. Justice, 394–5
Denmark: executions in, 208
Denning, Inspector Eleazar, 50, 591
Dennis, Florence, 451
Department of Crime, 90, 93–4; *see also* Criminal Investigation Department; Detective Department
Derby, Lord, 45
Derbyshire Courier, 209
Desmond, Timothy, 44, 46
Detective, The (penny-dreadful), 28
Detective Department: formed, 72, 77–8; officers interviewed by Dickens, 606; Swanson joins, 79; and Turf Fraud scandal, 81–2, 88–90; reorganised, 90, 92–5, 609; Trial of the Detectives, 91–2; *see also* Criminal Investigation Department; Department of Crime
Devonshire, Andrew Cavendish, 11th Duke of, 673
Devonshire, Georgiana, Duchess of, 69
Devonshire, William Cavendish, 5th Duke of, 69
Dick, Robert, 8
Dickens, Charles: interest in police detectives, 606; *Oliver Twist*, 72, 600
Dickenson, John, 549–50
Dicketts, Herbert, 177
Dickinson, Katherine, 127–9, 617
Diemschitz, Louis, 301–2
Dillon, Colonel (Chief Constable of Hertfordshire), 222
Disraeli, Benjamin, 45
dissection of bodies, 156, 159
DNA testing, 577–8
Docherty's School, Thurso, 15–16
Doctors' Commons (society of lawyers), 242, 633
Dodd, Chief Inspector (of X Division), 225
dog muzzling, 239, 575
Dolman, Mr. (Jermyn Street solicitor), 204
Don, Sergeant John, 379
Donald, Duncan, 11
Donner, Gerald, 651
Donovan, Timothy, 284–5, 286
'Don't take sweets from a stranger' (adage), 603
Doornkop, South Africa, 466
Dorset Street, Spitalfields: lodging houses, 270, 284–5, 286, 292,

378–9; Miller's Court, 321–2, 326–8; reputation, 322–3
Douglas, Joseph, 66, 604
Dover, 476, 542, 549
Dowdell, Detective Sergeant John, 112
Dowgate School, Bermondsey, 312
Dowling, Michael, 261
Dowty, P.C. (of N Division), 210
Doyle (greengrocer), 136
Doyle, Arthur Conan, 377, 483
Drage, Alice (*née* Goodwin), 212, 214, 629
Drage, Mary Ann, 212, 214
Drage, William, 212, 214
drains and sewers, 20
Dredge, Frederick, 382, 383
Drevar, Captain George: great sea serpent affair, 119–22, 616; invents water-velocipede, 122; sends threatening letters, 118–19; arrested and convicted, 121; paddle boat experiments, 122–3; death in Australia, 123
Drew, Mr. (coroner for West London), 453
Druitt, Ann, 684
Druitt, Montague John, 557, 566, 570, 572, 626, 684
Druitt, William, 684
Drummond, Maurice, 37, 599
Druscovich, Chief Inspector Nathaniel, 81, 84, 88–9, 91, 609
Drysdale, William, 479
Dublin, 84, 188–9, 451, 452; arrest of Davitt, 116; *see also* Phoenix Park murders (1882)
Dublin Castle, 116, 183, 188, 191
Dublin Express, 583
Duchess of Devonshire, The (painting): subject and early history, 69–70; exhibited at Agnew's gallery, 70, 491; theft of, 68–9, 491–2; police investigation, 69, 72, 486, 492; reward offered, 71; false sightings and public interest, 71–2; rumours of painting's whereabouts, 485–6; taken to America and hidden, 486, 493; handover plans, 484, 493–4; returned, 484–5, 494–5; and Gainsborough hat style, 495; sold to J. Pierpont Morgan, 495; displayed at Agnew's, 495; recent history, 673; booklet on theft of painting, 496–7; doubts over authenticity, 672–3
Duchess of Edinburgh's jewellery theft (1890), 370–2
Dudley, Frederica, 666
Duff, R. W., 174
Duffus, Alexander, 172
Duggan, Michael, 32
Duke's Place, Aldgate, 277
Dukes, Dr. William, 328
Dunecht grave robbery case: body entombed, 155–6; body stolen, 156, 159–60; aromas from vault, 163–5, 168; police investigations, 160–2; wild rumours, 161–2; Nabob letters, 164–6, 167, 170; reward offered, 166; arrests, 166–7; Soutar's version of theft, 167–8; body recovered, 168–9; re-interment at Haigh Hall, 169–70, 174; Soutar tried and convicted, 170; message in bottle hoax, 170–1; reward claimed, 171–2
Dunecht House: chapel and mausoleum, 155–6, 163–5, 169; search of house and estate, 160, 161; clairvoyant meeting at, 163; memorial cross, 174
dung: in streets, 21
Dunlop, William, 473, 474
Dunscombe, Rev. Mr., 313
Dupré, Dr. August, 199, 384, 385–6
Durness Street, Thurso, 6, 9, 513, 591
Dutfield, Arthur, 302
Dutfield's Yard, 301–2
Dutton, Thomas, 139, 146–7, 148
Dwarf (newspaper), 389
Dyer, Alfred, *The European Slave Trade in English Girls*, 324, 414–15
Dyer, Amelia, 620
dynamite campaign (1881–85), 180–3, 195–9, 201–4, 207–8, 217–20, 224–30
Dyson, Sergeant (of F Division), 451, 452–3

Earl family (of Green Lanes), 213, 214, 216, 629
East End: coroner districts, 291–2, 343; industry and employment, 270, 276–8; Jewish immigration, 271–9, 575; living conditions, 269–70, 277–8; population, 269, 275; poverty, 269–71; prostitution, 270–1; railway and Underground, 269
East End Dwelling Company, 274
East London Cemetery, Plaistow, 313–14, 352, 358, 380
East London Observer, 279
East London Railway, 269

Index

East London Union Workhouse, Homerton, 559
East Middlesex coronership elections (1886), 291, 292
Eastcote school, Hampton Wick, 449–50, 451
eating houses, 26
Eaton, Susanna, 541
Eayres, A. W., 262
Eddowes, Catherine: background and early life, 312; relationship with Thomas Conway, 312, 313; birth of children, 312; at Cooney's Lodging House, 298, 312; hop-picking in Kent, 298; last known movements, 298–9; arrested for drunkenness, 299; released, 301; gives false name to police, 301, 682; witness sightings, 305–6, 548; body discovered, 306–7; wounds and mutilations, 307; at Golden Lane Mortuary, 308; possessions, 308; apron, 308–9, 311, 556; body identified, 311–12; funeral procession and burial, 313; kidney supposedly removed from, 318; in Macnaghten memorandum, 569; shawl purportedly worn by, 577–8
Eddowes, Catherine (*née* Evans; Catherine's mother), 312
Eddowes, Elizabeth (Catherine's aunt), 312
Eddowes, George (Catherine's father), 312
Eddowes, William (Catherine's uncle), 312
Ede, Thomas, 296
Edinburgh, 176, 370, 371–2
Edinburgh High Court of Justiciary, 170, 240–1, 372
Edinburgh Police, 6
Education Act (1872), 10
Edward VII, King (*earlier* Prince of Wales): wedding procession mobbed, 39–40; opens Crossness pumping station, 20; opens Royal Albert Hall, 22; visits Thurso (1876), 512; death threat to, 194; opens Working Lads' Institute, 643; and Cleveland Street scandal, 431, 434; urges Monro not to resign commissionership, 366; and Royal Baccarat Scandal (1890), 628; assassination attempt in Brussels (1900), 504; announces death of Queen Victoria, 484; police planning for Coronation, 503–4; postponement of ceremony, 504; operation to remove stomach abscess, 504; Coronation, 504–5; congratulates police and approves issue of Coronation medals, 505; bestows knighthood on Anderson, 499
Edward VII Coronation Medal, 505
Edwards, Jeff, 524, 678
Edwards, Russell, *Naming Jack the Ripper*, 577
Edwin, Catherine, 606
Egypt, 176, 234, 235–7
'Elephant Man' (Joseph Merrick), 618
Elkins (betting man at Blue Posts Tavern), 98–9
Elliot, Hugh, 390, 391
Elliott, 'Little' Joe, 489, 490, 491, 492–3, 494
Ellis, Albert, 136
Ellis, Sir John Whittaker, 318–19
Ellis, William, 561
Ellis, Wynn: art collection, 69–70, 672
Ellisdon, Inspector Ernest, 639
Elms, Walter, 204
Englehart, Mr. (friend of Mrs. Hargreaves), 388, 389
Ericsson, Gustaf and Beata, 297
Etruria (steamer), 484, 485
Euston, Earl of (Henry James Fitzroy): at Cleveland Street brothel, 427, 437; alleged relations with Jack Saul, 435–6; named in the press, 432; sues for libel, 432–3, 434–6; targeted by blackmailers, 444
Evans, Alfred, 196
Evans, David, 392–4
Evans, Edwin, 247, 248
Evans, Frederick, 124
Evans, George de Lacy, 40
Evans, John, 286
Evans, Stewart, 533–4, 535
Eve, Frederick, 82
Evening Post, 360
Evening Telegraph, 122, 550
Ewer Street, Borough, 53–4
executions: Manchester Martyrs, 42–3; Michael Barrett, 46; Daniel Good, 76–7; Percy Lefroy, 148–50; Bishop and Williams, 159; Timothy Kelly, 192–3; Patrick O'Donnell, 194; Mary Pearcey, 376–7; as public events, 127; in Denmark, 208
Exploring Company Ltd, 460
Explosives Act (1875), 199

Index

Extra-Mural Cemetery, Brighton, 135

Fagan, Michael, 190
Fagan, William, 116
Fairchild, Frederick, 188
Fairfax, Malcolm *see* Graham, Lochiel Lorimer
Fairfax, Norman, 623
Fanny and Stella (cross-dressers), 421–3
Farmer, Annie, 344–6, 353, 527, 560, 651
Farndale, Joseph (Chief Constable of Birmingham), 222
Farnworth, William, 152, 616
Farr, Dr. George Frederick, 330, 333, 649–50
Farre, Frederick, 329, 330
Farson, Daniel, 526, 566
Farson's Guide to the British (TV programme), 566
Feasdale (solicitors), 102–3
Feilding, Colonel William, 45, 46
Felix, Elizabeth, 325
Fenian Office, 202–3
Fenians: formed, 41; raids (1866), 41; Skirmishers, 180–1; Manchester jailbreak and trial, 41–3, 181, 230; plot to kidnap Queen Victoria, 42; Clerkenwell Prison bombing, 43–4, 46, 179, 230; and Secret Service Department, 45, 46, 202; arms smuggling, 43, 115–16; dynamite campaign (1881–85), 180–3, 195–9, 201–4, 207–8, 217–20, 224–30; and Jubilee assassination plot, 249–51; *see also* Davitt, Michael; Fenian Office; Special Irish Branch
Fenwick, Collingwood, 650
Ferrari, Carlo, 158
Ferrett, Superintendent, 468
Fez, SS, 378, 379
Fiddymont, Mrs., 295
Fido, Martin, 526, 527–8, 529, 574–5, 582
Field, Inspector, 72, 606
Field, Mr. Justice, 432
Fielding, Henry, 605
Fingerprint Bureau, 507–8
fingerprinting, 499, 506–8
firearms: carried by burglars, 140; Fenian smuggling, 43, 115–16; Met officers armed, 143–4
First Home Rule Bill (1886), 239
First World War: origins, 478

Fish, William, 162
Fisher, Chief Superintendent (of A Division), 374
Fiske, John Safford, 423
Fitch (homosexual solicitor), 442
Fitzroy Square raid, London (12 August 1894), 438–40; list of men arrested, 440–1
fixed-point system, 56
flagstone industry, Caithness, 7, 513
Fleming, John, 224
Fleming, Joseph, 324
Fletcher, Assistant Judge, 411
Fletcher, Mr. (reporter), 354
Flowedean, William, 442
Flower and Dean Street, Whitechapel, 270, 351; lodging houses, 297, 298, 299, 312, 644
Flowers, Mr. (magistrate), 99, 421–2
Foam (steamship), 391
fog pollution, 21
Foley, Captain Cyril, 467
Forbes Winslow, Lyttleton *see* Winslow, Dr. L. Forbes
Ford (criminal associate of Henry Pollard), 101
Ford, Major (Majendie's assistant), 199, 207–8, 225–6, 229
Foreman, T. G., 446
Forensic Science Service, 531
Forster, William, 183
Forsyth, Kate, 449
Foster, Superintendent Alfred: and Mrs. Nunn assault case, 28; interviews John Kelly, 311–12; and Catherine Eddowes's funeral, 313; and Florence Osborne case, 392, 394
Foster, Elizabeth, Lady, 69, 672
Foster, Fred, 72
Fowler, Francis, 361
France: extradition treaty with Britain, 428
Francis, Sergeant David, 248
Francis, Jacob *see* Benson, Henry
Franklin, Margaret, 351
Franks, William, 129, 617
Fraser, Sir James, 39, 307, 318, 555
Freeman, Detective Sergeant, 396, 402
Freeman, Reverend Allan, 135
Freemasons' Hall, London, 457–8
Frewer, Robert, 542–3
Froest, Superintendent Frank: Pinchin Street murder, 354; Edward Pinter case, 384–5; Emily Smith case, 396, 400; Benjamin Judge case, 408–9;

escorts Jameson troopers to London, 468; Burden jewels case, 472–3; *Duchess of Devonshire* theft case, 494; praised by Cuffe, 477–8; as new school officer, 482; promoted Superintendent, 509, 658
Froggatt, Edward, 89, 91, 609
From Constable to Commissioner (Smith), 500–1
'From Hell' letter, 317–18
Frost, Robert Percival, 265
Fullagar, John, 289
Fullagar, Lewis Green, 288, 642
Fulton, Forrest, 288

Gadsden, Tryphena, 96
Galton, Sir Francis, 507
gaming, illegal, 205–6, 208–9
Gardiner, P.C. Arthur, 374
Gardner, P.C. William, 73–4
Gartly, Sergeant John, 167
Gascar, Jessie, 104
Geise Distillery, Caithness, 5–6, 590
Geoghegan, Gerald, 100
Geok, William, 442
George, Christopher T., 647
George IV tavern, Commercial Street, 397, 659
George Street, Spitalfields, 270, 325; No. 18, 344, 639; Satchell's Lodging House, 344, 345–6, 640
George Yard, 640, 685
George Yard Buildings, Wentworth Street, 284, 293, 570, 640
Germany: and origins of First World War, 478
Gerrett, Sergeant William, 77
Gerston Distilleries, Caithness, 5, 589–90
Gibraltar, 99, 176, 234, 513
Gibson, Richard, 130
Gibson, William, 129–30
Giffen, Robert, 274
Gigner, Robert, 265
Gilbart-Smith, Dr. Thomas, 268
Gilder, Rose, 506
Giles, Caroline (*later* Tindall), 411
Gill, Charles, 428
Gill, P.C. William, 379
Gillett, Rev. Mr., 459
Gladstone (barque), 187–8, 189
Gladstone, William, 183, 186, 194, 196, 199, 239
Glasgow: bomb attacks (1883), 195–6
Glass, Detective Inspector (of N Division), 212
Gleaves, James, 246, 247, 248
Glengall Road Rope Works: arson attack (1883), 206, 208
Globe (newspaper), 40, 215
Gloucester Citizen, 557
Goatley, Henry, 107
Goddard, Edward, 103–4, 611
Goddard, Henry, 103–4
Goff, P.C. Charles, 72, 77, 606
Gold, Eliza (*née* Eddowes; Catherine's sister), 312
Gold, Frederick Isaac: in London on business, 129; murdered, 129–30; body found in Balcombe tunnel, 130–1, 137; post mortem, 131; inquest, 132–5; funeral and burial, 135; crass joke about, 573
Golden Lane Mortuary, 308, 311, 312, 313
Goldesborough and Co. (Melbourne wool brokers), 114
Golding, Sergeant Robert, 347
Goldney, Beatrix, 389
Good, Daniel, 73–7
Good, Daniel, Jr., 74, 75
Good, Mary ('Old Molly'), 76
Goodfellow, J. W., 124
Goodman, Charles, 258
Goodman, Jonathan, 528
Goodwood Races, 374
Gordon, P.C. (of F Division), 447
Gore House, 22
Gosselin, Major Nicholas, 223
Gothenburg, 297
Goulston Street, 308; writing, 308–11, 556
Gower Street railway station, 451
Gower Street underground station: bomb attack (1885), 224–6
graffito, Goulston Street, 308–11
Graham, Fanny (Frederick Park) *see* Fanny and Stella
Graham, Lochiel Lorimer ('Sir Charles Cuffe'; 'Malcolm Fairfax'), 174–8, 623
Grainger, William Grant, 584
Grant, Inspector (of A Division), 50
Grant, Ulysses S.: visits Thurso, 512
Grantham, P.C. Joseph, 32
Graphic, The, 119–20, 276–7, 297, 491
Gravesend, 468–9; Pope's Head (public house), 296
Gray, William, 382, 383
Great Exhibition (1851), 22, 34
Great Pearl Case (1891–92), 388–95

Index

Great Scotland Yard, 48; origin of name, 31; response to Fenian kidnap plot, 42; headquarters, 50; reorganisation after Turf Fraud scandal, 90, 92–5; and Fenian bomb attack (1884), 219–20; Swanson transferred to Central Office, 258; relations with Home Office, 369–70; *see also* New Scotland Yard
Great Stink (1858), 20
Greek Gipsies, 320
Green, Edwin (fraudster), 166
Green, Edwin (visitor to Westminster Crypt), 227
Green, James, 280
Green, John, 108
Green, Walter, 510
Green Lanes, London, 213–14
Greenacre, Sergeant John, 274
'greeners' (sweatshop workers), 276
Greenham, Chief Inspector George: Harley Street murder mystery, 107; promoted Chief Inspector, 475; and Samuel Kosminski's application for naturalisation, 278; at Williamson's funeral, 361; at Roots's funeral, 377; at consecration of Justicia Lodge, 458; special duties to Royal family, 475; resigns from police, 475; publishes memoirs, 510
Greenwood, James, 85–6, 548
Gregson, William, 597
Grenadier Guards, 226, 255–6, 640
Grenfell, Lieutenant Harold, 467
Grey, Captain Rayleigh, 467, 472, 476
Grieve, John, 372
Griffiths, Major Arthur: sued for libel, 609; on Anderson's Polish Jew theory, 584; *Mysteries of Police and Crime*, 571–2, 574
Grimwood, Eliza, 72, 77, 606
Grosvenor, Lord Robert, 35–6, 599
Grove Cottages, Kennington, 98, 117
Guildhall, City of London, 392–4
Gumprecht, Louis, 640
Gunn, George, 10, 47, 513, 592
Guntrip, Albert, 603
Gustafsdotter, Elisabeth *see* Stride, Elisabeth
guys (effigies on Bonfire Night), 660

Habitual Criminals Act (1869), 58
Hagen, Detective Chief Inspector Charles, 95, 202, 264
Hagerty, Thomas, 58–9
Haigh Hall, Wigan, 155, 169–70, 174
Hailes, Mr. (reporter), 418
Halkirk, Caithness, 5–6
Hall, Dr. Benjamin, 130, 131
Hall, Esther, 346
Hall, Thomas, 442
Halse, Detective Constable Daniel, 307–8, 309
Hammersmith Road letter (19 October 1889), 357, 358
Hammond, Charles: Cleveland Street brothel keeper, 424, 425, 433; relations with Jack Saul, 435; flees to France, 426–7; efforts to extradite, 428; later life, 437
Hampshire Telegraph and Sussex Chronicle, 404
Hampstead mortuary, 376
Hampstead police station, 376
Hampstead Tragedy (1890), 374–7
Hanbury Street, Spitalfields: and Annie Chapman murder, 268, 279–82, 286–7, 292; Jack the Ripper letter sent to, 316
Hanbury Street School, 279
handcuffing of unconvicted prisoners, 560–1
Hands, John, 439
Handslip, Mr. (Metropolitan Police applicant), 249
hangings *see* executions
Hanks, P.C. Luke, 425–6, 427, 428, 433, 663
Hanlon, Joseph, 190
Hannay, Mr. (magistrate), 386, 439–40
Hanwell Asylum, 561, 563, 682
Harcourt, Sir William, 199, 223, 364; Lefroy case, 148, 152; Dunecht grave robbery case, 172; urges creation of Fenian Office, 202
Hardman, Mr. (magistrate), 409
Hardwicke, Dr. (coroner), 109
Hardy, Gathorne, 44, 46
Hare, Superintendent Arthur: and A. W. Eayres mystery, 262; Burden jewels case, 472–3; transferred to Central Office, 475; long-serving, 482; succeeds Swanson as Superintendent, 509
Hare, William and William Burke, 156–7
Hargreaves, Mrs., 388, 389, 394
Hargreaves, Major George, 388, 389, 390, 394
Harkins, Michael, 250

Harlech Castle (ship), 467–8
Harley Street murder mystery (1880), 107–9, 612
Harper, Rev. Henry, 456
Harper, Leonard, 456–7, 458–9
Harris (workhouse inmate), 559–60
Harris, Dr. George, 347
Harris, Harry, 305–6, 578, 583
Harris, Captain William, 37, 50, 55; retirement, 152
Harrison, Mary, 246
Hart, Bella, 57–8
Harvey, Daniel Whittle, 591
Harvey, P.C. James, 305, 306, 307
Harvey, Maria, 326, 649
Harvey, Robert, 15
Haslem, Rev. Mr., 214
Haslip, Dr. George, 639
Hassin (Malay seaman), 246–8
hat styles, ladies, 495
Hathaway, Henry, 575
Hatton Garden police court, 41, 600
Hawkes, Mr. (vestryman), 313
Hawkins, Edwin, 166
Hawkins, Mr. Justice Henry, 194, 229, 436, 445
Hay, Andrew, 113
Hay, Captain William, 33, 34–5, 36, 37
Haycraft and Gilfillan (underwriters), 213, 215–16
Haynes, Captain A. E., *Man-Hunting in the Desert*, 234
Haynes, Inspector John, 77
Hayter, P.C., 74
Headlam, Rev. Stewart, 261
Hearn, Detective Sergeant, 212
Hearn, William, 204–5
Hebbert, Dr. Charles, 260, 328, 335, 348
Helier, Stephen, 85
Helson, Inspector Joseph, 212, 284, 639
Henderson, Chief Constable (of Edinburgh Police), 371
Henderson, Lieutenant-Colonel Sir Edmund: background, 55; as Commissioner of Police, 55–6, 364; and Veiled Lady of Loughton mystery, 66; and creation of Department of Crime, 90, 93; and Fenian dynamite campaign, 218; resignation, 233; succeeded by Warren, 237, 310
Henriques, Jacob, 108
Henry, Edward: background, 499; introduces fingerprinting to Bengal police, 499, 507; appointed Assistant Commissioner (Crime), 499; and Henry Jackson trial, 507; establishes Fingerprint Bureau, 507–8; promoted Commissioner of Police, 508; signs Swanson's Pension Certificate, 509; concern over memoirs by ex-officers, 510
Herschel, Sir William, 507
Hewitt (telegraph boy), 426–7
'H.F.W.' (newspaper correspondent), 317
Hibbert, Charles ('Captain George'), 90–1, 609
Hickey, Ellen, 580
Higgins, Elizabeth, 103, 104
Higgins, Florence *see* Stanhope, Lillian
Higgins, John, 103
Hill, Brian, 524
Hilton, Henry (Chief Constable of Huddersfield Police), 1, 2–3
Hines, Edward ('Pudding'), 58–9
hoax bomb threats, 201–2
Hodges, Charles Clement, 419
Hodgkinson, Sarah Ann, 46
Hogg, Clara, 375–6
Hogg, Frank, 376
Hogg, Phoebe, 374–7
Hogg, Tiggie, 376
Holden, Captain C. C., 467
Holland: brothels in, 325
Holland, Emily, 162
Holland, P.C. Frederick, 306–7
Holland, Henry, 280
Holland and Holland (gun makers), 114, 613
Holland Park Road, Kensington, 446–7
Hollier, William, 451–2
Hollingsworth (workhouse inmate), 559
Holloway Gaol, 387, 394, 395, 419, 453, 454, 457, 458, 476–7
Holmes, Detective Sergeant George, 131–2, 574
Holmes, Dr. Timothy, 330
Holt, Thomas Lyttleton, 599
Home Office: relations with Scotland Yard, 369–70; disclosure rules for civil servants, 342, 498
Home Office files (Whitechapel Murders), 340–1, 650–1
Home Office Forensic Science Laboratory, Birmingham, 529
homosexuality: criminalisation, 420; in West End, 420–1; Fanny and Stella case, 421–3; Fitzroy Square raid, 438–40; and police intelligence-

gathering, 440–3, 445; theft and blackmail, 443–5; *see also* Cleveland Street scandal (1889)
Hooker, William, 204–5
hop-picking in Kent, 298
Hopkins, P.C., 124
Hopkins, Edward, 123
Horsens Correctional Institution, Denmark, 208
horseracing: scams, 80–1
horses, 20–1, 25, 594
Horsfall, Mr. (wool broker), 114
Hosking, Acting Inspector, 392
Hospital Saturday Fund, 539–40, 541, 542–3, 549
Houchin, Dr. Edmund, 576
Houghton, John, 73
House, Robert, *Jack the Ripper and The Case for Scotland Yard's Prime Suspect*, 574
House of Commons, 20, 29, 197, 274–5; bomb explosion (1885), 227–8
Hove Convalescent Home, Adelphi Terrace, 499
Howe, Thomas, 50
Howland, Detective Sergeant William, 131–2
Hoxton forgery case (1891), 381–3
Hoxton police station, 383
Huddersfield, 1, 3
Hudson River Railroad Express robbery (1869), 488
Hughes, Superintendent Samuel, 35–6
Huguenot settlers in East End, 271
Hull Daily Mail, 255–6
Hume, Inspector, 255
Humphreys, Sir John, 214, 216, 291
Hunt (seaman aboard *Lady Douglas*), 247
Hunt, Detective Constable Baxter, 309
Hunt, Detective Constable Frederick, 508
Hurt, Louis, 423
Hutchinson, George, 327
Hutchinson, J. T., 136, 152
Hutt, P.C. George, 301, 311
Hyde Park: protests and demonstrations, 232–3, 253, 254; riots, 35–8
Hyndman, Henry, 232, 233

Ibbetson, Sir Henry Selwyn, 94
Ibex (ship), 189
identification of prisoners, 545, 547–8
'If—' (poem), 460, 478–9

Illustrated London News, 121
Illustrated Police News, 314, 453, 614, 660
'Imbecile asylums', 563–4
Imperial Club, Duke Street, 305, 578
Indépendance Belge (newspaper), 486
'infernal machines' (clockwork and timed explosive devices), 201, 217–18, 219, 229
influenza epidemics (1892, 1895), 455
Ingham, Sir James, 117, 209, 233
Innes, George, 16
inquests: local jurisdiction of coroner, 291–2, 343
International Christian Police Association, 498–9
International Working Men's Educational Club, 300, 301–2, 576
Inverness, 18
Invincibles, the (Irish National Invincibles), 183, 184–7, 189–91, 192–3
Irish Republican Brotherhood, 41, 115, 180, 183; *see also* Fenians
Irish settlers in London, 19, 271
Isaacs, Sir Rufus, 501, 502
Isenschmid, Jacob, 295, 296
Islington burglary gang (1877), 85–6, 548
Islington Gazette, The, 212
Italian boy (murder victim), 158

Jack the Ripper: apron clue, 308–9, 311, 556; bloodhounds employed, 327; centenary books and articles, 526, 529; early possible victims (*see* Smith, Emma; Tabram, Martha); fear and panic inspired by, 314, 326, 555–6; handedness, 568, 572; Jews blamed, 279, 309–10, 500–1; Jill the Ripper theories, 377; later possible victims (*see* Coles, Frances; Farmer, Annie; McKenzie, Alice; Mylett, Catherine); letters/postcard from, 314–18, 357, 358, 521, 647; medical abilities, 294–5, 338–9; *modus operandi*, 294, 338; murder weapon, 339; origin of name, 315, 317; police investigation, 267–8, 282, 284, 307, 318, 319–21, 555; Polish Jew theory, 500–1, 520–1, 576, 584; press coverage, 321, 350; profile, 337–9; suspects and suspect theories, 295–7, 355–7, 570, 620, 626, 664, 686; Swanson's suspect,

381, 520–1, 522, 584–5 (*see also* 'Kosminski'); victim selection, 551–2; victims (*see* Chapman, Annie; Eddowes, Catherine; Kelly, Mary Jane; Nichols, Mary Ann; Stride, Elisabeth); Vigilance Committee established, 318; witness sightings, 287, 305–6, 548

Jack the Ripper: The Definitive Story (TV documentary), 533

Jackson, Harry, 506–7

Jacobs, Joseph, 271

Jacobson (Oxford Street fence), 91

Jacques, Sampson, 418

Jaggers, George, 210, 628

Jamaica, 490

James, Edwin, 491, 492

Jameson, Leander Starr: early life, 462; medical practice at Kimberley, 462; friendship with Cecil Rhodes, 462; wins concessions from Lobengula, 461; as colonial administrator, 464; prepares to invade Transvaal, 464–5; raid, 465–6; surrenders and jailed, 466; returns to London for trial, 466–7, 468–70; arrested by Swanson, 469; formally charged, 470; at Bow Street Magistrates' Court, 470–1, 472; public attitude toward, 471–2; committed for trial, 472; prison sentence, 476; illhealth, 476–7; released on medical grounds, 477; appears before Select Committee, 477; later political career in South Africa, 478; death and burial, 478; immortalised in Kipling's 'If—', 478–9

Jameson Raid (1896): raid, 464–6; list of senior officers involved, 466–7; trial, 476; government enquiry into, 477; aftermath, 478

Jarrett, Rebecca, 418

Jarvis, Detective Chief Inspector Frederick: and arrest of Lefroy, 124–6; escorts Lefroy to Lewes Gaol, 137–8; at committal hearing, 138–9; continuing enquiries, 151; rewarded, 154; at Williamson's funeral, 361; day at the races, 374; at dinner for Monro, 387–8; later career and retirement, 480

Jefferson, Thomas, 451

Jenkinson, Edward: and Phoenix Park murders, 188; replaces Anderson, 223; network of informers, 249; anti-terrorist strategy, 250; lack of communication with Metropolitan Police, 252, 634; removed as spymaster, 252, 253

Jenks, Captain, 205–6, 208–9

Jennings, Thomas, 130

Jennings, William, 130

Jermyn Street, London, 174–5, 177

Jersey, 456–7, 459

Jervois, Colonel Henry, 427, 437

Jewish Chronicle, 272

Jewish Standard, 578–9

Jewry, Mrs. (Harley Street cook), 108

Jews: anti-Semitism, 279, 309–10, 635; blamed for Jack the Ripper murders, 279, 309–10, 500–1; immigrants to London, 271–9, 575; industry and employment, 276–8; naturalisation process, 278–9, 578; pogroms, 271; refuges and shelters, 271–5; schools, 279; Whitechapel community, 275–6, 277–8, 279, 575; *see also* 'Kosminski'; Polish Jew theory

Jews' Free School, Spitalfields, 279

Jill the Ripper theories, 377

Jobson, William, 210

Jocus, Leopold, 91

Johannesburg, 465

John Bull (newspaper), 436

John O'Groat Journal, 6, 12, 513, 593, 615

Johnson, Florence Grace, 567

Johnson, George, 681

Johnson, P.C. Thomas, 82–3

Jones, Jane, 75–6

Jones, Mary, 580

Jones, Richard, 684–5

Jones, Rev. Samuel Flood, 455

Jubilee assassination plot (1887), 249–51

Judge, Benjamin, 408–10

Junior Carlton Club, Pall Mall: bomb blast (1884), 220

Justice, Anne, 44, 46

Justicia Masonic Lodge, 457–8

Kane, Detective Sergeant, 438–9

Kavanagh, Michael, 190

Keeble, Jasper, 642

Kelly, Inspector (of E Division), 225

Kelly, John (Catherine Eddowes's partner), 298–9, 311–12, 313, 644

Kelly, John (Mary Kelly's father), 324

Kelly, Mary Jane: background story, 324, 325; prostitution, 323, 324;

relationship with Joseph Barnett, 323, 325–6, 344; rent arrears at Miller's Court, 322; her fear of Jack the Ripper, 326; movements on night of murder, 326–7, 649; cry of 'Murder!' from Miller's Court, 327; body discovered, 322; murder scene, 328, 338; time of death, 338; crime scene photograph, 328, 569; body removed to mortuary, 328; autopsy notes, 335–7; inquest, 343, 651; funeral procession and burial, 343; reinterred, 651; in Macnaghten memorandum, 569
Kelly, Colonel Thomas J., 41–2, 230
Kelly, Tim, 186, 190, 192–3
Kendrick, John, 409–10
Kennedy, John, 660
Kennington Lane Section House, 48
Kenny, John, 184, 186
Kenny, Patrick, 232
Kensal Green cemetery, 55, 478
Kensington Cemetery, Hanwell, 454
Kensington Mortuary, 447, 449, 454
Kensington murder (1894), 446–55
Kent, Constance, 78
Kent, Francis, 78
Kent, James, 280
Kentish Town police station, 59, 376
Keppoch Hill Bridge, Glasgow: failed bombing (1883), 195–6
Kerley, Detective Sergeant Frederick, 421
Kerrison, P.C., 142
Kew, William, 345
Keyler, Mr. and Mrs. (of Miller's Court)., 327
kidnapping, child, 63–6, 604
Kidney, Michael, 298
Killeen, Dr. Timothy, 640
Kilmainham courthouse, 189
Kimberley, South Africa, 462
Kincaid-Smith, Lieutenant Kenneth, 467
King, Inspector George, 107
King Lud (public house), Ludgate Circus, 354, 402
King Street, 22, 23, 51
King Street Fire Station, 22, 594–5
King Street police station, 50–3, 57, 126–7, 137, 191, 197, 371
King Street Section House, 51
King's Arms (public house), Mayfair, 473
King's College School of Anatomy, Strand, 157–7, 159

King's Cross railway station, 18–19
King's Cross underground station: bomb attack (1885), 224–6
Kingston Cemetery, 517, 519
Kingston Hill: Knoll House murder case (1881), 140–2
Kingston police station, 141, 142
Kinlay, James, 522, 523
Kipling, Rudyard: 'If—' (poem), 460, 478–9
Kirkwood, Thomas, 166
Knightsbridge Barracks, 451, 455
Knoll House murder case (1881), 140–2
Knollys, Sir Francis, 251
Knox, Alexander, 45, 87–8, 608
Knox, Dr. Robert, 156
'Kosminski': seen with Catherine Eddowes, 305–6, 548; nearly captured in Mitre Square, 556–7; possibly sighted by P.C. Watkins, 556–7, 569, 570, 571; as police suspect, 538, 579–80, 585; sent to Morley House, 546, 548; identified by witness, 545–6; refusal of witness to testify, 546–7; returned to Whitechapel, 550; Butcher's Row address, 557, 583; under surveillance by City C.I.D., 550–1, 552–5, 557, 583; murders cease, 554–5; picked up as wandering lunatic, 560–1, 580, 583; in 'Stepney Workhouse', 558, 560; admitted to Colney Hatch, 565, 580–2, 583; named in Macnaghten memorandum, 526, 565, 570, 571, 584; as Swanson's suspect, 584–5; alluded to in Griffiths' memoirs, 571, 574; as Anderson's 'Polish Jew', 500–1, 574, 584; dissenting voices, 584; dismissed by Macnaghten in *Days of My Years*, 573; missing police file on, 574; named in Swanson marginalia, 521; initially underwhelming as suspect, 523, 525–6, 538; lack of biographical information about, 526, 527; compulsive masturbator, 574; as Aaron Kosminski, 575, 576–7, 578; as Martin Kosminski, 578–9; as David Cohen, 580–2; author's scenario, 582–5; as undiscovered 'Kosminski', 585
Kosminski, Aaron: biographical sources, 574; early research by Martin Fido, 527, 538, 574–5; Fido rejects as killer, 575; birth and early life,

575; fined for unmuzzled dog, 575; mental health problems, 575–6; as compulsive masturbator, 576; in Mile End Old Town Workhouse, 558, 575–6; in Colney Hatch, 576; in Leavesden, 576; death, 576; popularly conflated with 'Kosminski', 575; as 'Kosminski' suspect, 576–7; and shawl controversy, 577–8; unfairly maligned, 578
Kosminski, Abram (father), 575
Kosminski, Golda (née Lubnowski) (mother), 575
Kosminski, Isaac (brother), 575, 576
Kosminski, Martin, 578–9, 585
Kosminski, Samuel, 278, 578, 579, 585
Kosminski, Woolf (brother), 527, 575, 576
Kruger, Paul, 462, 466
Kruger telegram (1896), 478
Krugersdorp, South Africa, 465–6
Kurr, Frederick, 82, 84, 87, 88, 607–8
Kurr, William: criminal history, 608; telegraph ruse, 82; captured, 83–4; at police court, 84; on trial, 87; convicted and sentenced, 88; implicates Detective Department, 88; bribery, 88–9
Kyne, Thomas, 621

L Division (Lambeth), 331
Labalmondière, Captain Douglas: early life and marriage, 598; appointed Inspecting Superintendent, 33–4; witness at Boness trial, 34; attends Mayne's funeral, 55; imposes military drill, 34, 55; and Hyde Park riots (1855), 36; appointed Assistant Commissioner (Administrative), 37; and Clerkenwell bombing, 43; retirement, 223–4; death, 630
Labouchère Amendment (1885), 420
Lady Douglas (barque), 246–8
Laing, Allan Stewart, 600
Lakeman, J.B., 274
Lamb. P.C. Henry, 302
Lambert, P.C., 254
Lambert, William, 210
Lambeth Magistrates' Court, 409
Lancaster Asylum, 564
Land League, 116, 183
Landau, Hermann, 272
Lander, Mr. G. W. (pub landlord), 473
Lane, Catherine, 298
Langdon Down, Dr. John, 449–50, 667
Langdon Down, Mrs. Mary, 450
Langham, Charles, 70
Langham, Samuel, 291
Langton, Captain Henry Gore, 240
Larkin, Michael, 43
Lauver, Hermann, 446–7
Lawende, Joseph, 305, 307, 578, 583
Lawley, Detective George, 309
Le Caron, Henri, 223, 249
Leach, Chief Inspector Alfred: investigates Annie Chapman murder, 282; and Duchess of Edinburgh's jewellery theft, 371; Hoxton forgery case, 382, 383; transferred to Central Office, 475; later career, 482, 509
Leach, Sergeant Stephen, 282
Leahy, Jeff, 533
Leather Apron, 296–7, 309, 314, 316
'Leave Us Alone Club', 35, 599
Leavesden Asylum, 563, 576
Leeson, Benjamin: on City and Metropolitan police boundary, 40–1; on police drill, 48; on police uniform, 48–9
Lefroy, Arthur *see* Mapleton, Percy Lefroy
Leicester Square: bookshops, 407–8
Leman Street police station, 227, 274, 302, 309, 318, 379
Lemon, Captain Thomas, 232
Leopold and Loeb case (1924), 604
Letchworth, Edward, 458
letters/postcard claiming to be from Ripper, 314–18, 357, 358, 521, 647
Leverett, Arthur, 439
Levy, Joseph Hyam, 305–6, 578, 579, 583, 585
Lewer, William, 285
Lewes, Sussex, 287–8, 289, 642
Lewes Assizes, 445
Lewes Gaol, 138, 139, 148–50
Lewis, Angus, 468, 477
Lewis, P.C. George, 130–1
Lewis, Sir George, 411, 494
Lewis, Rosa ('The Duchess of Jermyn Street'), 623
Lewis, Sarah, 327
Lewis & Lewis (Ely Place solicitors), 208, 432, 494
Liddell, Sir Adolphus, 148
Life Guards, 1st Regiment, 255
life-saving equipment (marine), 122–3
Lighter Side of My Official Life, The (Anderson): publication, 500, 510; serialised in *Blackwood's Magazine*,

500–2, 502–3; dismissed as 'gross boastfulness', 502–3; on Polish Jew suspect, 500–1, 520–1, 574, 576; on identity of 'Dear Boss' letter-writer, 317, 521; names Powell as Worth's accomplice, 492; on telling tales, 512; on Seaside Home identification, 545, 557; quoted, 45–6, 116, 512

Lighter Side of My Official Life, The (Swanson's copy): annotations in, 317, 512, 520–1; marginalia discovered, 520, 521–2; borrowed by Charles Nevin, 526; examined by Totty, 529; photographed by Evans and Skinner, 533–4; red lines drawn in, 533–4; loaned to Crime Museum, 530; first examination by Davies, 531–3, 535–6; scans taken, 533; filmed for TV documentary, 533; returned to family, 534; second examination by Davies, 536; *see also* marginalia

Limehouse Workhouse, 62

Lincoln, 103–4

Lind, Montague, 442–3

Lindsell, Captain Charles, 467

Linenhall Barracks, Dublin, 452

Linnell, Alfred, 259–61, 635

Lion, The (public house), Stepney Green, 62

'Lipski' (derogatory epithet), 301

Lipski, Israel, 301, 618

Lisbon, 101

Lister, Lord, 504

Littlechild, Chief Inspector John: on facial hair for constables, 48; on Dolly Williamson, 79; and Turf Fraud case, 82, 83–4, 89; and Special Irish Branch, 202, 203; receives reward, 229; on Fenian Rising and dynamite campaign, 229–30; praised for Special Branch work, 251; at Williamson's funeral, 361; evidence to Committee of Enquiry into Police Superannuation (August 1889), 364; at Roots's funeral, 377; at dinner for Monro, 387–8; reputation, 614; publishes autobiography, 510; names author of 'Dear Boss' letter, 317; dismisses Anderson's Polish Jew theory, 584; names Tumblety as possible Ripper suspect, 686

Litton, Millicent, 103, 104

Liverpool Daily Post, 316

Liverpool police court, 121

Liverpool Town Hall: bomb attack (1881), 182

Llewellyn, Dr. Rees, 293–4

Lloyd, Major Clifford, 222

Lloyd's Weekly Newspaper, 153, 154, 418

Lobengula, Ndbele King, 461

Local Government Board offices, Whitehall: bomb attack (1883), 197–9, 203

Lock, John, 316

Lock Hospital, 57, 58, 602

Lockhart's Coffee House, Cheapside, 396

Lodge, H. B., 1, 589

lodging houses, 270, 320, 322; Buller's Lodging House, 323, 325; Cooney's Lodging House, 298, 299, 312, 644; Crossingham's Lodging House, 284–5, 286; Flower and Dean Street (No. 32), 297, 298; George Street (No. 18), 344, 639; Satchell's Lodging House, 344, 345–6, 640; Spitalfields Chambers, White's Row, 292, 378–9; Tenpenny's Lodging House, 351

Logan (criminal associate of Piano Charley), 100

Lomasney, William Mackey, 224

London: brothels in, 411–14, 416–18, 420, 424–6, 435–6; commuter routes, 24–6; crime statistics, 30, 33, 56–7; economic depression, 231; as finance centre, 24; homosexual scene in West End, 420–1; influenza epidemics (1892, 1895), 455; insanitary conditions, 19–21; Jewish immigration into East End, 271–9; size and population, 19, 24, 38–9; slums and slum clearance, 22–3, 268–9, 661; smoke and fog pollution, 21; transport developments and links, 19, 24, 268–9, 542; *see also* East End

London, Brighton and South Coast Railway, 153, 154

London, Chatham and Dover Railway, 139, 542, 549

London Board School, Berner Street, 300

London Bridge: as crossing-point, 21; bomb explosion (1884), 224

London Bridge railway station, 129

London Burkers (bodysnatching gang), 157–9

London Evening News, 317

London Evening Standard, 60, 381
London Hospital, 283, 292, 293, 379, 450, 639
London Underground, 19, 20, 24–5, 269, 595–6, 627; Fenian bombings (1883–85), 207–8, 224–6
London United Workmen's Committee, 232
London Weekend Television (L.W.T.), 529, 530
Long, P.C. Alfred, 308–9
Long, Edmund, 210
Long, Elizabeth, 286–7
Long Depression (1873–97) (worldwide price recession), 231
Loughton, Essex: Veiled Lady mystery (c.1875), 66–7, 604
Louvain Gaol, Belgium, 486, 493
Low, Detective, 82–3
Lowe, Edward, 86, 548
Lubnowski, Matilda (*née* Kosminski) (Aaron Kosminski's sister), 575, 576
Lucas, Inspector Stephen, 107
Ludgate Hill, 26
Ludgate Hill railway station: failed bombing (1884), 217–18
lunatics, wandering, 559–60
Lushington, Godfrey, 188, 340, 359–60, 457, 497–8, 655
Lusk, George, 317–18

MacDonald, Dr. Arthur, 340
Macdonald, Dr. Roderick, 291, 343
Macdonald, Somerled, 374
Machray, George, 167, 171, 172
Mackay (mermaid spotter), 615
Mackay, Hugh, 15
Mackay, John, *The Anarchists: A Picture of Civilization at the Close of the Nineteenth Century*, 270
Mackellar, Alexander: and Bond's role, 332, 333; examines Dolly Williamson, 264; post mortem on Catherine Mylett, 348; attends Alice McKenzie autopsy, 352; post mortem reporting and fees, 359; evidence to Committee of Enquiry into Police Superannuation (August 1889), 364
Macnaghten, Melville: friendship with Monro, 265; opposed as Assistant Chief Constable, 265; appointed Assistant Chief Constable (C.I.D.), 351; attested, 351; promoted Chief Constable (C.I.D.), 377; hosts dinner for Monro, 387–8; possibly borrows Home Office files on Ripper case, 341, 650–1; writes memorandum (February 1894), 565, 584; names 'Kosminski', 526, 565, 570, 571; source of information on 'Kosminski', 573–4; source of information on Druitt, 684; apprised of Harper extradition, 458; promoted Assistant Commissioner (Crime), 508; lends memorandum notes to Griffiths, 572; releases *Days Of My Years*, 572–3; dismisses 'Kosminski' as suspect, 573; on Swanson's 'synthetical turn of mind', 387
Macnaghten memorandum: official version (Scotland Yard), 565–6, 571; draft version (Aberconway version), 566–71
MacVeagh, Jeremiah, 502
Madeira, 468
Maginnis, Anne, 69, 673
Maguire (Liverpool private detective), 104
Maguire, Mr. (witness to Phoenix Park murders), 184
Maguire, Thomas, 43
Mahoney, Elizabeth (and husband), 640
'Maiden Tribute of Modern Babylon' (exposé of child sex trade), 411–14, 415–16
Maidstone Gaol, 139
Maier, Joseph (Tyrolese Jack the Ripper), 340, 341
Maitland, P.C. Thomas, 255
Majendie, Colonel Vivian Dering: background, 199, 626; Chief Inspector of Explosives, 199–201; and Fenian dynamite campaign, 201–2, 207–8, 225–6, 384; receives government reward, 229; related to Druitt, 626, 684; as Macnaghten's source on Druitt, 684
Major, M. and J. B., 140
Malcolm, John, *The Whitechapel Murders 1888: Another Dead End?*, 574
Malindidzimu Hill, Rhodesia, 478
Mallon, Superintendent John: police career, 614; and arrest of Davitt, 116; Phoenix Park murders, 183–4, 186–7, 188, 189; and Mary Ann Byrne, 192
Malone, Detective Inspector (of City Police), 391
Manchester: Fenian attack on police

Index

van, 41–2, 230; trial of Fenians, 42–3, 181; Salford Barracks bomb attack (1881), 179, 180–1
Mandelbaum, Fredericka, 487
Manor Park Cemetery, 295
Mansion House, London: Captain George committal hearing, 91; failed bombing (1881), 181–2
Mapleson, James, 361–2
Mapleton, Henry, 146
Mapleton, Percy Lefroy: swindles Albert Ellis, 136; takes revolver out of pawn, 139; boards Brighton express, 129, 617; switches carriage, 617; murders Frederick Gold, 129–30; claims attacked, 130; treated at Brighton hospital, 130; questioned and searched by police, 131–2; escorted to Wallington, 132; flees, 132; indicted for murder by coroner's jury, 135; in hiding at Smith Street, 124, 135, 136–7; description and 'wanted' sketch, 133–4, 135, 137, 150, 618; sends telegram to Frank Seale, 136, 140; arrested by Swanson, 124–6; makes voluntary statement, 126; detained at King Street, 126–7, 137; escorted to Lewes Gaol, 137–8; committal hearing, 138–9; transferred to Maidstone Gaol, 139; fake witness letter, 140; trial, 144–6; history of poor mental health, 146–7; reprieve refused, 146–7; writes autobiography, 148; confessions, 148; execution, 148–50; inquest and burial, 150; character, 150–1; reward issue, 151–4; notoriety of case, 573
marginalia: notes in margins, 520–1; notes on endpaper, 521; 'Kosminski' named in, 521; handwriting and physical description, 529, 535–6; use of initials, 535; when written, 537, 577; discovered, 520, 521–2; interest from *News of the World*, 522–3, 677; story not run, 523; Sandell's memo and draft of unused article, 524–6; story offered to *Daily Telegraph*, 526; story published, 527; reactions to, 527–8, 577; response from Jim Swanson, 528; publicised in Ripper books, 529; examined by Totty, 529; photographed by Evans and Skinner, 533–4; red lines made, 533–4; exhibited at Crime Museum, 530; first examination by Davies, 531–3, 535–6; scans taken, 533; filmed for TV documentary, 533; second examination by Davies, 536; authenticated, 536–7
Marine House, St. Margaret's-at-Cliffe (*later* Morley House), 540–1
Markowitz, Joseph, 274
Marks, Ellen, 345–6
Marlborough Street Magistrates' Court, 34, 84, 195, 233, 385–6, 426, 439–40, 473
Marley, Arthur, 439–40
Marriott, Detective Constable Edward, 307–8
Marsend, Mr. (journalist), 486, 493
Marsh, Ike, 488–9
Marshall, Detective Chief Inspector Henry, 98, 204, 410–11, 475, 480, 636
Marshall, Dr. W. G., 564
Marshall, William, 300
Martin, Charles, 90–1
Martin, Joseph (police photographer), 284, 328, 640
Martin Mill railway station, 542
Marwood, William, 148–50, 192
Mashonaland, 460, 464, 478
Mason, Mr. (solicitor), 154
masturbation, 574, 576
Matabele Rebellion (1896), 478
Matabeleland, 461
Mathews, Charles Willie, 428
Matthews, Henry: appointed Home Secretary, 239; work relationships, 239, 252, 253; and Jubilee assassination plot, 249, 251; issues Certificate of Naturalisation to Samuel Kosminski, 278; blocks appointment of Macnaghten, 265; and Ripper manhunt, 319; censures Warren, 342; and Warren's resignation, 342; criticised by press, 431; and police pensions, 365, 366; relations with Monro, 365, 367; announces appointment of Bradford as Commissioner, 367–8; petition from Edward Pinter, 387
Maule, Sir John Blossett, 209
May, James, 158, 159
May Laws (1882), 271
Maybrick, Florence, 620
Mayhew, Henry: on street dung, 20–1; on London Bridge traffic, 21; on St. Giles rookery, 22–3

Mayne, Katherine, 54–5
Mayne, Sir Richard: appointed first Joint Commissioner, 30, 597; creates Metropolitan Police, 30–1, 598; relationship with Hay, 34–5; and Hyde Park riots, 36–7, 38; appointed Chief Commissioner, 37; offers of resignation refused, 38, 44; and militarisation of police, 38, 42; on Fenian threat in London, 46, 233; illness and death, 55; funeral and memorial, 55; succeeded by Henderson, 55–6; on detective work, 72
Mayow, Thomas Newell, 442
McArthur, William, 182
McCarthy, John, 321–2, 328
McCarthy, Sergeant John, 567
McCawley, John, 621
McCormack, John, 351
McCormick, Alan, 530–1, 533
McCormick, Donald, 377; *The Identity of Jack the Ripper*, 566
McDonald, John, 59–60, 602
McEwan, Detective Inspector William, 371, 372
McIntyre, Detective Sergeant Patrick, 203, 251, 614, 626–7
McKay, Angus, 16
McKay, Donald, 8
McKenna, Edward, 296
McKenzie, Alice, 351–3, 355, 570
McKevitt, James, 182–3
McLaren, Rose, Lady, 566
McLeod, James, 47
McWilliam, Superintendent James, 307, 309, 318, 391–2, 555
Meade, Edward, 642
Meadow Well, Thurso, 9, 591
Meane, John, 240
Medium and Daybreak (spiritualist journal), 2–3, 589
Meikle, John, 24, 26
Meikle, Robert, 10, 24
Meikle & Co. (Commission Merchants), 24, 26
Meiklejohn, Inspector John: investigates theft of *Duchess of Devonshire*, 69, 72; investigates Turf Fraud gang, 81; corruption charges against, 88–9; convicted and sentenced, 91; later life, 609
Melachrino, John, 442
Melbourne, 114
Melhuish, Edward, 112

Mellor, Charlotte (*later* Meikle), 26
Melville, Inspector William, 250, 251
memoirs by retired police officers, 500, 501–2, 510–12; *see also Lighter Side of My Official Life, The* (Anderson)
mermaids, 121, 615
Merrick, Joseph ('Elephant Man'), 618
Merry, Jane, 558
Metropolis Management Amendment Act (1858), 20
Metropolitan and City Police Orphanage, 364
Metropolitan Commission of Sewers, 20
Metropolitan Convalescent Institution, Bexhill, 539, 540
Metropolitan Police: Anthropology Department, 507, 508; armed on night duty, 143–4; attestation, 49–50; beat patrols, 31, 53–4; and Bloody Sunday (13 November 1887), 253–8, 259, 310; City Police, relations and proposed amalgamation with, 30, 33, 39–41, 599; civil staff, 30, 31, 37, 252, 363–4, 599; and Coronation of Edward VII, 503–4, 505; corruption (*see* Trial of the Detectives; Turf Fraud scandal); created, 29–31; crime and performance statistics (1868), 56–7; criticised, 238, 263–4, 297; crowd and riot control, 34–8, 159, 232–3, 250–1, 254–8, 259, 264; detective branch (*see* Criminal Investigation Department; Department of Crime; Detective Department); divisional surgeons, 328–33; drill, 34, 38, 42, 48, 55, 239; drinking on duty, 32, 33; entrance requirements and examinations, 47, 600; evidence to House of Commons Immigration Committee (1888), 274–5; facial hair for officers, 48, 55–6; fingerprint evidence, 506–8; fixed-point system, 56; headquarters, 31; ineptness in early days, 31–2, 43, 44; intelligence-gathering on homosexuals, 440–3, 445; jurisdiction, 30, 39–40; killed or assaulted on duty, 32–3, 53, 140–3, 480, 619; leave allowance, 53; letters received from Jack the Ripper, 317; memoirs by retired officers, 500, 501–2, 510–12; militarisation of, 34, 38, 42, 55; nicknames, 32; organisation and structure, 30–1, 94–5; pay, 31, 56; pensions, 364–5,

366; photography, crime scene and mortuary, 284, 328, 569; police powers, 547; recruitment, 31, 41, 46–7, 249; Ripper investigation, liaison with City Police, 318, 555; section houses, 48, 51, 601; strength (1868), 38–9; training and instruction for constables, 31, 48; uniform and items of equipment, 31, 48–9, 598; unpopularity, 32; vetting of immigrants, 278; visibility, 70; 'wanted' portrait of Lefroy, 134, 135, 137, 618; Whitechapel Murders file, 284; *see also* Criminal Investigation Department; Great Scotland Yard; New Scotland Yard; Secret Service Department; Special Irish Branch; specific Divisions and individual stations and officers
Metropolitan Police Bill (1829), 30, 598
Metropolitan Police Convalescent Home, Hove, 538–9, 655
Metropolitan Police Forensic Science Laboratory, 531
Metropolitan Police Historical Collection, 530
Meyer & Co., Paris (bank), 490
Michaelston, P.C. Nicholas, 210
Mickle, Dr. William Julius, 295
'Micks' (ethnic slur), 46
Middlesbrough, 162–3
Middlesex Sessions, 246, 407
Mile End Old Town Workhouse, 558, 575–6
Millbank prison, 117
Millen, Frank, 249–50
Miller, Sergeant (of Thurso police), 175
Miller, Alexander, 11
Miller, Rev. Andrew, 15
Miller, John, 321
Miller, Inspector William, 452
Miller Institution, Thurso, 11–16, 512, 592
Miller's Court, Spitalfields, 321–2, 326–8
Mills, Thomas, 314
Millwood, Annie: attack on, 292, 560
Mitchell, Chief Constable (of Caithness Constabulary), 8
Mitchell, George, 85–6
Mitchelstown Massacre (1887), 254, 634
Mitre and Dove (public house), Westminster, 51
Mitre Square, 304, 305, 306–7

Moale, Evelyn, 472, 473
Mockett, Mary, 288
Moffatt, Ethel (*later* Vincent), 609
Moffatt, James, 657
Moir, John, 167
Molly Houses (homosexual brothels), 420
Molyneaux, Mr. Justice, 138
Monck, Rev. Dr. Francis Ward, 1–3, 84
Monro, Captain C. L. D., 467
Monro, James: background, 222–3; appointed Assistant Commissioner (Crime), 222; and Tower of London bomb attack (1885), 226–7; anti-Fenian career, 233; and Jubilee assassination plot, 249–51; relations with Jenkinson, 252, 253, 634; relations with Warren, 252, 253; takes command of 'Section D', 252–3; and Samuel Kosminski's application for naturalisation, 278; seeks to appoint Macnaghten as Assistant Chief Constable, 264–5; resigns as Assistant Commissioner (Crime), 265; appointed Commissioner of Police, 342; press reaction to appointment, 347; expedites post mortem reporting, 359–60; apprised of Cleveland Street affair, 426; complains of government inaction over Cleveland Street scandal, 430–1; criticised then defended by press, 431, 432; at Williamson's funeral, 361; and naming of new police headquarters, 363–4; recommends Macnaghten for Chief Constable position, 377; fights for improved pension scheme, 364, 365–6; relations with Matthews, 365, 367; resigns as Commissioner, 365–7; 'The Story of Police Pensions' (article), 367; not knighted, 367; Macnaghten hosts dinner for, 387–8; pension, 502; later life and death, 655
Monsell, Chief Constable Bolton, 468
Montagu, Samuel, 272
Montgomery, Andrew *see* Benson, Henry
Montsioa (Chief of Bechuanaland), 235
Moore, Chief Inspector Henry: John Broome Tower murder case, 212; at Miller's Court, 328; and burial of Pinchin Street remains, 358; at Williamson's funeral, 361; promoted

Detective Inspector, 377, 426; at dinner for Monro, 387–8; promoted Chief Inspector (Permanent), 475; career summary and retirement, 481, 482
Moore, James, 112
Morgan (sleuth-hound), 162–3
Morgan, J. Pierpont, 495–6, 673
Morgan, Octavius, 367
Morgenstern, Adrianus ('Morganstone'), 324, 325
Moriarty, P.C., 44
Morley, Samuel: background, 540; philanthropy, 540, 543; at opening of Morley House Convalescent Home, 542; and 'Maiden Tribute' exposures, 413, 416
Morley House Convalescent Home, St. Margaret's Bay: history, 540–1; location and rail links, 541–2; official opening, 542–3; funding, 543; City Police connections, 542, 543, 544, 548; extensions (1893), 543; admissions system, 544–5; patient population, 539, 545; recuperative benefits, 543–4; as 'Seaside Home', 548; and identification of Ripper suspect, 545–9; probable suicide of House Superintendent, 549–50; closes down, 550; later history and current use, 681
Morning Advertiser, 76–7
Morning Leader, 557
Morning Post, 579
Morris, George, 306–7
Morris, Joseph, 37
Morris, P.C. Richard, 288
Morris, William, 255, 261
Morrison, John, 651
Morrow, Detective Inspector (of Dublin Military Police), 188
Morton, Mrs. (thief), 103
Moser, Inspector Maurice: entrapment operations in Leicester Square, 407–8; on Fenian terrorism, 203–4
Mosher, Bill, 66, 604
Moss, P.C. (of City police), 28
Mozley, Herman, 561
Mugford, Joseph: relays information to police, 124, 136–7, 152; receives reward, 153; downfall, 154; life, 618–19
Muir, Richard, 507
Müller, Franz, 127
'Müller's Lights (train compartment portholes), 127
Mullett, James, 186
Munro, Rev. William, 615
Murder Act (1752), 156
Murdoch, Charles S., 458
Murphy, Mr. (barrister), 189
Murray, Edwin, 82, 87, 88, 608
Murray's Magazine, 341–2
Museum of London: Crime Museum Uncovered exhibition (2015–16), 612
Muswell Hill murder (1896), 480
muzzling of dogs, 239, 575
Myers, George, 562
Mylett, Catherine ('Rose'), 347–9, 350, 353
Myson, William, 258

'Nabob' letters, 165–6, 167, 170; pictured, 164
Nadin, Mary Ann, 179
naturalisation of Jewish immigrants, 278–9, 578
Neagle, Mr. (of Stepney Union), 61
Nearn, Sergeant James, 278, 579–80, 585
Nelson, Jans *see* Nielsen, Jens
Nelson's Column, Trafalgar Square: dynamite discovered at (1884), 219, 220
Nevill, Ada Eliza, 62, 96, 508, 517, 603; death, 519
Nevill, James, 62, 63, 96; death, 508
Nevill, James, Jr., 62, 63, 603
Nevill, Julia Ann *see* Swanson, Julia Ann
Nevill, Sarah Ann (*née* Turney), 62, 63, 96; illness and death, 258
Nevill, William, 62, 603
Nevin, Charles, 523, 526–7, 538, 678
New Bond Street, 472–3
New Oxford Street, 23
New Review, The, 367
New River Company, 210
New Scotland Yard, 361–2, 363–4; torso found in vault, 362–3
New Statesman, 566, 684
New York: Adam Worth in, 487–8; Captain Archer arrest (1883), 205; Commissioners' Plan of 1811, 8; Clan na Gael formed, 179–80; Brooklyn dynamite school, 180, 183; Stewart bodysnatching case (1878), 621; White Plains jail, 488
New York Herald:: Backchurch Lane murder story, 353–4; Forbes

Winslow interview, 355–6
New Zealand, 456, 458–9
Newbold, Charles, 407, 518
Newgate Prison, 46, 76, 159, 194, 423, 490
Newlands of Geise, Caithness, 5
Newlove, Henry: homosexual liaisons, 423–5; suspended and arrested, 426–7; accusations, 427, 429; trial, 428–30; later life, 438
Newlove, Mrs. (Henry's mother), 427, 438
News of the World: buys marginalia story, 522–3, 677; fails to publish, 523; Sandell's memo and draft of unused article, 524–6; waives exclusivity contract, 526
Newton, Mr. (magistrate), 426
Newton, Amelia, 372
Newton, Arthur: represents Newlove and Veck, 428; perverts course of justice, 430, 433–4; police press for arrest of, 431; arrested, 433; threatens to reveal royal involvement in Cleveland Street affair, 434; convicted and imprisoned, 434; Edward Pinter case, 387, 436; later career as solicitor, 436–7
Newton, William, 210
Nichols, Malen M., 91
Nichols, Mary Ann: murder of, 283; wounds, 293–4; inquest, 293–4; burial, 283; linked to Whitechapel murder series, 283–4, 293–4; in Macnaghten memorandum, 569
Nielsen, Jens, 206–7, 208
'night soil men', 19–20
Nineteenth Century and After, The (magazine), 497
Norfolk (ship), 118, 121
Norris, Mr. (parliamentary secretary), 177
North London Press, 429, 432, 434, 435
North Mail Coach service, 8, 18, 593
Northern Echo, 618, 661
Northern Ensign (newspaper), 12–15
Nova Scotia Gardens, 157, 158–9, 620
Nunn, Mary Ann, 27–8
Nursey, Sergeant Edward, 376
Nutkins, Detective Inspector Charles, 212, 480–1

Oakes, Charles, 474
Oath, 49–50
O'Brian, Superintendent Nassau Smith, 35–6
O'Brien, Kate, 84
O'Brien, Detective Sergeant Matthew, 204–5
O'Brien, Michael, 43
O'Brien, William, 614
Obscene Publications Act (1857), 406
O'Callaghan, Local Inspector, 95
Ocean National Bank robbery, Greenwich Village (1869), 488
O'Connor, Edward (and family), 204–5
O'Connor, Eustace William, 442
O'Connor, Feargus, 627
O'Connor, T. P., 502
Odell, Robin, 566
O'Donel, Chief Magistrate (of Dublin Metropolitan Police), 658
O'Donnell, Patrick, 193–4
O'Donnell, Samuel, 419
O'Donovan Rossa, Jeremiah, 180, 624
Offences Against the Person Act (1861), 420
offender profiling, 337–9
Ogle, Dr. William, 274
O'Harra, Sergeant: composes ballad, 235
Old Bailey trials: London Burkers (1831), 158; George Swain (1872, 1880), 240; Turf Fraud (1877), 86–8; Trial of the Detectives (1877), 91–2; Robert Cumming (1880), 113; Walter Selwyn (1881), 118; Captain Drevar (1881), 121; Jens Nielsen (1881), 208; Lochiel Graham (1882), 176–7, 178; John Crunden (1883), 194; Edward O'Connor (1883), 205; Burton and Cunningham (1885), 229; Benjamin Judge (1886), 410; crew of *Lady Douglas* (1887), 248; Burns and Cunninghame Graham (1888), 261–2; Mrs. Gordon Baillie (1888), 265; Cleveland Street scandal (1889), 428–30; Ernest Parke (1890), 433, 434–6; Hoxton forgery case (1891), 383; Edward Pinter (1891), 386; Florence Osborne (1892), 394–5; Reginald Saunderson (1895), 454; Robert Cliburn (1898), 445; Henry Jackson (1902), 506–7
Olive, James (Deputy Commissioner), 671
Ollive, Dr. Gustave, 340–1
Olsson, Lars Fredrik (and family), 297
Omaha Daily Bee, 437

omnibuses: routes, 25
O'Neil, James, 44, 46
Orchard Cottage, Edlesborough, 520, 521
Orrock, Thomas, 480
Osborn Street, Whitechapel, 283
Osborne, Captain Clarence, 388, 389, 390, 391, 394, 395-6
Osborne, Florence (*née* Elliot): background, 388; steals and sells jewellery, 388-9; sues Mrs. Hargreaves for slander, 389-90; flees to Continent, 390; returns to stand trial for fraud, 391-4; arrested for perjury, 394; on remand, 394; Old Bailey trial, 394-5; early release and birth of children, 395
Osborne, Phyllis, 395
Osborne House, 483-4
Ostend, 476
Ostrog, Michael, 570, 571-2, 684-5
Otway, Sergeant, 606
Oudemans, A. C., *The Great Sea-Serpent: An Historical and Critical Treatise*, 616
Outram, Detective Sergeant Robert, 307-8
Overend, Gurney & Co. (bank), 24
Owen, P.C., 99
Owen, P.C. Henry, 144
Oxford, Edward, 594
Oxford Music Hall, Westminster, 262-3

Packer, Matthew, 400, 660
Paddington railway station: construction, 19; arrest of Davitt, 116; failed bombing (1884), 217-18, 219; arrest of Stephen Smith, 371; Jameson's troops disembark, 468
Paddington underground line and station, 595-6, 627
Pale of Settlement, 271
Palestine Exploration Fund, 234
Pall Mall: unemployment demonstration (8 February 1886), 232
Pall Mall Gazette: on Alexander Knox, 45; on Fenian threat, 46; reviews Sanger's play at Astley's Theatre, 60; on Howard Vincent's resignation, 209, 221; on appointment of Charles Warren, 237-8; calls for prosecution of riot police, 259; on Linnell inquest, 260; on erasing of Goulston Street graffito, 310; on appointment of Edward Bradford, 369-70; on murder of Phoebe Hogg, 374-5; on Swanson's Jack the Ripper theory, 381, 584; on Emily Smith attack, 399-400; publishes Maiden Tribute articles, 411-14, 415-16; and Eliza Armstrong story, 416-18; on Swanson's promotion to Superintendent, 475; interviews Adam Worth in prison, 486, 493; interviews Abberline, 584; Stead as editor (1883-89), 661
Palmer, Amelia, 285, 286
Palmer, Professor Edward, 234
Palmer, Henry, 285
Palmer, Sergeant Samuel, 74
Palmer, Chief Inspector William: joins Detective Department, 78; investigates Turf Fraud gang, 81; corruption charges against, 88, 89; convicted and sentenced, 91; later life, 609
Palmerston, Lord, 35
Panic of 1873 (financial crisis), 231
Pankhurst, P.C. David, 82
Paris Detective Department *see* Sûreté Nationale
Parish School, Thurso, 10, 592
Park, Frederick *see* Fanny and Stella
Park Club, Mayfair, 205-6, 208-9
Parke, Ernest, 432-3, 434-6
Parker, George, *A View of Society and Manners in High and Low Life*, 420-1
Parnacott, Charles, 112
Parnell, Charles, 116, 180, 183, 186, 196, 529
Partridge, Ralph, 684
Partridge, Richard, 158
Passmore, Henry, 383
Patrick, P.C. John, 580, 583
Pattenden, Inspector (of H Division), 354
Patterson, P.C. William, 447
Paul, Dr. James, 422-3
Paul, Maurice Eden, 274
Pauline (barque), 119-21, 616
Payne, William John, 291
Peace, Charles, 140
Peacock and Goddard (Holborn solicitors), 401
Pearce, Inspector Nicholas, 73, 77, 605-6
Pearcey, Mary, 375-7
Pearl, The: A Magazine of Facetiae and Voluptuous Reading, 406, 409-10,

661
Pearson, Richard (Assistant Commissioner), 152, 351
peat burning, 9
Peel, Billy, 387–8
Peel, Lawrence, 597
Peel, Sir Robert: political career, 29, 596; proposes police force for London, 29–30; creates Metropolitan Police, 31, 597; liking for Gerston whisky, 5; death, 596
Pegler, P.C., 72
Pelham-Clinton, Lord Arthur, 423
Pelham Street, Whitechapel, 348
Pender, Inspector Peter, 456, 458, 668
Pennefather, Richard, 252, 363
Pennland, SS, 437
Penny, Rev. E. L., 120–1
penny-dreadfuls, 28
pensions, Metropolitan Police, 364–5, 366
Pentland Firth, 7
Pentonville Prison, 88, 173, 262, 386
Penzance police, 140
Perkins, William Meech, 425
Petticoat Lane Market, 277
Pharmaceutical Society, 84–5
Philadelphia, 63–6
Philadelphia Public Ledger (newspaper), 63–4
Philip, John, 166–7, 171
Phillips, Annie (*née* Conway; Catherine Eddowes's daughter), 299, 312–13
Phillips, Archie, 443–4, 665
Phillips, Dr. George Bagster: Annie Chapman case, 282, 293, 294; handed apron fragment, 309; Mary Kelly case, 327–8; Annie Farmer case, 346; Alice McKenzie case, 352; consulted on burial of Pinchin Street remains, 358
Phillips, John, 425
Phillips, John 'Junka', 491–2
Phillips, Louis, 313
Phoenix Park murders (1882): murders, 183–6; police investigation and arrests, 186–9, 191; trial of Invincibles, 189–91, 192; executions, 192–3; assassination of Carey, 193–4
photography: crime scene and mortuary, 284, 308, 328, 569; mugshots, 58, 479
Piano Charley (Charles Bullard), 100, 488–9, 490, 610
Pig and Whistle (public house),

Borough, 53
Pigburn, Frances, 158
'Pigeon Man' case, 374, 656
Pigott, William, 296
Pinchin Street, 302
Pinchin Street murder, 353–5, 568, 571; remains buried, 358
Pinkerton, Robert, 492, 494, 496
Pinkerton, William: meets Worth in Paris, 489; and recovery of *Duchess of Devonshire*, 484–5, 486, 493–5; correspondence with Agnew, 496; and Worth's autobiography (*Adam Worth*), 491–2, 494, 496–7; letter of gratitude from Swanson, 505–6
Pinkerton Detective Agency, 65, 474–5, 484–5, 488, 489, 492, 496–7
Pinter, Edward ('The Modern Alchemist'): intent to defraud, 384–6; extradition to Switzerland on fraud charges, 386–7, 396, 436; alleged theft of bonds, 387, 396; described by Windust, 483; lost photograph of, 658
'pipeman' (Berner Street witness), 301
Pizer, John, 297
Plaistow police station, 62
Play House Yard, Blackfriars: bomb explosion (1883), 196–7
Pless, Daisy, Princess of, 613
Plowman, P.C., 428
Poland, Harry, 194
Police Code, 360, 547, 654
Police Convalescent Home, Hove, 538–9, 655
Police Gazette, 288
police surgeons (divisional), 329–33; post mortem reporting, 359–60; post mortem fees, 360, 654
Polish Jew theory (Anderson), 500–1, 520–1, 576, 584; *see also* 'Kosminski'
Pollard, Henry (forger), 101
Pollard, Henry (lawyer), 385
Pollard, William, 88, 98
Poole, Joseph, 187
Poor Jews' Temporary Shelter, Leman Street, 272–5, 578, 580
Pope, Detective Inspector (of N Division), 203, 212
pornographic literature, 406–11, 617
Port of London Sanitary Authority, 271
Portal House, St. Margaret's-at-Cliffe (*formerly* Morley House), 681
Portland Place, Fitzrovia, 110, 113
Portland Prison, Weymouth, 410

post mortem reporting, 359–60
Potts, Detective William, 555, 682
poverty, in East End, 269–71
Powell (Worth's accomplice), 492, 672
Powell, R. Douglas, 484
Pownall, Henry, 562
Powys-Keck, Harry, 141
Praed Street underground station: bomb explosion (1883), 207–8; re-named Paddington, 627
Prater, Elizabeth, 326–7
Presburg Road (No. 3), New Malden, 514, 519, 520
Preston, Charles, 298
Preston, John, 439
Preston Park: railway station, 130; Mr. Gold's funeral procession, 135
Pretoria, 464
Prince, Dr. (of Kimberley), 462
Prince Albert (public house), Brushfield Street, 295
Princess Alice (public house), Commercial Street, 378, 379
Prinsep, Valentine, 446
Prison Commission, 477
profiling, criminal, 337–9
prostitution, 214, 270–1, 307, 580; *see also* brothels
Prudhoe, Robert, 443
Ptolomey, Charles, 348–9, 652
Pullman carriages, 127
Punch, 251, 316
Pupil Teachers, 16
Pycroft, Ella, 274

Queen Elizabeth's Walk, Stoke Newington, 209–10, 213–14
Quilter, Morris and Tod-Healey (property developers), 361
Quinn, Sergeant Patrick, 251
Quixley, Miss (Chelsea shop owner), 245

rabies outbreak in London (1886), 239
Raffles, Mr. (Liverpool magistrate), 121
Raikes, Henry Cecil, 426
Railway Act (1868), 127
Railway Arms (public house), Sutton Street, 399, 401–2, 660
Railway Inn, Balcombe, 131
railways: Brighton railway murder, 129–31, 153, 154; expansion across London, 19, 24, 269; first murder on, 127; Inverness–King's Cross service, 18, 594; Katherine Dickinson assault, 127–9; London–Dover service, 542; passenger safety concerns, 127; special train services, 127, 139, 142
Ramsay, Robert, 578
Rance, Henry, 642
Raymond, Henry J. *see* Worth, Adam
Read, Ada, 113
Read, James Canham, 451
Recollections of Forty Years (Forbes Winslow), 358
Reeves, John, 640
Reform League, 37–8
register of criminals, 58, 602
Reid, Inspector Edmund: police career, 283; report on Emma Smith, 639; at Miller's Court, 327, 328; and Frances Coles case, 378
Reid, James, 484
Reid, Samuel: jewellery shop, Oxford Street, 195
Resurrection Men (bodysnatchers), 156–9; *see also* Dunecht grave robbery case
Reuman, Oscar, 118
Reynolds, Henry, 387
Reynolds's Weekly Newspaper, 209, 360, 431, 449
Rhodes, Cecil: territorial ambitions and expansionism, 460–2, 464; friendship with Jameson, 462; prepares for invasion of Transvaal, 464–5; attempts to recall raiding party, 465; visits Jameson in nursing home, 477; death, 478
Rhodes, Miss (of Loughton), 66–7, 604
Rhodesia: created, 461; territorial divisions, 668; Malindidzimu Hill, 478
Richards, Captain George, 187, 188
Richardson, John, 316
Richardson, Thomas, 112
Rider, Walter Greenway, 98
riots, 34–8, 159, 232–3, 254–8, 259, 264
Rising Sun (public house), St. James's Square, 220
Ritchie Hunter, Andrew, 85
Robertson, Andrew, 513, 593
Robertson, Peterishea (*née* Alexander; Swanson's niece), 18, 513, 593, 675
Robertson Reid, James, 245–6
Robinson, Inspector (of Wellington Barracks), 48
Robinson, P.C. Edward, 140
Robinson, P.C. Louis, 299

Index

Robson, Inspector George, 82, 124, 166
Rogues Gallery, 479
Rollison, Francis, 449
Ronaldson, P.C. William, 8
rookeries (slums), 22–3, 50, 268–9, 661
Roots, Dr. (divisional surgeon), 141
Roots, Detective Inspector Thomas, 98, 101; death, 377
Roper, Lieutenant Percy, 148
Roper, P.C. Thomas, 229
Rose, Sergeant (of King Street police station), 197
Rose, Superintendent George, 47, 600
Rose, Thomas, 76
Rose Innes, Hugh, 173–4
Rosebery, Lord, 455
Ross, Charley Brewster: kidnapping case (1874), 63–6, 67, 604
Ross, Christian, 64, 65, 66
Ross, John, 182
Ross, Walter, 63, 604
Ross Gazette, 449
Rothery, H. C. (Wreck Commissioner), 118–19, 121
Rothschild, Henry de, Baron, 460
Rotterdam police, 82
Rowan, Sir Charles, 30–1, 33, 597, 598
Royal Albert Hall, 22
Royal Aquarium Pleasure Gardens, Sydney, 123
Royal Baccarat Scandal (1890), 628
'Royal Bank of London', 80–1
Royal Bounty Fund, 361
Royal Courts of Justice, 476
Royal Irish Constabulary, 203, 451, 452
Rudd, Henry, 575
Ruffell, Frank, 345
Ruggles-Brise, Sir Evelyn, 252
Rumbelow, Donald, 527, 528
Rush, James Blomfield, 127
Russell, Mary, 639
Russell, Rollo: writes on London fogs, 21
Russell, Lord William, 73, 77, 360, 606
Ryder, Betsy, 351, 352

Sadler, James Thomas, 378–80, 381, 571, 657
Sagar, Detective Inspector Robert, 392, 555–7, 583, 682
Sage, Richard, 292
St. Andrew's Home, Folkestone, 550
St. Anne's Church, Soho, 22, 595
St. Clair, George, 443–4
St. Giles' Christian Mission, 499–500
St. Giles rookery, 22–3, 50, 268
St. James's Gazette, 216, 316–17, 342–3, 377
St. James's Park, 42
St. John the Evangelist, Charlotte Street, 102, 103, 610
St. John's the Evangelist, Westminster, 361
St. Leonard's Church, Shoreditch, 343
St. Margaret's-at-Cliffe, Kent, 539, 542; *see also* Morley House Convalescent Home
St. Martin's Vestry Hall, 259–60
St. Maur, Edward, 102, 105, 106, 611–12
St. Maur, Lord Algernon (*later* 14th Duke of Somerset), 106, 612
St. Maur, Percy, 106, 612
St. Maur (Seymour) ancestry, 610–11
St. Patrick's Roman Catholic Cemetery, Leytonstone, 343, 651
St. Vincent, Mary Sawyer, 37
Sala, George Augustus, 599
Saleneskam, David, 559–60, 580
Salford Barracks bomb attack (1881), 179, 180–1
Salisbury, Lord, 239, 431, 434, 437
Sandell, Charles: crime reporter, 677, 678; negotiates purchase of marginalia story, 522–3; heart attack and death, 523–4; papers donated to Crime Museum, 524; internal memo and draft of unused article, 524–6, 538
Sanderson, Murray and Co. (wool merchants), 114
Sanger, 'Lord' George, 60–1
Satchell's Lodging House, Spitalfields, 344, 345–6, 640
'Saucy Jacky' postcard, 315–17
Saul, Jack, 435–6, 662, 665; *The Sins of the Cities of the Plain*, 406
Saunders, Mr. (magistrate), 314
Saunderson, Colonel Edward J., 451
Saunderson, Llewellyn (Reginald's father), 450–1, 454
Saunderson, Reginald: background and weak-mindedness, 450–1; absconds from Eastcote school, 449; murders Augusta Dawes, 446–7; movements after murder, 451–2; sends letter to police, 447–8, 449, 451, 452; apprehended and escorted back to Kensington, 452–3; remand hearing, 453; committal hearing, 454; unfit

to plead and detained at Broadmoor, 454–5
Schmalz, Herbert, 446
Schoenbein, Maximilian *see* Shinburn, Max
School of Military Engineering, Chatham, 234
Schwartz, Israel, 300–1
Science (journal), 577
Scotland Yard *see* Great Scotland Yard; New Scotland Yard
Scott, Benjamin, 415
Scott, Dr. James, 476
Scott, Sergeant John, 383
Scott, Rev. Thomas, 96
sea legends, 121, 615
sea serpents, 119–22, 615–16
Seale, Frank, 132, 136, 140
Seaside Home *see* Morley House Convalescent Home, St. Margaret's Bay
Secret Service Department, 45, 46, 202
'Section D' (Home Office Crime Department), 252–3
section houses, 48, 51, 601
Seething Lane, 24, 26
Seistrup, Jens, 208
Sellick, Ellen, 219
Selwyn, Walter (Walter Bailey), 117–18, 555, 615
Sequeira, Dr. George, 307
Sessiovitch, Carl, 490
Severs, John, 439–40
sewers and drains, 20
sex: Victorian attitude to, 406
sex trafficking, 324–5, 414–16
Seymour, Digby, 423
Seymour Scott & Co. (Dublin solicitors), 84
Shaddock, Detective Sergeant, 472–3
Shadwell police station, 400
Shaftesbury, Earl of, 413
Shaftesbury Avenue, 23, 268
Shamrock (yacht), 490
Shaw, Sergeant Frederick, 73, 77, 91, 606
Shaw, George Bernard, 255
shawl, purportedly worn by Catherine Eddowes, 577–8
Sheedy, Patrick, 494
Sheen, Edward, 558
Sheffield Central (parliamentary constituency), General Election (1885), 235, 630
Sheffield Hallam (parliamentary constituency), General Election (1885), 235
Shelden, Neal, 325
shelters and refuges, for Jewish immigrants, 271–5
Shepherd, Superintendent (of D Division), 438–9, 440
Sheppard, Dr. Edgar, 454, 564–5
Sheridan, Detective (of Dublin Police), 116, 192
Shields Daily Gazette, 162–3
Shiell, Quelez, 73
Shillito, Mr. (police surgeon), 74
Shinburn, Max (Maximilian Schoenbein), 487–8, 489
Shinnick, John, 634
Shipp, Charlotte, 383
Shipp, Frederick, 381–2
Shore, Detective Superintendent John: early police career, 670; raid on American Bar in Paris, 489; pursues Adam Worth, 490, 492; survives shake up of Detective Department, 94, 95, 671; old school copper, 95–6, 482; and arrest of Michael Davitt, 117; Jens Nielsen case, 208; promoted Superintendent and replaces Williamson, 264; writes his will, 264, 635; and Warren's 'Eyes and Ears' memorandum, 268; at Williamson's funeral, 361; and Duchess of Edinburgh's jewellery theft, 371; at Roots's funeral, 377; at dinner for Monro, 387–8; resigns from Metropolitan Police, 474, 475, 635; works for Pinkertons, 474; death, 635
Shoreditch mortuary, 328
Short, Mr. (Knoll House butler), 140–1
Shurm, Annie Collingwood (*later* Graham), 178
Simmons, P.C. George, 311
Simons, Detective Thomas, 184
Sims, George R., 557, 584
Sinclair, Sir George, 10, 12
Sinclair, Sir John, 7–8, 591
Sinclair, Sir Robert, 175–6
Sing Sing prison, 487
Sion Square, 527, 576
Sipido, Jean-Baptiste, 504
Sivvey, Annie *see* Chapman, Annie Elizabeth
sketch of Lefroy *see* 'wanted' portrait of Lefroy
Sketch, The, 201–2

Index

Skinner, Keith, 524, 530, 533–4, 535
Skinner, Tom, 58
Skirmishers, 180–1
Sladden, P.C. Richard, 428
sleuth-hounds, 162–3, 327
slums and slum clearance, 22–3, 268–9, 661
Smith, Arthur and Hector, 27–8
Smith, David, 11
Smith, Dr. Edward, 259, 260
Smith, Emily: background, 396; claims attacked in Whitechapel, 396–9; police response, 399–400; as victim of Jack the Ripper, 400–1; harassed by press, 401; sworn declaration, 401–4; as prostitute, 404–5; vanishes, 405
Smith, Emily (Annie Chapman's sister), 286
Smith, Emma: background, 639; at No. 18 George Street, 344; attack on, 283–4, 293, 639; taken to London Hospital, 639; inquest, 292
Smith, Fountain (Annie Chapman's brother), 641
Smith, G. Wentworth Bell, 355–7
Smith, George (Annie Chapman's father), 285
Smith, Gertrude, 580
Smith, Henry (Hanbury Street undertaker), 283
Smith, Henry (Harley Street butler), 108
Smith, Major Henry: and Catherine Eddowes murder, 308, 309, 311–12; and Florence Osborne case, 391, 392; writes memoirs, 500, 510; dismisses Anderson's Polish Jew theory, 500–1
Smith, J. Wells, 71
Smith, James, 51–3
Smith, Detective Inspector John, 447–8, 449
Smith, Miriam (Annie Chapman's sister), 286, 641
Smith, Oliver, 376
Smith, Ruth Chapman (Annie Chapman's mother), 285, 641
Smith, Sheriff Guthrie, 171
Smith, Stephen, 370–2
Smith, William (founder of Boys' Brigade), 16, 512
Smith, William (witness to Gower Street bombing), 225
Smith, P.C. William, 300, 302
Smith Street (No. 32), Stepney, 124–6,
135, 136, 151, 153, 616
smoke pollution, 21
Snagge, Thomas, 415
Snow Hill police station, 546
Snow Hill railway station, 542, 548
Social Democratic Federation (SDF), 232, 255
Society for the Suppression of Vice, 409
sodomy, 420, 421–2
Solomon, Lewis, 243, 244, 272
Somerset, Algernon, 14th Duke of *see* St. Maur, Lord Algernon
Somerset, Lord Arthur: at Cleveland Street brothel, 427, 437; monitored by police, 430; incriminating letters, 433; police press for arrest of, 431; abscondment, 431–2; named in press, 432; case dropped, 434; later life in exile, 437
Somerset, Edward Seymour, 12th Duke of, 102, 612
Somerset, Georgiana Seymour, Duchess of, 106
Sorata, SS, 101
Soutar, Charles: background, 167; involvement in Dunecht bodysnatching, 167–9; tried and convicted, 170, 188; rewards issue, 171–2; protests innocence, 172–3; later life, 173–4, 622
Soutar, Charlotte, 174
South Africa: Bechuanaland Protectorate, 235, 632; British imperialist expansion in, 460–2, 464; failed invasion of Transvaal, 465–6
South African Republic *see* Transvaal
South Grove workhouse, 292
Special Irish Branch, 203, 223, 224, 229, 251; surveillance of Frank Millen in France, 250
Speed, Robert, 73
Spelthorne Sanatorium, Feltham, 286
Spindlove (butler), 107
Spink and Son (goldsmiths), 389
spiritualism, 1–2, 163, 314
Spitalfields Chambers, White's Row, 292, 378–9
Spitalfields Market, 277
Spurgin, Dr. (police surgeon), 107
Stafford, Percy, 437
stagecoach: Thurso–Inverness service, 8, 18, 593
Stalker, P.C. John, 374
Standing, Detective Sergeant Arthur, 204, 205

Stanford, Leonard, 243-4
Stanhope, Lillian (*née* Florence Higgins; later Lady St. Maur), 102-6, 611
Stanley, Ted, 286
Staples, William, 47, 600
Star, The (newspaper), 296, 433, 452, 636, 647
Star and Garter (public house), Westminster, 51
Stark, Joseph, 130
Starr, Inspector (of A Division), 50
Station Place, Whitechapel, 399
Stead, W. T.: pallbearer at Alfred Linnell's funeral, 261; Maiden Tribute campaign, 411-14, 415-16; Eliza Armstrong case, 416-19; journalistic career and death, 661
Steadman, Detective Inspector Charles, 508
Steers, George, 76
Stenning, Harry, 84
Stephens, James, 41
Stephenson, Sir Augustus, 88, 434
Stepney Poor Law Union, 558
'Stepney Workhouse' (St. Leonard's Street Workhouse), Bromley-by-Bow, 558, 560, 577
Stevens, C. L. McCluer, *Famous Crimes and Criminals*, 486
Stewart, Alexander: theft of body, 621
Stewart, William, 377
Stickley, John, 683-4
Stoke Newington murder (1884), 209-17
Stracey, Major John, 467
Straight, Inspector (of A Division), 191
Strand Theatre, London, 421
strangulation, accidental, death from, 348, 349
Stratton brothers trial (1905), 507
Streeter (platelayer), 139
Streeter, Edward, 384-5, 472, 473-4, 483, 669
Stride, Elisabeth (*née* Gustafsdotter): early life in Sweden, 297-8; prostitute, 297; emigrates to England, 298; marriage to John Stride, 298; treated for bronchitis at Whitechapel Infirmary, 560; relationship with Michael Kidney, 298; last known movements, 297, 298, 299-301; body discovered, 301-2; murder scene, 302, 304; body examined, 302-4; inquest, 423; burial, 313-14; spirit summoned at *séance*, 314; in Macnaghten memorandum, 569
Stride, John, 298
Stuart-Wortley, Charles, 235, 330, 335, 498
Sturnham, Louisa, 218-19, 229
Suakin, 235-7
Sullivan, Alexander, 250
Sullivan, Mick, 216
Sullivan, William, 345
Sun (newspaper): accuses Thomas Cutbush, 565
Sunday Express, 522, 523
Sunday Telegraph, 526
Sunday trading legislation, 35, 36
Sûreté Nationale, 91, 94, 609
Surrey Assizes, 128
Sussex Agricultural Express, 455
Sutcliffe, Peter, 522, 677
Sutton Street, Whitechapel, 397, 399, 402
Swain, George, 240-1
Swainton, Mr. (of London Salvage Corps), 207
Swallow Gardens, 378, 379
Swansea, 188, 189
Swanson, Ada Mary (daughter; 'Sis'), 205, 241, 514, 519-20
Swanson, Alexander (first born brother), 590
Swanson, Alexander (third born brother), 10, 590
Swanson, Alice Julia (daughter; 'Lal'): birth, 350; inherits father's papers and effects, 519; moves to Orchard Cottage, 520; death, 520
Swanson, Charlotte (*née* Mister), 513
Swanson, Donald Gair (nephew), 591
Swanson, Donald Nevill (son; 'Donnie'): birth, 99; life, 513, 519; letter from father, 514-15; at father's funeral, 517; writes to Chief Constable Wensley, 517-18
SWANSON, DONALD SUTHERLAND:
Early life: family background, 5-6, 10; birth, 6; family moves to Thurso, 6; boyhood and early schooling, 10-11; at Miller Institution, 16; as Pupil Teacher and Second Master, 16, 512; glowing testimonial for, 16-18; leaves for London, 18; lodges with sister Mary, 22; employed as City clerk, 24, 25-6
Police career and family life; applies to join Metropolitan Police, 26-7,

Index

29, 47; examined and vetted, 47; police training and drill, 48; assigned A Division (Whitehall), 50; probationary constable at King Street, 51, 53; fined, 54; promoted Police Constable 3rd Class, 54; cautioned and fined again, 58; transferred to Y Division (Highgate), 59; promoted Sergeant, 61; transferred to K Division (Bow), 61; death of mother, 62; fined and reprimanded, 62; temporary posting to Plaistow, 62; brief romance with Ruth Darby, 62, 603; first meets Julia Nevill, 62; robbery tip-off story, 72; joins Detective Department, 72, 79; transferred back to A Division, 79; marries Julia, 96; rents house in Kennington, 97–8; promoted Detective Inspector 2nd Class, 98; wedding gift from colleagues, 98; birth of first son Donald Nevill, 99; death of father, 99–100; birth of second son James John, 117; presented with Tranter pistol, 113–14, 613–14, 678; moves to Camden Villas, Kennington, 205; birth of first daughter Ada Mary, 205; birth of third son Douglas Sutherland, 241; awarded Jubilee medal, 252, 634; transferred to Central Office, Scotland Yard, 258; death of mother-in-law, 258; promoted Detective Chief Inspector (Temporary), 264, 265–6; birth of twins and loss of William Alexander, 350; at Williamson's funeral, 361; evidence to Committee of Enquiry into Police Superannuation (August 1889), 364; complaint against, 372–4, 656; day at the races, 374; at Roots's funeral, 377; promoted Detective Chief Inspector (Permanent), 377; at dinner for Monro, 387–8; sick leave, 455; death prematurely reported (6 February 1892), 455; intelligence-gathering on homosexuals (Sods lists), 440–3, 445; at consecration of Justicia Lodge, 457–8; promoted Superintendent, 475, 482; visit from William Drysdale, 479; report on post mortem examinations, 654; at leaving celebrations for Nutkins and Moore, 481; congratulates Anderson on knighthood, 499; awarded King's Coronation Medal, 505, 674; writes to William Pinkerton, 505–6; resigns from Metropolitan Police, 508–9; police pension, 509; farewell dinner, 509

Retirement: trips to Thurso in retirement, 512; moves with family to Presburg Road, New Malden, 514; failing health in later years, 514–15; letters to family, 515, 536; death, 517; funeral and interment, 517–18; papers and effects, 519–20, 534–5; marginalia discovered, 520, 521–2 (*see also* marginalia)

Cases:
Jack Williams (petty theft) (1869), 57
Bella Hart (missing person) (1869), 57–8
Pudding Hines (attempted robbery) (1870), 58–9
George Sanger (unlawful performance of stage plays) (1871), 61
Maria Wheeler (child neglect) (1872), 61–2
Veiled Lady of Loughton mystery (c.1875), 66–7, 604
Hannah Thompson murder (1876), 82–3
Kate O'Brien (theft) (1877), 84
Dr. Monck (fraudulent medium) (1877), 2–3, 84
Ritchie Hunter and Colegrove (false representation) (1877), 84–5
Lowe, Anderson and Mitchell (Islington burglary gang) (1877), 85–6, 548
Captain George (forgery and robbery) (1877), 90–1
'Wheel of Beauty' fraud case (1878–79), 96, 97, 99, 100
William Virtue (forgery) (1878), 98
Blue Posts Tavern betting case (1878), 98–9
Piano Charley (robbery) (1879), 100
Henry Pollard (forgery), 101
Lillian Stanhope (forgery) (1880), 102–3, 105–6
Harley Street murder mystery (1880), 107–9
Countess of Bective jewellery heist (1880), 111–14, 151
Charles Newbold (selling obscene photographs) (1880), 407

Index

Caroline Thoriste (selling indecent pictures) (1880), 407
Captain Tempest (fraud) (1881), 114–15
Michael Davitt arrest (1881), 115, 116–17
Walter Selwyn (forgery) (1881), 117–18
Captain Drevar (sending threatening letters) (1881), 118–19, 121
Brighton railway murder (1881)
  arrests Lefroy, 124–6
  escorts Lefroy to Lewes Gaol, 137–8
  at committal hearing, 138–9
  continuing enquiries, 139–40, 151
  reward issue, 151, 152, 154
  discusses case with Macnaghten (c.1890), 573–4
Lochiel Graham (fraud) (1881–82), 175, 176–7
P.C. Atkins murder (1881), 142
Dunecht grave robbery case (1881–82), 160–2, 165, 166
Hawkins and Green (fraud) (1881), 166
Hannah Brannan (sex trafficking victim) (c1881–84), 324–5
Phoenix Park murders (1882–83)
  takes statements from crew of Gladstone, 188
  arrests Mary Ann Byrne, 191
John Crunden (threatening to murder and wilful damage) (1882–83), 194–5
Edward O'Connor (obtaining by false pretences) (1883), 204–5
Fenian bombing campaign (1883–85)
  inquiries at Waverley Hotel, 218–19, 229
  inspects Gower Street bomb damage, 225–6
  Westminster bombing investigation, 228
  Knightsbridge house search, 204
Captain Archer (forgery) (1883), 205
Park Club gaming investigation (1883–84), 205–6, 208–9
Jens Nielsen (arson) (1883), 206, 207, 208
Benjamin Judge (selling obscene literature) (1883), 408–9

John Broome Tower murder case (1884), 212, 217
Mary Cooper murder case (1884), 162–3
Arthur Tindall (selling obscene literature) (1885–86), 410–11
West End riots (1886), 233
Benjamin Judge (attempted extortion) (1886), 409–10
George Swain (forgery) (1886), 240–1
George Anderson (fraud) (1887), 241, 244–5
Arthur Ward (selling tickets for unauthorized lottery) (1887), 245
James Robertson Reid (fraud) (1887), 245–6
Captain James Cocks (murder on the high seas) (1887), 246, 248, 633
Trafalgar Square riots (1887)
  at committal hearing of leaders, 258–9
  at Linnell inquest, 260
A. W. Eayres mystery (1888), 262
Mrs. Gordon Baillie (fraud) (1888), 265
Jack the Ripper murders (1888)
  put in charge of investigation, 267–8, 295
  liaison with City Police, 318, 555
  progress report (19 October), 319–21
  Catherine Mylett case, 348–9
  list of victims, 353, 380, 527
  Swanson's suspect, 381, 520–1, 522, 584–5 (see also 'Kosminski'; marginalia)
Pinchin Street murder (1889), 353–5
  report on torso murders, 362–3
  Forbes Winslow enquiries, 355–8
Duchess of Edinburgh's jewellery theft (1890), 371
Mary Pearcey (murder) (1890), 375
Frances Coles murder (1891), 378, 379
Hoxton forgery case (1891), 381, 382
Edward Pinter
  intent to defraud (1891), 384, 385
  theft of bonds (1891–92), 387, 396

740

Index

Lochiel Graham (fraud) (1891), 178
The Great Pearl Case (1891–92), 388, 392–4
Emily Smith (alleged attack) (1892), 396, 399, 401, 404–5
Kensington murder (1894), 448, 449, 454
Leonard Harper (alleged fraud) (1895), 456–7, 458
Jameson Raid (1896)
   escorts troopers to London, 468
   arrests Jameson and fellow officers, 469
   brings to Court, 469–70
   evidence at remand hearing, 470
   mistaken for Jameson, 469, 471
   praised by Cuffe, 477–8
Burden jewels case (1896), 472, 473, 474
supposed mail packet robbery (1896), 475–6
Duchess of Devonshire theft (1897, 1899, 1901), 484, 486, 492, 494
Character and interests: appearance, 47, 56, 483; character, 18, 480, 483; fishing, 512; Freemasonry, 240, 632; habit of annotating books, 492, 512; hand tremors, 514–15, 535–6; manner and demeanour in court, 138–9; memory and mental alertness in older age, 577; nickname ('Lucky Swanson'), 151, 154; personal address book, 534–5; qualities as detective, 115, 264, 387, 518; reluctance to discuss police work in family circle, 512, 522, 677; reputation, 614; revolver carried in retirement, 679; rewards, awards and commendations, 84, 109, 113, 151, 154, 209, 229, 241, 248, 252, 262, 396, 473, 474; weight, 468–9, 514
Swanson, Donald (unrelated), 9–10, 47, 151, 591, 620
Swanson, Donald William (grandson): letter from grandfather, 515; discovers marginalia, 520
Swanson, Douglas Sutherland (son): birth, 241; life, 514; at father's funeral, 517; death, 519
Swanson, Elizabeth Gair (sister-in-law), 6, 161, 590
Swanson, Sergeant George, 8, 12
Swanson, Helen, 9, 47

Swanson, James (brother), 6, 10
Swanson, James Alexander (nephew): death, 455–6, 591
Swanson, James Douglas (grandson; 'Jim'): life, 676; and grandfather's revolver, 679; discovers marginalia, 520–2; negotiates with newspapers, 522–3, 677; offers story to *Daily Telegraph*, 526, 575; provides additional documents, 527; responds to reservations about marginalia, 528; appears on *Crime Monthly*, 529; visited by Skinner and Evans, 533–4; highlights marginalia with red lines, 534; filmed for *The Trial of Jack the Ripper*, 530; death, 530; on his grandfather's discretion, 512, 677
Swanson, James John (son; 'Jamie'), 117, 513–14, 675–6
Swanson, James and John (Gerston distillers), 5, 590
Swanson, Jannet Shearer (*later* Gunn; sister; 'Jessie'), 10, 513, 592, 675
Swanson, John (father), 5–6, 10; illness and death, 99–100
Swanson, John Thomson (brother), 6, 27, 160–1, 590–1, 621
Swanson, Julia Ann (*née* Nevill; wife): background, 62–3; marriage, 96; pregnancies and children, 98, 99, 109, 117, 194, 205, 241, 266, 350; in Aberdeen, 160, 161; cares for dying mother, 258; birth of twins and loss of William Alexander, 350; at husband's funeral, 517; death, 519
Swanson, Margaret Sutherland (*later* Alexander; sister), 10, 18, 99, 513, 590, 593
Swanson, Mary (*née* Thomson; mother), 5–6, 10; death, 62
Swanson, Mary Thomson (*later* Bailey; sister), 10, 18, 22, 26, 590, 592
Swanson, Nevill (great grandson): life, 678; seeks information on Tranter pistol, 530; agrees loan of Swanson material to Crime Museum, 530; and red pen lines, 534; collates great grandfather's papers and memorabilia, 534; on Great Aunts Alice and Lal, 520
Swanson, William Alexander (son), 350
Swanson marginalia *see* marginalia
'sweating system', 276, 552
Sweeney, Detective Inspector John: on Scotland Yard bomb attack, 219–20;

and London Bridge bomb attack (1884), 224; on living conditions of Jews in Whitechapel, 277; on applications for naturalisation, 278–9; on Swanson, 480; publishes memoirs, 510; *At Scotland Yard*, 219–20, 277, 278–9
Swell Mob, 127
Swinscow, Charles, 424, 425, 438
Switzerland: Edward Pinter extradition, 386–7, 396, 436
Sydney, Australia, 123

Tabram, Henry, 639
Tabram, Martha (*née* White): background, 639–40; at Satchell's Lodging House, 344; movements on night of death, 640, 685; murder of, 283–4, 293; body discovered, 640; wounds, 640; inquest, 292; in Macnaghten memorandum, 570
tailoring and clothing trade, 276
Talbot Hotel, Cuckfield, 138
Tamarama Beach, Sydney, 123
Tangier, 99
Tanner, Elizabeth, 297
Tanner, Richard, 50, 78
Taylor, Detective Inspector (of City Police), 391, 392, 394
Taylor, Alfred, 436
Taylorson, Frederick, 433, 434
Taylour, Evelyn, Lady, 111
Taylour, Olivia, Lady, 111, 613
Taylour, Thomas *see* Bective, Thomas Taylour, Earl of
telegraphy, 48
Tempany, Thomas, 351
Tempest, Captain Egerton (James Cheadle), 114–15
Templar, Eva, 389
Temple, James, 541
Tempted London: Young Men (anonymous series), 26
Tenpenny's Lodging House, Gun Street, 351
Thackray, George, 216–17
Thames, river: sewage disposal, 20
Thames Magistrates' Court, 208, 380, 560, 580, 583
Thames Police: Ripper enquiries, 320
Theatre of Anatomy, Windmill Street, 159
Thick, Sergeant William, 282
Thickbroom, Charles, 424, 426, 438
Thomas, David, 188

Thomas, George Danford, 683–4
Thomas, Superintendent Joseph, 158
Thomas Agnew and Sons (art gallery) *see* Agnew's art gallery
Thompson, Sarah (*later* Bickers), 616
Thompson, Mr. (solicitor), 260
Thompson, Sergeant (of F Division), 447, 451, 452–3
Thompson, P.C. Ernest, 378
Thompson, H. B., 215
Thompson, Hannah, 82–3
Thompson, Inspector James, 421
Thomson, Sheriff Comrie, 167
Thomson, Superintendent James, 50, 250
Thomson, Mary *see* Swanson, Mary
Thomson's Weekly News, 551, 552–4
Thoriste, Caroline, 407
Thorlby, John, 401–2, 660
Thornton, Sir Edward, 181
Thornton, Sergeant Stephen, 77, 606
Thow, David, 247
Thurso: crime and law enforcement, 8; education and schools, 10–16, 512, 592; gang rivalry between boys, 11, 15–16; housing and town planning, 7–8, 9; industry, 6–7, 8, 513; location, 6; Lochiel Graham ('Sir Charles Cuffe') at, 175–7; Masonic Lodge, 240, 632; population, 512; royal visit (1876), 512; sea legends, 121, 615; transport connections, 18, 512, 593; *see also* Durness Street; Meadow Well
Tillcock, P.C. (of City police), 28
Times, The: campaigns for amalgamation of Met and City forces, 39–40; on police inefficiency, 70; on death of Lady Edward St. Maur, 106; on Whitechapel murders, 284, 310; publishes letter from Warren, 319; on Annie Farmer attack, 345–6
The Times offices, Play House Yard, 196–7
Tinapp, William, 108
Tindall, Arthur Grey (aka John Ashley), 410–11
Titiens, Theresa, 361
Tobutt, Sergeant Charles, 132
Toronto, 100, 488
Torslanda, Sweden, 297
torso murders, 353–5, 362–3, 568
Tottenham Court Road police station, 439
Totty, Dr. Richard, 529

Index

Tower, Eliza, 212–13, 214, 629
Tower of London: bomb attack (1885), 226–7
Townsend, Dr. Meredith, 447, 448
Tradeston Gasworks, Glasgow: bomb attack (1883), 195
Trafalgar Square: Reform League demonstrations (1866), 37–8; dynamite discovered at (1884), 219, 220; as symbol of class struggle, 231; unemployment rally (8 February 1886), 232–3; Warren bans public meetings, 253–4; Bloody Sunday demonstration (13 November 1887), 253–8, 259, 310; demonstration (20 November 1887), 258, 259; and legality of Warren's proclamation, 264
transportation (penal), 38
Transvaal (South African Republic): independence from British rule, 464; Rhodes plans insurrection, 462, 464–5; failed invasion, 465–6
Tranter pistol, 113–14, 530, 613–14, 678–9
Travers, Mary Ann ('Curly Poll'), 58–9; similarity to Mary Ann Connelly, 602
Treves, Frederick, 504
Trial of Jack the Ripper, The (TV documentary), 530
Trial of the Detectives, 91–2; *see also* Turf Fraud scandal (1877)
Troup, Edward, 501, 510
Troutbeck, John, 259
Troyte, Joanna (*later* Harper), 456
Truly A Great Victorian (Constance Bradford), 368–9
Tucker, William, 244
Tumblety, Francis, 686
Tunbridge, John, 387–8
Turf Fraud scandal (1877), 80–2, 83–4, 86–90
Turner, Henry, 639, 640
Turner, Richard, 150
Turner, William, 473, 474
Turpin, Inspector, 139, 154, 205–6
Tustin, Charles Driscoll, 506
Tye, P.C., 74
Tyrolese Jack the Ripper case (Joseph Maier), 340, 341
Tysoe Street, Clerkenwell, 384

Uberfield, Thomas, 649
Uitlanders (outlanders), 464, 465
Umbrecht, Mr. (hotel manager), 371, 372
Underground railway, 19, 20, 24–5, 269, 595–6, 627; Fenian bombings (1883–85), 207–8, 224–6
United Irishmen of America, 180
University Life Assurance Society, 597

Vagrancy Act (1824), 1
Vaughan, Mr. (magistrate), 258, 456
Veck, George, 427–30, 433
Veiled Lady of Loughton mystery (c.1875), 66–7, 604
venereal disease, 602
Vestry Hall, Cable Street, 291, 423
Victoria, Queen: accession, 33; assassination attempts on, 22, 594; withdraws after Albert's death, 22; public appearances, 22; Fenian kidnap plot (1867), 42; writes to Katherine Dickinson, 129; and Jubilee assassination plot, 249–51; and Kruger telegram, 478; declining health and death, 483–4
Victoria, SS, 466–7, 468–9
Victoria Docks: arson attack (1881), 206, 208
Victoria railway station, London, 137; bomb attack (1884), 217–19
Villiers, Captain Charles, 467
Vincent, Edgar, 209
Vincent, Howard: background, 94, 609; appointed Director of Criminal Investigations, 93–4; access to Home Secretary, 252; and Harley Street murder case, 107; and arrest of Davitt, 117; and Lefroy case, 126, 153; and murder of P.C. Atkins, 142; and Phoenix Park murders, 188; visits scene of Whitehall bomb attack (1883), 199; anti-Fenian career, 202–3, 220, 233; and Jens Nielsen case, 206, 207; press criticism and speculation, 209; resignation from C.I.D., 220–2; political career, 235, 630; *Police Code*, 360, 547, 654; presented with findings of 'Maiden Tribute' Report, 413; mooted as Metropolitan Commissioner, 342, 651; writes to Swanson, 509; death, 630
Vine Street police station, 473
Virtue, William, 98
Volksrust, South Africa, 466
von Tornow, Detective Inspector Charles, 90, 202

Index

Wadge, Edward Harvey ('Captain Archer'), 205
Waglin, Hugh, 437
Wagner, Detective Sergeant, 387
Wainwright, George, 517
Wakefield Gaol, 3
Waldron, Superintendent (of Grimsby police), 217
Walker, Dr. Edward, 454
Walker, Chief Superintendent Robert, 50, 591
Waller, Maggie, 214–15
Wallington, East Sussex, 132, 136
Wallis, James, 635
Walpole, Spencer Horatio, 38
'Walter', *My Secret Life*, 406
Walters, William Henry, 607, 608
Walton-on-Thames, 142–3
wandering lunatics, 559–60
Wandsworth police station, 74
Wang, Charles, 96, 97, 99, 100
'wanted' portrait of Lefroy, 133–4, 135, 137, 150, 618
Wapping police station, 248
Warburton, Henry, 159
Ward, Mr. (and son Alfred), 122
Ward, Arthur, 245
Warren, Sir Charles: education and military training, 233–4; army career, 234–7; biblical archaeology, 234; Palmer search expedition, 234; knighted, 234, 367; Bechuanaland expedition, 235; fights election seat (1885), 235; appointed commander at Suakin, 235–7; considered for Fenian intelligence role, 223; becomes Metropolitan Police Commissioner, 237, 238–9; qualities, 237–8; relations with Matthews, 239; and militarisation of police, 239; tough stance on rabies and dog muzzling, 239, 575; Commissioner's Report (1886), 249, 252; triumphant handling of Jubilee Day, 251; conflict with Home Office, 252; relations with Monro, 252, 253; bans public meetings in Trafalgar Square, 253–4, 264, 310; and Bloody Sunday demonstrations, 258; warns of public disorder at Linnell funeral, 260–1; dispute with Bond, 329–33, 339; heckled at public lecture, 262–3; opposes appointment of Macnaghten, 265; puts Swanson in charge of Whitechapel murders investigation, 267–8, 295; and Anderson, 268; receives anonymous tip-off letter from brothel-keeper, 296, 580; orders graffito erased, 309–11; urges closer liaison with City force, 318; countenances drastic or illegal measures, 319, 548; and house-to-house search of Whitechapel, 319; and Bond's medico-legal expertise, 335; further press criticism of, 341; censured by Matthews, 342; resignation, 341–3; well wishes of colleagues, 346; press reaction to resignation, 347
Warren, Robert, 522–3, 526, 677
Warrilow, Thomas, 578, 685
Warrilow, Thomas Davis, 578, 685
Watch, The (Thames Police launch), 469
watchmen, 31, 598
Waters, James, 15, 480, 518; testimonial letter for Swanson, 16–18
Watkins, P.C. Edward: police beat, 304–5; possible sighting of Ripper, 556–7, 569, 570, 571; finds body of Catherine Eddowes, 306–7
Watlings, Harry, 124
Watson (Islington burglar), 86
Watson, Thomas, 130
Waverley Hotel, Great Portland Street, 218–19, 229
Weatherhead, Detective Sergeant Albert, 439
Webb, Beatrice, 274
Webster, John, 248
Weekly Welcome (magazine), 551
Welby, Captain (Deputy Governor of Pentonville Prison), 262
Weldon, Georgina, 620
Wellington, Duke of: lying-in-state, 34
Wellington Barracks, 38, 42, 48, 55
Wells, Dr. Arthur, 374
Wells, Charles H. *see* Bullard, Charles ('Piano Charley')
Wells, Mr. H. (City solicitor), 578
Wells, Kitty, 489
Wensley, Chief Constable Frederick Porter, 518
Wentworth Model Dwellings, 308–9, 311
West, Chief Inspector John, 274, 282
West, Henry, 419
West Ham Parish Church, 96
West London Police Court, 453
West London Union Workhouse, Upper

Holloway, 559
West Reservoir, Stoke Newington, 210, 213
Western Daily Press, 129
Western Mail, 357, 400-1, 402-4
Western Times, 184-5
Westgate, William, 187, 188-9
Westminster Abbey, 250-1, 504
Westminster Hall: bomb explosion (1885), 227-8
Westminster Magistrates' Court, 245
Westwood, Robert, 77, 605-6
Westwood, Sophia, 77
'Wheel of Beauty' fraud case (1878-9), 96, 97, 99, 100
Wheeler, Joseph, 61
Wheeler, Maria, 61-2
Wheeler, Rose and Clara, 61-2
Whelan, Captain William, 45, 46
Whicher, Detective Inspector Jonathan, 77-8, 606
whisky distilling, Halkirk, 5-6, 589-90
Whitby Gazette, 504-5
White, Detective Inspector, 371
White, Dr. (of Islington), 210-11
White, Arnold, 262, 274, 635
White, Major Henry, 466, 472, 476
White, Captain Robert, 467, 472, 476
White Horse Yard, off Drury Lane, 353-4
White Plains jail, New York, 488
white slave trade, 324-5, 414-16
Whitechapel: industry and employment, 276-8; Jewish immigrants, 275-6, 277-8, 279, 575; living conditions, 269-70, 277-8; population, 269, 275; railway and Underground, 269; schools, 279
Whitechapel Infirmary, 279, 292, 346, 560, 580-1
Whitechapel mortuary, Old Montague Street, 282, 283, 292, 295
Whitechapel murders, linked as series, 283-4, 293-4, 352-3
Whitechapel Vigilance Committee, 318
Whitechapel workhouse, 279
Whitehall: Local Government Board offices: bomb attack (1883), 197-9, 203
Whitehall (A Division), 50, 51, 53, 329-32
Whitehall Mystery (1888), 362-3
Whitehall Place, 31
White's Row *see* Spitalfields Chambers
Whittlestone, Mr. (caretaker), 197

Wick, Caithness, 8, 176
Wildbore (carpenter), 362
Wilde, Oscar, 436
Wilde, William, 514
Wildey, Detective Inspector Richard, 348-9
Wilhelm II, German Emperor (Kaiser), 478
Williams, Agnes (Sarah Wyath), 57
Williams, Jack, 57
Williams, Montagu: on Michael Barrett, 46; on Turf Fraud defendants, 86-7; on Lefroy, 144-6
Williams, Thomas, 158, 159
Williams-Wynn, Sir Watkin, 220
Williamson, Frederick Adolphus ('Dolly'): character and early life, 78-9; and Road Hill case, 78; at A Division (Whitehall), 50; moots reorganisation of Detective Department, 609; and Turf Fraud case, 79, 81, 88, 89-90, 92; appointed Chief Superintendent, 94; and arrest of Davitt, 115, 116-17; anti-Fenian activities, 202, 203, 220, 228; and Lefroy case, 126; receives reward, 229; serves summonses on leaders of West End riots, 233; and Jubilee assassination plot, 250, 251; promoted Chief Constable of C.I.D., 264; as Swanson's mentor, 264; sick leave, 264; returns to work, 265; and Annie Chapman murder, 282; recommends Swanson to Warren, 295; and Warren's 'Eyes and Ears' memorandum, 268; and 'Dear Boss' letter, 314; and house-to-house search of Whitechapel, 319; deteriorating health, 351; updates *Police Code*, 360, 654; death, tributes and funeral, 360-1; diaries, 360, 654
Willoughby, Major Sir John, 466, 472, 476
Wills, Mr. Justice, 410
Wilson, John, 116
Wilson, John Gleeson, 127
Wilton, Henry, 343
Winchester Music Hall, Islington, 60-1
Windsor Magazine, 584
Windust, Charles: *Some Crime Stories*, 483
Winn, Dr. J. M., 146
Winslow, Dr. L. Forbes: theories on insanity and crime, 619-20; and Lefroy case, 146, 147;

Jack the Ripper theory, 355–8; correspondence with Jack the Ripper, 357, 358; examines Reginald Saunderson, 454
Woking cemetery, 361
Wolf, Lucien, 'The Jews in London', 276–7
Wolverhampton, 312
Wood, Adam, 534, 536; researches Tranter pistol, 613–14, 678
Wood, Malcolm, 342
Woodroffee, Mr. (caretaker), 107
Woods, Thomas J, 70
workhouses, 279, 558–60
Working Lads' Institute, Whitechapel Road, 292, 643
Worsfold, Ellen, 649–50
Worship Street Magistrates' Court, 314, 383
Worswick, John Joseph, 105
Worth, Adam (alias Henry J. Raymond): as criminal mastermind, 486–7, 489; background and criminal career, 487–90; opens American Bar, 489; forgery scheme, 490; steals *Duchess of Devonshire*, 68–9, 491–2; betrayed by Joe Elliott, 492; decides to keep *Duchess*, 493; in Louvain prison, 486, 493; interviewed by *Pall Mall Gazette*, 486, 493; meeting with Pinkerton, 493–4; confesses to theft of painting, 494; returns *Duchess*, 493–4; death, 496; autobiography, 491–2, 494, 496–7
Worth, John, 490–1, 492
Wray, John, 30–1, 37, 597, 599
Wright, Detective Sergeant (of Thames Police), 248
Wright, Mr. (lawyer), 262
Wright, George Alma, 423–4, 426
Wright, Thomas, 244
Wright, Inspector Thomas, 374
Wyath, Mary, 57
Wyath, Sarah ('Agnes Williams'), 57

Yarrow, Dr. G. Eugene, 291
Yates, Mr. (handcuffed prisoner), 561
Yeats, William, 165
Young, Elizabeth, 8
Young, George Hay, 291
Young, Miss (Eastcote matron), 450
Young Apprentice, The (penny-dreadful), 28

Zambesia, 461

www.ingramcontent.com/pod-product-compliance
Lightning Source LLC
Chambersburg PA
CBHW031246230426
43670CB00005B/63